UNDERSTANDING HUMAN COMMUNICATION

EIGHTH EDITION

RONALD B. ADLER ■ GEORGE RODMAN
Santa Barbara City College

Brooklyn College
City University of New York

New York   Oxford
OXFORD UNIVERSITY PRESS
2003

D0126863

Oxford University Press

Oxford New York
Auckland Bangkok Buenos Aires Cape Town Chennai
Dar es Salaam Delhi Hong Kong Istanbul Karachi Kolkata
Kuala Lumpur Madrid Melbourne Mexico City Mumbai Nairobi
São Paulo Shanghai Singapore Taipei Tokyo Toronto

and an associated company in Berlin

Published by Oxford University Press, Inc.
198 Madison Avenue, New York, New York, 10016
http://www.oup-usa.org

Oxford is a registered trademark of Oxford University Press

ISBN: 0-19-521910-4

Printing number: 9 8 7 6 5 4 3 2 1

Printed in the United States of America
on acid-free paper

CONTENTS IN BRIEF

CONTENTS

PART THREE: COMMUNICATION IN GROUPS

CHAPTER 8: THE NATURE OF GROUPS 254

PART FOUR: PUBLIC COMMUNICATION

CHAPTER 10: CHOOSING AND DEVELOPING A TOPIC **318**

APPENDIXES

APPENDIX I: INTERVIEWING 447

APPENDIX II: MEDIATED COMMUNICATION 471

PREFACE

After eight editions we have come to realize that the title of this book may be misleading. It's presumptuous to suggest that any text or introductory course could enable readers to completely understand the complex phenomenon of human communication. So a more accurate title might be *Beginning to Understand Human Communication*. In another respect, the title doesn't reflect the promise of this book. If we have done our job—and if instructors and students do theirs—then readers should not only *understand* communication, they should also become more skillful, competent communicators in their everyday lives.

It's too late to change the title, but even a quick glance at *Understanding Human Communication* should make its goal clear: To provide a comprehensive, useful introduction to the academic study of person-to-person communication in interpersonal, small group, and public contexts; via face-to-face and electronic channels; and as it operates with family, friends, and strangers as well as in school and on the job.

You can evaluate this book by opening it to any page and asking three questions: Is its content important? Is the material clear? Is it useful? Our goal has been to focus on topics that are absolutely essential and present them so that every sentence delivers an informational payoff worth the space it occupies. You, of course, are the best judge of how well we have succeeded.

Basic Approach

This eighth edition of *Understanding Human Communication* retains the features that have served professors and students well in the past. A reader-friendly style presents material clearly without being simplistic. The handsome visual design of the book aims to make material inviting. A diverse array of photos, cartoons, marginal quotes, and readings give readers new perspectives on material in the text.

As in previous editions, *Understanding Human Communication* treats scholarship and skill development as mutually reinforcing. Virtually every page contains material that applies to the reader's everyday life, and the academic foundation for the suggestions about improving skill is described and documented.

The topics of cultural diversity and technology are given special emphasis. Along with being addressed throughout the text, *Understanding Diversity* sidebars highlight ways in which communication is influenced by the backgrounds people bring to their interaction. This edition contains diversity sidebars on topics including doing business across cultures, non-Western views of modern medicine, and how deafness shapes identity. Thanks to Ingrid Peternel, College of DuPage, cultural idioms are defined wherever they appear in the text, helping non-native speakers make sense of potentially confusing terms and reminding native speakers that familiar figures of speech can be puzzling to those from other cultures.

Understanding Communication Technology sidebars showcase the role played by electronic tools for keeping in touch. In this edition, these boxed inserts address topics including strategies for expressing emotions online, using the World Wide Web to deliver difficult messages, communicating in "virtual groups" via the Internet, and software that promises to improve group decision making.

Finally, the end-of-chapter Resource sections provide descriptions of high-interest feature films as well as print material. Since art often imitates life, these film listings help students see how communication concepts look and sound in a variety of situations.

Changes in the Eighth Edition

A number of changes in this edition should make it even more valuable to users. Each chapter now begins with cognitive and behavioral objectives, which make it clear to students precisely what they need to learn. Activities are now integrated into the text, adjacent to the concepts they help readers master. This connection will help students apply the material to their everyday lives.

New information in every chapter reflects the latest scholarship and the concerns of today's readers. For example, Chapter 1 explains how some communication aims at coordination, without necessarily seeking or needing understanding. Chapter 2 contains a new section describing how personal narratives shape perceptions and provide a framework for shared understanding. Information in Chapter 3 provides new perspectives on contemporary language use, as well as expanding the nonideological treatment of similarities and differences between male and female communication styles.

Chapter 4 presents new evidence of the importance of listening in career and personal life and new material on how cultural differences shape listening. It also contains a new section on personal listening styles and new material on the range of ways communicators can offer social support to others. Chapter 5 provides new material on deceptive communication, and Chapter 6 explains in greater depth when and why people disclose personal information.

Throughout the Public Communication section there is an increased emphasis on the role of human communication in contemporary world events. The public speaking chapters provide increased emphasis on the new student activism. This edition contains all new model student speeches, each of which is accompanied by marginal commentary that shows how the material follows the guidelines in the text. In addition, the speeches include commentary by the student speakers themselves.

Chapter 10 provides a new demographic analysis of today's audiences. Chapter 13 offers expanded guidelines for personalizing an informative speech, and Chapter 14 offers new material on persuasive speaking.

Appendixes on interviewing and mass media make this material accessible for those who want it while keeping the body of the text streamlined enough to be practical in a single academic term.

Ancillary Package

Understanding Human Communication is accompanied by a package of materials that help make teaching and learning as efficient and effective as possible.

The **Student Resource Manual**, developed by Jeanne M. Elmhorst of Albuquerque Technical-Vocational Institute, contains study guides, self-tests, activities, recommended readings, and Internet resources to help students understand and master the material in the text.

An **Instructor's Manual**, updated by Robert Dixon and Dennis Dufer of St. Louis Community College, provides a wide array of teaching strategies that should help both new and experienced instructors.

A **Test Bank**, refined and updated by Barbara Clinton of Highline Community College, provides several hundred questions.

An **Understanding Human Communication** website (www.oup-usa.org/highered/adlerrodman/uhc8) will provide a wealth of resources for students and instructors alike, as well as regularly updated descriptions of feature films that illustrate principles introduced in the text.

Acknowledgments

This book and its ancillary materials wouldn't exist without the contributions of many people. We are grateful for the skill and goodwill of our colleagues who developed each part of the instructional package. Our thanks go out to Jeanne Elmhorst, Bob Dixon and Denis Dufer, Barbara Clinton, Ingrid Peternel, and Russ Proctor.

We also thank the professors whose reviews helped us make sure this edition of *Understanding Human Communication* continues to meet the needs of faculty and students. Our sincere thanks to Bonne Doron, Des Moines Area Community College–Ankeny; Rebecca Anderson, Johnson County Community College; Marcia Dixson, Indiana-Purdue University at Fort Wayne; Bonnie Clark, St. Petersburg College; Shirley Maase, Chesapeake College; Elizabeth Willets, Ocean County College; Rosemary Gallick, Northern Virginia Community College–Woodbridge; Judith McKibbin, Jacksonville State University; Karen Holmes, Georgia State University; and Roberta Davila, University of Northern Iowa.

Long-time users will recognize that *Understanding Human Communication* is now published by Oxford University Press. We are delighted and honored to be part of the most venerable academic firm publishing in the English language. Our experience so far leaves us convinced that Oxford deserves its reputation. It has been a pleasure to work with Peter Labella, Chris Rogers, Robert Miller, Elyse Dubin, Karen Shapiro, Eve Siegel, Scott Burns, Valerie Hartman, Jeanne Ambrosio, Sunny Stimmler, and Sean Mahoney. We also express continuing gratitude to our designer and photo researcher, Janet Bollow Alleyn, whose talents are apparent in the handsome book you are now reading.

Finally, we thank our families, whose support and tolerance have made it possible for us to produce this book.

Ronald B. Adler
George Rodman

UNDERSTANDING HUMAN COMMUNICATION

EIGHTH EDITION

CONTENTS

KEY TERMS

behavior
channel
communication
communication competence
coordination
decoding
dyad
dyadic communication
encoding
environment
feedback
interpersonal communication
intrapersonal communication
linear communication model
mass communication
message
noise
public communication
receiver
sender
small group communication
symbol
transactional communication model

AFTER STUDYING
THE MATERIAL
IN THIS CHAPTER . . .

YOU SHOULD UNDERSTAND:

1. The working definition and characteristics of *communication*.

2. The types of communication covered in this book.

3. The needs satisfied by communication.

4. The characteristics of linear and transactional communication models.

5. The characteristics of competent communication.

6. Common misconceptions about communication.

YOU SHOULD BE ABLE TO:

1. Define *communication* and give specific examples of the various types of communication introduced in this chapter.

2. Describe the key needs you attempt to satisfy in your life by communicating.

3. Use the criteria in this chapter to identify the degree to which communication (yours or others') in a specific situation is competent and suggest ways of increasing the competence level.

4. Identify how misconceptions about communication can create problems and suggest how a more accurate analysis of the situations you describe can lead to better outcomes.

HUMAN COMMUNICATION: WHAT AND WHY

COMMUNICATION DEFINED

Because this is a book about *communication,* it makes sense to begin by defining that term. This is not as simple as it might seem because people use the term in a variety of ways that are only vaguely related:

- Family members, coworkers, and friends make such statements about their relationships as "We just can't communicate" or "We communicate perfectly."
- Business people talk about "office communications systems" consisting of computers, telephones, printers, and so on.
- Scientists study and describe communication among ants, dolphins, and other animals.
- Certain organizations label themselves "communications conglomerates," publishing newspapers, books, and magazines and owning radio and television stations.

There is clearly some relationship among uses of the term such as these, but we need to narrow our focus before going on. A look at the table of contents of this book shows that it obviously doesn't deal with animals, computers, or newspapers. Neither is it about Holy Communion, the bestowing of a material thing, or many of the other subjects mentioned in the *Oxford English Dictionary*'s 1,200-word definition of *communication.*

What, then, *are* we talking about when we use the term *communication?* A survey of the ways in which scholars use the word will show that there is no single, universally accepted usage. Some definitions are long and complex, whereas others are brief and simple. This isn't the place to explore the differences between these conceptions or to defend one against the others. What we need is a working definition that will help us in our study. For our purposes we will say that **communication** refers to the process of human beings responding to the symbolic behavior of other persons.

A point-by-point examination of this definition reveals some important characteristics of communication as we will be studying it.

Communication Is Human

In this book we'll be discussing communication between human beings. Animals clearly do communicate: Bees instruct their hive-mates about the location of food by a meaning-laden dance. Chimpanzees have been taught to express themselves with the same sign language used by deaf humans, and a few have developed impressive vocabularies. And on a more commonplace level, pet owners can testify to the variety of messages their animals can express. Although this subject of animal communication is fascinating and important, it goes beyond the scope of this book.[1]

Communication Is a Process

We often talk about communication as if it occurred in discrete, individual acts such as one person's utterance or a conversation. In fact, communication is a continuous, ongoing process. Consider, for example, a friend's compliment about your appearance. Your interpretation of those words will depend on a long series of experiences stretching far back in time: How have others judged your appearance? How do you feel about your looks? How honest has your friend been in the past? How have you been feeling about one another recently? All this history will help shape your response to the friend's remark. In turn, the words you speak and the way you say them will shape the way your friend behaves toward you and others—both in this situation and in the future.

This simple example shows that it's inaccurate to talk about "acts" of communication as if they occurred in isolation. To put it differently, communication isn't a series of incidents pasted together like photographs in a scrapbook; instead, it is more like a motion picture in which the meaning comes from the unfolding of an interrelated series of images. The fact that communication is a process is reflected in the transactional model introduced later in this chapter.

Communication Is Symbolic

Symbols are used to represent things, processes, ideas, or events in ways that make communication possible. Chapter 3 discusses the nature of symbols in more detail, but this idea is so important that it needs an introduction now. The most significant feature of symbols is their *arbitrary* nature. For example, there's no logical reason why the letters in the word *book* should stand for the object you're reading now. Speakers of Spanish call it a *libro,* and Germans call it a *Buch.* Even in English, another term would work just as well as long as everyone agreed to use it in the same way. We overcome the arbitrary nature of symbols by linguistic rules and customs. Effective communication depends on agreement among people about these rules. This is easiest to see when we observe people who don't follow linguistic conventions. For example, recall how unusual the speech of children and immigrant speakers of a language often sounds.

We've already talked about words as one type of symbol. In addition, nonverbal behavior can have symbolic meaning. As with words, some nonverbal behaviors, though arbitrary, have clearly agreed-upon meanings. For example, to most North Americans, nodding your head up and down means "yes" (although this meaning isn't universal). But even more than words, many nonverbal behaviors are ambiguous. Does a frown signify anger or unhappiness? Does a hug stand for a friendly greeting or a symbol of the hugger's romantic interest in you? One can't always be sure. We'll discuss the nature of nonverbal communication in Chapter 5.

CRITICAL
THINKING
PROBE

Must Communication Be Intentional?

Some theorists believe that any behavior that has meaning to others should be considered communication, whether it is intentional or not. To them, an involuntary grimace or overheard remark is worthy of studying. Other scholars believe that only messages that are intentionally sent and received should be considered communication. They argue that the broader definition means that the study of communication has no boundaries. Which position do you take? Be prepared to support your viewpoint in a discussion with others who hold the opposing viewpoint.

The Many Meanings of *Communication*

Few words have as many meanings as communication. *The term can refer to everything from messages on T-shirts to presidential speeches, from computer code to chimpanzee behavior. Communication has been the professional concern of philosophers, scientists (social, biological, and physical), poets, politicians, and entertainers, to name a few. Responding to this diversity, Brent Rubin asked, "How does being interested in communication differ from being interested in life?"*

There are several reasons why the term *communication* has so many different meanings. Understanding them will help explain how and why this word refers to a broad range of subjects.

Interdisciplinary Heritage   Unlike most subjects, communication has captured the interest of scholars from a wide range of fields. Ever since classical times, philosophers have studied the meaning and significance of messages. In the twentieth century, social scientists have joined the field: Psychologists examine the causes and effects of communication as it relates to individuals. Sociologists and anthropologists examine how communication operates within and between societies and cultures. Political scientists explore the ways communication influences governmental affairs. Engineers use their skill to devise methods of conveying messages electronically. Zoologists focus on communication between animals. With this kind of diversity, it's no surprise that *communication* is a broad and sometimes confusing term.

Field and Activity   Sometimes the word *communication* refers to a field of study (of nonverbal messages or effects of televised violence on children, for example). In other cases it denotes an activity that people do. This confusion doesn't exist in most disciplines.

People may study history or sociology, but they don't "historicate" or "sociologize." Having only one word that refers to both the field of study and the activity that it examines leads to confusion.

Humanity and Social Science   Unlike most disciplines, communication straddles two very different academic domains. It has one foot firmly planted in the humanities, where it shares concerns with disciplines like English and philosophy. At the same time, other scholars in the field take an approach like their colleagues in the social sciences, such as psychology, sociology, and anthropology. And to confuse matters even further, communication is sometimes associated with the performing arts, especially in the area of oral interpretation of literature.

Natural and Professional Communication   This is a natural activity that we all engage in unconsciously. At the same time, there are professional communication experts whose specialized duties require training and skill. Careers such as marketing, public relations, broadcasting, speechmaking, counseling, journalism, and management all call for talent that goes far beyond what is required for everyday speaking and listening.

Communication and Communications   Even the name of the field is confusing. Traditionally, *communications* (with an "s") has been used when referring to activities involving technology and the mass media. *Communication* is typically used to describe face-to-face and written messages, as well as the field as a whole. With the growth of communication technology, the two terms are being used interchangeably more often.

Brent Rubin
Communication and Human Behavior

TYPES OF COMMUNICATION

Within the domain of human interaction, there are several types of communication. Each occurs in a different context. Despite the features that all share, each has its own characteristics.

Intrapersonal Communication

By definition, **intrapersonal communication** means "communicating with oneself."[2] You can tune in to one way that each of us communicates internally by listening to the little voice that lives in your mind. Take a moment and listen to what it is saying. Try it now, before reading on. Did you hear it? It may have been saying something like "What little voice? I don't have any little voice!" This voice is the "sound" of your thinking.

We don't always think in verbal terms, but whether the process is apparent or not, the way we mentally process information influences our interaction with others. Thus, even though intrapersonal communication doesn't fit the "face-to-face" element of our definition of *communication,* it does affect those forms of interaction. You can understand the role of intrapersonal communication by imagining your thoughts in each of the following situations.

- You are planning to approach a stranger whom you would like to get to know better.
- You pause a minute and look at the audience before beginning a ten-minute speech.
- The boss yawns while you are asking for a raise.
- A friend seems irritated lately, and you're not sure whether you are responsible.

The way you handle all of these situations would depend on the intrapersonal communication that precedes or accompanies your overt behavior. Much of Chapter 2 deals with the perception process in everyday situations, and part of Chapter 12 focuses on the intrapersonal communication that can minimize anxiety when you deliver a speech.

Dyadic/Interpersonal Communication

Social scientists call two persons interacting a **dyad,** and they often use the term **dyadic communication** to describe this type of communication. Dyads are the most common communication setting. One study revealed that college students spend almost half of their total communication time interacting with one other person.[3] Observation in a variety of settings ranging from playgrounds, train depots, and shopping malls to other settings shows that most communication is dyadic in nature.[4] Even communication within larger groups (think of classrooms, parties, and families as examples) consists of multiple, often shifting dyadic encounters.

Dyadic interaction is sometimes considered as identical to **interpersonal communication;** but as Chapter 6 explains, not all two-person interaction can be considered interpersonal in the fullest sense of the word. In fact, you will learn that the qualities that characterize interpersonal communication aren't limited to twosomes. They can be present in threesomes or even in small groups.

Small Group Communication

In **small group communication** every person can participate actively with the other members. Small groups are a common fixture of everyday life. Your family is a group. So are an athletic team, a collection of fellow workers, and a group of students working on a class project.

Whatever their makeup, small groups possess characteristics that are not present in a dyad. For instance, two or more members of a group can form a coalition to defend their position against other members, whereas in a dyad the members face each other on their own, without support from others. In a group, the majority of members can put pressure on those in the minority to conform, either consciously or unconsciously; but in a dyad no such pressures exist. Conformity pressures can also be comforting, leading group members to take risks that they would not dare if they were alone or in a dyad. With their greater size, groups also have the ability to be more creative than dyads. Finally, communication in groups is affected strongly by the type of leader who is in a position of authority. Groups are such an important communication setting that Chapters 8 and 9 focus exclusively on them.

Public Communication

Public communication occurs when a group becomes too large for all members to contribute. One characteristic of public communication is an unequal amount of speaking. One or more people are likely to deliver their remarks to the remaining members, who act as an audience. This leads to a second characteristic of public settings: limited verbal feedback. The audience isn't able to talk back in a two-way conversation the way they might in a dyadic or small group setting. This doesn't mean that speakers operate in a vacuum when delivering their remarks. Audiences often have a chance to ask questions and offer brief comments, and their nonverbal reactions offer a wide range of clues about their reception of the speaker's remarks.

Public speakers usually have a greater chance to plan and structure their remarks than do communicators in smaller settings. For this reason, several chapters of this book describe the steps you can take to prepare and deliver an effective speech.

Mass Communicaton

Mass communication consists of messages that are transmitted to large, widespread audiences via electronic and print media: newspapers, magazines, television, radio, and so on. As Appendix II explains, mass communication differs from the interpersonal, small group, and public varieties in several ways. First, mass messages are aimed at a large audience without any personal contact between sender and receivers. Second, most of the messages sent via mass communication channels are developed, or at least financed, by large organizations. In this sense, mass communication is far less personal and more of a product than the other types we have examined so far. Finally, mass communication is almost always controlled by many gatekeepers who determine what messages

CULTURAL IDIOM

operate in a vacuum:
function as if there were
no others around

will be delivered to consumers, how they will be constructed, and when they will be delivered. Sponsors (whether corporate or governmental), editors, producers, reporters, and executives all have the power to influence mass messages in ways that don't affect most other types. Because of these and other unique characteristics, the study of mass communication raises special issues and deserves special treatment.

INVITATION
TO INSIGHT

Analyzing Your Communication Behavior

Prove for yourself that communication is both frequent and important by observing your interactions for a one-day period. Record every occasion in which you are involved in some sort of communication as it is defined on pages 2–4. Based on your findings, answer the following questions:

1. What percentage of your waking day is involved in communication?
2. What percentage of time do you spend communicating in the following contexts: intrapersonal, dyadic, small group, and public?
3. What percentage of your communication is devoted to satisfying each of the following types of needs: physical, identity, social, and practical? (Note that you might try to satisfy more than one type at a time.)

Based on your analysis, describe five to ten ways you would like to communicate more effectively. For each item on your list of goals, describe who is involved (e.g., "my boss," "people I meet at parties") and how you would like to communicate differently (e.g., "act less defensively when criticized," "speak up more instead of waiting for them to approach me"). Use this list to focus your studies as you read the remainder of this book.

FUNCTIONS OF COMMUNICATION

Now that we have a working understanding of the term *communication,* it is important to discuss why we will spend so much time exploring this subject. Perhaps the strongest argument for studying communication is its central role in our lives. The amount of time we spend communicating is staggering. In one study, researchers measured the amount of time a sample group of college students spent on various activities.[5] They found that the subjects spent an average of over 61 percent of their waking hours engaged in some form of communication. Whatever one's occupation, the results of such a study would not be too different. Most of us are surrounded by others, trying to understand them and hoping that they understand us: family, friends, coworkers, teachers, and strangers.

There's a good reason why we speak, listen, read, and write so much: Communication satisfies most of our needs.

Physical Needs

Communication is so important that it is necessary for physical health. In fact, evidence suggests that an absence of satisfying communication can even jeopardize life itself. Medical researchers have identified a wide range of hazards that result from a lack of close relationships.[6] For instance:

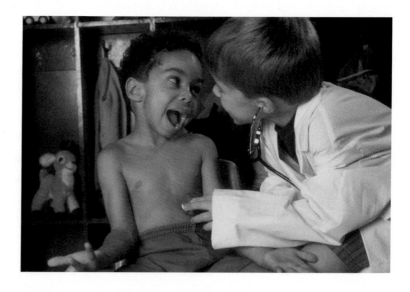

- People who lack strong relationships have two to three times the risk of early death, regardless of whether they smoke, drink alcoholic beverages, or exercise regularly.
- Terminal cancer strikes socially isolated people more often than those who have close personal relationships.
- Divorced, separated, and widowed people are five to ten times more likely to need hospitalization for mental problems than their married counterparts.
- Pregnant women under stress and without supportive relationships have three times more complications than pregnant women who suffer from the same stress but have strong social support.
- Socially isolated people are four times more susceptible to the common cold than those who have active social networks.[7]

Studies indicate that social isolation is a major risk factor contributing to coronary disease, comparable to physiological factors such as diet, cigarette smoking, obesity, and lack of physical activity.[8]

Research like this demonstrates the importance of having satisfying personal relationships. Remember: Not everyone needs the same amount of contact, and the quality of communication is almost certainly as important as the quantity. The important point here is that personal communication is essential for our well-being. To paraphrase a popular song, "people who need people" aren't "the luckiest people in the world," they're the *only* people!

Identity Needs

Communication does more than enable us to survive. It is the way—indeed, the *only* way—we learn who we are. As you'll read in Chapter 2, our sense of identity comes from the way we interact with other people. Are we smart or stupid, attractive or ugly, skillful or inept? The answers to these questions don't come from looking in the mirror. We decide who we are based on how others react to us.

Deprived of communication with others, we would have no sense of identity. In his book *Bridges, Not Walls,* John Stewart dramatically illustrates this fact by citing the case of the famous "Wild Boy of Aveyron," who spent his early childhood without any apparent human contact. The boy was discovered in January 1800 while digging for vegetables in a French village garden.[9] He showed no behaviors one would expect in a social human. The boy could not speak but uttered only weird cries. More significant than this absence of social skills was his lack of any identity as a human being. As author Roger Shattuck put it, "The boy had no human sense of being in the world. He had no sense of himself as a person related to other persons."[10] Only after the influence of a loving "mother" did the boy begin to behave—and, we can imagine, think of himself as a human. Contemporary stories support the essential role that communication plays in shaping identity. In 1970, authorities discovered a twelve-year-old girl (whom they called "Genie") who had spent virtually all her life in an otherwise empty, darkened bedroom with almost no human contact. The child could not speak and had no sense of herself as a person until she was removed from her family and "nourished" by a team of caregivers.[11]

Like Genie and the boy of Aveyron, each of us enters the world with little or no sense of identity. We gain an idea of who we are from the ways others define us. As Chapter 2 explains, the messages we receive in early childhood are the strongest, but the influence of others continues throughout life. Chapter 2 also explains how we use communication to manage the way others view us.

Some scholars have argued that we are most attracted to people who confirm our identity.[12] This confirmation can come in different forms, depending on the self-image of the communicator. People with relatively high self-esteem seek out others who confirm their value and, as much as possible, avoid those who treat them poorly. Conversely, people who regard themselves as unworthy may look for relationships in which others treat them badly. This principle offers one explanation for why some people maintain damaging or unsuccessful relationships. If you view yourself as a loser, you may associate with others who will confirm that self-perception. Of course, relationships can change a communicator's identity as well as confirm it. Supportive relationships can transform feelings of inadequacy into self-respect, and damaging ones can lower self-esteem.

The role of communication in shaping identity works in a second way. Besides others' messages shaping who we think we are, the messages we create often are attempts (some more conscious than others) to get others to view us the way we want to be seen. For example, the choices we make about how to dress and otherwise shape our appearance are almost always attempts to manage our identity.

Social Needs

Besides helping to define who we are, communication provides a vital link with others. Researchers and theorists have identified a range of social needs we satisfy by communicating: *pleasure* (e.g., "because it's fun," "to have a good time"); *affection* (e.g., "to help others," "to let others know I care"); *inclusion* (e.g., "because I need someone to talk to or be with," "because it makes me less lonely"); *escape* (e.g., "to put off doing something I should be doing"); *relaxation* (e.g., "because it allows me to unwind"); and *control* (e.g., "because I want someone to do something for me," "to get something I don't have").[13]

As you look at this list of social needs for communicating, imagine how empty your life would be if these needs weren't satisfied. Then notice that it would be impossible to fulfill them without communicating with others. Because relationships with others are so vital, some theorists have gone as far as to argue that communication is the primary goal of human existence. Anthropologist Walter Goldschmidt terms the drive for meeting social needs as the "human career."[14]

Whether the consequence of a mental attitude or a living condition, loneliness affects millions, usually for the worse. Death certificates read heart attack, cancer, or suicide; but coroners are missing the point. With no one to love or to love us, we tend to smoke, drink, brood, or simply cry ourselves into earlier graves.

Don E. Hamachek
Encounters with Others

Practical Needs

We shouldn't overlook the everyday, important functions that communication serves. Communication is the tool that lets us tell the hair stylist to take just a little off the sides, direct the doctor to where it hurts, and inform the plumber that the broken pipe needs attention *now!*

Beyond these obvious needs, a wealth of research demonstrates that communication is an important key to effectiveness in a variety of everyday settings. For example, a survey of over four hundred employers identified "communication skills" as the top characteristic that employers seek in job candidates.[15] It was rated as more important than technical competence, work experience, or academic background. In another survey, over 90 percent of the personnel officials at five hundred U.S. businesses stated that increased communication skills are needed for success in the twenty-first century.[16]

Communication is just as important outside of work. College roommates who are both willing and able to communicate effectively report higher satisfaction with one another than do those who lack these characteristics.[17] Married

---

UNDERSTANDING COMMUNICATION TECHNOLOGY

Uses of Answering Machines and Voice Mail

The first telephone answering machines were promoted as a tool for collecting messages that arrived when the phone's user wasn't available to receive them. Several decades later, answering machines (and their cousin, voice mail) serve many other uses. Notice how each of the following functions gives users a degree of control that isn't available in face-to-face or real-time telephone conversations.

Identity Management Your own experience will prove that answering machine greetings often reflect the public image their creators want to project. Some radiate friendliness, whereas others are businesslike, helpful, or humorous.

Call Screening Before answering machines, voice mail, and caller identification existed, phone users never knew who would be there when they answered a call. Now the technology provides a tool for sorting out desired calls from undesired ones.

Call Deterrence Beyond call screening, answering machine messages can discourage unwanted callers from even leaving a message. For example, most telephone solicitors hang up without leaving a message.

Time Shifting Even when they are available to take a phone call, answering machine users can record calls and return them later. Shifting lets users create phone-free blocks of time for work or social purposes, instead of forcing them to interrupt other activities to answer calls. The receiver gains control over his or her life.

Message Preparation Time shifting gives receivers time to plan answers to calls instead of being put on the spot. You can figure out how to gracefully decline an unwanted invitation, respond to an angry message without sounding defensive, or develop a counteroffer to a caller's proposal.

Information for Callers An answering machine greeting can provide callers with information that otherwise wouldn't be available. A business greeting might announce that the receiver is out of the office and tell callers who can be contacted for help. A residential greeting can inform callers that "Julie doesn't live here anymore" or that "the car has already been sold."

Users accustomed to using answering machines take these functions for granted. It's important to realize, though, that a simple kind of technology has significantly changed the way people communicate with one another.

couples who were identified as effective communicators reported happier relationships than did less skillful husbands and wives.[18] In school, the grade point averages of college students were related positively to their communication competence.[19] In "getting acquainted" situations, communication competence played a major role in whether a person was judged physically attractive, socially desirable, and good at the task of getting acquainted.[20]

"Richard, we need to talk. I'll E-mail you."

MODELING COMMUNICATION

So far we have introduced a basic definition of *communication* and seen the functions it performs. This information is useful, but it only begins to describe the process we will be examining throughout this book. One way to understand more about what it means to communicate is to look at some models that describe what happens when two or more people interact. As you will see, over the last half-century scholars have developed an increasingly accurate and sophisticated view of this process.

A Linear Model

Until about fifty years ago, researchers viewed communication as something that one person "does" to another.[21] In this **linear communication model**, communication is like giving an injection: a **sender encodes** ideas and feelings into some sort of **message** and then conveys them by means of a **channel** (speech, writing, and so on) into a **receiver**, who **decodes** the message (see Figure 1–1).

The linear model also introduces the concept of **noise**—a term used by social scientists to describe any forces that interfere with effective communication. Noise can occur at every stage of the communication process. Three types of noise can disrupt communication—external, physiological, and psychological. *External noise* (also called "*physical*") includes those factors outside the receiver that make it difficult to hear, as well as many other kinds of distractions. For instance, too much cigarette smoke in a crowded room might make it hard for you to pay attention to another person, and sitting in the rear of an auditorium might make a speaker's remarks unclear. External noise can disrupt

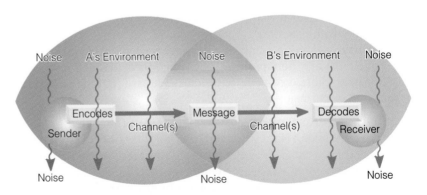

Figure 1–1   Linear Communication Model

communication almost anywhere in our model—in the sender, channel, message, or receiver. *Physiological noise* involves biological factors in the receiver or sender that interfere with accurate reception: illness, fatigue, and so on. *Psychological noise* refers to forces within a communicator that interfere with the ability to express or understand a message accurately. For instance, an outdoors person might exaggerate the size and number of the fish he caught in order to convince himself and others of his talents. In the same way, a student might become so upset upon learning that she failed a test that she would be unable (perhaps *unwilling* is a better word) to understand clearly where she went wrong.

A linear model shows that communicators often occupy different **environments**—fields of experience that help them understand others' behavior. In communication terminology, *environment* refers not only to a physical location but also to the personal experiences and cultural backgrounds that participants bring to a conversation.

Consider just some of the factors that might contribute to different environments:

- A might belong to one ethnic group and B to another;
- A might be rich and B poor;
- A might be rushed and B have nowhere to go;
- A might have lived a long, eventful life, and B might be young and inexperienced;
- A might be passionately concerned with the subject and B indifferent to it.

Environments aren't always obvious. For example, one study revealed that college students who have been enrolled in debate classes become more argumentative and verbally aggressive than those who have not been exposed to this environment.[22]

Notice how the model in Figure 1–1 shows that the environments of A and B overlap. This area represents the background that the communicators must have in common. As the shared environment becomes smaller, communication becomes more difficult. Consider a few examples in which different perspectives can make understanding difficult:

- Bosses who have trouble understanding the perspective of their employees will be less effective managers, and workers who do not appreciate the challenges of being a boss are more likely to be uncooperative (and probably less suitable for advancement).
- Parents who have trouble recalling their youth are likely to clash with their children, who have never known and may not appreciate the responsibility that comes with parenting.
- Members of a dominant culture who have never experienced how it feels to be "different" may not appreciate the concerns of people from nondominant cocultures, whose own perspectives make it hard to understand the cultural blindness of the majority.

Differing environments make understanding others challenging but certainly not impossible. Hard work and many of the skills described in this book provide ways to bridge the gap that separates all of us to a greater or lesser degree. For now, recognizing the challenge that comes from dissimilar environments is a good start. You can't solve a problem until you recognize that it exists.

SKILL BUILDER **Choosing the Most Effective Communication Channel**

Decide which communication channel would be most effective in each of the following situations. Be prepared to explain your answer.

1. In class, an instructor criticizes you for copying work from other sources when the work really was your own. You are furious, and you don't intend to accept the attack without responding. Which approach(es) would be best for you to use?
   a. Send your instructor an e-mail or write a letter explaining your objections.
   b. Telephone your instructor and explain your position.
   c. Schedule a personal meeting with your instructor.
2. You want to see whether the members of your extended family are able to view the photos you've posted on your family website. How can you find out how easily they can access the website?
   a. Demonstrate the website at an upcoming family get-together.
   b. Send them a link to the website as part of an e-mail.
   c. Phone family members and ask them about their ability to access websites.
3. You want to be sure the members of your office team are able to use the new voice mail system. Should you
   a. Send each employee an instruction manual for the system?
   b. Ask employees to send you e-mails or memos with any questions about the system?
   c. Conduct one or more training sessions where employees can try out the system and you can clear up any questions?
4. You've just been given two free tickets to tomorrow night's concert. How can you best find out whether your friend can go with you?
   a. Send her an e-mail and ask for a quick reply.
   b. Leave a message on your friend's answering machine asking her to phone you back.

UNDERSTANDING COMMUNICATION TECHNOLOGY

Choosing the Optimal Communication Channel

Different communication channels (such as e-mail, telephone, and face-to-face communication) can affect the way a receiver responds to a message. In certain contexts, the choice of a channel has symbolic meaning.[23] For example, a typewritten love letter just wouldn't have the same effect as a handwritten love letter. Likewise, ending a relationship by leaving a message on your ex-lover's answering machine would make a very different statement from delivering the bad news in person.

The information in the following table can help you answer some important questions about channel selection. Is it better to say, "I'm sorry" in person or over the phone? What channel is the best for expressing your anger? Should you approach the boss directly when asking for a raise or write a memo? Will asking a merchant for a refund work better than a personal request? Most communicators believe that face-to-face interaction is the best approach for personal communication.[24] As Table 1–1 suggests, each channel does have its individual characteristics.

TABLE 1–1 Factors to Consider When Choosing a Communication Channel

	Time required for feedback	Amount of information conveyed	Sender's control over how message is composed	Control over receiver's attention	Effectiveness for detailed messages
Face-to-Face	Immediate (after contact established)	Highest	Moderate	Highest	Weak
Telephone	Immediate (after contact established)	Vocal, but not visual	Moderate	Less than in face-to-face setting	Weakest
Voice Mail	Delayed	Vocal, but not visual	Higher (because receiver can't interrupt)	Low	Weak
E-Mail	Delayed	Lowest (text only, no formatting)	High	Low	Better
Hard Copy (e.g., handwritten or typed message)	Delayed	Words, numbers, and images, but no nonverbal cues	Highest	Low	Good

Adapted from R.B. Adler and J. M. Elmhorst, *Communicating at Work: Principles and Practices for Business and the Professions,* 7th ed. (New York: McGraw-Hill, 2002), pp. 32–33.

A Transactional Model

Despite its simplicity, the linear model doesn't do a very good job of representing the way most communication operates. The **transactional communication model** in Figure 1–2 presents a more accurate picture in several respects.

SIMULTANEOUS SENDING AND RECEIVING Although some types of mass communication (described in Appendix II) do flow in a one-way, linear manner, most types of personal communication are two-way exchanges.[25] The transactional model reflects the fact that we usually send and receive messages simultaneously. The roles of sender and receiver that

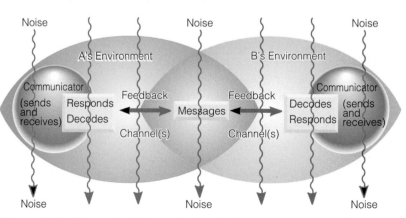

Figure 1–2 Transactional Communication Model

seemed separate in the linear model are now superimposed and redefined as those of "communicators." This new term reflects the fact that at a given moment we are capable of receiving, decoding, and responding to another person's behavior, while at the same time that other person is receiving and responding to ours.

Consider, for instance, the significance of a friend's yawn as you describe your romantic problems. Or imagine the blush you may see as you tell one of your raunchier jokes to a new acquaintance. Nonverbal behaviors like these show that most face-to-face communication is a two-way affair. The discernible response of a receiver to a sender's message is called **feedback.** Not all feedback is nonverbal, of course. Sometimes it is oral, as when you ask an instructor questions about an upcoming test or volunteer your opinion of a friend's new haircut. In other cases it is written, as when you answer the questions on a midterm exam or respond to a letter from a friend. Figure 1–2 makes the importance of feedback clear. It shows that most communication is, indeed, a two-way affair.

Another weakness of the traditional linear model is the questionable assumption that all communication involves encoding. We certainly do choose symbols to convey most verbal messages. But what about the many nonverbal cues that occur whether or not people speak: facial expressions, gestures, postures, vocal tones, and so on? Cues like these clearly do offer information about others, although they are often unconscious and thus don't involve encoding. For this reason, the transactional model replaces the term *encodes* in with the broader term *responds,* because it describes both intentional and unintentional actions that can be observed and interpreted.[26]

COMMUNICATION IS FLUID, NOT STATIC   Besides illustrating the simultaneous nature of face-to-face interaction, the example we just considered shows that it's difficult to isolate a single discrete "act" of communication from the events that precede and follow it. The way a friend or family member reacts to a sarcastic remark you make will probably depend on the way you have related to one another in the past. Likewise, the way you'll act toward each other in the future depends on the outcome of this conversation. Research conducted on partners in romantic relationships confirms the importance of context. As communication researcher Steve Duck put it, "Relationships are best conceived . . . as unfinished business".[27]

COMMUNICATION IS RELATIONAL, NOT INDIVIDUAL   The transactional model shows that communication isn't something we do *to* others; rather, it is something we do *with* them. In this sense, communication is rather like dancing—at least the kind of dancing we do with partners. Like dancing, communication depends on the involvement of a partner. And like good dancing, successful communication isn't something that depends just on the skill of one person. A great dancer who doesn't consider and adapt to the skill level of his or her partner can make both people look bad. In communication and dancing, even two talented partners don't guarantee success. When two talented dancers perform without coordinating their movements, the results feel bad to the dancers and look foolish to an audience. Finally, relational communication—like dancing—is a unique creation that arises out of the way in which the partners interact. The way you dance probably varies from one partner to another because of its cooperative, transactional nature. Likewise, the way you communicate almost certainly varies with different partners.

Psychologist Kenneth Gergen captures the relational nature of communication well when he points out how our success depends on interaction with others. As he says, ". . . one cannot be 'attractive' without others who are attracted, a 'leader' without others willing to follow, or a 'loving person' without others to affirm with appreciation."[28]

Because communication is transactional, it's often a mistake to suggest that just one person is responsible for a relationship. Consider the accompanying cartoon. Both Cathy and Irving had good intentions, and both probably could have handled the situation better. As the humorous outcome shows, trying to pin the blame for a disappointing outcome on one person or the other is fruitless and counterproductive. It would have been far better to ask, "How did *we* handle this situation poorly, and what can *we* do to make it better?"

The transactional nature of communication shows up in school, where teachers and students influence one another's behavior. For example, teachers who regard some students negatively may treat them with subtle or overt disfavor. As a result, these students are likely to react to their teachers' behavior negatively, which reinforces the teachers' original attitudes and expectations.[29] It isn't necessary to resolve the "who started it" issue here to recognize that the behaviors of teachers and students are part of a transactional relationship.

The transactional character of communication also figures dramatically in relationships between parents and their children. We normally think of "good parenting" as a skill that some people possess and others lack. We judge the ability of a mother and father in terms of how well their children turn out. In truth, the question of good parenting isn't quite so clear. Research suggests that the quality of interaction between parents and children is a two-way affair, that children influence parents just as much as the other way around.[30] For example, children who engage in what social scientists call "problematic behavior" evoke more high-control responses from their parents than do cooperative children. By contrast, youngsters with mild temperaments are less likely to provoke coercive reactions by their parents than are more aggressive children. Parents with low self-esteem tend to send more messages that weaken the self-esteem of their children, who in turn are likely to act in ways that make the parents feel even worse about themselves. Thus, a mutually reinforcing cycle arises in which parents and children shape one another's feelings and behavior. In cases like this it's at least difficult and probably impossible to identify who is the "sender" and who is the "receiver" of messages. It's more accurate to acknowledge that parents and children—just like husbands and wives, bosses and employees, teachers and students, or any other people who communicate with one another—act in ways that mutually influence one another. The transactional nature of relation-

CULTURAL IDIOM

pin the blame: claim the fault lies with

ships is worth reemphasizing: We don't communicate *to* others, we communicate *with* them.

By now you can see that a transactional model of communication should be more like a motion picture film than a gallery of still photographs. Although Figure 1–2 does a fair job of picturing the phenomenon we call communication, an animated version in which the environments, communicators, and messages constantly change would be an even better way of capturing the process.

COMMUNICATION COMPETENCE: WHAT MAKES AN EFFECTIVE COMMUNICATOR?

It's easy to recognize good communicators, and even easier to spot poor ones. But what are the characteristics that distinguish effective communicators from their less successful counterparts? Answering this question has been one of the leading challenges for communication scholars.[31] Although all the answers aren't yet in, research has identified a great deal of important and useful information about communication competence.

Communication Competence Defined

Defining **communication competence** isn't as easy as it might seem. Although scholars are still struggling to agree on a precise definition, most would agree that effective communication involves achieving one's goals in a manner that, ideally, maintains or enhances the relationship in which it occurs.[32] This definition may seem both vague and verbose, but a closer look shows that it suggests several important characteristics of communication competence.

THERE IS NO "IDEAL" WAY TO COMMUNICATE   Your own experience shows that a variety of communication styles can be effective. Some very successful people are serious, whereas others use humor; some are gregarious, whereas others are quiet; and some are straightforward, whereas others hint diplomatically. Just as there are many kinds of beautiful music and art, there are many kinds of competent communication.

The type of communication that succeeds in one situation might be a colossal blunder in another. The joking insults you routinely trade with a friend might be insensitive and discouraging if he or she had just suffered a personal setback. The language you use with your peers might offend a family member, and last Saturday night's romantic approach would probably be out of place at work on Monday morning. For this reason, being a competent communicator requires flexibility in understanding what approach is likely to work best in a given situation.[33]

Cultural differences also illustrate the principle that there is no single model of competence. What qualifies as competent behavior in one culture might be completely inept, or even offensive, in another.[34] On an obvious level, customs like belching after a meal or appearing nude in public, that might be appropriate in some parts of the world, would be considered outrageous in others. But there are more subtle differences in competent communication. For example, qualities like being self-disclosing and speaking clearly that are valued in the United States are likely to be considered overly aggressive and insensitive in many Asian cultures, where subtlety and indirectness are considered important.[35] Even within a single society, members of various cocultures may have different notions of appropriate behavior. One study revealed that ideas of how good friends should communicate varied from one ethnic group to another.[36] As a group, Latinos valued relational support most highly, whereas African Americans valued respect and acceptance. Asian Americans emphasized a caring, positive exchange of ideas, and Anglo Americans prized friends who recognized their needs as individuals. Findings like these mean that there can be no sure-fire list of rules or tips that will guarantee your success as a communicator. They also suggest that competent communicators are able to adapt their style to suit the individual and cultural preferences of others.[37]

Because many behaviors can work in a given situation, it's a mistake to suggest that any single approach is superior to others. Throughout this book, you will be introduced to a variety of communication skills. Although all of them are likely to be effective at one time or another, they aren't meant to replace other approaches that you already use. The skills you learn from this book will broaden your repertoire of choices about how to communicate. When you combine them with other approaches, you'll be likely to recognize a change for the better in your interactions with others.

COMPETENCE IS SITUATIONAL   Because competent behavior varies so much from one situation and person to another, it's a mistake to think that communication competence is a trait that a person either possesses or lacks. It's more accurate to talk about *degrees* or *areas* of competence.[38] You and the people you know are probably quite competent in some areas and less so in others. You might deal quite skillfully with peers, for example, but feel clumsy interacting with people much older or younger, wealthier or poorer, or more or less attractive than yourself. In fact, your competence with one person may vary from one situation to another. This means that it's an overgeneralization to say, in a moment of distress, "I'm a terrible communicator!" It would be more accurate to say, "I didn't handle this situation very well, even though I'm better in others."

COMPETENCE IS RELATIONAL   Because communication is transactional, something we do with others rather than to them, behavior that is competent in one relationship isn't necessarily competent in others.

A fascinating study on relational satisfaction illustrates that what constitutes satisfying communication varies from one relationship to another.[39] Researchers Brent Burleson and Wendy Sampter hypothesized that people with sophisticated communication skills (such as managing conflict well, giving ego-support to others, and providing comfort to relational partners) would be better at maintaining friendships than would be less skilled communicators. To their surprise, the results did not support this hypothesis. In fact, friendships were most satisfying when partners possessed matching skill levels. Apparently, relational satisfaction arises in part when our style matches those of the people with whom we interact.

The same principle holds true in the case of jealousy. Researchers have uncovered a variety of ways by which people deal with jealousy in their relationships.[40] The ways included keeping closer tabs on the partner, acting indifferent, decreasing affection, talking the matter over, and acting angry. The

CULTURAL IDIOM

sure-fire: certain to succeed

keeping closer tabs on: paying close attention to

UNDERSTANDING DIVERSITY

Front Porch Etiquette in Lake Wobegon

In this excerpt from his book Lake Wobegon Days, *Garrison Keillor explains one facet of small-town Minnesota etiquette. This section illustrates the degree to which communication competence involves understanding unwritten rules, which often vary from one region or coculture to another.*

■ Even if you're screened from public view, it's polite to call out hello to passersby you know. It's up to them to stop or not. It's up to you to invite them in or not. The porch is a room of your house, not part of the yard. Only peddlers or certain ministers would barge right in.

■ If you say "Why don't you come up and sit for a bit?," it is customary for them to decline politely. If the invite was legit, it should be repeated.

■ An invite to the porch is not an invite to the house. Its terms are limited to a brief visit on the porch, no refreshments necessarily provided unless the occupants have such at hand.

■ When the host stands up and stretches or says, "Well—," the visitor should need no further signal that the visit has ended. Only an oaf would remain longer. If the host says, "You don't have to run, do you?," this is not a question but a pleasantry.

Garrison Keillor

researchers found that no type of behavior was effective or ineffective in every relationship. They concluded that approaches that work with some people would be harmful to others. Findings like these demonstrate that competence arises out of developing ways of interacting that work for you and for the other people involved.[41]

COMPETENCE CAN BE LEARNED   To some degree, biology is destiny when it comes to communication style.[42] Studies of identical and fraternal twins suggest that traits including sociability, anger, and relaxation seem to be partially a function of our genetic makeup. Fortunately, biology isn't the only factor that shapes how we communicate: Communication is a set of skills that anyone can learn. As children grow, their ability to communicate effectively develops. For example, older children can produce more sophisticated persuasive attempts than can younger ones.[43] Along with maturity, systematic education (such as the class in which you are now enrolled) can boost communicative competence. Even a modest amount of training can produce dramatic results. After only thirty minutes of instruction, one group of observers became significantly more effective in detecting deception in interviews.[44] Even without systematic training, it's possible to develop communication skills through the processes of trial-and-error and observation. We learn from our own successes and failures, as well as from observing other models—both positive and negative. One study revealed that the passage of time does lead to improved communication skill: College students' communication competence increases over their undergraduate studies.[45]

Characteristics of Competent Communicators

Although competent communication varies from one situation to another, scholars have identified several common denominators that characterize effective communication in most contexts.

CULTURAL IDIOM

common denominators: similar or alike features

A WIDE RANGE OF BEHAVIORS   Effective communicators are able to choose their actions from a wide range of behaviors. To understand the importance of having a large communication repertoire, imagine that someone you know repeatedly tells jokes—perhaps discriminatory ones—that you find offensive. You could respond to these jokes in a number of ways. You could:

■ Say nothing, figuring that the risks of bringing the subject up would be greater than the benefits.
■ Ask a third party to say something to the joke teller about the offensiveness of the jokes.
■ Hint at your discomfort, hoping that your friend would get the point.
■ Joke about your friend's insensitivity, counting on humor to soften the blow of your criticism.
■ Express your discomfort in a straightforward way, asking your friend to stop telling the offensive jokes, at least around you.
■ Simply demand that your friend stop.

With this choice of responses at your disposal (and you can probably think of others as well), you could pick the one that had the best chance of success. But if you were able to use only one or two of these responses when raising a delicate issue—always keeping quiet or always hinting, for example—your chances of success would be much smaller. Indeed, many poor communicators are easy to spot by their limited range of responses. Some are chronic jokers. Others, like the character in the nearby cartoon, are always belligerent. Still others are quiet in almost every situation. Like a piano player who knows only one tune or a chef who can prepare only a few dishes, these people are forced to rely on a small range of responses again and again, whether or not they are successful.

ABILITY TO CHOOSE THE MOST APPROPRIATE BEHAVIOR   Simply possessing a large array of communication skills isn't a guarantee of effectiveness. It's also necessary to know which of these skills will work best in a particular situation. Choosing the best way to send a message is rather like choosing a gift: What is appropriate for one person won't be appropriate for another one at all. This ability to choose the best approach is essential because a response that works well in one setting would flop miserably in another one.

Although it's impossible to say precisely how to act in every situation, there are at least three factors to consider when you are deciding which response to choose: the context, your goal, and the other person.

SKILL AT PERFORMING BEHAVIORS   After you have chosen the most appropriate way to communicate, it's still necessary to perform the required skills effectively. There is a big difference between knowing *about* a skill and being able to put it into practice. Simply being aware of alternatives isn't much help, unless you can skillfully put these alternatives to work.

Just reading about communication skills in the following chapters won't guarantee that you can start using them flawlessly. As with any other skills—playing a musical instrument or learning a sport, for example—the road to competence in communication is not a short one. You can expect that your

CULTURAL IDIOM

counting on:
depending on

soften the blow of:
ease the effect of

"I SAID, "I have trouble developing close relationships with people!" For cryin' out loud, clean out your ears, fathead!"

first efforts at communicating differently will be awkward. After some practice you will become more skillful, although you will still have to think about the new way of speaking or listening. Finally, after repeating the new skill again and again, you will find you can perform it without conscious thought.

EMPATHY/PERSPECTIVE TAKING   People have the best chance of developing an effective message when they understand the other person's point of view. And because others aren't always good at expressing their thoughts and feelings clearly, the ability to imagine how an issue might look from the other's point of view is an important skill. The value of taking the other's perspective suggests one reason why listening is so important. Not only does it help us understand others, but also it gives us information to develop strategies about how to best influence them. Because empathy is such an important element of communicative competence, much of Chapter 4 is devoted to this topic.

COGNITIVE COMPLEXITY   Cognitive complexity is the ability to construct a variety of frameworks for viewing an issue. Cognitive complexity is an ingredient of communication competence because it allows us to make sense of people using a variety of perspectives. For instance, imagine that a longtime friend seems to be angry with you. One possible explanation is that your friend is offended by something you've done. Another possibility is that something upsetting has happened in another part of your friend's life. Or perhaps nothing at all is wrong, and you're just being overly sensitive. Researchers have found that the ability to analyze the behavior of others in a variety of ways leads to greater "conversational sensitivity," increasing the chances of acting in ways that will produce satisfying results.[46]

SELF-MONITORING   Psychologists use the term *self-monitoring* to describe the process of paying close attention to one's behavior and using these observations to shape the way one behaves. Self-monitors are able to separate a part of their consciousness and observe their behavior from a detached viewpoint, making observations such as:

"I'm making a fool out of myself."
"I'd better speak up now."
"This approach is working well. I'll keep it up."

Chapter 2 explains how too much self-monitoring can be problematic. Still, people who are aware of their behavior and the impression it makes are more skillful communicators than people who are low self-monitors.[47] For example, they are more accurate in judging others' emotional states, better at remembering information about others, less shy, and more assertive. By contrast, low self-monitors aren't even able to recognize their incompetence. (Calvin, in the nearby cartoon, does a nice job of illustrating this

I witnessed recently a striking and barely believable example of such [inappropriate] behavior at a wedding ceremony. One of the guests said loud enough for those of us on my side of the chapel to hear, "Think it through, Jerry" just at the point where the rabbi had asked Jerry if he took this woman to be his lawful wedded wife, according to (no less) the laws of Moses and Israel. So far as I could tell, the wedding guest was not drunk or embittered. He merely mistook the synagogue for Shea Stadium . . .

Neil Postman
Crazy Talk, Stupid Talk

Calvin and Hobbes   by Bill Watterson

Source: CALVIN and HOBBES © 1994 Watterson. Distributed by UNIVERSAL PRESS SYNDICATE. Reprinted with permission. All Rights Reserved.

problem.) One study revealed that poor communicators were blissfully ignorant of their shortcomings and more likely to overestimate their skill than were better communicators.[48] For example, experimental subjects who scored in the lowest quartile on joke-telling skill were more likely than their funnier counterparts to grossly overestimate their sense of humor.

COMMITMENT TO THE RELATIONSHIP   One feature that distinguishes effective communication in almost any context is commitment. People who seem to care about the relationship communicate better than those who don't.[49] This concern shows up in commitment to the other person and to the message you are expressing.

SKILL
BUILDER

Increasing Your Communicative Competence

Prove for yourself that communication competence can be increased by following these steps.

1. Identify a situation in which you are dissatisfied with your present communication skill.
2. Identify at least three distinct, potentially successful approaches you might take in this situation that are different from the one you have taken in the past. If you are at a loss for alternatives, consider how other people you have observed (both real and fictional characters) have handled similar situations.
3. From these three alternatives, choose the one you think would work best for you.
4. Consider how you could become more skillful at performing your chosen approach. For example, you might rehearse it alone or with friends, or you might gain pointers from watching others.
5. Consider how to get feedback on how well you perform your new approach. For instance, you might ask friends to watch you. In some cases, you might even be able to ask the people involved how you did.

This systematic approach to increasing your communicative competence isn't the only way to change, but it is one way to take the initiative in communicating more effectively.

CLARIFYING MISCONCEPTIONS ABOUT COMMUNICATION

Having spent time talking about what communication is, we ought also identify some things it is not.[50] Recognizing some misconceptions is important, not only because they ought to be avoided by anyone knowledgeable about the subject, but also because following them can get you into trouble.

Communication Does Not Always Require Complete Understanding

Most people operate on the implicit but flawed assumption that the goal of all communication is to maximize understanding between communicators. Although some understanding is necessary for us to comprehend one another's thoughts, there are some types of communication in which understanding as we usually conceive it isn't the primary goal.[51] Consider, for example:

- *Social rituals.* "How's it going?" you ask. "Great," the other person replies. The primary goal in exchanges like these is mutual acknowledgment: There's obviously no serious attempt to exchange information.
- *Many attempts to influence others.* A quick analysis of most television commercials shows that they are aimed at persuading viewers to buy products, not to understand the content of the commercial. In the same way, many of our attempts at persuading another to act as we want don't involve a desire to get the other person to understand what we want—just to comply with our wishes.
- *Deliberate ambiguity and deception.* When you decline an unwanted invitation by saying "I can't make it," you probably want to create the impression that the decision is really beyond your control. (If your goal was to be perfectly clear, you might say, "I don't want to get together. In fact, I'd rather do almost anything than accept your invitation.") As Chapters 3 and 6 explain in detail, we often equivocate precisely because we want to obscure our true thoughts and feelings.
- *Coordinate action.* Conversations where satisfaction doesn't depend on full understanding. The term **coordination** has been used to describe situations in which participants interact smoothly, with a high degree of satisfaction but without necessarily understanding one another well.[52] Coordination without understanding can be satisfying in far more important situations. Consider the words "I love you." This is a phrase that can have many meanings: Among other things, it can mean, "I admire you," "I feel great affection for you," "I desire you," "I am grateful to you," "I feel guilty," "I want you to be faithful to me," or even "I hope *you* love *me*."[53] It's not hard to picture a situation in which partners gain great satisfaction—even over a lifetime—without completely understanding that the mutual love they profess actually is quite different for each of them. The cartoon on this page reflects the fact that better understanding can sometimes lead to *less* satisfaction. "You mean you mostly love me because I've been there for you? Hey, a *dog* is there for you!"

"My wife understands me"

At the conversational level, some scholars have compared coordinated communication to what musicians call "jamming."[54] In this sort of musical interaction, musicians play off one another, improvising melodies and riffs based on what others have contributed. There's no plan, and no attempt at understanding. Some conversations resemble this sort of jamming in several respects:

- *Coordination is more important than understanding.* The players in a jam session gain satisfaction from making music together. They focus on what they are creating together, not on understanding one another. In coordinated conversations, satisfaction comes principally from being together—laughing, joking, exchanging confidences, and telling stories. The act of conversation is more important than its content.
- *Participants follow rules.* Musicians agree on fundamentals such as the key in which they will play, the tempo, and the overall structure of the music. Communicators tacitly agree on things like the level of seriousness, amount of time they will spend, and what topics are off limits. They may not understand the content of one another's messages, but they do understand how to behave with one another.
- *Everyone gets to solo.* In jamming, each member gets a time to take the lead, with others following. Conversations work only when the participants engage in turn-taking, giving each other time to talk.
- *Sessions go to new places.* In musical jamming, every session is unique. Likewise, no two conversations are identical in words or tone. One person's decision about what to say and how to say it triggers the other's response, which in turn results in a unique reaction. The communication is truly transactional, as described earlier.
- *Jamming builds rapport.* Musicians who jam with one another build unspoken bonds. In the same way, communicators who converse smoothly with one another feel a connection—even if the topic isn't very important or the participants don't completely understand one another.[55]

CULTURAL IDIOM

off limits: barred to a designated group

Communication Is Not Always a Good Thing

For most people, belief in the value of communication rates somewhere close to parenthood in their hierarchy of important values. In truth, communication is neither good nor bad in itself. Rather, its value comes from the way it is used. In this sense, communication is similar to fire: Flames in the fireplace on a cold night keep you warm and create a cozy atmosphere, but the same flames can kill if they spread into the room. Communication can be a tool for expressing warm feelings and useful facts, but under different circumstances the same words and actions can cause both physical and emotional pain.

No Single Person Or Event Causes Another's Reaction

Although communicative skill can often make the difference between pleasant and unpleasant outcomes, it's a mistake to suggest that any single thing we say or do causes an outcome. Many factors play a role in how others will react to your communication in a single situation. Suppose, for example, that you lose your temper and say something to a friend that you regret as soon as the words escape your lips. Your friend's reaction will depend on a whole host of events besides your unjustified remark: her frame of mind at the moment (uptight or mellow), elements of her personality (judgmental or forgiving), your relational history (supportive or hostile), and her knowledge of any factors in your life that might have contributed to your unfair remark. Because communication is a transactional, ongoing, collaborative process, it's usually a mistake to think that any event occurs in a vacuum.

Communication Will Not Solve All Problems

"If I could just communicate better . . ." is the sad refrain of many unhappy people who believe that if they could just express themselves better, their relationships would improve. Though this is sometimes true, it's an exaggeration to say that communicating—even communicating clearly—is a guaranteed panacea.

Meanings Rest in People, Not Words

We hinted that meanings rest in people, not in words, when we said earlier that the symbols we use to communicate are arbitrary. It's a mistake to think that, just because you use a word in one way, others will do so, too.[56] Sometimes differing interpretations of symbols are easily caught, as when we might first take the statement "He's loaded" to mean the subject has had too much to drink, only to find out that he is quite wealthy. In other cases, however, the ambiguity of words and nonverbal behaviors isn't so apparent, and thus has more far-reaching consequences. Remember, for instance, a time when someone said to you, "I'll be honest," and only later did you learn that those words hid precisely the opposite fact. In Chapter 3 you'll read a great deal more about the problems that come from mistakenly assuming that meanings rest in words.

Communication Is Not Simple

Most people assume that communication is an aptitude that people develop without the need for training—rather like breathing. After all, we've been swapping ideas with one another since early childhood, and there are lots of people who communicate pretty well without ever having had a class on the subject. Though this picture of communication as a natural ability seems accurate, it's actually a gross oversimplification.[57]

Throughout history there have been cases of infants raised without human contact. In all these cases the children were initially unable to communicate with others when brought into society. Only after extensive teaching (and not even then in some cases) were they able to speak and understand language in ways we take for granted. But what about the more common cases of effective communicators who have had no formal training yet are skillful at creating and understanding messages? The answer to this question lies in the fact that not all education occurs in a classroom: Many people learn to communicate skillfully because they have been exposed to models of such behavior by those around them. This principle of modeling explains why children who grow up in homes with stable relationships between family members have a greater chance of developing such relationships themselves. They know how to do so because they've seen effective communication in action.

Does the existence of these good communicators mean that certain people don't need courses like the one you're taking? Hardly. Even the best communicators aren't perfect: They often suffer the frustration of being unable to get a message across effectively, and they frequently misunderstand others. Furthermore, even the most successful people you know can probably identify ways in which their relationships could profit by better communication. These facts show that communication skills are rather like athletic ability: Even the most inept of us can learn to be more effective with training and practice, and those who are talented can always become better.

More Communication Is Not Always Better

Although it's certainly true that not communicating enough is a mistake, there are also situations when *too much* communication is a mistake. Sometimes excessive communication simply is unproductive, as when we "talk a problem to death," going over the same ground again and again without making any headway. And there are times when communicating too much can actually aggravate a problem. We've all had the experience of "talking ourselves into a hole"—making a bad situation worse by pursuing it too far. As McCroskey and Wheeless put it, "More and more negative communication merely leads to more and more negative results."[58]

"I'm so glad we had this little talk, Earl!"

There are even times when *no* communication is the best course. Any good salesperson will tell you that it's often best to stop talking and let the customer think about the product. And when two people are angry and hurt, they may say things they don't mean and will later regret. At times like these it's probably best to spend a little time cooling off, thinking about what to say and how to say it.

One key to successful communication, then, is to share an *adequate* amount of information in a *skillful* manner. Teaching you how to decide what information is adequate and what constitutes skillful behavior is one major goal of this book.

ETHICAL CHALLENGE

To Communicate or Not to Communicate?

The explanations on pages 23–25 make it clear that communication is not a panacea. Explaining yourself and understanding others will not solve all problems; in fact, sometimes more communication leads to more problems. Think of an occasion (real or hypothetical) where more interaction would make matters worse. Imagine that the other person (or people) involved in this situation is (are) urging you to keep the channels of communication open. You know that if you do communicate more the situation will deteriorate, yet you don't want to appear uncooperative. What should you do?

SUMMARY

This chapter began by defining *communication* as it will be examined in *Understanding Human Communication*: the process of human beings responding to the symbolic behavior of other persons.

It introduced four communication contexts that will be covered in the rest of the book: intrapersonal, dyadic, small group, and public. The chapter also identified several types of needs that communication satisfies: physical, identity, social, and practical.

A linear and a transactional communication model were developed, demonstrating the superiority of the transactional model in representing the process-oriented nature of human interaction.

The chapter went on to explore the difference between effective and ineffective exchanges by discussing communication competence, showing that there is no single correct way to behave and that competence is situational and relational in nature. Competent communicators were described as being able to choose and perform appropriately from a wide range of behaviors, as being cognitively complex self-monitors who can take the perspective of others and who have commitment to important relationships.

After spending most of the chapter talking about what communication *is*, the chapter concluded by discussing what it is *not* by refuting several common misconceptions. It demonstrated that communication is not always a good thing that will solve every problem. It showed that more communication is not always better; that meanings are in people, not in words; and that communication is neither simple nor easy.

RESOURCES

Print

Coupland, Nikolas, Howard Giles, and John M. Wiemann, eds. *Miscommunication and Problematic Talk.* Newbury Park, CA: Sage, 1991.

This collection of readings explores the many ways in which communication can be unsuccessful. Chapters focus on communication problems involving gender, age, physical disabilities, and culture. Other selections look at communication problems in different settings, such as medical, legal, and organizational.

Heath, Robert L., and Jennings Bryant. *Human Communication Theory and Research,* 2nd ed. Mawah, NJ: Erlbaum, 2000.

Separate chapters describe the body of research and theorizing on communication competence and new communication technologies.

Infante, Dominic A., Andrew S. Rancer, and Deanna F. Womack. *Building Communication Theory,* 4th ed. Prospect Heights, IL: Waveland Press, 1999.

This readable survey introduces the theoretical foundations upon which communication scholars base their research and advice about everyday interaction. A useful appendix describing communication research methods will help readers make sense of the experiments reported in major professional journals.

Stiebel, David. *When Talking Makes Things Worse! Resolving Problems When Communication Fails.* Kansas City, MO: Andrews and McMeel, 1997.

The author offers many examples from his experience as advisor to Fortune 500 companies, showing how even clear communication can create problems instead of solving them. Stiebel goes on to offer guidelines for deciding when talking will only make matters worse.

Films
Communication as a Defining Human Characteristic

The Wild Child (1969). Not rated. French with subtitles.

Jean-Pierre Cargol portrays the title character, a boy who grew up alone in the French woods, as a wild animal might, after being abandoned in early childhood. The film's director, Francois Truffaut, cast himself as the doctor who works with the boy to give him a sense of human identity—a self-concept—and the ability to communicate. Based closely on the true case discussed on page 8–9.

The Importance of Communication

Cast Away (2000). Rated PG.

Chuck Noland (Tom Hanks) is a hard-driving executive who is the only survivor of a plane crash.

Stranded for what may be the rest of his life on an otherwise uninhabited Pacific island, he creates a "companion" by drawing a face on a volleyball and naming him Wilson (based on the name of the sporting goods company that made the volleyball). He holds animated conversations with Wilson. Chuck seemed to be losing hope, faith, and the will to live. Even though Chuck is hungry, thirsty, sunbaked, and in physical pain, he retains his will to go on because he keeps talking and "interacting" to meet his communication needs.

Although the story is fictional, and the turning of a volleyball into a friend is a rather far-fetched and desperate means for meeting one's needs, many people can recall creating imaginary friends as a child, or holding "conversations" with others with whom they would like to speak but can't. As this chapter suggests, our physical, identity, and social needs are met through interpersonal communication—and for Chuck, communicating with something was better than communicating with no one. It also may have saved his life.

Communication as a Transactional Process

Parenthood (1989). Rated PG-13.

This serious, hilarious, poignant, chaotic film looks into the lives of a four-generation family, the mood of which is captured perfectly by the grandmother, who characterizes it as a roller-coaster ride—full of exhilarating highs and gut-wrenching plunges. Frank (Jason Robards) is a gruff patriarch who constantly badgers his mild-mannered wife Marilyn (Eileen Ryan). Each of their four children's families lives its own dramas. Gil (Steve Martin) and his wife Karen (Mary Steenburgen) are committed to living the dream of a wholesome life in the face of one obstacle after another: a neurotic nine-year-old and his head-banging three-year-old brother, an unexpected pregnancy, and the prospect of losing their income. Sister-in-law Helen (Diane Weist) is a single mom who is struggling with her ex-husband, who ran off with another woman, her secretive son (Joaquin Phoenix), her strong-willed teenage daughter Julie (Martha Plimpton), and Julie's boyfriend Tod (Keanu Reeves), whose dream is to become drag car racer. Susan (Harley Jane Kozak) and Nathan (Rick Moranis) are obsessed with raising their preschool

daughter to become a genius, so they bombard her with foreign languages, classical music, and literature. The last son, Larry (Tom Hulse), is a fast-talking swindler who takes advantage of his father's fondness by using the old man's gifts to pay off his gambling debts and finance futile get-rich-quick schemes.

We see how the life of each character is affected by the actions of the others. By the end of the film it is clear that each person's communication is both the cause and the effect of interactions with others—that communication is truly something we do *with* others, not *to* them.

Ordinary People (1980). Rated R.

Conrad (Timothy Hutton) is recovering from a suicide attempt triggered by guilt over surviving an accident in which his brother died. His low self-esteem is also shaped by the (correct) perception that his mother, Beth (Mary Tyler Moore), doesn't seem to love him, that she loved only his dead brother. The well-intentioned father, Calvin (Donald Sutherland), is ready to get on with his life but is caught in the middle between his wife and son. Conrad seeks help from a psychiatrist named Berger (Judd Hirsch), and after a difficult beginning he manages to get in touch with the source of his guilt. Despite this breakthrough, the film does not have a neat, happy ending: Calvin confronts Beth about her emotional sterility, and she leaves home. In the final scene, Conrad and Calvin affirm their love for each other.

Misconceptions About Communication

When a Man Loves a Woman (1994). Rated R.

Alice Green (Meg Ryan) is an alcoholic who has hidden her secret from everyone, even her husband, Michael (Andy Garcia). Only when she slaps their daughter and passes out does Alice realize how grave her problem has become. She confesses her secret to Michael—much to his shock and surprise—then checks into an alcohol treatment program. In the program, she learns to identify and talk about her thoughts, feelings, fears, and needs.

In some movies, this would lead to a happy ending. Instead, Alice's new levels of self-awareness and disclosure threaten her relationship with Michael. Their family system is thrown into upheaval, and his co-dependence is revealed. As

Alice describes some of her deepest fears, Michael is stunned and asks, "How come we haven't talked about this?" She replies, "How come we haven't talked about a lot of things?" Indeed, it seems the more they talk, the worse things get. After weeks of expressing hurt and anger at each other, they decide to separate.

There is hope in the movie's final scene. Michael acknowledges that they need different, not more, communication—specifically, he says, he needs to become a better listener. Although it is likely that listening will help him understand her better, anyone watching their relationship knows it will not solve all their problems.

CONTENTS

KEY TERMS

empathy
face
facework
impression management
narratives
perceived self
perception checking
personality
presenting self
reflected appraisal
self-concept
self-esteem
self-fulfilling prophecy
self-serving bias
significant others
sympathy

**AFTER STUDYING
THE MATERIAL
IN THIS CHAPTER . . .**

YOU SHOULD UNDERSTAND:

1. How common perceptual tendencies and situational factors influence perception.

2. The influence of culture on perception and the self-concept.

3. The importance of empathy in communication.

4. The communicative influences that shape the self-concept.

5. How self-fulfilling prophecies influence behavior.

6. How the process of identity management can result in presentation of multiple selves.

7. The reasons for and the ethical dimensions of identity management.

YOU SHOULD BE ABLE TO:

1. Identify how the perceptual tendencies in this chapter have led you to develop distorted perceptions of yourself and others.

2. Use perception checking to be more accurate in your perceptions of others' behavior.

3. Identify the ways you influence the self-concepts of others and the ways significant others influence your self-concept.

4. Identify the communication-related self-fulfilling prophecies that you have imposed on yourself, that others have imposed on you, and that you have imposed on others.

5. Describe the various identities you attempt to create and the ethical merit of your identity management strategies.

PERCEPTION, THE SELF, AND COMMUNICATION

■ Two classmates, one black and the other white, are discussing their latest reading assignment in an American history class. "Malcolm X was quite a guy," the white student says sincerely to the black one. "You must be very proud of him." The black student is offended at what sounds like a condescending remark.

■ A student is practicing his first speech for a public address class with several friends. "This is a stupid topic," he laments. The others assure him that the topic is interesting and that the speech sounds good. Later in class he becomes flustered because he believes that his speech is awful. As a result of his unenthusiastic delivery, the student receives a low grade on the assignment.

■ In biology class, a shy but earnest student mistakenly uses the term *orgasm* instead of *organism* when answering the professor's question. The entire class breaks into raucous laughter. The student remains quiet for the remainder of the semester.

■ Despite her nervousness, a graduating student does her best to look and sound confident in a job interview. Although she leaves the session convinced she botched a big chance, a few days later she is surprised to receive a job offer.

Stories like these probably sound familiar. Yet behind this familiarity lie principles that affect our communication more than almost any others discussed in this book.

■ Two or more people often perceive the world in radically different ways, which presents major challenges for successful communicating.

■ The beliefs each of us holds about ourselves—our self-concept—have a powerful effect on our own communication behavior.

■ The messages we send can shape others' self-concepts and thus influence their communication.

■ The image we present to the world varies from one situation to another.

These simple truths play a role in virtually all the important messages we send and receive. The goal of this chapter is to demonstrate the significance of these truths by describing the nature of perception and showing how it influences the way we view ourselves and how we relate to others.

PERCEIVING OTHERS

Suppose you woke up tomorrow in another person's body. Imagine how different the world would seem if you were fifteen years older or younger, a member of the opposite sex or a different ethnic group, far more or less intelligent, vastly more attractive or ugly, more wealthy or poverty-stricken. It doesn't take much imagination to understand that the world feels like a different place to each of us, depending on our physical condition as well as our social and personal backgrounds.

Narratives and Perception

We all have our own story of the world, and often our story is quite different from those of others. A family member or roommate might think your sense of humor is inappropriate, whereas you think you're quite clever. You might blame an unsatisfying class on the professor, who you think is a long-winded bore. On the other hand, the professor might characterize the students as superficial and lazy and blame the class environment on them. (Chapter 3 will talk about the sort of name-calling embedded in the previous sentences.)

Social scientists call the personal stories that we and others create to make sense of our personal world **narratives.**[1] In a few pages we will look at how a tool called "perception checking" can help bridge the gap between different narratives. For now, though, the important point is that differing narratives can lead to problematic communication.

After they take hold, narratives offer a framework for explaining behavior and shaping future communication. One study of sense making in organizations illustrates how the process operates on the job.[2] Researchers located employees who had participated in office discussions about cases where a fellow worker had received "differential treatment" from management about matters such as time off, pay, or work assignments. The researchers then analyzed the conversations that employees held with fellow workers about the differential treatment. The analysis revealed that these conversations were the occasion in which workers created and reinforced the meaning of the employee's behavior and management's response. For example, consider the way workers made sense of Jane Doe's habit of taking late lunches. As Jane's coworkers discuss her behaviors, they might decide that her late lunches aren't fair—or they might agree that late lunches aren't a big deal. Either way, the coworker's narrative of office events *defines* those events. Once they are defined, coworkers tend to seek reinforcement for their perceptions by keeping a mental scorecard rating their fellow employees and management. ("Did you notice that Bob came in late again today?" "Did you notice that the boss chose Jane to go on that trip to New York?") Although most of us like to think we make judgments about others on our own, this research suggests that sense making is an *interactive* process. In other words, reality in the workplace and elsewhere isn't "out there"; rather, we create it with others through communication.

Research on long-term happy marriages demonstrates that shared narratives don't have to be accurate to be powerful.[3] Couples who report being happily married after fifty or more years seem to collude in a relational narrative that doesn't always jibe with the facts. They agree that they rarely have conflict, although objective analysis reveals that they have had their share of disagreements and challenges. Without overtly agreeing to do so, they choose to blame outside forces or unusual circumstances for problems instead of attributing responsibility to one another. They offer the most charitable interpretations of one another's behavior, believing that their spouse acts with good intentions when things don't go well. They seem willing to forgive, or even forget, transgressions. Examining this research, one scholar concludes:

> Should we conclude that happy couples have a poor grip on reality? Perhaps they do, but is the reality of one's marriage better known by outside onlookers than by the players themselves? The conclusion is evident. One key to a long happy marriage is to tell yourself and others that you have one and then to behave as though you do![4]

INVITATION TO INSIGHT

Exploring Narratives

Think about a situation where relational harmony is due to you and the other people involved sharing the same narrative. Then think about another situation where you and the other person use different narratives to describe the same situation. What are the consequences of having different narratives in this situation?

Common Perceptual Tendencies

Shared narratives may be desirable, but they can be hard to achieve. Some of the biggest problems that interfere with understanding and agreement arise from errors in what psychologists call *attribution*—the process of attaching meaning to behavior. We attribute meaning to both our own actions and to the actions of others, but we often use different yardsticks. Research has uncovered several perceptual errors that can lead to inaccurate attributions—and to troublesome communication.[5] By becoming aware of these errors, we can guard against them and avoid unnecessary conflicts.

WE OFTEN JUDGE OURSELVES MORE CHARITABLY THAN WE JUDGE OTHERS   In an attempt to convince ourselves and others that the positive face we show to the world is true, we tend to judge ourselves in the most generous terms possible. Social scientists have labeled this tendency the **self-serving bias.**[6] When others suffer, we often blame the problem on their personal qualities. On the other hand, when we suffer, we find explanations outside ourselves. Consider a few examples:

- When they botch a job, we might think they weren't listening well or trying hard enough; when we botch a job, the problem was unclear directions or not enough time.
- When he lashes out angrily, we say he's being moody or too sensitive; when we blow off steam, it's because of the pressure we've been under.
- When she gets caught speeding, we say she should have been more careful; when we get caught, we deny we were driving too fast or say, "Everybody does it."

The egocentric tendency to rate ourselves more favorably than others see us has been demonstrated experimentally.[7] In one study, members of a random sample of men were asked to rank themselves on their ability to get along with others.[8] Defying mathematical laws, all subjects—every last one—put themselves in the top half of the population. Sixty percent rated themselves in the top 10 percent of the population, and an amazing 25 percent believed they were in the top 1 percent. In the same study, 70 percent of the men ranked their leadership in the top 25 percent of the population, whereas only 2 percent thought they were below average. Sixty percent said they were in the top 25 percent in athletic abilities, whereas only 6 percent viewed themselves as below average.

Evidence like this suggests how uncharitable attitudes toward others can affect communication. Your harsh opinions of others can lead to judgmental messages, and self-serving defenses of your own actions can result in a defensive response when others question your behavior.

WE ARE INFLUENCED BY WHAT IS MOST OBVIOUS   Every time we encounter another person, we are bombarded with more information than we can possibly manage. You can appreciate this by spending two or three minutes just reporting on what you can observe about another person through your five senses. ("Now I see you blinking your eyes . . . Now I notice you smiling . . . Now I hear you laugh and then sigh . . . Now I notice you're wearing a red shirt . . .") You will find that the list seems almost endless and that every time you seem to near the end, a new observation presents itself.

Faced with this tidal wave of sense data, we need to whittle down the amount of information we will use to make sense of others. There are three fac-

CULTURAL IDIOM

yardsticks: standards of comparison

lashes out: attacks with words

blow off steam: release excess energy or anger

tors that cause us to notice some messages and ignore others. For example, we pay attention to stimuli that are *intense* (loud music, brightly dressed people), *repetitious* (dripping faucets, persistent people), or *contrastive* (a normally happy person who acts grumpy or vice versa). *Motives* also determine what information we select from our environment. If you're anxious about being late for a date, you'll notice whatever clocks may be around you; if you're hungry, you'll become aware of any restaurants, markets, and billboards advertising food in your path. Motives also determine how we perceive people. For example, someone on the lookout for a romantic adventure will be especially aware of attractive potential partners, whereas the same person at a different time might be oblivious to anyone but police or medical personnel in an emergency.

If intense, repetitious, or contrastive information were the most important thing to know about others, there would be no problem. But the most noticeable behavior of others isn't always the most important. For example:

- When two children (or adults, for that matter) fight, it may be a mistake to blame the one who lashes out first. Perhaps the other one was at least equally responsible, by teasing or refusing to cooperate.
- You might complain about an acquaintance whose malicious gossiping or arguing has become a bother, forgetting that, by previously tolerating that kind of behavior, you have been at least partially responsible.
- You might blame an unhappy working situation on the boss, overlooking other factors beyond her control such as a change in the economy, the policy of higher management, or demands of customers or other workers.

Source: © Zits Partnership. Reprinted with special permission of King Features Syndicate.

WE CLING TO FIRST IMPRESSIONS, EVEN IF WRONG   Labeling people according to our first impressions is an inevitable part of the perception process. These labels are a way of making interpretations. "She seems cheerful." "He seems sincere." "They sound awfully conceited."

If they're accurate, impressions like these can be useful ways of deciding how to respond best to people in the future. Problems arise, however, when the labels we attach are inaccurate, because after we form an opinion of someone, we tend to hang on to it and make any conflicting information fit our image.

Suppose, for instance, you mention the name of your new neighbor to a friend. "Oh, I know him," your friend replies. "He seems nice at first, but it's all an act." Perhaps this appraisal is off-base. The neighbor may have changed since your friend knew him, or perhaps your friend's judgment is simply unfair. Whether the judgment is accurate or not, after you accept your friend's evaluation, it will probably influence the way you respond to the neighbor. You'll look for examples of the insincerity you've heard about—and you'll probably find them. Even if the neighbor were a saint, you would be likely to interpret his behavior in ways that fit your expectations. "Sure he *seems* nice," you might think, "but it's probably just a front." Of course, this sort of suspicion can create a self-fulfilling prophecy, transforming a genuinely nice person into someone who truly becomes an undesirable neighbor as he reacts to your suspicious behavior.

Given the almost unavoidable tendency to form first impressions, the best advice we can offer is to keep an open mind and be willing to change your opinion as events prove that the first impressions were mistaken.

WE TEND TO ASSUME THAT OTHERS ARE SIMILAR TO US   People commonly imagine that others possess the same attitudes and motives that they do. For example, research shows that people with low self-esteem imagine that others view them unfavorably, whereas people who like themselves imagine that others like them, too.[9] The frequently mistaken assumption that others' views are similar to our own applies in a wide range of situations. For example:

- You've heard a raunchy joke that you found funny. You might assume that it won't offend a somewhat conservative friend. It does.
- You've been bothered by an instructor's tendency to get off the subject during lectures. If you were a professor, you'd want to know if anything you were doing was creating problems for your students, so you decide that your instructor will probably be grateful for some constructive criticism. Unfortunately, you're wrong.
- You lost your temper with a friend a week ago and said some things you regret. In fact, if someone said those things to you, you would consider the relationship finished. Imagining that your friend feels the same way, you avoid making contact. In fact, your friend feels that he was partly responsible and has avoided you because he thinks you're the one who wants to end things.

Examples like these show that others don't always think or feel the way we do and that assuming that similarities exist can lead to problems. For example, one study revealed that men evaluate women who initiate first dates as being more interested in sex than do the women who initiated the dates.[10]

How can you find out the other person's real position? Sometimes by asking directly, sometimes by checking with others, and sometimes by making an educated guess after you've thought the matter out. All these alternatives are better than simply assuming that everyone would react the way you do.

WE TEND TO FAVOR NEGATIVE IMPRESSIONS OVER POSITIVE ONES What do you think about Harvey? He's handsome, hardworking, intelligent, and honest. He's also very conceited.

Did the last quality mentioned make a difference in your evaluation? If it did, you're not alone. Research shows that when people are aware of both the positive and negative traits of another, they tend to be more influenced by the negative traits. In one study, for example, researchers found that job interviewers were likely to reject candidates who revealed negative information even when the total amount of information was highly positive.[11]

Sometimes this attitude makes sense. If the negative quality clearly outweighs any positive ones, you'd be foolish to ignore it. A surgeon with shaky hands and a teacher who hates children, for example, would be unsuitable for their jobs whatever their other virtues. But much of the time it's a bad idea to pay excessive attention to negative qualities and overlook positive ones. This is the mistake some people make when screening potential friends or dates. They find some who are too outgoing or too reserved, others who aren't intelligent enough, and still others who have the wrong sense of humor. Of course, it's important to find people you truly enjoy, but expecting perfection can lead to much unnecessary loneliness.

WE BLAME INNOCENT VICTIMS FOR THEIR MISFORTUNES The blame we assign for misfortune depends on who the victim is. When others suffer, we often blame the problem on their personal qualities. On the other hand, when we suffer, we find explanations outside ourselves. Consider once more these telling examples:

- When *they* botch a job, we might think they weren't listening well or trying hard enough; when *we* botch a job, the problem was unclear directions or not enough time.
- When *he* lashes out angrily, we say he's being moody or too sensitive; when *we* lash out, it's because of the pressure we've been under.
- When *she* gets caught speeding, we say she should have been more careful; when *we* get caught, we deny we were driving too fast or say, "Everybody does it."

There are at least two explanations for this kind of behavior. Because most of us want other people to approve of us, we defend ourselves by finding explanations for our own problems that make us look good. Basically what we're doing here is saying, "It's not *my* fault." And because looking good is so often a personal goal, putting others down can be a cheap way to boost our own self-esteem, stating in effect, "I'm better than he is."

Don't misunderstand: We don't always commit the kind of perceptual errors described in this section. Sometimes, for instance, people *are* responsible for their misfortunes, and sometimes our problems are not our fault. Likewise, the most obvious interpretation of a situation may be the correct one. Nonetheless, a large amount of research has proved again and again that our perceptions of others are often distorted in the ways listed here. The moral, then, is clear: Don't assume that your first judgment of a person is accurate.

Situational Factors Influencing Perception

Along with the attribution errors described in the preceding pages, we consider a whole range of additional factors when trying to make sense of others' behavior.

I have heard students say things like, "It was John's fault, his speech was so confusing nobody could have understood it." Then, two minutes later, the same student remarked, "It wasn't my fault, what I said could not have been clearer. John must be stupid." Poor John! He was blamed when he was the sender and when he was the receiver. John's problem was that he was the other person, and that's who is always at fault.

Stephen W. King

Perceiving Others and Yourself

1. You can gain appreciation for the way perceptual errors operate by making two attributions for each situation that follows: Develop your first explanation for the behavior as if you were the person involved. Your second explanation for the behavior should be developed as if someone you dislike were the person described.

   - Dozing off in class
   - Getting angry at a customer on the job
   - Dressing sloppily in public
   - Being insensitive to a friend's distress
   - Laughing at an inappropriate or offensive joke

2. If your explanations for these behaviors differ, ask yourself why. Are the differing attributions justifiable, or do they support the tendency to make the perceptual errors listed on pages 34–37?

3. How do these perceptual errors operate in making judgments about others' behavior, especially when those others come from different social groups?

Relational Satisfaction   The behavior that seems positive when you are in a satisfying relationship might seem completely different when the relationship isn't going well. For example, you might regard the quirks of a housemate with amusement when things are going smoothly, but find them very annoying when you are unhappy with his other behavior. (In this sense, our willingness to tolerate the potentially bothersome behavior of people we like is rather like the amusement we get when a beloved cat climbs the Christmas tree or the dog sneaks a hamburger when nobody is looking.)

Degree of Involvement with the Other Person   We sometimes view people with whom we have or seek a relationship more favorably than those whom we observe from a detached perspective.[12] One study revealed how this principle operates in everyday life. A group of male subjects was asked to critique presentations by women who allegedly owned restaurants. Half of these presentations were designed to be competent and half incompetent. The men who were told they would be having a casual date with the female speakers judged their presentations—whether competent or not—more highly than did those who didn't expect any involvement with the speakers.[13]

Past Experience   What meaning have similar events held? If, for example, you've been gouged by landlords in the past, you might be skeptical about an apartment manager's assurances that careful housekeeping will assure the refund of your cleaning deposit.

Expectations   Anticipation shapes interpretations. If you imagine that your boss is unhappy with your work, you'll probably feel threatened by a request to "see me in my office first thing Monday morning." On the other hand, if you imagine that your work will be rewarded, your weekend will probably be pleasant.

CULTURAL IDIOM

been gouged by: was charged an excessive amount

Social Roles   A number of social relationships can influence the way we perceive others. For example, one recent study of communication in the workplace revealed that observers—both men and women—interpret facial expressions differently depending on their status relative to the other person.[14] Subjects were shown a photo of someone and asked to judge how that person was feeling. When the person pictured was a manager, subjects saw less fear than when they were told that the person pictured was an employee. Gender also makes a difference in how we perceive others: Seeing a woman and a man pose an anger display of the same intensity, subjects saw more anger and less fear in a man's expression than in a woman's, probably because gender stereotypes of emotion guided their interpretations.

Knowledge   If you know that a friend has just been jilted by a lover or been fired from a job, you'll interpret his aloof behavior differently than you would if you were unaware of what had happened. If you work in an environment where socializing is common and colleagues have friendly relationships, you may be less likely to perceive a fellow worker's remark as sexual harassment than you would if you were in an unfamiliar environment.[15]

Self-Concept   When you're feeling insecure, the world is a very different place from the world you experience when you're confident. For example, the recipient's self-concept has proved to be the single greatest factor in determining whether people who are on the receiving end of being teased interpret the teaser's motives as being friendly or hostile and whether they respond with comfort or defensiveness.[16] The same goes for happiness and sadness or any other opposing emotions. The way we feel about ourselves strongly influences how we interpret others' behavior.

Perception and Culture

Perceptual differences make communication challenging enough between members of the same culture. But when communicators come from different cultures, the potential for misunderstandings is even greater. Culture provides a perceptual filter that influences the way we interpret even the simplest events. This fact was demonstrated in studies exploring the domination of vision in one eye over the other.[17] Researchers used a binocular-like device that projects different images to each eye. The subjects were twelve Americans and twelve Mexicans. Each was presented with ten pairs of photographs, each pair containing one picture from U.S. culture (e.g., a baseball game) and one from Mexican culture (e.g., a bullfight). After viewing each pair of images, the subjects reported what they saw. The results clearly indicated the power of culture to influence perceptions: Subjects had a strong tendency to see the image from their own background.

The same principle causes people from different cultures to interpret similar events in different ways. Blinking while another person talks may be hardly noticeable to North Americans, but the same behavior is considered impolite in Taiwan. A "V" sign made with two fingers means "victory" in most of the Western world—as long as the palm is facing out. But in some European countries the same sign with the palm facing in roughly means "shove it." The beckoning finger motion that is familiar to Americans is an insulting gesture in most Middle and Far Eastern countries.

Even beliefs about the very value of talk differ from one culture to another.[18] North American culture views talk as desirable and uses it to achieve social purposes as well as to perform tasks. Silence in conversational situations has a negative value in this culture. It is likely to be interpreted as lack of interest, unwillingness to communicate, hostility, anxiety, shyness, or a sign of interpersonal incompatibility. Westerners are uncomfortable with silence, which they find embarrassing and awkward. Furthermore, the *kind* of talk that Westerners admire is characterized by straightforwardness and honesty. Being indirect or vague—"beating around the bush," it might be labeled—has a negative connotation.

On the other hand, most Asian cultures discourage the expression of thoughts and feelings. Silence is valued, as Taoist sayings indicate: "In much talk there is great weariness," or "One who speaks does not know; one who knows does not speak." Unlike Westerners, who are uncomfortable with silence, Japanese and Chinese believe that remaining quiet is the proper state when there is nothing to be said. To Easterners, a talkative person is often considered a show-off or insincere. And when an Asian does speak up on social matters, the message is likely to be phrased indirectly to "save face" for the recipient.

It is easy to see how these different views of speech and silence can lead to communication problems when people from different cultures meet. Both the talkative Westerner and the silent Easterner are behaving in ways they believe are proper, yet each views the other with disapproval and mistrust. Only when they recognize the different standards of behavior can they adapt to one another, or at least understand and respect their differences.

Perceptual differences are just as important right at home when members of different cocultures interact. Failure to recognize cocultural differences can lead to unfortunate and unnecessary misunderstandings. For example, an uninformed white teacher or police officer might interpret the downcast eyes of a Latino female as a sign of avoidance, or even dishonesty, when in fact this is the proper behavior in her culture for a female being addressed by an older man. To make direct eye contact in such a case would be considered undue brashness or even a sexual come-on.

Eye contact also differs in traditional black and white cultures. Whereas whites tend to look away from a conversational partner while speaking and at the partner while listening, blacks do just the opposite, looking at their partner more when talking and less when listening.[19] This difference can cause communication problems without either person's realizing the cause. For instance, whites are likely to use eye contact as a measure of how closely the other person is listening: The more others make eye contact, the more they seem to be paying attention. A white speaker, therefore, might interpret a black partner's lack of eye contact as a sign of inattention or rudeness when quite the opposite could be true.

> CULTURAL IDIOM
>
> **"save face":** protect one's dignity

When I meet someone from another culture, I behave in the way that is natural to me, while the other behaves in the way that is natural to him or her. The only problem is that our "natural" ways do not coincide.

Raymonde Carroll

UNDERSTANDING DIVERSITY

Non-Western Views of Western Medical Care

Author Anne Fadiman explains why Hmong emigrants from the mountains of Laos preferred their traditional shamanistic healers, called txiv neebs, to American doctors.[22] After the Hmong's objections are made explicit, it becomes clear why Western medicine can feel threatening and intrusive to patients who are already uncomfortable in a strange new environment.

A *txiv neeb* might spend as much as eight hours in a sick person's home; doctors forced their patients, no matter how weak they were, to come to the hospital, and then might spend only twenty minutes at their bedsides. *Txiv neebs* were polite and never needed to ask questions; doctors asked about their sexual and excretory habits. *Txiv neebs* could render an immediate diagnosis; doctors often demanded samples of blood (or even urine or feces, which they liked to keep in little bottles), took X rays, and waited for days for the results to come back from the laboratory—and then, after all that, sometimes they were unable to identify the cause of the problem. *Txiv neebs* never undressed their patients; doctors asked patients to take off all their clothes, and sometimes dared to put their fingers inside women's vaginas. *Txiv neebs* knew that to treat the body without treating the soul was an act of patent folly; doctors never even mentioned the soul.

Cross-cultural differences can be quite subtle. For example, when meeting with academic counselors, Latinos preferred to be respected as members of their own culture as well as individuals. On the other hand, blacks preferred to be acknowledged as individuals rather than being identified as members of an ethnic group.[20]

Along with ethnicity, geography also can influence perception. A fascinating series of studies revealed that climate and geographic latitude were remarkably accurate predictors of communication predispositions.[21] People living in southern latitudes of the United States are more socially isolated, less tolerant of ambiguity, higher in self-esteem, more likely to touch others, and more likely to verbalize their thoughts and feelings. This sort of finding helps explain why communicators who travel from one part of a country to another find that their old patterns of communicating don't work as well in their new location. A southerner whose relatively talkative, high-touch style seemed completely normal at home might be viewed as pushy and aggressive in a new northern home.

Empathy and Perception

By now it is clear that differing perceptions present a major challenge to communica-

We and They

Father, Mother, and Me,
Sister and Auntie say
All the people like us are We,
And everyone else is They.
And They live over the sea
While we live over the way,
But—would you believe it?—They look upon We
As only a sort of They!

We eat pork and beef
With cow-horn-handled knives.
They who gobble Their rice off a leaf
Are horrified out of Their lives;
While They who live up a tree,
Feast on grubs and clay,
(Isn't it scandalous?) look upon We
As a simply disgusting They!

We eat kitcheny food.
We have doors that latch.
They drink milk and blood
Under an open thatch. We have doctors to fee.
They have wizards to pay.
And (impudent heathen!) They look upon We
As a quite impossible They!

All good people agree,
And all good people say,
All nice people, like us, are We
And everyone else is They:
But if you cross over the sea,
Instead of over the way,
You may end by (think of it!) looking on We
As only a sort of They!

Rudyard Kipling

tors. One solution is to increase the ability to empathize. **Empathy** is the ability to re-create another person's perspective, to experience the world from the other's point of view.

INVITATION
TO INSIGHT
Experiencing Another Culture

Spend at least an hour in a culture that is unfamiliar to you and where you are a minority. Observe how communication practices differ from those of your own culture. Based on your experience, discuss what you can do to facilitate communication with people from other cultural backgrounds whom you may encounter in your everyday life. (As you develop a list of ideas, realize that what you might consider helpful behavior could make communicators from different cultures even more uncomfortable.)

DIMENSIONS OF EMPATHY   As we'll use the term here, *empathy* has three dimensions.[23] On one level, empathy involves *perspective taking*—the ability to take on the viewpoint of another person. This understanding requires a suspension of judgment, so that for the moment you set aside your own opinions and take on those of the other person. Besides cognitive understanding, empathy also has an *emotional* dimension that allows us to experience the feelings that others have. We know their fear, joy, sadness, and so on. When we combine the perspective-taking and emotional dimensions, we see that empathizing allows us to experience the other's perception—in effect, to become that person temporarily. A third dimension of empathy is a genuine *concern* for the welfare of the other person. When we empathize we go beyond just thinking and feeling as others do and genuinely care about their well-being.

It is easy to confuse empathy with **sympathy,** but the concepts are different in two important ways. First, sympathy means you feel compassion *for* another person's predicament, whereas empathy means you have a personal sense of what that predicament is like. Consider the difference between sympathizing with an unwed mother or a homeless person and empathizing with them—imagining what it would be like to be in their position. Despite your concern, sympathy lacks the degree of identification that empathy entails. When you sympathize, it is the other's confusion, joy, or pain. When you empathize, the experience becomes your own, at least for the moment. Both perspectives are important ones, but empathy is clearly the more complete of the two.

Empathy is different from sympathy in a second way. We only sympathize when we accept the reasons for another's

pain as valid, whereas it's possible to empathize without feeling sympathy. You can
empathize with a difficult relative, a rude
stranger, or even a criminal without feeling
much sympathy for that person.
Empathizing allows you to understand another person's motives without requiring you
to agree with them. After empathizing, you
will almost certainly understand a person
better, but sympathy won't always follow.

"How would you feel if the mouse did that to you?"

The ability to empathize seems to exist in
a rudimentary form in even the youngest
children.[24] Virtually from birth, infants become visibly upset when they hear another
infant crying, and children who are a few
months old cry when they observe another child crying. Young children have
trouble distinguishing others' distress from their own. If, for example, one child
hurts his finger, another child might put her own finger in her mouth as if she
was feeling pain. Researchers report cases in which children who see their parents crying wipe their own eyes, even though they are not crying.

Although infants and toddlers may have a basic capacity to empathize, studies
with twins suggest that the degree to which we are born with the ability to sense
how others are feeling varies according to genetic factors. Although some people
may have an inborn edge, environmental experiences are the key to developing
the ability to understand others. Specifically, the way in which parents communicate with their children seems to affect their ability to understand others' emotional states. When parents point out to children the distress that others feel from
their misbehavior ("Look how sad Jessica is because you took her toy. Wouldn't
you be sad if someone took away your toys?"), those children gain a greater appreciation that their acts have emotional consequences than they do when parents simply label behavior as inappropriate ("That was a mean thing to do!").

There is no consistent evidence that suggests that the ability to empathize is
greater for one sex or the other.[25] Some people, however, seem to have a heredi-
tary capacity for greater empathizing than do others.[26] Studies of identical and fraternal twins indicate that identical female twins are more similar to one another in
their ability to empathize than are fraternal twins. Interestingly, there seems to be
no difference between males. Although empathy may have a biological basis, environment can still play an important role. For example, parents who are sensitive
to their children's feelings tend to have children who reach out to others.[27]

Total empathy is impossible to achieve. Completely understanding another
person's point of view is simply too difficult a task for humans with different
backgrounds and limited communication skills. Nonetheless, it is possible to get
a strong sense of what the world looks like through another person's eyes.

The value of empathy is demonstrated by the results of a simple experiment.[28]
In a study, college students were asked to list their impressions of people either
shown in a videotaped discussion or described in a short story. Half the students
were instructed to empathize with the person shown as much as possible, and the
other half were not given any instructions about empathizing. The results were impressive: The students who did not practice empathy were prone to explain the
person's behavior in terms of personality characteristics. For example, they might
have explained a cruel statement by saying that the speaker was mean, or they

might have attributed a divorce to the partners' lack of understanding. The empathetic students, on the other hand, were more aware of possible elements in the situation that might have contributed to the reaction. For instance, they might have explained a person's unkind behavior in terms of job pressures or personal difficulties. In other words, practicing empathy seems to make people more tolerant.

A willingness to empathize can make a difference in everyday disputes. For example, communication researchers have spelled out how understanding opposing views can increase understanding and constructive problem solving in conflicts between environmentalists who want to preserve native species and landowners who want to earn a profit. After the parties begin to see one another's point of view, they can discover ways of protecting native species *and* allow landowners to carry on their enterprises.[29]

You might argue here, "Why should I be more tolerant? Maybe the other person's position or behavior isn't justified." Perhaps so, but research clearly shows that we are much more charitable when finding explanations for our own behavior.[30] When explaining our own actions, we are quick to suggest situational causes: "I was tired," "She started it," "The instructions weren't clear." In other words, we often excuse ourselves by saying, "It wasn't my fault!" As we've already said, we're less forgiving when we judge others. Perhaps becoming more empathetic can help even the score a bit, enabling us to treat others at least as kindly as we treat ourselves.

SKILL BUILDER

Empathy Exercise

Choose a disagreement you presently have with another person or group. The disagreement might be a personal one—such as an argument about how to settle a financial problem or who is to blame for a present state of affairs—or it might be a dispute over a contemporary public issue, such as the right of women to obtain abortions on demand or the value of capital punishment.

1. In three hundred words or so, describe your side of the issue. State why you believe as you do, just as if you were presenting your position to an important jury.
2. Now take three hundred words or so to describe in the first-person singular the other person's perspective of the same issue. For instance, if you are a religious person, write this section as if you were an atheist: For a short while get in touch with how the other person feels and thinks.
3. Now show the description you wrote to your "opponent," the person whose beliefs are different from yours. Have that person read your account and correct any statements that don't reflect his or her position accurately. Remember: You're doing this so that you can more clearly understand how the issue looks to the other person.
4. Make any necessary corrections in the account you wrote, and again show it to your partner. When your partner agrees that you understand his or her position, have your partner sign your paper to indicate this.
5. Now record your conclusions to this experiment. Has this perceptual shift made any difference in how you view the issue or how you feel about your partner?

PERCEPTION CHECKING   Good intentions and a strong effort to empathize are one way to understand others. Along with a positive attitude, however, there is a simple tool that can help you interpret the behavior of others more accurately. To see how this tool operates, consider how often others jump to mistaken conclusions about your thoughts, feelings, and motives:

"Why are you mad at me?" (Who said you were?)
"What's the matter with you?" (Who said anything was the matter?)
"Come on now. Tell the truth." (Who said you were lying?)

As you'll learn in Chapter 7, even if your interpretation is correct, a dogmatic, mind-reading statement is likely to generate defensiveness. The skill of **perception checking** provides a better way to handle your interpretations. A complete perception check has three parts:

- A description of the behavior you noticed
- At least two possible interpretations of the behavior
- A request for clarification about how to interpret the behavior.

Perception checks for the preceding three examples would look like this:

"When you stomped out of the room and slammed the door *[behavior]*, I wasn't sure whether you were mad at me *[first interpretation]* or just in a hurry *[second interpretation]*. How did you feel *[request for clarification]*?"

Cathy

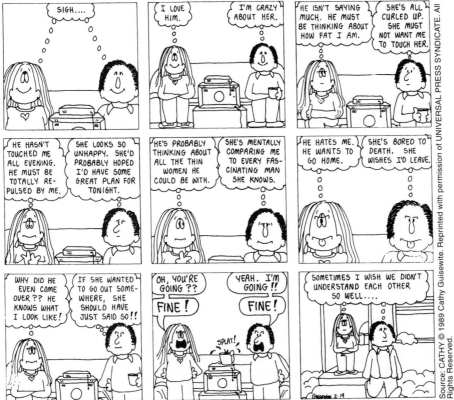

"You haven't laughed much in the last couple of days *[behavior]*. I wonder whether something's bothering you *[first interpretation]* or whether you're just feeling quiet *[second interpretation]*. What's up *[request for clarification]*?"

"You said you really liked the job I did *[behavior]*, but there was something about your voice that made me think you may not like it *[first interpretation]*. Maybe it's just my imagination, though *[second interpretation]*. How do you really feel *[request for clarification]*?"

Perception checking is a tool for helping us understand others accurately instead of assuming that our first interpretation is correct. Because its goal is mutual understanding, perception checking is a cooperative approach to communication. Besides leading to more accurate perceptions, it minimizes defensiveness by preserving the other person's face. Instead of saying in effect "I know what you're thinking . . ." a perception check takes the more respectful approach that states or implies "I know I'm not qualified to judge you without some help."

Sometimes a perception check won't need all of the parts listed earlier to be effective:

"You haven't dropped by lately. Is anything the matter *[single interpretation combined with request for clarification]*?"

"I can't tell whether you're kidding me about being cheap or if you're serious *[behavior combined with interpretations]*. Are you mad at me?"

"Are you *sure* you don't mind driving? I can use a ride if it's no trouble, but I don't want to take you out of your way *[no need to describe behavior]*."

Of course, a perception check can succeed only if your nonverbal behavior reflects the open-mindedness of your words. An accusing tone of voice or a hostile glare will contradict the sincerely worded request for clarification, suggesting that you have already made up your mind about the other person's - intentions.

CULTURAL IDIOM

dropped by: made an unplanned visit

SKILL BUILDER

Perception Checking Practice

Practice your perception-checking ability by developing three-part verifications for the following situations:

1. You made what you thought was an excellent suggestion to an instructor. The instructor looked uninterested but said she would check on the matter right away. Three weeks have passed, and nothing has changed.
2. A neighbor and good friend has not responded to your "Good morning" for three days in a row. This person is usually friendly.
3. You haven't received the usual weekly phone call from the folks back home in over a month. The last time you spoke, you had an argument about where to spend the holidays.
4. An old friend with whom you have shared the problems of your love life for years has recently changed when around you: The formerly casual hugs and kisses have become longer and stronger, and the occasions where you "accidentally" brush up against one another have become more frequent.

UNDERSTANDING DIVERSITY

Today's Lesson: Empathy

Time and time again, it was the bathroom stalls that got to Laura Manis and Kevin McCarthy.

"It's doable, but it's tight," said Manis, as she maneuvered a three-point turn into one stall.

"I should have come in forward," she observed after spending several minutes backing into another.

"I'm glad I didn't really have to go to the bathroom," said McCarthy after emerging from a third.

The pair, both second-year students in the University of Cincinnati's physical therapy assisting program, visited four suburban restaurants Thursday in an exercise that was part lesson in empathy and part consumer survey. Though neither has any physical disability, they and their classmates spent the day in wheelchairs to see how accessible 44 area restaurants were. Working off a checklist, 11 pairs of students tested the ramps, entrances, tables, salad bar and bathrooms of establishments.

"Students come away with the impression that there are a lot of barriers and obstacles for (disabled) people if they want to lead a normal life," said Tina Whalen, the instructor who organized a similar exercise two years ago. "I think it's really an eye-opener, too, as far as an energy expenditure. By the time they get into a restaurant, through the door and up to a table, some of them are too tired to eat."

Recent legislation such as the 1990 Americans with Disabilities Act has made it illegal for businesses to discriminate on the basis of physical handicaps, and most buildings are now required to have wheelchair access and other provisions for the disabled. But Thursday, the students found that legal doesn't always mean easy—or safe. Take, for instance, the wheelchair ramp into the front door of Wendy's fast-food restaurant near Tri-County Mall. It slopes out of a pair of wide doors—and into the restaurant's drive-through lane.

McCarthy and Manis found the excursion a reinforcement of lessons learned in the classroom. "This (exercise) allows us the opportunity to experience the reality of life of someone who's disabled, as opposed to just learning about it in a textbook," said Manis.

Julie Irwin

PERCEIVING THE SELF

It should be clear by now that our perceptions of others are subjective and that it takes a real effort to bridge the gap between our ideas about others and the way they view themselves. Now we will turn our examination inward, exploring the way we perceive ourselves and discussing how our self-perceptions affect our communication.

Self-Concept Defined

The **self-concept** is a set of relatively stable perceptions that each of us holds about ourselves. The self-concept includes our conception about what is unique about us and what makes us both similar to, and different from, others. To put it differently, the self-concept is rather like a mental mirror that reflects how we view ourselves: not only physical features, but also emotional states, talents, likes and dislikes, values, and roles.

We will have more to say about the nature of the self-concept shortly, but first you will find it valuable to gain a personal understanding of how this theoretical construct applies to you. You can do so by answering a simple question: "Who are you?"

How do you define yourself? As a student? A man or woman? By your age? Your religion? Occupation?

Retrospectively, one can ask "Who am I?" But in practice, the answer has come before the question.

J. M. Yinger

There are many ways of identifying yourself. Take a few more minutes and list as many ways as you can to identify who you are. You'll need this list later in this chapter, so be sure to complete it now. Try to include all the characteristics that describe you:

- Your moods or feelings
- Your appearance and physical condition
- Your social traits
- Talents you possess or lack
- Your intellectual capacity
- Your strong beliefs
- Your social roles

Even a list of twenty or thirty terms would be only a partial description. To make this written self-portrait complete, your list would have to be hundreds— or even thousands—of words long.

Of course, not all items on such a list would be equally important. For example, the most significant part of one person's self-concept might consist of social roles, whereas for another it might consist of physical appearance, health, friendships, accomplishments, or skills.

An important element of the self-concept is **self-esteem:** our evaluations of self-worth. One person's self-concept might include being religious, tall, or athletic. That person's self-esteem would be shaped by how he or she felt about these qualities: "I'm glad that I am athletic," or "I am embarrassed about being so tall," for example.

Self-esteem has a powerful effect on the way we communicate.[31] People with high self-esteem are more willing to communicate than people with low self-esteem. They are more likely to think highly of others and expect to be accepted by others. They aren't afraid of others' reactions and perform well when others are watching them. They work harder for people who demand high standards of performance, and they are comfortable with others whom they view as superior in some way. When confronted with critical comments, they are comfortable defending themselves. By contrast, people with low self-esteem are likely to be critical of others and expect rejection from them. They are also critical of their own performances. They are sensitive to possible disapproval of others and perform poorly when being watched. They work harder for undemanding, less critical people. They feel threatened by people they view as superior in some way and have difficulty defending themselves against others' negative comments.

Communication and Development of the Self

So far we've talked about what the self-concept is; but at this point you may be asking what it has to do with the study of human communication. We can begin to answer this question by looking at how you came to possess your own self-concept.

Our identity comes almost exclusively from communication with others. As psychologists Arthur Combs and Donald Snygg put it:

> The self is essentially a social product arising out of experience with people. . . . We learn the most significant and fundamental facts about ourselves from . . . "reflected appraisals," inferences about ourselves made as a consequence of the ways we perceive others behaving toward us.[32]

The term **reflected appraisal,** coined by Harry Stack Sullivan,[33] is a good one, because it metaphorically describes the fact that we develop an image of ourselves from the way we think others view us. This notion of the "looking-glass self" was

We are not only our brother's keeper; in countless large and small ways, we are our brother's maker.

Bonaro Overstreet

introduced in 1902 by Charles H. Cooley, who suggested that we put ourselves in the position of other people and then, in our mind's eye, view ourselves as we imagine they see us.[34]

As we learn to speak and understand language, verbal messages—both positive and negative—also contribute to the developing self-concept. These messages continue later in life, especially when they come from what social scientists term **significant others**—people whose opinions we especially value. A teacher from long ago, a special friend or relative, or perhaps a barely known acquaintance whom you respected can all leave an imprint on how you view yourself. To see the importance of significant others, ask yourself how you arrived at your opinion of you as a student, as a person attractive to the opposite sex, as a competent worker, and so on and you will see that these self-evaluations were probably influenced by the way others regarded you.

As we grow older, the influence of significant others is less powerful.[35] The evaluations of others still influence beliefs about the self in some areas, such as physical attractiveness and popularity. In other areas, however, the looking glass of the self-concept has become distorted, so that it shapes the input of others to make it conform with our existing beliefs. For example, if your self-concept includes the element "poor student," you might respond to a high grade by thinking "I was just lucky" or "The professor must be an easy grader."

You might argue that not every part of one's self-concept is shaped by others, insisting there are certain objective facts that are recognizable by self-observation. After all, nobody needs to tell you that you are taller than others, speak with an accent, can run quickly, and so on. These facts are obvious.

Though it's true that some features of the self are immediately apparent, the *significance* we attach to them—the rank we assign them in the hierarchy of our list and the interpretation we give them—depends greatly on the social environment. The interpretation of characteristics such as weight depends on the way people important to us regard them. Being anything less than trim and muscular is generally regarded as undesirable because others tell us that slenderness is an ideal. In one study, young women's perceptions of their bodies changed for the worse after watching just thirty minutes of televised images of the "ideal" female form.[36] Furthermore, these distorted self-images can lead to serious behavioral disorders such as depression, anorexia nervosa, bulimia, and other eating disorders. In cultures and societies where greater weight is considered beautiful, a Western supermodel would be considered unattractive. In the same way, the fact that one is single or married, solitary or sociable, aggressive or passive takes on meaning depending on the interpretation that society attaches to those traits. Thus, the importance of a given characteristic in your self-concept has as much to do with the significance that you and others attach to it as with the existence of the characteristic.

Culture and the Self-Concept

At the dawn of a new millennium, the challenges and opportunities that come from cultural diversity are becoming more apparent. But the power of culture is far more basic and pow-

Premier Artiste

Watch me perform!
I walk a tightrope of unique design.
I teeter, falter, recover and bow.
You applaud.
I run forward, backward, hesitate and bow.
You applaud.
If you don't applaud, I'll fall.
Cheer me! Hurray me!
Or you push me
Down.

Lenni Shender Goldstein

ETHICAL
CHALLENGE

Is Honesty the Best Policy?

By now it should be clear that each of us has the power to influence others' self-concepts. Even with the best of intentions, there are cases when an honest message is likely to reduce another person's self-esteem. Consider a few examples:

- Your friend, an aspiring artist, asks "What do you think of my latest painting?" You think it's terrible.
- After a long, hard week you are looking forward to spending the evening at home. A somewhat insecure friend who just broke off a long romantic relationship calls to ask if you want to get together. You don't.
- A good friend asks to use your name as a reference for a potential employer. You can't honestly tell the employer that your friend is qualified for the job.

In situations like these, how do you reconcile the desire to avoid diminishing another person's self-esteem with the need to be honest? Based on your conclusions, is it possible to always be both honest and supportive?

UNDERSTANDING DIVERSITY

Deafness and Identity³⁷

The experience of Howard offers a dramatic example of how reference groups and reflected appraisal can shape identity. Every member of Howard's immediate family—parents, brother, aunts, and uncles—was deaf. He spent his entire early childhood around deaf people and in his preschool life accepted this way of being as the natural state of affairs.

Even as a young child, Howard knew about deafness. The American Sign Language sign for "deaf" was part of his everyday vocabulary. But when he began school, Howard soon discovered that the same sign had a subtle but dramatically different meaning. Among his family, "deaf" meant "us—people who behave as expected."

But in a mostly hearing world, the same term meant "a remarkable condition—different from normal."

This sense of difference can shape the identity of a deaf child, especially in environments where sign language is discouraged in favor of communication forms that are favored in the hearing world, such as lip reading and speaking. In such an environment, it's not hard to imagine how the identity "I'm deaf" can come to mean "I'm different," and then "I'm deficient." Howard's physical condition didn't change when he began school, but his sense of himself shifted due to the reflected appraisal of his teachers and the broader reference groups he experienced in the hearing world.

erful than most people realize. Although we seldom recognize the fact, our whole notion of the self is shaped by the culture in which we have been reared.³⁸

The most obvious feature of a culture is the language its members use. If you live in an environment where everyone speaks the same tongue, then language will have little noticeable impact. But when your primary language is not the majority one, or when it is not prestigious, the sense of being a member of what social scientists call the "out-group" is strong. At this point the speaker of a nondominant language can react in one of two ways: either to feel pressured to assimilate by speaking the "better" language, or to refuse to accede to the majority

CULTURAL IDIOM

tongue: language

language and maintain loyalty to the ethnic language.[39] In either case, the impact of language on the self-concept is powerful. On one hand, the feeling is likely to be "I'm not as good as speakers of the native language," and on the other, the belief is "there's something unique and worth preserving in my language." A case study of Hispanic managers illustrates the dilemma of speaking a nondominant language.[40] The managers—employees in a predominantly Anglo organization—felt their "Mexican" identity threatened when they found that the road to advancement would be smoother if they deemphasized their Spanish and adopted a more colloquial English style of speaking.

Cultures affect the self-concept in more subtle ways, too. Most Western cultures are highly individualistic, whereas other cultures—most Asian ones, for example—are traditionally much more collective.[41] When asked to identify themselves, Americans, Canadians, Australians, and Europeans would probably respond by giving their first name, surname, street, town, and country. Many Asians do it the other way around.[42] If you ask Hindus for their identity, they will give you their caste and village as well as their name. The Sanskrit formula for identifying one's self begins with lineage and goes on to family and house and ends with one's personal name.[43]

These conventions for naming aren't just cultural curiosities: They reflect a very different way of viewing one's self. In collective cultures a person gains identity by belonging to a group. This means that the degree of interdependence among members of the society and its subgroups is much higher. Feelings of pride and self-worth are likely to be shaped not only by what the individual does, but also by the behavior of other members of the community. This linkage to others explains the traditional Asian denial of self-importance—a strong contrast to the self-promotion that is common in individualistic Western cultures. In Chinese written language, for example, the pronoun "I" looks very similar to the word for "selfish."[45] Table 2–1 summarizes some differences between individualistic Western cultures and more collective Asian ones.

In Japan, in fact, everything had been made level and uniform—even humanity. By one official count, 90 percent of the population regarded themselves as middle-class; in schools, it was not the outcasts who beat up the conformists, but vice versa. Every Japanese individual seemed to have the same goal as every other—to become like every other Japanese individual. The word for "different," I was told, was the same as the word for "wrong." And again and again in Japan, in contexts varying from the baseball stadium to the watercolor canvas, I heard the same unswerving, even maxim: "The nail that sticks out must be hammered down."

Pico Iyer
Video Night in Katmandu

TABLE 2–1   The Self in Individualistic and Collectivistic Cultures

Individualistic Cultures	Collectivistic Cultures
Self is separate, unique individual; should be independent, self-sufficient	People belong to extended families or in-groups; "we" or group orientation
Individual should take care of self and immediate family	Person should take care of extended family before self
Many flexible group memberships; friends based on shared interests and activities	Emphasis on belonging to a very few permanent in-groups, which have a strong influence over the person
Reward for individual achievement and initiative; individual decisions encouraged; individual credit and blame assigned	Reward for contribution to group goals and well-being; cooperation with in-group members; group decisions valued; credit and blame shared
High value on autonomy, change, youth, individual security, equality	High value on duty, order, tradition, age, group security, status, hierarchy

Adapted by Sandra Sudweeks from H. C. Triandis, "Cross-Cultural Studies of Individualism and Collectivism," in J. Berman, ed., *Nebraska Symposium on Motivation* 37 (Lincoln, NE: University of Nebraska Press, 1990), pp. 41–133, and E. T. Hall, *Beyond Culture* (Garden City, NY: Doubleday, 1976).

This sort of cultural difference isn't just an anthropological curiosity. It shows up in the level of comfort or anxiety that people feel when communicating. In societies where the need to conform is great, there is a higher degree of communication apprehension. For example, as a group, residents of China, Korea, and Japan exhibit significantly more anxiety about speaking out than do members of individualistic cultures such as the United States and Australia.[46] It's important to realize that different levels of communication apprehension don't mean that shyness is a "problem" in some cultures. In fact, just the opposite is true: In these cultures, reticence is valued. When the goal is to *avoid* being the nail that sticks out, it's logical to feel nervous when you make yourself appear different by calling attention to yourself. A self-concept that includes "assertive" might make a Westerner feel proud, but in much of Asia it would more likely be cause for shame.

The difference between individualism and collectivism shows up in everyday interaction. Communication researcher Stella Ting-Toomey has developed a theory that explains cultural differences in important norms, such as honesty and directness.[47] She suggests that in individualistic Western cultures where there is a strong "I" orientation, the norm of speaking directly is honored, whereas in collectivistic cultures where the main desire is to build connections between the self and others, indirect approaches that maintain harmony are considered more desirable. "I gotta be me" could be the motto of a Westerner, but "If I hurt you, I hurt myself" is closer to the Asian way of thinking.

The Self-Concept, Personality, and Communication

Whereas the self-concept is an internal image we hold of ourselves, the personality is the view others hold of us. We use the notion of **personality** to describe a relatively consistent set of traits people exhibit across a variety of situations.[48] We use the notion of personality to characterize others as friendly or aloof, energetic or lazy, smart or stupid, and in literally thousands of other ways. In fact, one survey revealed almost eighteen thousand trait words in the English language that can be used to describe a personality.[49] People do seem to possess some innate personality traits. Psychologist Jerome Kagan reports that 10 percent of all children seem to be born with a biological disposition toward shyness.[50] Babies who stop playing when a stranger enters the room, for example, are more likely than others to be reticent and introverted as adolescents. Likewise, Kagan found that another 10 percent of children seem to be born with especially sociable dispositions. Research with twins also suggests that personality may be at least partially a matter of physical destiny.[51] Biologically identical twins are much more similar in sociability than are fraternal twins. These similarities are apparent not only in infancy but also when the twins have grown to adulthood and are noticeable even when the twins have had different experiences.

Despite its common use, the term *personality* is often an oversimplification. Much of our behavior isn't consistent. Rather, it varies from one situation to another. You may be quiet around strangers but gregarious around friends and family. You might be optimistic about your schoolwork or career but pessimistic about your romantic prospects. The term *easygoing* might describe your behavior at home, whereas you might be a fanatic at work. This kind of diversity is not only common; it's also often desirable. The argumentative style you use with friends wouldn't be well received by the judge in traffic court when you appeal a citation. Likewise, the affectionate behavior you enjoy with a romantic partner at home probably wouldn't be appropriate in public. As you read in Chapter 1, a wide range of behaviors is an important ingredient of communication competence. In this sense, a consistent personality can be more of a liability than an asset—unless that personality is "flexible."

Figure 2–1 pictures the relationship between the self-concept and behavior. It illustrates how the self-concept both shapes much of our communication behavior and is shaped by it. We can begin to examine the process by considering the self-concept you bring to an event. Suppose, for example, that one element of your self-concept is "nervous with authority figures." That image probably comes from the evaluations of significant others in the past—perhaps teachers or former employers. If you view yourself as nervous with authority figures like these, you will probably behave in nervous ways when you encounter them in the future—in a teacher-student conference or a job interview. That nervous behavior is likely to influence how others view your personality, which in turn will shape how they respond to you—probably in ways that reinforce the self-concept you brought to the event. Finally, the responses of others will affect the way you interpret future events: other job interviews, meetings with professors, and so on. This cycle illustrates the chicken-and-egg nature of the self-concept, which is shaped by significant others in the past, helps to govern your present behavior, and influences the way others view you.

The Self-Fulfilling Prophecy

The self-concept is such a powerful force on the personality that it not only determines how we communicate in the present, but also can actually influence our behavior and that of others in the future. Such occurrences come about through a phenomenon called the self-fulfilling prophecy.

A **self-fulfilling prophecy** occurs when a person's expectation of an outcome makes the outcome more likely to occur than would otherwise have been true. Self-fulfilling prophecies occur all the time although you might never have given them that label. For example, think of some instances you may have known:

> **CULTURAL IDIOM**
>
> **the chicken-and-egg nature:** refers to the philosophical question, "Which came first, the chicken or the egg?"

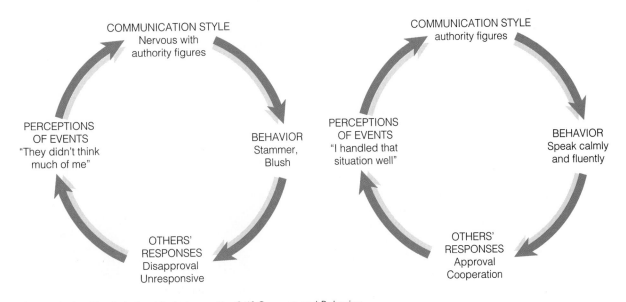

Figure 2–1   The Relationship Between the Self-Concept and Behavior

- You expected to become nervous and botch a job interview and later did so.
- You anticipated having a good (or terrible) time at a social affair and found your expectations being met.
- A teacher or boss explained a new task to you, saying that you probably wouldn't do well at first. You did not do well.
- A friend described someone you were about to meet, saying that you wouldn't like the person. The prediction turned out to be correct—you didn't like the new acquaintance.

In each of these cases, there is a good chance that the outcome happened because it was predicted to occur. You needn't have botched the interview, the party might have been boring only because you helped make it so, you might have done better on the new task if your boss hadn't spoken up, and you might have liked the new acquaintance if your friend hadn't given you preconceptions. In other words, what helped make each outcome occur was the expectation that it would happen.

There are two types of self-fulfilling prophecies. The first type occurs when your own expectations influence your behavior. Like the job interview and the party described earlier, there are many times when an outcome that needn't have occurred does occur because you expect it to. In sports you have probably psyched yourself into playing either better or worse than usual, so that the only explanation for your unusual performance was your attitude that you would behave differently. The same principle operates for anxious public speakers: Communicators who feel anxious about facing an audience often create self-fulfilling prophecies about doing poorly that cause them to perform less effectively.[52] (Chapter 13 offers advice on overcoming this kind of stage fright.)

Research has demonstrated the power of self-fulfilling prophecies. In one study, communicators who believed they were incompetent proved less likely than others to pursue rewarding relationships and more likely to sabotage their existing relationships than did people who were less critical of themselves.[53] On the other hand, students who perceived themselves as capable achieved more academically.[54] In another study, subjects who were sensitive to social rejection tended to expect rejection, perceive it where it might not have existed, and overreact to their exaggerated perceptions in ways that jeopardized the quality of their relationships.[55] The self-fulfilling prophecy also operates on the job. For example, salespeople who perceive themselves as being effective communicators are more successful than those who perceive themselves as less effective, despite the fact that there was no difference in the approach that members of each group used with customers. In other words, the apparent reason why some salespeople are successful is because they expect to succeed. As the nearby cartoon suggests, self-fulfilling prophecies can be physiologically induced: Researchers have found that putting a smile on your face, even if you're not in a good mood, can lead to a more positive disposition.[56]

"*I don't sing because I am happy. I am happy because I sing.*"

A second type of self-fulfilling prophecy occurs when the expectations of one person govern another's actions. The classic example was demonstrated by Robert Rosenthal and Lenore Jacobson:

> Twenty percent of the children in a certain elementary school were reported to their teachers as showing unusual potential for intellectual growth. The names of these 20 percent were drawn by means of a table of random numbers, which is to say that the names were drawn out of a hat. Eight months later these unusual or "magic" children showed significantly greater gains in IQ than did the remaining children who had not been singled out for the teachers' attention. The change in the teachers' expectations regarding the intellectual performance of these allegedly "special" children had led to an actual change in the intellectual performance of these randomly selected children.[57]

In other words, some children may do better in school, not because they are any more intelligent than their classmates, but because they learn that their teacher, a significant other, believes they can achieve.

To put this phenomenon in context with the self-concept, we can say that when a teacher communicates to students the message, "I think you're bright," they accept that evaluation and change their self-concepts to include that evaluation. Unfortunately, we can assume that the same principle holds for those students whose teachers send the message, "I think you're stupid."

This type of self-fulfilling prophecy has been shown to be a powerful force for shaping the self-concept and thus the behavior of people in a wide range of settings outside of the schools. In medicine, patients who unknowingly receive placebos—substances such as injections of sterile water or doses of sugar pills that have no curative value—often respond just as favorably to treatment as do people who actually receive a drug. The patients believe they have taken a substance that will help them feel better, and this belief actually brings about a "cure." In psychotherapy, Rosenthal and Jacobson describe several studies that suggest that patients who believe they will benefit from treatment do so, regardless of the type of treatment they receive. In the same vein, when a doctor believes a patient will improve, the patient may do so precisely because of this expectation, whereas another person for whom the doctor has little hope often fails to recover. Apparently the patient's self-concept as sick or well—as shaped by the doctor—plays an important role in determining the actual state of health.

The self-fulfilling prophecy operates in families as well. If parents tell their children long enough that they can't do anything right, the children's self-concepts will soon incorporate this idea, and they will fail at many or most of the tasks they attempt. On the other hand, if children are told they are capable or lovable or kind persons, there is a much greater chance of their behaving accordingly.[58]

The self-fulfilling prophecy is an important force in communication, but it doesn't explain all behavior. There are certainly times when the expectation of an event's outcome won't bring about that outcome. Your hope of drawing an ace in a card game won't in any way affect the chance of that card's turning up in an already shuffled deck, and your belief that good weather is coming won't stop the rain from falling. In the same way, believing you'll do well in a job interview when you're clearly not qualified for the position is unrealistic. Similarly, there will probably be people you don't like and occasions you won't enjoy, no matter what your attitude. To connect the self-fulfilling prophecy with the "power of positive thinking" is an oversimplification.

In other cases, your expectations will be borne out because you are a good predictor and not because of the self-fulfilling prophecy. For example, children are not equally well equipped to do well in school, and in such cases it would be wrong to say that a child's performance was shaped by a parent or teacher even though the behavior did match what was expected. In the same way, some workers excel and others fail, some patients recover and others don't—all according to our predictions but not because of them.

As we keep these qualifications in mind, it's important to recognize the tremendous influence that self-fulfilling prophecies play in our lives. To a great extent we are what we believe we are. In this sense we and those around us constantly create our self-concepts and thus ourselves.

CRITICAL THINKING PROBE	**Self-Fulfilling Prophecies**

Explore how self-fulfilling prophecies affect your communication by answering the following questions:

1. Identify three communication-related predictions you make about others. What are the effects of these predictions? How would others behave differently if you did not impose these predictions?
2. Identify three self-fulfilling prophecies you impose on yourself. What are the effects of these prophecies? How would you communicate differently if you did not subscribe to them?

IDENTITY MANAGEMENT: COMMUNICATION AS IMPRESSION MANAGEMENT

So far we have described how communication shapes the way communicators view themselves and others. In the remainder of this chapter we turn the tables and focus on **impression management**—the communication strategies people use to influence how others view them. In the following pages you will see that many of our messages aim at creating desired impressions.

Public and Private Selves

To understand why impression management exists, we have to discuss the notion of self in more detail. So far we have referred to the "self" as if each of us had only one identity. In truth, each of us possesses several selves, some private and others public. Often these selves are quite different.

The **perceived self** is a reflection of the self-concept. Your perceived self is the person you believe yourself to be in moments of honest self-examination. We can call the perceived self "private" because you are unlikely to reveal all of it to another person. You can verify the private nature of the perceived self by reviewing the self-concept list you developed while reading pages 47–48. You'll probably find some elements of yourself there that you would not disclose to many people, and some that you would not share with anyone. You might, for example, be reluctant to share some feelings about your appearance ("I think I'm rather unattractive"), your intelligence ("I'm not as smart as I wish I was"), your goals ("the most important thing to me is becoming rich"), or your motives ("I care more about myself than about others").

There is an old joke about a man who was asked if he could play a violin and answered, "I don't know. I've never tried." This is psychologically a very wise reply. Those who have never tried to play a violin really do not know whether they can or not. Those who say too early in life and too firmly, "No, I'm not at all musical," shut themselves off prematurely from whole areas of life that might have proved rewarding. In each of us there are unknown possibilities, undiscovered potentialities—and one big advantage of having an open self-concept rather than a rigid one is that we shall continue to discover more and more about ourselves as we grow older.

S. I. Hayakawa

CULTURAL IDIOM

turn the tables:
reverse the point of view

In contrast to the perceived self, the **presenting self** is a public image—the way we want to appear to others.

In most cases the presenting self we seek to create is a socially approved image: diligent student, loving partner, conscientious worker, loyal friend, and so on. Social norms often create a gap between the perceived and presenting selves. For instance, Table 2–2 shows that the self-concepts of the members of one group of male and female college students were quite similar, but that their public selves were different in several respects from both their private selves and from the public selves of the opposite sex.[59]

Sociologist Erving Goffman used the word **face** to describe the presenting self, and he coined the term **facework** to describe the verbal and nonverbal ways we act to maintain our own presenting image and the images of others.[60] He argued that each of us can be viewed as a kind of playwright, who creates roles that we want others to believe, as well as the performer who acts out those roles. Goffman suggested that all of us maintain face by putting on a *front* when we are around others whom we want to impress. By contrast, behavior in the *back* region when we are alone may be quite different. You can recognize the difference between front and backstage behavior by recalling a time when you observed a driver, alone in his or her car, behaving in ways that would never be acceptable in public. All of us engage in backstage ways of acting that we would never do in public. Just recall how you behave in front of the bathroom mirror when the

I know you would really like me if I could just be myself, but since this is our first date and, I'm incredibly nervous, you won't be seeing the real me because I can't be myself when I'm this nervous, so all I ask is that you try to like this me until I calm down and the real me emerges.

TABLE 2–2   Self-Selected Adjectives Describing Perceived and Presenting Selves of College Students

PERCEIVED SELF		PRESENTING SELF	
Men	**Women**	**Men**	**Women**
1. Friendly	1. Friendly	1. Wild	1. Active
2. Active	2. Responsible	2. Able	2. Responsible
3. Responsible	3. Independent	3. Active	3. Able
4. Independent	4. Capable	4. Strong	4. Bright
5. Capable	5. Sensible	5. Proud	5. Warm
6. Polite	6. Active	6. Smart	6. Funny
7. Attractive	7. Happy	7. Brave	7. Independent
8. Smart	8. Curious	8. Capable	8. Proud
9. Happy	9. Faithful	9. Responsible	9. Sensible
10. Funny	10. Attractive	10. Rough	10. Smart

Adapted from C. M. Shaw and R. Edwards, "Self-Concepts and Self-Presentations of Males and Females: Similarities and Differences," *Communication Reports* 10 (1997): 55–62.

door is locked and you will appreciate the difference between public and private behaviors. If you knew someone was watching, would you behave differently?

Characteristics of Identity Management

Now that you have a sense of what identity management is, we can look at some characteristics of this process.

"Hah! This is the Old King Cole nobody ever sees."

WE STRIVE TO CONSTRUCT MULTIPLE IDENTITIES   In the course of even a single day, most people play a variety of roles: respectful student, joking friend, friendly neighbor, and helpful worker, to suggest just a few. We even play a variety of roles with the same person. As you grew up you almost certainly changed characters as you interacted with your parents. In one context you acted as the responsible adult ("You can trust me with the car!"), and in another context you were the helpless child ("I can't find my socks!"). At some times—perhaps on birthdays or holidays—you were a dedicated family member, and at other times you may have played the role of rebel. Likewise, in romantic relationships we switch among many ways of behaving, depending on the context: friend, lover, business partner, scolding critic, apologetic child, and so on.

The ability to construct multiple identities is one element of communication competence. For example, the style of speaking or even the language itself can reflect a choice about how to construct one's identity. We recall an African-American colleague who was also minister of a Southern Baptist congregation consisting mostly of black members. On campus his manner of speaking was typically professorial; but a visit to hear him preach one Sunday revealed a speaker whose style was much more animated and theatrical, reflecting his identity in that context. Likewise, one scholar pointed out that bilingual Latinos in the United States often choose whether to use English or Spanish depending on the kind of identity they are seeking in a given conversation.[61]

IDENTITY MANAGEMENT IS COLLABORATIVE   As we perform like actors trying to create a front, our "audience" is made up of other actors who are trying to create their own characters. Identity-related communication is a kind of process theater in which we collaborate with other actors to improvise scenes in which our characters mesh.

You can appreciate the collaborative nature of identity management by thinking about how you might handle a gripe with a friend or family member who has failed to pass along a phone message that arrived while you were away from home. Suppose that you decide to raise the issue tactfully in an effort to avoid seeming like a nag (desired role for yourself: "nice person") and also to save the other person from the embarrassment of being confronted (hoping to avoid suggesting that the other person's role is "screw-up"). If your tactful bid is accepted, the dialogue might sound like this:

You: ". . . By the way, Jenny told me she called yesterday. If you wrote a note, I guess I missed seeing it."
Other: "Oh . . . sorry. I meant to write a note, but as soon as I hung up, the doorbell rang, and then I had to run off to class."

You (in friendly tone of voice): "That's okay. I sure would appreciate from now on if you'd leave me a note."
Other: "No problem."

In this upbeat conversation, both you and the other person accepted one another's bids for identity as basically thoughtful people. As a result, the conversation ran smoothly. Imagine, though, how different the outcome would be if the other person didn't accept your role as "nice person":

You: ". . .By the way, Jenny told me she called yesterday. If you wrote a note, I guess I missed seeing it."
Other (defensively): "Okay, so I forgot. It's not that big a deal. You're not perfect yourself, you know!"

Your first bid as "nice, face-saving person" was rejected. At this point you have the choice of persisting in trying to play the original role: "Hey, I'm not mad at you, and I know I'm not perfect!" Or, you might switch to the new role of "unjustly accused person," responding with aggravation "I never said I was perfect. But we're not talking about me here . . ."

As this example illustrates, *collaboration* doesn't mean the same thing as *agreement*.[62] The small issue of the phone message might mushroom into a fight in which you and the other person both adopt the role of combatants. The point here is that virtually all conversations provide an arena in which communicators construct their identities in response to the behavior of others. As you read in Chapter 1, communication isn't made up of discrete events that can be separated from one another. Instead, what happens at one moment is influenced by what each party brings to the interaction and by what happened in their relationship up to that point.

IDENTITY MANAGEMENT CAN BE CONSCIOUS OR UNCONSCIOUS   At this point you might object to the notion of strategic identity management, claiming that most of your communication is spontaneous and not a deliberate attempt to present yourself in a certain way. However, you might acknowledge that some of your communication involves a conscious attempt to manage impressions.

There's no doubt that sometimes we are highly aware of managing impressions. Most job interviews and first dates are clear examples of conscious identity management. But in other cases we unconsciously act in ways that are really small public performances.[63] For example, experimental subjects expressed facial disgust in reaction to eating sandwiches laced with a supersaturated saltwater solution only when there was another person present: When they were alone, they made no faces when eating the same sandwiches.[64] Another study showed that communicators engage in facial mimicry (such as smiling or looking sympathetic in response to another's message) in face-to-face settings only when their expressions can be seen by the other person. When they are speaking over the phone and their reactions cannot be seen, they do not make the same expressions.[65] Studies like these suggest that most of our behavior is aimed at sending messages to others—in other words, identity management.

The experimental subjects described in the last paragraph didn't consciously think, "Somebody is watching me eat this salty sandwich, so I'll make a face," or, "Since I'm in a face-to-face conversation I'll show I'm sympathetic by mimicking the facial expressions of my conversational partner." Reactions like these are often instantaneous and outside of our conscious awareness.

CULTURAL IDIOM

"face-saving person": person wishing to be thought of favorably

might mushroom: might escalate

In the same way, many of our choices about how to act in the array of daily interactions aren't deliberate, strategic decisions. Rather, they rely on "scripts" that we have developed over time. You probably have a variety of roles for managing your identity from which to choose in familiar situations such as dealing with strangers, treating customers at work, interacting with family members, and so on. When you find yourself in familiar situations like these, you probably slip into these roles quite often. Only when those roles don't seem quite right do you deliberately construct an approach that reflects how you want the scene to play out.

Despite the claims of some theorists, it seems like an exaggeration to suggest that *all* behavior is aimed at making impressions. Young children certainly aren't strategic communicators. A baby spontaneously laughs when pleased, and cries when sad or uncomfortable, without any notion of creating an impression in others. Likewise, there are almost certainly times when we, as adults, act spontaneously. But when a significant other questions the presenting self we try to present, the likelihood of acting to prop it up increases. This process isn't always conscious: At a nonconscious level of awareness we monitor others' reactions and swing into action when our face is threatened—especially by significant others.[66]

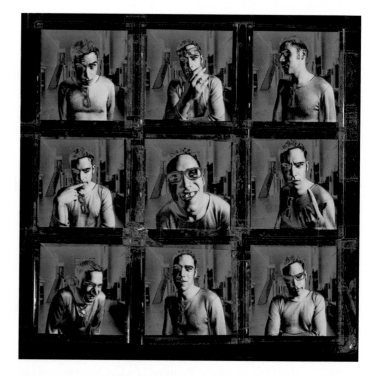

PEOPLE DIFFER IN THEIR DEGREE OF IDENTITY MANAGEMENT   Some people are much more aware of their impression management behavior than others. These high self-monitors have the ability to pay attention to their own behavior and others' reactions, adjusting their communication to create the desired impression. By contrast, low self-monitors express what they are thinking and feeling without much attention to the impression their behavior creates.[67]

There are certainly advantages to being a high self-monitor.[68] People who pay attention to themselves are generally good actors who can create the impression they want, acting interested when bored, or friendly when they really feel quite the opposite. This allows them to handle social situations smoothly, often putting others at ease. They are also good "people-readers" who can adjust their behavior to get the desired reaction from others. Along with these advantages, there are some potential disadvantages to being an extremely high self-monitor. The analytical nature of high self-monitors may prevent them from experiencing events completely, because a portion of their attention will always be viewing the situation from a detached position. High self-monitors' ability to act means that it is difficult to tell how they are really feeling. In fact, because high self-monitors change roles often, they may have a hard time knowing *themselves* how they really feel.

CULTURAL IDIOM

"scripts": practiced responses

to play out: to proceed to a conclusion

People who score low on the self-monitoring scale live life quite differently from their more self-conscious counterparts. They have a simpler, more focused idea of who they are and who they want to be. Low self-monitors are likely to have a narrower repertoire of behaviors, so that they can be expected to act in more or less the same way regardless of the situation. This means that low self-monitors are easy to read. "What you see is what you get" might be their motto. Although this lack of flexibility may make their social interaction less smooth in many situations, low self-monitors can be counted on to be straightforward communicators.

By now it should be clear that neither extremely high nor low self-monitoring is the ideal. There are some situations when paying attention to yourself and adapting your behavior can be useful, but there are other situations when reacting without considering the effect on others is a better approach. This need for a range of behaviors demonstrates again the notion of communicative competence outlined in Chapter 1: Flexibility is the key to successful relationships.

Why Manage Impressions?

Why bother trying to shape others' opinions? Sometimes we create and maintain a front to follow social rules. As children we learn to act polite, even when bored. Likewise, part of growing up consists of developing a set of manners for various occasions: meeting strangers, attending school, going to church services, and so on. Young children who haven't learned all the do's and don'ts of polite society often embarrass their parents by behaving inappropriately ("Mommy, why is that man so fat?"); but by the time they enter school, behavior that might have been excusable or even amusing just isn't acceptable. Good manners are often aimed at making others more comfortable. For example, able-bodied people often mask their discomfort upon encountering someone who is disabled by acting nonchalant or stressing similarities between themselves and the disabled person.[69]

Social rules govern our behavior in a variety of settings. It would be impossible to keep a job, for example, without meeting certain expectations. Salespeople are obliged to treat customers with courtesy. Employees need to appear reasonably respectful when talking to the boss. Some forms of clothing would be considered outrageous at work. By agreeing to take on a job, you are signing an unwritten contract that you will present a certain face at work, whether or not that face reflects the way you might be feeling at a particular moment.

Even when social roles don't dictate the proper way to behave, we often manage impressions for a second reason: to accomplish personal goals. You might, for example, dress up for a visit to traffic court in the hope that your front (responsible citizen) will convince the judge to treat you sympathetically. You might act sociable to your neighbors so they will agree to your request that they keep their dog off your lawn. We also try to create a desired impression to achieve one or more of the social needs described in Chapter 1: affection, inclusion, control, and so on. For instance, you might act more friendly and lively than you feel upon meeting a new person, so that you will appear likable. You could sigh and roll your eyes when arguing politics with a classmate to gain an advantage in an argument. You might smile and preen to show the attractive stranger at a party that you would like to get better acquainted. In situations like these you aren't being deceptive as much as putting "your best foot forward."

Prepare a face to meet the faces that you meet.

T. S. Eliot
"The Love Song of J. Alfred Prufrock"

CULTURAL IDIOM

putting "your best foot forward": making the best appearance possible

All these examples show that it is difficult—even impossible—*not* to create impressions. After all, you have to send *some* sort of message. If you don't act friendly when meeting a stranger, you have to act aloof, indifferent, hostile, or in some other manner. If you don't act businesslike, you have to behave in an alternative way: casual, goofy, or whatever. Often the question isn't whether or not to present a face to others; the question is only which face to present.

How Do We Manage Impressions?

How do we create a public face? In an age when technology provides many options for communicating, the answer depends in part on the communication channel chosen.

FACE-TO-FACE IMPRESSION MANAGEMENT   In face-to-face interaction, communicators can manage their front in three ways: manner, appearance, and setting.[70] *Manner* consists of a communicator's words and nonverbal actions. Physicians, for example, display a wide variety of manners as they conduct physical examinations. Some are friendly and conversational, whereas others adopt a brusque and impersonal approach. Still others are polite but businesslike. Much of a communicator's manner comes from what he or she says. A doctor who remembers details about your interests and hobbies is quite different from one who sticks to clinical questions. Along with the content of speech, nonverbal behaviors play a big role in creating impressions. A doctor who greets you with a friendly smile and a handshake comes across quite differently from one who gives nothing more than a curt nod. The same principle holds in personal relationships. Your manner plays a major role in shaping how others view you. Chapters 3 and 5 will describe in detail how your words and nonverbal behaviors create impressions. Because you *have* to speak and act, the question isn't whether or not your manner sends messages; rather, the question is whether or not these messages will be intentional.

Along with manner, a second dimension of impression management is *appearance*—the personal items people use to shape an image. Sometimes appearance is part of creating a professional image. A physician's white lab coat and a police officer's uniform both set the wearer apart as someone special. A tailored suit or a rumpled outfit create very different impressions in the business world. Off the job, clothing is just as important. We choose clothing that sends a message about ourselves, sometimes trendy and sometimes traditional. Some people dress in ways that accent their sexuality, whereas others hide it. Clothing can say "I'm an athlete," "I'm wealthy," or "I'm an environmentalist." Along with dress, other aspects of appearance play a strong role in impression management. Are you suntanned or pale? What is your hair style?

A third way to manage impressions is through the choice of *setting*—physical items we use to influence how others view us. Consider the artifacts that people use to decorate the space where they live. For example, the posters and other items a college student uses to decorate her dorm room function as a kind of "who I am" statement.[71] In modern Western society the automobile is a major part of impression management. This explains why many people lust after cars that are far more expensive and powerful than they really need. A sporty convertible or fancy imported coupe doesn't just get drivers from one place to another: It also makes statements about the kind of people they are. The physical setting we choose and the way we arrange it are other important ways to manage

CULTURAL IDIOM

sticks to: focuses solely on

lust after: strong desire to own

Not all messages are about identity, but identity is part of all messages.

Michael L. Hecht

impressions. What colors do you choose for the place you live? What artwork? What music do you play? Of course, we choose a setting that we enjoy; but in many cases we create an environment that will present the desired front to others. If you doubt this fact, just recall the last time you straightened up the house before important guests arrived. Backstage you might be comfortable with a messy place, but your public front—at least to some people—is quite different.

IMPRESSION MANAGEMENT IN MEDIATED COMMUNICATION   At first glance, computer-mediated communication (CMC) seems to have limited potential for identity management. E-mail messages, for example, appear to lack the "richness" of other channels. They don't convey the postures, gestures, or facial expressions that are an important part of face-to-face communication. They even lack the vocal information available in telephone messages. These limitations might seem to make it harder to create and manage an identity when communicating via computer.

"I loved your E-mail, but I thought you'd be older."

Recently, though, communication scholars have begun to recognize that what is missing in computer-mediated communication can actually be an *advantage* for communicators who want to manage the impressions they make.[72] E-mail authors can edit their messages until they create just the desired impression. They can choose the desired level of clarity or ambiguity, seriousness or humor, logic or emotion. Unlike face-to-face communication, electronic correspondence allows a sender to say difficult things without forcing the receiver to respond immediately, and it permits the receiver to ignore a message rather than give an unpleasant response. Options like these show that CMC can serve as a tool for impression management at least as well as face-to-face communication.

In CMC, communicators have much greater control over what kinds of information to reveal or hide. A webpage designer who doesn't want to be judged by his appearance (too young/old, not physically attractive, male or female) can hide or manipulate these characteristics in ways that aren't possible in face-to-face settings. A telecommuter working at home can close a big deal via computer while chomping on an apple, muttering about the client, or even belching—none of which is recommended in face-to-face interaction!

Along with providing greater control over *what* to say, mediated channels give communicators greater control over *how* to shape a message in ways that enhance the management of their own identity and preserve the face of others. On the Internet, it's possible to shape a message until it creates just the desired impression. You can edit remarks to get just the right tone of sincerity, humor, irony, or concern—or not send any message at all, if that is the best way to maintain face.

Recent research has revealed that communicators who are concerned with impression management don't always prefer computer-mediated channels. People are generally comfortable with face-to-face interaction when they feel

CULTURAL IDIOM

straightened up:
cleaned and/or
organized

"richness":
completeness

UNDERSTANDING COMMUNICATION TECHNOLOGY

Teen Identity Management on the Internet

A famous cartoon shows a mutt tapping on a computer keyboard and proclaiming, "On the Internet, nobody knows you're a dog." Behind the humor lies an important truth: Until "see you–see me" technology becomes common, electronic communicators have much more power to manage their identities than would be possible in face-to-face conversation, or even telephone interaction, where vocal cues reveal significant details about the sender.

A comprehensive survey conducted by the Pew Internet and American Life Project revealed the extent to which U.S. teenagers use Internet technology to create desired impressions. For example, 56 percent of online teens surveyed had more than one e-mail address or screen name. In many cases, teens reported that they used one or more of these names to hide their real identity from friends and strangers. A quarter of teens who used e-mail, instant messaging, or chat rooms confessed that they have pretended to be a different person when communicating with others. A third of the teens reported having been given fake personal information in an e-mail or instant message.

For some teens, the safe anonymity of the Internet is nothing more than an amusing way to have fun. For others, though, creating new identities is a way to explore who they are, or who they might become.

A. Lenhart, L. Rainie, and O. Lewis, "Teenage Life Online" (Washington, DC: Pew Internet and American Life Project, 2001).

---

confident that others support the image they want to present. On the other hand, people are more likely to prefer mediated channels when their own self-presentation is threatened.[73]

Impression Management and Honesty

After reading this far, you might think that impression management sounds like an academic label for manipulation or phoniness. If the perceived self is the "real" you, it might seem that any behavior that contradicts it would be dishonest.

There certainly are situations where impression management is dishonest. A manipulative date who pretends to be affectionate in order to gain sexual favors is clearly unethical and deceitful. So are job applicants who lie about academic records to get hired or salespeople who pretend to be dedicated to customer service when their real goal is to make a quick buck. But managing impressions doesn't necessarily make you a liar. In fact, it is almost impossible to imagine how we could communicate effectively without making decisions about which front to present in one situation or another. It would be ludicrous for you to act the same way with strangers as you do with close friends, and nobody would show the same face to a two-year-old as to an adult.

Each of us has a repertoire of faces—a cast of characters—and part of being a competent communicator is choosing the best role for the situation. Consider a few examples:

■ You offer to teach a friend a new skill: playing the guitar, operating a computer program, or sharpening a tennis

Public Selves on Parade

But in any case he took care to avoid catching anyone's eye. First of all, he had to make it clear to those potential companions of his holiday that they were of no concern to him whatsoever. He stared through them, round them, over them— eyes lost in space. The beach might have been empty. If by chance a ball was thrown his way, he looked surprised; then let a smile of amusement lighten his face (Kindly Preedy), looked round dazed to see that there were people on the beach, tossed it back with a smile to himself and not a smile at the people, and then resumed carelessly his nonchalant survey of space.

But it was time to institute a parade, the parade of the Ideal Preedy. By devious handling he gave any who wanted to look a chance to see the title of his book—a Spanish translation of Homer, classic thus, but not daring, cosmopolitan too— and then gathered together his beach-wrap and bag into a neat sand-resistant pile (Methodical and Sensible Preedy), rose slowly to stretch and ease his huge frame (Big-Cat Preedy), and tossed aside his sandals (Carefree Preedy, after all).

William Sansom
A Contest of Ladies

backhand. Your friend is making slow progress with the skill, and you find yourself growing impatient.

- At a party with a companion, you meet someone you find very attractive, and you are pretty sure that the feeling is mutual. You feel an obligation to spend most of your time with the person with whom you came, but the opportunity here is very appealing.
- At work you face a belligerent customer. You don't believe that anyone has the right to treat you this way.
- A friend or family member makes a joke about your appearance that hurts your feelings. You aren't sure whether to make an issue of the remark or pretend that it doesn't bother you.

In each of these situations—and in countless others every day—you have a choice about how to act. It is an oversimplification to say that there is only one honest way to behave in each circumstance and that every other response would be insincere and dishonest. Instead, impression management involves deciding which face—which part of yourself—to reveal. For example, when teaching a new skill you can choose to display the patient instead of the impatient side of yourself. In the same way, at work you have the option of acting hostile or nondefensive in difficult situations. With strangers, friends, or family you can choose whether or not to disclose your feelings. Which face to show to others is an important decision, but in any case you are sharing a real part of yourself. You may not be revealing *everything*—but, as you will learn in Chapter 6, complete self-disclosure is rarely appropriate.

> CULTURAL IDIOM
>
> **to make a quick buck:** to earn money with little effort

SUMMARY

Perceptions of others are always selective and are often distorted. The chapter began by describing how personal narratives shape our perceptions. It then outlined several perceptual errors that can affect the way we view and communicate with others. Along with universal psychological influences, cultural factors affect perceptions. Increased empathy is a valuable tool for increasing understanding of others and hence communicating more effectively with them. Perception checking is one tool for increasing the accuracy of perceptions and for increasing empathy.

Perceptions of one's self are just as subjective as perceptions of others, and they influence communication at least as much. Although individuals are born with some innate personality characteristics, the self-concept is shaped dramatically by communication with others, as well as by cultural factors. Once established, the self-concept can lead us to create self-fulfilling prophecies that determine how we behave and how others respond to us.

Impression management consists of strategic communication designed to influence others' perceptions of an individual. Impression management operates when we seek to present one or more public faces to others. These faces may be different from the private, spontaneous behavior that occurs outside of others' presence. Some communicators are high self-monitors who are highly conscious of their own behavior, whereas others are low self-monitors who are less aware of how their words and actions affect others.

Impression management occurs for two reasons. In many cases it aims at following social rules and conventions. In other cases it aims at achieving a variety of content and relational goals. In either case, communicators engage in creating impressions by managing their manner, appearance, and the settings in which they interact with others. Although impression management might seem manipulative, it can be an authentic form of communication. Because each person has a variety of faces that he or she can present, choosing which one to present need not be dishonest.

RESOURCES

Print

Blank, Peter D. *Interpersonal Expectations: Theory, Research, and Applications.* Cambridge, England: Cambridge University Press, 1993.

A thorough description of research that reveals how self-fulfilling prophecies can affect others' behavior. Chapters detail how what Blank terms the "interpersonal expectancy effect" operates in a variety of settings, including the perpetuation of racial inequality, education, health care, and organizations.

Cupach, William R., and Sandra Metts. *Facework.* Thousand Oaks, CA: Sage, 1994.

The authors summarize research on how communicators manage their own identity and maintain the face of others, especially in problematic situations.

Gergen, Kenneth. *The Saturated Self: Dilemmas of Identity in Contemporary Life.* New York: Basic Books, 1992.

Gergen's thesis is that in today's fast-paced society, traditional notions of the self are being crowded out by a variety of alternatives. Chapter 6, "From Self to Relationship," describes how creating (and communicating) any self-image one desires is becoming increasingly possible in emerging postmodern society.

Goss, Blaine. *The Psychology of Human Communication,* 2nd ed. Prospect Heights, IL: Waveland Press, 1995.

A brief, readable introduction to the perceptual factors that affect human communication. Chapters focus selectively on topics, including the physiology of perception, memory, and the self-concept.

Hamachek, Don E. *Encounters with the Self,* 4th ed. Ft. Worth, TX: Harcourt Brace Jovanovich, 1992.

This is a thorough, readable introduction to the self. Hamachek describes how communication shapes the self-concept, the accuracy and inaccuracy of self-perceptions, and how to change the self-concept. Individual chapters describe influences on formation of the self: developmental stages, parent-child relationships, and academic experiences.

Hattie, John. *Self-Concept.* Hillsdale, NJ: Lawrence Erlbaum, 1992.

A scholarly look at the self-concept. This book is a useful source for serious students who want to explore the self-concept in more detail.

Ickes, William E., ed. *Empathic Accuracy.* New York: Guilford, 1997.

This edited volume offers an array of scholarly articles describing the nature and importance of empathic accuracy. Chapters deal with topics including the evolutionary and social factors that contribute to empathy, the psychological characteristics and influes that affect empathic ability, and the relationship of empathy and gender.

Macrae, C. Neil, Charles Stangor, and Miles Hewstone, eds. *Stereotypes and Stereotyping.* New York: Guilford, 1996.

This collection of scholarly works provides a comprehensive look at stereotyping. Chapters deal with the formation and development of stereotypes, how stereotyping operates in everyday interaction, and how to minimize the harmful effects of stereotyping.

O'Brien, Jodi, and Peter Kollock, eds. *The Production of Reality: Essays and Readings on Social Interaction,* 3rd ed. Thousand Oaks, CA: Pine Forge Press, 2001.

Part III of this fascinating collection includes six selections describing how the self is a product of social interaction. Part IV offers five readings illustrating how the self-fulfilling prophecy operates in a variety of contexts ranging from first impressions in social situations to mental institutions.

Opposing Viewpoints series. San Diego: Greenhaven Press, 2002.

This series of pamphlets provides balanced, informative viewpoints on both sides of a series of hotly debated topics that often generate strong emotions. From a communication perspective, the contrasting views can serve as empathy-builders by illuminating perspectives that differ from one's own.

Films
Perception is Subjective

Shallow Hal (2001). Rated PG-13.

Hal Larsen (Jack Black) is an aging, out-of-shape lounge lizard who foolishly thinks he can seduce attractive women. After being hypnotized by self-help guru Tony Robbins, Hal begins to look beyond appearances and see the inner beauty of people. When Hal first sees Rosemary (Gwyneth Paltrow), her beauty takes his breath away. But whereas Hal sees Rosemary as a willowy beauty, in reality she is a grossly obese woman who draws snickers and stares from clear-eyed spectators.

Although the film will never be considered a classic, it does illustrate in an exaggerated way that perception is subjective, showing that what we think about one another (and ourselves) is more powerful than a more objective perspective. The film also illustrates the power we have to shape one another's self concept: As Hal treats Rosemary well, she starts to feel better about herself.

Building Empathy

The Doctor (1991). Rated PG.

Jack McKee (William Hurt) is an ace surgeon who regards his patients more as props than as human beings with real concerns. His arrogance is deflated when an equally callous colleague matter of factly diagnoses him as having cancer. As a patient, McKee learns the fears and frustrations of being on the receiving end of an often indifferent medical care system. By the film's end, McKee has become a far more empathic physician. The film is a clear, entertaining example of the value of viewing the world from another person's perspective.

Rashomon (1950). Not rated. Japanese with English subtitles.

Set in eighth-century Japan, this is the story of a samurai and his wife who are ambushed by a bandit, who kills the man and rapes the woman. At the bandit's trial, the incident is told from four points of view: the bandit's, the wife's, the dead man's (speaking through a medium), and a woodcutter's (who has stolen the dead man's knife, and so has his own self-interest to protect). The event seems radically different from each perspective. Director Akira Kurosawa's first film is an outstanding illustration of how the same event can be perceived in many ways.

Influences on the Self-Concept

Welcome to the Dollhouse (1996). Rated R.

Dawn Weiner (Heather Matarazzo) is an unpopular seventh-grader who personifies all the gawkiness and lack of social skills that afflict so many young adolescents. Most of her classmates relentlessly tease, harass, and humiliate Dawn, calling her "Weiner Dog" in a cruel takeoff on her family name. When she asks one fellow student why she hates her, the other girl replies "Because you're ugly." Dawn has a nerdish older brother, Mark (Matther Waber), and a precocious younger sister, Missy (Daria Kalinina), who constantly dances around the house dressed in a ballerina's costume. The parents claim they love all the children equally, but the way they dote on Missy raises doubts about their claim.

Welcome to the Dollhouse is a dark comedy. Those who suffered or witnessed the incredible cruelty that is common in junior high school will be painfully reminded of their own experiences. At the same time, Dawn's resilience under the onslaught of her peers offers an encouraging hint that she may survive her adolesence and, as an adult, find an environment in which significant others appreciate her wit, intelligence, and grit.

Self-Fulfilling Prophecy

Class Act (1992). Rated PG-13.

Class Act follows the lives of brilliant, nerdish high school student Duncan Pinderhughes (Christopher Reid) and delinquent Blade Brown (Christopher Martin), who has been given the alternative of staying in school or going to jail. A mixup in school records puts Pinderhughes into the remedial program with troublemakers and losers, while Brown winds up in the gifted students.

The story is a case study in self-fulfilling prophecies: After the students are labeled, they wind up matching the expectations that are imposed on them. Because Brown has the reputation of being smart, he gets better grades no matter what he does. By contrast, when Pinderhughes is labeled as a loser, he gets poor evaluations no matter how hard he tries. Expectations also influence behavior in the characters' social lives: When girls view Pinderhughes as excitingly dangerous, he begins to get dates. Brown, on the other hand, loses his allure when he is labeled as a nerd. The film is an obvious satire, but behind the humor is a valid point: Perceptions can create reality.

Pay It Forward (2000). Rated PG-13.

Trevor (Haley Joel Osment) is a junior high schooler whose father has disappeared. His mother, Arlene (Helen Hunt), is a recovering alcoholic who makes ends meet by working as a Las Vegas cocktail waitress. On the first day of school, Trevor's new teacher, Mr. Simonet (Kevin Spacey), gives a provocative assignment: Think of an idea that could change the world. Trevor's idea is simple but profound: You have to do something that really helps people. It has to be something they can't do by themselves. The recipients of the favor "pay it forward" by doing the same thing for three other people.

Trevor's "pay it forward" acts become powerful self-fulfilling prophecies, helping to transform formerly hopeless and cynical people into powerful agents who really do help make the world a better place. One of his schemes is to get his mom and Mr. Simonet together. Simonet, whose face is covered with scars from burns, is reluctant. It's clear that the emotional scars are more painful than his physical ones, and he resists the idea that he could be lovable. Still, Trevor's persistence guides his teacher and mother into a relationship in which each of them helps boost the self-esteem of the other.

The film ends on a sad note, but its message comes through strongly: Each of us has the power to communicate in ways that shape ourselves, others, and the world. The only questions are whether we will use that power consciously and whether we use it to make life better or worse.

Identity Management

In and Out (1997). Rated PG-13.

Howard Brackett (Kevin Kline) is a high school English teacher in an idyllic small Indiana town.

While watching the Academy Awards telecast with his friends, family, and fiancée Emily (Joan Cusack), Brackett is dumbfounded to hear one of his former students accept an Oscar by publicly thanking him and then announcing—to most of the world—that Brackett is gay.

Not surprisingly, pandemonium ensues as Brackett feverishly defends his heterosexual identity, often with macho posturing that is so overdone that it becomes a parody of traditional male behavior. This lighthearted comedy provides an entertaining illustration of how much communication is dedicated to managing one's identity. As a contrast to Brackett, watch how television journalist Peter Malloy (Tom Selleck), who is openly gay, handles his sexual identity.

You've Got Mail (1999). Rated PG.

Joe Fox (Tom Hanks) and Kathleen Kelly (Meg Ryan) are thirty-something New Yorkers who detest each other—or at least they think they do. Face-to-face, Kathleen despises Joe because his discount bookstore chain threatens to bankrupt Kathleen's family-owned bookshop. She also hates Joe's arrogant, self-absorbed style of communicating.

But in cyberspace, Joe seems like a different person. Unknown to both Joe and Kathleen, they have been communicating anonymously for months after meeting in an online chat room, using the names "NY152" and "Shopgirl." The e-mail messages Joe sends Kathleen are tender and self-disclosing. She falls for NY152 without knowing that the same man she can't stand in person writes the enchanting messages.

Joe learns of Kathleen's cyber identity before she learns of his, and he realizes the need to change his face-to-face presentational style. He begins revealing his softer side in their in-person encounters. In true Hollywood fashion, Kathleen and Joe ultimately find love in person. For students of communication, this romance demonstrates that each of us has many identities and that the way we present ourselves can shape the fate of our relationships.

CONTENTS

KEY TERMS

abstract language
abstraction ladder
behavioral description
convergence
divergence
emotive language
equivocal words
equivocation
euphemism
factual statement
high-context culture
inferential statement
jargon
language
linguistic determinism
linguistic relativism
low-context culture
opinion statement
phonological rules
pragmatic rules
relative words
semantic rules
sex role
slang
symbol
syntactic rules
Whorf-Sapir hypothesis

CHAPTER 3

AFTER STUDYING THE MATERIAL IN THIS CHAPTER

YOU SHOULD UNDERSTAND:

1. The symbolic, person-centered nature of language.

2. Phonological, semantic, syntactic, and pragmatic rules that govern language.

3. The ways in which language shapes and reflects perceptions.

4. The types of troublesome language and the skills to deal with each.

5. The relationship between language use and gender.

6. The relationship between language and culture.

YOU SHOULD BE ABLE TO:

1. Identify at least two ways in which language has shaped your perceptions.

2. Identify at least two ways in which language reflects your perceptions.

3. Discuss how you and others use syntactic, semantic, phonological, and pragmatic rules and how their use affects a message's comprehension.

4. Recognize and suggest alternatives for equivocal language, relative terms, and overly abstract language.

5. Identify and suggest alternatives for fact-inference and fact-opinion confusion and for emotive statements.

6. Suggest appropriate alternatives for unnecessary or misleading euphemisms and equivocal statements.

LANGUAGE

At one time or another, every one of us has suffered the limits and traps of language. Even though we are using familiar words, it's clear that we often don't use them in ways that allow us to communicate smoothly with one another.

In the following pages we will explore the nature of linguistic communication. By the time you have finished reading this chapter, you will better appreciate the complexity of language, its power to shape our perception of people and events, and its potential for incomplete and inaccurate communication. Perhaps more importantly, you will be better equipped to use the tool of language more skillfully to improve your everyday interaction.

THE NATURE OF LANGUAGE

Humans speak about ten thousand dialects.[1] Although most of these sound different from one another, all possess the same characteristics of **language**: a collection of symbols governed by rules and used to convey messages between individuals. A closer look at this definition can explain how language operates and suggest how we can use it more effectively.

Language Is Symbolic

There's nothing natural about calling your loyal four-footed companion a "dog" or the object you're reading right now a "book." These words, like virtually all language, are **symbols**—arbitrary constructions that represent a communicator's thoughts. Not all linguistic symbols are spoken or written words. Speech and writing aren't the only forms of language. Sign language, as "spoken" by most deaf people, is symbolic in nature and not the pantomime it might seem. There are literally hundreds of different sign languages spoken around the world that represent the same ideas differently.[2] These distinct languages include American Sign Language, British Sign Language, French Sign Language, Danish Sign Language, Chinese Sign Language—even Australian Aboriginal and Mayan sign languages.

Symbols are more than just labels: They are the way we experience the world. You can prove this fact by trying a simple experiment.[3] Work up some saliva in your mouth, and then spit it into a glass. Take a good look, and then drink it up. Most people find this process mildly disgusting. But ask yourself why this is so. After all, we swallow our own saliva all the time. The answer arises out of the symbolic labels we use. After the saliva is in the glass, we call it *spit* and think of it in a different way. In other words, our reaction is to the *name,* not the thing.

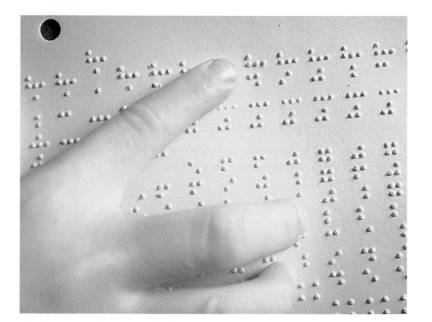

. . . words strain,

Crack and sometimes break, under the burden

Under the tension, slip, slide, perish,

Decay with imprecision, will not stay in one place,

Will not stay still.

T. S. Eliot
"Burnt Norton" in Four Quartets

The naming process operates in virtually every situation. How you react to a stranger will depend on the symbols you use to categorize him or her: gay (or straight), religious (or not), attractive (or unattractive), and so on.

Meanings Are in People, Not Words

Calvin and Hobbes   **by Bill Watterson**

Ask a dozen people what the same symbol means, and you are likely to get twelve different answers. Does an American flag bring up associations of patriots giving their lives for their country? Fourth of July parades? Cultural imperialism? How about a cross: What does it represent? The message of Jesus Christ? Fire-lit rallies of Ku Klux Klansmen? Your childhood Sunday school? The necklace your sister always wears?

As with physical symbols, the place to look for meaning in language isn't in the words themselves, but rather in the way people make sense of them. One unfortunate example of this fact occurred in Washington, DC, when the newly appointed city ombudsman used the word "niggardly" to describe an approach to budgeting.[4] Some African-American critics accused him of uttering an unforgivable racial slur. His defenders pointed out that the word, which means "miserly," is derived from Scandinavian languages and that it has no link to the racial slur it resembles. Even though the criticisms eventually died away, they illustrate that, correct or not, the meanings people associate with words have far more significance than do their dictionary definitions.

Linguistic theorists C. K. Ogden and I. A. Richards illustrated the fact that meanings are social constructions in their well-known "triangle of meaning" (Figure 3–1).[5] This model shows that there is only an indirect relationship—indicated by a broken line—between a word and the thing it claims to represent. Some of these "things" or referents do not exist in the physical world. For instance, some referents are mythical (such as unicorns), some are no longer tangible (such as Elvis, if he really is dead), and others are abstract ideas (such as "love").

Problems arise when people mistakenly assume that others use words in the same way they do. It's possible to have an argument about *feminism* without ever realizing that you and the other person are using the word to represent entirely different things. The same goes for *environmentalism, Republicans, rock music,* and thousands upon thousands of other symbols. Words don't mean; people do—and often in widely different ways.

Despite the potential for linguistic problems, the situation isn't hopeless. We do, after all, communicate with one another reasonably well most of the time. And with enough effort, we can clear up most of the misunderstandings that do occur. The key to more accurate use of

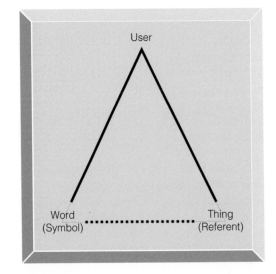

Figure 3–1   Ogden and Richards's Triangle of Meaning

language is to avoid assuming that others interpret words the same way we do. In truth, successful communication occurs when we *negotiate* the meaning of a statement. [6] As one French proverb puts it: The spoken word belongs half to the one who speaks it and half to the one who hears.

Language Is Rule-Governed

Languages contain several types of rules. **Phonological rules** govern how words sound when pronounced. For instance, the words *champagne, double,* and *occasion* are spelled identically in French and English, but all are pronounced differently. Nonnative speakers learning English are plagued by inconsistent phonological rules, as a few examples illustrate:

He could lead if he would get the lead out.
A farm can produce produce.
The dump was so full it had to refuse refuse.
The present is a good time to present the present.
I did not object to the object.
The bandage was wound around the wound.
I shed a tear when I saw the tear in my clothes.

Phonological rules aren't the only ones that govern the way we use language to communicate. **Syntactic rules** govern the structure of language—the way symbols can be arranged. For example, correct English syntax requires that every word contain at least one vowel and prohibits sentences such as "Have you the cookies brought?" which is a perfectly acceptable word order in German. Although most of us aren't able to describe the syntactic rules that govern our language, it's easy to recognize their existence by noting how odd a statement that violates them appears.

Technology has spawned subversions of English with their own syntactic rules.[7] For example, users of instant messaging on the Internet have devised a streamlined version of English that speeds up typing in real-time communication (although it probably makes teachers of composition grind their teeth in anguish):

A: Hey
B: r u at home?
A: yup yup
B: ok I'm getting offline now
A: no! why?
B: i need t study for finals u can call me tho bye
A: kbye

Semantic rules deal with the meaning of specific words. Semantic rules are what make it possible for us to agree that "bikes" are for riding and "books" are for reading; they also help us to know whom we will and won't encounter when we open doors marked "men" or "women." Without semantic rules, communication would be impossible, because each of us would use symbols in unique ways, unintelligible to one another.

Pragmatic rules are the final type of rules that governs how we use language. We use them to figure out what interpretation of a message is appropriate in a given context. Table 3–1 illustrates how pragmatic rules help communicators

TABLE 3–1   Pragmatic Rules Govern the Use and Meaning of a Statement

Notice how the same message ("You look very pretty today") takes on different meanings depending on which of a variety of rules are used to formulate and interpret it.

Statement	Boss "You look very pretty today."	Employee
Self-concept "Who am I?" "Who is she [or he]?"	Friendly guy	Woman determined to succeed on own merits
Episode "What's going on in this exchange?"	Casual conversation	Possible come-on by boss?
Relationship "Who are we to one another?"	Boss who treats employees like family members	Subordinate employee, dependent on boss's approval for advancement
Culture "What does my background say about the meaning here?"	Middle-class American	Middle-class American

Adapted from W. B. Pearce and V. Cronen, *Communication, Action, and Meaning* (New York: Praeger, 1980), and E. M. Griffin, *A First Look at Communication Theory*, 5th ed. (New York: McGraw-Hill, 2003).

UNDERSTANDING COMMUNICATION TECHNOLOGY

Translation on the Web

Can technology solve the ages-old problem of allowing us to understand people who speak different languages? Several sites on the World Wide Web offer automatic computerized translations. One such program is available free through AltaVista at http://world.altavista.com/.

How effective are programs like AltaVista's? The standard way to test the accuracy of a translator is to convert a message from one language to another, and then back. This approach demonstrates that computerized translations are useful, but far from perfect.

AltaVista's software works well enough for most simple messages. For example, the request "Please send me information on travel in Latin America." came through almost perfectly when first translated into Spanish and then back to English.

A translation of the announcement "My flight from Miami arrives at 9:00 P.M." changed prepositions, but it was understandable when it came back as "My flight of Miami arrives 9:00 P.M."

Translation software begins to show its limitations when literal conversions fail to capture the colloquial meaning of a word. For example, the message "This is a tricky job" came back from AltaVista after an Italian translation as "This is a deceptive job." It's easy to imagine how this sort of error could lead to ill feelings.

Idioms are especially prone to bungled translations. For example, the English expression "That's easier said than done" was translated in an English-Spanish-English conversion into the confusing statement "That one is the this easiest one that done." An English-French-English translation of "I'm down in the dumps" came back as "I am feeling downwards in emptyings."

Computerized translations aren't advised for communicators who want to build and maintain personal relationships. A simple example shows why: The flattering confession "I would like to get to know you better" was transformed into the confusing statement "It wanted to familiarize to me with him better"—not the kind of message that is likely to win friends and influence people.

Despite their shortcomings, computerized translation programs can provide at least a sense of what is being expressed in an unfamiliar language. At the same time, their flaws demonstrate that understanding semantic and pragmatic rules is a uniquely human ability—at least for now.

make sense of a message—and how the same statement can have quite different meanings when communicators use different pragmatic rules. The semantic meaning of the statement "You look very pretty today" is clear enough, yet the statement could be taken in several ways. The "Understanding Communication Technology" box on page 75 shows that understanding pragmatic rules is vitally important when mastering a new language and that learning vocabulary and syntactic rules is no guarantee of linguistic proficiency.

Pragmatic rules can be quite complex. Consider the use of humor: One study identified twenty-four different functions humor can serve in conversations.[8] These include showing the speaker's sense of humor, entertaining others, decreasing another person's aggressive behavior, easing the disclosure of difficult information, expressing feelings, protecting the speaker's ego from attack, avoiding self-disclosure, and expressing aggression. It's easy to imagine how a joke aimed at serving one of these functions—reducing boredom, for example— might be interpreted by the recipient as an attack.

INVITATION
TO INSIGHT

Discovering Linguistic Rules

You can understand the types and importance of linguistic rules by interviewing someone who is familiar with a language besides English. (If you speak a second language, use your own experience to complete this exercise.)

1. For each type of rule that follows, identify examples of the differences between English and the other language:
   a. phonological rules
   b. semantic rules
   c. syntactic rules
   d. pragmatic rules
2. Now answer the following questions:
   a. What kinds of communication challenges arise when each type of rule is broken? How do these challenges differ?
   b. Are there any cases when one or more types of these rules vary within the same language?

THE POWER OF LANGUAGE

On the most obvious level, language allows us to satisfy basic functions such as describing ideas, making requests, and solving problems. But beyond these functions, the way we use language also influences others and reflects our attitudes in more subtle ways, which we will examine now.

Language Shapes Attitudes

The power of language to shape ideas has been recognized throughout history. The first chapters of the Bible report that Adam's dominion over animals was demonstrated by his being given the power to give them names.[9] As we will now see, our speech—sometimes consciously and sometimes not—shapes others' values, attitudes, and beliefs in a variety of ways.

The most powerful stimulus for changing minds is not a chemical. Or a baseball bat. It is a word.

George A. Miller, past president, American Psychological Association

Source: © Zits Partnership. Reprinted with special permission of King Features Syndicate.

NAMING "What's in a name?" Juliet asked rhetorically. If Romeo had been a so-cial scientist, he would have answered, "A great deal." Research has demon-strated that names are more than just a simple means of identification: They shape the way others think of us, the way we view ourselves, and the way we act.

At the most fundamental level, some research suggests that even the phonetic sound of a person's name affects the way we regard him or her, at least when we don't have other information available. One recent study revealed that reason-ably accurate predictions about who will win an election can be made on the ba-sis of some phonetic features of the candidates' surnames.[10] Names that were simple, easily pronounced, and rhythmic were judged more favorably than ones that lack these qualities. For example, in one series of local elections, the win-ning candidates had names that resonated with voters: Sanders beat Pekelis, Rielly defeated Dellwo, Grady outpolled Schumacher, Combs trounced Bernsdorf, and Golden prevailed over Nuffer. Names don't guarantee victory, but in seventy-eight elections, forty-eight outcomes supported the value of hav-ing an appealing name.

The book of Proverbs (22:1) proclaims "a good name is rather to be chosen than great riches." Social science research confirms this position.[11] In one study, psychologists asked college students to rate over a thousand names according to their likability, how active or passive they seemed, and their masculinity or fem-ininity. The names Michael, John, and Wendy were viewed as likable and active and were rated as possessing the masculine or feminine traits of their sex. The names Percival, Isadore, and Alfreda were less likable, and their sexual identity was less clear.

The preconceptions we hold about people because of their names influence our behavior toward them. In another study, researchers asked a number of teachers to read several essays supposedly written by fifth-grade students. The researchers found that certain names—generally the most popular ones, such as Lisa, Michael, and Karen—received higher grades regardless of which essay they were attached to, whereas less popular names—Elmer, Bertha, Hubert—were consistently graded as inferior. There was one exception to the link between popular names and high grades: Unpopular Adelle received the highest evalua-tion of all. The researchers speculated that the teachers saw her as more "schol-arly." The impact of names does affect first impressions, but the effect doesn't seem so powerful after communicators become more familiar with one an-other.[12]

Choosing a newborn's name can be especially challenging for people from nondominant cultures with different languages. One writer from India describes the problem he and his wife faced when considering names for their first child:

> How will the child's foreign name sound to American ears? (That test ruled out Shiva, my family deity; a Jewish friend put her foot down.) Will it provoke bullies to beat him up on the school playground? (That was the end of Karan, the name of a warrior from the Mahabharata, the Hindu epic. A boy called "Karen" wouldn't stand a chance.) Will it be as euphonic in New York as it is in New Delhi? (That was how Sameer failed to get off the ground. "Like a bagel with a schmear!" said one ruthless well-wisher.)[13]

Parents who adopt children from different cultures face even greater challenges when choosing names.[14] Some adoptive parents have chosen "American" names in order to help their children fit comfortably into society. One set of parents followed this advice and chose the familiar-sounding name Jae for their six-year-old son. By the time the boy was eight, he complained that they should have given him a *more* American-sounding name, "like Hulk Hogan!"[15] On the other hand, there are compelling reasons to let children keep the names from their cultures of origin. Doing so gives them a connection with their heritage and emphasizes that their roots can be a source of pride. There's no easy answer to the cross-cultural naming dilemma, but its very existence shows the importance of naming.

First names aren't the only linguistic elements that may shape attitudes about men and women. As the reading on page 84 suggests, the choice of what last name to use after marriage can influence others' perceptions.

CREDIBILITY   Scholarly speaking is a good example of how speech style influences perception. We refer to what has been called the Dr. Fox hypothesis.[16] "An apparently legitimate speaker who utters an unintelligible message will be judged competent by an audience in the speaker's area of apparent expertise." The Dr. Fox hypothesis got its name from one Dr. Myron L. Fox, who delivered a talk followed by a half-hour discussion on "Mathematical Game Theory as Applied to Physical Education." The audience included psychiatrists, psychologists, social workers, and educators. Questionnaires collected after the session revealed that these educated listeners found the lecture clear and stimulating.

Despite his warm reception by this learned audience, Fox was a complete fraud. He was a professional actor whom researchers had coached to deliver a lecture of double-talk—a patchwork of information from a *Scientific American* article mixed with jokes, non sequiturs, contradictory statements, and meaningless references to unrelated topics. When wrapped in a linguistic package of high-level professional jargon, however, the meaningless gobbledygook was judged as important information. In other words, Fox's audience reaction was based more on the credibility that arose from his use of impressive-sounding language than from the ideas he expressed.

The same principle seems to hold for academic writing.[17] A group of thirty-two management professors rated material according to its complexity rather than its content. When a message about consumer behavior was loaded with unnecessary words and long, complex sentences, the professors rated it highly. When the same message was translated into more readable English, with shorter words and clearer sentences, the professors judged the same research as less competent.

STATUS In the classic musical *My Fair Lady,* Professor Henry Higgins transformed Eliza Doolittle from a lowly flower girl into a high-society woman by replacing her cockney accent with an upper-crust speaking style. Decades of research have demonstrated that the power of speech to influence status is a fact.[18] Several factors combine to create positive or negative impressions: accent, choice of words, speech rate, and even the apparent age of a speaker. In most cases, speakers of standard dialect are rated higher than nonstandard speakers in a variety of ways: They are viewed as more competent and more self-confident, and the content of their messages is rated more favorably. The unwillingness or inability of a communicator to use the standard dialect fluently can have serious consequences. For instance, speakers of Black English, a distinctive dialect with its own accent, grammar, syntax, and semantic rules, are rated as less intelligent, professional, capable, socially acceptable, and employable by speakers of standard English.[19]

SEXISM AND RACISM By now it should be clear that the power of language to shape attitudes goes beyond individual cases and influences how we perceive entire groups of people. For example, Casey Miller and Kate Swift argue that some aspects of language suggest women are of lower status than men. Miller and Swift contend that, except for words referring to females by definition, such as *mother* and *actress,* English defines many nonsexual concepts as male. Most dictionaries, in fact, define *effeminate* as the opposite of *masculine,* although the opposite of *feminine* is closer to *unfeminine.*

Miller and Swift also argue that incorrect use of the pronoun *he* to refer to both men and women can have damaging results.

> On the television screen, a teacher of first-graders who has just won a national award is describing her way of teaching. "You take each child where you find him," she says. "You watch to see what he's interested in, and then you build on his interests."
> A five-year-old looking at the program asks her mother, "Do only boys go to that school?"
> "No," her mother begins, "she's talking about girls too, but—"
> But what? The teacher being interviewed on television is speaking correct English. What can the mother tell her daughter about why a child, in any generalization, is always he rather than she? How does a five-year-old comprehend the generic personal pronoun?[20]

It's usually easy to use nonsexist language. For example, the term *mankind* may be replaced by *humanity, human beings, human race,* or *people; man-made* may be replaced by *artificial, manufactured,* and *synthetic; manpower* may be replaced by *human power, workers,* and *workforce;* and *manhood* may be replaced by *adulthood.* Likewise,

"No, I'm not a salesgirl. Are you a salesboy?"

- *Congressmen* may be called *members of Congress.*
- *Firemen* may be called *firefighters.*
- *Foremen* may be called *supervisors.*
- *Policemen* and *policewomen* are both *police officers.*

The use of labels for racist purposes has a long and ugly past. Names have been used throughout history to stigmatize groups that other groups have disapproved of.[21] By using derogatory terms to label some people, the out-group is set apart and pictured in an unfavorable light. Diane Mader provides several examples of this:

> We can see the process of stigmatization in Nazi Germany when Jewish people became vermin, in the United States when African Americans became "niggers" and chattel, in the military when the enemy became "gooks."[22]

"When you're on their flowers, you're a snail. When they want to eat you, suddenly you're an escargot."

The power of racist language to shape attitudes is difficult to avoid, even when it is obviously offensive. In one study, experimental subjects who heard a derogatory label used against a member of a minority group expressed annoyance at this sort of slur; but despite their disapproval, the negative emotional terms did have an impact.[23] Not only did the unwitting subjects rate the minority individual's competence lower when that person performed poorly, but also they found fault with others who associated socially with the minority person—even members of the subject's own ethnic group.

ETHICAL CHALLENGE

Sexist and Racist Language

One of the most treasured civil liberties is freedom of speech. At the same time, most people would agree that some forms of racist and sexist speech are hateful and demeaning to their targets. As you have read in these pages, language shapes the attitudes of those who hear it.

How do you reconcile the principle of free speech and the need to minimize hateful and discriminatory messages? Do you think laws and policies can and should be made that limit certain types of communication? If so, how should those limits be drafted to protect civil liberties? If not, can you justify the necessary protection of even sexist and racist language?

Language Reflects Attitudes

Besides shaping the way we view ourselves and others, language reflects our attitudes. Feelings of control, attraction, commitment, responsibility—all these and more are reflected in the way we use language.

POWER   Communication researchers have identified a number of language patterns that add to, or detract from, a speaker's ability to influence others, as well as reflecting how a speaker feels about his or her degree of control over a situation.[24] Table 3–2 summarizes some of these findings by listing several types of "powerless" language.

You can see the difference between powerful language and powerless language by comparing the following statements:

> "Excuse me, sir, I hate to say this, but I . . . uh . . . I guess I won't be able to turn in the assignment on time. I had a personal emergency and . . . well . . . it was just impossible to finish it by today. I'll have it in your mailbox on Monday, okay?"

> "I won't be able to turn in the assignment on time. I had a personal emergency, and it was impossible to finish it by today. I'll have it in your mailbox on Monday."

Although the powerless speech described in Table 3–2 can often lead to unsatisfying results, don't assume that the best goal is always to sound as powerful as you can. Along with gaining compliance, another conversational goal is often building a supportive, friendly relationship; and sharing power with the other person can help you in this regard. For this reason, many everyday statements will contain a mixture of powerful speech and powerless speech. Our student-teacher example illustrates how this combination of powerless mannerisms and powerful mannerisms can help the student get what she wants while staying on good terms with the professor:

> "Excuse me, Professor Rodman. I want you to know that I won't be able to turn in the assignment on time. I had a personal emergency, and it was impossible to finish it by today. I'll definitely have it in your mailbox on Monday."

Whether or not the professor finds the excuse acceptable, it's clear that this last statement combines the best features of powerful speech and powerless speech: a combination of self-assurance and goodwill.

Simply counting the number of powerful or powerless statements won't always reveal who has the most control in a relationship. Social rules often mask the real distribution of power. Sociolinguist Deborah Tannen describes how politeness can be a face-saving way of delivering an order:

> I hear myself giving instructions to my assistants without actually issuing orders: "Maybe it would be a good idea to . . .;" "It would be great if you could . . . " all the while knowing that I expect them to do what I've asked right away . . . This rarely creates problems, though, because the people who work for me know that there is only one reason I mention tasks—because I want them done. I *like* giving instructions in this way; it appeals to my sense of what it means to be a good person . . . taking others' feelings into account.[25]

As this quote suggests, high-status speakers often realize that politeness is an effective way to get their needs met

---

The power which comes from names and naming is related directly to the power to define others— individuals, races, sexes, ethnic groups. Our identities, who and what we are, how others see us, are greatly affected by the names we are called and by the words with which we are labeled. The names, labels, and phrases employed to "identify" a people may in the end determine their survival.

Haig A. Bosmajian
The Language of Oppression

CULTURAL IDIOM

face-saving: protective of one's dignity

TABLE 3–2   Powerless Language

Type of Usage	Example
Hedges	"I'm kinda disappointed . . ." "I think we should . . ." "I guess I'd like to . . ."
Hesitations	"Uh, can I have a minute of your time?" "Well, we could try this idea . . ." "I wish you would—er—try to be on time."
Intensifiers	"So that's how I feel . . ." "I'm not very hungry."
Polite forms	"Excuse me, sir . . ."
Tag questions	"It's about time we got started, isn't it?" "Don't you think we should give it another try?"
Disclaimers	"I probably shouldn't say this, but . . ." "I'm not really sure, but . . ."

while protecting the face of the less powerful person. The importance of achieving both content goals and relational goals helps explain why a mixture of powerful speech and polite speech is usually most effective.[26] Of course, if the other person misinterprets politeness for weakness, it may be necessary to shift to a more powerful speaking style.

Powerful speech that gets the desired results in mainstream North American and European culture doesn't succeed everywhere with everyone.[27] In Japan, saving face for others is an important goal, so communicators there tend to speak in ambiguous terms and use hedge words and qualifiers. In most Japanese sentences the verb comes at the end of the sentence so the "action" part of the statement can be postponed. Traditional Mexican culture, with its strong emphasis on cooperation, makes a priority of using language to create harmony in interpersonal relationships rather than taking a firm or oppositional stance in order to make others feel more at ease. Korean culture represents yet another group of people who prefers "indirect" (for example, "perhaps," "could be") to "direct" speech.

SKILL BUILDER

Powerful Speech and Polite Speech

Increase your ability to achieve an optimal balance between powerful speech and polite speech by rehearsing one of the following scenarios:

- Describing your qualifications to a potential employer for a job that interests you.
- Requesting an extension on a deadline from one of your professors.
- Explaining to a merchant why you want a cash refund on an unsatisfactory piece of merchandise when the store's policy is to issue credit vouchers.
- Asking your boss for three days off so you can attend a friend's out-of-town wedding.
- Approaching your neighbors whose dog barks while they are away from home.

Your statement should gain its power by avoiding the types of powerless language listed in Table 3–2. You should not become abusive or threatening, and your statement should be completely honest.

AFFILIATION Power isn't the only way language reflects the status of relationships. Language can also be a way of building and demonstrating solidarity with others. An impressive body of research has demonstrated that communicators who want to show affiliation with one another adapt their speech in a variety of ways, including their choice of vocabulary, rate of talking, number and placement of pauses, and level of politeness.[28] On an individual level, close friends and lovers often develop special terms that serve as a way of signifying their relationship.[29] Using the same vocabulary sets these people apart from others, reminding themselves and the rest of the world of their relationship. The same process works among members of larger groups, ranging from street gangs to military personnel. Communication researchers call this linguistic accommodation **convergence.**

When two or more people feel equally positive about one another, their linguistic convergence will be mutual. But when communicators want or need the approval of others they often adapt their speech to suit the others' style, trying to say the "right thing" or speak in a way that will help them fit in. We see this process when immigrants who want to gain the rewards of material success in a new culture strive to master the prevalent language. Likewise, employees who seek advancement tend to speak more like their superiors: supervisors adopt the speech style of managers, and managers converge toward their bosses.

The principle of speech accommodation works in reverse, too. Communicators who want to set themselves apart from others adopt the strategy of **divergence,** speaking in a way that emphasizes their difference from others. For example, members of an ethnic group, even though fluent in the dominant language, might use their own dialect as a way of showing solidarity with one another—a sort of "us against them" strategy. Divergence also operates in other settings. A physician or attorney, for example, who wants to establish credibility with his or her client might speak formally and use professional jargon to create a sense of distance. The implicit message here is "I'm different (and more knowledgeable) than you."

ATTRACTION AND INTEREST   Social customs discourage us from expressing like or dislike in many situations. Only a clod would respond to the question "What do you think of the cake I baked for you?" by saying, "It's terrible." Bashful or cautious suitors might not admit their attraction to a potential partner. Even when people are reluctant to speak candidly, the language they use can suggest their degree of interest and attraction toward a person, object, or idea. Morton Weiner and Albert Mehrabian outline a number of linguistic clues that reveal these attitudes.[30]

- **Demonstrative pronoun choice.** *These* people want our help (positive) versus *Those* people want our help (less positive).
- **Negation.** It's *good* (positive) versus It's *not bad* (less positive).
- **Sequential placement.** Dick and Jane (Dick is more important) versus Jane and Dick (Jane is more important). However, sequential placement isn't always significant. You may put "toilet bowl cleaner" at the top of your shopping list simply because it's closer to the market door than is champagne.

RESPONSIBILITY   In addition to suggesting liking and importance, language can reveal the speaker's willingness to accept responsibility for a message.

- **"It" versus "I" statements.** *It's* not finished (less responsible) versus *I* didn't finish it (more responsible).
- **"You" versus "I" statements.** Sometimes *you* make me angry (less responsible) versus Sometimes *I* get angry when you do that (more responsible). "I" statements are more likely to generate positive reactions from others when compared to accusatory ones.[31]
- **"But" statements.** It's a good idea, *but* it won't work. You're really terrific, *but* I think we ought to spend less time together. (*But* cancels everything that went before the word.)
- **Questions versus statements.** Do you think we ought to do that? (less responsible) versus I don't think we ought to do that (more responsible).

CULTURAL IDIOM

a clod: a dull or stupid person

In the Name of Love

It used to be a non-issue. When Jane Doe married Joe Snow, she became Jane Snow. But as gender roles change, more couples are breaking with tradition.

These days, a married woman might remain Jane Doe or become Jane Doe Snow, or Jane Doe-Snow—or even Joe Doe. Some couples are choosing to merge their last names, becoming Jane and Joe Snowdoe.

"There's been all kinds of engineering with names," says Rae Moses, a linguistics professor at Northwestern University. Moses surveyed an Illinois grade school with 302 students and found that 32% of them—most of whose mothers were working professionals—had non-traditional last names.

As more options become acceptable, many couples are asking themselves: What's in a name?

There's no shortage of answers. To some, the traditional method is a sexist vestige of the days when a woman literally became her husband's property. To others, the tradition has long since shed that stigma and has become a romantic symbol of the bond between two people. To still others, it's a convenient way to dump an unwieldy name. At least 90% of Americans still follow tradition, says Laurie Scheuble, a sociologist at Doane College in Nebraska. But, she says, as more women establish careers and marry later in life, many are choosing to keep their names.

"I don't think it's ever going to be the norm, but I think we're going to see more of it in the future," says Scheuble. She adds, people with more education and higher incomes are more likely to be tolerant of a woman keeping her name, as are people who grew up in large cities. Political and religious leanings also seemed to affect attitudes.

When Jeff Nicholson of Champaign, Ill., married Dawn Owens, he became Nicholson-Owens; she became Owens-Nicholson. "I felt it would make me feel a lot closer to her," says Jeff, 24. "And it seemed fairest. Neither of us loses our heritage in the family tree." Dawn, 31, says her family wasn't thrilled when she broke the news. "My mom was really looking forward to saying 'Mr. and Mrs. Jeffrey Nicholson.'" So, apparently, was the Illinois Department of Motor Vehicles. "We had to fight them tooth and nail to get a hyphen on our driver's licenses," Dawn says. "They said their software wouldn't take it."

Nancy Herman of Minneapolis and her husband, Don Perlmutter, came up with yet another variation: They merged their names, becoming the Perlmans.

Several other countries do have different naming methods. In some Scandinavian and Latin American countries, married women often keep their names. In Japan, if a woman with no siblings marries into a family that has several sons, her husband will sometimes take her family name. "It's kind of a gift that the groom's family gives to the bride's family," Moses says.

Suzanne Schlosberg
Los Angeles Times

TROUBLESOME LANGUAGE

Besides being a blessing that enables us to live together, language can be something of a curse. We have all known the frustration of being misunderstood, and most of us have been baffled by another person's overreaction to an innocent comment. In the following pages we will look at several kinds of troublesome language, with the goal of helping you communicate in a way that makes matters better instead of worse.

The Language of Misunderstandings

The most obvious kind of language problems are semantic: We simply don't understand others completely or accurately. Most misunderstandings arise from some common problems that are easily remedied—after you recognize them.

EQUIVOCAL LANGUAGE   **Equivocal words** have more than one correct dictionary definition. Some equivocal misunderstandings are simple, at least after they are exposed. A nurse once told her patient that he "wouldn't be needing" the materials he requested from home. He interpreted the statement to mean he was near death when the nurse meant he would be going home soon. A colleague of ours mistakenly sent some confidential materials to the wrong person after his boss told him to "send them to Richard," without specifying *which* Richard. Some equivocal misunderstandings can be embarrassing, as one woman recalls:

> In the fourth grade the teacher asked the class what a period was. I raised my hand and shared everything I had learned about girls' getting their period. But he was talking about the dot at the end of a sentence. Oops![32]

Equivocal misunderstandings can have serious consequences. Communication researchers Michael Motley and Heidi Reeder suggest that equivocation at least partially explains why men may sometimes persist in attempts to become physically intimate when women have expressed unwillingness to do so.[33] Interviews and focus groups with college students revealed that women often use ambiguous phrases to say "no" to a man's sexual advances: "I'm confused about this." "I'm not sure that we're ready for this yet." "Are you sure you want to do this?" "Let's be friends" and even "That tickles." (The researchers found that women were most likely to use less direct phrases when they hoped to see or date the man again. When they wanted to cut off the relationship, they were more likely to give a direct response.) Whereas women viewed indirect statements as equivalent to saying "no," men were more likely to interpret them as less clear-cut requests to stop. As the researchers put it, "male/female misunderstandings are not so much a matter of males hearing resistance messages as "go," but rather their not hearing them as "stop." Under the law, "no" means precisely that, and anyone who argues otherwise can be in for serious legal problems.

RELATIVE WORDS **Relative words** gain their meaning by comparison. For example, is the school you attend large or small? This depends on what you compare it to: Alongside a campus like UCLA, with an enrollment of over thirty thousand students, it probably looks small; but compared to a smaller institution, it might seem quite large. In the same way relative words like *fast* and *slow, smart* and *stupid, short* and *long* depend for their meaning upon what they're compared to. (The "large" size can of olives is the smallest you can buy; the larger ones are "giant," "colossal," and "supercolossal.")

Some relative words are so common that we mistakenly assume that they have a clear meaning. In one study, graduate students were asked to assign numerical values to terms such as

> **CULTURAL IDIOM**
>
> **a period:** occurrence of menstruation

doubtful, toss-up, likely, probable, good chance, and *unlikely.*[34] There was a tremendous variation in the meaning of most of these terms. For example, the responses for *possible* ranged from 0 to 99 percent. *Good chance* meant between 35 and 90 percent, whereas *unlikely* fell between 0 and 40 percent.

Using relative words without explaining them can lead to communication problems. Have you ever responded to someone's question about the weather by saying it was warm, only to find out that what was warm to you was cold to the other person? Or have you followed a friend's advice and gone to a "cheap" restaurant, only to find that it was twice as expensive as you expected? Have you been disappointed to learn that classes you've heard were "easy" turned out to be hard, that journeys you were told would be "short" were long, that "unusual" ideas were really quite ordinary? The problem in each case came from failing to anchor the relative word used to a more precisely measurable word.

SLANG   **Slang** is language used by a group of people whose members belong to a similar co-culture or other group. Some slang is related to specialized interests and activities. For instance, cyclists who talk about "bonking" are referring to running out of energy. Rapsters know that "bling bling" refers to jewelry and a "whip" is a nice-looking car.

Other slang consists of *regionalisms*—terms that are understood by people who live in one geographic area but that are incomprehensible to outsiders. This sort of use illustrates how slang defines insiders and outsiders, creating a sense of identity and solidarity.[35] Residents of the fiftieth U.S. state know that when a fellow Alaskan says "I'm going outside," he or she is leaving the state. In the East End of London, cockney dialect uses rhyming words as substitutes for everyday expressions: "bacon and eggs" for "legs," and "Barney Rubble" for "trouble." This sort of use also illustrates how slang can be used to identify insiders and outsiders: With enough shared rhyming, slang users could talk about outsiders without the clueless outsiders knowing that they were the subject of conversation ("Lovely set of bacons, eh?" "Stay away from him. He's Barney.").

Slang can also be age-related. Most college students know that drinkers wearing "beer goggles" have consumed enough alcohol that they find almost everyone of the opposite—or sometimes the same—sex attractive. At some schools, a "monkey" is the "other" woman or man in a boyfriend's or girlfriend's life: "I've heard Mitch is cheating on me. When I find his monkey, I'm gonna do her up!"[36]

JARGON   Almost everyone uses some sort of **jargon**: the specialized vocabulary that functions as a kind of shorthand by people with common backgrounds and experience. Skateboarders have their own language to describe maneuvers: "ollie," "grind," and "shove it." Some jargon consists of *acronyms*—initials of terms that are combined to form a word. Stock traders refer to the NASDAQ (pronounced "naz-

"He's, like, 'To be or not to be,' and I'm, like, 'Get a life.'"

The little second grader's family had just moved and she was going to her school for the first time. When she came home that afternoon she said to her mother, "What's sex?" Her mother had been expecting that question for some time and she was ready for her tiny daughter. So, for the next half hour she explained about the birds and the bees. Then she said to her, "Now, do you understand what I have been telling you?" "Yes," her daughter said, "I think I do." Then she showed her mother a school registration card that she had brought home from school and said, "But how am I going to get all of that into this little square?"

Winston K. Pendelton

dak") securities index, and military people label failure to serve at one's post as being AWOL (absent without leave). The digital age has spawned its own vocabulary of jargon. For instance, computer users know that "viruses" are malicious programs that migrate from one computer to another, wreaking havoc. Likewise, "cookies" are tiny files that remote observers can use to monitor a user's computer habits. Some jargon goes beyond being descriptive and conveys attitudes. For example, cynics in the high-tech world sometimes refer to being fired from a job as being "uninstalled." They talk dismissively about the nonvirtual world as the "carbon community" and to books and newspapers as "treeware." Some technical support staffers talk of "banana problems," meaning those that could be figured out by monkeys, as in "This is a two-banana problem at worst."[37]

Jargon can be a valuable kind of shorthand for people who understand its use. The trauma team in a hospital emergency room can save time, and possibly lives, by speaking in shorthand, referring to "GSWs" (gunshot wounds), "chem 7" lab tests, and so on; but the same specialized vocabulary that works so well among insiders can mystify and confuse family members of the patient, who don't understand the jargon. The same sort of misunderstandings can arise in less critical settings when insiders use their own language with people who don't share the same vocabulary. Jeffrey Katzman of the William Morris Agency's Hollywood office experienced this sort of problem when he met with members of a Silicon Valley computer firm to discuss a joint project.

> When he used the phrase "in development," he meant a project that was as yet merely an idea. When the techies used it, on the other hand, they meant designing a specific game or program. Ultimately, says Katzman, he had to bring in a blackboard and literally define his terms. "It was like when the Japanese first came to Hollywood," he recalls. "They had to use interpreters, and we did too."[38]

SKILL BUILDER

Slang and Jargon

Find a classmate, neighbor, coworker, or other person whose background differs significantly from yours. In an interview, ask this person to identify the slang and jargon terms that you take for granted but that he or she has found confusing. Explore the following types of potentially confusing terms:

1. regionalisms
2. age-related terms
3. technical jargon
4. acronyms

OVERLY ABSTRACT LANGUAGE Most objects, events, and ideas can be described with varying degrees of specificity. Consider the material you are reading. You could call it:

A book
A textbook
A communication textbook
Understanding Human Communication
Chapter 3 of *Understanding Human Communication*
Page 87 of Chapter 3 of *Understanding Human Communication*

UNDERSTANDING COMMUNICATION TECHNOLOGY

E-Mail Abbreviations

E-mail users have adopted abbreviations with enthusiasm, primarily because they enable users to insert common phrases into their correspondence quickly and easily. Notice that several abbreviations (such as <G>, LOL, TIC) also serve the function of clarifying the sender's intentions, which aren't always clear in the sterile format of e-mail text.

AAMOF	As a matter of fact	OTOH	On the other hand
BFN	Bye for now	ROF	Rolling on the floor (laughing)
BTW	By the way	TIA	Thanks in advance
CMII	Correct me if I'm wrong	TIC	Tongue in cheek
FAQ	Frequently asked question(s)	TTYL	Talk to you later
FWIW	For what it's worth	WYSIWYG	What you see is what you get
FYI	For your information	<G>	Grinning
HTH	Hope this helps	<J>	Joking
IMHO	In my humble opinion (usually ironic)	<L>	Laughing
IOW	In other words	<S>	Smiling
LOL	Laughing out loud	<Y>	Yawning

In each case your description would be more and more specific. Semanticist S. I. Hayakawa created an **abstraction ladder** to describe this process.[39] This ladder consists of a number of descriptions of the same thing. Lower items focus specifically on the person, object, or event, whereas higher terms are generalizations that include the subject as a member of a larger class. To talk about "college," for example, is more abstract than to talk about a particular school. Likewise, referring to "women" is more abstract than referring to "feminists," or more specifically naming feminist organizations or even specific members who belong to them.

Higher-level abstractions are a useful tool, because without them language would be too cumbersome to be useful. It's faster, easier, and more useful to talk about *Europe* than to list all of the countries on that continent. In the same way, using relatively abstract terms like *friendly* or *smart* can make it easier to describe people than listing their specific actions.

Abstract language serves a second, less obvious function. At times it allows us to avoid confrontations by deliberately being unclear.[40] Suppose, for example, your boss is enthusiastic about a new approach to doing business that you think is a terrible idea. Telling the truth might seem too risky, but lying—saying "I think it's a great idea"—wouldn't feel right either. In situations like this an abstract answer can hint at your true belief without a direct confrontation: "I don't know . . . It's sure unusual . . . It *might* work." The same sort of abstract language can help you avoid embarrassing friends who ask for your opinion with questions like "What do you think of my new haircut?" An abstract response like "It's really different!" may be easier for you to deliver—and for your friend to receive—than the clear, brutal truth: "It's really ugly!" We will have more to say about this linguistic strategy of equivocation later in this chapter.

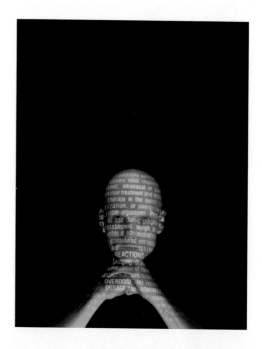

Although vagueness does have its uses, highly abstract language can cause several types of problems. The first is *stereotyping*. Consider claims like "All whites are bigots," "Men don't care about relationships," "The police are a bunch of goons," or "Professors around here care more about their research than they do about students." Each of these claims ignores the very important fact that abstract descriptions are almost always too general, that they say more than we really mean.

Besides creating stereotypical attitudes, abstract language can lead to the problem of *confusing others*. Imagine the lack of understanding that results from imprecise language in situations like this:

A: We never do anything that's fun anymore.

B: What do you mean?

A: We used to do lots of unusual things, but now it's the same old stuff, over and over.

B: But last week we went on that camping trip, and tomorrow we're going to that party where we'll meet all sorts of new people. Those are new things.

A: That's not what I mean. I'm talking about really unusual stuff.

B: *(becoming confused and a little impatient)* Like what? Taking hard drugs or going over Niagara Falls in a barrel?

A: Don't be stupid. All I'm saying is that we're in a rut. We should be living more exciting lives.

B: Well, I don't know what you want.

The best way to avoid this sort of overly abstract language is to use **behavioral descriptions** instead. (See Table 3–3.) Behavioral descriptions move down the abstraction ladder to identify the specific, observable phenomenon being discussed. A thorough description should answer three questions:

1. **Who Is Involved?** Are you speaking for just yourself or for others as well? Are you talking about a group of people ("the neighbors," "women") or specific individuals ("the people next door with the barking dog," "Lola and Lizzie")?

2. **In What Circumstances Does the Behavior Occur?** Where does it occur: everywhere or in specific places (at parties, at work, in public)? When does it occur: When you're tired or when a certain subject comes up? The behavior you are describing probably doesn't occur all the time. In order to be understood, you need to pin down what circumstances set this situation apart from other ones.

3. **What Behaviors Are Involved?** Though terms such as *more cooperative* and *helpful* might sound like concrete descriptions of behavior, they are usually too vague to do a clear job of explaining what's on your mind. Behaviors must be *observable*, ideally both to you and to others. For instance, moving down the abstraction ladder from the relatively vague term *helpful*, you might come to behaviors such as *does the dishes every other day, volunteers to help me with my studies,* or *fixes dinner once or twice a week without being asked*. It's easy to see that terms like these are easier for both you and others to understand than are more vague abstractions.

Behavioral descriptions can improve communication in a wide range of situations, as Table 3–3 illustrates. Research also supports the value of specific language. One study found that well-adjusted couples had just as many conflicts as poorly adjusted couples, but the way the well-adjusted couples handled their problems was significantly different. Instead of blaming one another by using emotive language, the well-adjusted couples expressed their complaints in behavioral terms.[41]

CULTURAL IDIOM

goons: those who intimidate others

in a rut: having fixed and monotonous routines and habits

TABLE 3–3 Abstract and Behavioral Descriptions

	Abstract Description	Behavioral Description			Remarks
		Who Is Involved	In What Circumstances	Specific Behaviors	
Problem	I talk too much.	People I find intimidating	When I want them to like me	I talk (mostly about myself) instead of giving them a chance to speak or asking about their lives.	Behavioral description more clearly identifies behaviors to change.
Goal	I want to be more constructive.	My roommate	When we talk about household duties	Instead of finding fault with her ideas, suggest alternatives that might work.	Behavioral description clearly outlines how to act; abstract description doesn't.
Appreciation	"You've really been helpful lately."	(Deliver to fellow worker)	"When I've had to take time off work because of personal problems"	"You took my shifts without complaining."	Give both abstract and behavioral descriptions for best results.
Request	"Clean up your act!"	(Deliver to target person)	"When we're around my family"	"Please don't tell jokes that involve sex."	Behavioral description specifies desired behavior.

Low-Level Abstractions

You can develop your ability to use low-level abstractions by following these steps:

1. Use your own experience to write each of the following:
   a. a complaint or gripe
   b. one way you would like someone with whom you interact to change
   c. one reason why you appreciate a person with whom you interact
2. Now translate each of the statements you have written into a low-level abstraction by including:
   a. the person or people involved
   b. the circumstances in which the behavior occurs
   c. the specific behaviors to which you are referring
3. Compare the statements you have written in Steps 1 and 2. How might the lower-level abstractions in Step 2 improve the chances of having your message understood and accepted?

You can dismiss an abstraction . . . You can mistreat an object . . . But as soon as you come upon a human being, you will be moved to share yourself with him, to care for him. It will be far more difficult to hurt his feelings or ignore him or simply analyze him. It will be almost impossible to kill him or cheer his death, which is why this sort of orientation can put armies out of business.

Alfie Kohn

Disruptive Language

Not all linguistic problems come from misunderstandings. Sometimes people understand one another perfectly and still end up in conflict. Of course, not all disagreements can, or should be, avoided. But eliminating three bad linguistic habits from your communication repertoire can minimize the kind of clashes that don't need to happen, allowing you to save your energy for the unavoidable and important struggles.

CONFUSING FACTS AND OPINIONS   **Factual statements** are claims that can be verified as true or false. By contrast, **opinion statements** are based on the speaker's beliefs. Unlike matters of fact, they can never be proved or disproved. Consider a few examples of the difference between factual statements and opinion statements:

FACT	OPINION
It rains more in Seattle than in Portland.	The climate in Portland is better than in Seattle
Kareem Abdul Jabar is the all-time leading scorer in the National Basketball Assocation.	Kareem is the greatest basketball player in the history of the game.
Per capita income in the United States is lower than in several other countries.	The United States is not the best model of economic success in the world.

When factual statements and opinion statements are set side by side like this, the difference between them is clear. In everyday conversation, we often present our opinions as if they were facts, and in doing so we invite an unnecessary argument. For example:

- "That was a dumb thing to say!"
- "Spending that much on _____ is a waste of money!"
- "You can't get a fair shake in this country unless you're a white male."

Notice how much less antagonistic each statement would be if it was prefaced by a qualifier like "In my opinion . . ." or "It seems to me . . ."

CONFUSING FACTS AND INFERENCES   Labeling your opinions can go a long way toward relational harmony, but developing this habit won't solve all linguistic problems. Difficulties also arise when we confuse factual statements with **inferential statements**—conclusions arrived at from an interpretation of evidence. Consider a few examples:

FACT	INFERENCE
He hit a lamppost while driving down the street.	He was daydreaming when he hit the lamppost.
You interrupted me before I finished what I was saying.	You don't care about what I have to say.
You haven't paid your share of the rent on time for the past three months.	You're trying to weasel out of your responsibilities.
I haven't gotten a raise in almost a year.	The boss is exploiting me.

There's nothing wrong with making inferences as long as you identify them as such: "She stomped out and slammed the door. It looked to me as if she were furious." The danger comes when we confuse inferences with facts and make them sound like the absolute truth.

One way to avoid fact-inference confusion is to use the perception-checking skill described in Chapter 2 to test the accuracy of your inferences. Recall that a perception check has three parts: a description of the behavior being discussed, your interpretation of that behavior, and a request for verification. For instance, instead of saying, "Why are you laughing at me?" you could say, "When you laugh like that [description of behavior], I get the idea you think something I did was stupid [interpretation]. Are you laughing at me [question]?"

EMOTIVE LANGUAGE   **Emotive language** contains words that sound as if they're describing something when they are really announcing the speaker's attitude toward something. Do you like that old picture frame? If so, you would probably call it "an antique," but if you think it's ugly, you would likely describe it as "a piece of junk." Emotive words may sound like statements of fact but are always opinions.

Barbra Streisand pointed out how some people use emotive language to stigmatize behavior in women that they admire in men:

A man is commanding—a woman is demanding.
A man is forceful—a woman is pushy.
A man is uncompromising—a woman is a ball-breaker.
A man is a perfectionist—a woman's a pain in the ass.
He's assertive—she's aggressive.
He strategizes—she manipulates.
He shows leadership—she's controlling.
He's committed—she's obsessed.
He's persevering—she's relentless.
He sticks to his guns—she's stubborn.
If a man wants to get it right, he's looked up to and respected.
If a woman wants to get it right, she's difficult and impossible.[42]

Source: © 1999 Marian Henley from cartoonbank.com. All Rights Reserved.

The reading on page 94 illustrates how emotive language can escalate conflicts and make constructive dialogue difficult, or even impossible.

As this reading suggests, problems occur when people use emotive words without labeling them as such. You might, for instance, have a long and bitter argument with a friend about whether a third person was "assertive" or "obnoxious," when a more accurate and peaceable way to handle the issue would be to acknowledge that one of you approves of the behavior and the other doesn't.

SKILL BUILDER

Emotive Language

Test your ability to identify emotive language by playing the following word game.

1. Take an action, object, or characteristic and show how it can be viewed either favorably or unfavorably, according to the label it is given. For example:
   a. I'm casual.
      You're careless.
      He's a slob.
   b. I read adult love stories.
      You read erotic literature.
      She reads pornography.
2. Now create three-part descriptions of your own, using the following statements as a start:
   a. I'm tactful.
   b. She's a liar.
   c. I'm conservative.
   d. You have a high opinion of yourself.
   e. I'm quiet.
   f. You're pessimistic.
3. Now recall two situations in which you used emotive language as if it were a description of fact. How might the results have differed if you had used more objective language?

Evasive Language

None of the troublesome language habits we have described so far is a deliberate strategy to mislead or antagonize others. Now, however, we'll consider euphemisms and equivocations, two types of language that speakers use by design to avoid communicating clearly. Although both of these have some very legitimate uses, they also can lead to frustration and confusion.

EUPHEMISMS   A euphemism (from the Greek word meaning "to use words of good omen") is a pleasant term substituted for a more direct but potentially less pleasant one. We are using euphemisms when we say "restroom" instead of "toilet" or "plump" instead of "fat" or "overweight." There certainly are cases where the euphemistic pulling of linguistic punches can be face-saving. It's probably more constructive to question a possible "statistical misrepresentation" than to call someone a liar, for example. Likewise, it may be less disquieting to some to refer to people as "senior citizens" than "old."

Becoming Desensitized to Hate Words

The ceremonies are over, but I would like to suggest one last way to commemorate the golden anniversary of the defeat of the Nazis. How about a moratorium on the current abuse of terms like storm trooper, swastika, Holocaust, Gestapo, and Hitler? How about putting the language of the Third Reich into mothballs?

The further we are removed from the defeat of the Nazis, the more this vocabulary seems to be taking over our own. It's become part of the casual, ubiquitous, inflammatory speech Americans use to turn each other into monsters. Which, if I recall correctly, was a tactic favored by Goebbels himself.

The NRA attacked federal agents as "jackbooted government thugs who wear Nazi bucket helmets and black storm trooper uniforms." In the ratcheting up of the rhetorical wars, it wasn't enough for the NRA to complain that the agents had overstepped their bounds; they had to call them Nazis.

Republican congressmen have compared environmentalist agencies with Hitler's troops. Pennsylvania's Bud Shuster talked about EPA officials as an "environmental Gestapo." Missouri's Bill Emerson warned about the establishment of an "eco-Gestapo force."

On the Democratic side, Sen. John Kerry recently suggested that a proposed new kind of tax audit, on "lifestyles," would produce an "IRS Gestapo-like entity." And John Lewis and Charles Rangel compared silence in the face of the new conservative agenda to silence in the early days of the Third Reich. They didn't just disagree with conservatives; they Nazified them.

Then there are the perennial entries on the Hitler log. Anti-abortion groups talk about the abortion holocaust—comparing the fetuses to Jews and the doctors to Mengele. As for pinning the Nazi label on supporters of abortion rights, the propagandists surely know that Hitler was a hard-line opponent of abortion. (Did that make him pro life?)

Even when Nazi-speak isn't historically dumb, it's rhetorically dumb. The Hitlerian language has become a [sic] indiscriminate shorthand for every petty tyranny. I [sic] this vocabulary, every two-bit boss becomes a "little Hitler." Every domineering high school principal is accused of running a "concentration camp." Every overbearing piece of behavior becomes a "Gestapo" tactic. And every political disagreement becomes a fight against evil.

Crying Hitler in our time is like crying wolf. The charge immediately escalates the argument, adding verbal fuel to fires of any dimension, however minor. But eventually, yelling Nazi at environmentalists and Gestapo at federal agents diminishes the emotional power of these words should we need them. In time, these epithets even downgrade the horror of the Third Reich and the immensity of World War II. They cheapen history and insult memory, especially the memory of the survivors.

Fifty years ago, Americans learned, with a fresh sense of horror, about the crematoriums, about man's inhumanity, about the trains that ran on time to the gas chambers. This was Nazism. This was the Gestapo. This was the Holocaust. This was Hitler. If you please, save the real words for the real thing.

Source: "Becoming Desensitized to Hate Words" by Ellen Goodman in *The Boston Globe*, June 6, 1995. Copyright © 1995, The Boston Globe Newspaper Co./Washington Post Writer's Group. Reprinted with permission.

putting . . . into mothballs: retiring.
two-bit: unimportant, minor.
crying wolf: issuing a false alarm.

Like many businesses, the airline industry uses euphemisms to avoid upsetting already nervous flyers.[43] For example, rather than saying "turbulence," pilots and flight attendants use the less frightening term "bumpy air." Likewise, they refer to thunderstorms as "rain showers," and fog as "mist" or "haze." And savvy flight personnel never use the words "your final destination."

Despite their occasional advantages, many euphemisms are not worth the effort it takes to create them. Some are pretentious and confusing, such as the renaming of one university's Home Economics Department as the Department of Human Ecology or a middle school's labeling of hallways as "behavior transition corridors." Other euphemisms are downright deceptive, such as the U.S. Senate's labeling of a $23,200 pay raise a "pay equalization concept."

EQUIVOCATION It's 8:15 P.M., and you are already a half-hour late for your dinner reservation at the fanciest restaurant in town. Your partner has finally finished dressing and confronts you with the question "How do I look?" To tell the truth, you hate your partner's outfit. You don't want to lie, but on the other hand you don't want to be hurtful. Just as importantly, you don't want to lose your table by waiting around for your date to choose something else to wear. You think for a moment and then reply, "You look amazing. I've never seen an outfit like that before. Where did you get it?"

"Be honest with me Roger. By 'mid-course correction' you mean divorce, don't you."

Your response in this situation was an **equivocation**—a deliberately vague statement that can be interpreted in more than one way. Earlier in this chapter we talked about how *unintentional* equivocation can lead to misunderstandings. But our discussion here focuses on *intentionally ambiguous speech* that is used to avoid lying on one hand and telling a painful truth on the other. Equivocations have several advantages. They spare the receiver from the embarrassment that might come from a completely truthful answer, and it can be easier for the sender to equivocate than to suffer the discomfort of being honest.

Despite its benefits, there are times when communicators equivocate as a way to weasel out of delivering important but unpleasant messages. Suppose, for example, that you are unsure about your standing in one of your courses. You approach the professor and ask how you're doing. "Not bad," the professor answers. This answer isn't too satisfying. "What grade am I earning?" you inquire. "Oh, lots of people would be happy with it" is the answer you receive. "But will I receive an A or B this semester?" you persist. "You *could*," is the reply. It's easy to see how this sort of evasiveness can be frustrating.

As with euphemisms, high-level abstractions, and many other types of communication, it's impossible to say that equivocation is always helpful or harmful. As you learned in Chapter 1, competent communication behavior is situational. Your success in relating to others will depend on your ability to analyze yourself, the other person, and the situation when deciding whether to be equivocal or direct.

ETHICAL CHALLENGE

Euphemisms and Equivocations

For most people, "telling it like it is" is usually considered a virtue and "beating around the bush" is a minor sin. You can test the function of indirect speech by following these directions:

1. Identify five examples of euphemisms and equivocations in everyday interaction.
2. Imagine how matters would have been different if the speakers or writer had used direct language in each situation.
3. Based on your observations, discuss whether equivocation and euphemisms have any place in face-to-face communication.

CULTURAL IDIOM

to weasel out of: to get out of doing something

GENDER AND LANGUAGE

So far we have discussed language use as if it were identical for both sexes. Some theorists and researchers, though, have argued that there are significant differences between the way men and women speak, whereas others have argued that any differences are not significant.[44] What are the similarities and differences between male and female language use?

Content

Although there is a great deal of variation within each gender, on the average, men and women discuss a surprisingly different range of topics. The first research on conversational topics was conducted over sixty years ago. Despite the changes in male and female roles since then, the results of more recent studies are remarkably similar.[45] In these studies, women and men ranging in age from seventeen to eighty described the range of topics each discussed with friends of the same sex. Certain topics were common to both sexes: work, movies, and television proved to be frequent for both groups. Both men and women reserved discussions of sex and sexuality for members of the same gender. The differences between men and women were more striking than the similarities, however. Female friends spent much more time discussing personal and domestic subjects, relationship problems, family, health and reproductive matters, weight, food and clothing, men, and other women. Men, on the other hand, were more likely to discuss music, current events, sports, business, and other men. Both men and women were equally likely to discuss personal appearance, sex, and dating in same-sex conversations. True to one common stereotype, women were more likely to gossip about close friends and family. By contrast, men spent more time gossiping about sports figures and media personalities. Women's gossip was no more derogatory than men's.

These differences can lead to frustration when men and women try to converse with one another. Researchers report that *trivial* is the word often used by both sexes to describe topics discussed by the opposite sex. "I want to talk about important things," a woman might say, "like how we're getting along. All he wants to do is talk about the news or what we'll do this weekend."

Reasons for Communicating

Research shows that the notion that men and women communicate in dramatically different ways is exaggerated. Both men and women, at least in the dominant cultures of the United States and Canada, use language to build and maintain social relationships. Regardless of the sex of the communicators,

the goals of almost all ordinary conversations include making the conversation enjoyable by being friendly, showing interest in what the other person says, and talking about topics that interest the other person.[46] *How* men and women accomplish these goals is often different, though. Although most communicators try to make their interaction enjoyable, men are more likely than women to emphasize making conversation fun. Their discussions involve a greater amount of joking and good-natured teasing. By contrast, women's conversations focus more frequently on feelings, relationships, and personal problems. In fact, communication researcher Julia Wood flatly states that "for women, talk *is* the essence of relationships."[47] When a group of women was surveyed to find out what kinds of satisfaction they gained from talking with their friends, the most common theme mentioned was a feeling of empathy—"To know you're not alone," as some put it. [48] Whereas men commonly described same-sex conversations as something they *liked,* women characterized their woman-to-woman talks as a kind of contact they *needed.* The greater frequency of female conversations reflects their importance. Nearly 50 percent of the women surveyed said they called friends at least once a week just to talk, whereas less than half as many men did so. In fact, 40 percent of the men surveyed reported that they never called another man just to talk.

Because women use conversation to pursue social needs, female speech typically contains statements showing support for the other person, demonstrations of equality, and efforts to keep the conversation going. With these goals, it's not surprising that traditionally female speech often contains statements of sympathy and empathy: "I've felt just like that myself," "The same thing happened to me!" Women are also inclined to ask lots of questions that invite the other person to share information: "How did you feel about that?" "What did you do next?" The importance of nurturing a relationship also explains why female speech is often somewhat powerless and tentative. Saying, "This is just my opinion . . ." is less likely to put off a conversational partner than a more definite "Here's what I think . . ."

Men's speech is often driven by quite different goals than women's. Men are more likely to use language to accomplish the job at hand than to nourish relationships. This explains why men are less likely than women to disclose their vulnerabilities, which would be a sign of weakness. When someone else is sharing a problem, instead of empathizing, men are prone to offer advice: "That's nothing to worry about . . ." or "Here's what you need to do . . ." Besides taking care of business, men are more likely than women to use conversations to exert control, preserve their independence, and enhance their status. This explains why men are more prone to dominate conversations and one-up their partners. Men interrupt their conversational partners to assert their own experiences or point of view. (Women interrupt too, but they usually do so to offer support: quite a different goal.) Just because male talk is competitive doesn't mean it's not enjoyable. Men often regard talk as a kind of game: When researchers asked men what they liked best about their all-male talk, the most frequent answer was its ease.[49] Another common theme was appreciation of the practical value of conversation: new ways to solve problems. Men also mentioned enjoying the humor and rapid pace that characterized their all-male conversations.

Differences like these begin early in childhood. Sociolinguist Deborah Tannen summarizes a variety of studies showing that boys use talk to assert control over one another, whereas girls use talk to maintain harmony.[50] Transcripts of conversations between preschoolers aged two to five showed that girls are far more cooperative than boys.[51] They preceded their proposals for action by saying, "let's," as in "Let's go find some" or "Let's turn back." By contrast, boys gave orders like "Lie down" or "Gimme your arm."

CULTURAL IDIOM

to grease the wheels:
to facilitate

Conversational Style

Women behave differently in conversations than do men.[52] For example, women ask more questions in mixed-sex conversations than do men—nearly three times as many, according to one study. Other research has revealed that in mixed-sex conversations, men interrupt women far more than the other way around. Some theorists have argued that differences like these result in women's speech that is less powerful and more emotional than men's. Research has supported these theories—at least in some cases. Even when clues about the speakers' sex were edited out, raters found clear differences between transcripts of male speech and female speech. In one study women's talk was judged more aesthetic, whereas men's talk was seen as more dynamic, aggressive, and strong. In another, male job applicants were rated more fluent, active, confident, and effective than female applicants.

Other studies have revealed that men and women behave differently in certain conversational settings. For example, in mixed-sex dyads men talk longer than women, whereas in same-sex situations women speak for a longer time. In larger groups, men talk more, whereas in smaller groups, women talk more. In same-sex conversations there are other differences between men and women: women use more questions, justifiers, intensive adverbs, personal pronouns, and adverbials. Men use more directives, interruptions, and filler words to begin sentences.[53]

Given these differences, it's easy to wonder how men and women manage to communicate with one another at all. One reason why cross-sex conversations do run smoothly is because women accommodate to the topics men raise. Both men and women regard topics introduced by women as tentative, whereas topics that men introduce are more likely to be pursued. Thus, women seem to grease the wheels of conversation by doing more work than men in maintaining conversations. A complementary difference between men and women also promotes cross-sex conversations: Men are more likely to talk about themselves

with women than with other men; and because women are willing to adapt to this topic, conversations are likely to run smoothly, if one-sidedly.

An accommodating style isn't always a disadvantage for women. One study revealed that women who spoke tentatively in were actually more influential with men than those who used more powerful speech.[54] On the other hand, this tentative style was less effective in persuading women. (Language use had no effect on men's persuasiveness.) This research suggests that women who are willing and able to be flexible in their approach can persuade both other women and men—as long as they are not dealing with a mixed-sex audience.

Nongender Variables

Despite the differences in the ways men and women speak, the link between gender and language use isn't as clear-cut as it might seem. Despite the differences identified earlier, several research reviews have found that the ways women and men communicate are much more similar than different. For example, one analysis of over twelve hundred research studies found that only 1 percent of variance in communication behavior resulted from sex difference.[55] There is no significant difference between male speech and female speech in areas such as use of profanity, use of qualifiers such as "I guess" or "This is just my opinion," tag questions, and vocal fluency.[56] Some on-the-job research shows that male and female supervisors in similar positions behave the same way and are equally effective. In light of the considerable similarities between the sexes and the relatively minor differences, some communication scholars suggest that the "men are from Mars, women are from Venus" claim should be replaced by the metaphor that "men are from North Dakota, women are from South Dakota."[57]

A growing body of research explains some of the apparent contradictions between the similarities and differences between male speech and female speech. They have revealed other factors that influence language use as much or more than does gender. For example, social philosophy plays a role. Feminist wives talk longer than their partners, whereas nonfeminist wives speak less than their husbands. Orientation toward problem-solving also plays a role in conversational style. The cooperative or competitive orientations of speakers have more influence on how they interact than does their gender.

The speaker's occupation and social role also influence speaking style. For example, male day-care teachers' speech to their students resembles the language of female teachers more closely than it resembles the language of fathers at home. Overall, doctors interrupt their patients more often than the reverse, although male patients do interrupt female physicians more often than their male counterparts. At work, task differences exert more powerful effects on whether speakers use gender-inclusive language (such as "he or she" instead of just "he") than does biological sex.[58] A close study of trial transcripts showed that the speaker's experience on the witness stand and occupation had more to do with language use than did gender. If women generally use "powerless" language, this may possibly reflect their social role in society at large. As the balance of power grows more equal between men and women, we can expect many linguistic differences to shrink.

Sex Roles

Why is the research on gender differences so confusing? In some studies, male speech and female speech seem identical, whereas other studies reveal important differences. As we have already said, one reason for the confusion is that factors besides gender influence the way people speak: the setting in which conversation takes place, the expertise of the speakers, their social roles (husband/wife, boss/employee, and so on). Also, female roles are changing so rapidly that many women simply don't use the conversational styles that characterized their older sisters and mothers. But in addition to these factors, another powerful force that influences the way individual men and women speak is their **sex role**—the social orientation that governs behavior—rather than their biological gender. Researchers have identified three sex roles: masculine, feminine, and androgynous. These sex roles don't always line up neatly with gender. There are "masculine" females, "feminine" males, and androgynous communicators who combine traditionally masculine and feminine characteristics.

Research shows that linguistic differences are often a function of these sex roles more than the speaker's biological sex. Masculine sex-role communicators—whether male or female—use more dominant language than either feminine or androgynous speakers. Feminine speakers have the most submissive speaking style, whereas androgynous speakers fall between these extremes. When two masculine communicators are in a conversation, they often engage in a one-up battle for dominance, responding to the other's bid for control with a counterattempt to dominate the relationship. Feminine sex-role speakers are less predictable. They use dominance, submission, and equivalent behavior in an almost random fashion. Androgynous individuals are more predictable: They most frequently meet another's bid for dominance with a symmetrical attempt at control, but then move quickly toward an equivalent relationship.

All this information suggests that, when it comes to communicating, "masculinity" and "femininity" are culturally recognized sex roles, not biological traits. Research suggests that neither a stereotypically male style nor female style is the best choice. For example, one study showed that a "mixed gender strategy" that balanced the stereotypically male task-oriented approach with the stereotypically female relationship-oriented approach received the highest marks by both male and female respondents.[59] As opportunities for men and women become more equal, we can expect that the differences between male and female use of language will become smaller.

If women speak and hear a language of connection and intimacy, while men speak and hear a language of status and independence, then communication between men and women can be like cross-cultural communication, prey to a clash of conversational styles. Instead of different dialects, it has been said they speak different genderlects.

Deborah Tannen
You Just Don't Understand: Women and Men in Conversation

INVITATION
TO INSIGHT
Gender and Language

1. Note differences in the language use of three men and three women you know. Include yourself in the analysis. Your analysis will be most accurate if you tape record the speech of each person you analyze. Consider the following categories:

   conversational content   conversational style
   reasons for communicating   use of powerful/powerless speech

2. Based on your observations, answer the following questions:
   a. How much does gender influence speech?
   b. What role do other variables play? Consider occupational or social status, cultural background, social philosophy, competitive-cooperative orientation, and other factors in your analysis.

CULTURE AND LANGUAGE

Anyone who has tried to translate ideas from one language to another knows that communication across cultures can be a challenge.[60] Sometimes the results of a bungled translation can be amusing. For example, the American manufacturers of *Pet* condensed milk unknowingly introduced their product in French-speaking markets without realizing that the word *pet* in French means "to break wind."[61] Likewise, the naive English-speaking representative of a U.S. soft drink manufacturer drew laughs from Mexican customers when she offered free samples of Fresca soda pop. In Mexican slang, the word *fresca* means "lesbian."

Even choosing the right words during translation won't guarantee that non-native speakers will use an unfamiliar language correctly. For example, Japanese insurance companies warn their policyholders who are visiting the United States to avoid their cultural tendency to say "excuse me" or "I'm sorry" if they are involved in a traffic accident.[62] In Japan, apologizing is a traditional way to express goodwill and maintain social harmony, even if the person offering the apology is not at fault. But in the United States, an apology can be taken as an admission of guilt and may result in Japanese tourists' being held accountable for accidents for which they may not be responsible.

Difficult as it may be, translation is only a small part of the communication challenges facing members of different cultures. Differences in the way language is used and the very worldview that a language creates make communicating across cultures a challenging task.

Verbal Communication Styles

Using language is more than just choosing a particular group of words to convey an idea. Each language has its own unique style that distinguishes it from others. Matters like the amount of formality or informality, precision or vagueness, and brevity or detail are major ingredients in speaking competently. And when a communicator tries to use the verbal style from one culture in a different one, problems are likely to arise.[63]

One way in which verbal styles vary is in their *directness*. Anthropologist Edward Hall identified two distinct cultural ways of using language.[64] **Low-context cultures** use language primarily to express thoughts, feelings, and ideas as clearly and logically as possible. To low-context communicators, the meaning of a statement is in the words spoken. By contrast, **high-context cultures** value language as a way to maintain social harmony. Rather than upset others by speaking clearly, communicators in these cultures learn to discover meaning from the context in which a

message is delivered: the nonverbal behaviors of the speaker, the history of the relationship, and the general social rules that govern interaction between people. Table 3–4 summarizes some key differences between the way low- and high-context cultures use language.

North American culture falls towards the low-context end of the scale. Residents of the United States and Canada value straight talk and grow impatient with "beating around the bush." By contrast, most Asian and Middle Eastern cultures fit the high-context pattern. In many Asian cultures, for example, maintaining harmony is important, and so communicators will avoid speaking clearly if that would threaten another person's face. For this reason, Japanese or Koreans are less likely than Americans to offer a clear "no" to an undesirable request. Instead, they would probably use roundabout expressions like "I agree with you in principle, but . . ." or "I sympathize with you . . ."

Low-context North Americans may miss the subtleties of high-context messages, but people raised to recognize indirect communication have little trouble decoding them. A look at Japanese child-rearing practices helps explain why. Research shows that Japanese mothers rarely deny the requests of their young children by saying "no." Instead, they use other strategies: ignoring a child's requests, raising distractions, promising to take care of the matter later, or explaining why they can or will not say "yes."[65] Sociolinguist Deborah Tannen explains how this indirect approach illustrates profound differences between high-and low-context communications:

> . . . saying no is something associated with children who have not yet learned the norm. If a Japanese mother spoke that way, she would feel she was lowering herself to her child's level precisely because that way of speaking is associated with Japanese children.[66]

Tannen goes on to contrast the Japanese notion of appropriateness with the very different one held by dominant North American society:

> Because American norms for talk are different, it is common, and therefore expected, for American parents to "just say no." That's why an American mother feels authoritative when she talks that way: because it fits her image of how an authoritative adult talks to a child.[67]

The clash between cultural norms of directness and indirectness can aggravate problems in cross-cultural situations such as encounters between straight-talking low-context Israelis, who value speaking clearly, and Arabs, whose high-context culture stresses smooth interaction. It's easy to imagine how the clash of cultural styles could lead to misunderstandings and conflicts between Israelis and their Palestinian neighbors. Israelis could view their Arab counterparts as evasive, whereas the Palestinians could perceive the Israelis as insensitive and blunt.

Even within a single country, subcultures can have different notions about the value of direct speech. For example, Puerto Rican language style resembles high-context Japanese or Korean more than low-context English.[68] As a group, Puerto Ricans value social harmony and avoid confrontation, which leads them to systematically speak in an indirect way to avoid giving offense. Asian Americans are more offended by indirectly racist statements than are African Americans, Hispanics, and Anglo Americans.[69] Researchers Laura Leets and Howard Giles suggest that the traditional Asian tendency to favor high-context messages explains the difference: Adept at recognizing hints and nonverbal cues, high-context communicators are more sensitive to messages that are overlooked by people from cultural groups that rely more heavily on unambiguous, explicit low-context messages.

It's worth noting that even generally straight-talking residents of the United States raised in the low-context Euro-American tradition often rely on context to make their point. When you decline an unwanted invitation by saying "I can't make it," it's likely that both you and the other person know that the choice of attending isn't really beyond your control. If your goal was to be perfectly clear, you might say, "I don't want to get together."

Another way in which language styles can vary across cultures is in terms of whether they are *elaborate* or *succinct*. Speakers of Arabic, for instance, commonly use language that is much more rich and expressive than most communicators who use English. Strong assertions and exaggerations that would sound ridiculous in English are a common feature of Arabic. This contrast in linguistic style can lead to misunderstandings between people from different backgrounds. As one observer put it,

> First, an Arab feels compelled to overassert in almost all types of communication because others expect him [or her] to. If an Arab says exactly what he [or she] means without the expected assertion, other Arabs may still think that he [or she] means the opposite. For example, a simple "no" to a host's requests to eat more or drink more will not suffice. To convey the meaning that he [or she] is actually full, the guest must keep repeating "no" several times, coupling it with an oath such as "By God" or "I swear to God." Second, an Arab often fails to realize that others, particularly foreigners, may mean exactly what they say even though their language is simple. To the Arabs, a simple "no" may mean the indirectly expressed consent and encouragement of a coquettish woman. On the other hand, a simple consent may mean the rejection of an hypocritical politician.[70]

Succinctness is most extreme in cultures where silence is valued. In many American Indian cultures, for example, the favored way to handle ambiguous social situations is to remain quiet.[71] When you contrast this silent style to the talkativeness common in mainstream American cultures when people first meet, it's easy to imagine how the first encounter between an Apache or Navajo and a white person might feel uncomfortable to both people.

Along with differences such as directness-indirectness and elaborate-succinct styles, a third way languages differ from one culture to another involves *formality* and *informality*. The informal approach that characterizes relationships in countries like the United States, Canada, and Australia is quite different from the great concern for using proper speech in many parts of Asia and Africa. Formality isn't so much a matter of using correct grammar as of defining social position. In Korea, for example, the language reflects the Confucian system of relational hierarchies.[72] It has special vocabularies for different sexes, for different levels of social status, for different degrees of intimacy, and for different types of social occasions. For example, there are different degrees of formality for speaking with old friends, nonacquaintances whose background one knows, and complete strangers. One sign of being a learned person in Korea is the ability to use language that recognizes these relational distinctions. When you contrast these sorts of distinctions with the casual friendliness many North Americans use even when talking with complete strangers, it's easy to see how a Korean might view communicators in the United States as boorish and how an American might view Koreans as stiff and unfriendly.

TABLE 3–4 Low- and High-Context Communication Styles	
Low Context	**High Context**
Majority of information carried in explicit verbal messages, with less focus on the situational context.	Important information carried in contextual clues (time, place, relationship, situation). Less reliance on explicit verbal messages.
Self-expression valued. Communicators state opinions and desires directly and strive to persuade others.	Relational harmony valued and maintained by indirect expression of opinions. Communicators refrain from saying "no" directly.
Clear, eloquent speech considered praiseworthy. Verbal fluency admired.	Communicators talk "around" the point, allowing others to fill in the missing pieces. Ambiguity and use of silence admired.

LANGUAGE AND WORLDVIEW

Different linguistic styles are important, but there may be even more fundamental differences that separate speakers of various languages. For almost 150 years, some theorists have put forth the notion of **linguistic determinism**: the notion that the worldview of a culture is shaped and reflected by the language its members speak. The best-known example of linguistic determinism is the notion that Eskimos have a large number of words (estimated from seventeen to one hundred) for what we simply call "snow." Different terms are used to describe conditions like a driving blizzard, crusty ice, and light powder. This example suggests how linguistic determinism operates. The need to survive in an Arctic environment led Eskimos to make distinctions that would be unimportant to residents of warmer environments, and after the language makes these distinctions, speakers are more likely to see the world in ways that match the broader vocabulary.

Even though there is some doubt that Eskimos really do have one hundred words for snow,[73] other examples do seem to support the principle of linguistic determinism.[74] For instance, bilingual speakers seem to think differently when they change languages. In one study, French Americans were asked to interpret a series of pictures. When they spoke in French, their descriptions were far more romantic and emotional than when they used English to describe the same kind of pictures. Likewise, when students in Hong Kong were asked to complete a values test, they expressed more traditional Chinese values when they answered in Cantonese than when they answered in English. In Israel, both Arab and Jewish students saw bigger distinctions between their group and "outsiders" when using their native language than when they used English, a neutral tongue. Examples like these show the power of language to shape cultural identity—sometimes for better and sometimes for worse.

"The Eskimos have eighty-seven words for snow and not one for malpractice."

Linguistic influences start early in life. English-speaking parents often label the mischievous pranks of their children as "bad," implying that there is something immoral about acting wild. "Be good!" they are inclined to say. On the other hand, French parents are more likely to say *"Sois sage!"*—"Be wise." The linguistic implication is that misbehaving is an act of foolishness. Swedes would correct the same action with the words *"Var snall!"*—"Be friendly, be kind." By contrast, German adults would use the command *"Sei artig!"*—literally, "Be of your own kind"—in other words, get back in step, conform to your role as a child.[75]

The best-known declaration of linguistic determinism is the **Whorf-Sapir hypothesis,** formulated by Benjamin Whorf, an amateur linguist, and anthropologist Edward Sapir.[76] Following Sapir's theoretical work, Whorf found that the language spoken by the Hopi represents a view of reality that is dramatically different from more familiar tongues. For example, the Hopi language makes no distinction between nouns and verbs. Therefore, the people who speak it describe the entire world as being constantly in process. Whereas we use nouns to characterize people or objects as being fixed or constant, the Hopi view them more as verbs, constantly changing. In this sense our language represents much of the world rather like a snapshot camera, whereas Hopi reflects a worldview more like a motion picture.

Although the Whorf-Sapir hypothesis originally focused on foreign languages, Neil Postman illustrates the principle with an example closer to home. He describes a hypothetical culture where physicians identify patients they treat as "doing" arthritis and other diseases instead of "having" them and where criminals are diagnosed as "having" cases of criminality instead of "being" criminals.[77]

The implications of such a linguistic difference are profound. We believe that characteristics people "have"—what they "are"—are beyond their control, whereas they are responsible for what they "do." If we changed our view of what people "have" and what they "do," our attitudes would most likely change as well. Postman illustrates the consequences of this linguistic difference as applied to education:

> In schools, for instance, we find that tests are given to determine how smart someone is or, more precisely, how much smartness someone "has." If one child scores a 138, and another a 106, the first is thought to "have" more smartness than the other. But this seems to me a strange conception—every bit as strange as "doing" arthritis or "having" criminality. I do not know anyone who *has* smartness. The people I know sometimes *do* smart things (as far as I can judge) and sometimes *do* stupid things—depending on what circumstances they are in, and how much they know about a situation, and how interested they are. "Smartness," so it seems to me, is a specific performance, done in a particular set of circumstances. It is not something you *are* or have in measurable quantities. In fact, the assumption that smartness is something you *have* has led to such nonsensical ideas as "over-" and "underachievers." As I understand it, an overachiever is someone who doesn't have much smartness but does a lot of smart things. An underachiever is someone who *has* a lot of smartness but does a lot of stupid things.
>
> Although I have not heard of them, there may be good reasons to imagine that smartness or honesty or sensitivity are "qualities" that people *have* in measurable proportions and that exist independently of what people actually do. What I am driving at is this: All language is metaphorical, and often in the subtlest ways. In the simplest sentence, sometimes in the simplest word, we do more than merely express ourselves. We construct reality along certain lines. We make the world according to our own imagery.[78]

Although there is little support for the extreme linguistic deterministic viewpoint that it is *impossible* for speakers of different languages to view the world identically, the more moderate notion of **linguistic relativism**—the notion that language exerts a strong influence on perceptions—does seem valid. As one scholar put it, "the differences between languages are not so much in what *can* be said, but in what it is *relatively easy* to say."[79] Some languages contain terms that have no exact English equivalents.[80] For example, consider a few words in other languages that have no exact English equivalents:

- *Nemawashi* (Japanese) The process of informally feeling out all the people involved with an issue before making a decision
- *Lagniappe* (French) An extra gift given in a transaction that wasn't expected by the terms of a contract
- *Lao* (Mandarin) A respectful term used for older people, showing their importance in the family and in society
- *Dharma* (Sanskrit) Each person's unique, ideal path in life and the knowledge of how to find it
- *Koyaanisquatsi* (Hopi) Nature out of balance; a way of life so crazy it calls for a new way of living

After words like these exist and become a part of everyday life, the ideas that they represent are easier to recognize. But even without such words, each of the concepts mentioned earlier is still possible to imagine. Thus, speakers of a language that includes the notion of *lao* would probably treat older members respectfully, and those who are familiar with *lagniappe* might be more generous. Despite these differences, the words aren't essential to follow these principles. Although language may shape thoughts and behavior, it doesn't dominate them absolutely.

Language Use in North American Culture

The importance of language as a reflection of worldview isn't just a matter of interest for anthropologists and linguists. The labels we use in everyday conversa-

UNDERSTANDING DIVERSITY

Language and Perception

English speakers can often draw shades of distinction unavailable to non-English speakers. The French, for instance, cannot distinguish between house and home, between mind and brain, between man and gentleman, between "I wrote" and "I have written." The Spanish cannot differentiate a chairman from a president, and the Italians have no equivalent of wishful thinking. In Russia there are no native words for efficiency, challenge, engagement ring, have fun, or take care.

On the other hand, other languages have facilities that we lack. Both French and German can distinguish between knowledge that results from recognition (respectively, *connaitre* and *kennen*) and knowledge that results from understanding (*savior* and *wissen*).

Portuguese has words that differentiate between an interior angle and an exterior one. All the Romance languages can distinguish between something that leaks into and something that leaks out of. The Italians even have a word for the mark left on a table by a moist glass (*culacino*) while the Gaelic speakers of Scotland, not to be outdone, have a word for the itchiness that overcomes the upper lip just before taking a sip of whiskey. It's *sgirob*. And we have nothing in English to match the Danish *hygge* (meaning "instantly satisfying and cozy"), the French *sang-froid*, the Russian *glasnost*, or the Spanish *macho*, so we must borrow the term from them or do without the sentiment.

Bill Bryson
The Mother Tongue

tion both reflect and shape the way we view ourselves and others. This explains why businesses often give employees impressive titles and why a woman's choice of the label "Ms." or "Mrs." can be a statement about her identity. Women in Western society face a conscious choice about how to identify themselves when they marry. They may follow the tradition of taking their husband's last name, or hyphenate their birth name with their husband's, or keep their birth name. A fascinating study revealed that a woman's choice is likely to reveal a great deal about herself and her relationship with her husband.[81] Surveys revealed that women who have taken their husbands' names place the most importance on relationships, with social expectations of how they should behave placing second, and issues of self coming last. By contrast, women who have kept their birth names put their personal concerns ahead of relationships and social expectations. Women with hyphenated names fall somewhere between the other groups, valuing self and relationships equally.

In the same way, the labels that members of an ethnic group choose to define themselves say a great deal about their sense of identity. Over the years labels of racial identification have gone through cycles of popularity.[82] In North America, the first freed slaves preferred to be called "Africans." In the late nineteenth and early twentieth centuries *colored* was the term of choice; but later *Negro* became the respectable word. Then, in the 1960s, the term *black* grew increasingly popular—first as a label for militants and later as a term preferred by more moderate citizens of all colors. More recently *African American* has gained popularity.[83] Decisions about which name to use reflect a person's attitude. For example, one survey revealed that individuals who prefer the label *black* choose it because it is "acceptable" and "based on consensus" of the larger culture.[84] They describe themselves as patriotic, accepting of the status quo, and attempting to assimilate into the larger culture. By contrast, people who choose the term *Afro-American* derive their identity from their ethnicity and do not want to assimilate into the larger culture, only to succeed in it. The label others choose can also be revealing. Political liberals are more likely to use the term *African American* than are conservatives.[85]

SUMMARY

Language is both one of humanity's greatest assets and the source of many problems. This chapter highlighted the characteristics that distinguish language and suggested methods of using it more effectively.

Any language is a collection of symbols governed by a variety of rules and used to convey messages between people. Because of its symbolic nature, language is not a precise tool: Meanings rest in people, not in words themselves. In order for effective communication to occur, it is necessary to negotiate meanings for ambiguous statements.

Language not only describes people, ideas, processes, and events; it also shapes our perceptions of them in areas including status, credibility, and attitudes about gender and ethnicity. Along with influencing our attitudes, language reflects them. The words we use and our manner of speech reflect power, status, affiliation, attraction, and interest.

Many types of language have the potential to create misunderstandings. Other types of language can result in unnecessary conflicts. In other cases, speech and writing can be evasive, avoiding expression of unwelcome messages.

The relationship between gender and language is a confusing one. There are many differences in the ways men and women speak: The content of their conversations varies, as do their reasons for communicating and their conversational styles. Not all differences in language use can be accounted for by the speaker's gender, however.

Occupation, social philosophy, and orientation toward problem solving also influence the use of language, and psychological sex role can be more of an influence than biological sex.

Language operates on a broad level to shape the consciousness and communication of an entire society. Different languages often shape and reflect the views of a culture. Low-context cultures like that of the United States use language primarily to express feelings and ideas as clearly and unambiguously as possible, whereas high-context cultures avoid specificity to promote social harmony. Some cultures value brevity and the succinct use of language, whereas others value elaborate forms of speech. In some societies formality is important, whereas in others informality is important. Beyond these differences, there is evidence to support linguistic relativism—the notion that language exerts a strong influence on the worldview of the people who speak it.

RESOURCES

Print

Canary, Daniel J., and Tara M. Emmers-Sommer. *Sex and Gender Differences in Personal Relationships.* New York: Guilford Press, 1997.

This book surveys the substantial body of research exploring the relationship among sex, gender, and language. It provides a balanced view of the subject, showing that the "Men are from Mars, Women are from Venus" portrayal isn't completely accurate. Chapters cover topics including male and female emotional expression, intimacy styles, and conversational control.

Ellis, Donald G. *From Language to Communication,* 2nd ed. Hillsdale, NJ: Lawrence Erlbaum, 1999.

Ellis provides a comprehensive tour of the ways in which scholars have examined language. The book covers a wide range of topics, including the origins of language, a review of the field of linguistics, a look at the mental processes that govern language use, and how language operates in everyday conversations. Along with providing a thorough introduction to the topic, the book's references will guide serious students to resources for further study.

Henley, Nancy M., and Cheris Kramarae. "Gender, Power, and Miscommunication," in Nikolas Coupland, Howard Giles, and John M. Wiemann, eds., *Miscommunication and Problematic Talk.* Newbury Park, CA: Sage, 1991.

The authors explore several explanations for differences and problems that arise when men and women communicate across the gender barrier. After considering the "female deficit" notion (that women need to gain skill in stereotypical male speech) and the "two cultures" theory (that men and women operate side-by-side in significantly different cultures), the authors argue that a study of the relationship between gender and communication involves other issues such as failure to recognize similarities between the sexes, an excessive focus on white, North American behavior to the exclusion of other cultures, and social biases against women.

Rheingold, Howard. *They Have a Word for It.* Los Angeles: Jeremy P. Tarcher, 1988.

Rheingold has collected a lexicon of words and phrases from languages around the world that lend support to the Whorf-Sapir hypothesis. This entertaining two-hundred-page compendium of "untranslatable phrases" illustrates that speaking a new language does, indeed, prompt a different worldview. Imagine how life might be different to speakers of Bantu, whose word *mbuki-mvuki* means "to shuck off clothes in order to dance." Entertainment aside, the bibliography at the end of this book contains a valuable list of sources for exploring the notion of linguistic relativism.

Tannen, Deborah. *Gender and Discourse.* New York: Oxford University Press, 1995.

This collection of essays provides a more scholarly look at the connection between gender and communication than do Tannen's trade books, described next. One chapter describes how social class interacts with gender to affect the interaction between men and women.

Tannen, Deborah. *You Just Don't Understand: Women and Men in Conversation.* New York: Morrow, 1990. *Talking from 9 to 5.* New York: Morrow, 1994.

You Just Don't Understand summarizes a large amount of research in a readable manner, concluding that, from early childhood, there are some fundamental differences in male and female communication styles. *Talking from 9 to 5* zeroes in on how differences in stereotypical male and female communications operate on the job.

Wood, Julia. *Gendered Communication* 4th ed. Belmont, CA: Wadsworth, 2001.

Chapter 4, "Gendered Verbal Communication," offers a good survey of the relationship between language and the way we think about men and women in society.

Films
Jargon and Slang

Clueless (1995). Rated PG-13.

Cher (Alicia Silverstone) and her friend Dionne (Stacey Dash) are teen queens at a posh Beverly Hills high school. This clever parody exaggerates the lifestyle of privileged teens in the context of Cher's plot to woo Christian (Justin Walker), a new kid at school, and boost the popularity of a new girl named Tai (Brittany Murphy). The opening line in this film is "So, okay, you're probably like—what is this, a Noxzema commercial?" From beginning to end, the teens in this film offer a clever, if exaggerated, illustration of how jargon and slang operate in youth culture.

The Nature of Language

Nell (1994). Rated PG.

Deep in the mountains of North Carolina, physician Jerome Lovell (Liam Neeson) discovers Nell (Jodie Foster), a young woman who has had no contact with the outside world for virtually her entire life. In her seclusion, Nell developed her own language. Lovell and psychologist Paula Olsen (Natasha Richardson) struggle to learn Nell's language and her unique way of perceiving the world.

Language and Perception

Being There (1980). Rated PG.

Chance (Peter Sellers) is a mentally retarded gardener who has lived and worked his entire life inside the walls of an elegant Washington townhouse. His only exposure to the world is through television. When the owner of the house dies, Chance is expelled into a society he does not un-

derstand. Through a fluke, Chance is adopted by Ben Rand (Melvyn Douglas), a dying millionaire industrialist, and his wife, Eve (Shirley MacLaine), who introduce him to the elite of Washington's social and political world, including the president of the United States. Although Chance the gardener (his hosts mistakenly call him Chauncey Gardner) knows nothing about anything, his hosts, the president, and eventually the nation misinterpret his simple, literal statements about his trade (e.g., "Spring is a time for planting") as profound observations about society and human nature. He becomes a national sensation, and as the film ends he appears destined to succeed his millionaire host as husband to Eve and head of an industrial empire. Based on the novella by Jerzy Kosinski.

Language and Social Class

My Fair Lady (1964). Rated G.

In this Academy Award-winning musical, linguistics professor Henry Higgins (Rex Harrison) takes on the professional challenge of his life: teaching cockney flower girl Eliza Doolittle (Audrey Hepburn) to masquerade as royalty by learning proper elocution. The film illustrates—albeit in a romanticized manner—the importance of language as a marker of social status. Also available on videocassette is a nonmusical 1938 version, titled *Pygmalion* after the original comedy by George Bernard Shaw.

Language and Culture

Children of a Lesser God (1986). Rated R.

John Leeds (William Hurt) takes a job at a boarding school for deaf children, where he meets Sarah (Marlee Matlin). John is both attracted to and frustrated by Sarah's passionate refusal to learn lipreading, which she views as a concession to the hearing world and a compromise of the integrity and value of sign language. The story chronicles Leeds's changes in attitudes about the relationship of deaf and hearing people, as well as following the development of his relationship with Sarah. This film introduces viewers to the linguistic and cultural world of the deaf. Through it we learn some fundamental differences between sign and spoken language, as well as learning more about how the deaf suffer from many misunderstandings and stereotypes.

CONTENTS

KEY TERMS

action-oriented listeners
advising
ambushers
analyzing
attending
content-oriented listeners
counterfeit question
critical listening
defensive listening
empathic listening
hearing
informational listening
insensitive listeners
insulated listeners
judging response
listening
paraphrasing
people-oriented listeners
prompting
pseudolistening
questioning
remembering
residual message
responding
selective listening
sincere question
stage hogs
supporting
time-oriented listeners
understanding

**AFTER STUDYING
THE MATERIAL
IN THIS CHAPTER . . .**

YOU SHOULD UNDERSTAND:

1. The most common misconceptions about listening.

2. The five components of the listening process.

3. The most common types of ineffective listening.

4. The challenges that make effective listening difficult.

5. The skills necessary to listen effectively in informational, critical, and empathic settings.

YOU SHOULD BE ABLE TO:

1. Identify situations where you listen ineffectively and explain the reasons for your lack of effectiveness.

2. Identify the consequences of your ineffective listening.

3. Follow the guidelines for informational listening.

4. Analyze an argument or claim by evaluating the credibility of its proponent, the quality of evidence offered, and the soundness of its reasoning.

5. Apply appropriate response styles in an empathic listening context.

LISTENING

In a world where almost everyone acknowledges the importance of better communication, the need for good listening is obvious. On the most basic level, listening is just as important as speaking. After all, it's impossible for communication to occur without someone receiving a sender's message. (Imagine how ridiculous it would be to speak to an empty room or talk into a disconnected telephone.)

If frequency is a measure of importance, then listening easily qualifies as the most prominent kind of communication. We spend more time in listening to others than in any other type of communication. One study (summarized in Figure 4–1) revealed that of their total communicating time, college students spent an average of 14 percent writing, 16 percent speaking, 17 percent reading, and a whopping 53 percent listening.[1] On the job, listening is by far the most common form of communication. On average, employees of major corporations in North America spend about 60 percent of each working day listening to others.[2]

Besides being the most frequent form of communication, listening is arguably just as important as speaking. A survey of personnel managers identified listening as the most critical skill for working effectively in teams.[3] In small groups, other members view people who listen well as leaders.[4] Listening is just as important in personal relationships. In one survey, marital counselors identified "failing to take the other's perspective when listening" as one of the most frequent communication problems in the couples with whom they work.[5] When another group of adults was asked which communication skills were most important in family and social settings, listening was ranked first.[6] In committed relationships, listening to personal information in everyday conversations is considered an important ingredient of satisfaction.[7] For this reason, some theorists have argued that effective listening is an essential ingredient in effective relational communication.[8]

When a group of adults was asked to identify the most important on-the-job communication skills, listening again ranked at the top of the list. A study examining the link between listening and career success revealed that better listeners rose to higher levels in their organizations.[9] When one thousand human resource executives were asked to identify the skills of the ideal manager, the ability to listen effectively ranked at the top of the list.[10]

Despite the importance of listening, experience shows that much of the listening we and others do is not at all effective. We misunderstand others and are misunderstood in return. We become bored and feign attention while our minds wander. We engage in a battle of interruptions where each person fights to speak without hearing the other's ideas.

Some of this poor listening is inevitable, perhaps even justified. But in other cases we can be better receivers by learning a few basic listening skills. The purpose of this chapter is to help you become a better listener by giving you some important information about the subject. We'll talk about some common misconceptions concerning listening and show you what really happens

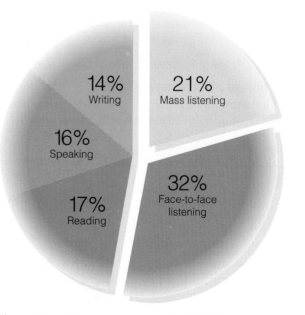

Figure 4–1 Types of Communication Activities

when listening takes place. We'll discuss some poor listening habits, explain why they occur, and suggest better alternatives.

CLARIFYING MISCONCEPTIONS ABOUT LISTENING

In spite of its importance, listening is misunderstood by most people. Because these misunderstandings so greatly affect our communication, we need to take a look at four common misconceptions that many communicators hold.

Listening and Hearing Are Not the Same Thing

Hearing is the process in which sound waves strike the eardrum and cause vibrations that are transmitted to the brain. **Listening** occurs when the brain reconstructs these electrochemical impulses into a representation of the original sound and then gives them meaning. Barring illness, injury, or earplugs, hearing can't be stopped. Your ears will pick up sound waves and transmit them to your brain whether you want them to or not. Listening, however, isn't automatic. Many times we hear but do not listen. Sometimes we deliberately tune out unwanted signals: everything from a neighbor's power lawn mower or the roar of nearby traffic to a friend's boring remarks or a boss's unwanted criticism.

A closer look at listening—at least the successful variety—shows that it consists of several stages. The first is **attending**—the act of paying attention to a signal. An individual's needs, wants, desires, and interests determine what is attended to, or selected, to use the term introduced in Chapter 2. If you're hungry, you are more likely to attend to the message about restaurants in the neighborhood from the person next to you than the competing message on the importance of communication from the speaker in front of the room. Table 4–1 lists several factors that influence how closely a listener attends to a message.

The next step in listening is **understanding**—the process of making sense of a message. Chapter 3 discussed many of the ingredients that combine to make understanding possible: a grasp of the syntax of the language being spoken, semantic decoding, and knowledge of the pragmatic rules that help you figure out a speaker's meaning from the context. In addition to these steps, understanding often depends on the ability to organize the information we hear into recognizable form. As early as 1948, Ralph Nichols related successful understanding to a large number of factors, most prominent among which were verbal ability, intelligence, and motivation.[11]

Responding to a message consists of giving observable feedback to the speaker. Offering feedback serves two important functions: It helps you clarify

TABLE 4–1   Some Factors Affecting Information Reception

1. The Receiver
   - Needs
   - Attitudes, beliefs, values
   - Goals
   - Experience and habit
   - Verbal ability and intelligence
2. The Message
   - Channel
   - Organization
   - Novelty
   - Grammatical and linguistic rules

1. Source
   - Proximity
   - Attractiveness
   - Similarity
   - Credibility
   - Perceived motivation and intent
   - Delivery
   - Status, power, and authority
4. Environment
   - Social context
   - Physical factors
   - Familiarity

Adapted from Brent Ruben, *Communication and Human Behavior,* 2nd ed. (New York: MacMillan, 1988).

UNDERSTANDING COMMUNICATION TECHNOLOGY

Deafness/Hard of Hearing Resources

What is it like to be deaf or have a hearing loss? You can find out by exploring some of the many resources about the subject on the World Wide Web. A good starting place is the Deafness/Hard of Hearing site at http://deafness.miningco.com/. You will find links to information on deaf culture, deaf studies programs, sign language, medical tips, and much more.

your understanding of a speaker's message, and it shows that you care about what that speaker is saying.

Listeners don't always respond visibly to a speaker—but research suggests that they should. One study of 195 critical incidents in banking and medical settings showed that a major difference between effective listening and ineffective listening was the kind of feedback offered.[12] Good listeners showed that they were attentive by nonverbal behaviors such as keeping eye contact and reacting with appropriate facial expressions. Their verbal behavior—answering questions and exchanging ideas, for example—also demonstrated their attention. It's easy to imagine how other responses would signal less effective listening. A slumped posture, bored expression, and yawning send a clear message that you are not tuned in to the speaker.

Adding responsiveness to our listening model demonstrates the fact, discussed in Chapter 1, that communication is transactional in nature. Listening isn't just a passive activity. As listeners we are active participants in a communication transaction. At the same time that we receive messages we also send them.

The final step in the listening process is **remembering**.[13] Research has revealed that people remember only about half of what they hear *immediately after* hearing it.[14] This is true even if people work hard at listening. This situation would probably not be too bad if the half remembered right after were retained,

I can't help hearing, but I don't always listen.

George Burns

CULTURAL IDIOM

tuned in: focused, paying attention

TABLE 4–2 Comparison of Communication Activities

	Listening	Speaking	Reading	Writing
Learned	First	Second	Third	Fourth
Used	Most	Next to most	Next to least	Least
Taught	Least	Next to least	Next to most	Most

but it isn't. Within two months half of the half is forgotten, bringing what we remember down to about 25 percent of the original message. This loss, however, doesn't take two months: People start forgetting immediately (within eight hours the 50 percent remembered drops to about 35 percent). Given the amount of information we process every day—from instructors, friends, the radio, TV, and other sources—the **residual message** (what we remember) is a small fraction of what we hear.

Listening Is Not a Natural Process

Another common myth is that listening is like breathing: a natural activity that people do well. The truth is that listening is a skill much like speaking: Everybody does it, though few people do it well. One study illustrates this point: 144 managers in a study were asked to rate their listening skills. Astonishingly, not one of the managers described himself or herself as a "poor" or "very poor" listener, whereas 94 percent rated themselves as "good" or "very good."[15] The favorable self-ratings contrasted sharply with the perceptions of the managers' subordinates, many of whom said their boss's listening skills were weak. As we have already discussed, some poor listening is inevitable. The good news is that listening can be improved through instruction and training.[16] Despite this fact, the amount of time devoted to teaching listening is far less than that devoted to other types of communication. Table 4–2 reflects this upside-down arrangement.

Your own experience should prove that communication often suffers owing to poor listening. How many times have others misunderstood directions or explanations because they didn't seem to be receiving your ideas clearly? And how often have you failed to understand others accurately because you weren't receiving their thoughts accurately? The answers to these questions demonstrate the need for effective training in listening.

Listening Requires Effort

Most people assume that listening is fundamentally a passive activity in which the receiver absorbs a speaker's ideas in rather the way a sponge absorbs water. As you will soon read, every kind of listening requires mental effort by the receiver.

And experience shows that passive listening almost guarantees that the respondent will fail to grasp at least some of the speaker's ideas and misunderstand others.

Sometimes the responsibility for incomplete and inaccurate decoding rests with the speaker, and sometimes with the listener.[17] In either case, it takes hard work and a fair amount of back-and-forth interaction by both parties to clarify messages.

All Listeners Do Not Receive the Same Message

When two or more people are listening to a speaker, we tend to assume that they all are hearing and understanding the same message. In fact, such uniform comprehension isn't the case. Recall the discussion of perception in Chapter 2, where we pointed out the many factors that cause each of us to perceive an event differently. Physiological factors, social roles, cultural background, personal interests, and needs all shape and distort the raw data we hear into uniquely different messages.

INVITATION TO INSIGHT

Recognizing Listening Misconceptions

You can see how listening misconceptions affect your life by identifying important situations when you have fallen for each of the following assumptions. In each case, describe the consequences of believing these erroneous assumptions.

- Thinking that, because you were hearing a message, you were listening to it.
- Believing that listening effectively is natural and effortless.
- Assuming that other listeners were understanding a message in the same way as you.

OVERCOMING CHALLENGES TO EFFECTIVE LISTENING

Despite the importance of good listening, people seem to get worse at the skill as they grow older.[18] Teachers at various grade levels were asked to stop their lectures periodically and ask students what they were talking about. Ninety percent of first-grade children could repeat what the teacher had been saying, and 80 percent of the second-graders could do so; but when the experiment was repeated with teenagers, the results were much less impressive. Only 44 percent of junior high students and 28 percent of senior high students could repeat their teachers' remarks.

Research suggests that adults listen even more poorly—at least in some important relationships. One experiment found that people listened more attentively and courteously to strangers than to their spouses. When faced with decision-making tasks, couples interrupted one another more frequently and were generally less polite than they were to strangers.[19]

What kinds of poor listening habits plague communication? To find out, read on.

Faulty Listening Behaviors

Although we can't listen effectively all the time, most people possess one or more habits that keep them from understanding truly important messages.

PSEUDOLISTENING

Pseudolistening is an imitation of the real thing. "Good" pseudolisteners give the appearance of being attentive: They look you in the eye, nod and smile at the right times, and even may answer you occasionally. Behind that appearance of interest, however, something entirely different is going on, because pseudolisteners use a polite facade to mask thoughts that have nothing to do with what the speaker is saying.

"Stanley, we need to talk, so please don't interrupt."

SELECTIVE LISTENING   **Selective listeners** respond only to the parts of a speaker's remarks that interest them, rejecting everything else. All of us are selective listeners from time to time as, for instance, when we screen out media commercials and music while keeping an ear cocked for a weather report or an announcement of time. In other cases, selective listening occurs in conversations with people who expect a thorough hearing but get their partner's attention only when the conversation turns to the partner's favorite topic—perhaps money, sex, a hobby, or some particular person. Unless and until you bring up one of these pet topics, you might as well talk to a tree.

DEFENSIVE LISTENING   **Defensive listeners** take innocent comments as personal attacks. Teenagers who perceive parental questions about friends and activities as distrustful snooping are defensive listeners, as are insecure breadwinners who explode when their mates mention money and touchy parents who view any questioning by their children as a threat to their authority and parental wisdom. Many defensive listeners are suffering from shaky public images and avoid admitting this by projecting their insecurities onto others.

AMBUSHING   **Ambushers** listen carefully, but only because they are collecting information to attack what you have to say. The cross-examining prosecution attorney is a good example of an ambusher. Using this kind of strategy will justifiably initiate defensiveness on the other's behalf.

INSULATED LISTENING   **Insulated listeners** are almost the opposite of their selective-listening cousins. Instead of looking for something specific, these people avoid it. Whenever a topic arises they'd rather not deal with, insulated listeners simply fail to hear it or, rather, to acknowledge it. If you remind them about a problem—perhaps an unfinished job, poor grades, or the like—they'll nod or answer you and then promptly forget what you've just said.

> **CULTURAL IDIOM**
>
> **keeping an ear cocked:** listening alertly
>
> **pet:** favorite
>
> **breadwinners:** those who support their families with their earnings

Not comprehending, they hear like the deaf.

Heraclitus

INSENSITIVE LISTENING **Insensitive listeners** are the final example of people who don't receive another person's messages clearly. People often don't express their thoughts or feelings openly but instead communicate them through subtle and unconscious choice of words or nonverbal clues or both. Insensitive listeners aren't able to look beyond the words and behavior to understand their hidden meanings. Instead, they take a speaker's remarks at face value.

STAGE HOGGING **Stage hogs** (sometimes called "conversational narcissists") try to turn the topic of conversations to themselves instead of showing interest in the speaker.[20] Interruptions are a hallmark of stage hogging. Besides preventing the listener from learning potentially valuable information, stage hogging can damage the relationship between the interrupter and the speaker. For example, applicants who interrupt the questions of an employment interviewer are likely to be rated less favorably than job seekers who wait until the interviewer has finished speaking before they respond.[21]

When confronted with stage hogs, people respond in one of two ways. Sometimes the strategy is passive: talking less, tuning out the speaker, showing boredom nonverbally, and leaving the conversation. Other strategies are more active: trying to recapture the floor, hinting about the stage hog's dominance, or confronting the speaker about his or her narcissism. Reactions like these give stage hogs a taste of their own medicine, turning the conversation into a verbal tug-of-war.

INVITATION TO INSIGHT

Your L.Q. (Listening Quotient)

Explain the poor listening behaviors listed on pages 117–118 to someone who knows you well. Then ask your informant to describe which, if any, of them, you use. Also explore the consequences of your listening behavior.

Reasons For Poor Listening

What causes people to listen poorly? There are several reasons, some of which can be avoided and others that are sad but inescapable facts of life.

EFFORT Listening effectively is hard work. The physical changes that occur during careful listening show the effort it takes: Heart rate quickens, respiration increases, and body temperature rises.[22] Notice that these changes are similar to the body's reaction to physical effort. This is no coincidence, because listening carefully to a speaker can be just as taxing as more obvious efforts. You can manage the effort that's required to listen well if you prepare yourself for the task. If you know that passive listening won't be enough, you can invest the energy to understand others.

MESSAGE OVERLOAD The amount of speech most of us encounter every day makes careful listening to everything we hear impossible. As we've already seen, many of us spend as much as one-third of the time we're awake listening to verbal messages—from teachers, coworkers, friends, family, salespeople, and total strangers. This means we often spend five hours or more a day listening to peo-

---

A father once told me, "I can't understand my kid. He just won't listen to me at all."

"Let me restate what you just said," I replied. "You don't understand your son because he won't listen to you?"

"That's right," he replied.

"Let me try again," I said. "You don't understand your son because he won't listen to you?"

"That's what I said," he impatiently replied.

"I thought that to understand another person, you needed to listen to him," I suggested.

Steven R. Covey
The 7 Habits of Highly Effective People

Easy listening is a style of music, not communication.

Harvey Mackay

CULTURAL IDIOM

tuning out: not listening

a taste of their own medicine: retaliating by responding in a similar manner

tug-of-war: contest or struggle

ple talk. If you add this to the amount of time we tune in radio and television, you can see that it's impossible for us to keep our attention totally focused for that amount of time. Therefore, we have to let our attention wander at times. If you can consciously decide which messages are worth your attention, you can devote the time it takes to understand them.

RAPID THOUGHT   Listening carefully is also difficult for a physiological reason. Although we are capable of understanding speech at rates up to 600 words per minute, the average person speaks between 100 and 140 words per minute.[23] Thus, we have a great deal of mental "spare time" to spend while someone is talking. And the temptation is to use this time in ways that don't relate to the speaker's ideas, such as thinking about personal interests, daydreaming, planning a rebuttal, and so on. The trick is to use this spare time to understand the speaker's ideas better rather than to let your attention wander. Try to rephrase the speaker's ideas in your own words. Ask yourself how the ideas might be useful to you. Consider other angles that the speaker might not have mentioned.

PSYCHOLOGICAL NOISE   Another reason why we don't always listen carefully is that we're often wrapped up in personal concerns that are of more immediate importance to us than the messages others are sending. It's hard to pay attention to someone else when you're anticipating an upcoming test or thinking about the wonderful time you had last night with good friends. Yet, we still feel we have to "listen" politely to others, and so we continue with our charade. It usually takes a conscious effort to set aside your personal concerns if you expect to give others' messages the attention they deserve.

Figure 4–2 illustrates four ways in which preoccupied listeners lose focus when distracted by psychological noise. Everyone's mind wanders at one time or another, but excessive preoccupation is both a reason for and a sign of poor listening.

PHYSICAL NOISE   The world in which we live often presents distractions that make it hard to pay attention to others. The sound of traffic, music, others' speech, and the like interfere with our ability to hear well. Also, fatigue or other forms of discomfort can distract us from paying attention to a speaker's remarks. Consider, for example, how the efficiency of your listening decreases when you are seated in a crowded, hot, stuffy room that is surrounded by traffic and other noises. In such circumstances even the best intentions aren't enough to ensure clear understanding. You can often listen better by insulating yourself from outside distractions. This may involve removing the sources of noise: turning off the television, shutting the book you were reading, closing the window, and so on. In some cases, you and the speaker may need to find a more hospitable place to speak in order to make listening work.

HEARING PROBLEMS   Sometimes a person's listening ability suffers from a hearing problem—the most obvious sort of physiological noise, as defined in Chapter 1. After a hearing problem has been diagnosed, it's often possible to

CULTURAL IDIOM

charade: pretending or covering up

Figure 4–2   Four Thought Patterns. *Source:* A. D. Wolvin and C. G. Coakley, *Perspectives on Listening* (Norwood, NJ: Ablex, 1993), p. 115.

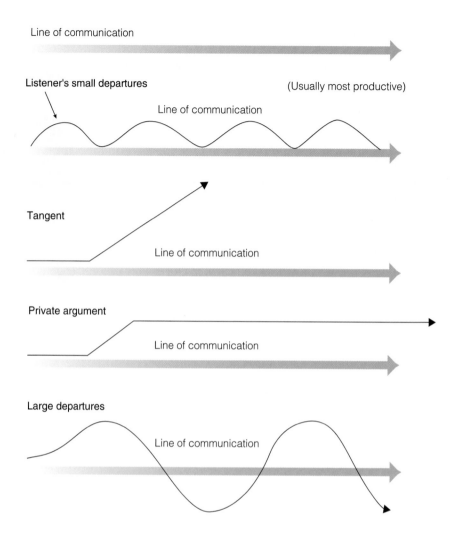

treat it. The real tragedy occurs when a hearing loss goes undetected. In such cases, both the person with the defect and others can become frustrated and annoyed at the ineffective communication that results. If you suspect that you or someone you know suffers from a hearing loss, it's wise to have a physician or audiologist perform an examination.

FAULTY ASSUMPTIONS   We often make incorrect assumptions that lead us to believe that we're listening attentively when quite the opposite is true. If the subject is a familiar one, it's easy to think that you've "heard it all before" when, in fact, the speaker is offering new information. A related problem arises if you assume that a speaker's thoughts are too simple or obvious to deserve careful attention when the truth is that you ought to be listening carefully. At other times, just the opposite occurs: You think that another's comments are too complex to possibly understand (as in some lectures) and so give up trying to make sense of them. A final mistake people often make is to assume that a subject is unimportant and to stop paying attention when they ought to be listening carefully. If you follow the guidelines listed in the section on informational listening on pages 124–132, you may be surprised to discover that comments that first seemed familiar, simplistic, or too complicated to understand turn out to be quite valuable. Of course, you'll never know unless you try.

TALKING HAS MORE APPARENT ADVANTAGES   It often appears that we have more to gain by speaking than by listening. Whatever the goal—to have a prospective boss hire you, to convince others to vote for the candidate of your choice, or to describe the way you want your hair cut—the key to success seems to be the ability to speak well. Another apparent advantage of speaking is the chance it provides to gain the admiration, respect, or liking of others—or so you may think. Tell jokes, and everyone may think you're a real wit. Offer advice, and they might be grateful for your help. Tell them all you know, and they could be impressed by your wisdom.

Although speaking at the right time can lead people to appreciate you, talking too much can result in the kind of stage hogging described on page 118. Not all interruptions are attempts at stage hogging. One study revealed a difference between male and female interrupters.[24] Men typically interrupted conversations far more than women. Their goal was usually to control the discussion. Women interrupted for very different reasons: to communicate agreement, to elaborate on the speaker's idea, or to participate in the topic of conversation. These sorts of responses are more likely to be welcomed as a contribution to the conversation and not as attempts to grab the stage.

If you find yourself hogging the conversation, try a simple experiment. Limit the frequency and length of your responses to a fraction of their usual amount. If you were speaking 50 percent of the time, cut back to 25 percent—or even less. If you interrupt the speaker every fifteen seconds, try to let him or her talk for closer to a minute. You are likely to discover that you're learning more—and probably gaining the appreciation of the other person.

CULTURAL DIFFERENCES   The way members of different cultures communicate can affect listening.[25] For instance, one study of young adults in various countries showed marked differences in listening preferences. Young Germans favored an action-oriented approach: They engaged speakers directly and were highly inquisitive. This style contrasts with the indirect approach of high-context Japanese listeners. Young Israelis were also less vocal than Germans and focused on careful analysis of others' statements. By contrast, young Americans emphasized the social dimension of a conversation and were more focused on how much time a conversation was taking.

MEDIA INFLUENCES   A final challenge to serious listening is the influence of contemporary mass media, especially television and radio. A growing amount of programming consists of short segments: news items, commercials, music videos, and so on. (Think of *Sesame Street* and MTV.) In the same vein, news

Deafness Lite

So slight is the bereftness of my belated ear-fault
that "Deafness Lite" became the name that I call it.

In a simpler word: things heard are blurred
on the left as well (or as weakly) as right.
Neither half's loss is a matter too drastic
both partly "cured" by batteries in plastic.

But if eyeing such signs of silence, Hearer,
or (harder to do) spying a less visible clue
try, by turning your speech slow and clearer
to reach those few who must communicate anew.

And so
that is why
as their advocate I
ask you unafflicted this:
Make me your talking's target
and practice, practice, practice.
Address then the wise assistive eyes
of sisters and brothers with hindered ear
and so come to know, then to de-stranger-ize
those kindred other souls who less than I can hear.

Repeat. Reword. For patience may reward your
self, not by some sense of the charity kind
but by sharing the very daringest adventure:
eyes meeting eyes and mind mating with mind.

Sal Parlato, Jr.

stories (for example, *USA Today* and the television news) consist of brief stories with a declining portion of text and a growing amount of graphical information. These trends discourage the kind of focused attention that is necessary for careful listening, especially to complicated ideas and feelings.

While the right to talk may be the beginning of freedom, the necessity of listening is what makes that right important.

Walter Lippmann

ETHICAL CHALLENGE

How Carefully Should You Listen?

What responsibility do communicators have to listen as carefully and thoughtfully as possible? Are there ever cases where we are justified in pseudolistening? Stage hogging? Defensive listening? Selective attention? Responding defensively? Ambushing? Insensitivity?

Is it dishonest to fake careful listening when you are not doing so, or do communicators have an obligation to confess that they are not listening? How would you feel if you knew others weren't listening to you?

What Good Is Free Speech If No One Listens?

It is the law in this country, as in no other, that the individual has an extraordinary right to personal expression. The First Amendment to the Constitution protects the right to speak and to publish; these rights and the degree to which they are safeguarded are the distinguishing characteristics of American society.

For that we have only the courts to thank. Americans seem to be almost completely uninterested in any point of view other than their individual own. We are absolutely up to our necks in groups and blocs and religious and economic interests certain beyond all reason that they are correct and actively interested in imposing their rules and values and self-selected morals on the rest of us. They prattle about democracy, and use it when it suits them without the slightest regard or respect for what it means and costs and requires. These people are—please believe me—dangerous.

The right to speak is meaningless if no one will listen, and the right to publish is not worth having if no one will read. It is simply not enough that we reject censorship and will not countenance suppression; we have an affirmative responsibility to hear the argument before we disagree with it.

I think that you think that you agree with me, that you are fair and open-minded and good citizens. But if we put it to the test—if I make up some speeches about gun control, abortion, gay rights, racial and ethnic characteristics, political terrorism and genocide—I believe that I can make you boo and jeer or at least walk out in protest.

We cannot operate that way. It's not difficult to listen to the philosophy you agree with or don't care about. It's the one that galls that must be heard. No idea is so repugnant that it must not be advocated. If we are not free to speak heresy and utter awful thoughts, we are not free at all. And if we are unwilling to hear that with which we most violently disagree, we are no longer citizens but have become part of the mob.

Nowhere is the willingness to listen more important than at a university, and nowhere is our failure more apparent than at the university whose faculty members or students think that it's legitimate to parade their own moral or political purity by shouting down the unpopular view of the day.

It will not be a week, and certainly not a month, before you will become aware that someone in your own circle of influence is saying something or thinking something very wrong. I think you have to do something about that. I think you have to help them be heard. I think you are required to listen.

Kurt Luedtke

PERSONAL LISTENING STYLES

Not everyone listens the same way. Communication researchers have identified four styles, each of which has both strengths and weaknesses.[26]

CULTURAL IDIOM

give weight to: give priority to

tune into: pay attention to

Content-Oriented

As the label that characterizes them suggests, **content-oriented listeners** are most interested in the quality of messages they hear. They want to seek details and are good at analyzing an issue from several perspectives. They give weight to the messages of experts and other credible sources of information. Content-oriented listeners often enjoy ideas for their own sake and are willing to spend time exploring them in thorough exchanges of ideas.

A content-oriented approach is valuable when the goal is to evaluate the quality of ideas and when there is value in looking at issues from a wide range of perspectives. It is especially valuable when the topic is a complicated one. On the other hand, a content-oriented approach risks annoying people who don't have the same sort of analytical orientation. A content-oriented approach can take more time than others may be willing to give, and the challenging of ideas that comes with it can be perceived as overly critical or even hostile.

People-Oriented

People-oriented listeners are especially concerned with creating and maintaining positive relationships. They tune into others' moods, and they respond to speakers' feelings as well as their ideas. People-oriented listeners are typically less judgmental about what others have to say than are content-oriented types: They are more interested in understanding and supporting people than in evaluating them.[27]

A people orientation has obvious strengths. But a strong concern for relationships has some less obvious drawbacks. It is easy to become overly involved with others' feelings. People-oriented listeners may lose their detachment and ability to assess the quality of information others are giving in an effort to be congenial and supportive. Less personally oriented communicators can view them as overly expressive and even intrusive.

Action-Oriented

Unlike people-oriented listeners, who focus on relationships, and content-oriented listeners, who are fascinated with ideas for their own sake, **action-oriented listeners** are most concerned with the task at hand. Their main concern is to figure out what sort of response is required by a message. They want to get to the heart of the matter quickly, and so they appreciate clear, concise messages and often translate others' remarks into well-organized mental outlines.

Action-oriented listening is most appropriate when taking care of business is the primary concern: Such listeners keep a focus on the job at hand and encourage others to be organized and concise. But their no-nonsense approach isn't always appreciated by speakers who lack the skill or inclination to be clear and direct. Action-oriented listeners seem to minimize emotional issues and concerns, which may be an important part of business and personal transactions.

Time-Oriented

Time-oriented listeners are most concerned with efficiency. They view time as a scarce and valuable commodity. They grow impatient when they view others as wasting it. A time orientation can be an asset when deadlines and other pressures demand fast action. On the other hand, a time orientation can put off others when it seems to disregard their feelings. Also, an excessive focus on time can hamper the kind of thoughtful deliberation that some jobs require.

As you read the preceding descriptions, you may have found that you use more than one of the listening styles. If so, you aren't alone: 40 percent of the people who have used this instrument indicate at least two strong listening preferences.[28] Whichever styles you use, it is important to recognize that you can control the way you listen and to use the styles that best suit the situation at hand. When your relationship with the speaker needs attention, adopt a people-oriented approach. When clarity is the issue, be an action-oriented listener. If analysis is called for, put on your content-oriented persona. And when the clock is what matters most, become a model of time orientation. You can also boost your effectiveness by assessing the listening preferences of your conversational partners and adapting your style to them.

The Chinese characters that make up the verb "to listen" tell us something significant about this skill

---

INVITATION TO INSIGHT

YOUR LISTENING STYLE PREFERENCES

You can analyze your effectiveness as a listener by answering the following questions.

1. Which of the listening styles described earlier do you use?
2. Does your listening style change in various situations, or do you use the same style most or all of the time?
3. What are the consequences (beneficial and harmful) of the listening styles you use?
4. How could you adapt your listening styles to improve your communication effectiveness?

INFORMATIONAL LISTENING

Informational listening is the approach to take when you want to understand another person. When you are an informational listener, your goal is to make sure you are receiving the same thoughts the other person is trying to convey—not always an easy feat when you consider the forces listed on pages 118–122 that interfere with understanding.

The situations that call for informational listening are endless and varied: following an instructor's comments in class, listening to a friend's account of a night on the town, hearing a description of a new piece of equipment that you're thinking about buying, learning about your family history from a relative's tales, swapping ideas in a discussion about religion or politics—the list goes on and on. You can become more effective as an informational listener by approaching others with a constructive attitude and by using some simple but effective skills.

Let the wise listen and add to their learning and let the discerning get guidance.

Proverbs 1:5

Learn to listen. Opportunity could be knocking at your door very softly.

Frank Tyger

Don't Argue or Judge Prematurely

Ever since ancient Greece and later Rome, Western civilization has admired the ability to persuade others.[29] This tradition has led us to measure the success of much communication in terms of whether it changes the way others think and act. Recall, for example, what often happens when people encounter someone with differing opinions. Rather than try to understand one another, their conversation often turns into an argument or debate (sometimes friendly, and sometimes not) in which the participants try to change one another's minds.

Persuasion is certainly one important goal of communication, but it isn't the *only* one. Most people would agree with the principle that it's essential to understand a speaker's ideas before judging them. Despite this commonsense fact, all of us are guilty of forming snap judgments, evaluating others before hearing them out. This tendency is greatest when the speaker's ideas conflict with our own.

It's especially tempting to counterattack when others criticize you, even when those criticisms might contain valuable truths and when understanding them might lead to a change for the better. Even if there is no criticism or disagreement, we tend to evaluate others based on sketchy first impressions, forming snap judgments that aren't at all valid. Not all premature judgments are negative. It's also possible to jump to overly favorable conclusions about the quality of a speaker's remarks when we like that person or agree with the ideas being expressed. The lesson contained in these negative examples is clear: Listen first. Make sure you understand. *Then* evaluate or argue, if you choose.

Separate the Message from the Speaker

The first recorded cases of blaming the messenger for an unpleasant message occurred in ancient Greece. When messengers would arrive reporting losses in battles, their generals were known to respond to the bad news by having the messengers put to death. This sort of irrational reaction is still common (though fortunately less violent) today. Consider a few situations in which there is a tendency to get angry with a communicator bearing unpleasant news: An instructor tries to explain why you did poorly on a major paper; a friend explains what you did to make a fool of yourself at the party last Saturday night; the boss points out how you could do your job better. At times like this, becoming irritated with the bearer of unpleasant information not only can cause you to miss important information, but also can harm your relationships.

There's a second way that confusing the message and the messenger can prevent you from understanding important ideas. At times you may mistakenly discount the value of a message because of the person who is presenting it. Even the most boring instructors, the most idiotic relatives, and the most demanding bosses occasionally make good points. If you write off everything a person says before you consider it, you may be cheating yourself out of some valuable information.

Be Opportunistic

Even if you listen with an open mind, sooner or later you will end up hearing information that is either so unimportant or so badly delivered that you're tempted to tune out. Although making a quick escape from such tedious

We can communicate an idea around the world in seventy seconds but it sometimes takes years for an idea to get through $\frac{1}{4}$ inch of human skull.

Charles Kettering
inventor and General Motors executive

Be not arrogant because of your knowledge. Take counsel with the ignorant as with the wise. You can learn something from everyone. Error enters early for those who do not hear. There is no one who can do anything for them. They regard knowledge as ignorance and what is beneficial as harmful.

Egyptian Vizier Ptahhotep, 3000 B.C.

situations is often the best thing to do, there are times when you can profit from paying close attention to apparently worthless communication. This is especially true when you're trapped in a situation where the only alternatives to attentiveness are pseudolistening or downright rudeness.

As an opportunistic listener you can find *some* value in even the worst situations, if you are willing to invest the effort. Consider how you might listen opportunistically when you find yourself locked in a boring conversation with someone whose ideas are worthless. Rather than torture yourself until escape is possible, you could keep yourself amused—and perhaps learn something useful—by listening carefully until you can answer the following (unspoken) questions:

> "Is there anything useful in what this person is saying?"
> "What led the speaker to come up with ideas like these?"
> "What lessons can I learn from this person that will keep me from sounding the same way in other situations?"

Listening with a constructive attitude is important, but even the best intentions won't always help you understand others. The following skills can help you figure out messages that otherwise might be confusing, as well as help you see how those messages can make a difference in your life.

Look for Key Ideas

It's easy to lose patience with long-winded speakers who never seem to get to the point—or *have* a point, for that matter. Nonetheless, most people do have a central idea, or what we will call a "thesis" in Chapter 12. By using your ability to think more quickly than the speaker can talk, you may be able to extract the thesis from the surrounding mass of words you're hearing. If you can't figure out what the speaker is driving at, you can always ask in a tactful way by using the skills of questioning and paraphrasing, which we'll examine now.

Ask Questions

Questioning involves asking for additional information to clarify your idea of the sender's message. If you ask directions to a friend's house, typical questions might be "Is your place an apartment?" or "How long does it take to get there from here?" In more serious situations, questions could include "What's bothering you?" or "Why are you so angry?" or "Why is that so important?" Notice that one key element of these questions is that they request the speaker to elaborate on information already given.

Despite their apparent benefits, not all questions are equally helpful. Whereas **sincere questions** are aimed at understanding others, **counterfeit questions** are really disguised attempts to send a message, not receive one. Counterfeit questions come in several varieties:

- Questions that make statements. "Are you finally off the phone?" is more of a statement than a question—a fact unlikely to be lost on the targeted person. Emphasizing certain words can also turn a question into a statement: "You lent money to *Tony*?" We also use questions to offer advice. The person who responds with, "Are you going to stand up to him and give him what he deserves?" clearly has stated an opinion about what should be done.

There is no such thing as an uninteresting subject. There are only uninterested people.

G. K. Chesterton

Know how to listen and you will profit even from those who talk badly.

Plutarch

CULTURAL IDIOM

long-winded: speaking for a long time

- Questions that carry hidden agendas. "Are you busy Friday night?" is a dangerous question to answer. If you say, "No," thinking the person has something fun in mind, you won't like hearing, "Good, because I need some help moving my piano." Obviously, such questions are not designed to enhance understanding; they are set-ups for the proposal that follows. Other examples include "Will you do me a favor?" and "If I tell you what happened, will you promise not to get mad?"

- Questions that seek "correct" answers. Most of us have been victims of question-askers who want to hear only a particular response. "Which shoes do you think I should wear?" can be a sincere question—unless the asker has a predetermined preference. When this happens, the asker isn't interested in listening to contrary opinions, and "incorrect" responses get shot down. Some of these questions may venture into delicate territory. "Honey, do you think I look ugly?" can be a request for a "correct" answer.

- Questions that are based on unchecked assumptions. "Why aren't you listening to me?" assumes the other person isn't paying attention. "What's the matter?" assumes that something *is* wrong. As Chapter 2 explains, perception checking is a much better way of checking out assumptions. As you recall, a perception check offers a description and interpretations, followed by a sincere request for clarification: "When you kept looking over at the TV, I thought you weren't listening to me, but maybe I was wrong. *Were* you paying attention?"

Unlike the counterfeit questions we've just examined, sincere questions are genuine requests for new information that clarifies a speaker's thoughts or feelings. Although the value of sincere questioning might seem obvious, people don't use this information-seeking approach enough. Communicators are often reluctant to show their ignorance by asking for explanation of what seems like it should be an obvious point. At times like this it's a good idea to recall a quote attributed to Confucius: "He who asks a question is a fool for five minutes. He who does not ask is a fool for life."

Paraphrase

Questioning is often a valuable tool for increasing understanding. Sometimes, however, it won't help you receive a speaker's ideas any more clearly, and it can even lead to further communication breakdown. To see how this can be so, consider our example of asking directions to a friend's home. Suppose the instructions you've received are to "drive about a mile and then turn left at the traffic signal." Now imagine that a few common problems exist in this simple message. First, suppose that your friend's idea of a mile is different from

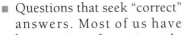

CULTURAL IDIOM

to stand up to: to confront courageously

shot down: rejected or defeated

yours: Your mental picture of the distance is actually closer to two miles, whereas hers is closer to three hundred yards. Next, consider the very likely occurrence that though your friend said "traffic signal," she meant "stop sign"; after all, it's common for us to think one thing and say another. Keeping these problems in mind, suppose you tried to verify your understanding of the directions by asking, "After I turn at the light, how far should I go?" to which your friend replied that her house is the third from the corner. Clearly, if you parted after this exchange, you would encounter a lot of frustrations before finding the elusive residence.

It's easy to see that questioning didn't help, because your original ideas of how far to drive and where to turn were mistaken. And contained in such mistakes is the biggest problem with questioning, because such inquiries don't tell you whether you have accurately received the information that has *already* been sent.

Now consider another kind of feedback—one that would tell you whether you understood what had already been said before you asked additional questions. This sort of feedback, termed **paraphrasing**, involves restating in your own words the message you thought the speaker had just sent, without adding anything new. In the example of seeking directions that we've been using, such rephrasing might sound like this: "So you're telling me to drive down to the traffic light by the high school and turn toward the mountains, is that it?" Immediately sensing the problem, your friend could then reply, "Oh no, that's way too far. I meant that you should drive to the four-way stop by the park and turn there. Did I say 'stop light'? I always do that when I mean 'stop sign'!"

Sometimes a paraphrase will reflect the *ideas* you think a speaker has expressed:
(*To a direction-giver*) "You're telling me to drive down to the traffic light by the high school and turn toward the mountains, is that it?"
(*To the boss*) "So you need me both this Saturday *and* next Saturday—right?"
(*To a professor*) "When you said, 'Don't worry about the low grade on the quiz,' did you mean it won't count against my grade?"

In other cases, a paraphrase will reflect your understanding of the speaker's *feelings*:

"You said you understand, but you look confused. Are you?"
"You seem to be in a hurry. I get the idea you don't want to talk now. Is that right?"
"You said 'Forget it,' but it sounds like you're mad. Are you?"

Figure 4–3 Asking Questions Doesn't Guarantee Understanding

CULTURAL IDIOM

parroting: repeating without understanding

bleeding-heart liberals: persons motivated by sympathy rather than practicality

boosts the odds: increases the chances of success

Whether your paraphrasing reflects a speaker's thoughts or feelings, and whether it focuses on a specific comment or a general theme, the key to success is to restate the other person's comments in your own words as a way of cross-checking the information. If you simply repeat the speaker's comments verbatim, you will sound foolish—and you still might well be misunderstanding what has been said. Notice the difference between simply parroting a statement and really paraphrasing:

Speaker: "I'd like to go, but I can't afford it."
Parroting: "You'd like to go, but you can't afford it."
Paraphrasing: "So if we could find a way to pay for you, you'd be willing to come. Is that right?"
Speaker: "Gawd, do you look awful!"
Parroting: "You think I look terrible."
Paraphrasing: "You think I've put on too much weight?"

As these examples suggest, effective paraphrasing is a skill that takes time to develop. You can make your paraphrasing sound more natural by taking any of three approaches, depending on the situation:

1. Change the speaker's wording.

Speaker: "Bilingual education is just another failed idea of bleeding-heart liberals."
Paraphrase: "Let me see if I've got this right. You're mad because you think bilingual ed sounds good, but it doesn't work?" (*Reflects both the speaker's feeling and the reason for it.*)

2. Offer an example of what you think the speaker is talking about.   When the speaker makes an abstract statement, you may suggest a specific example or two to see if your understanding is accurate.

Speaker: "Lee is such a jerk. I can't believe the way he acted last night."
Paraphrase: "You think those jokes were pretty offensive, huh?" (*Reflects the listener's guess about speaker's reason for objecting to the behavior.*)

3. Reflect the underlying theme of the speaker's remarks.   When you want to summarize the *theme* that seems to have run through another person's conversation, a complete or partial perception check is appropriate:

Paraphrase: "You keep reminding me to be careful. Sounds like you're worried that something might happen to me. Am I right?" (*Reflects both the speaker's thoughts and feelings and explicitly seeks clarification.*)

Learning to paraphrase isn't easy, but it can be worth the effort, because it offers two very real advantages. First, it boosts the odds that you'll accurately and fully understand what others are saying. We've already seen that using one-way listening or even asking questions may lead you to think that you've understood a speaker when, in fact, you haven't. Paraphrasing, on the other hand, serves as a way of double-checking your interpretation for accuracy. Second, paraphrasing guides you toward sincerely trying to understand another person instead of using nonlistening styles such as stage hogging, selective listening, and so on. If you force yourself to reflect the other person's ideas in your own words, you'll spend your mental energy trying to understand that speaker instead of using less constructive listening styles. For this reason, some communication experts suggest that the ratio of questioning and paraphrasing to confronting should be at least 5:1, if not more.[30]

Take Notes

Understanding others is crucial, of course, but comprehending their ideas doesn't guarantee that you will remember them. As you read earlier in this chapter, listeners usually forget almost two-thirds of what they hear.

Sometimes recall isn't especially important. You don't need to retain many details of the vacation adventures recounted by a neighbor or the childhood stories told by a relative. At other times, though, remembering a message—even minute details—is important. The lectures you hear in school are an obvious example. Likewise, it can be important to remember the details of plans that involve you: the time of a future appointment, the name of a phone caller whose message you took for someone else, or the orders given by your boss at work.

At times like these it's smart to take notes instead of relying on your memory. Sometimes these notes may be simple and brief: a phone number jotted on a scrap of paper or a list of things to pick up at the market. In other cases—a lecture, for example—your notes need to be much longer. When detailed notes are necessary, a few simple points will help make them effective:

1. *Don't wait too long before beginning to jot down ideas.* If you don't realize that you need to take notes until five minutes into a conversation, you're likely to forget much of what has been said and miss out on other information as you scramble to catch up.
2. *Record only key ideas.* Don't try to capture every word of long messages. If you can pin down the most important points, your notes will be easier to follow and much more useful.
3. *Develop a note-taking format.* The exact form you choose isn't important. Some people use a formal outlining scheme with headings designated by Roman numerals, letters, and numbers, whereas others use simple lists. You might come up with useful symbols: boxes around key names and numbers or asterisks next to especially important information. After you develop a consistent format, your notes will not only help you remember information, but also help you whip others' ideas into a shape that's useful to you.

UNDERSTANDING COMMUNICATION TECHNOLOGY

High Speed Listening

As a student and as a lifelong learner, you can use the knowledge of "spare time" in listening to your advantage. People generally speak between 125 and 150 words per minute, but the brain can process and understand up to 300 words in the same amount of time. The more familiar you are with a topic, the faster you may be able to understand.

You can take advantage of your ability to process information quickly by using some simple technology.

Many variable-speed tape recorders are available in microcassette size. Some have pitch control to keep the speeded-up playback from sounding ridiculously high pitched.

You can use one of these devices for taping lectures and playing them back at a faster speed. If you listen to and tape a lecture as it is given, you may find that you can increase the playback speed and still understand and review the lecture.

Informational Listening Practice

Effective informational listening isn't easy. It takes hard work and concentration. You can improve your skill in this important area and convince yourself of the difference good informational listening makes by following these steps.

1. Find a partner with whom you have an important relationship. This may be a family member, lover, friend, fellow worker, or even an "enemy" with whom you interact frequently.

2. Invite your partner to explain his or her side of an issue that the two of you have difficulty discussing. Your job during this conversation is to understand your partner. You should not even attempt to explain your position. (If you find the prospect of trying to understand the other person distressing, consider how this attitude might interfere with your ability to listen carefully.)

3. As your partner explains his or her point of view, use the skills outlined on pages 129–130 to help you understand. You can discover how well you are grasping your partner's position by occasionally paraphrasing what you think he or she is saying. If your partner verifies your paraphrase as correct, go on with the conversation. If not, try to listen again and play back the message until the partner confirms your understanding.

4. After the conversation is over, ask yourself the following questions:
   - As you listened, how accurate was your first understanding of the speaker's statements?
   - How did your understanding of the speaker's position change after you used paraphrasing?
   - Did you find that the gap between your position and that of your partner narrowed as a result of your both using paraphrasing?
   - How did you feel at the end of your conversation? How does this feeling compare to your usual emotional state after discussing controversial issues with others?
   - How might your life change if you used paraphrasing at home? At work? With friends?

Calvin and Hobbes

by Bill Watterson

Finding Common Ground through Listening

The reports from the front lines of the abortion wars are as dispiriting as ever. Hostilities have only escalated and opponents have now become enemies.

But in a vine-covered building behind a wooden fence in suburban Boston, a small group of family therapists is trying to establish a demilitarized zone. The Public Conversations Project they have created is on a leading edge of the nascent movement struggling to defuse the civil wars.

Their project grew out of a question that director Laura Chasin asked herself and her colleagues in 1990: "Do we as family therapists have skills that can be helpfully applied 'out there'?"

Over the past year and a half, they invited groups of people to join a different sort of conversation. Some of their names were provided by Planned Parenthood and Massachusetts Citizens for Life; all identified themselves as pro-choice or pro-life.

Under the ground rules, people were not allowed to try to persuade each other. Instead, over three hours and under the guidance of a project member, they talked and listened. They explored stereotypes of each other, acknowledged ambivalence and watched what emerged from this process.

Some questions indeed led down hopeless, dead ends. When does life begin? Is the fetus a person? Who should decide? But of the fifty people who went through the process, only two were totally unable to find new ways of talking.

"The main thing that happened was the way these people perceived each other," says Chasin. "They came in thinking, oh my God, I'm going to be meeting with them. They went out thinking these people are compassionate, principled and share concerns that I have."

Indeed at moments in the videotaped conversations, it is impossible to know the opponents without a label. Which side said, for example, "How do we get people who are in the business of making laws to start thinking about a world in which there would be no need for abortion?"

"These people were in such pitched battles," said another project member, "they didn't have a clue what they had in common." But gradually they uncovered a shared concern about the well-being of children and mothers. Both sides agreed that using abortion as a form of birth control was wrong. They agreed as well about the importance of preventing unintended pregnancy and about the need for sex education.

Chasin and her colleagues harbor no grand illusions that this process will forge A Great Compromise on abortion—take your placards and go home.

But, once a pattern has been "busted," once people are no longer defined as demons, they hope that the public, like the family, may be able to come up with some solutions. Indeed, there are hints of this success in other parts of this movement.

In Missouri, Wisconsin, Texas and California, pro-life and pro-choice people are meeting and talking—carefully.

Ellen Goodman

CRITICAL LISTENING

Whereas the goal of informational listening is to understand a speaker, the goal of **critical listening** (also called "evaluative listening") is to judge the quality of a message in order to decide whether to accept or reject it. At first the words *critical* and *evaluative* may put you off, because both words carry the negative connotations of carping and fault finding. But critical listeners needn't be hostile. Critical listening—at least in the sense we're discussing here—involves evaluating an idea to test its merit. In this sense, we could say that noncritical listeners are unquestioning, or even naive and gullible. Critical listening is appropriate when someone is trying to persuade you to buy a product, to act in a certain way, or to accept a belief—to cite a few examples. You will be most effective as a critical listener if you follow several guidelines:

Listen for Information Before Evaluating

The principle of listening for information before evaluating seems almost too obvious to mention, yet all of us are guilty of judging a speaker's ideas before we completely understand them. The tendency to make premature judgments is especially strong when the idea you are hearing conflicts with your own beliefs.

You can avoid the tendency to judge before understanding by following the simple rule of paraphrasing a speaker's ideas before responding to them. The effort required to translate the other person's ideas into your own words will keep you from arguing, and if your interpretation is mistaken, you'll know immediately.

Evaluate the Speaker's Credibility

The acceptability of an idea often depends on its source. If your longtime family friend, the self-made millionaire, invited you to invest your life savings in jojoba fruit futures, you might be grateful for the tip. If your deadbeat brother-in-law made the same offer, you would probably laugh off the suggestion.

Chapter 14 discusses credibility in detail, but two questions provide a quick guideline for deciding whether or not to accept a speaker as an authority:

1. *Is the speaker competent?* Does the speaker have the experience or the expertise to qualify as an authority on this subject? Note that someone who is knowledgeable in one area may not be as well qualified to comment in another area. For instance, your friend who can answer any question about computer programming might be a terrible advisor when the subject turns to romance.
2. *Is the speaker impartial?* Knowledge alone isn't enough to certify a speaker's ideas as acceptable. People who have a personal stake in the outcome of a topic are more likely to be biased. The unqualified praise a commission-earning salesperson gives a product may be more suspect than the mixed review you get from a user. This doesn't mean you should disregard any comments you hear from an involved party—only that you should consider the possibility of intentional or unintentional bias.

Examine the Speaker's Evidence and Reasoning

Speakers usually offer some kind of support to back up their statements. A car dealer who argues that domestic cars are just as reliable as imports might cite frequency-of-repair statistics from *Consumer Reports* or refer you to satisfied customers, for example; and a professor arguing that students don't work as hard as they used to might tell stories about then and now to back up the thesis.

Chapter 11 describes several types of supporting material that can be used to prove a point: definitions, descriptions, analogies, statistics, and so on. Whatever form the support takes, you can ask two fundamental questions to judge its quality. First, ask whether the evidence is true. Most people won't tell deliberate lies, but they may misquote the facts or even distort them out of enthusiasm—rather like an angler who exaggerates the size of a fish in a desire to make the story more impressive. Second, be sure to ask whether enough evidence is given. A small number of examples may not prove a point. For example, one or two bad experiences don't necessarily make it true that "all men (or women) are jerks."

Whatever form the support takes, you can ask several questions to determine the quality of a speaker's evidence and reasoning:[31]

1. *Is the evidence recent enough?* In many cases, ranging from trivial to important, old evidence is worthless. If the honors were earned several years ago, the cuisine from an "award-winning" restaurant may be barely edible today. The claim "Tony is a jerk" may have been true in the past, but people do change. Before you accept even the most credible evidence, be sure it isn't obsolete.

2. *Is enough evidence presented?* One or two pieces of support may be exceptions and not conclusive evidence. You might have heard this example of generalizing from limited evidence: "I never wear seat belts. I knew somebody who wasn't wearing them in an accident, and his life was saved because he was thrown clear from the car." Although not wearing seat belts might have been safer in this instance, on the average, experts agree when you consider *all* vehicle accidents, the chances of avoiding serious injury are much greater if you wear seat belts.

3. *Is the evidence from a reliable source?* Even a large amount of recent evidence may be worthless if the source is weak. Your cousin, the health-food fanatic, might not have the qualifications to talk about the poisonous effects of commercially farmed vegetables. On the other hand, the opinion of an impartial physician, nutritionist, or toxologist would carry more weight.

4. *Can the evidence be interpreted in more than one way?* A piece of evidence that supports one claim might also support others. For example, you might hear someone argue that statistics showing women are underrepresented in the management of a company as part of a conspiracy to exclude them from positions of power. The same statistics, though, could have other explanations: Perhaps fewer women have been with the company long enough to be promoted, or perhaps this is a field that has not attracted large numbers of women. Alternative explanations don't necessarily mean that the one being argued is wrong, but they do raise questions that need to be answered before you accept an argument.

Besides taking a close look at the evidence a speaker presents, a critical listener will also look at how that evidence is put together to prove a point. Logicians have identified a number of logical fallacies—errors in reasoning that can lead to false conclusions. Logicians have identified over one hundred fallacies.[32] Chapter 14 identifies some of the most common ones.

Examine Emotional Appeals

Sometimes emotion alone may be enough reason to persuade you. You might lend your friend $20 just for old time's sake even though you don't expect to see the money again soon. In other cases, it's a mistake to let yourself be swayed by

UNDERSTANDING DIVERSITY

Council: Reviving the Art of Listening

Not too long ago, before our ears became accustomed to an increasing barrage of stimulation, many people knew how to listen attentively, while tracking an animal or hearing the approach of rain—or sitting in council with a group of their peers.

We know of no more effective way to invoke this state of listening than in what we have come to call the "council process." The origin of this process can be traced to the League of the Iroquois (which had a powerful influence on the beginnings of our present governmental system) and the peoples of the plains and of the Southwestern pueblos. More recently, the traditional practice of council has emerged in contemporary form through the Native American Church. The roots of council also can be found in Homer's *Iliad,* where a talking wand was used by a gathering of men to resolve the bitter dispute between Achilles and Agamemnon.

As we have practiced it, the basic form of council is simple. In order to empower each person to speak in turn, a "talking" object or "stick" is chosen to be passed around the circle—traditionally clockwise, in the "sun direction." The talking stick can be as innocent as a flower just picked for the occasion or as venerable as a traditional hand-crafted artifact familiar to the group.

Many councils that meet regularly use the same object over a period of months or even years, so that it becomes a symbol of the group's integrity and its capability for spirited communication.

We often set three simple rules for council: Speak honestly, be brief, and listen from the heart. One of the great challenges is to not be thinking about what you're going to say until it's your turn to speak. Preparing your contribution before you receive the talking stick obviously diminishes its spontaneity and its responsiveness to what others have said. A good practice is to wait until the talking stick is in your hands and then pause to see what springs to mind. Often we are surprised at the humor, tears, wisdom, or vision that comes forth.

We share the concern many people have today about the superficial "playing Indian"—that is, the appropriation of another culture's traditions. We want to acknowledge how much we have learned from the teachings of Native American peoples and our own ancestors. Council for us is a spiritual practice growing out of all our history, and a practice in which we seek to express these roots in a contemporary context.

Jack Zimmerman and Virginia Coyle

emotion when the logic of a point isn't sound. The excitement or fun in an ad or the lure of low monthly payments probably aren't good enough reasons to buy a product you can't afford. Again, the fallacies described in Chapter 14 will help you recognize flaws in emotional appeals.

EMPATHIC LISTENING

We listen both informationally and critically out of self-interest. In **empathic listening,** however, the goal is to build a relationship or help the speaker solve a problem.[33] Empathic listening is the approach to use when others seek help for personal dilemmas. Sometimes the problem is a big one: "I don't know whether to split up or stay with him." At other times the problem is more modest. A friend might be trying to decide what birthday gift to buy or whether to switch jobs. Empathic listening is also a good approach to take when you simply want to become better acquainted with others and to show them that their opinions and feelings matter to you.

The two goals of helping others and building a relationship aren't mutually exclusive. Empathic listening can accomplish both of them, because when listening helps another person, the relationship between speaker and listener

CULTURAL IDIOM

to split up: to separate from one another in a relationship

improves.[34] For example, couples who communicate in ways that show they understand one another's feelings and ideas are more satisfied with their marriages than couples who express less understanding. The opposite is also true: In marriages where husbands do not give emotional responses to their wives, the stress level grows.

Whatever the relationship and topic, there are several styles by which you can respond empathically to another person's remarks.[35] Each of these styles has its advantages and disadvantages. As you read them, you can aim toward choosing the best style for the situation at hand.

Advising

When approached with another's problem, the most common tendency is an **advising** response: to help by offering a solution.[36] Although such a response is sometimes valuable, often it isn't as helpful as you might think.[37]

It is hard to tell when the other person wants to hear the helper's idea of a solution.[38]

"The days of the bartender psychologist are over, but I can help if you have any software problems."

Sometimes the request is clear: "What do you think I should do?" At other times, though, it isn't clear whether certain statements are requests for direct advice. Ambiguous statements include requests for opinions ("What do you think of Jeff?"), soliciting information ("Would that be an example of sexual harassment?"), and announcement of a problem ("I'm really confused . . .").

Even when someone with a problem asks for advice, offering it may not be helpful. Your suggestion may not offer the best course to follow, in which case it can even be harmful. There's often a temptation to tell others how we would behave in their place, but it's important to realize that what's right for one person may not be right for another. A related consequence of advising is that it often allows others to avoid responsibility for their decisions. A partner who follows a suggestion of yours that doesn't work out can always pin the blame on you. Finally, often people simply don't want advice: They may not be ready to accept it, needing instead simply to talk out their thoughts and feelings.

Advice is most welcome under two conditions: when it has been requested and when the advisor seems concerned with respecting the face needs of the recipient.[39]

Before offering advice, you need to be sure that three conditions are present:

1. *Be confident that the advice is correct.* You may be certain about some matters of fact, such as the proper way to solve a school problem or the cost of a piece of merchandise, but resist the temptation to act like an authority on matters you know little about. Furthermore, it is both unfair and risky to make suggestions when you aren't positive that they are the best choice. Realize that just

---

CULTURAL IDIOM

pin the blame on: claim the fault lies with

respecting the face needs: protecting one's dignity

Many receive advice, few profit by it.

Publilius Syrus

because a course of action worked for you doesn't guarantee that it will work for everybody.

2. *Ask yourself whether the person seeking your advice seems willing to accept it.* In this way you can avoid the frustration of making good suggestions, only to find that the person with the problem had another solution in mind all the time.

3. *Be certain that the receiver won't blame you if the advice doesn't work out.* You may be offering the suggestions, but the choice and responsibility for accepting them are up to the recipient of your advice.

Judging

A **judging response** evaluates the sender's thoughts or behaviors in some way. The judgment may be favorable—"That's a good idea" or "You're on the right track now"—or unfavorable—"An attitude like that won't get you anywhere." But in either case it implies that the person doing the judging is in some way qualified to pass judgment on the speaker's thoughts or behaviors.

Sometimes negative judgments are purely critical. How many times have you heard such responses as "Well, you asked for it!" or "I *told* you so!" or "You're just feeling sorry for yourself"? Although comments like these can sometimes serve as a verbal slap that brings problem-holders to their senses, they usually make matters worse.

At other times negative judgments are less critical. These involve what we usually call *constructive criticism,* which is intended to help the problem-holder improve in the future. This is the sort of response given by friends about everything from the choice of clothing to jobs to friends. Another common setting for constructive criticism occurs in school, where instructors evaluate students' work to help them master concepts and skills. But whether it's justified or not, even constructive criticism runs the risk of arousing defensiveness because it may threaten the self-concept of the person at whom it is directed.

Judgments have the best chance of being received when two conditions exist:

1. *The person with the problem should have requested an evaluation from you.* Occasionally an unsolicited judgment may bring someone to his or her senses, but more often this sort of uninvited evaluation will trigger a defensive response.

2. *Your judgment is genuinely constructive and not designed as a put-down.* If you are tempted to use judgments as a weapon, don't fool yourself into thinking that you are being helpful. Often the statement "I'm telling you this for your own good" simply isn't true.

If you can remember to follow these two guidelines, your judgments will probably be less frequent and better received.

Analyzing

In an **analyzing** statement, the listener offers an interpretation of a speaker's message. Analyses like these are probably familiar to you:

CULTURAL IDIOM

bring someone to his or her senses: cause someone to think more rationally

a put down: an insult, degrading remark

- "I think what's really bothering you is . . ."
- "She's doing it because . . ."
- "I don't think you really meant that."
- "Maybe the problem started when she . . ."

Interpretations are often effective ways to help people with problems to consider alternative meanings—meanings they would have never thought of without your help. Sometimes a clear analysis will make a confusing problem suddenly clear, either suggesting a solution or at least providing an understanding of what is occurring.

At other times, an analysis can create more problems than it solves. There are two problems with analyzing. First, your interpretation may not be correct, in which case the speaker may become even more confused by accepting it. Second, even if your interpretation is correct, telling it to the problem-holder might not be useful. There's a chance that it will arouse defensiveness (because analysis implies superiority and evaluativeness), and even if it doesn't, the person may not be able to understand your view of the problem without working it out personally.

How can you know when it's helpful to offer an analysis? There are several guidelines to follow:

1. *Offer your interpretation in a tentative way rather than as absolute fact.* There's a big difference between saying, "Maybe the reason is . . ." or "The way it looks to me . . ." and insisting, "This is the truth."
2. *Your analysis ought to have a reasonable chance of being correct.* An inaccurate interpretation—especially one that sounds plausible—can leave a person more confused than before.
3. *You ought to be sure that the other person will be receptive to your analysis.* Even if you're completely accurate, your thoughts won't help if the problem-holder isn't ready to consider them.
4. *Be sure that your motive for offering an analysis is truly to help the other person.* It can be tempting to offer an analysis to show how brilliant you are or even to make the other person feel bad for not having thought of the right answer in the first place. Needless to say, an analysis offered under such conditions isn't helpful.

Questioning

A few pages ago we talked about questioning as one way to understand others better. A **questioning** response can also be a way to help others think about their problems and understand them more clearly.[40] For example, questioning can help a problem-holder define vague ideas more precisely. You might respond to a friend with a line of questioning: "You said Greg has been acting 'differently' toward you lately. What has he been doing?" Another example of a question that helps clarify is as follows: "You told your roommates that you wanted them to be more helpful in keeping the place clean. What would you like them to do?"

Questions can also encourage a problem-holder to examine a situation in more detail by talking either about what happened or about personal feelings, for example, "How did you feel when they turned you down? What did you do then?" This type of questioning is particularly helpful when you are dealing with someone who is quiet or is unwilling under the circumstances to talk about the problem very much.

Although questions have the potential to be helpful, they also run the risk of confusing or distracting the person with the problem. The best questioning follows these principles:

1. *Don't ask questions just to satisfy your own curiosity.* You might become so interested in the other person's story that you will want to hear more. "What did he say then?" you might be tempted to ask. "What happened next?" Responding to questions like these might confuse the person with the problem, or even leave him or her more agitated than before.

2. *Be sure your questions won't confuse or distract the person you're trying to help.* For instance, asking someone, "When did the problem begin?" might provide some clue about how to solve it—but it could also lead to a long digression that would only confuse matters. As with advice, it's important to be sure you're on the right track before asking questions.

3. *Don't use questions to disguise your suggestions or criticism.* We've all been questioned by parents, teachers, or other figures who seemed to be trying to trap us or indirectly to guide us. In this way, questioning becomes a strategy that can imply that the questioner already has some idea of what direction the discussion should take but isn't willing to tell you directly.

Supporting

A **supporting** response can take several forms:

Agreement	"You're right—the landlord is being unfair."
	"Yeah, that class was tough for me, too."
Offers to help	"I'm here if you need me."
	"Let me try to explain it to him."
Praise	"I don't care what the boss said: I think you did a great job!"
	"You're a terrific person! If she doesn't recognize it, that's her problem."
Reassurance	"The worst part is over. It will probably get easier from here."
	"I know you'll do a great job."
Diversion	"Let's catch a movie and get your mind off this."
	"That reminds me of the time we . . ."
Acknowledgment	"I can see that really hurts."
	"I know how important that was to you."
	"It's no fun to feel unappreciated."

There's no question about the value of receiving support when faced with personal problems. "Comforting ability" and social support have been shown to be among the most important communication skills a friend—or a teacher or a parent—can have.[41] In other instances, this kind of comment isn't helpful at all; in fact, it can even make things worse. Telling a person who is obviously upset that everything is all right, or joking about a serious matter, can trivialize the problem. People might see your comments as a put-down, leaving them feeling worse than before.

It is hard to know what to say to a person who has been struck by tragedy, but it is easier to know what not to say. Anything critical of the mourner ("don't take it so hard," "try to hold back your tears, you're upsetting people") is wrong. Anything which tries to minimize the mourner's pain ("it's probably for the best," "it could be a lot worse," "she's better off now") is likely to be misguided and unappreciated. Anything which asks the mourner to disguise or reject his feelings ("we have no right to question God," "God must love you to have selected you for this burden") is wrong as well.

Harold S. Kushner
When Bad Things Happen to Good People

Source: © Zits Partnership. Reprinted with special permission of King Features Syndicate.

As with the other styles we'll discuss, supporting can be helpful, but only in certain circumstances.[42] For the occasions when supporting is an appropriate response, follow these guidelines:

1. *Make sure your expression of support is sincere.* Phony agreement or encouragement is probably worse than no support at all, because it adds the insult of your dishonesty to whatever pain the other person is already feeling.
2. *Be sure the other person can accept your support.* Sometimes we become so upset that we aren't ready or able to hear anything positive.

Even if your advice, judgments, and analysis are correct and your questions are sincere, and even if your support comes from the best motives, these responses often fail to help. As the cartoon above illustrates, even the most sincere supportive efforts don't always help. One recent survey demonstrates how poorly such traditional responses work.[43] Mourners who had recently suffered from the death of a loved one reported that 80 percent of the statements made to them were unhelpful. Nearly half of the "helpful" statements were advice: "You've got to get out more." "Don't question God's will." Despite their frequency, these responses were helpful only 3 percent of the time. The next most frequent response was reassurance, such as "She's out of pain now." Like advice, this kind of support was helpful only 3 percent of the time. Far more helpful were expressions that acknowledged the mourner's feelings.

One American Red Cross grief counselor explained to survivors of the September 11, 2001, terrorist attacks on the United States how simply being present can be more helpful than trying to reassure grief-stricken family members who had lost loved ones in the tragedy:

> Listen. Don't say anything. Saying "it'll be okay," or "I know how you feel" can backfire. Right now that's not what a victim wants to hear. They want to know people are there and care about them. Be there, be present, listen. The clergy refer to it as a "ministry of presence." You don't need to do anything, just be there or have them know you're available.[44]

Prompting

Advising, judging, analyzing, questioning, and supporting are all active approaches to helping that call for a great deal of input from the respondent. Another approach to problem solving is more passive. **Prompting** involves using silences and brief statements of encouragement to draw others out, and in so doing to help them solve their own problems. Consider this example:

Pablo: Julie's dad is selling a complete computer system for only $1,200, but if I want it I have to buy it now. He's got another interested buyer. It's a great deal. But buying it would wipe out my savings. At the rate I spend money, it would take me a year to save up this much again.

Tim: Uh huh.

Pablo: I wouldn't be able to take that ski trip over winter break . . . but I sure could save time with my schoolwork . . . and do a better job, too.

Tim: That's for sure.

Pablo: Do you think I should buy it?

Tim: I don't know. What do *you* think?

Pablo: I just can't decide.

Tim: *(silence)*

Pablo: I'm going to do it. I'll never get a deal like this again.

Prompting works especially well when you can't help others make a decision. At times like this your presence can act like a catalyst to help others find their own answers. Prompting will work best when it's done sincerely. Your nonverbal behaviors—eye contact, posture, facial expression, tone of voice—have to show that you are concerned with the other person's problem. Mechanical prompting is likely to irritate instead of help.

Paraphrasing

A few pages ago you read about the value of paraphrasing to understand others. The same skill can be used as a helping tool. When you use this approach, be sure to reflect both the *thoughts* and the *feelings* you hear being expressed. This conversation between two friends shows how reflecting can offer support and help a person find the answer to her own problem:

Jill: I've had the strangest feeling about my boss lately.

Mark: What's that? *(A simple question invites Jill to go on.)*

Jill: I'm starting to think maybe he has this thing about women—or maybe it's just about me.

Mark: You mean he's coming on to you? *(Mark paraphrases what he thinks Jill has said.)*

Jill: Oh no, not at all! But it seems like he doesn't take women—or at least me—seriously. *(Jill corrects Mark's misunderstanding and explains herself.)*

Mark: What do you mean? *(Mark asks another simple question to get more information.)*

Jill: Well, whenever we're in a meeting or just talking around the office and he asks for ideas, he always seems to pick men. He gives orders to women—men, too—but he never asks the women to say what they think.

Mark: So you think maybe he doesn't take women seriously, is that it? *(Mark paraphrases Jill's last statement.)*

Jill: Yeah. Well, he sure doesn't seem interested in their ideas. But that doesn't mean he's a total woman-hater or a male chauvinist pig. I know he counts on some women in the office. Our accountant Teresa has been there forever, and he's always saying he couldn't live without her. And when Brenda got the new computer system up and running last month, I know he

CULTURAL IDIOM

wipe out: deplete

coming on to: making a sexual advance to

a male chauvinist pig: a male who believes that men are superior to women

The reality of the other person is not in what he reveals to you, but in what he cannot reveal to you. Therefore, if you would understand him, listen not to what he says but rather to what he does not say.

Kahlil Gibran

appreciated that. He gave her a day off and told everybody how she saved our lives.

Mark: Now you sound confused. (*Reflects her apparent feeling.*)

Jill: I am confused. I don't think it's just my imagination. I mean I'm a good producer, but he has never—not once—asked me for my ideas about how to improve sales or anything. And I can't remember a time when he's asked any other women. But maybe I'm overreacting.

Mark: You're not positive whether you're right, but I can tell that this has you concerned. (*Mark paraphrases both Jill's central theme and her feeling.*)

Jill: Yes. But I don't know what to do about it.

Mark: Maybe you should . . . (*Starts to offer advice but catches himself and decides to ask a sincere question instead.*) So what are your choices?

Jill: Well, I could just ask him if he's aware that he never asks women's opinions. But that might sound too aggressive and angry.

Mark: And you're not angry? (*Tries to clarify how Jill is feeling.*)

Jill: Not really. I don't know whether I should be angry because he's not taking ideas seriously, or whether he just doesn't take my ideas seriously, or whether it's nothing at all.

Mark: So you're mostly confused. (*Reflects Jill's apparent feeling again.*)

Jill: Yes! I don't know where I stand with my boss, and not being sure is starting to get to me. I wish I knew what he thinks of me. Maybe I could just tell him I'm confused about what is going on here and ask him to clear it up. But what if it's nothing? Then I'll look insecure.

Mark: (*Mark thinks Jill should confront her boss, but he isn't positive that this is the best approach, so he paraphrases what Jill seems to be saying.*) And that would make you look bad.

Jill: I'm afraid maybe it would. I wonder if I could talk it over with anybody else in the office and get their ideas . . .

Mark: . . . see what they think . . .

Jill: Yeah. Maybe I could ask Brenda. She's easy to talk to, and I do respect her judgment. Maybe she could give me some ideas about how to handle this.

Mark: Sounds like you're comfortable with talking to Brenda first.

Jill: (*Warming to the idea.*) Yes! Then if it's nothing, I can calm down. But if I do need to talk to the boss, I'll know I'm doing the right thing.

Mark: Great. Let me know how it goes.

Reflecting a speaker's ideas and feelings in this way can be surprisingly helpful.[45] First, paraphrasing helps the problem-holder to sort out the problem. In the dialogue you just read, Mark's paraphrasing helped Jill pin down the real source of her concern: what her boss thinks of her, not whether he doesn't take women seriously. The clarity that comes from this sort of perspective can make it possible to find solutions that weren't apparent before. Paraphrasing is also helpful because it helps the problem-holder to unload more of the concerns he or she has been carrying around, often leading to the relief that comes from catharsis. Finally, listeners who reflect the speaker's thoughts and feelings (instead of judging or analyzing, for example) show their involvement and concern.

Paraphrasing can be helpful, but it is no panacea. A study by noted researcher John Gottman revealed that "active listening" (a term sometimes used to describe paraphrasing) by itself was not a trait that distinguished happily married couples from troubled ones.[46] Because empathy is the ingredient that

CULTURAL IDIOM

where I stand with:
how I am perceived by

makes paraphrasing thoughts and feelings helpful, it is a mistake to think of reflective listening as a technique that you can use mechanically. Carl Rogers, the psychologist generally considered the foremost advocate of active listening, made the case against mechanical paraphrasing strongly: "I am *not* trying to 'reflect feelings.' I am trying to determine whether my understanding of the client's inner world is correct—whether I am seeing it as he or she is experiencing it at this moment."[47] In other words, reflecting is not an end in itself; rather, it is one way to help others by understanding them better.

There are several factors to consider before you decide to paraphrase:

1. *Is the problem complex enough?* Sometimes people are simply looking for information and not trying to work out their feelings. At times like this, paraphrasing would be out of place. If someone asks you for the time of day, you'd do better simply to give her the information than to respond by saying, "You want to know what time it is." If you're fixing dinner, and someone wants to know when it will be ready, it would be exasperating to reply "You're interested in knowing when we'll be eating."

2. *Do you have the necessary time and concern?* The kind of paraphrasing we've been discussing here takes a good deal of time. Therefore, if you're in a hurry to do something besides listen, it's wise to avoid starting a conversation you won't be able to finish. Even more important than time is concern. It's not necessarily wrong to be too preoccupied to help or even to be unwilling to exert the considerable effort that active listening requires: You can't help everyone with every problem. It's far better to state honestly that you're unable or unwilling to help than to pretend to care when you really don't.

3. *Are you genuinely interested in helping the other person?* Sometimes as you listen to others, it's easy to relate their thoughts to your own life or to seek more information just to satisfy your own curiosity. Remember that paraphrasing is a form of helping someone else. The general obligation to reciprocate the other person's self-disclosure with information of your own isn't necessary when the goal is to solve a problem. Research shows that speakers who reveal highly intimate personal information don't expect, or even appreciate, the same kind of disclosure from a conversational partner.[48] Rather, the most competent and socially attractive response is one that sticks to the same topic but is lower in intimacy. In other words, when we are opening up to others, we don't appreciate their pulling a conversational take-away such as "You're worried? So am I! Let me tell you about how I feel . . ."

4. *Can you withhold judgment?* You've already seen that paraphrasing allows other people to find their own answers. You should use this style only if you can comfortably paraphrase without injecting your own judgments. It's sometimes tempting to rephrase others' comments in a way that leads them toward the solution you think is best without ever clearly stating your intentions. As you will read in Chapter 9, this kind of strategy is likely to backfire by causing defensiveness if it's discovered. If you think the situation meets the criteria for advice described earlier in this chapter, you should offer your suggestions openly.

5. *Is your paraphrasing in proportion to other responses?* Although active listening can be a very helpful way of responding to others' problems, it can become

artificial and annoying when it's overused. This is especially true if you suddenly begin to use it as a major response. Even if such responses are potentially helpful, this sudden switch in your behavior will be so out of character that others might find it distracting. A far better way to use paraphrasing is gradually to introduce it into your repertoire of helpfulness, so that you can become comfortable with it without appearing too awkward. Another way to become more comfortable with this style is to start using it on real but relatively minor problems, so that you'll be more adept at knowing how and when to use it when a big crisis does occur.

When and How to Help?

Before committing yourself to helping another person—even someone in obvious distress—make sure your help is welcome. There are many cases in which others prefer to keep their concerns to themselves. In these cases your efforts to get involved may not be useful and can even be harmful. In one survey, some people reported occasions when social support wasn't necessary, because they felt capable of handling the problem by themselves.[49] Many regarded uninvited help as an intrusion, and some said it left them feeling more nervous than before. The majority of respondents expressed a preference for being in control of whether their distressing situation should be discussed with even the most helpful friend.

When help is welcome, there is no single best way to provide it. Research shows that *all* styles can help others accept their situation, feel better, and have a sense of control over their problems.[50] But there is enormous variability in which style will work with a given person.[51] This fact explains why communicators who are able to use a wide variety of helping styles are usually more effective than those who rely on just one or two styles.[52]

You can boost the odds of choosing the best helping style in each situation by considering three factors. First, think about the *situation* and match your response to the nature of the problem. Sometimes people need your advice. At other times your encouragement and support will be most helpful, and at still other times your analysis or judgment may be truly useful. And, as you have seen, there are times when your probes and paraphrasing can help others find their own answer.

Second, besides considering the situation, you should also think about the *other person* when deciding which style to use. Some people are able to consider advice thoughtfully, whereas others use suggestions to avoid making their own decisions. Many communicators are extremely defensive and aren't capable of receiving analysis or judgments without lashing out. Still others aren't equipped to think through problems clearly enough to profit from paraphrasing and probing. Sophisticated helpers choose a style that fits the person.

Third, think about *yourself* when deciding how to respond. Most of us reflexively use one or two helping styles. You may be best at listening quietly, offering a prompt from time to time. Or perhaps you are especially insightful and can offer a truly useful analysis of the problem. Of course, it's also possible to rely on a response style that is *unhelpful*. You may be overly judgmental or too eager to advise, even when your suggestions aren't invited or productive. As you think about how to respond to another's problems, consider both your strengths and weaknesses.

SKILL
BUILDER

Empathic Response Styles

This exercise will help improve your ability to listen empathically in the most successful manner. For each of the following statements:

1. Write separate responses, using each of the following styles:
   - Advising
   - Judging
   - Analyzing
   - Questioning
   - Supporting
   - Prompting
   - Paraphrasing

2. Discuss the pros and cons of using each response style.

3. Identify which response seems most effective, explaining your decision.

   a. At a party, a guest you have just met for the first time says, "Everybody seems like they've been friends for years. I don't know anybody here. How about you?"

   b. Your best friend has been quiet lately. When you ask if anything is wrong, she snaps "no!" in an irritated tone of voice.

   c. A fellow worker says, "The boss keeps making sexual remarks to me. I think it's a come-on, and I don't know what to do."

   d. It's registration time at college. One of your friends asks if you think he should enroll in the communication class you've taken.

   e. Someone with whom you live remarks, "It seems like this place is always a mess. We get it cleaned up, and then an hour later it's trashed."

SUMMARY

Even the best message is useless if it goes unreceived or if it is misunderstood. For this reason, listening—the process of giving meaning to an oral message—is a vitally important part of the communication process. We began our look at the subject by identifying and refuting several myths about listening. Our conclusion here was that effective listening is a skill that needs to be developed in order for us to be truly effective in understanding others.

We next took a close look at five steps in the process of listening: hearing, attending, understanding, responding, and remembering. We examined several types of ineffective listening and then identified several challenges that make listening effectively difficult.

The chapter concluded by examining three types of listening. Informational listening is the proper approach to take when the goal is to understand another person's ideas. Information can be best gained with an active approach to listening. This active approach can involve either questioning or paraphrasing—restating the speaker's message in your own words.

Critical listening is appropriate when the goal is to judge the quality of an idea. A critical analysis will be most successful when the listener ensures correct understanding of a message before passing judgment, when the speaker's credibility is taken into account, when the quality of supporting evidence is examined, and when the logic of the speaker's arguments is examined carefully.

The aim of empathic listening is to help the speaker, not the receiver. Various helping responses include advising, judging, analyzing, supporting, and paraphrasing the speaker's thoughts and feelings. Listeners can be most helpful when they use a variety of styles, focus on the emotional dimensions of a message, and avoid being too judgmental.

RESOURCES

Print

Albrecht, Terence L., Brant R. Burleson, and Deana Goldsmith. "Supportive Communication," in *Handbook of Interpersonal Communication,* 2nd ed., Mark L. Knapp and Gerald R. Miller, eds. Newbury Park, CA: Sage, 1994.

This chapter describes the damaging consequences that come from a lack of social support, as well as describing how communicators can provide support for one another in a variety of ways, including listening.

Burleson, Brant R. "Comforting Messages: Features, Functions, and Outcomes," in *Strategic Interpersonal Communication,* John A. Daly and John M. Wiemann, eds. Hillsdale, NJ: Erlbaum, 1994.

Burleson is a leading researcher on comforting communication. This survey describes the nature and results of supportive responses.

Foss, Sonja, and Cindy L. Griffn. "Beyond Persuasion: A Proposal for an Invitational Rhetoric." *Communication Monographs* 62 (1995): 2–18.

The authors suggest that most communication scholars view human interaction in terms of persuasion, influence, and power. They propose a different mode of communication, which they term "invitational rhetoric." In this mode the goal is to *understand* the other communicator, rather than to try to change his or her point of view. The article provides a clear argument for more informational listening.

Freeman, Sally A., Stephen W. Littlejohn, and W. Barnett Pearce. "Communication and Moral Conflict." *Western Journal of Communication* 56 (Fall 1992): 311–329.

This article uses two case studies to illustrate the poor listening behavior that often occurs when people who hold radically different viewpoints on highly charged moral issues face one another. It also describes two programs that have been used to help disputants listen more constructively to one another. The authors acknowledge that neither program will eliminate conflict, but they suggest that both can help to transform hostile debates into constructive dialogues.

Leeds, Dorothy. *The Seven Powers of Questions: Secrets to Successful Communication in Life and Work.* New York: Penguin, 2001.

This practical book shows the many ways in which questions can be useful. In addition to getting the information we need from others, questions can stimulate others' thinking, get people to open up, and even enhance our control over a situation. Leeds shows how questions can work in both personal and career situations.

Purdy, Michael, and Deborah Borisoff. *Listening in Everyday Life: A Personal and Professional Approach.* Lanham, MD: University Press of America, 1997.

As its title suggests, this collection of readings offers practical information about listening in a variety of contexts, including the health care, legal, and service industries. In addition, chapters discuss the influences of gender, culture, and group settings on listening.

Spacapan, Shirlynn, and Stuart Oskamp. *Helping and Being Helped.* Newbury Park, CA: Sage, 1992.

Chapter 4—titled "When are Attempts to Help Effective?"—offers insights into why the most intuitive listening response to another's problem may not always be the most helpful one. This information can be useful in becoming a more empathic listener.

Films
Ineffective Listening

Jerry Maguire (1996). Rated R.

Jerry Maguire (Tom Cruise) is a high-powered pro sports agent with a bulging Rolodex and a stable of multimillionaire athletes. Jerry is so successful that he doesn't have time to truly listen to any of his clients. In an early scene, we see him juggle the callers on his multiline office phone, slinging clichés as he switches between athletes. At this point we think that success is the reason why Jerry is such an awful listener; but after he loses his job and scrambles to keep his last client, we learn that he is just as inattentive and insensitive when desperate as when successful. Rich or poor, the egocentric Maguire treats people in his life as props.

In true Hollywood fashion, Jerry learns the importance of listening only when he is close to losing the most important people in his life. As the film ends, Jerry is redeemed by the love of a good woman (Renée Zellweger), a young boy (Jonathan Lipnicki), and good friends (Cuba Gooding, Jr., and Regina King).

Kramer vs. Kramer (1979). Rated PG.

Ted Kramer (Dustin Hoffman) is an advertising executive whose involvement in his career excludes his wife, Joanna (Meryl Streep), driving her to leave him and their seven-year-old son, Billy (Justin Henry). The early scenes illustrate how Ted's failure to listen to Joanna has been the major cause of the breakup. As the film goes on, we discover that characters who truly listen to one another develop rewarding relationships, whereas those who don't live isolated lives.

Supportive Listening

Good Will Hunting (1997). Rated R.

Will Hunting (Matt Damon) is a janitor who spends most of his free time hanging around with his friends from their lower-middle-class Boston neighborhood, boozing and fighting. It soon becomes apparent that Will is a natural-born mathematical genius who can intuitively solve problems that have baffled some of the best minds in the world. Will turns down offers of jobs that take advantage of his gift, preferring a lifestyle of brawling and boozing that seems to point him toward jail, or worse.

The film depicts the efforts of four people who try to head Will away from a life of self-destruction: Will's best friend, Chuckie (Ben Affleck); his girlfriend, Skylar (Minnie Driver); MIT professor Lambeau (Stellan Skarsgard), who discovered Will's talents; and Lambeau's college roommate, Sean Maguire (Robin Williams), a gifted counselor.

From a communication perspective, it is instructive to see the array of communication styles and strategies these four characters use to help Will turn his life around. As in real life, no single approach is the best. Will's breakthrough occurs in response to Maguire's skilled counseling, but it is clear that his hope for change and growth depends on the genuine concern of all four characters—each of whom offers help in a highly personal way.

CONTENTS

KEY TERMS

affect blends
chronemics
disfluencies
emblems
illustrators
intimate distance
kinesics
manipulators
nonverbal communication
paralanguage
personal distance
proxemics
public distance
social distance
territory

AFTER STUDYING THE MATERIAL IN THIS CHAPTER . . .

YOU SHOULD UNDERSTAND:

1. Five characteristics of nonverbal communication.

2. Three differences between verbal and nonverbal communication.

3. Six functions that nonverbal communication can serve.

4. How the types of nonverbal communication described in this chapter function.

YOU SHOULD BE ABLE TO:

1. Identify and describe nonverbal behavior of yourself and others in various contexts.

2. Identify nonverbal behaviors that repeat, substitute for, complement, accent, regulate, and contradict verbal messages.

3. Recognize the emotional and relational dimensions of your own nonverbal behavior.

4. Share your interpretation of another person's nonverbal behavior in a tentative manner when such sharing is appropriate.

NONVERBAL COMMUNICATION

There is often a big gap between what people say and what they feel. An acquaintance says, "I'd like to get together again" in a way that leaves you suspecting the opposite. (But how do you know?) A speaker tries to appear confident but acts in a way that almost screams out, "I'm nervous!" (What tells you this?) You ask a friend what's wrong, and the "nothing" you get in response rings hollow. (Why does it sound untrue?)

Then, of course, there are times when another's message comes through even though there are no words at all. A look of irritation, a smile, a sigh—signs like these can say more than a torrent of words.

All situations like these have one point in common—the message was sent nonverbally. The goal of this chapter is to introduce you to this world of nonverbal communication. Although you have certainly recognized nonverbal messages before, the following pages should introduce you to a richness of information you have never noticed. And though your experience won't transform you into a mind reader, it will make you a far more accurate observer of others—and yourself.

We need to begin our study of *nonverbal communication* by defining this term. At first this might seem like a simple task. If *non* means "not" and *verbal* means "words," then *nonverbal communication* appears to mean "communication without words." This is a good starting point after we distinguish between vocal communication (by mouth) and verbal communication (with words). After this distinction is made, it becomes clear that some nonverbal messages are vocal, and some are not. Likewise, although many verbal messages are vocal, some aren't. Table 5–1 illustrates these differences.

What about languages that don't involve words? Does American Sign Language, for example, qualify as nonverbal communication? Most scholars would say not.[1] Keeping this fact in mind, we arrive at a working definition of **nonverbal communication:** "oral and nonoral messages expressed by other than linguistic means." This rules out not only sign languages but also written words, but it includes messages transmitted by vocal means that don't involve language—sighs, laughs, and other utterances we will discuss soon.

CULTURAL IDIOM

rings hollow: sounds insincere

CHARACTERISTICS OF NONVERBAL COMMUNICATION

Our brief definition only hints at the richness of nonverbal messages. You can begin to understand their prevalence by trying a simple experiment. Spend

TABLE 5–1 Types of Communication		
	Vocal Communication	**Nonvocal Communication**
Verbal Communication	Spoken words	Written words
Nonverbal Communication	Tone of voice, sighs, screams, vocal qualities (loudness, pitch, and so on)	Gestures, movement, appearance, facial expression, and so on

Adapted from John Stewart and Gary D'Angelo, *Together: Communicating Interpersonally,* 2nd ed. (Reading, MA: Addison-Wesley, 1980), p. 22. Copyright © 1993 by McGraw-Hill. Reprinted/adapted by permission.

an hour or so around a group of people who are speaking a language you don't understand. (You might find such a group in the foreign students' lounge on campus, in an advanced language class, or in an ethnic neighborhood.) Your goal is to see how much information you can learn about the people you're observing from means other than the verbal messages they transmit. This experiment will reveal several characteristics of nonverbal communication.

Nonverbal Communication Exists

Your observations in the experiment show clearly that even without understanding speech it is possible to get an idea about how others are feeling. You probably noticed that some people were in a hurry, whereas others seemed happy, confused, withdrawn, or deep in thought. The point is that without any formal experience you were able to recognize and to some degree interpret messages that other people sent nonverbally. In this chapter, we want to sharpen the skills you already have and to give you a better grasp of the vocabulary of nonverbal language.

Nonverbal Behavior Has Communicative Value

The pervasiveness of nonverbal communication brings us to its second characteristic. Suppose you were instructed to avoid communicating any messages at all. What would you do? Close your eyes? Withdraw into a ball? Leave the room? You can probably see that even these behaviors communicate messages, suggesting that you are avoiding contact. A moment's thought will show that there is no way to avoid communicating nonverbally.

Of course, we don't always intend to send nonverbal messages. Unintentional nonverbal behaviors differ from intentional ones.[2] For example, we often stammer, blush, frown, and sweat without meaning to do so. Some theorists argue that unintentional behavior may provide information, but it shouldn't count as communication. Others draw the boundaries of nonverbal communication more broadly, suggesting that even unconscious and unintentional behavior conveys messages and thus is worth studying as communication.[3] We take the broad view here because, whether or not our nonverbal behavior is intentional, others recognize it and take it into account when responding to us.

Although nonverbal behavior reveals information, we aren't always conscious of what we are communicating nonverbally. In one study, less than a quarter of experimental subjects who had been instructed to show increased or decreased liking of a partner could

No matter how eloquently a dog may bark, he cannot tell you that his parents were poor but honest.

Bertrand Russell

Writer (to movie producer Sam Goldwyn): Mr. Goldwyn, I'm telling you a sensational story. I'm only asking for your opinion, and you fall asleep.
Goldwyn: Isn't sleeping an opinion?

describe the nonverbal behaviors they used. Furthermore, just because communicators are nonverbally expressive doesn't mean that others will tune into the abundance of unspoken messages that are available. One study comparing the richness of e-mail to in-person communication confirmed the greater amount of information available in face-to-face conversations, but it also showed that some communicators (primarily men) failed to recognize these messages.[4]

The fact that you and everyone around you are constantly sending nonverbal clues is important because it means that you have a constant source of information available about yourself and others. If you can tune into these signals, you will be more aware of how those around you are feeling and thinking, and you will be better able to respond to their behavior.

Sometimes you can observe a lot by watching.

Yogi Berra

INVITATION TO INSIGHT ## Observing and Reporting Nonverbal Behavior

This exercise will give you a clear idea of the many nonverbal behaviors that are available to you whenever you encounter another person. It will also help prevent you from jumping to conclusions about the meaning of those behaviors without checking out your interpretations. You can try the exercise either in or outside of class, and the period of time over which you do it is flexible, from a single class period to several days. In any case, begin by choosing a partner, and then follow these directions:

1. For the first period of time (however long you decide to make it), observe the way your partner behaves. Notice how he or she moves; his or her mannerisms, postures, way of speaking; how he or she dresses; and so on. To remember your observations, jot them down. If you're doing this exercise out of class over an extended period of time, there's no need to let your observations interfere with whatever you'd normally be doing: Your only job here is to compile a list of your partner's behaviors. In this step, you should be careful not to interpret your partner's actions; just record what you see.

2. At the end of the time period, share what you've seen with your partner. He or she will do the same with you.

3. For the next period of time, your job is not only to observe your partner's behavior but also to interpret it. This time in your conference you should tell your partner what you thought his or her actions revealed. For example, if your partner dressed carelessly, did you think this meant that he or she overslept, that he or she is losing interest in his or her appearance, or that he or she was trying to be more comfortable? If you noticed him or her yawning frequently, did you think this meant that he or she was bored, tired from a late night, or sleepy after a big meal? Don't feel bad if your guesses weren't all correct. Remember that nonverbal clues tend to be ambiguous. You may be surprised how checking out the nonverbal clues you observe can help build a relationship with another person.

CULTURAL IDIOM

tune in to: pay attention to

Nonverbal Communication Is Primarily Relational

Some nonverbal messages serve utilitarian functions. For example, a police officer directs the flow of traffic, and a team of street surveyors uses hand motions to coordinate its work. But nonverbal communication also serves a far more common (and more interesting) series of social functions.[5]

One important social function of nonverbal communication involves identity management. Chapter 2 discussed how we strive to create an image of ourselves as we want others to view us. Nonverbal communication plays an important role in this process—in many cases more important than verbal communication. Consider, for example, what happens when you attend a party where you are likely to meet strangers you would like to get to know better. Instead of projecting your image verbally ("Hi! I'm attractive, friendly, and easygoing"), you behave in ways that will present this identity. You might smile a lot, and perhaps try to strike a relaxed pose. It's also likely that you dress carefully—even if the image involves looking as if you hadn't given a lot of attention to your appearance.

Along with identity management, nonverbal communication allows us to define the kind of relationships we want to have with others. You can appreciate this fact by thinking about the wide range of ways you could behave when greeting another person. You could wave, shake hands, nod, smile, clap the other person on the back, give a hug, or avoid all contact. Each one of these decisions would send a message about the nature of your relationship with the other person.

Nonverbal communication performs a third valuable social function: conveying emotions that we may be unwilling or unable to express—or ones we may not even be aware of. In fact, nonverbal communication is much better suited to expressing attitudes and feelings than ideas.[6] You can prove this for yourself by imagining how you could express each item on the following list nonverbally:

- You're bored.
- You are opposed to capital punishment.
- You are attracted to another person in the group.
- You want to know if you will be tested on this material.
- You are nervous about trying this experiment.

The first, third, and fifth items in this list all involve attitudes; you could probably imagine how each could be expressed nonverbally. By contrast, the second and fourth items involve ideas, and they would be quite difficult to convey without using words. The same principle holds in everyday life: Nonverbal behavior offers many cues about the way people feel—often more than we get from their words alone. In fact, some research suggests that one important element of communicative competence is nonverbal expressiveness.[7]

Nonverbal Communication Is Ambiguous

Before you get the idea that this book will turn you into a mind reader, it is important to realize that nonverbal communication is often difficult to interpret accurately. To appreciate the ambiguous nature of nonverbal communication, study the photo on page 154. What emotions do you imagine the couple are feeling: grief? anguish? agony? In fact, none of these is even close. The couple have just learned that they won $1 million in the New Jersey state lottery!

Nonverbal communication can be just as ambiguous in everyday life, as Table 5–2 illustrates. This ambiguity can create some serious problems. For example, relying on nonverbal cues in romantic situations can lead to inaccurate guesses about a partner's interest in a sexual relationship.[8] Workers of the Safeway supermarket chain discovered firsthand the problems with nonverbal ambiguity when they tried to follow the company's new "superior customer service" policy that required them to smile and make eye contact with cus-

UNDERSTANDING COMMUNICATION TECHNOLOGY

Expressiveness in Online Communication

Communication scholars have characterized face-to-face interaction as "rich" in nonverbal cues that convey feelings and attitudes. Even telephone conversations carry a fair amount of emotional information via the speakers' vocal qualities. By comparison, most text-based communication on the Internet, such as e-mail and instant messaging, is relatively lean in relational information. With only words, subtlety is lost. This is why hints and jokes that might work well in person or on the phone often fail when communicated online.

Ever since the early days of e-mail, Internet correspondents have devised a series of "emoticons" using typed characters to convey feelings. The most common of these is the symbol :) , which, of course, represents humorous intent. Less commonly used emoticons convey other emotions: :-(is a frown, :-0 surprise, and so on.

Even though you can't make your voice louder or softer or change its tone in type, you can use regular keyboard characters to convey a surprisingly large range of feelings.

Asterisks   Not all e-mail and instant messaging systems allow the use of italics, which are useful for emphasizing a point. Enclosing a statement in asterisks can add the same sort of light emphasis. Instead of saying
`I really want to hear from you,` you can say

`I *really* want to hear from you.`
Notice how changing the placement of asterisks produces a different message:
`I really want to hear from *you.*`

Capitalization   Capitalizing a word or phrase can also emphasize the point:
`I hate to be a pest, but I need the $20 you owe me TODAY.`
Overuse of capitals can be offensive. Be sure to avoid typing messages in all uppercase letters, which creates the impression of shouting:
`HOW ARE YOU DOING? WE ARE HAVING A GREAT TIME HERE. BE SURE TO COME SEE US SOON.`

Multiple Methods of Emphasis   When you *really* want to emphasize a point, you can use multiple methods:
`I can't believe you told the boss that I sleep with a teddy bear! I wanted to *die* of embarrassment. Please don't *EVER* **EVER** do that kind of thing again.`
Use this type of emphasis sparingly, and only where you want to make your point very strongly.

Adapted from K. Baker and S. Baker, *How to Say It Online.* (New York: Prentice Hall, 2001).

TABLE 5–2	**Some Meanings of Silence**
Agreement	Disagreement ("silent treatment")
Thoughtfulness	Ignorance
Revelation (We often say much about the people we are describing by what we choose to omit.)	Secrecy ("If he didn't have something to hide, he'd speak up.")
Warmth ("Bind the participants.")	Coldness ("Separate the participants.")
Submission	Attack ("Not answering a letter—or worse, not answering a comment directed at you.")
Gaining attention	Boredom
Consideration	Inconsideration

Source: "Some Meanings of Silence" by Mark L. Knapp and Anita L. Vangelisti from *Interpersonal Communication and Human Relationships,* 3rd ed. Copyright © 1996 by Allyn & Bacon. Reprinted by permission.

tomers. Twelve employees filed grievances over the policy, reporting that several customers had propositioned them, misinterpreting their actions as come-ons.[9]

Although all nonverbal behavior is ambiguous, some emotions are easier to decode accurately than others. In laboratory experiments, subjects are better at identifying positive facial expressions such as happiness, love, surprise, and interest than negative ones such as fear, sadness, anger, and disgust.[10] In real life, however, spontaneous nonverbal expressions are so ambiguous that observers are able to identify the emotions they convey no more accurately than by blind guessing.[11]

Some people are more skillful than others at accurately decoding nonverbal behavior.[12] Those who are better senders of nonverbal messages also are better receivers. Decoding ability also increases with age and training, although there are still differences in ability owing to personality and occupation. For instance, extroverts are relatively accurate judges of nonverbal behavior, whereas dogmatists are not. Interestingly, women seem to be better than men at decoding nonverbal messages. Over 95 percent of the studies examined in one analysis

CULTURAL IDIOM

come-ons: sexual advances

blind guessing: coming to a conclusion without any factual basis for judgment

"That was unkind, darling. When their mouths turn up at the corners they want to be friends."

showed that women are more accurate at interpreting nonverbal signals.[13] Despite these differences, even the best nonverbal decoders do not approach 100 percent accuracy.

When you do try to make sense out of ambiguous nonverbal behavior, you need to consider several factors: the context in which they occur (e.g., smiling at a joke suggests a different feeling from what is suggested by smiling at another's misfortune); the history of your relationship with the sender (friendly, hostile, etc.); the other's mood at the time; and your feelings (when you're feeling insecure, almost anything can seem like a threat). The important idea is that when you become aware of nonverbal messages, you should think of them not as facts, but rather as clues that need to be checked out.

CULTURAL IDIOM

wind up in: end up being in

Much Nonverbal Communication Is Culture-Bound

Cultures have different nonverbal languages as well as verbal ones. Fiorello LaGuardia, legendary mayor of New York from 1933 to 1945, was fluent in English, Italian, and Yiddish. Researchers who watched films of his campaign speeches with the sound turned off found that they could tell which language he was speaking by the changes in his nonverbal behavior.[14]

The meaning of some gestures varies from one culture to another. The "okay" gesture made by joining thumb and forefinger to form a circle is a cheery affirmation to most Americans, but it has less positive meanings in other parts of the world.[15] In France and Belgium it means "You're worth zero." In Greece and Turkey it is a vulgar sexual invitation, usually meant as an insult. Given this sort of cross-cultural ambiguity, it's easy to imagine how an innocent tourist might wind up in serious trouble.

Less obvious cross-cultural differences can damage relationships without the parties ever recognizing exactly what has gone wrong. Edward Hall points out that whereas Americans are comfortable conducting business at a distance of roughly four feet, people from the Middle East stand much closer.[16] It is easy to visualize the awkward advance and retreat pattern that might occur when two diplomats or business people from these cultures meet. The Middle Easterner would probably keep moving forward to close the gap that feels so wide, whereas the American would continually back away. Both would feel uncomfortable, probably without knowing why.

Like distance, patterns of eye contact vary around the world.[17] A direct gaze is considered appropriate for speakers in Latin America, the Arab world, and southern Europe. On the other hand, Asians, Indians, Pakistanis, and northern Europeans gaze at a listener peripherally or not at all. In either case, deviations from the norm are likely to make a listener uncomfortable.

BUILD A BETTER LIFE BY STEALING OFFICE SUPPLIES Dogbert's Big Book of Business 9

Even within a culture, various groups can have different nonverbal rules. For example, many white teachers use quasi questions that hint at the information they are seeking. An elementary teacher might encourage the class to speak up by making an incorrect statement that demands refutation: "So twelve divided by four is six, right?" Most white students would recognize this behavior as a way of testing their understanding. But this style of questioning is unfamiliar to many students raised in traditional black cultures, who aren't likely to respond until they are directly questioned by the teacher.[18] Given this difference, it is easy to imagine how some teachers might view minority children as unresponsive or slow, when in fact they are simply playing by a different set of rules.

Communicators become more tolerant of others after they understand that unusual nonverbal behaviors are the result of cultural differences. In one study, American adults were presented with videotaped scenes of speakers from the United States, France, and Germany.[19] When the sound was cut off, viewers judged foreigners more negatively than their fellow citizens. But when the speakers' voices were added (allowing viewers to recognize that they were from a different country), the critical ratings dropped.

Despite differences like these, many nonverbal behaviors are universal. Certain expressions have the same meanings around the world. Smiles and laughter are a universal signal of positive emotions, for example, whereas the same sour expressions convey displeasure in every culture.[20] Charles Darwin believed that expressions like these are the result of evolution, functioning as survival mechanisms that allowed early humans to convey emotional states before the development of language. The innateness of some facial expressions becomes even more clear when we examine the behavior of children born deaf and blind.[21] Despite a lack of social learning, these children display a broad range of expressions. They smile, laugh, and cry in ways virtually identical to seeing and hearing infants.

Although nonverbal expressions like these may be universal, the way they are used varies widely around the world. In some cultures display rules discourage the overt demonstration of feelings like happiness or anger. In other cultures the same feelings are perfectly appropriate. Thus, a Japanese might appear much more controlled and placid than an Arab when in fact their feelings might be identical.[22]

The same principle operates closer to home among cocultures. For example, observations have shown that black women in all-black groups are nonverbally

Once identified and analyzed, nonverbal communication systems can be taught, like a foreign language. Without this training, we respond to nonverbal communications in terms of our own culture; we read everyone's behavior as if it were our own, and thus we often misunderstand it. . . .
The language of behavior is extremely complex. Most of us are lucky to have under control one subcultural system—the one that reflects our sex, class, generation, and geographic region.

Edward and Mildred Hall

INVITATION
TO INSIGHT

Culture and Nonverbal Communication

1. Identify at least three significant differences between nonverbal practices in two cultures or cocultures (e.g., ethnic, age, or socioeconomic groups) within your own society.
2. Describe the potential difficulties that could arise out of the differing nonverbal practices when members from the cultural groups interact. Are there any ways of avoiding these difficulties?
3. Now describe the advantages that might come from differing cultural nonverbal practices. How might people from diverse backgrounds profit by encountering one another's customs and norms?

more expressive and interrupt one another more than do white women in all-white groups.[23] This doesn't mean that black women always feel more intensely than their white counterparts. A more likely explanation is that the two groups follow different cultural rules. The researchers found that in racially mixed groups both black and white women moved closer to the others' style. This nonverbal convergence shows that skilled communicators can adapt their behavior when interacting with members of other cultures or cocultures in order to make the exchange more smooth and effective.

DIFFERENCES BETWEEN VERBAL AND NONVERBAL COMMUNICATION

The features described in the preceding section suggest some ways in which nonverbal communication differs from the spoken and written word. By examining the key differences between these two forms of communication, you will get a clearer idea of what each type can and can't accomplish.

Single versus Multiple Channels

Most verbal messages—words, sentences, and paragraphs—reach us one at a time, rather like pearls on a string. In fact, it's physically impossible for a person to speak more than one word at a time. Unlike the spoken word, however, nonverbal messages don't arrive in such an orderly, sequential manner. Instead, they bombard us simultaneously from a multitude of channels. Consider the everyday act of meeting a stranger for the first time. On a verbal level there's relatively little information exchanged in the clichés that occupy the first few minutes of most conversations ("How's it going . . . ." "Great weather we've been having . . ." "What's your major?"). But at the same moment, the number of nonverbal messages available to you is overwhelming: the other person's facial expressions, postures, gestures, the clothing he or she wears, the distance he or she stands from you, and so on. In one way, this multichannel onslaught of nonverbal messages is a boon because it provides so many ways of learning about others. In another way, however, the number of simultaneous messages is a problem, because it's difficult to recognize the overwhelming amount of nonverbal information we receive from others every moment.

Discrete versus Continuous

Verbal messages—words, sentences, and paragraphs—form messages with clear beginnings and endings. In this sense, it's possible to say that someone either is or isn't communicating verbally by seeing whether or not he or she is speaking or writing. Unlike the written and spoken word, however, nonverbal communication is continuous and never ending. As we've already said, it's impossible not to communicate nonverbally: The postures, gestures, and other types of messages described in the following pages provide a constant flow of messages.

Conscious versus Unconscious

Whereas we usually think about what we want to say before speaking or writing, most nonverbal messages aren't deliberate.[25] Of course, we do pay attention

UNDERSTANDING COMMUNICATION TECHNOLOGY

Misunderstandings on the Internet

In recent years, computer-mediated communication (CMC) has become a common channel for personal interaction. A growing number of people around the world exchange e-mail messages as effortlessly and frequently as they use the telephone. Computer-based news and discussion groups provide a forum for exchanging information on literally thousands of topics.

At first, theorists predicted that computer-mediated messages would be more prone to misunderstanding than face-to-face ones. Without nonverbal cues, it seemed that CMC couldn't match the rich kind of interaction that happens in person, or even over the phone where tone of voice can provide cues about the speaker's feelings and intentions. Recent scholarship, however, suggests that CMC can be as accurate and satisfying as the face-to-face variety. In one survey, e-mail users acknowledged that the absence of nonverbal cues was a source of misunderstandings in CMC, but they were likely to use both e-mail and other forms of communication (such as the telephone and face-to-face meetings) to clear up those misunderstandings.[24] Perhaps most tellingly, the users reported a high degree of satisfaction with their mediated interaction.

to some of our nonverbal behavior: smiling when we want to convince others we're happy or making sure our handshakes are firm to show that we're straightforward, decisive people. But there are so many nonverbal channels that it's impossible to think about and control all of them. Thus, our slumping shoulders might contradict our smiles, and our sweating palms might cancel out all the self-confidence of our firm handshakes. The unconscious nature of most nonverbal behavior explains why it offers so many useful cues about how others are feeling.

ETHICAL
CHALLENGE

The Power of Nonverbal Insight

The awareness of the communicative power of nonverbal behavior can often give you an edge in understanding and influencing it. Suppose that your skill at controlling your own nonverbal behavior became great enough that you were able to present yourself to others in precisely the way you desire (even if that image wasn't completely accurate), and your ability to analyze others' nonverbal behavior gave you a high degree of accuracy in interpreting others' unexpressed feelings.

What ethical obligations would come with your increased nonverbal skill? Would you be obliged to disclose your ability to others? To reveal your motives when trying to influence them? To share your analysis of their behavior?

FUNCTIONS OF NONVERBAL COMMUNICATION

Although verbal and nonverbal messages differ in many ways, the two forms of communication operate together on most occasions. The following discussion explains the many functions nonverbal communication can serve and shows how nonverbal messages relate to verbal ones.

Repeating

If someone asked you for directions to the nearest drug-
store, you could say, "North of here about two blocks" and
then repeat your instructions by pointing north. Pointing is
an example of what social scientists call **emblems**—deliberate nonverbal behaviors that have precise meanings
known to everyone within a cultural group. For example,
we all know that a head nod means "yes," a head shake
means "no," a wave means "hello" or "good-bye," and a
hand to the ear means "I can't hear you."

Substituting

Emblems can also replace a verbal message. When a friend
asks you what's new, you might shrug your shoulders instead
of answering in words. Not all substituting consists of emblems, however. Sometimes substituting responses are more
ambiguous and less intentional. A sigh, smile, or frown may
substitute for a verbal answer to your question, "How's it going?" As this example suggests, nonverbal substituting is especially important when people are reluctant to express their feelings in words.

Complementing

Sometimes nonverbal behaviors match the content of a verbal message.
Consider, for example, a friend apologizing for forgetting an appointment with
you. Your friend's sincerity would be reinforced if the verbal apology were
accompanied by the appropriate nonverbal behaviors: the right tone of voice, facial expression, and so on. We often recognize the significance of complementary nonverbal behavior when it is missing. If your friend's apology were delivered with a shrug, a smirk, and a light tone of voice, you probably would doubt
its sincerity, no matter how profuse the verbal explanation was.

Much complementing behavior consists of **illustrators**—nonverbal behaviors that accompany and support spoken words. Scratching the head when
searching for an idea and snapping your fingers when it occurs are examples of
illustrators that complement verbal messages. Research shows that North
Americans use illustrators more often when they are emotionally aroused—trying to explain ideas that are difficult to put into words—when they are furious,
horrified, very agitated, distressed, or excited.[26]

Accenting

Just as we use italics to emphasize an idea in print, we use nonverbal devices to
emphasize oral messages. Pointing an accusing finger adds emphasis to criticism
(as well as probably creating defensiveness in the receiver). Stressing certain
words with the voice ("It was *your* idea!") is another way to add nonverbal accents.

Regulating

Nonverbal behaviors can control the flow of verbal communication. For example, parties in a conversation often unconsciously send and receive turn-taking

cues.[27] When you are ready to yield the floor, the unstated rule is: Create a rising vocal intonation pattern, then use a falling intonation pattern, or draw out the final syllable of the clause at the end of your statement. Finally, stop speaking. If you want to maintain your turn when another speaker seems ready to cut you off, you can suppress the attempt by taking an audible breath, using a sustained intonation pattern (because rising and falling patterns suggest the end of a statement), and avoiding any pauses in your speech. Other nonverbal cues exist for gaining the floor and for signaling that you do not want to speak.

Contradicting

People often simultaneously express different and even contradictory messages in their verbal and nonverbal behaviors. A common example of this sort of mixed message is the experience we've all had of hearing someone with a red face and bulging veins yelling, "Angry? No, I'm not angry!"

Even though some of the ways in which people contradict themselves are subtle, mixed messages have a strong impact. Research suggests that when a receiver perceives an inconsistency between verbal and nonverbal messages, the nonverbal one carries more weight—more than 12.5 percent more, according to some research.[28]

Deliberately sending mixed messages might sound foolish at first, but there are times when we do just this. One deliberate use of mixed messages is to send a message politely but clearly that might be difficult to handle if it were expressed in words. For instance, think of a time when you became bored with a conversation while your companion kept rambling on. At such a time the most straightforward statement would be, "I'm tired of talking to you and want to go meet someone else." Although it might feel good to be so direct, this kind of honesty is impolite for anyone over five years of age. Instead of being blunt in situations like this, a face-saving alternative is to express your disinterest nonverbally. While nodding politely and murmuring, "uh-huh" and "no kidding?" at the appropriate times, you can signal a desire to leave by looking around the room, turning slightly away from the speaker, or even making a point of yawning. In most cases such clues are enough to end the conversation without the awkwardness of expressing outright what's going on.

Deceiving

Deception is perhaps the most interesting type of nonverbal communication and one that social scientists have studied extensively. As Chapter 6 explains, most of the messages we exchange are not completely truthful. As you will read there, not all deception is self-serving or malicious: Much of it is aimed at saving the face of the communicators involved. For example, you might tell a "white lie" to avoid hurting the feelings of a friend who asks your opinion: "That new tattoo looks, uh, really nice." In a situation like this, it's easy to see how nonverbal factors can make the face-saving deception either succeed or fail.

Some people are better at hiding deceit than others. For example, most people—especially women—become more successful liars as they grow older.[29] High self-monitors are usually better at hiding their deception than communicators who are less self-aware, and raters judge highly expressive liars as more honest than those who are more subdued.[30] Not surprisingly, people whose jobs require them to act differently than they feel, such as actors, lawyers,

What you are stands over you
. . . and thunders so that I cannot hear what you say to the contrary.

Ralph Waldo Emerson

CULTURAL IDIOM

the floor: the right or privilege to speak

to cut you off: to interrupt you in order to stop you from proceeding with your remarks

face saving: protecting one's dignity

a white lie: harmless untruth

diplomats, and salespeople, are more successful at deception than the general population.[31]

It's easiest to catch liars when they haven't had a chance to rehearse, when they feel strongly about the information being hidden, or when they feel anxious or guilty about their lies.[32] Imagine, for example, that you want to decline an unwanted invitation with a face-saving lie. Your chances of getting away with the deception are best if you have had advance notice of the invitation. If you are caught unprepared, your excuse for not attending is likely to be less persuasive. Trust (or lack of it) also plays a role in which deceptive messages are successful: People who are suspicious that a speaker may be lying pay closer attention to the speaker's nonverbal behavior (e.g., talking faster than normal, shifted posture) than do people who are not suspicious.[33] Still, asking questions—even if you are suspicious—isn't especially effective at uncovering detection.[34] As you read earlier, people who focus their attention on catching liars are less effective than those who are busy with other mental tasks.[35] Table 5–3 lists situations in which deceptive messages are most likely to be obvious.

Decades of research have revealed that there are no surefire nonverbal cues that indicate deception. Nonetheless, there are some cues that may reveal less-than-totally-honest communication. For example, deceivers typically make more speech errors than truth-tellers: stammers, stutters, hesitations, false starts, and so on. Vocal pitch often rises when people tell lies, and liars hesitate more.[36] Deceivers tend to blink their eyes more often, fidget with their hands, and more rapidly shift their posture. Despite cues like these, it's a mistake to assume that every tongue-tied, fidgeting, eye-blinking person is a liar.

How good are people at detecting lies? The range of effectiveness in uncovering deceptive messages is broad, ranging from 45 to 70 percent.[37] As we grow older we become better at interpreting contradictory messages. Children between the ages of six and twelve use a speaker's words to make sense of a message. But as

CULTURAL IDIOM
sure-fire: certain to succeed

TABLE 5–3   Leakage of Nonverbal Clues to Deception

Deception Clues Are Most Likely When the Deceiver	Deception Clues Are Least Likely When the Deceiver
Wants to hide emotions being experienced at the moment.	Wants to hide information unrelated to his or her emotions.
Feels strongly about the information being hidden.	Has no strong feelings about the information being hidden.
Feels apprehensive about the deception.	Feels confident about the deception.
Feels guilty about being deceptive.	Experiences little guilt about the deception.
Gets little enjoyment from being deceptive.	Enjoys the deception.
Needs to construct the message carefully while delivering it.	Knows the deceptive message well and has rehearsed it.

Based on material from "Mistakes When Deceiving" by Paul Ekman, in Thomas A. Sebok and Robert Rosenthal (eds.), *The Clever Hans Phenomenon: Communication with Horses, Whales, Apes and People* (New York: New York Academy of Sciences, 1981), pp. 269–278.

adults, we rely more on nonverbal cues to form many impressions. For example, audiences put more emphasis on nonverbal cues than on words to decide whether speakers are honest.[38] They also use nonverbal behaviors to judge the character of speakers as well as their competence and composure; and differences in nonverbal behavior influence how much listeners are persuaded by a speaker.[39]

Even with an awareness of nonverbal clues, it isn't always easy to detect lies. Training can improve the ability to catch deceivers.[40] Again, the range of effectiveness in uncovering deceptive messages is broad, ranging from 45 to 70 percent.[41] Sometimes the very suspicion that someone is lying can improve the deceiver's attempts to hide the truth. Research shows that people who probe the messages of deceptive communicators are no better at detecting lies than those who don't investigate the truth of a message. One explanation for this surprising finding is that deceivers who are questioned become more vigilant about revealing the truth and their greater vigilance results in a better cover-up of deception cues.

Some people are better than others at uncovering deception. For example, women are consistently more accurate than men at detecting lying and what the underlying truth is.[42] The same research showed that, as people become more intimate, their accuracy in detecting lies actually declines. This is a surprising fact: Intuition suggests that we ought to be better at judging honesty as we become more familiar with others. Perhaps an element of wishful thinking interferes with our accurate decoding of these messages. After all, we would hate to think that a lover would lie to us. When intimates *do* become suspicious, however, their ability to recognize deception increases.[43] Despite their overall accuracy at detecting lies, women are more inclined to fall for the deception of intimate partners than are men. No matter how skillful or inept we may be at interpreting nonverbal behavior, training can make us better.[44]

Technology may be gaining ground on deceivers. In 2002, Mayo Clinic researchers reported developing a facial imaging device that detected heat patterns in deceivers' skins.[45] Like more familiar polygraph lie detectors, the device seems to actually be measuring anxiety rather than deception itself. The device has more potential benefits for security providers than in personal situations. Still, the notion of using technology to catch liars is appealing.

Before we finish considering how nonverbal behaviors can deceive, it is important to realize that not all deceptive communication is aimed at taking advantage of the recipient. Some are a polite way to express an idea that would be difficult to handle if expressed in words. In this sense, the ability to deliberately send nonverbal messages that contradict your words can be a kind of communication competence.

TYPES OF NONVERBAL COMMUNICATION

Now that you understand how nonverbal messages operate as a form of communication, we can look at the various forms of nonverbal behavior. The following pages explain how our bodies, artifacts, environments, and the way we use time all send messages.

Posture and Gesture

Stop reading for a moment and notice how you are sitting. What does your position say nonverbally about how you feel? Are there other people near you now?

> **CULTURAL IDIOM**
>
> **cover-up:** a plan to escape discovery

What messages do you get from their posture and movements? Tune your television to any program, and without turning up the sound, see what messages are communicated by the movements and body position of the people on the screen. These simple experiments illustrate the communicative power of **kinesics,** the study of body movement, gesture, and posture.

Posture is a rich channel for conveying nonverbal information. From time to time postural messages are obvious. If you see a person drag through the door or slump over while sitting in a chair, it's apparent that something significant is going on. But most postural cues are more subtle. For instance, the act of mirroring the posture of another person can have positive consequences. One experiment showed that career counselors who used "posture echoes" to copy the postures of clients were rated as more empathic than those who did not reflect the clients' postures.[46] Researchers have also found that partners in romantic relationships mirror one another's behaviors.[47]

Posture can communicate vulnerability in situations far more serious than mere social or business settings. One study revealed that rapists sometimes use postural clues to select victims that they believe will be easy to intimidate.[48] Easy targets are more likely to walk slowly and tentatively, stare at the ground, and move their arms and legs in short, jerky motions.

Gestures are a fundamental element of communication—so fundamental, in fact, that people who have been blind from birth use them.[49] One group of ambiguous gestures consists of what we usually call fidgeting—movements in which one part of the body grooms, massages, rubs, holds, fidgets, pinches, picks, or otherwise manipulates another body part. Social scientists call these behaviors **manipulators.**[50] Social rules may discourage us from performing most manipulators in public, but people still do so without noticing. For example, one study revealed that deceivers bob their heads more often than truth-tellers.[51] Research confirms what common sense suggests—that increased use of

INVITATION TO INSIGHT **Kinesics in Action**

You can appreciate the many ways kinesic cues operate by identifying examples from your own experience when body movement served each of the following nonverbal functions:

- Repeating
- Substituting
- Complementing
- Accenting
- Regulating
- Contradicting

Fie, fie upon her! There's language in her eyes, her cheek, her lip. Nay, her foot speaks; her wanton spirits look out at every joint and motive in her body.

William Shakespeare
Troilus and Cressida

UNDERSTANDING DIVERSITY

Expressive Italians Let Hands Do the Talking

A recipe for trouble in Italy: Make a fist, extend index finger and pinkie, thrust forward and up. A snarl is optional. The gesture—an insult suggesting an unfaithful wife—is part of the array of hand jabs, facial tics and arm movement that add significance and sentiment to nearly every conversation among Italians.

"There are gestures for everything from making love to making dinner. The hands can often say things better than words," said Milan design artist Bruno Munari, who compiled a book illustrating some of the most popular Italian gestures. Munari's *Dictionary of Italian Gestures* contains dozens of examples stretching from early 19th century Naples to modern signals for a cellular telephone call.

Squeezing your chin between thumb and index finger signifies cuteness. Pulling slightly on the skin under the right eye with an index finger shows an agreement has been reached. Consider something foolish? Place hands together as if in prayer and then lower the pinkies.

Technology has added new gestures. The first telephone gesture was a rotating finger, simulating dialing. It was replaced by a push-button movement. Now, with cellular phones widely popular in Italy, the latest phone gesture is a palm pressed to an ear.

With gestures, entire conversations could be conducted in silence.

"What do you want?" (Fingertips pinched together.)

"I'm hungry." (A curving motion of the hand above the top of the stomach.)

"And something to drink?" (Thumb tipped down toward the mouth.)

"No, everything's fine. It was delicious." (Shake hand with palm down. Then stick index finger in cheek and rock side to side.)

Some gestures are obvious in their intent. A threat is a thumb slashing across the neck. I'm angry: curl your index finger and bite down.

Others need translation. Rubbing two index fingers together represents an affair or secret meeting. Tapping your forehead with your finger means something is too strange to believe.

"A foreigner can come to Italy and learn the language perfectly, but without knowing the gestures you are not really fluent," said Munari.

Brian Murphy

manipulators is often a sign of discomfort.[52] But not all fidgeting signals uneasiness. People also are likely to use manipulators when relaxed. When they let their guard down (either alone or with friends), they will be more likely to fiddle with an earlobe, twirl a strand of hair, or clean their fingernails. Whether or not the fidgeter is hiding something, observers are likely to interpret manipulators as a signal of dishonesty. Because not all fidgeters are liars, it's important not to jump to conclusions about the meaning of manipulators.

Face and Eyes

The face and eyes are probably the most noticed parts of the body, and their impact is powerful. For example, smiling cocktail waitresses earn larger tips than unsmiling ones, and smiling nuns collect larger donations than ones with glum expressions.[53] The influence of facial expressions and eye contact doesn't mean that their nonverbal messages are always easy to read. The face is a tremendously complicated channel of expression for several reasons. One reason is the number of expressions people can produce. Another is the speed with which they can change. For example, slow-motion films have been taken that show expressions fleeting across a subject's face in as short a time as a fifth of a second. Finally, it seems that different emotions show most clearly in

CULTURAL IDIOM

let their guard down: saying boldly what one thinks

to fiddle with: to manipulate in a playful manner

different parts of the face: happiness and surprise in the eyes and lower face, anger in the lower face and brows and forehead, fear and sadness in the eyes, and disgust in the lower face.

Ekman and Friesen have identified six basic emotions that facial expressions reflect—surprise, fear, anger, disgust, happiness, and sadness.[54] Expressions reflecting these emotions seem to be recognizable in and between members of all cultures. Of course, **affect blends**—the combination of two or more expressions showing different emotions—are possible. For instance, it's easy to imagine how someone would look who is fearful and surprised or disgusted and angry.

Research indicates that people are quite accurate at judging facial expressions of these emotions.[55] Accuracy increases when judges know the "target" or have knowledge of the context in which the expression occurs or when they have seen several samples of the target's expressions.

"Spare a little eye contact?"

The eyes themselves can send several kinds of messages. In mainstream Euro-American culture, meeting someone's glance with your eyes is usually a sign of involvement whereas looking away signals a desire to avoid contact. This is why solicitors on the street—panhandlers, salespeople, petitioners—try to catch our eye. After they've managed to establish contact with a glance, it becomes harder for the approached person to draw away.

INVITATION TO INSIGHT

The Eyes Have It

Prove for yourself the role eye contact plays in social influence by trying a simple experiment.

1. Choose a situation where you can make simple requests from a series of strangers. You might, for example, ask to cut in line to use a photocopying machine, or you could ask passersby for a small amount of change to make an important phone call.
2. Make such a request to at least twenty people. Use the same words for each request but alternate your nonverbal behavior. Half the time make direct eye contact, and the other half of the time avoid looking directly at the other person when you make your request.
3. Record your results, and see if your eye behavior played any role in generating compliance to your request.
4. If eye contact does make a difference, describe how you could apply your findings to real-life situations.

It was terribly dangerous to let your thoughts wander when you were in any public place or within range of a telescreen. The smallest thing could give you away. A nervous tic, an unconscious look of anxiety, a habit of muttering to yourself—anything that carried with it the suggestion of abnormality, of having something to hide. In any case, to wear an improper expression on your face (to look incredulous when a victory was announced, for example) was itself a punishable offense. There was even a word for it in Newspeak: facecrime, it was called.

George Orwell
1984

Voice

The voice itself is another form of nonverbal communication. Social scientists use the term **paralanguage** to describe nonverbal, vocal messages. You can begin to understand the power of vocal cues by considering how the meaning of a simple sentence can change just by shifting the emphasis from word to word:

- *This* is a fantastic communication book.
  (Not just any book, but this one in particular.)
- This is a *fantastic* communication book.
  (This book is superior, exciting.)
- This is a fantastic *communication* book.
  (The book is good as far as communication goes; it may not be so good as literature or drama.)
- This is a fantastic communication *book.*
  (It's not a play or a compact disc; it's a book.)

There are many other ways the voice communicates—through its tone, speed, pitch, volume, number and length of pauses, and **disfluencies** (such as stammering, use of "uh," "um," "er," and so on). All these factors can do a great deal to reinforce or contradict the message our words convey.

Sarcasm is one instance in which both emphasis and tone of voice help change a statement's meaning to the opposite of its verbal message. Experience this yourself with the following three statements. The first time through, say them literally, and then say them sarcastically.

- Thanks for waking me up.
- I really had a wonderful time on my blind date.
- There's nothing I like better than waking up before sunrise.

Researchers have identified the communicative value of paralanguage through the use of content-free speech—ordinary speech that has been electronically manipulated so that the words are unintelligible, but the paralanguage remains unaffected. (Hearing a foreign language that you do not understand has the same effect.) Subjects who hear content-free speech can consistently recognize the emotion being expressed, as well as identifying its strength.[56]

The impact of paralinguistic cues is strong. In fact, research shows that listeners pay more attention to the vocal messages than to the words that are spoken when asked to determine a speaker's attitudes.[57] Furthermore, when vocal factors contradict a verbal message, listeners judge the speaker's intention from the paralanguage, not from the words themselves.[58]

Paralanguage can affect behavior in many ways, some of which are rather surprising. Researchers have discovered that communicators were most likely to comply with requests delivered by speakers whose rate was similar to their own.[59] Besides complying with same-rate speakers, listeners also feel more positively about people who seem to talk at their own rate. Vocal intensity also can affect how willing people are to respond to another person's requests.[60]

Vocal changes that contradict spoken words are not easy to conceal. If the speaker is trying to conceal fear or anger, the voice will probably sound higher and louder, and the rate of talk may be faster than normal. Sadness produces the opposite vocal pattern: quieter, lower-pitched speech delivered at a slower rate.[61]

Women also have a distinctive style of speaking: "I was shopping last night? And I saw this wonderful dress?" It's hard to convey intonation in print, but the question marks indicate a rise in pitch at the end of the sentence, as in a question. Many women, especially younger women, use this intonation in declarative sentences: "This is Sally Jones? I have an appointment with Dr. Smith? And I'd like to change it to another day?"

I cringe when I hear this. The rising intonation sounds timid and lacking in self-confidence; the speaker seems to be asking for approval or permission to speak when there's no need to. And I worry that rising intonation harms women. It gets them taken less seriously than they should be . . .

Thomas Hurka

Besides reinforcing or contradicting messages, some vocal factors influence the way a speaker is perceived by others. For example, communicators who speak loudly and without hesitations are viewed as more confident than those who pause and speak quietly.[62] People who speak more slowly are judged as having greater conversational control than fast talkers.[63] Research has also demonstrated that people with more attractive voices are rated more highly than those whose voice sounds less attractive.[64] Just what makes a voice attractive can vary. As Figure 5–1 shows, culture can make a difference. Surveys show that there are both similarities and differences between what Mexicans and Americans view as the "ideal" voice.

Touch

Besides being the earliest means we have of making contact with others, touching—or haptics—is essential to our healthy development. During the nineteenth and early twentieth centuries many

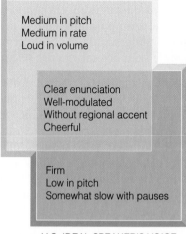

MEXICAN IDEAL SPEAKER'S VOICE

Medium in pitch
Medium in rate
Loud in volume

Clear enunciation
Well-modulated
Without regional accent
Cheerful

Firm
Low in pitch
Somewhat slow with pauses

U.S. IDEAL SPEAKER'S VOICE

Figure 4–1   Ideal Speaker's Voice Types in Mexico and the United States

---

SKILL BUILDER

Building Vocal Fluency

You can become more adept at both conveying and interpreting vocal messages by following these directions.

1. Join with a partner and designate one person A and the other B.
2. Partner A should choose a passage of twenty-five to fifty items from the telephone directory, using his or her voice to convey one of the following attitudes:
   a. Egotism
   b. Friendliness
   c. Insecurity
   d. Irritation
   e. Confidence
3. Partner B should try to detect the emotion being conveyed.
4. Switch roles and repeat the process. Continue alternating roles until each of you has both conveyed and tried to interpret at least four emotions.
5. After completing the preceding steps, discuss the following questions:
   a. What vocal cues did you use to make your guesses?
   b. Were some emotions easier to guess than others?
   c. Given the accuracy of your guesses, how would you assess your ability to interpret vocal cues?
6. How can you use your increased sensitivity to vocal cues to improve your everyday communication competence?

babies died from a disease then called *marasmus,* which, translated from Greek, means "wasting away." In some orphanages the mortality rate was quite high, but even children in "progressive" homes, hospitals, and other institutions died regularly from the ailment. When researchers finally tracked down the causes of this disease, they found that many infants suffered from lack of physical contact with parents or nurses rather than poor nutrition, medical care, or other factors. They hadn't been touched enough, and as a result they died. From this knowledge came the practice of "mothering" children in institutions—picking babies up, carrying them around, and handling them several times each day. At one hospital that began this practice, the death rate for infants fell from between 30 and 35 percent to below 10 percent.[65]

As a child develops, the need for being touched continues. In his book *Touching: The Human Significance of the Skin,* Ashley Montagu describes research that suggests that allergies, eczema, and other health problems are, in part, caused by a person's lack of contact as an infant with his or her mother.[66] Although Montagu says that these problems develop early in life, he also cites cases where adults suffering from conditions as diverse as asthma and schizophrenia have been successfully treated by psychiatric therapy that uses extensive physical contact.

Touch seems to increase a child's mental functioning as well as physical health. L. J. Yarrow has conducted surveys that show that babies who have been given plenty of physical stimulation by their mothers have significantly higher IQs than those receiving less contact.[67]

Touch also plays a large part in how we respond to others and to our environment.[68] For example, touch increases self-disclosure, verbalization of psychiatric patients, and the preference children have for their counselors. Touch also increases compliance.[69] In one study, subjects were approached by a female confederate who requested that they return a dime left in the phone booth from which they had just emerged. When the request was accompanied by a light touch on the subject's arm, the probability that the subject would return the dime increased significantly.[70] In a similar experiment, subjects were asked by a male or female confederate to sign a petition or complete a rating scale. Again, subjects were more likely to cooperate when they were touched lightly on the arm. In the rating-scale variation of the study, the results were especially dramatic: 70 percent of those who were touched complied, whereas only 40 percent of the untouched subjects complied (indicating a predisposition not to comply).[71] An additional power of touch is its on-the-job utility. One study showed that fleeting touches on the hand and shoulder resulted in larger tips for restaurant waiters.[72]

Touch can communicate many messages. Researchers have catalogued twelve different kinds of touches, including "positive," "playful," "control," and "ritualistic."[73] Some kinds of touch indicate varying degrees of aggression. Others signify types of relationships.[74]

- Functional/professional (dental examination, haircut)
- Social/polite (handshake)
- Friendship/warmth (clap on back, Spanish *abrazo*)
- Love/intimacy (some caresses, hugs)
- Sexual arousal (some kisses, strokes)

You might object to the examples following each of these categories, saying that some nonverbal behaviors occur in several types of relationships. A kiss, for

In our now more than slightly cockeyed world, there seems to be little provision for someone to get touched without having to go to bed with whomever does the touching. And that's something to think about. We have mixed up simple, healing, warm touching with sexual advances. So much so, that it often seems as if there is no middle way between "Don't you dare touch me!" and "Okay, you touched me, so now we should make love!"

A nation which is able to distinguish the fine points between offensive and defensive pass interference, bogies, birdies, and par, a schuss and a slalom, a technical, a personal, and a player-control foul should certainly be able to make some far more obvious distinctions between various sorts of body contact.

Sidney Simon
Caring, Feeling, Touching

example, can mean anything from a polite but superficial greeting to the most intense arousal. What makes a given touch more or less intense? Researchers have suggested a number of factors:

- What part of the body does the touching
- What part of the body is touched
- How long the touch lasts
- How much pressure is used
- Whether there is movement after contact is made
- Whether anyone else is present
- The situation in which the touch occurs
- The relationship between the persons involved

In traditional U.S. culture, touching is generally more appropriate for women than for men.[75] Males touch their male friends less than they touch their female friends and also less than females touch their female friends. Fear of homosexuality seems to be a strong reason why many men are reluctant to touch one another. Although females are more comfortable about touching than men, gender isn't the only factor that shapes contact. In general, the degree of touch comfort goes along with openness to expressing intimate feelings, an active interpersonal style, and satisfactory relationships.[76]

> *The unconscious parental feelings communicated through touch or lack of touch can lead to feelings of confusion and conflict in a child. Sometimes a "modern" parent will say all the right things but not want to touch his child very much. The child's confusion comes from the inconsistency of levels: if they really approve of me so much like they say they do, why won't they touch me?*
>
> William Schutz
> *Here Comes Everybody*

INVITATION TO INSIGHT

The Rules of Touch

Like most types of nonverbal behavior, touching is governed by cultural and social rules. Imagine you are writing a guidebook for visitors from another culture. Describe the rules that govern touching in the following relationships. In each case, describe how the gender of the participants affects the rules.

- An adult and a five-year-old
- An adult and a twelve-year-old
- Two good friends
- Boss and employee

Physical Attractiveness

Most people claim that looks aren't the best measure of desirability or character, but they typically prefer others who they find attractive.[77] For example, women who are perceived as attractive have more dates, receive higher grades in college, persuade males with greater ease, and receive lighter court sentences. Both men and women whom others view as attractive are rated as being more sensitive, kind, strong, sociable, and interesting than their less-fortunate brothers and sisters. Who is most likely to succeed in business? Place your bet on the attractive job applicant. For example, shorter men have more difficulty finding jobs in the first place, and men over six-foot-two receive starting salaries that average 12.4 percent higher than comparable applicants under six feet.

The influence of attractiveness begins early in life. Preschoolers were shown photographs of children their own age and asked to choose potential friends and enemies. The researchers found that children as young as three agreed as to

CULTURAL IDIOM

lighter: lesser in duration

place your bet on: predict with confidence

who was attractive ("cute") and unattractive ("homely"). Furthermore, they valued their attractive counterparts—both of the same and the opposite sex—more highly. Also, preschool children rated by their peers as pretty were most liked, and those identified as least pretty were least liked. Children who were interviewed rated good-looking children as having positive social characteristics ("He's friendly to other children") and unattractive children as having negative ones ("He hits other children without reason").

Teachers also are affected by students' attractiveness. Physically attractive students are usually judged more favorably—more intelligent, friendly, and popular than their less attractive counterparts.[78] Fortunately, attractiveness is something we can control without having to call a plastic surgeon. We view others as beautiful or ugly not just on the basis of the "original equipment" they come with, but also on how they use that equipment. Posture, gestures, facial expressions, and other behaviors can increase the attractiveness of an otherwise unremarkable person. Exercise can improve the way each of us looks. Finally, the way we dress can make a significant difference in the way others perceive us, as you'll now see.

Clothing

Besides protecting us from the elements, clothing is a means of nonverbal communication, providing a relatively straightforward (if sometimes expensive) method of impression management. Clothing can be used to convey economic status, educational level, social status, moral standards, athletic ability and/or interests, belief system (political, philosophical, religious), and level of sophistication.

Research shows that we do make assumptions about people based on their clothing. Communicators who wear special clothing often gain persuasiveness. For example, experimenters dressed in uniforms resembling police officers were more successful than those dressed in civilian clothing in requesting pedestrians to pick up litter and in persuading them to lend a dime to an overparked motorist.[79] Likewise, solicitors wearing sheriff's and nurse's uniforms increased the level of contributions to law enforcement and healthcare campaigns.[80] Uniforms aren't the only kind of clothing that carries influence. In one study, a male and female were stationed in a hallway so that anyone who wished to go by had to avoid them or pass between them. In one condition, the conversationalists wore "formal daytime dress"; in the other, they wore "casual attire." Passersby behaved differently toward the couple depending on the style of clothing: They responded positively with the well-dressed couple and negatively when the same people were casually dressed.[81] Similar results in other situations show the influence of clothing. We are more likely to obey people dressed in a high-status manner. Pedestrians were more likely to return lost coins to well-dressed people than to those dressed in low-status clothing.[82] We are also more likely to follow the lead of high-status dressers even when it comes to violating social rules. Eighty-three percent of the pedestrians in one study followed a well-dressed jaywalker who violated

"Tell me about yourself, Kugelman— your hopes, dreams, career path, and what that damn earring means."

a "wait" crossing signal, whereas only 48 percent followed a confederate dressed in lower-status clothing.[83] Women who are wearing a jacket are rated as being more powerful than those wearing only a dress or skirt and blouse.[84]

As we get to know others better, the importance of clothing shrinks.[85] This fact suggests that clothing is especially important in the early stages of a relationship, when making a positive first impression is necessary in order to encourage others to get to know us better. This advice is equally important in personal situations and in employment interviews. In both cases, your style of dress (and personal grooming) can make all the difference between the chance to progress further and outright rejection.

ETHICAL CHALLENGE

Clothing and Impression Management

Using clothing as a method of creating impressions is a fact of life. Discover for yourself how dressing can be a type of deception.

1. Identify three examples from your experience when someone dressed in a manner that disguised or misrepresented his true status or personal attributes. What were the consequences of this misrepresentation for you or others?
2. Now identify three occasions in which you successfully used clothing to create a favorable but inaccurate impression. What were the consequences of this deception for others?
3. Based on your conclusions, define any situations when clothing may be used as an unethical means of impression management. List both "misdemeanors," in which the consequences are not likely to cause serious harm, and "felonies," in which the deception has the potential to cause serious harm.

Distance

The study of the way people and animals use space has been termed **proxemics**. Preferred spaces are largely a matter of cultural norms. For example, people living in hyperdense Hong Kong manage to live in crowded residential quarters that most North Americans would find intolerable.[86] Anthropologist Edward T. Hall has defined four distances used in mainstream North American culture.[87] He says that we choose a particular distance depending on how we feel toward the other person at a given time, the context of the conversation, and our personal goals.

Intimate distance begins with skin contact and ranges out to about eighteen inches. The most obvious context for intimate distance involves interaction with people to whom we're emotionally close—and then mostly in private situations. Intimate distance between individuals also occurs in less intimate circumstances: visiting the doctor or dentist, at the hairdresser's, and during some athletic contests. Allowing someone to move into the intimate zone usually is a sign of trust.

Personal distance ranges from eighteen inches at its closest point to four feet at its farthest. Its closer range is the distance at which most relational partners stand in public. We are uncomfortable if someone else "moves in" to this area

UNDERSTANDING DIVERSITY

Marked: Women in the Workplace

Some years ago I was at a small working conference of four women and eight men. Instead of concentrating on the discussion, I found myself looking at the three other women at the table.

One woman had dark brown hair in a classic style that was a cross between Cleopatra and Plain Jane. The severity of her straight hair was softened by wavy bangs and ends that turned under. Because she was beautiful, the effect was more than plain. The second woman was older, full of dignity and composure. Her hair was cut in a fashionable style that left her with only one eye, thanks to a side part that let a curtain of hair fall across half her face. The third woman's hair was wild, a frosted blond avalanche falling over and beyond her shoulders. When she spoke, she frequently tossed her head, thus calling attention to her hair and away from her lecture.

Then there was makeup. The first woman wore facial cover that made her skin smooth and pale. The second wore only a light gloss on her lips and a hint of shadow on her eyes. The third had blue bands under her eyes, dark blue shadow, mascara, bright red lipstick, and rouge; her fingernails also flashed red.

I considered the clothes each woman had worn on the three days of the conference: In the first case, man-tailored suits in primary colors with solid-color blouses. In the second, casual but stylish black T-shirt, a floppy collarless jacket and baggy slacks or skirt in neutral colors. The third wore a sexy jumpsuit; tight sleeveless jersey and tight yellow slacks; a dress with gaping armholes and an indulged tendency to fall off one shoulder.

As I amused myself finding patterns and coherence in these styles and choices, I suddenly wondered why I was scrutinizing only the women. I scanned the table to get a fix on the styles of the eight men. And then I knew why I wasn't studying them. The men's styles were unmarked. I was able to identify the styles and types of the women at the conference because each of us had to make decisions about hair, clothing, makeup and accessories, and each of those decisions carried meaning. Every style available to us was marked. Of course, the men in our group had to make decisions too, but their choices carried far less meaning. Each style available to us was marked. The men could have chosen styles that were marked, but they didn't have to, and in this group, none did. Unlike the women, they had the option of being unmarked.

There could have been a cowboy shirt with string tie or a three-piece suit or a necklaced hippie in jeans. But there wasn't. All eight men wore brown or blue slacks and standard-style shirts of light colors. No man wore sandals or boots; their shoes were dark, closed, comfortable, and flat. In short, unmarked.

I asked myself what style we women could have adopted that would have been unmarked, like the men's. The answer was: none. There is no unmarked woman.

There is no woman's hairstyle that could be called "standard," that says nothing about her. The range of women's hairstyles is staggering, but if a woman's hair has no particular style, this in itself is taken as a statement that she doesn't care how she looks—an eloquent message that can disqualify a woman for many positions.

Women have to choose between shoes that are comfortable and shoes that are deemed attractive. If a woman's clothes are tight or revealing (in other words, sexy), it sends a message—-an intended one of wanting to be attractive but also a possibly unintended one of availability. But if her clothes are not sexy, that too sends a message, lent meaning by the knowledge that they could have been.

Looking at the men and women sitting around the conference table, I was amazed at how different our worlds were. Though men have to make choices too, and men's clothing styles may be less neutral now than they once were, nonetheless the parameters within which men must choose when dressing for work are much narrower than the riotous range of colors and styles from which women must choose. But even this contrast in the range from which men and women must choose is irrelevant to the crucial point: A man can choose a style that will not attract attention or subject him to any particular interpretation, but a woman can't.

This does not mean that men have complete freedom when it comes to dress. Quite the contrary—they have much less freedom than women have to express their personalities in their choice of fabrics, colors, styles, and jewelry. But one freedom they have that women don't is the point of this discussion—the freedom to be unmarked.

Deborah Tannen
Talking from 9 to 5

without invitation. The far range of personal distance runs from about two-and-one-half to four feet. This is the zone just beyond the other person's reach—the distance at which we can keep someone "at arm's length." This term suggests the type of communication that goes on at this range: Interaction is still reasonably personal, but less so than communication that occurs a foot or so closer.

Social distance ranges from four to about twelve feet. Within it are the kinds of communication that usually occur in business situations. Its closer range, from four to seven feet, is the distance at which conversations usually occur between salespeople and customers and between people who work together. We use the far range of social distance—seven to twelve feet—for more formal and impersonal situations. This is the range at which we generally sit from the boss.

Public distance is Hall's term for the farthest zone, running outward from twelve feet. The closer range of public distance is the one most teachers use in the classroom. In the farther range of public space—twenty-five feet and beyond—two-way communication becomes difficult. In some cases it's necessary for speakers to use public distance owing to the size of their audience, but we can assume that anyone who voluntarily chooses to use it when he or she could be closer is not interested in having a dialogue.

Choosing the optimal distance can have a powerful effect on how we regard others and how we respond to them. For example, students are more satisfied with teachers who reduce the distance between themselves and their classes. They also are more satisfied with the course itself, and they are more likely to follow the teacher's instructions.[88] Likewise, medical patients are more satisfied with physicians who are not standoffish.[89]

Distance Violations

You can test the importance of distance for yourself by violating the cultural rules for use of the proxemic zones outlined on pages 172–174.

1. Join with a partner. Choose which one of you will be the experimenter and which will be the observer.
2. In three situations, the experimenter should deliberately use the "wrong" amount of space for the context. Make the violations as subtle as possible. You might, for instance, gradually move into another person's intimate zone when personal distance would be more appropriate. (Be careful not to make the violations too offensive!)
3. The observer should record the verbal and nonverbal reactions of others when the distance zones are violated. After each experiment, inform the people involved about your motives and ask whether they were consciously aware of the reason for any discomfort they experienced.

Time

Social scientists use the term **chronemics** for the study of how human beings use and structure time. The way we handle time can express both intentional and unintentional messages.[90] Social psychologist Robert Levine describes several ways that time can communicate.[91] For instance, in a culture like ours that values time highly, waiting can be an indicator of status. "Important" people (whose time is supposedly more valuable than that of others) may be seen by appointment only, whereas it is acceptable to intrude without notice on lesser beings. To see how this rule operates, consider how natural it is for a boss to drop into a subordinate's office unannounced, whereas some employees would never intrude into the boss's office without an appointment. A related rule is that low-status people must never make more important people wait. It would be a serious mistake to show up late for a job interview, although the interviewer might keep you cooling your heels in the lobby. Important people are often whisked to the head of a restaurant or airport line, whereas the presumably less exalted are forced to wait their turn.

The use of time depends greatly on culture.[92] In some cultures, punctuality is critically important, whereas in others it is barely considered. Punctual mainlanders often report welcoming the laid-back Hawaiian approach to time. One psychologist discovered the difference between North and South American attitudes when teaching at a university in Brazil.[93] He found that some students arrived halfway through a two-hour class and that most of them stayed put and kept asking questions when the class was scheduled to end. A half-hour after the official end of the class, the professor finally closed off discussion, because there was no indication that the students intended to leave. This flexibility of time is quite different from what is common in most North American colleges!

Even within a culture, rules of time vary. Sometimes the differences are geographic. In New York City, the party invitation may say "9 P.M.," but nobody would think of showing up before 9:30. In Salt Lake City, guests are expected to show up on time, or perhaps even a bit early.[94] Even within the same geographic area, different groups establish their own rules about the use of time. Consider your own experience. In school, some instructors begin and end class punctually, whereas others are more casual. With some people you feel comfortable talking for hours in person or on the phone, whereas with others time seems to be precious and not meant to be "wasted."

Territoriality

Whereas personal space is the invisible bubble we carry around as an extension of our physical being, **territory** is fixed space. Any area, such as a room, house, neighborhood, or country, to which we assume some kind of "rights" is our territory. Not all territory is permanent. We often stake out space for ourselves in the library, at the beach, and so on by using markers such as books, clothing, or other personal possessions.

The way people use space can communicate a good deal about power and status relationships. Generally, we grant people with higher status more personal territory and greater privacy.[95] We knock before entering the boss's office, whereas a boss can usually walk into our work area without hesitating. In traditional schools, professors have offices, dining rooms, and even toilets that are private, whereas the students, who are presumably less important, have no such sanctuaries. In the military, greater space and privacy usually come with rank: Privates sleep forty to a barracks, sergeants have their own private rooms, and generals have government-provided houses.

Status distinctions are sometimes remarkably precise. In many universities, for example, there is an unwritten rule that students must wait 10 minutes for an assistant professor who is late for class, 20 minutes for an associate professor, and 30 minutes for a full professor. Such standards establish comparative worth: I'm permitted to waste my students' time without explanation, but they must not trespass on mine. The higher my rank, the more time I can waste.

This is peculiar since the students must pay my salary. From a monetary standpoint, they own my time, rather than the other way around. But, along with my professorship, I've been granted control of their grades, which to some degree determines their future. In the end, our rules of waiting make it clear just who's running the show.

Robert Levine

CULTURAL IDIOM

cooling your heels: waiting impatiently

mainlanders: people who live in the continental United States

laid-back: relaxed, calm

stayed put: remained in space

UNDERSTANDING DIVERSITY

Doing Business across Cultures

In a world where international business is becoming increasingly more common, communicators who don't understand and adapt to cultural differences are likely to encounter problems that can disrupt their relationships. In this scenario, two businesspeople from different backgrounds fail to recognize and appreciate each other's cultural norms. Mike is from the United States, and is used to a "time is money" task-oriented approach. Miguel is from Latin America, where personal understanding and trust must develop before business takes place.

If Mike and Miguel understood each other's cultural communication styles, they would have been more able to adapt to them and less upset by what seemed to each to be inappropriate behavior.

Mike

(To himself) Why aren't we getting on with it?

(To himself) It's a quarter to twelve. I've been here with Miguel for forty-five minutes already, and I haven't even begun to talk business. I know that both me and this proposal are new to Miguel, but how can I count on this guy when all he does is ask me questions about myself, my background, my interests, my family, and my "philosophy"! Why does he have to be so nosy? I don't know him well enough yet to get into that personal stuff. I know he's just invited me to have lunch with him, but it's a thirty minute drive to the one o'clock appointment I scheduled, and I have to be on time. All I wanted to do was run through this proposal quickly the first time, see if he had any interest and if he did come back again to see about doing business. Sometimes I think that all these Hispanics want to do is talk about anything but business.

(To himself) Oh, well, I've never had any luck doing business with Hispanics before. Why should it be any different this time?

Thanks for the invitation to have lunch with you, Miguel, but I've got to get along to my next appointment. Here's my card. Maybe we can do business next time.

Miguel

(To himself) Why aren't we getting on with it?

(To himself) It's a quarter to twelve. I've been here with Mike for forty-five minutes already, and I haven't even begun to talk business. How can I know if I want to do business with him unless I know something about him and the kind of man he is? But I feel like a dentist pulling teeth. And he doesn't want to know anything about me! Where I come from, we don't like to do business with strangers. We like to know something about the other person and feel we can at least begin to trust them before we start to talk business seriously. It's too bad he turned me down for lunch. I think I can trust him and really am interested in his product line. With a little more time, I think we could do business. But first I've got to feel at least a little sure about who I'm doing business with. Sometimes I think that all these Anglos want to talk about is business.

(To himself) Oh, well, I've never had any luck doing business with gringos before. Why should it be any different this time?

Oh, that's all right, Mike. We'll have lunch another time. Come back again. I'd like to get to know you better. Maybe we can do business next time.

Adapted from John F. Kikoski and Catherine Kano Kikoski, *Reflexive Communication in the Culturally Diverse Workplace.* (Westport, CT: Quorum, 1996), pp. 2–3.

Environment

The physical environment people create can both reflect and shape interaction. This principle is illustrated right at home. The impressions that home designs communicate can be remarkably accurate. Researchers showed ninety-nine students slides of the insides or outsides of twelve upper-middle-class homes and then asked them to infer the personality of the owners from their impressions.[96] The students were especially accurate after glancing at interior photos. The decorating schemes communicated accurate information about the homeowners' intellectualism, politeness, maturity, optimism, tenseness, willingness to take adventures, family orientations, and reservedness. The home exteriors also gave viewers accurate perceptions of the owners' artistic interests, graciousness, privacy, and quietness.

Besides communicating information about the designer, an environment can shape the kind of interaction that takes place in it. In one experiment, researchers found that the attractiveness of a room influenced the happiness and energy of the people working in it.[97] The experimenters set up three rooms: an "ugly" one, which resembled a janitor's closet in the basement of a campus building; an "average" room, which was a professor's office; and a "beautiful" room, which was furnished with carpeting, drapes, and comfortable furniture. The subjects in the experiment were asked to rate a series of pictures as a way of measuring their energy and feelings of well-being while at work. Results of the experiment showed that while in the ugly room the subjects became tired and bored more quickly and took longer to complete their task. When they moved to the beautiful room, however, they rated the faces they were judging higher, showed a greater desire to work, and expressed feelings of importance, comfort, and enjoyment. The results teach a lesson that isn't surprising: Workers generally feel better and do a better job when they're in an attractive environment.

In a more therapeutic and less commercial way, physicians have also shaped environments to improve communication. Psychologist Robert Sommer found that redesigning the convalescent ward of a hospital greatly increased the interaction among patients. In the old design, seats were placed shoulder to shoulder around the edges of the ward. When the chairs were grouped around small tables so that patients faced each other at a comfortable distance, the number of conversations doubled.[98]

The design of an entire building can shape communication among its users. Architects have learned that the way housing projects are designed controls to a great extent the contact neighbors have with each other. People who live in apartments near stairways and mailboxes have many more neighbor contacts than do those living in less heavily traveled parts of the building, and tenants generally have more contacts with immediate neighbors than with people even a few doors away.[99] Architects now use this information to design buildings that either encourage communication or increase privacy, and house hunters can use the same knowledge to choose a home that gives them the neighborhood relationships they want.

So far we have talked about how designing an environment can shape communication, but there is another side to consider. Watching how people use an already existing environment can be a way of telling what kind of relationships they want. For example, Sommer watched students in a college library and found that there's a definite pattern for people who want to study alone. While the library was uncrowded, students almost always chose corner seats at one of the empty rectangular tables.[100] Finally, each table was occupied by one reader. New readers would then choose a seat on the opposite side and far end of an occupied table, thus keeping the maximum distance between themselves and the other readers. One of Sommer's associates tried violating these "rules" by sitting next to, and across from, other female readers when more distant seats were available. She found that the approached women reacted defensively, either by signaling their discomfort through shifts in posture or gesturing or by eventually moving away.

A team of social scientists studying United Nations deliberations was puzzled by the unexpected and influential role that the ambassador from Ireland was playing in Middle East negotiations. It wasn't until communication patterns were considered that the answer became clear. The Irish ambassador, it turns out, sits alphabetically among delegates from Iran, Israel, Jordan, and Kuwait. This arrangement facilitated communicative ties and, as a result, Ireland discovered itself playing the role of Mideast peace broker.

Aaron Cargile

A good house is planned from the inside out. First, you decide what it has to do for its occupants. Then, you let the functions determine the form. The more numerous and various those functions, the more responsive and interesting the house should be. And it may not look at all like you expect.

Dan MacMasters
Los Angeles *Times*

SUMMARY

Nonverbal communication consists of messages expressed by nonlinguistic means. Thus, it is inaccurate to say that all wordless expressions are nonverbal or that all spoken statements are totally verbal.

There are several important principles of nonverbal communication. First is the simple fact that it exists—that communication occurs even in the absence of language. This leads to the second principle: It is impossible not to communicate nonverbally; humans constantly send messages about themselves that are available for others to receive. The third principle is that nonverbal communication is ambiguous; there are many possible interpretations for any behavior. This ambiguity makes it important for the receiver to verify any interpretation before jumping to conclusions about the meaning of a nonverbal message. The fourth principle states that much nonverbal communication is culture-bound. In other words, behaviors that have special meanings in one culture may express different messages in another. Finally, we stated that

nonverbal communication serves many functions: repeating, substituting, complementing, accenting, regulating, and contradicting verbal behavior, as well as deceiving.

We also examined the differences between verbal and nonverbal communications. Whereas verbal messages occupy a single channel and must be received one at a time, many nonverbal messages occur simultaneously in everyday situations. Nonverbal messages are also continuous, whereas verbal ones are discrete, having beginnings and endings. Verbal messages are usually intentional, whereas nonverbal ones are often expressed unintentionally. Finally, verbal messages are less ambiguous than nonverbal ones, which are almost always open to more than one interpretation.

The remainder of this chapter introduced the many ways in which humans communicate nonverbally: through posture, gesture, use of the face and eyes, voice, touch, clothing, distance, time, territoriality, and physical environment.

RESOURCES

Print

Buller, David B. "Deception," in *Communicating Strategically: Strategies in Interpersonal Communication,* John A. Daly and John M. Wiemann, eds. Hillsdale, NJ: Erlbaum, 1994.

This chapter summarizes the nonverbal and verbal behaviors that characterize both intentional and unintentional deception, as well as discussing the role of deception in interpersonal relationships.

Burgoon, Judee K. "Nonverbal Signals," in *Handbook of Interpersonal Communication,* Mark L. Knapp and Gerald R. Miller, eds. Newbury Park, CA: Sage, 1994.

Burgoon offers a definition of *nonverbal communication* that is more restricted than the one in this chapter. She focuses on the ways communicators both produce and process nonverbal messages, as well as describing the functions nonverbal communication performs. The chapter also describes

how culture and gender influence the production and interpretation of nonverbal messages.

Jones, Stanley. *The Right Touch: Understanding and Using the Language of Physical Contact.* Creskill, NJ: Hampton Press, 1994.

Jones uses research findings to offer advice on how to use touch in a variety of settings and contexts. Topics include seven "taboos" of touch, the most commonly violated cultural norms of touching, rules for touch on the job, and ways in which men and women use touching.

Knapp, Mark L., and Judy Hall. *Nonverbal Communication in Human Interaction,* 3rd ed. Fort Worth, TX: Harcourt Brace Jovanovich, 1992.

This comprehensive survey of the field discusses various types of nonverbal communication and then concludes with chapters that describe how various nonverbal signals combine in everyday life and how nonverbal behavior is acquired.

Levine, Robert. *A Geography of Time, Or How Every Culture Keeps Time Just a Little Differently*. New York: Basic Books, 1997.

Levine's central argument is that a lack of understanding of time is one of the biggest barriers between cultures. He describes how the meaning of time varies around the world by comparing the effects of time in thirty-six U.S. cities and thirty-one countries. This brief, readable book demonstrates many ways in which differing senses of time affect the flow of communication.

Films
Making Sense of Nonverbal Behavior

At First Sight (1998). Rated PG-13.

Virgil Adamson (Val Kilmer) has been blind since he was three years old. He works as a massage therapist in a small resort town where he meets and falls in love with Amy Benic (Mira Sorvino).

Amy learns of a surgical procedure that can restore Virgil's sight, and he reluctantly agrees to undergo the procedure. When the bandages are removed, he opens his eyes to a world that is confusing and terrifying. (He cries, "There's something wrong—this can't be seeing!"). A therapist (Nathan Lane) explains that Virgil lacks a "visual vocabulary," which keeps him from making connections between the foreign things he sees, the familiar things he hears and touches, and the words that represent them.

The movie, based on a true story, illustrates how sighted people can take for granted their understanding of nonverbal messages. Virgil often asks Amy, "What does that face mean?" He is unfamiliar with the relational cues being sent in a coy smile, a pained grimace, or an embarrassed blush. Amy even has to teach Virgil when not to look, such as when he stares at a homeless person on the street. Ultimately, they both learn that assigning meaning to sensory information and nonverbal behavior is not a natural ability—it is a skill that must be learned and honed.

The Communicative Value of Nonverbal Behavior

For a better understanding of nonverbal communication, there is value in watching any film (without subtitles) in which the characters speak an unfamiliar language. The surprising amount of information that can be gained from visual and vocal behavior will give an appreciation for the communicative value of nonverbal behavior, and the details that cannot be understood will show its limitations.

Quest for Fire (1982). Rated R.

This story takes place at the dawn of humanity, before speech has developed to any degree. It follows the adventures of three men who seek fire for their tribe. Anthropologists can certainly find fault with the many inaccuracies of Neolithic life. Nonetheless, viewers who are willing to accept these flaws may find a moving account of how Neolithic people began to acquire the qualities that made them truly human. From a communication perspective, the way a very rudimentary language limits the characters reinforces both the power and limitations of nonverbal communication. (The embryonic languages spoken by the characters were specially created for the film by novelist Anthony Burgess, while the actors' nonverbal communication was choreographed by Desmond Morris.)

The Nuances of Nonverbal Behavior

The Man in the Iron Mask (1998). Rated PG-13.

This film, loosely based on the Dumas novel, is set in prerevolutionary France. King Louis XIV (Leonardo DiCaprio) is a heartless despot who presides over his decadent court, indifferent to the fate of his starving subjects. In an attempt to protect his sovereignty, Louis has banished his twin brother, Philippe, (also DiCaprio) to a prison where he wears the notorious iron mask.

The Man in the Iron Mask isn't likely to go down in history as a film gem, but it does provide a good illustration of the subtleties of nonverbal behavior. DiCaprio's acting gives Louis and Philippe different identities. Identifying the different behaviors of each character provides good practice in observing and recording nonverbal communication.

Masculine and Feminine Nonverbal Behavior

The Birdcage (1996). Rated R.
Mrs. Doubtfire (1993). Rated PG-13.
Tootsie (1982). Rated PG.

One way to recognize differences between masculine and feminine styles of nonverbal communication is to observe the same person playing different gender-related roles. Filmmakers have found this notion intriguing enough to produce several movies in which characters disguise themselves with makeup and costumes—and nonverbal cues—related to masculine and feminine roles.

In *Tootsie,* Michael Dorsey (Dustin Hoffman) is an aspiring New York actor who can't get any roles—at least as a man. In a flash of inspiration, he transforms himself into Dorothy Michaels, a middle-aged woman, and wins a part in a daytime soap opera. Along the way, he learns that cabs will stop for Michael's bass-voiced commands but not for Dorothy's soprano requests. He also becomes attentive to apparel, appearance, and attractiveness in ways he never experienced as a man. Michael becomes a richer person for seeing the world from Dorothy's perspective.

Robin Williams takes on a *Tootsie*-like role in *Mrs. Doubtfire*. He plays Daniel Hillard, a divorced man who cannot bear to live without his children. His ex-wife (Sally Field) needs a housekeeper for the kids, so Daniel asks his gay, makeup-artist brother (Harvey Fierstein) to turn him into Mrs. Doubtfire. Although the makeup is terrific and the costumes assist the ruse, neither gets changed in the climactic scene where Daniel must play both roles in the same restaurant. It is primarily nonverbal cues—voice, gestures, mannerisms—that differentiate Daniel from Doubtfire.

In yet another twist on the masculine/feminine theme, Robin Williams plays a man who teaches his gay partner to be more macho in *The Birdcage*. The goal, once again, is disguise: The partners want their soon-to-be in-laws to believe they are brothers, not lovers. Armand (Williams), the more masculine of the two, instructs the more effeminate Albert (Nathan Lane) on the "manly" way to walk, drink tea (no pinkie finger raised), and spread butter on toast. Again, the focus of the differences is on nonverbal mannerisms and nuances.

From *Some Like It Hot* to *Victor/Victoria* (where a woman plays a man playing a woman), films through the years have capitalized on masculine/feminine differences to entertain and intrigue. In each case, the success of the characters is not determined just by what they say; it's also determined by how they say it.

CONTENTS

KEY TERMS

breadth (of self-disclosure)
content messages
contextual interpersonal communication
depth (of self-disclosure)
developmental models (of relational maintenance)
dialectical model (of relational maintenance)
dialectical tensions
equivocal language
impersonal communication
intimacy
Johari Window
metacommunication
qualitative interpersonal communication
relational messages
self-disclosure
social penetration model
white lies

CHAPTER 6

AFTER STUDYING THE MATERIAL IN THIS CHAPTER . . .

YOU SHOULD UNDERSTAND:

1. The characteristics that distinguish interpersonal relationships from impersonal ones.
2. The content and relational dimensions of every message.
3. The role of metacommunication in conveying relational messages.
4. Dimension of and influences of intimacy in relationships.
5. Knapp's model of relational development and deteriorations.
6. Tension in relationships.
7. Reasons for self-disclosure and the Johari Window model of self-disclosure.
8. Characteristics of and guidelines for effective and appropriate self-disclosure.
9. The functions served by lies, equivocation, and hints.

YOU SHOULD BE ABLE TO:

1. Identify interpersonal and impersonal communication.
2. Identify the content and relational dimensions of a message.
3. Distinguish among types of intimacy and influences on intimacy.
4. Identify the stages of relationships and the dialectical tensions present in a relationship.
5. Identify the degree of self-disclosure in your relationships and the functions this serves.
6. Compose effective and appropriate disclosing messages.
7. Identify the types of nondisclosing messages you use, the functions these messages serve, and their ethical validity.

UNDERSTANDING INTERPERSONAL RELATIONSHIPS

In this chapter we will take a first look at the vitally important topic of interpersonal relationships. We will begin by exploring what kinds of communication make a relationship interpersonal. Next, we will look at some ways—both subtle and obvious—that we show others how we regard them and what kind of relationship we are seeking with them. We will go on to explore two approaches that characterize how communication operates throughout the lifetime of relationships. Finally, we will look at the role of self-disclosure in interpersonal communication.

CHARACTERISTICS OF INTERPERSONAL RELATIONSHIPS

What is interpersonal communication? How does it differ from other types of interaction? When and how are interpersonal messages communicated? Read on and see.

What Makes Communication Interpersonal?

The most obvious way to define *interpersonal communication* is by **context**, looking at the number of people involved. In this sense we could say that all dyadic communication—all two-person interaction—is interpersonal. In many ways, dyadic communication *is* different from the kind that goes on in other contexts, such as the kinds of small groups discussed in Chapters 8 and 9 of this book. For example, unlike threesomes and other groups, dyads are complete and cannot be subdivided. If one person withdraws from the other, the relationship is finished. This indivisibility means that, unlike groups, the partners in a dyad can't form coalitions to get their needs met: They must work matters out with one another. Likewise, dyadic communication differs from the kinds of public speeches described in Chapters 10–14 and from most types of mass communication described in Appendix II.

Although looking at communication by context is useful, this approach raises some problems. Consider, for example, a routine transaction between a sales clerk and customer, or the rushed exchange when you ask a stranger on the street for directions. Communication of this sort hardly seems interpersonal—or personal in any sense of the word. In fact, after transactions like this we commonly remark, "I might as well have been talking to a machine."

The impersonal nature of some two-person exchanges has led some scholars to say that quality, not quantity, is what distinguishes interpersonal communication. In a **qualitative** sense, interpersonal communication occurs when people treat one another as unique individuals, regardless of the context in which the

"I'm your wife, Arthur. You talk to me. You don't touch base with me."

interaction occurs or the number of people involved.[1] When quality of interaction is the criterion, the opposite of interpersonal communication is **impersonal** interaction, not group, public, or mass communication.

The majority of our communication, even in dyadic contexts, is relatively impersonal. We chat pleasantly with shopkeepers or fellow passengers on the bus or plane; we discuss the weather or current events with most classmates and neighbors; we deal with coworkers in a polite way. Considering the number of people we communicate with, qualitatively interpersonal interaction is rather scarce. This scarcity isn't necessarily unfortunate: Most of us don't have the time or energy to create personal relationships with everyone we encounter—or even to act in a personal way all the time with the people we know and love best. In fact, the scarcity of qualitatively interpersonal communication contributes to its value. Like precious jewels and one-of-a-kind artwork, qualitatively interpersonal relationships are special because of their scarcity. You can get a sense of how interpersonal your relationships are by trying the following exercise.

> *Half of all telephone calls do not involve a two-way conversation anymore. The human dimensions of the phenomenon are everywhere, suggested by a bizarre question surfacing in Hollywood where people often conduct business by voice mail, fax and modem rather than in person. "Do you need face on that?" people will ask.*
>
> Karen Brandon

INVITATION TO INSIGHT   ## Interpersonal Communication: Context and Quality

1. Examine your interpersonal relationships in a contextual sense by making two lists. The first should contain all the two-person relationships in which you have participated during the past week. The second should contain all your relationships that have occurred in small-group and public contexts. Are there any important differences that distinguish dyadic interaction from communication with a larger number of people?

2. Now make a second set of two lists. The first one should describe all of your relationships that are interpersonal in a qualitative sense, and the second should describe all the two-person relationships that are more impersonal. Are you satisfied with the number of qualitatively interpersonal relationships you have identified?

3. Compare the lists you developed in Steps 1 and 2. See what useful information each one contains. What do your conclusions tell you about the difference between contextual and qualitative definitions of interpersonal communication?

Content and Relational Messages

Virtually every verbal statement contains two kinds of messages. **Content messages**, which focus on the subject being discussed, are the most obvious. The content of such statements as "It's your turn to do the dishes" or "I'm busy Saturday night" is obvious.

Content messages aren't the only kind that are exchanged when two people interact. In addition, virtually all communication—both verbal and nonverbal—contains **relational messages**, which make statements about how the parties feel toward one another.[2] These relational messages deal with one or more social needs, most often inclusion, control, affection, or respect.

Consider the two examples we just mentioned. Imagine two ways of saying "It's your turn to do the dishes": one that is demanding and another that is matter-of-fact. Notice how the different nonverbal messages make statements about how the sender views control in this part of the relationship. The demanding tone says, in effect, "I have a right to tell you what to do around the house," whereas the matter-of-fact one suggests, "I'm just reminding you of something you might have overlooked." You can easily visualize two ways to deliver the statement "I'm busy Saturday night": one with little affection and the other with much liking.

Notice that in each of these examples the relational dimension of the message was never discussed. In fact, most of the time we aren't conscious of the relational messages that bombard us every day. Sometimes we are unaware of relational messages because they match our belief about the amount of respect, inclusion, control, and affection that is appropriate. For example, you probably won't be offended if your boss tells you to do a certain job, because you agree that supervisors have the right to direct employees. In other cases, however, conflicts arise over relational messages even though content is not disputed. If your boss delivers the order in a condescending, sarcastic, or abusive tone of voice, you probably will be offended. Your complaint wouldn't be with the order itself but rather with the way it was delivered. "I may work for this company," you might think, "but I'm not a slave or an idiot. I deserve to be treated like a human being."

How are relational messages communicated? As the boss-employee example suggests, they are usually expressed nonverbally. To test this fact for yourself, imagine how you could act while saying, "Can you help me for a minute?" in a way that communicates each of the following attitudes:

superiority	aloofness	friendliness
helplessness	sexual desire	irritation

Although nonverbal behaviors are a good source of relational messages, remember that they are ambiguous. The sharp tone you take as a personal insult might be due to fatigue, and the interruption you take as an attempt to ignore your ideas might be a sign of pressure that has nothing to do with you. Before you jump to conclusions about relational clues, it's a good idea to practice the skill of perception checking that you learned in Chapter 2: "When you use that tone of voice to tell me it's my turn to do the dishes, I get the idea you're mad at me. Is that right?" If your interpretation was indeed correct, you can talk about the problem. On the other hand, if you were overreacting, the perception check can prevent a needless fight.

Metacommunication

As the preceding example of perception checking shows, not all relational messages are nonverbal. Social scientists use the term **metacommunication** to describe messages that refer to other messages.[3] In other words, metacommunication is communication about communication. Whenever we discuss a

---

SKILL BUILDER

Identifying Relational Messages

To complete this exercise, you will need the help of a partner with whom you communicate on an ongoing basis.

1. Pick three recent exchanges between you and your partner. Although any exchanges will do, the most interesting ones will be those in which you sense that something significant (positive or negative) was going on that wasn't expressed overtly.

2. For each exchange, identify both the content and relational messages that you were expressing. Identify relational messages in terms of dimensions such as affection, respect, inclusion, and/or control.

3. Explain the concept of relational messages to your partner, and ask him or her to identify the relational messages received from you during the same exchanges. How closely does your partner's perception match your analysis of the relational messages?

4. Now identify the relational messages you interpreted your partner as sending during the three exchanges.

5. Ask your partner to describe the relational messages he or she believed were sent to you on these occasions. How closely did your interpretation match your partner's explanation?

Based on your analysis of these three exchanges, answer the following questions:

1. What significant kinds of relational messages are exchanged in your relationship?

2. How accurate are you in decoding your partner's relational messages? How accurate is your partner in decoding your relational messages?

3. What lessons have you learned from this exercise that can improve the quality of your relationship?

---

relationship with others, we are metacommunicating: "It sounds like you're angry at me" or "I appreciate how honest you've been." Metacommunication is an essential ingredient in successful relationships. Sooner or later there are times when it becomes necessary to talk about what is going on between you and the other person. The ability to focus on the kinds of issues described in this and the following chapter can be the tool for keeping the relationship on track.

Metacommunication is an important method of solving conflicts in a constructive manner. It provides a way to shift discussion from the content level to relational questions, where the problem often lies. For example, consider a couple bickering because one partner wants to watch television, whereas the other wants to talk. Imagine how much better the chances of a positive outcome would be if they used metacommunication to examine the relational problems that were behind their quarrel: "Look, it's not the TV watching itself that bothers me. It's that I imagine you watch so much because you're mad at me or bored. Are you feeling bad about us?"

Metacommunication isn't just a tool for handling problems. It is also a way to reinforce the good aspects of a relationship: "I really appreciate it when you

UNDERSTANDING COMMUNICATION TECHNOLOGY
Interpersonal Communication and the Internet

Is online communication a poor substitute for face-to-face contact, or is it a rich medium for developing close personal relationships? In one survey, approximately 25 percent of the respondents who used the Internet regularly spent less time talking in person and on the phone with friends and family members.[4] Another survey revealed that people who relied heavily on the Internet to meet their communication needs grew to rely less and less on their face-to-face networks. More significantly, they tended to feel more lonely and depressed as their online communication increased.[5]

Despite findings like these, a growing body of research disputes the notion that mediated communication lacks quality.[6] Writing (online, of course) in *CMC Magazine,* Brittney G. Chenault summarized research, concluding that e-mail, chat rooms, Internet newsgroups, and computer conferences can and do allow electronic correspondents to develop a degree of closeness similar to what can be achieved in person.[7] Research confirms this claim. Over 75 percent of the Internet users in a UCLA survey said they never felt ignored by another household member's spending time online.[8] The majority of the Internet users said that e-mail websites and chat rooms had a "modestly positive impact" on their ability to communicate more

with family members and make new friends. Another survey of over three thousand adults in the United States showed how relationships can prosper online.[9] In that study, 72 percent of the Internet users had communicated with a relative or a friend within the past day, compared with 61 percent for nonusers. Surprisingly, the Internet users were also more likely to have phoned friends and relatives. Even more significant than the amount of communication that occurs online is its quality. Fifty-five percent of Internet users said e-mail had improved communications with family, and 66 percent reported that their contact with friends had increased because of e-mail. Among women, the rate of satisfaction was even higher: 60 percent reported better contact with family and 71 percent with friends.

Findings like these suggest that, rather than weakening opportunities for communication, CMC provides rich opportunities for establishing and maintaining relationships. An Internet connection makes it possible to send and receive messages at any time of the day or night from people around the world. While face-to-face contact is impossible and telephone conversations difficult due to cost or time differences, computer-mediated messages are cheap, quick, and easy.

---

compliment me about my work in front of the boss." Comments like this serve two functions: First, they let others know that you value their behavior. Second, they boost the odds that the other people will continue the behavior in the future.

Despite the benefits of metacommunication, bringing relational issues out in the open does have its risks. Discussing problems can be interpreted in two ways. On the one hand, the other person might see it in a positive light—"Our relationship is working because we can still talk things out." On the other hand, your desire to focus on the relationship might look like a bad omen—"Our relationship isn't working if we have to keep talking it over." Furthermore, metacommunication does involve a certain degree of analysis ("It seems like you're angry at me"), and some people resent being analyzed. These cautions don't mean verbal metacommunication is a bad idea. They do suggest, though, that it's a tool that needs to be used carefully.

Sociolinguist Deborah Tannen describes two situations where e-mail's lack of immediacy enhanced relationships that wouldn't have developed to the same degree in person:

CULTURAL IDIOM

on the other hand:
from the other point of view

E-mail deepened my friendship with Ralph. Though his office was next to mine, we rarely had extended conversations because he is shy. Face to face he mumbled so, I could barely tell he was speaking. But when we both got on e-mail, I started receiving long, self-revealing messages; we poured our hearts out to each other. A friend discovered that e-mail opened up that kind of communication with her father. He would never talk much on the phone (as her mother would), but they have become close since they both got on line.[10]

As Tannen's accounts suggest, electronic communication isn't identical to the face-to-face variety. For one thing, mediated relationships seem to develop more slowly than the ones that are nurtured by face-to-face interaction. Furthermore, mediated communication isn't for everyone: Heavy computer users are more likely to develop online relationships than people who log on less often. Heavy computer use also seems to have pitfalls.

INTIMACY IN INTERPERSONAL RELATIONSHIPS

Even the closest relationships involve a mixture of personal and interpersonal communication. We alternate between a "we" and a "me" orientation, sometimes focusing on connecting with others and at other times focusing on our own needs and interests. In the next few pages we will examine how our communication is affected by these apparently conflicting drives for intimacy and distance.

Dimensions of Intimacy

The dictionary defines *intimacy* as arising from "close union, contact, association, or acquaintance." This definition suggests that the key element of intimacy is closeness, one element that "ordinary people" have reported as characterizing their intimate relationships.[11] However, it doesn't explain what *kinds* of closeness can create a state of intimacy. In truth, **intimacy** can have several qualities. The first is *physical.* Even before birth, the developing fetus experiences a kind of physical closeness with its mother that will never happen again, "floating in a warm fluid, curling inside a total embrace, swaying to the undulations of the moving body and hearing the beat of the pulsing heart."[12] As they grow up, fortunate children are continually nourished by physical intimacy: being rocked, fed, hugged, and held. As we grow older, the opportunities for physical intimacy are less regular, but still possible and important. Some, but by no means all, physical intimacy is sexual. In one survey, only one-quarter of the respondents (who were college students) stated that intimacy necessarily contained a romantic or sexual dimension.[13] Other forms of physical intimacy include affectionate hugs, kisses, and even struggles. Companions who have endured physical challenges together—in athletics or emergencies, for example—form a bond that can last a lifetime.

In other cases, intimacy comes from *intellectual* sharing. Not every exchange of ideas counts as intimacy, of course.

Talking about next week's midterm with your professor or classmates isn't likely to forge strong relational bonds. But when you engage another person in an exchange of important ideas, a kind of closeness develops that can be powerful and exciting.

A third quality of intimacy is *emotion*: exchanging important feelings. This chapter will offer several guidelines for disclosing your thoughts and feelings to others. If you follow those guidelines, you will probably recognize a qualitative change in your relationships.

If we define *intimacy* as being close to another person, then *shared activities* can provide another way to achieve this state. Shared activities can include everything from working side by side at a job to meeting regularly for exercise workouts. Although shared activities are no guarantee of intimacy, people who spend time together can develop unique ways of relating that transform the relationship from an impersonal one that could be done with anybody to one with interpersonal qualities. For example, both same-sex friendships and opposite-sex romantic relationships are often characterized by several forms of play. Partners invent private codes, fool around by acting like other people, tease one another, and play games—everything from having punning contests to arm wrestling.[14]

Some intimate relationships exhibit all four qualities: physical intimacy, intellectual exchanges, emotional disclosure, and shared activities. Other intimate relationships exhibit only one or two. Some relationships, of course, aren't intimate in any way. Acquaintances, roommates, and coworkers may never become intimate. In some cases even family members develop smooth but relatively impersonal relationships.

Not even the closest relationships always operate at the highest level of intimacy. At some times you might share all of your thoughts or feelings with a friend, family member, or lover; and at other times you might withdraw. You might freely share your feelings about one topic and stay more aloof in another one. The same principle holds for physical intimacy, which waxes and wanes in most relationships. The dialectical view of relational maintenance described later in this chapter explains how intimacy can wax and wane, even in the closest relationships.

Before I built a wall I'd ask to know
What I was walling in or walling out.
And to whom I was like to give offense.
Something there is that doesn't love a wall
That wants it down.

Robert Frost

Male and Female Intimacy Styles

Until recently most social scientists believed that women are better at developing and maintaining intimate relationships than men.[15] This belief grew from the assumption that the disclosure of personal information is the most important ingredient of intimacy. Most research *does* show that women (taken as a group, of course) are more willing to share their thoughts and feelings than men.[16] In terms of the amount and depth of information exchanged, female-female relationships are at the top of the disclosure list. Male-female relationships come in second, whereas relationships between men have less disclosure than any other type. At every age, women disclose more than men, and the information they disclose is more personal and more likely to involve feelings. Although both sexes are equally likely to reveal negative information, men are less likely to share positive feelings.[17]

Through the mid-1980s many social scientists interpreted the relative lack of male self-disclosure as a sign that men are unwilling or even unable to develop

CULTURAL IDIOM

fool around: spend time joking

Sally Forth

Source: Reprinted by special permission of King Features Syndicate.

close relationships. Some argued that the female trait of disclosing personal information and feelings makes them more "emotionally mature" and "interpersonally competent" than men. Personal growth programs and self-help books urge men to achieve closeness by learning to open up and share their feelings.

But scholarship conducted in roughly the last decade has begun to show that emotional expression isn't the *only* way to develop close relationships. Unlike women who value personal talk, men grow close to one another by doing things. In one study more than 75 percent of the men surveyed said that their most meaningful experiences with friends came from activities other than talking.[18] They reported that through shared activities they "grew on one another," developed feelings of interdependence, showed appreciation for one another, and demonstrated mutual liking. Likewise, men regarded practical help from other men as a measure of caring. Research like this shows that, for many men, closeness grows from activities that don't depend heavily on disclosure: A friend is a person who does things *for* you and *with* you.

The difference between male and female measures of intimacy helps explain some of the stresses and misunderstandings that can arise between the sexes. For example, a woman who looks for emotional disclosure as a measure of affection may overlook an "inexpressive" man's efforts to show he cares by doing favors or spending time together. Fixing a leaky faucet or taking a hike may look like ways to avoid getting close, but to the man who proposes them, they may be measures of affection and bids for intimacy. Likewise, differing ideas about the timing and meaning of sex can lead to misunderstandings. Whereas many women think of sex as a way to express intimacy that has already developed, men are more likely to see it as a way to *create* that intimacy.[19] In this sense, the man who encourages sex early in a relationship or after a fight may not just be a testosterone-crazed lecher: He may view the shared activity as a way to build closeness. By contrast, the woman who views personal talk as the pathway to intimacy may resist the idea of physical closeness before the emotional side of the relationship has been discussed.

Cultural Influences on Intimacy

The notion of how much intimacy is desirable and how to express it varies from one culture to another.[20] In one study, researchers asked residents of Britain, Japan, Hong Kong, and Italy to describe their use of thirty-three rules that governed interaction in a wide range of communication behaviors: everything from the use of humor to hand shaking to the management of money.[21] The results

CULTURAL IDIOM

to open up: to talk about subjects that otherwise might be withheld

showed that the greatest differences between Asian and European cultures focused on the rules for dealing with intimacy: showing emotions, expressing affection in public, engaging in sexual activity, respecting privacy, and so on. Culture also plays a role in shaping how much intimacy we seek in different types of relationships. For instance, the Japanese seem to expect more intimacy in friendships, whereas Americans look for more intimacy in romantic relationships with a boy or girlfriend, fiancée, or spouse.[22]

Disclosure is especially high in mainstream North American society. In fact, natives of the United States are more disclosing than members of any other culture studied.[23] They are likely to disclose more about themselves to acquaintances and even strangers. By contrast, Germans and Japanese tend to disclose little about themselves except in personal relationships with a select few. Within American culture, intimacy varies from one group to another. For example, working-class black men are much more disclosing than their white counterparts.[24] By contrast, upwardly mobile black men communicate more like white men with the same social agenda, disclosing less with their male friends.

In some collectivist cultures such as Taiwan and Japan there is an especially great difference in the way members communicate with members of their "in-groups" (such as family and close friends) and with those they view as outsiders.[25] They generally do not reach out to strangers, often waiting until they are properly introduced before entering into a conversation. Once introduced, they address outsiders with a degree of formality. They go to extremes to hide unfavorable information about in-group members from outsiders, on the principle that one doesn't wash dirty laundry in public. By contrast, members of more individualistic cultures like the United States and Australia make less of a distinction between personal relationships and casual ones. They act more familiar with strangers and disclose more personal information, making them excellent "cocktail party conversationalists." Social psychologist Kurt Lewin captured the difference nicely when he noted that Americans are easy to meet but difficult to get to know, whereas Germans are difficult to meet but then easy to know well.[26]

Differences like these mean that the level of self-disclosure that is appropriate in one culture may seem completely inappropriate in another one. If you were

> ### CULTURAL IDIOM
>
> **wash dirty laundry in public:** disclose personal and private problems and concerns beyond one's family or group

---

INVITATION TO INSIGHT

Your I.Q. (Intimacy Quotient)

Answer the following questions as you think about your relationship with a person important in your life.

1. What is the level of physical intimacy in your relationship?
2. What intellectual intimacy do you share?
3. How emotionally intimate are you? Is your emotional intimacy deeper in some ways than in others?
4. Has your intimacy level changed over time? If so, in what ways?

After answering these questions, ask yourself how satisfied you are with the amount of intimacy in this relationship. Identify any changes you would like to occur, and describe the steps you could take to make them happen.

UNDERSTANDING DIVERSITY

Intimacy Through the Ages

The concept of intimacy—at least as we think of it—is a relatively new one. A time traveler who visited almost any era before the nineteenth century would not find much resembling today's notions of intimacy in either the physical or emotional sense.

If physical intimacy meant only close proximity and little privacy, then it was more common in the past than it is today, especially in less-privileged social classes. In many preindustrial societies, families usually used a common room for bathing, eating, and sleeping. Often a household lacked even a bed, and in one writer's phrase, an entire American colonial family "pigg'd lovingly together" on the floor.

Despite a high degree of physical proximity, in many other times and places there was little emotional intimacy, in even close relationships. Most communities—at least in North America, England, and northern Europe—were too concerned with meeting their economic needs to worry about feelings. The family was primarily an economic unit, with members bound together by the mutual task of survival. In seventeenth-century America and England, the customary level of communication among spouses was rather formal: not much different from the way acquaintances or neighbors spoke with one another. One might regard a husband or wife with affection, but the concept of romantic love as we know it did not flourish until the nineteenth century.

In nineteenth-century bourgeois society, extreme differences between public and private behavior emerged. In public, privacy was the rule. It was considered selfish to burden others with details of your personal life. By contrast, the home was viewed as a refuge from the outside world—a place where the family could support and nourish one another. Love and marriage changed from the pragmatic business they were a century earlier and became highly romanticized. Intimate self-disclosure was expected to be an ingredient in any loving partnership. Not only did sharing one's deepest feelings strengthen the marriage bond, but also it provided support that was lacking in the restrained, private public world.

Emotional intimacy may have become valued in nineteenth-century bourgeois society, but sexual relationships still were characterized by repression. In the early years of the century, "petting" was considered unacceptable. By the 1870s, sexual restraint had reached a peak: Some popular marriage manuals recommended female frigidity "as a virtue to be cultivated, and sexual coldness as a condition to be desired." The term *nymphomania* was used to describe degrees of sexual expression that would be considered commonplace today. One doctor even referred to his patient as a "virgin nymphomaniac."

The concept of emotional intimacy has also changed in the last hundred years. The nineteenth-century approval of self-disclosure has expanded considerably, so that the distinction between public and private relationships is a fuzzy one. As etiquette writer "Miss Manners" points out, we live in a time when waiters introduce themselves by name and sign our checks with a personal "thank you" and when clerks urge us to "have a nice day." In contemporary society it is common to share details of one's personal life with new acquaintances or even total strangers—behavior that would have astonished and offended our great-grandparents.

Understanding the changing concept of intimacy can help show us that notions we take for granted are not universal and are often shaped by economic and social conditions. A sense of perspective can also give us an appreciation for communication practices that are a part of everyday life and give us a sense of other possibilities.

The material in this reading was drawn from several sources: Stephanie Coontz, *The Social Origins of Private Life* (New York: Verso, 1988); John F. Kasson, *Rudeness and Civility: Manners in Nineteenth-Century Urban America* (New York: Hill and Wang, 1990); and Sara Trenholm and Arthur Jensen, "The Guarded Self: Toward a Social History of Interpersonal Styles," a paper presented to the Speech Communication Association's meeting in San Juan, Puerto Rico, December 1990.

raised in the United States or Canada you might view people from other cultures as undisclosing, or even standoffish. But the amount of personal information that the nonnatives reveal might actually be quite personal and revealing according to the standards of their culture. The converse is also true: To members of other cultures, North Americans probably appear like exhibitionists who spew personal information to anyone within earshot.

RELATIONAL DEVELOPMENT AND MAINTENANCE

Qualitatively interpersonal relationships aren't stable. Instead, they are constantly changing. Communication scholars have described the way relationships develop and shift in two ways. We will examine each of them now.

Developmental Models

One of the best-known explanations of how communication operates in relationships was created by Mark Knapp, whose **developmental model** broke down the rise and fall of relationships into ten stages, contained in the two broad phases of "coming together" and "coming apart."[27] Other researchers have suggested that any model of relational communication ought to contain a third part of relational maintenance—communication aimed at keeping relationships operating smoothly and satisfactorily.[28] Figure 6–1 shows how Knapp's ten stages fit into this three-part view of relational communication.

The following stages are especially descriptive of intimate, romantic relationships and close friendships. The pattern for other intimate relationships, such as families, would follow different paths. Some valuable relationships don't require a high level of intimacy. They are based on other, equally important foundations: career activities, shared political interests, and religion, to mention just a few.[29]

INITIATING   The stage of initiation involves the initial making of contact with another person. Knapp restricts this stage to conversation openers, both in initial contacts and in contacts with acquaintances: "Nice to meet you," "How's it going?" and so on.

Although an initial encounter is necessary to the succeeding interaction, its importance is overemphasized in books advising how to pick up men and women. These books suggest fail-proof openers ranging from "Excuse me, I'm from out of town, and I was wondering what people do around here at night" to "How long do you cook a leg of lamb?" Whatever your preference for opening

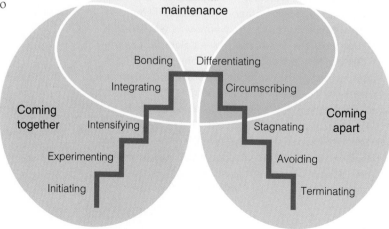

Figure 6–1   Stages of Relational Development

remarks, this stage is important because you are formulating your first impressions and presenting yourself as interested in the other person.

CULTURAL IDIOM

"small talk":
unimportant or trivial
conversation

EXPERIMENTING   In the stage of experimenting, the conversation develops as the people get acquainted by making "small talk." We ask: "Where are you from?" or "What do you do?" or "Do you know Josephine Mandoza? She lives in San Francisco, too."

Though small talk might seem meaningless, Knapp points out that it serves four purposes:

■ It is a useful process for uncovering integrating topics and openings for more penetrating conversation.
■ It can be an audition for a future friendship or a way of increasing the scope of a current relationship.
■ It provides a safe procedure for indicating who we are and how another can come to know us better (reduction of uncertainty).
■ It allows us to maintain a sense of community with our fellow human beings.

The relationship during this stage is generally pleasant and uncritical, and the commitments are minimal. Experimenting may last ten minutes or ten years.

The willingness to pursue relationships with strangers is partly a matter of personal style. Some people are outgoing and others more shy. But culture also plays a role in orientations to newcomers, especially ones from a different background. Research suggests that members of some cultures—Chinese and Japanese, for example—are more cautious in their first encounters with strangers and make more assumptions about them based on their backgrounds than do North Americans and most Europeans.[30] This fact might explain why people from certain backgrounds appear unfriendly, when in fact they are simply operating by a set of rules different from those common in the outgoing United States.

INTENSIFYING   At the next stage the kind of truly interpersonal relationship defined earlier in this chapter begins to develop. Several changes in communication patterns occur during intensifying. The expression of feelings toward the other becomes more common. Dating couples use a wide range of communication strategies to describe their feelings of attraction.[31] About a quarter of the time they express their feelings directly, using metacommunication to discuss the state of the relationship. More often they use less-direct methods of communication: spending an increasing amount of time together, asking for support from one another, doing favors for the partner, giving tokens of affection, hinting and flirting, expressing feelings non-

verbally, getting to know the partner's friends and family, and trying to look more physically attractive. Touching is more common during this stage than in either earlier or later ones.[32] Other changes mark the intensifying stage. Forms of address become more familiar. The parties begin to see themselves as "we" instead of separate individuals. It is during the intensifying stage that we begin to express directly feelings of commitment to one another: "I'm sure glad we met." "You're the best thing that's happened to me in a long time."

INTEGRATING   As the relationship strengthens, the parties begin to take on an identity as a social unit. Invitations begin to come addressed to the couple. Social circles merge. The partners begin to take on each other's commitments: "Sure, we'll spend Thanksgiving with your family." Common property may begin to be designated—our apartment, our car, our song.[33] Partners develop their own rituals for everything from expressing intimacy to handling daily routines.[34] They even begin to speak alike, using common words and sentence patterns.[35] In this sense, the integration stage is a time when we give up some characteristics of our old selves and become different people.

As we become more integrated with others, our sense of obligation to them grows.[36] We feel obliged to provide a variety of resources such as class notes and money, whether or not the other person asks for them. When intimates do make requests of one another, they are relatively straightforward. Gone are the elaborate explanations, inducements, and apologies. In short, partners in an integrated relationship expect more from one another than they do in less-intimate associations.

BONDING   During the bonding stage, the parties make symbolic public gestures to show the world that their relationship exists. The most common form of bonding in romantic relationships is a wedding ceremony and the legal ties that come with it. Bonding generates social support for the relationship. Both custom and law impose certain obligations on partners who have officially bonded.

Bonding marks a turning point in a relationship. Up to now the relationship may have developed at a steady pace: Experimenting gradually moved into intensifying and then into integrating. Now, however, there is a spurt of commitment. The public display and declaration of exclusivity make this a critical period in the relationship.

DIFFERENTIATING   Now that the two people have formed this commonalty, they need to reestablish individual identities. This is the point where the "hold me tight" orientation that has existed shifts, and "put me down" messages begin to occur. Partners use a variety of strategies to gain privacy from one another.[37] Sometimes they confront the other party directly, explaining that they don't want to continue a discussion. At other times they are less direct, offering nonverbal cues, changing the topic, or leaving the room.

"And do you, Rebecca, promise to make love only to Richard, month after month, year after year, and decade after decade, until one of you is dead?"

Differentiation is likely to occur when a relationship begins to experience the first, inevitable stress. This need for autonomy needn't be a negative experience, however. People need to be individuals as well as parts of a relationship, and differentiation is a necessary step toward autonomy. The key to successful differentiation is maintaining a commitment to the relationship while creating the space for being an individual as well.

CIRCUMSCRIBING   So far we have been looking at the growth of relationships. Although some reach a plateau of development, going on successfully for as long as a lifetime, others pass through several stages of decline and dissolution. In the circumscribing stage, communication between members decreases in quantity and quality. Restrictions and restraints characterize this stage, and dynamic communication becomes static. Rather than discuss a disagreement (which requires some degree of energy on both parts), members opt for withdrawal: either mental (silence or daydreaming and fantasizing) or physical (where people spend less time together). Circumscribing doesn't involve total avoidance, which comes later. Rather, it entails a certain shrinking of interest and commitment.

STAGNATING   If circumscribing continues, the relationship begins to stagnate. Members behave toward each other in old, familiar ways without much feeling. No growth occurs. The relationship is a shadow of its former self. We see stagnation in many workers who have lost enthusiasm for their job yet continue to go through the motions for years. The same sad event occurs for some couples who unenthusiastically have the same conversations, see the same people, and follow the same routines without any sense of joy or novelty.

AVOIDING   When stagnation becomes too unpleasant, parties in a relationship begin to create distance between each other. Sometimes this is done under the guise of excuses ("I've been sick lately and can't see you"), and sometimes it is done directly ("Please don't call me; I don't want to see you now"). In either case, by this point the handwriting about the relationship's future is clearly on the wall.

TERMINATING   Characteristics of this final stage include summary dialogues about where the relationship has gone and the desire to dissociate. The relationship may end with a cordial dinner, a note left on the kitchen table, a phone call, or a legal document stating the dissolution. Depending on each person's feelings, this stage can be quite short, or it may be drawn out over time, with bitter jabs at one another. In either case, termination doesn't have to be totally negative. Understanding one another's investments in the relationship and needs for personal growth may soften the hard feelings.

The deterioration of a relationship from bonding to circumscribing, stagnating, and avoiding isn't inevitable. One of the key differences between marriages that end in separation and those that are restored to their former intimacy is the communication that occurs when the partners are unsatisfied.[38] Unsuccessful couples deal with their problems by avoidance, indirectness, and less involvement with one another. By contrast, couples who "repair" their relationship communicate much more directly. They confront one another with their concerns and spend time and effort negotiating solutions to their problems.

CRITICAL THINKING PROBE **Stages in Nonromantic Relationships**
Knapp's model of relational development and decline offers a good description of communication stages in traditional romantic relationships. Some critics have argued that it doesn't characterize other sorts of relationships so well. Identify your position in this debate by following these steps:

1. Explain how well (or poorly) the model describes one other type of relationship: among coworkers, friends (either close or more distant), parent and child, or another relational context of your choosing.
2. Construct a model describing communication stages in the relationship type you just identified. How does this model differ from Knapp's?

Dialectical Perspectives

Developmental models like the one described in the preceding pages suggest that communication differs in important ways at various points in the life of a relationship. According to these stage-related models, the kinds of interaction that happen during initiating, experimenting, or intensifying are different from the interaction that occurs during differentiating, circumscribing, or avoiding.

Not all theorists agree that a stage-related model is the best way to explain interaction in relationships. Some suggest that communicators grapple with the same kinds of challenges whether a relationship is brand new or has lasted decades. They argue that communicators seek important but inherently incompatible goals throughout virtually all of their relationships. These **dialectical models** suggest that struggling to achieve these goals creates **dialectical tensions**: conflicts that arise when two opposing or incompatible forces exist simultaneously. In recent years, communication scholars have identified the dialectical tensions that make successful communication challenging.[39] They suggest that the struggle to manage these dialectical tensions creates the most powerful dynamics in relational communication. In the following pages we will discuss three powerful dialectical tensions.

CONNECTION VERSUS AUTONOMY   No one is an island. Recognizing this fact, we seek out involvement with others. But, at the same time, we are unwilling to sacrifice our entire identity to even the most satisfying relationship. The conflicting desires for connection and independence are embodied in the *connection-autonomy dialectic*. Research on relational breakups demonstrates the consequences for relational partners who can't find a way to manage these very different personal needs.[40] Some of the most common reasons for relational breakups involve failure of partners to satisfy one another's needs for connection: "We barely spent any time together"; "He wasn't committed to the relationship"; "We had different needs." But other relational complaints involve excessive demands for connection: "I was feeling trapped"; "I needed freedom."

The levels of connection and autonomy that we seek can change over time. In his book *Intimate Behavior,* Desmond Morris suggests that each of us repeatedly goes through three stages: "Hold me tight," "Put me down," and "Leave me

[Porcupines] huddle together for warmth, but their sharp quills prick each other, so they pull away. But then they get cold. They have to keep adjusting their closeness and distance to keep from freezing and from getting pricked by their fellow porcupines— the source of both comfort and pain.

We need to get close to each other to have a sense of community, to feel we're not alone in the world. But we need to keep our distance from each other to preserve our independence, so others don't impose on or engulf us. This duality reflects the human condition. We are individual and social creatures. We need other people to survive, but we want to survive as individuals.

Deborah Tannen
That's Not What I Meant!

alone."[41] This cycle becomes apparent in the first years of life when children move from the "hold me tight" stage that characterizes infancy into a new "put me down" stage of exploring the world by crawling, walking, touching, and tasting. This move for independence isn't all in one direction: The same three-year-old who insists "I can do it myself" in August may cling to parents on the first day of preschool in September. As children grow into adolescents, the "leave me alone" orientation becomes apparent. Teenagers who used to happily spend time with their parents now may groan at the thought of a family vacation or even the notion of sitting down at the dinner table each evening. More time is spent with friends or alone. Although this time can be painful for parents, most developmental experts recognize it as a necessary stage in moving from childhood to adulthood.

As the need for independence from family grows, adolescents take care of their "hold me tight" needs by associating with their peers. Friendships during the teenage years are vital, and the level of closeness with contemporaries can be a barometer of happiness. This is the time when physical intimacy becomes an option, and sexual exploration may provide a new way of achieving closeness.

In adult relationships, the same cycle of intimacy and distance repeats itself. In marriages, for example, the "hold me tight" bonds of the first year are often followed by a desire for independence. This need for autonomy can manifest itself in a number of ways, such as the desire to make friends or engage in activities that don't include the spouse, or the need to make a career move that might disrupt the relationship. As the discussion of relational stages later in this chapter will explain, this movement from closeness to autonomy may lead to the breakup of relationships; but it can also be part of a cycle that redefines the relationship in a new form that can recapture or even surpass the intimacy that existed in the past.

PREDICTABILITY VERSUS NOVELTY   Stability is an important need in relationships, but too much of it can lead to feelings of staleness. The *predictability-novelty dialectic* reflects this tension. Humorist Dave Barry exaggerates only slightly when he talks about the boredom that can come when husbands and wives know each other too well:

> After a decade or so of marriage, you know *everything* about your spouse, every habit and opinion and twitch and tic and minor skin growth. You could write a seventeen-pound book solely about the way your spouse *eats*. This kind of intimate knowledge can be very handy in certain situations—such as when you're on a TV quiz show where the object is to identify your spouse from the sound of his or her chewing—but it tends to lower the passion level of a relationship.[42]

Although too much familiarity can lead to the risk of boredom and stagnation, nobody wants a completely unpredictable relational partner. Too many surprises can threaten the foundations upon which the relationship is based ("You're not the person I married!").

The challenge for communicators is to juggle the desire for predictability with the need for novelty that keeps the relationship fresh and interesting. People differ in their need and desire for stability and surprises, so there is no optimal mixture of the two. As you will read shortly, there are a number of strategies people can use to manage these contradictory drives.

A SEMI-PRIVATE PERSON

OPENNESS VERSUS PRIVACY   As Chapter 1 explained, disclosure is one characteristic of interpersonal relationships. Yet, along with the need for intimacy, we have an equally important need to maintain some space between ourselves and others. These sometimes-conflicting drives create the *openness-privacy dialectic.*

Even the strongest interpersonal relationships require some distance. On a short-term basis, the desire for closeness waxes and wanes. Lovers may go through periods of much sharing and times of relative withdrawal. Likewise, they experience periods of passion and then periods of little physical contact. Friends have times of high disclosure where they share almost every feeling and idea and then disengage for days, months, or even longer. Figure 6–2 illustrates some patterns of variation in openness uncovered in a study of college students' communication patterns.[43] The students reported the degree of openness in one of their important relationships—a friendship, romantic relationship, or marriage—over a range of thirty conversations. The graphs show a definite pattern of fluctuation between disclosure and privacy in every stage of the relationships.

STRATEGIES FOR MANAGING DIALECTICAL TENSIONS   Managing the dialectical tensions outlined in these pages presents communication challenges. There are a number of strategies by which these challenges can be managed.[44] One of the least functional is *denial* that tensions exist. People in denial insist that "everything is fine," that the inevitable tugs of dialectical tensions really aren't a problem. For example, coworkers who claim that they're *always* happy to be members of the team and *never* see con-

Love one another, but make not a bond of love:
Let it rather be a moving sea between the shores of your souls.
Fill each other's cup but drink not from one cup.
Give one another of your bread but eat not of the same loaf.
Sing and dance together and be joyous, but let each one of you be alone,
Even as the strings of a lute are alone though they quiver with the same music.

Kahlil Gibran
The Prophet

INVITATION
TO INSIGHT

Striking a Balance between Intimacy and Distance

Choose an important interpersonal relationship with someone you encounter on a frequent, regular basis. You might choose a friend, family member, or romantic partner.

For at least a week, chart how your communication with this relational partner reflects your desire for either intimacy or distance. Use a seven-point scale, in which behavior seeking high intimacy receives a 7, whereas behavior seeking to avoid physical, intellectual, and/or emotional contact receives a 1. Use ratings from 2 through 6 to reflect intermediate stages. Record at least one rating per day, making more detailed entries if your desire for intimacy or distance changes during that period.

After charting your communication, reflect on what the results tell you about your personal desire for intimacy and distance. Consider the following questions:

1. Which state—intimacy or distance—seemed most desirable for you?
2. To the degree that you seek intimacy, which variety or varieties are most important to you: intellectual, emotional, and/or physical?
3. Was the pattern you charted during this week typical of your communication in this relationship over a longer period of time?
4. Do you seek the same mixture of intimacy and distance in other relationships?
5. Most importantly, are you satisfied with the results you discovered in this exercise? If not, how would you like to change your communication behavior?

---

flicts between their personal goals and the organization's are probably operating in a state of denial.

Disorientation is another response to dialectical tensions. In this response, communicators feel so overwhelmed and helpless that they are unable to confront their problems. In the face of dialectical tensions they might fight, freeze, or even leave the relationship. A couple who discover soon after the honeymoon that living a "happily ever after" conflict-free life is impossible might become so terrified that they would come to view their marriage as a mistake.

In the strategy of *selection*, communicators respond to one end of the dialectical spectrum and ignore the other. For example, a couple caught between the conflicting desires for stability and novelty might find their struggle to change too difficult to manage and choose to stick with predictable, if unexciting, patterns of relating to one another.

Communicators choose the strategy of *alternation* to alternate between one end of the dialectical spectrum at some times and the other end at other times. Friends, for example, might manage the autonomy-connection dialectic by alternating between times when they spend a large amount of time together and other times when they live independent lives.

A fifth strategy is *segmentation*, a tactic in which partners compartmentalize different areas of their relationship. For example, a couple might manage the

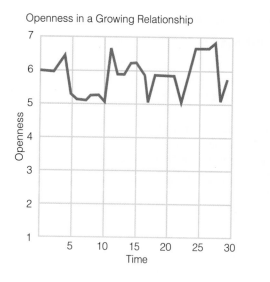

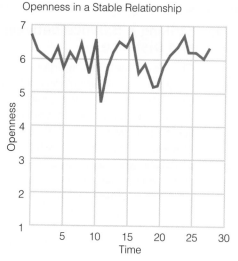

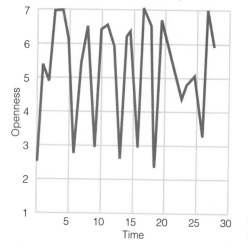

Figure 6–2   Cyclical Phases of Openness and Withdrawal in Relationships

openness-closedness dialectic by sharing almost all their feelings about mutual friends with one another but keep certain parts of their past romantic histories private.

Moderation is a sixth strategy. This strategy is characterized by compromises, in which communicators choose to back off from expressing either end of the dialectical spectrum. Adult children, for example, might manage the revelation-concealment dialectic with their inquisitive parents by answering some (though not all) unwelcome parental questions.

Communicators can also respond to dialectical challenges by *reframing* them in terms that redefine the situation so that the apparent contradiction disappears. Consider a couple who wince when their friends characterize them as a "perfect couple." On one hand, they want to escape from the "perfect couple" label that feels confining, but on the other hand, they enjoy the admiration that comes with this identity. By pointing out to their friends that "ideal couples" aren't always blissfully happy, they can both be themselves and keep the admiration of their friends.

A final strategy for handling dialectical tensions is *reaffirmation*—acknowledging that dialectical tensions will never disappear, accepting or even embracing the challenges they present. The metaphorical view of relational life as a kind of roller coaster reflects this orientation, and communicators who use reaffirmation view dialectical tensions as part of the ride.

INVITATION
TO INSIGHT

Juggling Dialectical Tensions

Identify one situation in which you are trying to manage dialectical tensions in your life. (Describe which of the dialectical forces described in this chapter are in operation.) Then answer these questions:

1. Which of the strategies for managing dialectical tensions listed on pages 200–203 do you use?
2. How effective is the strategy (or strategies) that you have chosen?
3. Would an alternative strategy be more effective for managing the tensions in this situation?
4. How might things go differently if you choose the alternative strategy?

Characteristics of Relational Development and Maintenance

Whether you analyze a relationship in terms of stages or dialectical dynamics, two characteristics are true of every interpersonal relationship. As you read about each, consider how it applies to your own experience.

RELATIONSHIPS ARE CONSTANTLY CHANGING Relationships are certainly not doomed to deteriorate. But even the strongest ones are rarely stable for long periods of time. In fairy tales a couple may live "happily ever after," but in real life this sort of equilibrium is less common. Consider a husband and wife who have been married for some time. Although they have formally bonded, their relationship will probably shift from one dimension of a relational dialectic to another, and forward or backward along the spectrum of stages. Sometimes the partners will feel the need to differentiate from one another, and at other times they will seek intimacy. Sometimes they will feel secure in the predictable patterns they have established, and at other times one or both will be hungry for novelty. The relationship may become more circumscribed, or even stagnant. From this point the marriage may fail, but this fate isn't certain. With effort, the partners may move from the stage of stagnating to experimenting, or from circumscribing to intensifying.

Communication theorist Richard Conville describes the constantly changing, evolving nature of relationships as a cycle in which partners move through a series of stages, returning to ones they previously encountered—although at a new level[45] (see Figure 6–3). In this cycle, partners move from security (integration, in Knapp's terminology) to disintegration (differentiating) to alienation (circumscribing) to resynthesis (intensifying, integrating) to a new level of security. This process repeats itself again and again.

MOVEMENT IS ALWAYS TO A NEW PLACE   Even though a relationship may move back to a stage it has experienced before, it will never be the same. For example, most healthy long-term relationships will go through several phases of experimenting, when the partners try out new ways of behaving with one another. Though each phase is characterized by the same general features, the specifics will feel different each time. As you learned in Chapter 1, communication is irreversible. Partners can never go back to "the way things were." Sometimes this fact may lead to regrets: It's impossible to take back a cruel comment or forget a crisis. On the other hand, the irreversibility of communication can make relationships exciting, because it lessens the chance for boredom.

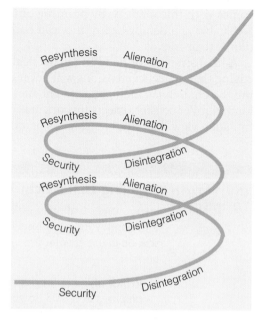

Figure 6–3   A Helical Model of Relational Cycles

SELF-DISCLOSURE IN INTERPERSONAL RELATIONSHIPS

One way we judge the strength of interpersonal relationships is by the amount of information we share with others. "We don't have any secrets," some people proudly claim. Opening up certainly is important. Earlier in this chapter you learned that one ingredient in qualitatively interpersonal relationships is disclosure. You've also read that we find others more attractive when they share certain private information with us. Given the obvious importance of self-disclosure, we need to take a closer look at the subject. Just what is it? When is it desirable? How can it best be done?

The best place to begin is with a definition. **Self-disclosure** is the process of deliberately revealing information about oneself that is significant and that would not normally be known by others. Let's take a closer look at some parts of this definition. Self-disclosure must be *deliberate*. If you accidentally mentioned to a friend that you were thinking about quitting a job or proposing marriage, that information would not fit into the category we are examining here. Self-disclosure must also be *significant*. Revealing relatively trivial information—the fact that you like fudge, for example—does not qualify as self-disclosure. The third requirement is that the information being revealed would *not be known by others*. There's nothing noteworthy about telling others that you are depressed or elated if they already know how you're feeling.

Polishing and Peeling

The personality of man is not an apple that has to be polished, but a banana that has to be peeled. And the reason we remain so far from one another, the reason we neither communicate nor interact in any real way, is that most of us spend our lives in polishing rather than peeling.

Man's lifelong task is simply one, but it is not simple: To remove the discrepancy between his outer self and his inner self, to get rid of the "persona" that divides his authentic self from the world. This persona is like the peeling on a banana: It is something built up to protect from bruises and injury. It is not the real person, but sometimes (if the fear of injury remains too great) it becomes a lifelong substitute for the person. The "authentic personality" knows that he is like a banana, and knows that only as he peels himself down to his individuated self can he reach out and make contact with his fellows.

Most of us, however, think in terms of the apple, not the banana. We spend our lives in shining the surface, in making it rosy and gleaming, in perfecting the "image." But the image is not the apple, which may be wormy and rotten to the taste. Almost everything in modern life is devoted to the polishing process, and little to the peeling process. It is the surface personality that we work on—the appearance, the clothes, the manners, the geniality. In short, the salesmanship: We are selling the package, not the product.

Sydney J. Harris

TABLE 6–1 Reasons for Self-Disclosure

Self-disclosure has the potential to improve and expand interpersonal relationships, but it serves other functions as well. As you read each of the following reasons why people reveal themselves, see which apply to you.

Reason	Example/Explanation
Catharsis	"I need to get this off my chest . . ."
Self-Clarification	"I'm really confused about something I did last night. If I tell you, maybe I can figure out why I did it . . ."
Self-Validation	" I think I did the right thing. Let me tell you why I did it . . ."
Reciprocity	"I really like you..." (Hoping for a similar disclosure by other person.)
Impression management	Salesperson to customer: "My boss would kill me for giving you this discount . . ." (Hoping disclosure will build trust.)
Relationship maintenance and enhancement	"I'm worried about the way things are going between us. Let's talk." *or* "I sure am glad we're together!"
Control	(Employee to boss, hoping to get raise) "I got a job offer yesterday from our biggest competitor."

Adapted from V. J. Derlega and J. Grezlak, "Appropriateness of Self-Disclosure," in G. J. Chelune, ed., *Self-Disclosure* (San Francisco, CA: Jossey-Bass, 1979).

As Table 6–1 shows, people self-disclose for a variety of reasons. Some involve developing and maintaining relationships, but other reasons often drive revealing personal information. The reasons for disclosing vary from one situation to another, depending on several factors. The first important factor in whether we disclose seems to be how well we know the other person.[46] When the target of disclosure is a friend, the most frequent reason people give for volunteering personal information is relationship maintenance and enhancement. In other words, we disclose to friends in order to strengthen the relationship. The second important reason is self-clarification—to sort out confusion to understand ourselves better.

With strangers, reciprocity becomes the most common reason for disclosing. We offer information about ourselves to strangers to learn more about them, so we can decide whether and how to continue the relationship. The second most common reason is impression formation. We often reveal information about ourselves to strangers to make ourselves look good. This information, of course, is usually positive—at least in the early stages of a friendship.

Although our definition of *self-disclosure* is helpful, it doesn't reveal the important fact that not all self-disclosure is equally revealing—that some disclosing messages tell more about us than others.

Social psychologists Irwin Altman and Dalmas Taylor describe two ways in which communication can be more or less disclosing.[47] Their **social penetration model** is pictured in Figure 6–4. The first dimension of

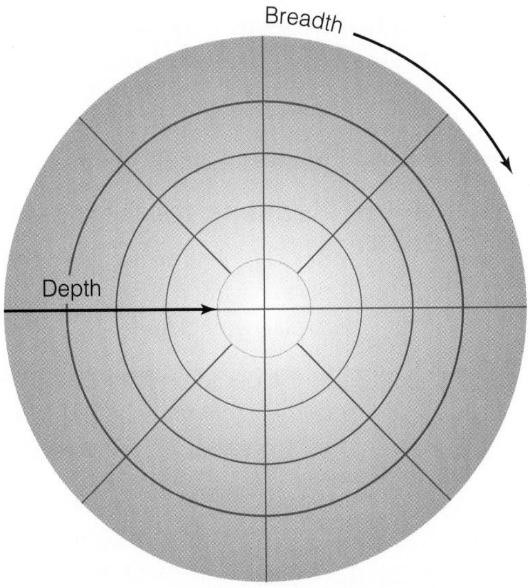

CULTURAL IDIOM

opening up: talking about subjects that might otherwise be withheld

Figure 6–4 Social Penetration Model

self-disclosure in this model involves the **breadth** of information volunteered—the range of subjects being discussed. For example, the breadth of disclosure in your relationship with a fellow worker will expand as you begin revealing information about your life away from the job, as well as on-the-job details. The second dimension of disclosure is the **depth** of the information being volunteered, the shift from relatively nonrevealing messages to more personal ones.

Depending on the breadth and depth of information shared, a relationship can be defined as casual or intimate. In a casual relationship, the breadth may be great, but not the depth. A more intimate relationship is

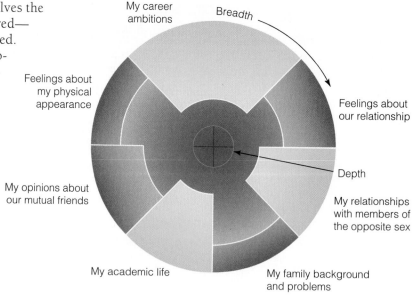

Figure 6–5   Sample Model of Social Penetration

likely to have high depth in at least one area. The most intimate relationships are those in which disclosure is great in both breadth and depth. Altman and Taylor see the development of a relationship as a progression from the periphery of their model to its center, a process that typically occurs over time. Each of your personal relationships probably has a different combination of breadth of subjects and depth of disclosure. Figure 6–5 pictures a student's self-disclosure in one relationship.

What makes the disclosure in some messages deeper than others? One way to measure depth is by how far it goes on two of the dimensions that define self-disclosure. Some revelations are certainly more *significant* than others. Consider the difference between saying "I love my family" and "I love you." Other statements qualify as deep disclosure because they are *private*. Sharing a secret you've told to only a few close friends is certainly an act of self-disclosure, but it's even more revealing to divulge information that you've never told anyone.

Reasons for Disclosing

Recall recent personal examples of times when you have disclosed personal information for each of the reasons listed in Table 6–1. Explain your answer by describing:

- the person who was the target of your self-disclosure
- the information you disclosed
- your reason(s) for disclosing

Based on your findings, decide which of the reasons for self-disclosure are most characteristic of your communication. *Note:* In order to protect privacy, this exercise can be conducted in class by having each member submit anonymous entries.

The Johari Window Model of Self-Disclosure

One way to look at the important part self-disclosure plays in interpersonal communication is by means of a device called the **Johari Window.**[48] (The window takes its name from the first names of its creators, Joseph Luft and Harry Ingham.) Imagine a frame inside which is everything there is to know about you: your likes and dislikes, your goals, your secrets, your needs—everything. (See Figure 6–6.)

Of course, you aren't aware of everything about yourself. Like most people, you're probably discovering new things about yourself all the time. To represent this, we can divide the frame containing everything about you into two parts: the part you know about and the part you don't know about, as in Figure 6–7.

We can also divide this frame containing everything about you in another way. In this division the first part contains the things about you that others know, and the second part contains the things about you that you keep to yourself. Figure 6–8 represents this view.

When we impose these two divided frames one atop the other, we have a Johari Window. By looking at Figure 6–9 you can see the *everything about you* window divided into four parts.

Part 1 represents the information of which both you and the other person are aware. This part is your *open area.* Part 2 represents the *blind area:* information of which you are unaware but the other person knows. You learn about information in the blind area primarily through feedback. Part 3 represents your *hidden area:* information that you know but aren't willing to reveal to others. Items in this hidden area become public primarily through self-disclosure, which is the focus of this chapter. Part 4 represents information that is *unknown* to both you and others. At first, the unknown area seems impossible to verify. After all, if neither you nor others know what it contains, how can you be sure it exists? We can deduce its existence because we are constantly discovering new things about ourselves. It is not unusual to discover, for example, that you have an unrecognized talent, strength, or weakness. Items move from the unknown area into the open area either directly when you disclose your insight or through one of the other areas first.

Interpersonal communication of any depth is virtually impossible if the individuals involved have little open area. Going a step further, you can see that a relationship is limited by the individual who is less open, that is, who possesses the smaller open area. Figure 6–10 illustrates this situation with Johari

Figure 6–6   The Johari Window: Everything About You

Figure 6–7   The Johari Window: Known to Self; Not Known to Self

Figure 6–8   The Johari Window: Known to Others; Not Known to Others

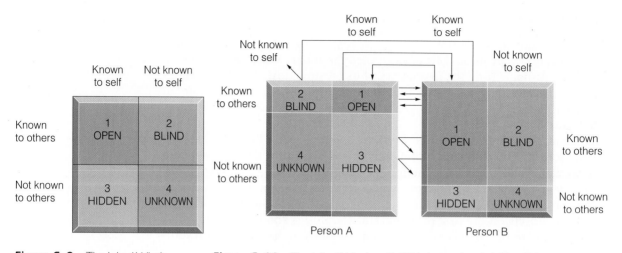

Figure 6–9   The Johari Window: Open; Blind; Hidden; Unknown

Figure 6–10   The Johari Window: Self-Disclosure Levels in Two-Way Communication

Windows. A's window is set up in reverse so that A's and B's open areas are adjacent. Notice that the amount of communication (represented by the arrows connecting the two open areas) is dictated by the size of the smaller open area of A. The arrows originating from B's open area and being turned aside by A's hidden and blind areas represent unsuccessful attempts to communicate.

You have probably found yourself in situations that resemble Figure 6–10. Perhaps you have felt the frustration of not being able to get to know someone who was too reserved. Perhaps you have blocked another person's attempts to build a relationship with you in the same way. Whether you picture yourself more like Person A or Person B, the fact is that self-disclosure on both sides is necessary for the development of any interpersonal relationship. This chapter will describe just how much self-disclosure is optimal and of what type.

Characteristics of Effective Self-Disclosure

The Johari Window suggests several characteristics of self-disclosure:

SELF-DISCLOSURE IS INFLUENCED BY CULTURE   The level of self-disclosure that is appropriate in one culture may seem completely inappropriate in another one. Disclosure is especially high in mainstream North American society. In fact, natives of the United States are more disclosing than members of any other culture studied.[49] They are likely to disclose more about themselves to acquaintances and even strangers. By contrast, Germans tend to disclose little about themselves except in intimate relationships with a select few, and Japanese reveal very little about themselves in even their closest relationships.

Cultural differences like this mean that what counts as disclosing communication varies from one culture to another. If you were raised in the United States, you might view people from certain other cultures as undisclosing or even standoffish. But the amount of personal information that the nonnatives reveal might actually be quite personal and revealing according to the standards of their culture. The converse is also true: To members of some other cultures, North Americans probably appear like exhibitionists who spew personal information to anyone within earshot.

> **CULTURAL IDIOM**
>
> **standoffish:** unfriendly
>
> **earshot:** the distance at which one can hear something or someone

When communicating with people from different cultures it's important to consider their standards for appropriate disclosure. Don't mistakenly judge them according to your own standards. Likewise, be sensitive about honoring their standards when talking about yourself. In this sense, choosing the proper level of self-disclosure isn't too different from choosing the appropriate way of dressing or eating when encountering members of a different culture: What seems familiar and correct at home may not be suitable with strangers. As you read on, realize that the characteristics and guidelines that suit mainstream North American culture may not apply in other contexts.

SELF-DISCLOSURE USUALLY OCCURS IN DYADS   Although it is possible for people to disclose a great deal about themselves in groups, such communication usually occurs in one-to-one settings. Because revealing significant information about yourself involves a certain amount of risk, limiting the disclosure to one person at a time minimizes the chance that your disclosure will lead to unhappy consequences.

EFFECTIVE SELF-DISCLOSURE IS USUALLY SYMMETRICAL   Note in Figure 6–10 that the amount of successful, two-way communication (represented by the arrows connecting the two open areas) is dictated by the size of the smaller open area of A. The arrows that are originating from B's open area and being turned aside by A's hidden and blind areas represent unsuccessful attempts to communicate. In situations such as this, it's easy to imagine how B would soon limit the amount of disclosure to match that of A. On the other hand, if A were willing to match the degree of disclosure given by B, the relationship would move to a new level of intimacy. In either case, we can expect that most often the degree of disclosure between partners will soon stabilize at a symmetrical level.

EFFECTIVE SELF-DISCLOSURE OCCURS INCREMENTALLY   Although instances occur in which partners start their relationship by telling everything about themselves to each other, such instances are rare. In most cases, the amount of disclosure increases over time. We begin relationships by revealing relatively little about ourselves; then if our first bits of self-disclosure are well received and bring on similar responses from the other person, we're willing to reveal more. This principle is important to remember. It would usually be a mistake to assume that the way to build a strong relationship would be to reveal the most private details about yourself when first making contact with another person. Unless the circumstances are unique, such baring of your soul would be likely to scare potential partners away rather than bring them closer.

RELATIVELY FEW TRANSACTIONS INVOLVE HIGH LEVELS OF SELF-DISCLOSURE   Just as it's unwise to seek great self-disclosure too soon, it's also unwise to reveal yourself too much. Except for unique settings—such as in therapy—there's usually no need to disclose frequently or steadily. When used properly, self-disclosure may strengthen relationships, but like most medicines, using large amounts of disclosure is not necessary.

SELF-DISCLOSURE IS RELATIVELY SCARCE   Most conversations—even among friends—focus on everyday mundane topics and disclose little or no personal information.[50] Even partners in intimate relationships rarely talk about personal information.[51] Whether or not we open up to others is based on several criteria, some of which are listed in Table 6–2.

What is the optimal amount of self-disclosure? You might suspect that the correct answer is "the more, the better," at least in personal relationships. Research has showed that the matter isn't this simple, however.[52] For example, there seems to be a curvilinear relationship between openness and satisfaction in marriage, so that a moderate amount of openness produces better results than either extreme disclosure or withholding. One good measure of happiness is how well the level of disclosure matches the expectations of communicators: If we get what we believe is a reasonable amount of candor from oth-

---

TABLE 6–2   Some Criteria Used to Reveal Family Secrets

Intimate Exchange
Does the other person have a similar problem?
Would knowing the secret help the other person feel better?
Would knowing the secret help the other person manage her problem?

Exposure
Will the other person find out this information, even if I don't' tell her?
Is the other person asking me directly to reveal this information?

Urgency
Is it very important that the other person know this information?
Will revealing this information make matters better?

Acceptance
Will the other person still accept me if I reveal this information?

Conversational Appropriateness
Will my disclosure fit into the conversation?
Has the topic of my disclosure come up in this conversation?

Relational Security
Do I trust the other person with this information?
Do I feel close enough to this person to reveal the secret?

Important Reason
Is there a pressing reason to reveal this information?

Permission
Have other people involved in the secret given their permission for me to reveal it?
Would I feel okay telling the people involved that I have revealed the secret?

Membership
Is the person to whom I'm revealing the secret going to join this group (i.e., family)?

Adapted from A. L. Vangelisti, J. P. Cauglhin, and L. Timmerman, "Criteria for Revealing Family Secrets," *Communication Monographs* 68 (2001): 1–27.

ers, we are happy. If they tell us too little—or even too much—we become less satisfied.

Guidelines for Appropriate Self-Disclosure

One fear we've had while writing this chapter is that a few overenthusiastic readers may throw down their books and begin to share every personal detail of their lives with whomever they can find. As you can imagine, this kind of behavior isn't an example of effective interpersonal communication.

No single style of self-disclosure is appropriate for every situation. Let's take a look at some guidelines that can help you recognize how to express yourself in a way that's rewarding for you and the others involved.[53]

IS THE OTHER PERSON IMPORTANT TO YOU?   There are several ways in which someone might be important. Perhaps you have an ongoing relationship deep enough so that sharing significant parts of yourself justifies keeping your present level of togetherness intact. Or perhaps the person to whom you're considering disclosing is someone with whom you've previously related on a less personal level. But now you see a chance to grow closer, and disclosure may be the path toward developing that personal relationship.

IS THE RISK OF DISCLOSING REASONABLE?   Take a realistic look at the potential risks of self-disclosure. Even if the probable benefits are great, opening yourself up to almost certain rejection may be asking for trouble. For instance, it might be foolhardy to share your important feelings with someone you know is likely to betray your confidences or ridicule them. On the other hand, knowing that your partner is trustworthy and supportive makes the prospect of speaking out more reasonable.

Revealing personal thoughts and feelings can be especially risky on the job.[54] The politics of the workplace sometimes requires communicators to keep feelings to themselves in order to accomplish both personal and organizational goals. You might, for example, find the opinions of a boss or customer personally offensive but decide to bite your tongue rather than risk your job or lose goodwill for the company.

ARE THE AMOUNT AND TYPE OF DISCLOSURE APPROPRIATE?   A third point to realize is that there are degrees of self-disclosure. Telling others about yourself isn't an all-or-nothing decision you must make. It's possible to share some facts, opinions, or feelings with one person while reserving riskier ones for others. In the same vein, before sharing very important information with someone who does matter to you, you might consider testing reactions by disclosing less personal data.

IS THE DISCLOSURE RELEVANT TO THE SITUATION AT HAND?   The kind of disclosure that is often a characteristic of highly personal relationships usually isn't appropriate in less personal settings. For instance, a study of classroom communication revealed that sharing all feelings—both positive and negative—and being completely honest resulted in less cohesiveness than having a "relatively" honest climate in which pleasant but superficial relationships were the norm.[55]

Even in personal relationships—with close friends, family members, and so on—constant disclosure isn't a useful goal. The level of sharing in successful

> **CULTURAL IDIOM**
>
> **to bite your tongue:**
> to remain silent
>
> **in the same vein:**
> related to this idea

relationships rises and falls in cycles. You may go through a period of great disclosure and then spend another period of relative nondisclosure. Even during a phase of high disclosure, sharing *everything* about yourself isn't necessarily constructive. Usually the subject of appropriate self-disclosure involves the relationship rather than personal information. Furthermore, it is usually most constructive to focus your disclosure about the relationship on the "here and now" as opposed to "there and then." "How am I feeling now?" "How are we doing now?" These are appropriate topics for sharing personal thoughts and feelings. There are certainly times when it's relevant to bring up the past but only as it relates to what's going on in the present.

IS THE DISCLOSURE RECIPROCATED?   There's nothing quite as disconcerting as talking your heart out to someone only to discover that the other person has yet to say anything to you that is half as revealing as what you've been saying. And you think to yourself, "What am I doing?" Unequal self-disclosure creates an unbalanced relationship, one doomed to fall apart.

There are few times when one-way disclosure is acceptable. Most of them involve formal, therapeutic relationships in which a client approaches a trained professional with the goal of resolving a problem. For instance, you wouldn't necessarily expect to hear about a physician's personal ailments during a visit to a medical office. Nonetheless, it's interesting to note that one frequently noted characteristic of effective psychotherapists, counselors, and teachers is a willingness to share their feelings about a relationship with their clients.

WILL THE EFFECT BE CONSTRUCTIVE?   Self-disclosure can be a vicious tool if it's not used carefully. Psychologist George Bach suggests that every person has a psychological "belt line." Below that belt line are areas about which the person is extremely sensitive. Bach says that jabbing at a "below-the-belt" area is a surefire way to disable another person, although usually at great cost to the relationship. It's important to consider the effects of your candor before opening up to others. Comments such as "I've always thought you were pretty unintelligent" or "Last year I made love to your best friend" *may* sometimes resolve old business and thus be constructive, but they also can be devastating—to the listener, to the relationship, and to your self-esteem.

IS THE SELF-DISCLOSURE CLEAR AND UNDERSTANDABLE?   When you express yourself to others, it's important that you share yourself in a way that's intelligible. This means describing the *sources* of your message clearly. For instance, it's far better to describe another's behavior by saying, "When you don't answer my phone calls or drop by to visit anymore . . ." than to complain vaguely, "When you avoid me. . . ."

It's also vital to express your *thoughts* and *feelings* explicitly. "I feel worried because I'm afraid you don't care about me" is more understandable than "I don't like the way things have been going."

Alternatives to Self-Disclosure

At first glance, our moral heritage leads us to abhor anything less than the truth. Ethicists point out that the very existence of a society seems based on a foundation of truthfulness.[56] Although isolated cultures do exist where deceit is a norm, they are dysfunctional and on the verge of breakdown.

CULTURAL IDIOM

talking your heart out: revealing your innermost thoughts and feelings

Hateful to me as are the gates of hell
Is he, who hiding one thing in his heart,
Utters another.

Homer
Iliad

Although honesty is desirable in principle, it often has risky, potentially unpleasant consequences. This explains why communicators—even those with the best intentions—aren't always completely honest when they find themselves in situations when honesty would be uncomfortable.[57] Three common alternatives to self-disclosure are lies, equivocation, and hinting. We will take a closer look at each one.

LIES   To most people, lying appears to be a breach of ethics. Although lying to gain unfair advantage over an unknowing victim seems clearly wrong, another kind of untruth—the "white lie"—isn't so easy to dismiss as completely unethical. **White lies** are defined (at least by the people who tell them) as being harmless, or even helpful, to the person to whom they are told. As Table 6–3 shows, at least some of the lies we tell are indeed intended to be helpful, or at least relatively benign. Whether or not they are innocent, white lies are certainly common. In one study, 130 subjects were asked to keep track of the truthfulness of their everyday conversational statements.[58] Only 38.5 percent of these statements—slightly more than a third—proved to be totally honest.

What are the consequences of discovering that you've been lied to? In an interpersonal relationship, the discovery can be traumatic. As we grow closer to others, our expectations about their honesty grow stronger. After all, discovering that you've been deceived requires you to redefine not only the lie you just uncovered, but also many of the messages you previously took for granted. Was last week's compliment really sincere? Was your joke really funny, or was the other person's laughter a put-on? Does the other person care about you as much as he or she claimed?

Research has shown that deception does, in fact, threaten relationships.[59] Not all lies are equally devastating, however. Feelings like dismay and betrayal are greatest when the relationship is most intense, when the importance of the subject is high, and when there was previous suspicion that the other person wasn't

The injunction against bearing false witness, branded in stone and brought down by Moses from the mountaintop, has always provoked ambivalent, conflicting emotions. On the one hand, nearly everyone condemns lying. On the other, nearly everyone does it every day.

Paul Gray

CULTURAL IDIOM

a put-on: a false show of emotion

TABLE 6–3   Some Reasons for Lying

REASON	EXAMPLE
Acquire resources	"Oh, please let me add this class. If I don't get in, I'll never graduate on time!"
Protect resources	"I'd like to lend you the money, but I'm short myself."
Initiate and continue interaction	"Excuse me, I'm lost. Do you live around here?"
Avoid conflict	"It's not a big deal. We can do it your way. Really."
Avoid interaction or take leave	"That sounds like fun, but I'm busy Saturday night." "Oh, look what time it is! I've got to run!"
Present a competent image	"Sure, I understand. No problem."
Increase social desirability	"Yeah, I've done a fair amount of skiing."

Adapted from categories originally presented in C. Camden, M. T. Motley, and A. Wilson, "White Lies in Interpersonal Communication: A Taxonomy and Preliminary Investigation of Social Motivations," *Western Journal of Speech Communication* 48 (1984): 315.

being completely honest. Of these three factors, the importance of the information lied about proved to be the key factor in provoking a relational crisis. We may be able to cope with "misdemeanor" lying, but "felonies" are a grave threat. In fact, the discovery of major deception can lead to the end of the relationship. More than two-thirds of the subjects in one study reported that their relationship had ended since they discovered a lie. Furthermore, they attributed the breakup directly to the lie. If preserving a relationship is important, honesty—at least about important matters— really does appear to be the best policy.

EQUIVOCATION   Lying isn't the only alternative to self-disclosure. When faced with the choice between lying and telling an unpleasant truth, communicators can—and often do—equivocate. As Chapter 3 explained, **equivocal language** has two or more equally plausible meanings. Sometimes people send equivocal messages without meaning to, resulting in confusion. "I'll meet you at the apartment," could refer to more than one place. But other times we are deliberately vague. For instance, when a friend asks what you think of an awful outfit, you could say, "It's really unusual—one of a kind!" Likewise, if you are too angry to accept a friend's apology but don't want to appear petty, you might say, "Don't mention it."

"Believe me when I tell you that I'm not that honest."

The value of equivocation becomes clear when you consider the alternatives. Consider the dilemma of what to say when you've been given an unwanted present—an ugly painting, for example—and the giver asks what you think of it. How can you respond? On the one hand, you need to choose between telling the truth and lying. On the other hand, you have a choice of whether to make your response clear or vague. Figure 6–11 displays these choices. After considering the alternatives, it's clear that the first choice—an equivocal, true response—is far preferable to the other choices in several respects. First, it spares the receiver from embarrassment. For example, rather than flatly saying "no" to an unappealing invitation, it may be kinder to say "I have other plans"—even if those plans are to stay home and watch TV.

Besides saving face for the recipient, honest equivocation can be less stressful for the sender than either telling the truth bluntly or lying. Because equivocation is often easier to take than the cold, hard truth, it spares the teller from feeling guilty. It's less taxing on the conscience to say, "I've never tasted anything like this" than to say, "this meal tastes terrible," even though the latter comment is more precise. Few people *want* to lie, and equivocation provides an alternative to deceit.[60]

A study by communication researcher Sandra Metts and her colleagues shows how equivocation can save face in difficult situations.[61] Several hundred college students where asked how they would turn down the unwanted sexual overtures

---

CULTURAL IDIOM

less taxing on: less demanding of

from a person whose feelings were important to them: either a close friend, a prospective date, or a dating partner. The majority of students chose a diplomatic reaction ("I just don't think I'm ready for this right now") as being more face-saving and comfortable than a direct statement like "I just don't feel sexually attracted to you." The diplomatic reaction seemed sufficiently clear to get the message across but not so blunt as to embarrass or even humiliate the other person. (Interestingly, men said they would be able to handle a direct rejection more comfortably than women. The researchers suggest that one reason for the difference is that men stereotypically initiate sexual offers and thus are more likely to expect rejection.)

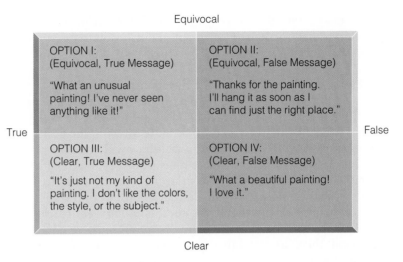

Figure 6–11 Dimensions of Truthfulness and Equivocation

Besides preventing embarrassment, equivocal language can also save the speaker from being caught lying. If a potential employer asks about your grades during a job interview, you would be safe saying, "I had a B average last semester," even though your overall grade average is closer to C. The statement isn't a complete answer, but it is honest as far as it goes. As one team of researchers put it, "Equivocation is neither a false message nor a clear truth, but rather an alternative used precisely when both of these are to be avoided."[62]

Given these advantages, it's not surprising that most people will usually choose to equivocate rather than tell a lie. In a series of experiments, subjects chose between telling a face-saving lie, telling the truth, and equivocating. Only 6 percent chose the lie, and between 3 and 4 percent chose the hurtful truth. By contrast, over 90 percent chose the equivocal response.[63] People *say* they prefer truth-telling to equivocating,[64] but given the choice, they prefer to finesse the truth.

HINTING Hints are more direct than equivocal statements. Whereas an equivocal message isn't necessarily aimed at changing others' behavior, a hint seeks to get the desired response from others. Some hints are designed to save the receiver from embarrassment:[65]

FACE-SAVING HINT	**DIRECT STATEMENT**
These desserts are terribly overpriced.	You're too overweight to be ordering dessert.
I know you're busy; I'd better let you go.	I'm bored. I want to get out of this conversation.

Other hints are strategies for saving the sender from embarrassment:

FACE-SAVING HINT	**DIRECT STATEMENT**
I'm pretty sure that smoking isn't permitted here.	Your smoking bothers me.

CULTURAL IDIOM

face-saving: protective of one's dignity

Gee, it's almost lunchtime. Have you ever eaten at that new Italian restaurant around the corner?

I'd like to invite you out for lunch, but I don't want to risk a "no" answer to my invitation.

CULTURAL IDIOM

go right over the head of: be difficult for someone to understand

The success of a hint depends on the other person's ability to pick up the unexpressed message. Your subtle remarks might go right over the head of an insensitive receiver—or one who chooses not to respond to them. If this does happen, you still have the choice to be more direct. If the costs of a straightforward message seem too high, you can withdraw without risk.

It's easy to see why people choose hints, equivocations, and white lies instead of complete self-disclosure. These strategies provide a way to manage difficult situations that is easier than the alternatives for both the speaker and the receiver of the message. In this sense, successful liars, equivocators, and hinters can be said to possess a certain kind of communicative competence. On the other hand, there are certainly times when honesty is the right approach, even if it's painful. At times like these, evaders could be viewed as lacking the competence or the integrity to handle a situation most effectively.

Are hints, benign lies, and equivocations an ethical alternative to self-disclosure? Some of the examples in these pages suggest the answer is a qualified "yes." Many social scientists and philosophers agree. Some argue that the morality of a speaker's *motives* for lying ought to be judged, not the deceptive act itself.[66] Others ask whether the *effects* of a lie will be worth the deception. Ethicist Sissela Bok offers some circumstances where deception may be justified: doing good, avoiding harm, and protecting a larger truth.[67] Perhaps the right questions to ask, then, are whether an indirect message is truly in the interests of the receiver, and whether this sort of evasion is the only effective way to behave. Bok suggests another way to check the justifiability of a lie: Imagine how others would respond if they knew what you were really thinking or feeling. Would they accept your reasons for not disclosing?

ETHICAL CHALLENGE

The Ethics of Lying and Equivocating

Research shows that virtually everyone hints, lies, and equivocates for a variety of reasons. Explore the ethical legitimacy of your lies and equivocations by following these directions:

1. For a two-day period, keep track of:
   a. Your hints, lies, and equivocations.
   b. Your reason for taking one of these approaches in each situation.
   c. The consequences (for you and the other person) of avoiding self-disclosure.
2. Based on your analysis of the information collected in Step 1, identify the ethical legitimacy of each type of nondisclosing communication. Are any sorts of deception justifiable? Which sorts are not? How would you feel if you discovered the other person had not been straightforward with you under similar circumstances?

SKILL
BUILDER

Effective Self-Disclosure

Choose a self-disclosing message that is important enough for you to consider sharing. Use the guidelines on pages 211–212 to craft the message in a way that maximizes the chances of having it received successfully. Share your message strategy with classmates, and get their opinion of whether it needs refinement.

SUMMARY

An interpersonal relationship is one in which two or more people meet one another's social needs to a greater or lesser degree. Communication can be considered interpersonal either according to the context or the quality of interaction. Regardless of which definition is used, communication in relationships consists of both content and relational messages. Explicit relational messages are termed *metacommunication*.

Intimacy is a powerful need for most people. Intimacy can be created and expressed in a variety of ways: physically, emotionally, intellectually, and through shared activities. The notion of levels of intimacy has varied according to historical period, culture, and gender. Along with the desire for closeness, a need for distance is equally important. These opposing drives lead to conflicting communication behavior at different stages in people's lives and their relationships. The challenge is to communicate in a way that strikes a balance between intimacy and distance.

Some communication theorists suggest that intimate relationships pass through a series of stages, each of which is characterized by a unique mode of communication. These stages fall into three broad phases: coming together, relational maintenance, and coming apart. Although the movement within and between these stages does follow recognizable patterns, the amount and direction of movement are not predetermined. Some relationships move steadily toward termination, whereas others shift backward and forward as the partners redefine their desires for intimacy and distance.

Self-disclosure is the process of deliberately revealing significant information about oneself that would not normally be known. The breadth and depth of self-disclosure can be described by the social penetration model. The Johari Window model reveals an individual's open, blind, hidden, and unknown areas. Complete self-disclosure is not common, nor is it always desirable. The chapter listed several guidelines to help determine when it is and is not appropriate. The chapter concluded by describing three widely used alternatives to self-disclosure: lies, equivocation, and hints. It discussed the conditions under which these alternatives can be appropriate.

RESOURCES

Print

Canary, Daniel J., and Laura Stafford. *Communication and Relational Maintenance*. San Diego: Academic Press, 1993.

This book helps to answer the question, "How do people communicate in order to maintain their personal relationships?" Several chapters address how communication operates in friendships, romances, and marriages. The book does an excellent job of showing that communication—both planned and unplanned—plays an essential role in keeping relationships operating successfully.

Chovil, Nicole. "Equivocation as an Interactional Event," in *The Dark Side of Interpersonal*

Communication, William R. Cupach and Brian H. Spitzberg, eds. Hillsdale, NJ: Erlbaum, 1994.

This chapter describes how equivocation can be a form of strategic ambiguity that greases the wheels of social interaction. It outlines the types of equivocal messages and identifies situations that elicit them.

Conville, Richard, and L. Edna Rogers, eds. *The Meaning of "Relationship" in Interpersonal Communication.* Westport, CT: Praeger, 1998.

The readings in this volume offer an excellent resource for exploring the nature of interpersonal relationships. Besides offering insights, the references in each chapter will direct serious students to more information on various dimensions of relational communication.

Knapp, Mark L., and Anita L. Vangelisti. *Interpersonal Communication and Human Relationships,* 4th ed. Boston: Allyn and Bacon, 2003.

This book provides a thorough model of Knapp's theory of relational stages, described in this chapter. It is an excellent source for readers interested in learning more about the rise and fall of interpersonal relationships.

Miller, Gerald R., and James B. Stiff. *Deceptive Communication.* Newbury Park, CA: Sage, 1993.

This brief book surveys the extensive research on deceptive messages, showing their pervasiveness in everyday communication. Separate chapters explore topics such as the characteristics of deceptive behavior and the inaccuracy of humans as lie detectors.

Montgomery, Barbara M., and Leslie A. Baxter, eds. *Dialectical Approaches to Studying Personal Relationships.* New York: Erlbaum, 1998.

This edited collection provides a useful look at how dialectics operate in a variety of interpersonal relationships.

Redmond, Mark V. *Interpersonal Communication: Readings in Theory and Research.* Fort Worth, TX: Harcourt Brace, 1995.

For serious students, this book is a valuable resource on information about communication in interpersonal relationships. Chapters by an impressive array of scholars address topics including relational stages, self-disclosure, communicative competence, interpersonal attraction, and interpersonal conflict.

Tannen, Deborah. *I Only Say This Because I Love You: How the Way We Talk Can Make or Break Family Relationships throughout Our Lives.* New York: Random House, 2001.

Tannen explains why talking about even the most innocuous subjects with family members can sometimes be so painful. She looks behind content issues and highlights relational themes that often trigger criticism, disapproval, and rejection on the one hand and pain on the other. Tannen also explains how some of the dialectical tensions described in this chapter operate, focusing especially on how family communication must balance the need for connection with the desire for control.

Wood, Julia T. *Gendered Relationships.* Mountain View, CA: Mayfield, 1996.

A useful collection of readings shows how gender affects relational communication in a variety of contexts and ways. Chapters examine the influence of gender on various types of relationships: personal (including friendship), romantic, and professional. Other chapters examine topics including interpersonal violence, sexual harassment, and communicating across class and race.

Films
Relational Stages

Annie Hall (1977). Rated PG.

Annie Hall is Woody Allen's autobiographical comedy of the rise and fall of the relationship between neurotic, intellectual comedian Alvie Singer (Allen) and the flaky Annie Hall (Diane Keaton). The film is ideally suited to illustrate the development and deterioration of an interpersonal relationship as it traces the romance between Alvie and Annie from their first meeting through courtship, bonding, disenchantment, and breakup. Seen through the eyes of Allen, the story makes two points: Enduring relationships are difficult to the point of near-impossibility, yet life without the search for relationships is unthinkable.

When Harry Met Sally (1989). Rated R.

The film follows Harry (Billy Crystal) and Sally (Meg Ryan) from their first meeting during college until they get together as a couple fifteen years later. When they first meet, Sally loathes Harry for his egotism and chauvinistic attitude toward women. Many years later they become friends and eventually fall in love. The story poses the question of whether men and women can be friends, or whether sex is bound to enter into the relationship. The treatment is humorous, but the question is a serious one. The development of Harry and Sally's relationship provides a good opportunity to compare Knapp's model of relational stages with Baxter and Montgomery's dialectical approach. The film is also useful for illustrating the progression of a relationship from impersonal to interpersonal.

Impersonal and Interpersonal Communication

Rain Man (1989). Rated R.

Charlie Babitt (Tom Cruise) is a fast-dealing car importer who, in his early thirties, discovers that he has an institutionalized autistic brother, Raymond (Dustin Hoffman). In an effort to get a share of their late father's estate, Charlie kidnaps Raymond, and the two drive across the country. As the journey progresses, Charlie's sensitivity and love toward Raymond grow. The film offers a moving portrait of the development of a relationship from an impersonal to an interpersonal level. At first, Charlie views Raymond only as an obstacle to acquiring his father's fortune, but as their journey progresses he grows to love his brother. The bond is especially touching because it requires Charlie to abandon his self-centered lifestyle. (Raymond also grows to care for Charlie, at least as much as his emotionally limited capabilities permit.) As Charlie's feelings change, his manner of treating other people as objects changes to a far more personally confirming style.

Intimacy

Shall We Dance? (1997). Rated PG (Japanese with English subtitles).

As the film opens, a narrator explains that in Japan couples don't go out hand in hand or say "I love you." As a result, ballroom dancing is regarded with great suspicion. Dancing with a spouse seems like a shockingly public display of personal behavior, and dancing with a stranger has overtones of intimacy that are virtually absent in the West.

The cultural significance of ballroom dancing sets the stage for this story. One night as he takes the train home from the office, a married salaryman, Shohei Sugiyama (Koji Yakusyo), spots a beautiful woman gazing pensively from the window of a dance school. Captivated by her mysterious allure, he signs up for ballroom dancing lessons and enters a world that is considered slightly illicit by the standards of Japanese society. Ashamed of his fascination with the beautiful and mysterious Mai (Tamiyo Kusakari) and his involvement in the world of ballroom dancing, Sugiyama tries to hide his activities from his loving wife, who soon hires a private investigator to discover an explanation for her husband's increasingly suspicious behavior.

As the story develops, Sugiyama and Mai slowly break through personal and cultural barriers to become close friends and confidants. Sugiyama (and the audience) also grows more fond and understanding of the other characters in the dance school, who first appeared rather odd. By the end of the film, these characters reach a degree of mutual understanding and closeness that is especially surprising and rewarding, given the cultural norms in Japan that discourage self-disclosure.

Besides telling a delightful story, *Shall We Dance?* not only introduces us to the ways in which notions of intimacy can vary from one culture to another; but also suggests that people everywhere flourish when they are able to develop close personal relationships.

Smoke (1995). Rated R.

This film about friendship shows that intimacy, especially between men, can be like smoke: sometimes barely visible, elusive, yet powerful. It introduces us to the connections among a variety of characters: Augie Wren (Harvey Keitel), who owns a New York cigar shop; Paul Benjamin (William Hurt), a forlorn writer still recovering from the death of his wife; Rashid Cole (Harold Perrineau

Jr.), a bright young man searching for his father and on the run from local thugs; Cyrus Cole (Forest Whitaker), the boy's father; and Ruby McNutt (Stockard Channing), who reappears in Augie's life after an eighteen-year absence to ask for help for their crack-addicted daughter.

These motley characters prove to be surprisingly decent people who grow to care for one another deeply, although they rarely disclose their feelings directly. They demonstrate that self-disclosure is not the only way to develop or express intimacy.

Self-Disclosure

The Breakfast Club (1985). Rated R.

Five high school students have broken school rules. As a punishment, they have to spend a full Saturday together in the school library. The students are quite different: John (Judd Nelson) is a swaggering tough guy, Brian (Michael Anthony Hall) a studious nerd, Andrew (Emilio Estevez) an all-star wrestler, Claire (Molly Ringwald) a social queen, and Allison (Ally Sheedy) an insecure neurotic. At first the students squabble, but as the day goes on they reveal personal truths to one another and gradually come to appreciate each other's uniqueness. The pressures to avoid self-disclosure and the contrast between impersonal and interpersonal communication are well illustrated.

Il Postino (1995). Not rated (Italian with English subtitles).

Mario Ruoppolo (Massimo Troilsi) is a shy man whose provincial world on a small Italian island expands when he begins delivering mail to Nobel Prize-winning poet Pablo Neruda (played by Philippe Noiret). Quoting Neruda's poetry and mimicking the great man's style, Ruoppolo wins the heart of the beautiful Beatrice Russo (Maria Grazia Cucinotta).

But the victory seems hollow: Does Beatrice love the real Ruoppolo, or has she fallen for an actor playing a role? Will her feelings change if she discovers the source of Ruoppolo's poetry? But the story is not over: Although Ruoppolo is not a creative genius himself, his own gifts develop as he is bathed in Neruda's poetry and friendship. This beautiful, touching film raises interesting questions about the nature of self-disclosure and personal identity.

CONTENTS

KEY TERMS

assertive
certainty
communication climate
compromise
confirming responses
conflict
controlling message
crazymaking
deescalatory conflict spiral
descriptive communication
direct aggression
disconfirming responses
empathy
equality
escalatory conflict spirals
evaluative communication
Gibb categories
"I" language
indirect communication
lose–lose problem solving
neutrality
nonassertion
passive aggression
problem orientation
provisionalism
spiral
spontaneity
strategy
superiority
win–lose problem solving
win–win problem solving
"you" language

AFTER STUDYING THE MATERIAL IN THIS CHAPTER . . .

YOU SHOULD UNDERSTAND:

1. The role of communication climate in interpersonal relationships.

2. Types of messages that contribute to confirming and disconfirming climates.

3. The unavoidable, but potentially problematic, role of conflict in interpersonal relationships.

4. Characteristics of nonassertive, directly aggressive, passive-aggressive, indirect, and assertive communications.

5. The influence of culture and gender on conflict styles.

6. The differences between win–lose, lose–lose, compromising, and win–win approaches to conflict resolution.

YOU SHOULD BE ABLE TO:

1. Identify disconfirming messages and replace them with confirming ones, using the Gibb categories of supportive communication.

2. Describe the degree to which you use nonassertive, directly aggressive, passive-aggressive, indirect, and assertive messages and choose more satisfying responses as necessary.

3. Compose and deliver an assertive message, using the behavior-interpretation-feeling-consequence-intention format.

4. Apply the win–win approach to an interpersonal conflict.

IMPROVING INTERPERSONAL RELATIONSHIPS

No matter how satisfying your relationships, there are almost certainly ways they could be better. At times even the best of friends, the closest of families, and the most productive coworkers become dissatisfied. Sometimes the people involved are unhappy with each other. At other times, one person's problem is unrelated to the relationship. In either case, there's a desire to communicate in a way that makes matters better.

The ideas in this chapter can help you improve the important relationships in your life. We'll begin by talking about the factors that make communication "climates" either positive or negative. Next we'll focus on methods for understanding and resolving interpersonal conflicts.

COMMUNICATION CLIMATES IN INTERPERSONAL RELATIONSHIPS

Personal relationships are a lot like the weather. Some are fair and warm, whereas others are stormy and cold; some are polluted, and others healthy. Some relationships have stable climates, whereas others change dramatically—calm one moment and turbulent the next. You can't measure the interpersonal climate by looking at a thermometer or glancing at the sky, but it's there nonetheless. Every relationship has a feeling, a pervasive mood that colors the interactions of the participants. The term **communication climate** refers to the emotional tone of a relationship. A climate doesn't involve specific activities as much as the way people feel about each other as they carry out those activities. Consider two interpersonal communication classes, for example. Both meet for the same length of time and follow the same syllabus. It's easy to imagine how one of these classes might be a friendly, comfortable place to learn, whereas the other might be cold and tense—even hostile. The same principle holds for families, coworkers, and other relationships: Communication climates are a function more of the way people feel about one another than of the tasks they perform.

Confirming and Disconfirming Messages

What makes some climates positive and others negative? A short but accurate answer is that the *communication climate is determined by the degree to which people see themselves as valued.* When we believe others view us as important, we are likely to feel good about our relationship. On the other hand, the relational climate suffers when we think others don't appreciate or care about us.

Messages that show you are valued have been called **confirming responses.**[1] In one form or another, confirming responses say "you exist," "you matter," "you're important." Actually, it's an oversimplification to talk about one type of confirming message. In truth, confirming communication occurs on three increasingly positive levels:[2]

■ *Recognition* The most fundamental act of confirmation is to recognize the other person. Recognition seems easy and obvious, and yet there are many times when we do not respond to others on this basic level. Failure to write or visit a friend is a common example. So is failure to return a phone message. Avoiding eye contact and not approaching someone you know on campus, at a party, or on the street send a negative message. Of course, this lack of recognition may simply be an oversight. You might not notice your friend, or the pressures of work and school might prevent you from staying in touch. Nonetheless, if the other person *perceives* you as avoiding contact, the message has the effect of being disconfirming.

- *Acknowledgment* Acknowledging the ideas and feelings of others is a stronger form of confirmation. Listening is probably the most common form of acknowledgment. Of course, counterfeit listening—ambushing, stage hogging, pseudolistening, and so on—has the opposite effect of acknowledgment. More active acknowledgment includes asking questions, paraphrasing, and reflecting. Not surprisingly, employees rate managers who solicit their suggestions highly—even when the managers don't accept every suggestion.[3] As you read in Chapter 7, reflecting the speaker's thoughts and feelings can be a powerful way to offer support when others have problems.

- *Endorsement* Whereas acknowledgment means you are interested in another's ideas, endorsement means that you agree with them. It's easy to see why endorsement is the strongest type of confirming message, because it communicates the highest form of valuing. The most obvious form of endorsement is agreeing. Fortunately, it isn't necessary to agree completely with another person in order to endorse her or his message. You can probably find something in the message that you endorse. "I can see why you were so angry," you might reply to a friend, even if you don't approve of his outburst. Of course, outright praise is a strong form of endorsement and one you can use surprisingly often after you look for opportunities to compliment others. Nonverbal endorsement can also enhance the quality of a relational climate. For example, women rate men who agree with them as more physically attractive than those who fail to do so.[4]

It's hard to overstate the importance of confirming messages. For instance, a positive climate is the best predictor of marital satisfaction.[5] Satisfied couples have a 5:1 ratio of positive to negative statements, whereas the ratio for dissatisfied partners is 1:1.[6] Positive, confirming messages are just as important in families. For example, the satisfaction that siblings feel with one another drops sharply as aggressive, disconfirming messages increase.[7]

In contrast to confirming communication, messages that deny the value of others have been labeled **disconfirming responses.** These show a lack of regard for the other person either by disputing or ignoring some important part of that person's message.[8] *Disagreement* can certainly be disconfirming, especially if it goes beyond disputing the other person's ideas and attacks the speaker personally. However, disagreement is not the most damaging kind of disconfirmation. It may be tough to hear someone say, "I don't think that's a good idea," but a personal attack like "You're crazy" is even tougher to hear. Far worse than disagreements are responses that *ignore* others' ideas—or even their existence.

As you read in Chapter 6, every message has a relational dimension along with its content. This means that, whether or not we are aware of the fact, we send and receive confirming and disconfirming messages virtually whenever we communicate. Serious conversations about our relationships may not be common, but we convey our attitudes about one another even when we talk about everyday matters. In other words, it isn't *what* we communicate about that shapes a relational climate so much as *how* we speak and act toward one another.

It's important to note that disconfirming messages, like virtually every other kind of communication, are a matter of perception. Communicators are likely to downplay the significance of a potentially hurtful message that they consider to be unintentional.[9] On the other hand, even messages that aren't intended to devalue the other person can be interpreted as disconfirming. Your failure to return a phone call or respond to the letter of an out-of-town friend might simply be the result of a busy schedule; but if the other person views the lack of contact as a sign that you don't value the relationship, the effect can be powerful.

> *The worst sin towards our fellow creatures is not to hate them, but to be indifferent to them; that's the essence of inhumanity.*
>
> George Bernard Shaw

> *Listening, not imitation, may be the sincerest form of flattery.*
>
> Dr. Joyce Brothers

INVITATION TO INSIGHT

Your Confirming and Disconfirming Messages

You can gain an understanding of how confirming and disconfirming messages create communication spirals by trying the following exercise.

1. Identify the communication climate of an important personal relationship. Using weather metaphors (sunny, gloomy, calm) may help.
2. Describe several confirming or disconfirming messages that have helped create and maintain the climate. Be sure to identify both verbal and nonverbal messages.
3. Show how the messages you have identified have created either escalatory or deescalatory conflict spirals. Describe how these spirals reach limits and what events cause them to stabilize or reverse.
4. Describe what you can do to either maintain the existing climate (if positive) or change it (if negative). Again, list both verbal and nonverbal behaviors.

How Communication Climates Develop

As soon as two people start to communicate, a relational climate begins to develop. If the messages are confirming, the climate is likely to be a positive one. If they disconfirm one another, the climate is likely to be hostile, cold, or defensive.

Verbal messages certainly contribute to the tone of a relationship, but many climate-shaping messages are nonverbal. The very act of approaching others is confirming, whereas avoiding them can be disconfirming. Smiles or frowns, the presence or absence of eye contact, tone of voice, the use of personal space—all these and other cues send messages about how the parties feel toward one another.

After a climate is formed, it can take on a life of its own and grow in a self-

"*I need a more interactive you.*"

perpetuating **spiral**: a reciprocating communication pattern in which each person's message reinforces the other's.[10] In positive spirals, one partner's confirming message leads to a similar response from the other person. This positive reaction leads the first person to be even more reinforcing. Negative spirals are just as powerful, though they leave the partners feeling worse about themselves and each other. Research shows how spirals operate in relationships to reinforce the principle that "what goes around comes around." In one study of married couples, each spouse's response in conflict situations was similar to the other's statement.[11] Conciliatory statements (for example, supporting, accepting responsibilities, agreeing) were likely to be followed by conciliatory responses. Confrontational acts (such as criticism, hostile questions, and faultfinding) were likely to trigger aggressive responses. The same pattern held for other kinds of messages: Avoidance begat avoidance, analysis begat analysis, and so on.

Escalatory conflict spirals are the most visible way that disconfirming messages reinforce one another.[12] One attack leads to another until a skirmish escalates into a full-fledged battle. Although they are less obvious, **deescalatory conflict spirals** can also be destructive.[13] Rather than fighting, the parties slowly lessen their dependence on one another, withdraw, and become less invested in the relationship.

Spirals rarely go on indefinitely. Most relationships pass through cycles of progression and regression. If the spiral is negative, partners may find the exchange growing so unpleasant that they switch from negative to positive messages without discussing the matter. In other cases they may engage in metacommunication. "Hold on," one might say. "This is getting us nowhere." In some cases, however, partners pass the "point of no return," leading to the breakup of a relationship. Even positive spirals have their limit: Even the best relationships go through periods of conflict and withdrawal, although a combination of time and communication skills can eventually bring the partners back into greater harmony.

Creating Positive Communication Climates

It's easy to see how disconfirming messages can pollute a communication climate. But what are some alternative ways of communicating that encourage positive relationships? The work of Jack Gibb gives a picture of what kinds of messages lead to both positive and negative spirals.[14]

After observing groups for several years, Gibb was able to isolate six types of defense-arousing communication and six contrasting behaviors that seemed to reduce the level of threat and defensiveness. The **Gibb categories** are listed in Table 7–1. Using the supportive types of communication and avoiding the defensive ones will increase the odds of creating and maintaining positive communication climates in your relationships.

EVALUATION VERSUS DESCRIPTION The first type of defense-provoking behavior Gibb noted was **evaluative**

> **CULTURAL IDIOM**
>
> **"what goes around, comes around":** expect to be treated the way you treat others
>
> **"hold on":** wait
>
> **the "point of no return":** the stage in a process after which there is no possibility of stopping or turning back

TABLE 7–1 The Gibb Categories of Defensive and Supportive Behaviors

Defensive Behaviors	Supportive Behaviors
1. Evaluation	1. Description
2. Control	2. Problem Orientation
3. Strategy	3. Spontaneity
4. Neutrality	4. Empathy
5. Superiority	5. Equality
6. Certainty	6. Provisionalism

communication. Most people become irritated at judgmental statements, which they are likely to interpret as indicating a lack of regard. Evaluative language has often been described as **"you" language** because most such statements contain an accusatory use of that word. For example,

- You don't know what you're talking about.
- You're not doing your best.
- You smoke too much.

Unlike evaluative "you" language, **descriptive communication** focuses on the speaker's thoughts and feelings instead of judging the listener. One form of descriptive communication is **"I" language.**[15] Instead of putting the emphasis on judging another's behavior, the descriptive speaker simply explains the personal effect of the other's action. For instance, instead of saying, "You talk too much," a descriptive communicator would say, "When you don't give me a chance to say what's on my mind, I get frustrated." Notice that statements such as this include an account of the other person's behavior plus an explanation of its effect on the speaker and a description of the speaker's feelings.

CONTROL VERSUS PROBLEM ORIENTATION   A second defense-provoking message involves some attempt to control another. A **controlling message** occurs when a sender seems to be imposing a solution on the receiver with little regard for the receiver's needs or interests. The object of controls can range from where to eat dinner or what TV show to watch to whether to remain in a relationship or how to spend a large sum of money. Whatever the situation, people who act in controlling ways create a defensive climate. Researchers have found that the communication of abusive couples was characterized by opposition to one another's viewpoints.[16] None of us likes to feel that our ideas are worthless and that nothing we say will change other people's determination to have their way—yet this is precisely the attitude a controller communicates. Whether done with words, gestures, tone of voice, or some other channel; whether control is accomplished through status, insistence on obscure or irrelevant rules, or physical power, the controller generates hostility wherever he or she goes. The unspoken message such behavior communicates is "I know what's best for you, and if you do as I say, we'll get along."

Source: © 1994 by NAS. Reprinted by special permission of North America Syndicate.

A Comparison of Dialogue and Debate

People will always have disagreements. The way they handle them both creates and reflects relational climates. The following list contrasts the very different types of communication that characterize dialogue and debate. As you review them, consider how dialogue confirms the other person, even in the face of disagreement, whereas debate is fundamentally disconfirming.

Dialogue is collaborative: Two or more sides work together toward common understanding.
Debate is oppositional: Two sides oppose each other and attempt to prove each other wrong.

In dialogue, finding common ground is the goal.
In debate, winning is the goal.

Dialogue enlarges and possibly changes the participants' points of view.
Debate affirms the participants' own points of view.

Dialogue reveals assumptions for reevaluation.
Debate defends assumptions as truth.

Dialogue causes introspection about one's own position.
Debaters critique the others' positions.

Dialogue opens the possibility of reaching a better solution than any of the original ones.
Debate defends one's own positions as the best and excludes other positions.

Dialogue involves a genuine concern for the other person and seeks not to alienate or offend.
Debate involves countering the other position without focusing on feelings or relationships and often belittles or deprecates the other position.

By contrast, in **problem orientation,** communicators focus on finding a solution that satisfies both their needs and those of the others involved. The goal here isn't to "win" at the expense of your partner but rather to work out some arrangement in which everybody feels like a winner. The sidebar "A Comparison of Dialogue and Debate" above shows several important differences between controlling and problem-oriented communication. The last section of this chapter has a great deal to say about "win–win" problem solving as a way to find problem-oriented solutions.

STRATEGY VERSUS SPONTANEITY   The third communication behavior that Gibb identified as creating a poor communication climate is **strategy.** A more accurate term to describe this type of behavior is *manipulation.* Manipulation explains why most people detest coworkers who act friendly to peers while acting friendly and helpful to the boss.[17] One of the surest ways to make people defensive is to get caught trying to manipulate them. The fact that you tried to trick them instead of just asking for what you wanted is enough to build mistrust. Nobody likes to be a guinea pig or a sucker, and even well-meant manipulation can cause bad feelings.

Spontaneity is the label Gibb used as a contrast to strategy. A better term might be *honesty.* Despite the misleading label, spontaneous communication needn't be blurted out as soon as an idea comes to you. You might want to plan the wording of your message carefully so that you can express yourself clearly. The important thing is to be honest. A straightforward message may not always get what you want, but in the long run it's likely to pay dividends in a positive relational climate.

> **CULTURAL IDIOM**
>
> **to be a guinea pig or a sucker:** to be taken advantage of
>
> **in the long run:** over a period of time

NEUTRALITY VERSUS EMPATHY   Gibb used the term **neutrality** to describe a fourth behavior that arouses defensiveness. Probably a more descriptive term would be *indifference*. A neutral attitude is disconfirming because it communicates a lack of concern for the welfare of another and implies that the other person isn't very important to you.

The damaging effects of neutrality become apparent when you consider the hostility that most people have for the large, impersonal organizations with which they have to deal: "They think of me as a number instead of a person"; "I felt as if I were being handled by computers and not human beings." These two common statements reflect reactions to being handled in an indifferent way.

Empathy is an approach that confirms the other person. Having empathy means accepting another's feelings, putting yourself in another's place. This doesn't mean you need to agree with that person. Gibb noted the importance of nonverbal messages in communicating empathy. He found that facial and bodily expressions of concern are often more important to the receiver than the words used.

SUPERIORITY VERSUS EQUALITY   **Superiority** is a fifth type of communication that creates a defensive climate. When it seems that people believe they are better than we are, a defensive response is likely. We turn them off, justify ourselves, or argue with them in our minds. Sometimes we choose to change the subject verbally or even walk away. Another common reaction to superiority is to counterattack in an attempt to cut the offender down to size.

We often meet people who possess knowledge or talents greater than ours. But your own experiences will tell you that it isn't necessary for these people to project an attitude of superiority. Gibb found ample evidence that many who have superior skills and talents are capable of conveying an attitude of **equality** rather than superiority. Such people communicate that, although they may have greater talent in certain areas, they see others as having just as much worth as human beings.

SKILL
BUILDER

Constructing Supportive Messages

This exercise will give you practice in sending confirming messages that exhibit Gibb's categories of supportive behavior. You will find that you can communicate in a constructive way—even in conflict situations.

1. Begin by recalling at least two situations in which you found yourself in an escalatory conflict spiral.
2. Using the Gibb categories, identify your defense-arousing messages, both verbal and nonverbal.
3. Now reconstruct the situations, writing a script in which you replace the defense-arousing behaviors with the supportive alternatives outlined by Gibb.
4. If it seems appropriate, you may choose to approach the other people in each of the situations you have described here and attempt to replay the exchange. Otherwise, describe how you could use the supportive approach you developed in Step 3 in future exchanges.

CERTAINTY VERSUS PROVISIONALISM   *Dogmatism* is another term for the behavior Gibb calls **certainty.** Messages that suggest the speaker's mind is already made up are likely to generate defensiveness.

In contrast to dogmatic communication is **provisionalism,** in which people may have strong opinions but are willing to acknowledge that they don't have a corner on the truth and will change their stand if another position seems more reasonable.

There is no guarantee that using Gibb's supportive, confirming approach to communication will build a positive climate. The other person may simply not be receptive. But the chances for a constructive relationship will be greatest when communication consists of the kind of constructive approach described here. Besides boosting the odds of getting a positive response from others, supportive communication can leave you feeling better in a variety of ways: more in control of your relationships, more comfortable, and more positive toward others.

MANAGING INTERPERSONAL CONFLICT

Even the most supportive communication climate won't guarantee complete harmony. Regardless of what we may wish for or dream about, a conflict-free world just doesn't exist. Even the best communicators, the luckiest people, are bound to wind up in situations when their needs don't match the needs of others. Money, time, power, sex, humor, aesthetic taste, as well as a thousand other issues, arise and keep us from living in a state of perpetual agreement.

For many people the inevitability of conflict is a depressing fact. They think that the existence of ongoing conflict means that there's little chance for happy relationships with others. Effective communicators know differently, however. They realize that although it's impossible to *eliminate* conflict, there are ways to *manage* it effectively. And those effective communicators know the subject of this chapter—that managing conflict skillfully can open the door to healthier, stronger, and more satisfying relationships.

The Nature of Conflict

Whatever forms they may take, all interpersonal conflicts share certain similarities. Joyce Frost and William Wilmot provide a thorough definition of *conflict.* They state that **conflict** is an *expressed struggle between at least two interdependent parties who perceive incompatible goals, scarce rewards, and interference from the other parties in achieving their goals.*[18] A closer look at the various parts of this definition helps to develop a clearer idea of how conflicts operate.

EXPRESSED STRUGGLE   A conflict doesn't exist unless both parties know that some disagreement exists. You may be upset for months because a neighbor's loud stereo keeps you from getting to sleep at night, but no conflict exists between the two of you until the neighbor learns about your problem. Of course, the expressed struggle doesn't have to be verbal. You can show your displeasure with somebody without saying a word. Giving a dirty look, using the silent

CULTURAL IDIOM

mind is already made up: will not waiver from one's opinion

boosting the odds of: increasing the chances of success

to wind up in: to end up being in

open the door to: remve barriers to

Coming out of a meeting they had attended together, the Anglican Archbishop offered the Roman Catholic Cardinal a ride in his limousine. "After all," said the Anglican Archbishop, "we are both engaged in God's work." "Yes," replied the Cardinal, "you in your way and I in His!"

treatment, and avoiding the other person are all ways of expressing yourself. But one way or another, both parties must know that a problem exists before they're in conflict.

PERCEIVED INCOMPATIBLE GOALS All conflicts look as if one party's gain will be another's loss. For instance, consider the neighbor whose stereo keeps you awake at night. Does somebody have to lose? A neighbor who turns down the noise loses the enjoyment of hearing the music at full volume; but if the neighbor keeps the volume up, then you're still awake and unhappy.

But the goals in this situation really aren't completely incompatible—solutions do exist that allow both parties to get what they want. For instance, you could achieve peace and quiet by closing your windows and getting the neighbor to do the same. You might use a pair of earplugs. Or perhaps the neighbor could get a set of earphones and listen to the music at full volume without bothering anyone. If any of these solutions proves workable, then the conflict disappears.

Unfortunately, people often fail to see mutually satisfying answers to their problems. And as long as they *perceive* their goals to be mutually exclusive, then, although the conflict is unnecessary, it is still very real.

PERCEIVED SCARCE REWARDS In a conflict, people believe there isn't enough of something to go around. The most obvious example of a scarce resource is money—a cause of many conflicts. If a person asks for a raise in pay and the boss would rather keep the money or use it to expand the business, then the two parties are in conflict.

Time is another scarce commodity. As authors and family men, both of us are constantly in the middle of struggles about how to use the limited time we have to spend. Should we work on this book? Visit with our wives? Play with our kids? Enjoy the luxury of being alone? With only twenty-four hours in a day we're bound to end up in conflicts with our families, editors, students, and friends—all of whom want more of our time than we have available to give.

INTERDEPENDENCE However antagonistic they might feel toward each other, the parties in a conflict are usually dependent on each other. The welfare and satisfaction of one depend on the actions of another. If this weren't true, then even in the face of scarce resources and incompatible goals there would be no need for conflict. Interdependence exists between conflicting nations, social groups, organizations, friends, and lovers. In each case, if the two parties didn't need each other to solve the problem, both would go their separate ways. In fact, many conflicts go unresolved because the parties fail to understand their interdependence. One of the first steps toward resolving a conflict is to take the attitude that "we're all in this together."

Styles of Expressing Conflict

Communication scholars have identified a wide range of ways communicators handle conflicts.[19] Table 7–2 describes five ways people can act when their needs are not met. Each one has very different characteristics.

NONASSERTION **Nonassertion** is the inability or unwillingness to express thoughts or feelings in a conflict. Sometimes nonassertion comes from a lack of

The history of man is replete with mechanisms and attempts to control aggression. People have tried to pray it away, wish it away, or play it away. More recently they have tried to psychoanalyze it away. But it does not seem to go away.

George Bach and Herb Goldberg
Creative Aggression

TABLE 7–2 Individual Styles of Conflict					
	Nonassertive	**Directly Aggressive**	**Passive Aggressive**	**Indirect**	**Assertive**
Approach to Others	I'm not okay, you're okay.	I'm okay, you're not okay.	I'm okay, you're not okay.	I'm okay, you're not okay. (But I'll let you think you are.)	I'm okay, you're okay.
Decision Making	Lets others choose.	Chooses for others. They know it.	Chooses for others. They don't know it.	Chooses for others. They don't know it.	Chooses for self.
Self-Sufficiency	Low	High or low	Looks high but usually low	High or low	Usually high
Behavior in Problem Situations	Flees; gives in	Outright attack	Concealed attack	Strategic, oblique	Direct confrontation
Response of Others	Disrespect, guilt, anger, frustration	Hurt, defensiveness, humiliation	Confusion, frustration, feelings of manipulation	Unknowing compliance or resistance	Mutual respect
Success Pattern	Succeeds by luck or charity of others	Beats out others	Wins by manipulation	Gains unwitting compliance of others	Attempts "win–win" solutions

Adapted with permission from *The Assertive Woman* © 1970, 1987, 1997, and 2000, by Stanlee Phelps and Nancy Austin, San Luis Obispo, CA: *Impact,* 1975, p. 11; and Gerald Piaget, American Orthopsychiatric Association, 1975. Further reproduction prohibited.

confidence. At other times, people lack the awareness or skill to use a more direct means of expression. Sometimes people know how to communicate in a straightforward way but choose to behave nonassertively.

Nonassertion is a surprisingly common way of dealing with conflicts. One survey examined the conflict level of husbands and wives in normal "nondistressed" marriages. Over a five-day period, spouses reported that their partner engaged in an average of thirteen behaviors that were "displeasurable" to them but that they had only *one* confrontation during the same period.[20]

Nonassertion can take a variety of forms. One is *avoidance*—either physical (steering clear of a friend after having an argument) or conversational (changing the topic, joking, or denying that a problem exists). People who avoid conflicts usually believe it's easier to put up with the status quo than to face the problem head-on and try to solve it. *Accommodation* is another type of nonassertive response. Accommodators deal with conflict by giving in, putting the other's needs ahead of their own.

Despite the obvious drawbacks of nonassertion, there are situations when accommodating or avoiding is a sensible approach. Avoidance may be the best course if a conflict is minor and short-lived. For example, you might let a friend's annoying grumpiness pass without saying anything, knowing that he is having one of his rare bad days. Likewise, you might not complain to a neighbor whose lawn sprinklers occasionally hit your newly washed car. You may also reasonably choose to keep quiet if the conflict occurs in an unimportant relationship, as with an acquaintance whose language you find offensive but whom you don't see often. Finally, you might choose to keep quiet if the risk of speaking up is too great: getting fired from a job you can't afford to lose, being humiliated in public, or even risking physical harm.

Like avoidance, accommodation can also be appropriate, especially in cases when the other person's needs may be more important than yours. For instance, if a friend wants to have a serious talk and you feel playful, you'd most likely honor your friend's request, particularly if that person is facing some kind of crisis and wants your help. In most cases, however, nonassertive accommodators fail to assert themselves either because they don't value themselves sufficiently or because they don't know how to ask for what they want.

DIRECT AGGRESSION   Whereas nonasserters avoid conflicts, communicators who use **direct aggression** embrace them. A directly aggressive message confronts the other person in a way that attacks his or her position—and even the dignity of the receiver. Many directly aggressive responses are easy to spot: "You don't know what you're talking about." "That was a stupid thing to do." "What's the matter with you?" Other forms of direct aggression come more from nonverbal messages than from words. It's easy to imagine a hostile way of expressing statements like "What is it now?" or "I need some peace and quiet."

PASSIVE AGGRESSION   **Passive aggression** is far more subtle than its directly aggressive cousin. It occurs when a communicator expresses hostility in an obscure way. Psychologist George Bach terms this behavior **"crazymaking"**[21] and identifies several varieties. For example, "pseudoaccommodators" pretend to agree with you ("I'll be on time from now on") but don't comply with your request for change. "Guiltmakers" try to gain control by making you feel responsible for changing to suit them: "I really should be studying, but I'll give you a ride." "Jokers" use humor as a weapon and then hide behind the complaint ("Where's your sense of humor?") when you object. "Trivial tyrannizers" do small things to drive you crazy instead of confronting you with their complaints: "forgetting" to take phone messages, playing the music too loud, and so on. "Withholders" punish their partners by keeping back something valuable, such as courtesy, affection, or humor.

INDIRECT COMMUNICATION   The clearest communication is not necessarily the best approach. **Indirect communication** conveys a message in a roundabout manner, in order to save face for the recipient.[22] Although indirect com-

UNDERSTANDING COMMUNICATION TECHNOLOGY

Anonymous Messages via the Internet

Delivering unpleasant messages about matters such as personal hygiene, annoying habits, and _____ can be unpleasant and risky. The Internet now provides a way to deliver unpleasant messages anonymously to fellow workers, friends, family members, and lovers. All of the following sites operate in a similar manner: They send an untraceable e-mail to the target person without revealing your identity.

CoWorkerHints.com (www.coworkerhints.com) will send compassionate letters that aim to save face for the recipient. Justatip (www.justatip.com) has the capability to send messages—some serious and some gags—on a variety of topics including personal hygiene and annoying habits. Finally, give-a-hint.com (www.give-a-hint.com) attempts to lighten the tone of messages with cartoons and humor.

For most communicators, anonymous message sites like these are more of a curiosity than a legitimate way to deliver important messages. Still, they provide a tempting tool for those occasions where straightforward honesty is definitely not the best policy.

munication lacks the clarity of an aggressive or assertive message, it involves more initiative than nonassertion. It also has none of the hostility of passive-aggressive crazymaking. The goal is to get what you want without arousing the hostility of the other person. Consider the case of the neighbor's annoying dog. One indirect approach would be to strike up a friendly conversation with the owners and ask if anything you are doing is too noisy for them, hoping they would get the hint.

Because it saves face for the other party, indirect communication is often kinder than blunt honesty. If your guests are staying too long, it's probably kinder to yawn and hint about your big day tomorrow than to bluntly ask them to leave. Likewise, if you're not interested in going out with someone who has asked you for a date, it may be more compassionate to claim that you're busy than to say "I'm not interested in seeing you."

At other times we communicate indirectly in order to protect ourselves. You might, for example, test the waters by hinting instead of directly asking the boss for a raise, or by letting your partner know indirectly that you could use some affection instead of asking outright. At times like these, an oblique approach may get the message across while softening the blow of a negative response.

The advantages of protecting oneself and saving face for others help explain why indirect communication is the most common way people make requests.[23] The risk of an indirect message, of course, is that the other party will misunderstand you or fail to get the message at all. There are also times when the importance of an idea is so great that hinting lacks the necessary punch. When clarity and directness are your goals, an assertive approach is in order.

ASSERTION   **Assertive** people handle conflicts skillfully by expressing their needs, thoughts, and feelings clearly and directly but without judging others or dictating to them. They have the attitude that most of the time it is possible to resolve problems to everyone's satisfaction. Possessing this attitude and the skills to bring it about doesn't guarantee that assertive communicators will always get what they want, but it does give them the best chance of doing so. An additional benefit of such an approach is that whether or not it satisfies a particular need, it maintains the self-respect of both the assertors and those with

Not everything that is faced can be changed, but nothing can be changed until it is faced.

James Baldwin

whom they interact. As a result, people who manage their conflicts assertively may experience feelings of discomfort while they are working through the problem. They usually feel better about themselves and each other afterward—quite a change from the outcomes of no assertiveness or aggression.

ETHICAL CHALLENGE

Choosing an Ethical Conflict Style

At first glance, assertiveness seems like the most ethical communication style to use when you are faced with a conflict. The matter might not be so clear, however. Find out for yourself by following these steps.

1. Decide for yourself whether it is ever justifiable to use each of the other conflict styles: nonassertion, direct aggression, passive aggression, and indirect communication. Support your position on each style with examples from your own experience.
2. Explain your answer to classmates who disagree, and listen to their arguments.
3. After hearing positions that differ from yours, work with your classmates to develop a code of ethics for expressing conflict messages.

Characteristics of an Assertive Message

Knowing *about* assertive messages isn't the same as being able to express them. The next few pages will describe a method for communicating assertively. It works for a variety of messages: your hopes, problems, complaints, and appreciations. Besides giving you a way to express yourself directly, this format also makes it easier for others to understand you. A complete assertive message has five parts:

1. BEHAVIORAL DESCRIPTION   As you learned in Chapter 3, a behavioral description is an objective picture of the behavior in question, without any judging or editorializing. Put in terms of Gibb's categories, it uses descriptive rather than evaluative language. Notice the difference between a behavioral description and an evaluative judgment:

- *Behavioral description:* "You asked me to tell you what I really thought about your idea, and then when I gave it to you, you told me I was too critical."
- *Evaluative judgment:* "Don't be so touchy! It's hypocritical to ask for my opinion and then get mad when I give it to you."

Judgmental words like "touchy" and "hypocritical" invite a defensive reaction. The target of your accusation can reply "I'm not touchy or hypocritical!" It's harder to argue with the facts stated in an objective, behavioral description. Furthermore, the neutral language reduces the chances of a defensive reaction.

2. YOUR INTERPRETATION OF THE OTHER PERSON'S BEHAVIOR   After describing the behavior in question, an assertive message expresses the communicator's interpretation. The important thing to realize about interpretations is that they

CULTURAL IDIOM

touchy: quickly offended with little provocation

are *subjective*. That is, there is more than one interpretation that we can attach to any behavior. For example, look at these two interpretations of each of the preceding behavioral descriptions.

- *Interpretation A:* "Maybe you reacted defensively because my criticism sounded too detailed—because my standards seemed too high."
- *Interpretation B:* "Your reaction made me think that you really didn't want to know my opinion: You were just fishing for a compliment when you asked my opinion."

There's nothing wrong with making an interpretation. The key is to label it as such instead of suggesting that your interpretation is the correct one.

3. A DESCRIPTION OF YOUR FEELINGS   Reporting behavior and sharing your interpretations are important, but expressing your feelings adds a new dimension to a message. For example, consider the difference between these two responses:

- "When you kiss me and nibble on my ear while we're watching television *[behavior]*, I think you probably want to make love *[interpretation]*, and *I feel excited.*"
- "When you kiss me and nibble on my ear while we're watching television *[behavior]*, I think you probably want to make love *[interpretation]*, and *I feel disgusted.*"

Likewise, adding feelings to the situation we have been examining makes the assertive message more clear:

- "When you said I was too critical after you asked me for my honest opinion *[behavior]*, it seemed to me that you really didn't want to hear a critical remark, *and that made me feel stupid for being honest [feeling].*"

4. A DESCRIPTION OF THE CONSEQUENCES   A consequence statement explains what happens as a result of the behavior you have described, your interpretation, and the ensuing feeling. There are three kinds of consequences:

- *What happens to you, the speaker:*
  "When you forgot to give me the phone message yesterday *[behavior]*, I didn't know that my doctor's appointment was delayed, and I wound up sitting in the office for an hour when I could have been studying or working *[consequences]*. It seems to me that you don't care enough about how busy I am to even write a simple note *[interpretation]*, and that really makes me mad *[feeling]*."
  "I appreciate *[feeling]* the help you've given me on my term paper *[behavior]*. It tells me you think I'm on the right track *[interpretation]*, and *this gives me a boost to keep working on the idea [consequences].*"
- *What happens to the person you're addressing:*
  "When you have four or five drinks at a party after I've warned you to slow down *[behavior], you start to act strange: You make crude jokes that offend everybody, and on the way home you drive poorly [consequences].* For instance, last night you almost hit a phone pole while you were backing out of the driveway *[more behavior]*. I don't think you realize how differently you act *[interpretation]*, and I'm worried *[feeling]* about what will happen if you don't drink less."

CULTURAL IDIOM

fishing for: trying to get another to say what one wants to hear

- *What happens to others:*

  "You probably don't know because you couldn't hear her cry *[interpretation]*, but when you rehearse your lines for the play without closing the doors *[behavior], the baby can't sleep [consequence].* I'm especially concerned *[feeling]* about her because she's had a cold lately."

  "I thought you'd want to know *[interpretation]* that when you kid Bob about his height *[behavior],* he gets embarrassed *[feeling]* and *usually quiets down or leaves [consequences]."*

  A consequence statement for our ongoing example might sound like this:

- "When you said I was too critical after you asked me for my honest opinion *[behavior],* it seemed to me that you really didn't want to hear a critical remark. That made me feel stupid for being honest *[feeling]. Now I'm not sure whether I should tell you what I'm really thinking the next time you ask [consequence]."*

5. A STATEMENT OF YOUR INTENTIONS   Intention statements are the final element in the assertive format. They can communicate three kinds of messages:

- *Where you stand on an issue:*

  "When you call us 'girls' after I've told you we want to be called 'women' *[behavior],* I get the idea you don't appreciate how important the difference is to us *[interpretation]* and how demeaning it feels *[feeling].* Now I'm in an awkward spot: Either I have to keep bringing the subject up, or else drop it and feel bad *[consequence]. I want you to know how much this bothers me [intention]."*

  "I'm really grateful *[feeling]* to you for speaking up for me in front of the boss yesterday *[behavior].* That must have taken a lot of courage *[interpretation].* Knowing that you're behind me gives me a lot of confidence *[consequence],* and *I want you to know how much I appreciate your support [intention]."*

- *Requests of others:*

  "When you didn't call last night *[behavior]* I thought you were mad at me *[interpretation].* I've been thinking about it ever since *[consequence],* and I'm still worried *[feeling]. I'd like to know whether you are angry [intention]."*

  "I really enjoyed *[feeling]* your visit *[behavior],* and I'm glad you had a good time, too *[interpretation]. I hope you'll come again [intention]."*

- *Descriptions of how you plan to act in the future:*

  "I've asked you to repay the twenty-five dollars I lent you three times now *[behavior].* I'm getting the idea that you've been avoiding me *[interpretation],* and I'm pretty angry about it *[feeling].* I want you to know that unless we clear this up now, *you shouldn't expect me ever to lend you anything again [intention]."*

  "I'm glad *[feeling]* you liked *[interpretation]* the paper I wrote. *I'm thinking about taking your advanced writing class next term [intention]."*

Why is it so important to make your intentions clear? Because failing to do so often makes it hard for others to know what you want from them or how to act. Consider how confusing the following statements are because they lack a clear statement of intention.

- "Wow! A frozen Snickers. I haven't had one of those in years." (Does the speaker want a bite, or is she just making an innocent remark?)
- "Thanks for the invitation, but I really should study Saturday night." (Does the speaker want to be asked out again, or is he indirectly suggesting that he doesn't ever want to go out with you?)

- "To tell you the truth, I was asleep when you came by, but I should have been up anyway." (Is the speaker saying that it's okay to come by in the future, or is she hinting that she doesn't appreciate unannounced visitors?)

You can see from these examples that it's often hard to make a clear interpretation of another person's ideas without a direct statement of intention. Notice how much more direct statements become when the speakers make their position clear.

- "Wow! A frozen Snickers. I haven't had one of those in years. *If I hadn't already eaten, I'd sure ask for a bite.*"
- "Thanks for the invitation, but I really should study Saturday night. *I hope you'll ask me again soon.*"
- "To tell you the truth, I was asleep when you came by, but I should have been up anyway. *Maybe the next time you should phone before dropping in so I'll be sure to be awake.*"

In our ongoing example, adding an intention statement would complete the assertive message:

- "When you said I was too critical after you asked me for my honest opinion *[behavior]*, it seemed to me that you really didn't want to hear a critical remark. That made me feel stupid for being honest *[feeling]*. Now I'm not sure whether I should tell you what I'm really thinking the next time you ask *[consequence]*. I'd like to get it clear right now: Do you really want me to tell you what I think or not *[intention]*?"

Before you try to deliver messages using the assertive format outlined here, there are a few points to remember. First, it isn't necessary or even wise always to put the elements in the order described here. As you can see from reviewing the examples on the preceding pages, it's sometimes best to begin by stating your feelings. In other cases, you can start by sharing your intentions or interpretations or by describing consequences.

You also ought to word your message in a way that suits your style of speaking. Instead of saying, "I interpret your behavior to mean," you might choose to say, "I think . . ." or "It seems to me . . ." or perhaps "I get the idea. . . ." In the same way, you can express your intentions by saying, "I hope you'll understand (or do) . . ." or perhaps "I wish you would. . . ." It's important that you get your message across, but you should do it in a way that sounds and feels genuine to you.

Realize that there are some cases in which you can combine two elements in a single phrase. For instance, the statement ". . . and ever since then I've been wanting to talk to you" expresses both a consequence and an intention. In the same way, saying, ". . . and after you said that, I felt confused" expresses a consequence and a feeling. Whether you combine elements or state them separately, the important point is to be sure that each one is present in your statement.

Finally, you need to realize that it isn't always possible to deliver messages such as the ones here all at one time, wrapped up in neat paragraphs. It will often be necessary to repeat or restate one part many times before your receiver truly understands what you're saying. As you've already read, there are many types of psychological and physical noise that make it difficult for us to understand each other. Just remember: You haven't communicated successfully until the receiver of your message understands everything you've said. In communication, as in many other activities, patience and persistence are essential.

SKILL
BUILDER **Constructing Assertive Messages**

Develop your skill at expressing assertive messages by composing responses for each of the following situations:

1. A neighbor's barking dog is keeping you awake at night.
2. A friend hasn't repaid the twenty dollars she borrowed two weeks ago.
3. Your boss made what sounded like a sarcastic remark about the way you put school before work.
4. An out-of-town friend phones at the last minute to cancel the weekend you planned to spend together.

Now develop two assertive messages you could send to a real person in your life. Discuss how you could express these messages in a way that is appropriate for the situation and that fits your personal style.

Gender and Conflict Style

Men and women often approach conflicts differently. Even in childhood, males are more likely to be overtly aggressive, demanding, and competitive, whereas females are more cooperative, or at least less directly aggressive. Studies of children from preschool to early adolescence have shown that boys typically try to get their way by ordering one another around: "Lie down." "Get off my steps." "Gimme your arm." By contrast, girls are more likely to make proposals for action, beginning with the word "Let's." "Let's go find some." "Let's ask her, 'Do you have any bottles?'" "Let's move *these* out *first.*"[24] Whereas boys tell each other what role to take in pretend play ("Come on, be a doctor"), girls more commonly ask each other what role they want ("Will you be the patient for a few minutes?") or make a joint proposal ("We can both be doctors"). Furthermore, boys often make demands without offering

an explanation ("Look, man, I want the wire cutters right now"). By contrast, girls often give reasons for their suggestions ("We gotta *clean* 'em first . . .'cause they got germs"). When girls do have conflicts and disagreements, they are more likely to handle them via indirect aggression such as excluding someone from peer groups and complaining to others.[25] Gender isn't the only variable that determines how children will handle conflict. For example, girls are more likely to assert themself with boys when their friends are also present.[26]

Differences like these often persist into adulthood. One survey of college students revealed that men and women viewed conflicts in contrasting ways.[27] Regardless of their cultural background, female students described men as being concerned with power and more interested in content than relational issues. Phrases used to describe male conflict styles included "The most important thing to males in conflict is their egos"; "Men don't worry about feelings"; "Men are more direct." By contrast, women were described as being more concerned with maintaining the relationship during a conflict. Phrases used to describe female conflict styles included "Women are better listeners"; "Women try to solve problems without controlling the other person"; and "Females are more concerned with others' feelings."

Research confirms some of these reports.[28] Limited evidence suggests that women are more likely than men to use indirect strategies instead of confronting conflict head-on. They are also more likely to compromise and give in to maintain relational harmony. Men, by contrast, are more likely to use aggression to get their way.

After a relational conflict begins, men are often more likely than women to withdraw if they become uncomfortable or fail to get their way. The reason why men tend to avoid and women assert may have little to do with gender stereotypes: Women may demand more from their partners because they have more to gain by complaining.[29] In many cases, women make more demands because they have more to gain by doing so. When men benefit from the status quo, they protect their situation by withdrawing. To understand this "demand-withdraw" dynamic, consider a stereotypical housekeeping situation in which the woman complains because the man doesn't do his share. Speaking up has the potential to change the woman's plight for the better, whereas avoiding the discussion enables the man to maintain his situation.

Differences like these don't mean that men are incapable of forming good relationships. Instead, the stereotypical male notion of what a good relationship is differs from the stereotypical female notion. For some men, friendship and aggression aren't mutually exclusive. In fact, many strong male relationships are built around competition—at work or in athletics, for example. Women can be competitive, too, but they also are more likely to use logical reasoning and bargaining than aggression.[30] When men communicate with women, they become less aggressive and more cooperative than they are in all-male groups.

Most theorists suggest that the primary reason for differences in conflict style is socialization.[31] Some social scientists have proposed that a "threshold of assertiveness" may exist for people, especially women, allowing them to behave in an assertive way up to a point, but no further. Because women have been typically perceived as more compliant and cooperative, they may have seen themselves as reaching this threshold sooner than men, at which time they would back off. Because men have been expected to be more assertive—or even aggressive—they find it more comfortable to persist in seeking to meet their needs. As sex-role stereotyping becomes less common, it is likely that the differences between male and female conflict styles may become smaller.

Cultural Influences on Conflict

The ways in which people communicate during conflicts vary widely from one culture to another. The kind of rational, straight-talking, calm yet assertive approach that characterizes Euro-American disagreements is not the norm in other cultures.[32] For example, in traditional African-American culture, conflict is characterized by a greater tolerance for expressions of intense emotions than is the rational, calm model taught in mainstream U.S. culture.[33] Ethnicity isn't the only factor that shapes a communicator's preferred conflict style: The degree of assimilation also plays an important role. For example, Latino Americans with strong cultural identities tend to seek accommodation and compromise more than those with weaker cultural ties.[34]

Not surprisingly, people from different regions often manage conflict quite differently. In individualistic cultures like that of the United States, the goals, rights, and needs of each person are considered important, and most people would agree that it is an individual's right to stand up for himself or herself. By contrast, collectivist cultures (more common in Latin America and Asia) consider the concerns of the group to be more important than those of any individual. In these cultures, the kind of assertive behavior that might seem perfectly appropriate to a North American would seem rude and insensitive.

Another factor that distinguishes the assertiveness that is so valued by North Americans and northern Europeans from other cultures is the difference between high- and low-context cultural styles.[35] Low-context cultures like that of the United States place a premium on being direct and literal. By contrast, high-context cultures like that of Japan value self-restraint and avoid confrontation. Communicators in these cultures derive meaning from a variety of unspoken rules, such as the context, social conventions, and hints. Preserving and honoring the face of the other person are prime goals, and communicators go to great lengths to avoid any communication that might risk embarrassing a conversational partner. For this reason, what seems like "beating around the bush" to an American would be polite to an Asian. In Japan, for example, even a simple request like "close the door" would be too straightforward.[36] A more indirect statement like "it is somewhat cold today" would be more appropriate. To take a more important example, Japanese are reluctant to simply say "no" to a request. A more likely answer would be "Let me think about it for a while," which anyone familiar with Japanese culture would recognize as a refusal. When indirect communication is a cultural norm, it is unreasonable to expect more straightforward approaches to succeed.

It isn't necessary to look at Eastern cultures to encounter cultural differences in conflict. The style of some other familiar cultures differs in important ways from the northern European and North American norm. These cultures see verbal disputes as a form of intimacy and even a game. Americans visiting Greece, for example, often think they are witnessing an argument when they are overhearing a friendly conversation.[37] A comparative study of American and Italian nursery school children showed that one of the Italian children's favorite pastimes was a kind of heated debating that Italians call *discussione,* which Americans would regard as arguing. Likewise, research has shown that working-class Jewish speakers of eastern European origin used arguments as a means of being sociable.

Within the United States, the ethnic background of communicators also plays a role in their ideas about conflict. When African-American, Mexican-American, and white American college students were asked about their views regarding conflict, some important differences emerged.[38] For example, white Americans seem more willing to accept conflict as a natural part of relationships, whereas Mexican Americans describe the short- and long-term dangers of disagreeing. Whites' willingness to experience conflicts may be part of their individualistic, low-context communication style of speaking directly and avoiding uncertainty. It's not surprising that people from more collective, high-context cultures that emphasize harmony among people with close relationships tend to handle conflicts in less direct ways. With differences like these, it's easy to imagine how two friends, lovers, or fellow workers from different cultural backgrounds might have trouble finding a conflict style that is comfortable for them both.

> **CULTURAL IDIOM**
>
> **"beating around the bush":** approaching something in an indirect way

CRITICAL THINKING PROBE

Valuing Diversity in Conflict Styles

The preceding section made it clear that conflict styles are shaped by social and cultural influences. Choose a conflict style different from yours—by virtue of gender or culture—and identify the assumptions on which it is based. Next, suggest how people with different styles can adapt their assumptions and behaviors to communicate in a more satisfying manner.

Methods of Conflict Resolution

No matter what the relational style, gender, or culture of the participants, every conflict is a struggle to have one's goals met. Sometimes that struggle succeeds, and at other times it fails. In the remainder of this chapter we'll look at various approaches to resolving conflicts and see which ones are most promising.

WIN–LOSE Win–lose conflicts are ones in which one party achieves its goal at the expense of the other. People resort to this method of resolving disputes when they perceive a situation as being an "either-or" one: Either I get what I want, or you get your way. The most clear-cut examples of win–lose situations are certain games, such as baseball or poker, in which the rules require a winner and a loser. Some interpersonal issues seem to fit into this win–lose framework: two coworkers seeking a promotion to the same job, for instance, or a couple who disagree on how to spend their limited money.

Power is the distinguishing characteristic in win–lose problem solving, because it is necessary to defeat an opponent to get what you want. The most obvious kind of power is physical. Some parents threaten their children with warnings such as "Stop misbehaving, or I'll send you to your room." Adults who use physical power to deal with each other usually aren't so blunt, but the legal system is the implied threat: "Follow the rules, or we'll lock you up."

Real or implied force isn't the only kind of power used in conflicts. People who rely on authority of many types engage in win–lose methods without ever threatening physical coercion. In most jobs, supervisors have the potential to use authority in the assignment of working hours, job promotions, desirable or undesirable tasks and, of course, in the power to fire an

"Just another of our many disagreements. He wants a no-fault divorce whereas I would prefer to have the bastard crucified."

unsatisfactory employee. Teachers can use the power of grades to coerce students to act in desired ways.

Even the usually admired democratic principle of majority rule is a win–lose method of resolving conflicts. However fair it may be, this system results in one group's getting its way and another group's being unsatisfied.

There are some circumstances when win–lose problem solving may be necessary, such as when there are truly scarce resources and where only one party can achieve satisfaction. For instance, if two suitors want to marry the same person, only one can succeed. And to return to an earlier example, it's often true that only one applicant can be hired for a job. But don't be too willing to assume that your conflicts are necessarily win–lose: As you'll soon read, many situations that seem to require a loser can be resolved to everyone's satisfaction.

There is a second kind of situation when win–lose is the best method. Even when cooperation is possible, if the other person insists on trying to defeat you, then the most logical response might be to defend yourself by fighting back. "It takes two to tango," the old cliché goes, and it also often takes two to cooperate.

A final and much less frequent justification for trying to defeat another person occurs when the other person is clearly behaving in a wrong manner and when defeating that person is the only way to stop the wrongful behavior. Few people would deny the importance of restraining a person who is deliberately harming others even if the aggressor's freedom is sacrificed in the process. Forcing wrongdoers to behave themselves is dangerous because of the wide difference in opinion between people about who is wrong and who is right. Given this difference, it would seem justifiable to coerce others into behaving as we think they should only in the most extreme circumstances.

LOSE–LOSE In **lose–lose problem solving**, neither side is satisfied with the outcome. Although the name of this approach is so discouraging that it's hard to imagine how anyone could willingly use it, in truth lose–lose is a fairly common way to handle conflicts. In many instances the parties will both strive to be winners, but as a result of the struggle, both end up losers. On the international scene many wars illustrate this sad point. A nation that gains military victory at the cost of thousands of lives, large amounts of resources, and a damaged national consciousness hasn't truly won much. On an interpersonal level the same principle holds true. Most of us have seen battles of pride in which both parties strike out and both suffer.

COMPROMISE Unlike lose–lose outcomes, a **compromise** gives both parties at least some of what they wanted, though both sacrifice part of their goals. People usually settle for compromises when they see partial satisfaction as the best they can hope for. Although a compromise may be better than losing everything, this approach hardly seems to deserve the positive image it has with some people. In his valuable book on conflict resolution, management consultant Albert Filley makes an interesting observation about our attitudes toward this approach.[39] Why is it, he asks, that if someone says, "I will compromise my values," we view the action unfavorably, yet we talk admiringly about parties in a conflict who compromise to reach a solution? Although compromises may be the best obtainable result in some conflicts, it's important to realize that both people in a dispute can often work together to find much better solutions. In such cases *compromise* is a negative word.

The Navajo definition of conflict resolution is to restore harmony. Their experience has convinced them that if one ends a dispute by having a winner and a loser, one dispute may have been ended but another dispute surely will have been started because harmony will not have been restored. Behind this is the Navajo recognition that coercion is not an effective way to bring about genuine change in any individual's long-term behavior or attitude. Coercion works only as long as one is willing and able to continue the coercion. When the coercion stops, people generally revert to their prior ways, the only real difference being that by then they will have become angry and resentful. Coercion is a short-term, not a long-term answer.

Anne Kaas
The Better Way: Navajo Peacemaking

CULTURAL IDIOM

"it takes two to tango": it takes two people to do something

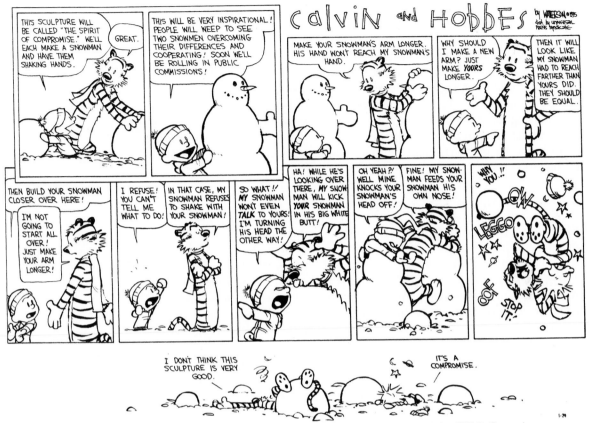

Most of us are surrounded by the results of bad compromises. Consider a common example: the conflict between one person's desire to smoke cigarettes and another's need to breathe clean air. The win–lose outcomes of this conflict are obvious: Either the smoker abstains, or the nonsmoker gets polluted lungs—neither very satisfying. But a compromise in which the smoker gets to enjoy only a rare cigarette or must retreat outdoors and in which the nonsmoker still must inhale some fumes or feel like an ogre is hardly better. Both sides have lost a considerable amount of both comfort and goodwill. Of course, the costs involved in other compromises are even greater. For example, if a divorced couple compromise on child care by haggling over custody and then finally grudgingly agree to split the time with their children, it's hard to say that anybody has won.

> **CULTURAL IDIOM**
>
> **haggling over:** arguing about

WIN–WIN   In **win–win problem solving,** the goal is to find a solution that satisfies the needs of everyone involved. Not only do the parties avoid trying to win at the other's expense, but also they believe that by working together it is possible to find a solution that allows both to reach their goals.

Some compromises approach this win–win ideal. You and the seller might settle on a price for a used car that is between what the seller was asking and what you wanted to pay. Although neither of you got everything you wanted, the outcome would still leave both of you satisfied. Likewise, you and your companion might agree to see a film that is the second choice for both of you in order to spend an evening together. As long as everyone is satisfied with an outcome, it's accurate to describe it as a win–win solution.

Although compromises can be a type of win–win outcome, the best solutions are ones in which all the parties get everything they want.

Although a win–win approach sounds ideal, it is not always possible, or even appropriate. Table 7–3 suggests some factors to consider when deciding which approach to take when facing a conflict. There will certainly be times when compromising is the most sensible approach. You will even encounter instances when pushing for your own solution is reasonable. Even more surprisingly, you will probably discover that there are times when it makes sense to willingly accept the loser's role.

Steps in Win–Win Problem Solving

Although win–win problem solving is often the most desirable approach to managing conflicts, it is also one of the hardest to achieve. In spite of the challenge, it is definitely possible to become better at resolving conflicts. The following pages outline a method to increase your chances of being able to handle your conflicts in a win–win manner, so that both you and others have your needs met. As you learn to use this approach, you should find that more and more of your conflicts end up with win–win solutions. And even when total satisfaction isn't possible, this approach can preserve a positive relational climate.

As it is presented here, win–win problem solving is a highly structured activity. After you have practiced the approach a number of times, this style of managing conflict will become almost second nature to you. You'll then be able to approach

---

TABLE 7–3   Choosing the Most Appropriate Method of Conflict Resolution

1. Consider deferring to the other person:
- When you discover you are wrong
- When the issue is more important to the other person than it is to you
- To let others learn by making their own mistakes
- When the long-term cost of winning may not be worth the short-term gains

2. Consider compromising:
- When there is not enough time to seek a win–win outcome
- When the issue is not important enough to negotiate at length
- When the other person is not willing to seek a win–win outcome

3. Consider competing:
- When the issue is important and the other person will take advantage of your noncompetitive approach

4. Consider cooperating:
- When the issue is too important for a compromise
- When a long-term relationship between you and the other person is important
- When the other person is willing to cooperate

CULTURAL IDIOM

second nature: easy and natural

rolling in: possessing large amounts of

INVITATION TO INSIGHT

Problem Solving in Your Life

1. Recall as many conflicts as possible that you have had in one relationship. Identify which approach best characterizes each one: win–lose, lose–lose, compromise, or win–win.
2. For each conflict, describe the consequences (for both you and the other person) of this approach.
3. Based on your analysis, decide for yourself how successful you and your partner are at managing conflicts. Describe any differences in approach that would result in more satisfying outcomes. Discuss what steps you and your partner could take to make these changes.

your conflicts without the need to follow the step-by-step approach. But for the time being, try to be patient, and trust the value of the following pattern. As you read on, imagine yourself applying it to a problem that's bothering you now.

IDENTIFY YOUR PROBLEM AND UNMET NEEDS Before you speak out, it's important to realize that the problem that is causing conflict is yours. Whether you want to return an unsatisfactory piece of merchandise, complain to noisy neighbors because your sleep is being disturbed, or request a change in working conditions from your employer, the problem is yours. Why? Because in each case *you* are the person who is dissatisfied. You are the one who has paid for the defective article; the merchant who sold it to you has the use of your good money. You are the one who is losing sleep as a result of your neighbors' activities; they are content to go on as before. You, not your boss, are the one who is unhappy with your working conditions.

Realizing that the problem is yours will make a big difference when the time comes to approach your partner. Instead of feeling and acting in an evaluative way, you'll be more likely to share your problem in a descriptive way, which will not only be more accurate but also will reduce the chance of a defensive reaction.

After you realize that the problem is yours, the next step is to identify the unmet needs that leave you feeling dissatisfied. Sometimes a relational need underlies the content of the issue at hand. Consider these cases:

- A friend hasn't returned some money you lent long ago. Your apparent need in this situation might be to get the cash back. But a little thought will probably show that this isn't the only, or even the main, thing you want. Even if you were rolling in money, you'd probably want the loan repaid because of your most important need: *to avoid feeling victimized by your friend's taking advantage of you.*

■ Someone you care about who lives in a distant city has failed to respond to several letters. Your apparent need may be to get answers to the questions you've written about, but it's likely that there's another, more fundamental need: *the reassurance that you're still important enough to deserve a response.*

As you'll soon see, the ability to identify your real needs plays a key role in solving interpersonal problems. For now, the point to remember is that before you voice your problem to your partner, you ought to be clear about which of your needs aren't being met.

MAKE A DATE   Unconstructive fights often start because the initiator confronts a partner who isn't ready. There are many times when a person isn't in the right frame of mind to face a conflict: perhaps owing to fatigue, being in too much of a hurry to take the necessary time, upset over another problem, or not feeling well. At times like these, it's unfair to "jump" a person without notice and expect to get full attention for your problem. If you do persist, you'll probably have an ugly fight on your hands.

After you have a clear idea of the problem, approach your partner with a request to try to solve it. For example: "Something's been bothering me. Can we talk about it?" If the answer is "yes", then you're ready to go further. If it isn't the right time to confront your partner, find a time that's agreeable to both of you.

DESCRIBE YOUR PROBLEM AND NEEDS   Your partner can't possibly meet your needs without knowing why you're upset and what you want. Therefore, it's up to you to describe your problem as specifically as possible. When you do so, it's important to use terms that aren't overly vague or abstract. Recall our discussion of behavioral descriptions in Chapter 3 when clarifying your problem and needs.

PARTNER CHECKS BACK   After you've shared your problem and described what you need, it's important to make sure that your partner has understood what you've said. As you can remember from the discussion of listening in Chapter 4, there's a good chance—especially in a stressful conflict situation—of your words being misinterpreted.

It's usually unrealistic to insist that your partner paraphrase your problem statement, and fortunately there are more tactful and subtle ways to make sure you've been understood. For instance, you might try saying, "I'm not sure I expressed myself very well just now—maybe you should tell me what you heard me say so I can be sure I got it right." In any case, be absolutely sure that your partner understands your whole message before going any further. Legitimate agreements are tough enough, but there's no point in getting upset about a conflict that doesn't even exist.

SOLICIT PARTNER'S NEEDS   After you've made your position clear, it's time to find out what your partner needs in order to feel satisfied about this issue. There are two reasons why it's important to discover your partner's needs. First, it's fair. After all, the other person has just as much right as you to feel satisfied, and if you expect help in meeting your needs, then it's reasonable that you behave in the same way. Second, just as an unhappy partner will make it hard for you to become satisfied, a happy one will be more likely to cooperate in letting you reach your goals. Thus, it is in your own self-interest to discover and meet your partner's needs.

Let us begin anew, remembering on both sides that civility is not a sign of weakness.

John F. Kennedy

CULTURAL IDIOM

frame of mind: mood, mental state

to "jump": to attack

to keep on top of: to be in control of

You can learn about your partner's needs simply by asking about them: "Now I've told you what I want and why. Tell me what you need to feel okay about this." After your partner begins to talk, your job is to use the listening skills discussed earlier in this book to make sure you understand.

CHECK YOUR UNDERSTANDING OF PARTNER'S NEEDS   Paraphrase or ask questions about your partner's needs until you're certain you understand them. The surest way to accomplish this is to use the paraphrasing skills you learned in Chapter 4.

NEGOTIATE A SOLUTION   Now that you and your partner understand each other's needs, the goal becomes finding a way to meet them. This is done by trying to develop as many potential solutions as possible and then evaluating them to decide which one best meets the needs of both. The following steps can help communicators develop a mutually satisfying solution.

1. **Identify and Define the Conflict.** We've discussed this process in the preceding pages. It consists of discovering each person's problem and needs, setting the stage for meeting all of them.
2. **Generate a Number of Possible Solutions.** In this step the partners work together to think of as many means as possible to reach their stated ends. The key word here is *quantity*: It's important to generate as many ideas as you can think of without worrying about which ones are good or bad. Write down every thought that comes up, no matter how unworkable; sometimes a far-fetched idea will lead to a more workable one.
3. **Evaluate the Alternative Solutions.** This is the time to talk about which solutions will work and which ones won't. It's important for all concerned to be honest about their willingness to accept an idea. If a solution is going to work, everyone involved has to support it.
4. **Decide on the Best Solution.** Now that you've looked at all the alternatives, pick the one that looks best to everyone. It's important to be sure everybody understands the solution and is willing to try it out. Remember: Your decision doesn't have to be final, but it should look potentially successful.

FOLLOW UP ON THE SOLUTION   You can't be sure the solution will work until you try it out. After you've tested it for a while, it's a good idea to set aside some time to talk over how things are going. You may find that you need to make some changes or even rethink the whole problem. The idea is to keep on top of the problem, to keep using creativity to solve it.

Win–win solutions aren't always possible. There will be times when even the best-intentioned people simply won't be able to find a way of meeting all their needs. In cases like this, the process of negotiation has to include some compromising. But even then the preceding steps haven't been wasted. The genuine desire to learn what the other person wants and to try to satisfy those desires will build a climate of goodwill that can help you find the best solution to the present problem and also improve your relationship in the future.

Letting Go

One typical comment people have after trying the preceding method of handling conflicts is "This is a helpful thing sometimes, but it's so rational!

We struggled together, knowing. We prattled, pretended, fought bitterly, laughed, wept over sad books or old movies, nagged, supported, gave, took, demanded, forgave, resented—hating the ugliness in each other, yet cherishing that which we were. . . . Will I ever find someone to battle with as we battled, love as we loved, share with as we shared, challenge as we challenged, forgive as we forgave? You used to say that I saved up all of my feelings so that I could spew forth when I got home. The anger I experienced in school I could not vent there. How many times have I heard you chuckle as you remembered the day I would come home from school and share with you all of the feelings I had kept in. "If anyone had been listening they would have thought you were punishing me, striking out at me. I always survived and you always knew that I would still be with you when you were through." There was an honesty about our relationship that may never exist again.

Vian Catrell

Sometimes I'm so uptight I don't care about defensiveness or listening or anything . . . I just want to yell and get it off my chest!"

When you feel like this, it's almost impossible to be rational. At times like these, probably the most therapeutic thing to do is to get your feelings off your chest in what Bach calls a "Vesuvius"—an uncontrolled, spontaneous explosion. A Vesuvius can be a terrific way of blowing off steam, and after you do so, it's often much easier to figure out a rational solution to your problem.

So we encourage you to have a Vesuvius with the following qualifications: Be sure your partner understands what you're doing and realizes that whatever you say doesn't call for a response. He or she should let you rant and rave for as long as you want without getting defensive or "tying in." Then, when your eruption subsides, you can take steps to work through whatever still troubles you.

CULTURAL IDIOM
uptight: anxious
get it off my chest: talk about something that is worrying or upsetting one
blowing off steam: releasing excess energy or anger

SUMMARY

This chapter explored several factors that help make interpersonal relationships satisfying or unsatisfying. We began by defining *communication climate* as the emotional tone of a relationship as it is expressed in the messages being sent and received. We examined factors that contribute to positive and negative climates, learning that the underlying factor is the degree to which a person feels valued by others. We examined types of confirming and disconfirming messages, and then looked in detail at Gibb's categories of defensiveness-arousing and supportive behaviors.

The second half of the chapter dealt with interpersonal conflict. We saw that conflict is a fact of life in every relationship and that the way conflicts are handled plays a major role in the quality of a relationship. There are five ways people can behave when faced with a conflict: nonassertive, directly aggressive, passive-aggressive, indirect, and assertive. Each of these approaches can be appropriate at times, but the chapter focused on assertive communication skills because of their value and novelty for most communicators. We saw that conflict styles are affected by both gender and culture.

There are four outcomes to conflicts: win–lose, lose–lose, compromise, and win–win. Win–win outcomes are often possible, if the parties possess the proper attitudes and skills. The final section of the chapter outlined the steps in win–win problem solving.

RESOURCES

Print

Cissna, Kenneth N., and Evelyn Seiburg. "Patterns of Interactional Confirmation and Disconfirmation," in *Interpersonal Communication: Readings in Theory and Research.* Fort Worth, TX: Harcourt Brace, 1995.

Cissna and Seiburg provide the theoretical basis for messages that either validate or attack others. They go on to provide a dismally comprehensive catalogue of the many ways it is possible to express disconfirming messages.

Hocker, Joyce L., and William W. Wilmot. *Interpersonal Conflict,* 6th ed. New York: McGraw-Hill, 2001.

A thorough survey of the nature of interpersonal conflict and how it can be resolved. This is an ideal second step for readers who want to explore the subject in further detail.

Kohn, Alfie. *No Contest: The Case against Competition.* Boston: Houghton Mifflin, 1986.

Kohn offers extensive evidence suggesting that competition is inherently destructive, both in society at large and in personal relationships. He goes on to demonstrate how cooperation can make people happier, more productive, and secure.

Stone, Douglas, Bruce Patton, and Sheila Heen. *Difficult Conversations: How to Discuss What Matters Most.* New York: Penguin, 2000.

This outstanding book was developed by members of the famous Harvard Negotiation Project. It offers a comprehensive, readable, and (most importantly) effective approach to understanding the potential dangers of unproductive conflicts and how to avoid them. Examples are drawn from a variety of contexts, including work, family, and friendships.

Tannen, Deborah. *The Argument Culture.* New York: Random House, 1998.

Sociolinguist Tannen argues (note the combative metaphor) that our culture is suffused with an orientation toward combat that often pushes personal relationships away from cooperation and toward conflict. She offers examples from areas such as the media, politics, and law to support her points. Tannen also profiles other cultures with more collaborative approaches toward managing differences.

Films
Confirming and Disconfirming Behavior

Mr. Holland's Opus (1996). Rated PG.

Glenn Holland (Richard Dreyfuss) is a brand-new high school teacher. His first day on the job is hardly promising: His students are bored, in great part because he is boring. Holland slowly learns to change the climate in his classroom. He begins teaching lessons from the students' music, rock and roll. He spends countless hours working one-on-one with those who need extra help. Most importantly, he confirms his students' worth and dignity by investing himself in their lives.

An interesting subplot involves Mr. Holland's son, Cole (Joseph Anderson). When Holland learns his young son is virtually deaf, Holland is devastated because he believes they will never share a passion for music. Holland begins pouring more time and energy into his students, with little left over for Cole. He barely learns the basics of sign language, which further stifles his communication with his son. Although his students feel his constant confirmation, Holland continually dis-

confirms Cole by ignoring him and the events of his life.

Fortunately, Holland is awakened to the problem and addresses it in a variety of ways (including the sharing of music). By movie's end, their relationship is repaired. The story thus has many morals: A person can send both confirming and disconfirming messages; disconfirmation can be unintentional; patterns of disconfirmation can be reversed. Ultimately, *Mr. Holland's Opus* is a testimony to the transforming power of confirming communication.

Dead Man Walking (1995). Rated R.

Dead Man Walking begins as Sister Helen Prejean (Susan Sarandon), a nun who works in an inner-city neighborhood, receives a letter from death row inmate Matthew Poncelet (Sean Penn). She visits Poncelet in the penitentiary and finds that he fills the profile for everything she is not: He is uneducated, angry, unattractive, rude, and insecure. Nonetheless, Sister Helen agrees to help Poncelet appeal his conviction and death sentence.

As time goes on, Sister Helen comes to realize that Poncelet is, indeed, guilty of the awful crimes for which he has been convicted. We feel her pain as she confronts the grieving families of his victims, none of whom can understand or accept why she is willing to defend a murderer.

As the film progresses, we see Sister Helen as the paradigm of a Gibb's supportive behavior. She never wavers in her abhorrence for Poncelet's deeds, but she remains steadfast in separating her hate for the sin from her love for the sinner. As such, she provides viewers with proof that unconditional positive regard can be achieved and have healing power.

Patch Adams (1998). Rated PG-13.

Hunter "Patch" Adams (Robin Williams) is one of the top students in his medical school class, but his unconventional methods get him in trouble. Adams clowns around with children, sings songs to dying patients, and acts silly during serious moments. This doesn't mean that Adams isn't serious about becoming a doctor. His mission is to create a medical climate where people are more important than regimen, where concern is valued over technique, where patients' emotional conditions matter as much as their vital signs, and where laughter is indeed the best medicine.

Adams works to change the school's climate by altering traditional medical communication patterns. He doesn't talk down to patients or nurses; he calls them by name and values their input. He fights against "the most terrible disease of all—indifference" by showing kindness and empathy to those around him. Early on, he identifies one of his primary professional goals: "I want to listen—really listen."

The film is based on the true story of a doctor who is developing "Gesundheit Hospital" in the hills of West Virginia. As the name suggests, it will be a medical center with nontraditional methods and a sense of humor. It also will have a warm and cheery communication climate.

Win–Lose and Lose–Lose Conflict Outcomes

He Got Game (1998). Rated R.

Jesus Shuttlesworth (Ray Allen) is a high school basketball star who has received offers to play for universities and pro teams across the country. Jesus becomes a pawn in a greedy bidding war between coaches, agents, friends, and family members. The most significant of Jesus' conflicts is with his father, Jake (Denzel Washington). Jake is in prison for accidentally killing his wife, and his son has never forgiven him. Jake is given a one-week parole because the governor wants him to convince Jesus to attend Big State University. If Jake succeeds, his prison sentence will be reduced—but this leads to more father-son conflict.

Competition is Jesus' preferred approach to managing conflict with Jake. He walks away from conversations with his father, even though he holds the power to commute Jake's sentence in his hands. In a symbolic moment near the end of the story, the two men play a one-on-one basketball game to determine the fate of their relationship.

Jesus and Jake ultimately learn that win–lose solutions can end up hurting both parties and that forgiveness can be an important part of repairing relationships damaged by years of unresolved conflict.

The War of the Roses (1989). Rated R.

The War of the Roses was billed as a black comedy, but there is little to laugh about in this grim story. Oliver and Barbara Rose (Michael Douglas and Kathleen Turner) are a couple whose "perfect marriage" falls apart when they encounter their respective midlife crises. Their decision to divorce is not nearly as depressing as their escalating hostility: Oliver and Barbara would rather die than sacrifice either their egos or their possessions.

The Roses' battles soon escalate to the point of absurdity, but anyone who has seen the self-defeating lengths to which some people will go in a dysfunctional conflict will find the film's theme sadly familiar. A civil divorce is hardly the goal to which any couple aspires, but after viewing the mutual destruction that arises from situations like the Roses', couples who can handle their breakups decently seem as deserving of admiration as sympathy.

Culture and Conflict

The Joy Luck Club (1993). Rated R.

The Joy Luck Club is not one story but many, told in film through flashbacks, narrations, and gripping portrayals. The primary stories involve four Chinese women and their daughters. The mothers all flee difficult situations in China to start new lives in the United States, where they raise their daughters with a mixture of Chinese and American styles. Many of the movie's conflicts arise out of differing cultural values.

The mothers were raised in the high-context, collectivist environment of China, where open conflict is discouraged and individual needs (particularly of women) are submerged for the larger good. To achieve their goals, the mothers use a variety of indirect and passive-aggressive methods. Their daughters, raised in the United States, adopt a more low-context, direct form of communication. They are also more assertive and aggressive in their conflict styles, particularly when dealing with their mothers.

The daughters have a hard time dealing with the men in their lives. For example, Rose (Rosalind Chao) begins her relationship with Ted (Andrew McCarthy) very assertively, telling him candidly what she thinks and how she feels about him (he is charmed by her directness). They marry, and she becomes an accommodator, constantly submerging her needs for his. Rather than liking Rose's accommodating, Ted comes to despise it. He exhorts her to be more assertive: "Once in awhile, I would like to hear what you want. I'd like to hear your voice, even if we disagree." He then suggests that they separate.

Several of the stories have happy endings. In Rose's case, she fights for her rights with Ted—and ultimately they reconcile. In fact, each woman in the movie takes a stand on an important issue in her life, and most of the outcomes are positive. The women in *The Joy Luck Club* learn to both embrace and reject aspects of their cultural heritage as they attempt to manage their conflicts effectively.

CONTENTS

KEY TERMS

all-channel network
chain network
collectivistic orientation
consensus
dysfunctional roles
formal roles
gatekeeper
group
group goals
growth groups
hidden agenda
individual goals
individualistic orientation
informal roles
learning group
norms
power distance
problem-solving groups
procedural norms
roles
rules
social groups
social norms
social orientation
social roles
sociogram
task norms
task orientation
task roles
uncertainty avoidance
wheel network

**AFTER STUDYING
THE MATERIAL
IN THIS CHAPTER . . .**

YOU SHOULD UNDERSTAND:

1. The characteristics that distinguish groups from other collections of people.

2. The types of goals that operate in groups.

3. The various types of groups.

4. The characteristics of groups described in this chapter.

5. The advantages and disadvantages of the decision-making methods introduced in this chapter.

6. The cultural influences that shape communication in groups.

THE NATURE OF GROUPS

YOU SHOULD BE ABLE TO:

1. Identify the groups you presently belong to and those you are likely to join in the future.

2. List the personal and group goals in groups you observe or belong to.

3. Identify the norms, roles, and interaction patterns in groups you observe or belong to.

4. Choose the most effective decision-making methods for a group task.

How important are groups?

You can answer this question for yourself by trying a simple experiment. Start by thinking of all the groups you belong to now and have belonged to in the past: the family you grew up with, the classes you have attended, the companies you have worked for, the teams you have played on, the many social groups you have been a member of—the list is a long one. Now, one by one, imagine that you had never belonged to each of these groups. Start with the less important ones, and the results aren't too dramatic; but very soon you will begin to see that a great deal of the information you have learned, the benefits you have gained—even your very identity have all come from group membership.

On the job, groups are the setting in which most work takes place. In one survey, 75 percent of the professionals surveyed reported that they "always" or "often" worked in teams.[1] In the growing multimedia field, the ability to work effectively as a team has been identified as the top nontechnical job skill.[2] When negotiating is conducted by teams instead of individuals, the results are better for everyone involved.[3]

This doesn't mean that every group experience is a good one. Some are vaguely unrewarding, rather like eating food that has no taste and gives no nourishment. And others are downright miserable. Sometimes it is easy to see why a group succeeds or fails, but in other cases matters aren't so clear.[4]

This chapter will help you understand better the nature of group communication. It will start by explaining just what a group is—because not every collection of people qualifies. It will go on to examine the reasons why people form groups and then look at several types of groups. Finally, it will conclude by looking at some common characteristics all groups share.

> Most of the decisions that affect our lives are not made by individuals, but by small groups of people in executive boardrooms, faculty meetings, town councils, quality circles, dormitory rooms, kitchens, locker rooms, and a host of other meeting places. In a democracy, the small group is the most basic way to get work done.
>
> Arthur Jensen

WHAT IS A GROUP?

Imagine that you are taking a test on group communication. Which of the following would you identify as groups?

- A crowd of onlookers gawking at a burning building
- Several passengers at an airline ticket counter discussing their hopes to find space on a crowded flight
- An army battalion

Because all these situations seem to involve groups, your experience as a canny test taker probably tells you that a commonsense answer will get you in trouble here—and you're right. When social scientists talk about *groups*, they use the word in a special way that excludes each of the preceding examples.

What are we talking about when we use the word *group*? For our purposes a **group** consists of a *small collection of people who interact with each other, usually face to face, over time in order to reach goals*. A closer examination of this definition will show why none of the collections of people described in the preceding quiz qualifies as a group.

Interaction

Without interaction, a collection of people isn't a group. Consider, for example, the onlookers at a fire. Though they all occupy the same area at a given time, they have virtually nothing to do with each other. Of course, if they should begin interacting—working together to give first aid or to rescue victims, for example—the situation would change. This requirement of interaction highlights the difference between true groups and collections of individuals who merely coact—simultaneously engaging in a similar activity without communicating with one another. For example, students who passively listen to a lecture don't technically constitute a group until they begin to exchange messages with each other and their instructor. (This explains why some students feel isolated even though they spend so much time on a crowded campus. Despite being surrounded by others, they really don't belong to any groups.)

As you read in Chapters 3 and 5, there are two types of interaction that go on in any communication setting. The most obvious type is verbal, in which group members exchange words either orally or in writing. But people needn't talk to each other in order to communicate as a group: Nonverbal channels can do the job, too. We can see how by thinking again about a hypothetical classroom. Imagine that the course is in its tenth week and that the instructor has been lecturing nonstop for the entire time. During the first few meetings there was very little interaction of any kind: Students were too busy scribbling notes and wondering how they would survive the course with grade-point averages and sanity intact. But as they became more used to the class, the students began to share their feelings with each other. Now there's a great amount of eye rolling and groaning as the assignments are poured on, and the students exchange resigned signs as they hear the same tired jokes for the second and third time. Thus, even though there's no verbal exchange of sentiments, the class has become a group—interestingly, in this sense a group that doesn't include the professor.

The explosion of communication technologies has led to the growth of "virtual groups"—people who interact with one another without meeting face to face. For a small cost (at least compared with in-person meetings), people, whether within the same office or around the world, can swap ideas via computer networks, speak with one another via telephone conference calls, and even have visual contact thanks to teleconferencing.[5] Despite the lack of personal contact between members, virtual teams actually can be superior to face-to-face teams in at least two ways. First, getting together is fast and easy. A virtual team can meet whenever necessary, even if the members are widely separated. This ease of interaction isn't just useful in the business world. For most groups of students working on class projects, finding a convenient time to meet can be a major headache. Virtual groups don't face the same challenges.

A second advantage of virtual teams is the leveling of status differences. When people connect via computer networks, rank is much less prominent than when groups meet face to face.[6] Because fear of authority figures can squelch creative thinking, virtual teams are a good device for making sure groups find the best solutions to problems.

Interdependence

In groups, members don't just interact: Their members are *interdependent*.[7] The behavior of one person affects all the others in what can be called a "ripple effect."[8] Consider your own experience in family and work groups: When one member behaves poorly, his or her actions shape the way the entire group functions. The ripple effect can be positive as well as negative: Beneficial actions by some members help everyone.

UNDERSTANDING COMMUNICATION TECHNOLOGY

Communicating With Your Own Virtual Group

Groups don't have to meet in person. Setting up a telephone conference call is easy and affordable. (Ask your phone company for details.) Also, you can create your own virtual group on the Internet.

Yahoo! Groups (http://groups.yahoo.com/) will host your own virtual team at no charge, providing a surprising array of services. You and your groupmates can

- Send and receive e-mail messages
- Upload and download files
- Create and use your own private chat for real-time conferencing
- Add and edit photos

- Link to other Web pages using bookmarks
- Conduct votes and polls online
- Schedule events and reminders on a group calendar
- Create a roster of group members, complete with personal profiles

Sometimes there is no good substitute for face-to-face meetings. But you may be surprised how quick, easy, and effective it can be for a group to work online.

Time

A collection of people who interact for a short while doesn't qualify as a group. As you'll soon read, groups who work together for any length of time begin to take on characteristics that aren't present in temporary aggregations. For example, certain standards of acceptable behavior begin to evolve, and the way individuals feel about each other begins to affect their behavior toward the group's task and toward each other. According to this criterion, onlookers at a fire might have trouble qualifying as a group even if they briefly cooperated with one another to help out in the emergency. The element of time clearly excludes temporary gatherings such as the passengers gathered around the airline ticket counter. Situations like this simply don't follow many of the principles you'll be reading about in the next two chapters.

Size

Our definition of *groups* included the word *small*. Most experts in the field set the lower limit of group size at three members. This decision isn't arbitrary, because there are some significant differences between two- and three-person communication. For example, the only ways two people can resolve a conflict are to change one another's minds, give in, or compromise; in a larger group, however, there's a possibility of members' forming alliances either to put increased pressure on dissenting members or to outvote them.

There is less agreement about when a group stops being small.[9] Though no expert would call a five hundred-member army battalion a group in our sense of the word (it would be labeled an organization), most experts are reluctant to set an arbitrary upper limit. Probably the best description of smallness is the ability for each member to be able to know and react to every other member. It's sufficient to say that our focus in these pages will be on collections of people ranging in size from three to between seven and twenty.

In task-oriented groups, bigger usually isn't better. Research suggests that the optimal size for a group is the smallest number of people capable of performing the task at hand effectively.[10] This definition makes it clear that there is no magic number or formula for choosing the best group size. The optimal number will change according to the task, as well as contextual factors such as politics, legal requirements, and institutional norms.[11] But generally speaking, as a group becomes larger, it is harder to schedule meetings, the members have less access to important information, and they have fewer chances to participate—three ingredients in a recipe for dissatisfaction.

Goals

Group membership isn't always voluntary, as some family members and most prison inmates will testify. But whether or not people choose to join groups, they usually hope to achieve one or more goals. At first the goal-related nature of group membership seems simple and obvious. In truth, however, there are several types of goals, which we will examine in the following pages.

THE FAR SIDE By GARY LARSON

Larson ©1987 Universal Press Syndicate 7-15

"And so you just threw everything together? ... Mathews, a posse is something you have to *organize*."

INVITATION TO INSIGHT **Your Membership in Groups**

To find out what roles groups play in your life, complete the following steps:

1. Use the criteria of size, interaction, time, and goals to identify the small groups to which you belong.
2. Describe the importance of each group to you, and evaluate how satisfying the communication is in each one.

As you read the remainder of this chapter, develop a list of insights that help you understand how communication operates in your groups and how you can improve your satisfaction in them.

GOALS OF GROUPS AND THEIR MEMBERS

We can talk about two types of goals when we examine groups. The first type involves **individual goals**—the motives of individual members—whereas the second involves **group goals**—the outcome the group seeks to accomplish.

Individual Goals

The most obvious reason why individuals join groups is to meet their personal needs. **Task orientation**—getting the job done—is the most obvious type of individual motive for belonging to a group. Some people join study groups, for example, in order to improve their knowledge. Sometimes a member's task-related goals will have little to do with a group's stated purpose. Many merchants, for example, join service clubs such as Kiwanis, Rotary, or Lions primarily because doing so is good for business. The fact that these groups help achieve worthy

goals such as helping the blind or disabled is fine, of course, but for many people it is not the prime motive for belonging.[12]

What about groups with no specifically defined purpose? Consider, for instance, gatherings of regulars at the beach on sunny weekends or a group of friends whose members eat lunch together several times a week. Collections such as these meet the other criteria for being groups: They interact, meet over time, and have the right number of members. But what are the members' reasons for belonging? In our examples here, the goals can't be sunbathing or eating because these activities could be carried out alone. The answer to our question introduces **social orientation.** In many cases people join together in order to seek a sense of belonging, to exercise influence over others, and to gain the liking of others. Notice that none of these factors necessarily has much to do with the task: It's possible to get social needs met without getting the job done. Likewise, a group can be efficient—at least for a short while—without meeting the social needs of its members.

We join many, if not most, groups in order to accomplish both task and social goals. School becomes a place both to learn important information and to meet desirable friends. Our work becomes a means of putting food on the table and getting recognition for being competent. The value of making a distinction between task and social goals comes from recognizing that the latter are usually important but often not stated or even recognized by group members. Thus, asking yourself whether social goals are being met can be one way of identifying and overcoming blocks to group effectiveness.

Group Goals

So far we have discussed the forces that motivate individual group members. In addition to these individual forces, there also exist group goals. For example, athletic teams exist to compete with each other, and academic classes strive to transmit knowledge.

Sometimes there is a close relationship between group and individual goals. In athletic teams the group goal is to win, whereas individual members' goals include helping the group succeed. If you think about it for a moment, however, you'll see that the individual members have other goals as well: improving their physical ability, having a good time, overcoming the personal challenges of competition, and often gaining the social benefits that come from being an athlete. The difference between individual and group goals is even more pronounced when the two are incompatible. Consider, for instance, the case of an athletic team that has one player more interested in being a "star" (satisfying personal needs for recognition) than in helping the team win. Or recall classes you have known in which a lack of student enthusiasm made the personal goal of many students—getting by with the smallest possible amount of work—hardly consistent with the stated group goal of conveying information. Sometimes the gap between individual and group goals is public, whereas at other times an individual's goal becomes a **hidden agenda.** In either case, this discrepancy can be dangerous for the well-being of the group and needs to be dealt with. We'll have more to say about this subject in Chapter 10.

As long as the members' individual goals match those of the group, no conflicts are likely to arise. But when there is a clash between what members seek for themselves and what the group seeks, the collective goal is likely to suffer. The risk of individuals putting their own interests ahead of the group's is especially great when there is less need for interdependence. John Krakauer captures this situation clearly in his account of a team of climbers seeking to reach the peak of Mount Everest:

> There were more than fifty people camped on the Col that night, huddled in shelters pitched side by side, yet an odd feeling of isolation hung in the air. We were a team in name only, I'd sadly come to realize. Although in a few hours we would leave camp as a group, we would ascend as individuals, linked to one another by neither rope nor any deep sense of loyalty. Each client was in it for himself or herself, pretty much. And I was no different: I sincerely hoped Doug got to the top, for instance, yet I would do everything in my power to keep pushing on if he turned around.[13]

INVITATION TO INSIGHT   **Group and Individual Goals**

Think about two groups to which you belong.

1. What are your task-related goals in each?
2. What are your social goals?
3. Are your personal goals compatible or incompatible with those of other members?
4. Are they compatible or incompatible with the group goals?
5. What effect does the compatibility or incompatibility of goals have on the effectiveness of the group?

TYPES OF GROUPS

So far we have seen that groups fulfill a variety of goals. Another way of examining groups is to look at some of the functions they serve.

Learning Groups

When the term **learning group** comes up, most people think first about school. Although academic settings certainly qualify as learning groups, they aren't the only ones. Members of a scuba-diving class, friends who form a Bible study group, and members of a League of Women Voters chapter all belong to learning groups. Whatever the setting or subject, the purpose of learning groups is to increase the knowledge or skill of each member.

Growth Groups

Unlike learning groups, in which the subject matter is external to the members, **growth groups** focus on teaching the members more about themselves. Consciousness-raising groups, marriage encounter workshops, counseling, and group therapy are all types of growth groups. These are unlike most other types of groups in that there is no real collective goal: The entire purpose of the group is to help the members identify and deal with their personal concerns.

"So, does anyone in the group feel like responding to what Richard has just shared with us?"

Problem-Solving Groups

Problem-solving groups work to resolve a mutual concern of members. Sometimes the problem involves the group itself, as when a family decides how to handle household chores or when coworkers meet to coordinate vacation schedules. At other times, the problem is external to the group. For instance, neighbors who organize themselves to prevent burglaries or club members who plan a fund-raising drive are focusing on external problems.

Problem-solving groups can take part in many activities: One type is gathering information, as when several students compile a report for a class assignment. At other times, a group makes policy—a club's deciding whether or not to admit the public to its meetings being an example. Some groups make individual decisions; an interview committee who decides which candidate to hire is fulfilling this function.

Social Groups

We have already mentioned that some groups serve strictly to satisfy the social needs of their participants. Some **social group**s are organized, whereas others are informal. In either case, the inclusion, control, and affection that such groups provide are reason enough for belonging.

Groups don't always fall neatly into just one category. For example, learning groups often have other functions. Consider the class in which you are reading this book as an example: Besides becoming more knowledgeable about communication, many of the students in your class are probably satisfying social needs by making new friends. Some are probably growing personally by applying the principles to their own lives. Groups of students—fellow employees or teammates, for instance—may even take the class together to focus on solving a collective problem. Despite the multiplicity of goals, it's usually possible to characterize a group as primarily focused on learning, growth, problem-solving, or social goals.

ETHICAL CHALLENGE

Motives for Group Membership

Members often join a group for reasons unrelated to the group's stated purpose for existing. For example, some people belong to growth groups to achieve social needs, and others speak out in task-oriented groups to satisfy their egos more than to help solve the stated problem. Develop a set of ethical guidelines that describes when you believe it is and is not ethical to participate in groups without stating any hidden agendas.

CHARACTERISTICS OF GROUPS

Whatever their function, all groups have certain characteristics in common. Understanding these characteristics is a first step to behaving more effectively in your own groups.

Rules and Norms

Many groups have formal **rules**—explicit, officially stated guidelines that govern what the group is supposed to do and how the members should behave. In a classroom, these rules include how absences will be treated, whether papers must be typed or may be handwritten, and so on. Alongside the official rules, an equally powerful set of standards also operates, often without ever being discussed. Sociologists call these unstated rules **norms.** Norms are shared values, beliefs, behaviors, and procedures that govern a group's operation. For instance, you probably won't find a description of what jokes are and aren't acceptable in the bylaws of any groups you belong to, yet you can almost certainly describe the unstated code if you think about it. Is sexual humor acceptable? How much, and what types? What about religious jokes? How much kidding of other members is proper? Matters such as these vary from one group to another, according to the norms of each one.[14]

There are three categories of group norms: social, procedural, and task. **Social norms** govern the relationship of members to each other. How honest and direct will members be with one another? What emotions will and won't be expressed, and in what ways? Matters such as these are handled by the establishment of social norms, usually implicit ones. **Procedural norms** outline how the group should operate. Will the group make decisions by accepting the vote of the majority, or will the members keep talking until consensus is reached? Will one person run meetings, or will discussion be leaderless? **Task norms** focus on how the job itself should be handled. Will the group keep working on a problem until everyone agrees that its solution is the best one possible, or will members settle for an adequate, if imperfect, solution? The answer to this question results in a task-related norm. All groups have social norms, whereas problem-solving, learning, and growth groups also have procedural and task norms.

Table 8–1 lists some typical rules and norms that operate in familiar groups. It is important to realize that the actual rules and norms that govern a group don't always match the idealized ones that embody cultural standards. Consider the matter of punctuality, for example. A cultural norm in our society is that meetings should begin at the scheduled time, yet some groups soon generate the usually unstated agreement that the real business won't commence until ten or so minutes later. On a more serious level, one cultural norm is that other people should be treated politely and with respect, but in some groups failure to listen, sarcasm, and even outright hostility make the principle of civility a sham.

It is important to understand a group's norms. Following them is one way to gain acceptance into the group, and sometimes recognizing norms that cause problems can be a way to help the group operate more effectively. For instance, in some groups a norm is to discourage new ideas by criticism, sarcasm, or in-

---

TABLE 8–1 Typical Rules and Norms in Two Types of Groups

Family

Rules (Explicit)

- If you don't do the chores, you don't get your allowance.
- If you're going to be more than a half-hour late, phone home so the others don't worry about you.
- If the gas gauge reads "empty," fill up the tank before bringing the car home.
- Don't make plans for Sunday nights. That's time for the family to spend together.
- Daniel gets to watch *Sesame Street* from 5 to 6 P.M.

Norms (Unstated)

- When Dad is in a bad mood, don't bring up problems.
- Don't talk about Sheila's divorce.
- It's okay to tease Lupe about being short, but don't make comments about Shana's complexion.
- As long as the kids don't get in trouble, the parents won't ask detailed questions about what they do with their friends.
- At family gatherings, try to change the subject when Uncle Max brings up politics.

On-the-Job Meetings

Rules (Explicit)

- Regular meetings are held every Monday morning at 9 A.M.
- The job of keeping minutes rotates from person to person.
- Meetings last no more than an hour.
- Don't leave the meetings to take phone calls except in emergencies.

Norms (Unstated)

- Use first names.
- It's okay to question the boss's ideas, but if she doesn't concede after the first remark, don't continue to object.
- Tell jokes at the beginning of the meeting, but avoid sexual or ethnic topics.
- It's okay to talk about "gut feelings," but back them up with hard facts.
- Don't act upset when your ideas aren't accepted, even if you're unhappy.

difference. Pointing this out to members might be a way to change the unwritten rules and thereby improve the group's work.

If norms are rarely stated, how is it possible to identify them? There are two sets of clues that can help you pin down norms. First, look for behaviors that occur often.[15] For instance, notice what time meetings begin. Observe the amount of work members are willing to contribute to the group. See what kinds of humor are and aren't used. Habitual behaviors like these suggest the unspoken rules that the group lives by. Second, look for clues that members are being punished for violating norms. Most punishments are subtle, of course: pained expressions from other members when a speaker talks too much, no laughter following an inappropriate joke, and so on.

CULTURAL IDIOM

pin down: identify specifically

SKILL
BUILDER

Norms and Rules in Action

Describe the desirable norms and explicit rules you would like to see established in the following new groups, and describe the steps you could take to see that they are established.

1. A group of classmates formed to develop and present a class research project
2. A group of neighbors who is meeting for the first time to persuade the city to install a stop sign at a dangerous intersection
3. A group of eight-year-olds you will be coaching in a team sport
4. A group of fellow employees who will be sharing new office space

---

"Rules Are the Only Thing We've Got"

"What are we? Humans? Or animals? Or savages? What's grownups going to think? Going off—hunting pigs—letting fires out—and now!"

A shadow fronted him tempestuously.

"You shut up, you fat slug!"

There was a moment's struggle and the glimmering conch jigged up and down. Ralph leapt to his feet.

"Jack! Jack! You haven't got the conch! Let him speak."

Jack's face swam near him.

"And you shut up! Who are you, anyway? Sitting there telling people what to do. You can't hunt, you can't sing—"

"I'm chief. I was chosen."

"Why should choosing make any difference? Just giving orders that don't make any sense—"

"Piggy's got the conch."

"That's right—favor Piggy as you always do—"

"Jack!"

Jack's voice sounded in bitter mimicry.

"Jack! Jack!"

"The rules!" shouted Ralph. "You're breaking the rules!"

"Who cares?"

Ralph summoned his wits.

"Because the rules are the only thing we've got!"

William Golding
Lord of the Flies

Roles

Whereas norms define acceptable group standards, **roles** define patterns of behavior expected of members. Just like norms, some roles are officially recognized. These **formal roles** are assigned by an organization or group partly to establish order. Formal roles usually come with a label, such as "assistant coach," "treasurer," or "customer service representative." Unlike these formal classifications, **informal roles** (sometimes called "functional roles") are rarely acknowledged by the group.[16] Table 8–2 lists some of the most common informal roles in task-oriented groups. As the list shows, informal roles describe the functions members can fill rather than their formal positions. You can probably think of many groups in which members occupy functional roles. For example, you can probably think of many groups in which some members were clearly leaders and others followers.

Informal roles are not formally assigned to members. In fact, they are rarely even recognized as existing. Many of the roles may be filled by more than one member, and some of them may be filled by different people at different times. The important fact is that, at crucial times, each of the informal roles must be filled by someone.

Notice that the informal roles listed in Table 8–2 fall into two categories: task and maintenance. **Task roles** help the group accomplish its goals, and **social roles** (also called "maintenance roles") help the relationships

TABLE 8–2 Functional Roles of Group Members		
Task Roles	**Typical Behaviors**	**Examples**
1. Initiator/Contributor	Contributes ideas and suggestions; proposes solutions and decisions; proposes new ideas or states old ones in a novel fashion.	"How about taking a different approach to this chore? Suppose we . . ."
2. Information Seeker	Asks for clarification of comments in terms of their factual adequacy; asks for information or facts relevant to the problem; suggests information is needed before making decisions.	"Do you think the others will go for this?" "How much would the plan cost us?" "Does anybody know if those dates are available?"
3. Information Giver	Offers facts or generalizations that may relate to the group's task.	"I bet Chris would know the answer to that." *Newsweek* ran an article on that a couple of months ago. It said . . ."
4. Opinion Seeker	Asks for clarification of opinions made by other members of the group and asks how people in the group feel.	"Does anyone else have an idea about this?" "That's an interesting idea, Ruth. How long would it take to get started?"

TABLE 8-2	**Functional Roles of Group Members—cont'd**	
5. Opinion Giver	States beliefs or opinions having to do with suggestions made; indicates what the group's attitude should be.	"I think we ought to go with the second plan. It fits the conditions we face in the Concord plant best. . . ."
6. Elaborator/Clarifier	Elaborates ideas and other contributions; offers rationales for suggestions; tries to deduce how an idea or suggestion would work if adopted by the group.	"If we followed Lee's suggestion, each of us would need to make three calls." "Let's see . . . at thirty-five cents per brochure, the total cost would be $525.00."
7. Coordinator	Clarifies the relationships among information, opinions, and ideas or suggests an integration of the information, opinions, and ideas of sub-groups.	"John, you seem most concerned with potential problems. Mary sounds confident that they can all be solved. Why don't you list the problems one at a time, John, and Mary can respond to each one."
8. Diagnostician	Indicates what the problems are.	"But you're missing the main thing, I think. The problem is that we can't afford . . ."
9. Orienter/Summarizer	Summarizes what has taken place; points out departures from agreed-on goals; tries to bring the group back to the central issues; raises questions about the direction in which the group is heading.	"Let's take stock of where we are. Helen and John take the position that we should act now. Bill says, 'Wait.' Rusty isn't sure. Can we set that aside for a moment and come back to it after we . . ."
10. Energizer	Prods the group to action.	"Come on, guys. We've been wasting time. Let's get down to business."
11. Procedure Developer	Handles routine tasks such as seating arrangements, obtaining equipment, and handing out pertinent papers.	"I'll volunteer to see that the forms are printed and distributed." "I'd be happy to check on which of those dates are free."
12. Secretary	Keeps notes on the group's progress.	"Just for the record, I'll put these decisions in the memo and get copies to everyone in the group."
13. Evaluator/Critic	Constructively analyzes group's accomplishments according to some set of standards; checks to see that consensus has been reached.	"Look, we said we only had two weeks, and this proposal will take at least three. Does that mean that it's out of the running, or do we need to change our original guidelines?"

Continued

TABLE 8–2   Functional Roles of Group Members—cont'd

Social/Maintenance Roles

1. Supporter/Encourager	Praises, agrees with, and accepts the contributions of others; offers warmth, solidarity, and recognition.	"I really like that idea, John." "Priscilla's suggestion sounds good to me. Could we discuss it further?"
2. Harmonizer	Reconciles disagreements; mediates differences; reduces tensions by giving group members a chance to explore their differences.	"I don't think you two are as far apart as you think. Henry, are you saying _____? Benson, you seem to be saying _____. Is that what you mean?"
3. Tension Reliever	Jokes or in some other way reduces the formality of the situation; relaxes the group members.	"Let's take a break . . . maybe have a drink." "You're a tough cookie, Bob. I'm glad you're on our side!"
4. Conciliator	Offers new options when his or her own ideas are involved in a conflict; willing to admit errors so as to maintain group cohesion.	"Looks like our solution is halfway between you and me, John. Can we look at the middle ground?"
5. Gatekeeper	Keeps communication channels open; encourages and facilitates interaction from those members who are usually silent.	"Susan, you haven't said anything about this yet. I know you've been studying the problem. What do you think about _____?"
6. Feeling Expresser	Makes explicit the feelings, moods, and relationships in the group; shares own feelings with others.	"I'm really glad we cleared things up today." "I'm just about worn out. Could we call it a day and start fresh tomorrow?"
7. Follower	Goes along with the movement of the group passively, accepting the ideas of others, sometimes serving as an audience.	"I agree. Yes, I see what you mean. If that's what the group wants to do, I'll go along."

among the members run smoothly. Not all roles are constructive. Table 8–3 lists several **dysfunctional roles** that prevent a group from working effectively. Research suggests that the presence of positive social roles and the absence of dysfunctional ones are key ingredients in the effectiveness of groups.[17]

What is the optimal balance between task and social functions? According to Robert Bales, one of the earliest and most influential researchers in the area, the ideal ratio is 2:1, with task-related behavior dominating.[18] This ratio allows the

TABLE 8–3   Dysfunctional Roles of Group Members

Dysfunctional Roles	Typical Behaviors	Examples
1. Blocker	Interferes with progress by rejecting ideas or taking a negative stand on any and all issues; refuses to cooperate.	"Wait a minute! That's not right! That idea is absurd." "You can talk all day, but my mind is made up."
2. Aggressor	Struggles for status by deflating the status of others; boasts, criticizes.	"Wow, that's really swell! You turkeys have botched things again." "Your constant bickering is responsible for this mess. Let me tell you how you ought to do it."
3. Deserter	Withdraws in some way; remains indifferent, aloof, sometimes formal; daydreams; wanders from the subject, engages in irrelevant side conversations.	"I suppose that's right . . . I really don't care."
4. Dominator	Interrupts and embarks on long monologues; is authoritative; tries to monopolize the group's time.	"Bill, you're just off base. What we should do is this. First . . ."
5. Recognition Seeker	Attempts to gain attention in an exaggerated manner; usually boasts about past accomplishments; relates irrelevant personal experiences, usually in an attempt to gain sympathy.	"That reminds me of a guy I used to know . . ." "Let me tell you how I handled old Marris . . ."
6. Joker	Displays a lack of involvement in the group through inappropriate humor, horseplay, or cynicism.	"Why try to convince these guys? Let's just get the mob to snuff them out." "Hey, Carla, wanna be my roommate at the sales conference?"
7. Cynic	Discounts chances for group's success.	"Sure, we could try that idea, but it probably won't solve the problem. Nothing we've tried so far has worked."

Source: "Functional Roles of Group Members" and "Dysfunctional Roles of Group Members" adapted from *GROUPS IN CONTEXT: Leadership and Participation in Decision-Making Groups* by Gerald Wilson and Michael Hanna, pp. 144–146. © 1986. Reprinted by permission of McGraw-Hill Companies, Inc.

group to get its work done while at the same time taking care of the personal needs and concerns of the members.

ROLE EMERGENCE   We said earlier that most group members aren't aware of the existence of informal roles. You will rarely find members saying things like "You ask most of the questions, I'll give opinions, and she can be the summarizer." Yet it's fairly obvious that over time certain members do begin to fulfill specific roles. How does this process occur?

There are two answers to this question. One factor in role differentiation is certainly the personal characteristics of each member. But by themselves, personal skills and traits aren't enough to earn a member acceptance as possessor of a role, especially in newly formed groups where no formal leader exists. The process of role emergence has been studied extensively by communication scholar Ernest Bormann, who has identified a predictable series of stages groups go through in role designation.[19] (Remember that this process is almost never discussed and is rarely performed consciously.)

At first, members will make bids for certain roles. A particularly analytical communicator might audition for the role of critic by pointing out flaws in a proposal, for example. In order for this role to "take," the group members must endorse the bid by acknowledging and accepting it verbally and nonverbally—giving the would-be critic their attention and making positive comments about the observations. If the group does not support the first few initial bids, a sensitive member is likely to try another role.

ROLE-RELATED PROBLEMS AND SOLUTIONS   Groups can suffer from at least three role-related problems. The first occurs when one or more important informal roles—either task or social—go unfilled. For instance, there may be no information giver to provide vital knowledge or no harmonizer to smooth things over when members disagree.

There are other cases when the problem isn't an absence of candidates to fill certain roles, but rather an overabundance of them. This situation can lead to unstated competition between members, which gets in the way of group effectiveness. You have probably seen groups in which two people both want to be the tension-relieving comedian. In such cases, the problem arises when the members become more concerned with occupying their pet position than with getting the group's job done.

Even when there's no competition over roles, a group's effectiveness can be threatened when one or more members suffer from "role fixation"—acting out a specific role whether or not the situation requires it.[20] As you learned in Chapter 1, a key ingredient of communication competence is flexibility—the ability to choose the right behavior for a given situation. Members who always take the same role—even a constructive one—lack competence, and they hinder the group. As in other areas of life, too much of a good thing can be a problem. You can overcome the potential role-related problems by following these guidelines:

- Look for unfilled roles. When a group seems to be experiencing problems, use the list in Table 8–2 as a kind of checklist to diagnose what roles might be unfilled.
- Make sure unfilled roles are filled. After you have identified unfilled roles, you may be able to help the group by filling them yourself. If key facts are missing, take the role of information seeker and try to dig them out. If nobody is keeping track of the group's work, offer to play secretary and take notes. Even if you are not suited by skill or temperament to a job, you can often encourage others to fill it.
- Avoid role fixation. Don't fall into familiar roles if they aren't needed. You may be a world-class coordinator or critic, but these talents will only annoy others if you use them when they aren't needed. In most cases your natural inclination to be a supporter might be just the ticket to help a group succeed; but if

you find yourself in a group where the members don't need or want this sort of support, your encouragement might become a nuisance.

■ Avoid dysfunctional roles. Some of these roles can be personally gratifying, especially when you are frustrated with a group; but they do nothing to help the group succeed, and they can damage your reputation as a team player. Nobody needs a blocker, a joker, or any other of the dysfunctional roles listed in Table 8–3. Resist the temptation to indulge yourself by taking on any of them.

CRITICAL THINKING PROBE	**Functional and Dysfunctional Roles**
	Identify the functional and dysfunctional roles in an established group. You might analyze a group to which you belong (e.g., an athletic team or class group), a group who can be observed (e.g., city council, faculty senate), or even a fictional group (such as those described in the books and films listed at the end of this chapter). How do the roles in the group you are analyzing contribute to the group's success (or lack of it)? How might members take on different roles to make the group more effective?

Patterns of Interaction

In Chapter 1 we said that communication involves the exchange of information between and among people. It almost goes without saying that this exchange needs to be complete and efficient for the communicators to reach their goals. In interpersonal and public speaking settings, information exchange is relatively uncomplicated, taking basically two routes: either between the two individuals in an interpersonal dyad or between the speaker and the audience in a public speaking situation. (Actually, this is a slight oversimplification. In public speaking situations, members of an audience also exchange messages with one another with their laughter, restless movements, and so on. It's still fair to say, however, that the exchange of information is basically two-way.) In groups, however, things aren't so simple. The mathematical formula that identifies the number of possible interactions between individuals is

$$\frac{N(N-1)}{2}$$

where N equals the number of members in a group. Thus, in even a relatively small five-member group, there are ten possible combinations of two-person conversations and seventy-five possible multiperson interactions. Besides the sheer quantity of information exchanged, the more complex structure of groups affects the flow of information in other ways, too.

A look at Figure 8–1 (usually called a **sociogram**) will suggest the number and complexity of interactions that can occur in a group. Arrows connecting members indicate remarks shared between them. Two-headed arrows represent two-way conversations, whereas one-headed arrows represent remarks that did not arouse a response. Arrows directed to the center of the circle indicate remarks made to the group as a whole. A network analysis of this sort can reveal both the amount of participation by each member and the recipients of every member's remarks. As such, it provides a graphic look at who seems to be making the most significant contributions (at least in terms of their quantity), as well as who is not contributing.

In the group pictured in Figure 8–1, person E appears to be connected to the group only through a relationship with person A; E never addressed any other members, nor did they address E. Also notice that Person A is the most active and best-connected member. A addressed remarks to the group as a whole and to every other member and was the object of remarks from three individuals as well.

Sociograms don't tell the whole story, because they do not indicate the quality of the messages being exchanged. Nonetheless, they are a useful tool in diagnosing group communication.

Physical arrangement influences communication in groups. It's obviously easier to interact with someone you can see well. Lack of visibility isn't a serious problem in dyadic settings, but it can be troublesome in groups. For example, group members seated in a cir-

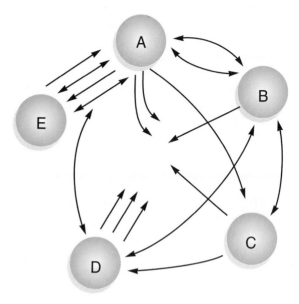

Figure 8–1 Patterns of Interaction in a Five-Person Group

cle are more likely to talk with persons across from them than with those on either side.[21] Different things happen when members are seated in rectangular arrangements. Research with twelve-person juries showed that those sitting at either end of rectangular tables participated more in discussions and were viewed by other members as having more influence on the decision-making process.[22] Rectangular seating patterns have other consequences as well. Research conducted on six-person groups seated at rectangular tables showed that as distance between two persons increased, other members perceived them as being less friendly, less talkative, and less acquainted with each other.[23]

If group members always stayed together and shared every piece of information with one another, their interaction would resemble the pattern in Figure 8–2—what communication theorists have called an **all-channel network.** But

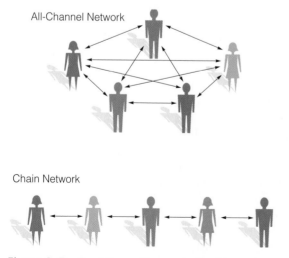

Figure 8–2 Small Group Communication Networks

not all groups meet face to face. The crew who waits tables and prepares the food at a restaurant and the group of nurses, aids, and technicians who staff an eight- or ten-hour hospital shift rarely sit down together to discuss their work. When group members aren't in immediate contact with one another, information can flow through a variety of other networks (see Figure 8–2). Some follow a **chain network,** moving sequentially from one member to another. Chains are an efficient way to deliver simple verbal messages or to circulate written information when members can't manage to attend a meeting at one time. You might use this approach to route an important message to members of a team at work, asking each person to initial a memo and pass it along to the next person on a routing slip. Chain networks are not very reliable for lengthy or complex verbal messages, because the content of the message can change as it passes from one person to another.

Another communication pattern is the **wheel network,** in which one person acts as a clearinghouse, receiving and relaying messages to all other members. Like chains, wheel networks are sometimes a practical choice, especially if one member is available to communicate with others all or most of the time. In a class group, you might use a wheel network if one of your members is usually near a telephone. This person can become the informational hub who keeps track of messages and people. Groups sometimes use wheel networks when relationships are strained between two or more members. In cases like this, the central member can serve as a mediator or facilitator who manages messages as they flow between others.

The success of a wheel network depends heavily on the skill of the **gatekeeper**—the person through whom information flows. If he or she is a skilled communicator, these mediated messages may help the group function effectively. But if the gatekeeper consciously or unconsciously distorts messages to suit personal goals or plays members off against one another, the group is likely to suffer.

Decision-Making Methods

Another way to classify groups is according to the approach they use to make decisions. There are several approaches a group can use to make decisions. We'll look at each of them now, examining their advantages and disadvantages.[24]

CONSENSUS **Consensus** occurs when all members of a group support a decision. The advantages of consensus are obvious: Full participation can increase the quality of the decision as well as the commitment of the members to support it. Consensus is especially important in decisions on critical or complex matters; in such cases, methods using less input can diminish the quality of or enthusiasm for a decision. Despite its advantages, consensus also has its disadvantages. It takes a great deal of time, which makes it unsuitable for emergencies. In addition, it is often very frustrating: Emotions can run high on important matters, and patience in the face of such pressures is difficult. Because of the need to deal with these emotional pressures, consensus calls for more communication skill than do other decision-making approaches. As with many things in life, consensus has high rewards, which come at a proportionately high cost.

MAJORITY CONTROL A naive belief of many people (perhaps coming from overzealous high school civics teachers) is that the democratic method of

During a [second-grade] science project . . . one of the 7-year-olds wondered out loud whether the baby squirrel they had in class was a boy or a girl. After pondering the issue for a few minutes, one budding scientist offered the suggestion that they have a class discussion about it and then take a vote.

Cal Downs, Wil Linkugel, and David M. Berg

Source: DILBERT reprinted by permission of United Feature Syndicate, Inc.

majority rule is always superior. This method does have its advantages in matters where the support of all members isn't necessary, but in more important matters it is risky. Remember that even if a 51 percent majority of the members favors a plan, 49 percent might still oppose it—hardly sweeping support for any decision that needs the support of all members in order to work.

Besides producing unhappy members, decisions made under majority rule often are of a quality inferior to that of decisions hashed out by a group until the members reach consensus.[25] Under majority rule, members who recognize that they are outvoted often participate less, and the deliberations usually end after a majority opinion has formed—even though minority viewpoints might be worthwhile.

EXPERT OPINION Sometimes one group member will be defined as an expert and, as such, will be given the power to make decisions. This method can work well when that person's judgment is truly superior. For example, if a group of friends is

*"Now that you've all put in your two cents' worth,
I should like to interject my fifty-one per cent controlling interest."*

backpacking in the wilderness, and one becomes injured, it would probably be foolish to argue with the advice of a doctor in the group. In most cases, however, matters aren't so simple. Who is the expert? There is often disagreement on this question. Sometimes a member might think he or she is the best qualified to make a decision, but others will disagree. In a case like this, the group probably won't support that person's advice, even if it is sound.

MINORITY CONTROL   Sometimes a few members of a group will decide matters. This approach works well with noncritical questions that would waste the whole group's time. In the form of a committee, a minority of members also can study an issue in greater detail than can the entire group. When an issue is so important that it needs the support of everyone, it's best at least to have the committee report its findings for the approval of all members.

AUTHORITY RULE   Authority rule is the approach most often used by autocratic leaders (see Chapter 9). Though it sounds dictatorial, there are times when such an approach has its advantages. This method is quick: There are cases when there simply isn't time for a group to decide what to do. The approach is also perfectly acceptable with routine matters that don't require discussion in order to gain approval. When overused, however, this approach causes problems. As Chapter 9 will show, much of the time group decisions are of higher quality and gain more support from members than those made by an individual. Thus, failure to consult with members can lead to a decrease of effectiveness even when the leader's decision is a reasonable one.

When the person in authority consults members before making a decision, the results gain some of the quality and commitment that come from group interaction while also enjoying the speed that comes from avoiding extensive discussion. This approach has its disadvantages, however. In some cases other group members will be tempted to tell the leader what they think he or she wants to hear, and in other cases they will compete to impress the decision maker.

Which of these decision-making approaches is best? The answer can vary from one culture to another. In Japan, consensus is highly valued. British and Dutch businesspeople also value the "team must be aboard" approach. On the other hand, Germans, French, and Spanish communicators depend more on the decision of a strong leader and view a desire for consensus as somewhat wishy-washy.[26]

Culture notwithstanding, the most effective approach in a given situation depends on the circumstances:

- **The type of decision** Some decisions can best be made by an expert, whereas others will benefit from involving the entire group.
- **The importance of the decision** If the decision is relatively unimportant, it's probably not worth involving all members of the group. By contrast, critical decisions probably require the participation, and ideally the buy-in, of all members.
- **Time available** If time is short, it may not be possible to assemble the entire group for deliberations.[27]

When choosing a decision-making approach, weigh the pros and cons of each before you decide which one has the best chance of success in the situation your group is facing.

CULTURAL IDIOM
buy-in: support

Choosing the Best Decision-Making Approach

Describe which of the decision-making approaches listed on pages 273–276 would be most appropriate in each of the following situations. Explain why your recommended approach is the best one for this situation.

1. Four apartment mates must decide how to handle household chores.
2. A group of hikers and their experienced guide become lost in a snowstorm and debate whether to try to find their way to safety or to pitch camp and wait for the weather to clear.
3. After trying unsuccessfully to reach consensus, the partners in a new business venture cannot agree on the best name for their enterprise.
4. A twenty-five-member ski club is looking for the cheapest airfare and lodging for its winter trip.
5. A passenger falls overboard during an afternoon sail on your friend's twenty-foot sailboat. The wind is carrying the boat away from the passenger.

CULTURAL INFLUENCES ON GROUP COMMUNICATION

Groups don't operate in isolation. They are influenced by a variety of factors, some obvious and others less obvious. One of the most subtle and yet profound forces that shapes group communication is the culture in which they exist. Culture provides a set of unstated assumptions and rules that determines how members will behave toward one another and how they will tackle the job at hand. After surveying over 160,000 members of organizations in sixty countries, Geert Hofstede identified four cultural forces that shape the attitudes and behaviors of groups and individuals.[28] We will examine each of them in the following pages.

Individualism versus Collectivism

Some cultures value the individual, whereas others value the group. As Table 8–4 shows, the United States is one of the world's more individualistic societies, along with Canada, Australia, and Britain. By contrast, Latin American and Asian societies are generally more collectivistic.

UNDERSTANDING DIVERSITY

Baseball in Japan and the USA

The concept and practice of group harmony or *wa* is what most dramatically differentiates Japanese baseball from the American game. It is the connecting thread running through all Japanese life and sports. While "Let It All Hang Out" and "Do Your Own Thing" are mottoes of contemporary American society, the Japanese have their own credo in the well-worn proverb, "The Nail That Sticks Up Shall Be Hammered Down." It is practically a national slogan.

Holdouts, for example, are rare in Japan. A player usually takes what the club deigns to give him and that's that. Demanding more money is evidence that a player is putting his own interests before those of the team.

In the pressure-cooker world of U.S. pro sports, temper outbursts are considered acceptable, and at times even regarded as a salutary show of spirit. In Japan, however, a player's behavior is often considered as important as his batting average. Batting slumps are usually accompanied by embarrassed smiles. Temper tantrums—along with practical joking, bickering, complaining, and other norms of American clubhouse life—are viewed in Japan as unwelcome incursions into the team's collective peace of mind.

When [Tokyo] Giants top pitcher Takashi Nishimoto ignored the instructions of a coach in practice one summer day in 1985, the coach punched him between the eyes. Nishimoto was also forced to apologize and pay a one-hundred thousand yen fine for insubordination.

Moreover, untoward behavior is also seen as a sign of character weakness and a "small heart," as well as being detrimental to the team's image overall. In Japan, a "real man" is one who keeps his emotions to himself and thinks of others' feelings.

Robert Whiting
You Gotta Have Wa

Members of individualistic cultures view their primary responsibility as being to themselves, whereas members of collectivistic societies feel loyalties and obligations to the groups of which they are members: the family, the community, the organization they work for, and their working teams. Members of individualistic societies gain most of their identity and self-esteem from their own accomplishments, whereas members of collectivistic societies are identified with the groups to which they belong. Individualistic cultures are also characterized by self-reliance and competition, whereas collectivistic cultures are more attentive to and concerned with the opinions of significant others.[29] Individualistic and collectivistic cultures have very different approaches to communication. For example, individualistic cultures are relatively tolerant of conflicts, using a direct, solution-oriented approach. By contrast, members of collectivistic cultures are less direct.[30]

It's easy to see how a culture's **individualistic** or **collectivistic orientation** can affect group communication. Members of collectivistic cultures are more likely to be team players, whereas members of individualistic ones are far more likely to produce and reward stars. As members of highly individualistic cultures, North Americans often need to control their desires to dominate group discussions and to "win" in problem-solving situations. Consensus may be a desirable outcome, but it doesn't always come easily to individualists. By contrast, members of collectivistic cultures need to consider when speaking out—even if it means disagreeing—is always in the best interests of the group.

CULTURAL IDIOM

holdouts: those who refuse to participate until they receive a satisfactory contract offer

speaking out: saying boldly what one thinks

Power Distance

Some cultures accept differences in power and status, whereas others accept them grudgingly, if at all. Most members of U.S. and Canadian cultures are firm believers in the principle of equality, which means that the notion that some people are entitled to greater power or privilege doesn't come easily. In other cultures, inequality is accepted as a fact of life.[31] **Power distance** refers to the degree to which members are willing to accept a difference in power and status between members of a group. In a culture with a high power distance, group members might willingly subordinate themselves to a leader—especially one whose title comes from socially accepted sources such as age, experience, training, or status. By contrast, members of cultures where low power distance is the norm would probably be less likely to feel that many groups need a leader or that people who do occupy that role automatically deserve unquestioning obedience. Supervisors, bosses, teachers, and so on certainly have the respect of the members they lead in cultures where low power distance is the norm—but mostly because they earn it. In low power distance cultures, group members expect leaders to be more considerate of their interests and needs. "After all," they assume, "we're basically equal."

TABLE 8–4   Cultural Values in Selected Countries

(Countries ranked lower on each list are closer to the mean)

Individualistic	Collectivistic
U.S.A.	Venezuela
Australia	Taiwan
Great Britain	Mexico
Canada	Philippines

Low Power Distance	High Power Distance
Israel	Philippines
New Zealand	Mexico
Germany	India
U.S.A.	France

Low Uncertainty Avoidance	High Uncertainty Avoidance
Singapore	Greece
India	Japan
Philippines	Peru
U.S.A.	Mexico

High Task Orientation	High Social Orientation
Japan	Sweden
Austria	Norway
Italy	Chile
Mexico	Portugal

Long-Term Focus	Short-Term Focus
China (includes Hong Kong and Taiwan)	Pakistan
Japan	Canada
South Korea	Great Britain
Brazil	U.S.A.
India	Australia

Source: Based on research summarized in G. Hofstede, *Culture and Organizations: Software of the Mind* (New York: McGraw-Hill, 1997).

Uncertainty Avoidance

Some cultures accept—and even welcome—risk, uncertainty, and change.[32] Others, characterized by **uncertainty avoidance**, are uncomfortable with these unavoidable trends. Instead, they favor stability and tradition. Geography offers no clue to a culture's tolerance of uncertainty. Countries whose members tend to avoid surprises include Greece, Portugal, Turkey, Mexico, and Israel. Among those who are more comfortable with change are Denmark, Hong Kong, Ireland, and India.

It should come as no surprise that uncertainty avoidance affects the way members of groups communicate. They are uncomfortable with ambiguous tasks and reluctant to take risks. They worry more about the future, are more loyal to employers, and accept seniority as the basis for leadership. They view conflict as undesirable and are also less willing to compromise when disagreements arise. By contrast, members of groups who come from cultures with a higher tolerance for uncertainty are more willing to take risks, more accepting of change, and more willing to break rules for pragmatic reasons. They accept conflict as natural and are willing to compromise when disagreements occur.

Task versus Social Orientation

The categories of task and social orientation were originally labeled "masculine" and "feminine," based on traditional views that men are assertive and results oriented, whereas women are nurturing. In an era of increasingly flexible sex roles these labels are considered sexist and misleading, so we have substituted different labels. Groups in societies with a strong task orientation (Japan, Austria, Switzerland, and Mexico are examples) focus heavily on getting the job done. By contrast, groups in societies with a high degree of social orientation (including all the Scandinavian countries, Chile, Portugal, and Thailand) are more likely to be concerned about the feelings of members and their smooth functioning as a team. When compared to other countries, the United States falls slightly toward the task-oriented end of the spectrum, and Canada is almost exactly in the middle, balanced between task and social concerns.[33]

Task-oriented societies are characterized by a focus on making the team more competent through training and the use of up-to-date methods. In task-oriented societies members are highly concerned with individual success: advancing to more responsible jobs, better training, and so on. By contrast, groups in socially oriented societies focus more on collective concerns: cooperative problem solving, a friendly atmosphere, and good physical working conditions. Members may still be interested in solving the problem at hand, but they are reluctant to do so if the personal costs to members—in stress and hard feelings—may be high.

It's easy to see how a society's orientation toward task or social aspects of groups, uncertainty, individuality, and power distance can make a tremendous difference in how a group operates. Whether the group is an athletic team, a military unit, a working group, or a family, the principle is the same. Cultural values shape what groups communicate about and how they interact. Cultural differences don't account for every difference in group functioning, of course, but they do provide a common set of assumptions that exerts a subtle yet powerful effect on communication.

Short- versus Long-Term Orientation

Members of some cultures look for quick payoffs, whereas members of other cultures are willing to defer gratification in pursuit of long-range goals. The willingness to work hard today for a future payoff is especially common in East Asian cultures, including China, Japan, and South Korea. Western industrialized cultures are much more focused on short-term results.

As long as all group members share the same orientation toward payoffs, the chances for harmony are good. When some people push for a quick fix, while others urge patience, conflicts are likely to arise.

A fighter pilot soon found he wanted to associate only with other fighter pilots. Who else could understand the nature of the little proposition (right stuff/death) they were all dealing with? And what other subject could compare with it? It was riveting! To talk about it in so many words was forbidden, of course. The very words death, danger, bravery, fear were not to be uttered except in the occasional specific instance or for ironic effect. Nevertheless, the subject could be adumbrated in code or by example . . . They diced that righteous stuff up into little bits, bowed ironically to it, stumbled blindfolded around it, groped, lurched, belched, staggered, bawled, sang, roared, and feinted at it with self-deprecating humor. Nevertheless!—they never mentioned it by name.

Tom Wolfe
The Right Stuff

CULTURAL IDIOM

work in a vacuum:
function as if there are
no other individuals or
influences

SUMMARY

Groups play an important role in many areas of our lives—families, education, employment, and friendships, to name a few. Groups possess several characteristics that distinguish them from other communication contexts. They involve interaction over time among a small number of participants with the purpose of achieving one or more goals. Groups have their own goals, as do individual members. Member goals fall into two categories: task-related and social. Sometimes individual and group goals are compatible, and sometimes they conflict.

Groups can be put into several classifications—learning, growth, problem solving, and social. All these types of groups share certain characteristics: the existence of group norms, individual roles for members, patterns of interaction that are shaped by the group's structure, and the choice of one or more ways of reaching decisions.

Groups don't work in a vacuum. The culture in which they work influences the way members communicate with one another. The chapter examined four ways in which culture influences interaction: individualism versus collectivism, power distance, uncertainty avoidance, and task versus social orientation.

RESOURCES

Print

Golding, William. *Lord of the Flies.* London: Faber and Faber, 1954.

A group of schoolboys is marooned on an uninhabited island when their plane crashes there. The boys are forced to create their own society, which serves as a disturbing metaphor for the way adults have managed the larger world. The book (which has been filmed twice) offers many examples of the principles that influence communication in groups.

Frey, Lawrence R., ed. *Handbook of Group Communication Theory and Research.* Newbury Park, CA: Sage, 1999.

In this volume, leading communication scholars provide state-of-the-art reviews on a variety of group-related topics, including influence, creativity, technology, and socialization.

Larson, Carl E., and Frank M. J. LaFusto. *Team Work: What Must Go Right/What Can Go Wrong.* Newbury Park, CA: Sage, 1989.

Larson and LaFusto interviewed members of a variety of successful teams: cardiac surgeons, members of a Mount Everest climbing expedition, a championship football team, and the developers of the IBM personal computer. Based on their findings, the authors offer a list of the principles that are essential for successful teams.

Rothwell, J. Dan. *In Mixed Company,* 4th ed. Fort Worth, TX: Harcourt Brace, 2001.

This is a readable, comprehensive look at the process of communication in small groups. The book does an excellent job of summarizing literally hundreds of research studies in a manner that makes their value in everyday interaction clear. This book is ideal for readers looking for more information on group communication.

Films
Group Formation and Maintenance

The Full Monty (1997). Rated PG-13.

In Sheffield, England, six unemployed steelworkers band together to become amateur male strippers, which is the only alternative they can devise to welfare. The film offers a good example of the interaction between group and individual goals. All of the men share the desire to earn some desperately needed money, and all struggle in varying degrees with issues of self-esteem arising from the prospect of displaying their less-than-perfect bodies to the public. Gaz (Robert Carlyle) is a hapless but devoted divorced father trying to meet his support payments so his son will trust him. Gerald (Tom Wilkinson) is a former manager who has not found the nerve to tell his wife that he has been unemployed for six months. Dave (Mark Addy) juggles his need for cash with the potential humiliation of baring his flabby body to the public. This touching film shows how belonging to a group can help members gain strength and solve challenges that they could never tackle alone.

Group Goals and Power Distribution

One Flew over the Cuckoo's Nest. (1975). Rated R.

R. P. McMurphy (Jack Nicholson) is a perfectly sane convict who is sent to a mental institution as a punishment for troublemaking. As he begins to rally the patients' self-confidence, cohesiveness, and assertiveness, the control-hungry Nurse Ratched (Louise Fletcher) recognizes McMurphy is a threat to her dominion. The film offers vivid examples of many concepts discussed in this chapter, including norms, roles, and group and individual goals.

Conflict in Groups

Almost Famous (2000). Rated R.

This film is the semiautobiographical tale of writer-director Cameron Crowe's life as a teenage correspondent for *Rolling Stone* magazine in the early 1970s. In the movie, the Crowe-like character (his name is William Miller in the movie, and he is played by Patrick Fugit) tours with a band named Stillwater. Through Miller's eyes, we get a picture of the forces that affect the band as it goes on tour. For example, the group's vocalist and the lead guitarist, each of whom wants maximum recognition, illustrate the clash between individual and group goals.

Platoon (1986). Rated R.

This movie gives a soldier's view of the Vietnam War. Narrated by Chris Taylor (Charlie Sheen), a middle-class kid who enlisted to join the infantry, the film follows the life of an army platoon for several months in 1967–68. In addition to giving a feel for jungle fighting, *Platoon* profiles the personal conflicts of the soldiers in the platoon. The film portrays a small group under constant pressure. Its setting makes interpersonal conflicts more intense and the stakes higher than in more familiar surroundings, but the same principles that affect the platoon members are present in everyday groups.

Group Norms

Dangerous Minds (1995). Rated R.

Louanne Johnson (Michelle Pfeiffer) takes over as English teacher for a class of tough inner-city students. At first they challenge her, but soon Johnson's toughness (she is an ex-marine), teaching savvy, and genuine concern have the students excited about literature and learning. Although the focus is on Johnson's role in this transformation, the shift in the class's norms nicely illustrates how groups have their own standards of what counts as appropriate behavior.

The Right Stuff (1983). Rated PG.

This film (like Tom Wolfe's book, upon which it was based) chronicles the history of the original seven U.S. astronauts in the early days of America's space exploration program. More than detailing the astronauts' physical accomplishments, the film examines the attitudes that led them to risk death and their reactions to being treated as heroes. It contains many examples of the unspoken norms that these men developed to govern their approach to their jobs, one another, and the world at large.

CONTENTS

KEY TERMS

authoritarian leadership style
brainstorming
buzz group
coercive power
cohesiveness
conflict stage
democratic leadership style
emergence stage
expert power
focus group
force field analysis
forum
groupthink
information overload
information underload
laissez-faire leadership style
leader
Leadership Grid
legitimate power
nominal leader
orientation stage
panel discussion
parliamentary procedure
participative decision making
probative question
problem census
referent power
reinforcement stage
reward power
situational leadership
symposium
trait theories of leadership

AFTER STUDYING
THE MATERIAL
IN THIS CHAPTER . . .

YOU SHOULD UNDERSTAND:

1. The advantages of solving problems in groups.

2. The characteristics of several common discussion formats.

3. The steps in the rational problem-solving method.

4. The developmental stages in a problem-solving group.

5. The factors that contribute to group cohesiveness.

6. The factors that contribute to balanced participation in a group.

7. The various approaches to studying leadership.

YOU SHOULD BE ABLE TO:

1. Use the problem-solving steps outlined in this chapter in solving a group task.

2. Suggest ways to build the cohesiveness and participation in a group.

3. Analyze the sources of leadership and power in a group.

4. Suggest the most effective leadership approach for a specific task.

5. Identify the obstacles to effective functioning of a specific group and suggest more effective ways of communicating.

SOLVING
PROBLEMS
IN GROUPS

Chapter 8 described various types of groups—learning, growth, social, and problem-solving groups. Of all these, problem-solving groups have been studied most intensively by social scientists. After we understand the nature of problem solving, the reason becomes clear. *Solving problems,* as we define it here, doesn't refer only to situations where something is wrong. Perhaps *meeting challenges* and *performing tasks* are better terms. After you recognize this fact, you can see that problem solving occupies a major part of working life. The figures from just one company illustrate the scope of group problem solving: At 3M Corporation, managers spend a total of 4.4 million hours per year in meetings, at a cost to the company of $78.8 million in salaries.[1] Away from work, groups also meet to solve problems: Nonprofit organizations plan fund-raisers, athletic teams work to improve their collective performance, neighbors meet to improve the quality of life where they live, educators and parents work together to improve schools—the list is almost endless.

This chapter will focus on both the task and the relational aspects of problem-solving groups. In addition, it will explore the nature of *leadership,* defining that important term and suggesting how groups can be led most effectively. Finally, it will list several common problems task-oriented groups can encounter and describe how to overcome them.

PROBLEM SOLVING IN GROUPS: WHEN AND WHY

To many people, groups are to communication what Muzak is to music or Twinkies are to food—a joke. The snide remark, "A camel is a horse designed by a committee" reflects this attitude, as does this ditty:

> Search all your parks in all your cities . . .
> You'll find no statues to committees![2]

This unflattering reputation is at least partly justified. Most of us would wind up with a handsome sum if we had a dollar for every hour wasted in groups. On the other hand, it's unfair to view all groups as bad, especially when this accusation implies that other types of communication are by nature superior. After all, we also have wasted time listening to boring lectures, reading worthless books, and making trivial conversation.

So what's the truth? Is group problem solving a waste of effort, or is it the best way to manage a task? As with most matters, the truth falls somewhere between these two extremes. Groups do have their shortcomings, which we will discuss in a few pages. But extensive research has shown that when these shortcomings can be avoided, groups are clearly the most effective way to handle many tasks.

Advantages of Group Problem Solving

Research over fifty years that has compared problem solving by groups to that by individuals shows that, in most cases, groups can produce more solutions to a problem than individuals working alone—and that the solutions will be of higher quality.[3] Groups have proved superior at a wide range of tasks—everything from assembling jigsaw puzzles to solving complex reasoning problems. There are several reasons why groups are effective.

RESOURCES For many tasks, groups possess a greater collection of resources than do most individuals. Sometimes the resources are physical. For example, three or four people can put up a tent or dig a ditch better than a lone person. But on other problems the pooled resources lead to qualitatively better solutions. Think, for instance, about times when you have studied with other students for a test, and you will remember how much better the group was at preparing for all the questions that might be asked and at developing answers to them. (This, of course, assumes that the study group members cared enough about the exam to have studied for it before the group meeting.) Groups not only have more resources than individuals, but also through interaction among the members they are better able to mobilize them. Talking about an upcoming test with others can jog your memory about items you might not have thought of if you had been working alone.

ACCURACY Another benefit of group work is the increased likelihood of catching errors. At one time or another, we all make stupid mistakes, like the man who built a boat in his basement and then wasn't able to get it out the door. Working in a group increases the chance that foolish errors like this won't slip by. Sometimes, of course, errors aren't so obvious, which makes groups even more valuable as an error-checking mechanism. Another side to the error-detecting story is the risk that group members will support each other in a bad idea. We'll discuss this problem when we focus on conformity later in this chapter.

COMMITMENT Besides coming up with superior solutions, groups also generate a higher commitment to carrying them out. Members are most likely to accept solutions they have helped create, and they will work harder to carry out those solutions. This fact has led to the principle of **participative decision making,** in which the people who will live with a plan help make it. This is an especially important principle for those in authority, such as supervisors, teachers, and parents. As professors, we have seen the difference between the sullen compliance of students who have been forced to accept a policy with which they disagree and the much more willing cooperation of students who have helped develop it. Though the benefits of participative decision making are great, we need to insert a qualification here: There are times when an autocratic approach of imposing a decision without discussion is most effective. We will discuss this question of when to be democratic and when to be directive in the section on leadership later in this chapter.

When to Use Groups for Problem Solving

Despite their advantages, groups aren't always the best way to solve a problem. Many jobs can be tackled more quickly and easily—even more efficiently—by one or more people working independently. Answering the following questions will help you decide when to solve a problem using a group and when to tackle it alone.[4]

CULTURAL IDIOM

jog your memory:
remind yourself

IS THE JOB BEYOND THE CAPACITY OF ONE PERSON? Some jobs are simply too big for one person to manage. They may call for more information than a single person possesses or can gather. For example, a group of friends planning a large New Year's party will probably have a better event if they pool their ideas than if one person tries to think of everything. Some jobs also require more time and energy than one person can spare. Putting on the New Year's party could involve a variety of tasks: inviting the guests, hiring a band, finding a place large enough to hold the party, buying food and drinks, and so on. It's both unrealistic and unfair to expect one or two people to do all this work.

CULTURAL IDIOM

cut-and-dried: the usual thing

ARE INDIVIDUALS' TASKS INTERDEPENDENT? Remember that a group is more than a collection of individuals working side by side. The best tasks for groups are ones where the individuals can help one another in some way. Think of a group of disgruntled renters considering how to protest unfair landlords. In order to get anywhere, they realize that they have to assign areas of responsibility to each member: researching the law, getting new members, publicizing their complaints, and so on. It's easy to see that these jobs are all interdependent: Getting new members, for example, will require publicity; and publicizing complaints will involve showing how the renters' legal rights are being violated.

One manager let employees know how valuable they are with the following memo:

```
YOU ARX A KXY PXRSON

Xvxn though my typxwritxr is an old modxl, it works vxry
wxll—xxcxpt for onx kxy. You would think that with all
thx othxr kxys functioning propxrly, onx kxy not working
would hardly bx noticxd; but just onx kxy out of whack
sxxms to ruin thx wholx xffort.
    You may say to yoursxlf—Wxll I'm only onx pxrson. No
onx will noticx if I don't do my bxst. But it doxs makx a
diffxrxncx bxcausx to bx xffxctivx an organization nxxds
activx participation by xvxry onx to thx bxst of his or
hxr ability.
    So thx nxxt timx you think you arx not important,
rxmxmbxr my old typxwritxr. You arx a kxy pxrson.
```

Even when everyone is working on the same job, there can be interdependence if different members fulfill the various functional roles described in Chapter 8. Some people might be better at task-related roles like information giving, diagnosing, and summarizing. Others might contribute by filling social roles such as harmonizing, supporting, or relieving tension. People working independently simply don't have the breadth of resources to fill all these functions.

IS THERE MORE THAN ONE DECISION OR SOLUTION? Groups are best suited to tackling problems that have no single, cut-and-dried answer: What's the best way to boost membership in a campus organization? How can funds be raised for a charity? What topic should the group choose for a class project? Gaining the perspectives of every member boosts the odds of finding high-quality answers to questions like these.

By contrast, a problem with only one solution won't take full advantage of a group's talents. For example, phoning merchants to get price quotes and looking up a series of books in the library don't require much creative thinking. Jobs like these can be handled by one or two people working alone. Of course, it may take a group meeting to decide how to divide the work to get the job done most efficiently.

Once upon a September Day—

Another meeting! One after another without coming up with a proposal that would fly.

This one took place in early September and (not surprisingly) only a few people showed up—12, to be precise. And so they talked for some days and finally came up with a plan for still another meeting, eight months hence. It was hoped this would offer sufficient time to generate interest in the matter.

They also moved the location. It was not that the September site had been unpleasant—on the contrary, the facilities were quite good—but variety in meeting places might induce more individuals to attend.

Of the 74 invitees, 55 showed up. But they didn't all come at once. They were supposed to convene on Monday, May 14, but it wasn't until Friday, May 25, that enough were present to conduct business. They decided to work diligently from that day on until they finished their proposal. They even agreed to put a lid on their deliberations.

They were a relatively young group; the average age was 42. The youngest was 30 and the oldest 82 and prone to nod during long meetings. Although some were lackluster in ability, most were able and would later move to high executive positions.

They were together for 116 days, taking off only Sundays and 12 other days. And you might have guessed it: During a very hot summer they were with-out air conditioning. In addition to the formal sessions of the entire group, much of their work was done in committee and after hours.

The formal sessions sometimes got out of hand. One faction had come with a proposal that was almost the reverse of an outline offered by another group. The advocates of each seemed unwilling to bend, and by the end of June tempers were flaring so much that the oldest participant suggested beginning each session with an invocation.

By early June, they got wind of a way out of their impasse: Adopt a portion of each plan. By compromising, they might be better able to sell their product to a broad market. Yet even this task of drawing the line between two extremes was not easy, and so some decided to go home or back to their offices. It simply was not worth the effort.

Even among those who remained there was still criticism of the final proposal. It was much too short, some argued—only 4,000 words. Four months of work and only 4,000 words! It was scarcely enough to fill a few sheets of paper. But 39 of them felt it was the best they could come up with. It was good enough to sign, which they did on the 17th day of September, 1787.

And they called their proposal the Constitution of the United States.

Thomas V. DiBacco

When to Use Group Problem Solving

Explain which of the following tasks would best be managed by a group.

1. Collecting and editing a list of films illustrating communication principles
2. Deciding what the group will eat for lunch at a one-day meeting
3. Choosing the topic for a class project
4. Finding which of six companies had the lowest auto insurance rates
5. Designing a survey to measure community attitudes toward a subsidy for local artists

> **CULTURAL IDIOM**
>
> **to put a lid on:** to limit the time spent
>
> **to nod:** to fall asleep
>
> **out of hand:** out of control
>
> **got wind of:** learned about

IS THERE POTENTIAL FOR DISAGREEMENT?   Tackling a problem as a group is essential if you need the support of everyone involved. Consider a group of friends planning a vacation trip. Letting one or two people choose the destination, schedule, and budget would be asking for trouble, because their decisions would almost certainly disappoint at least some of the people who weren't consulted. It would be far smarter to involve everyone in the most important decisions, even if doing so took more time. After the key decisions were settled, it might be fine to delegate relatively minor issues to one or two people.

TYPES OF PROBLEM-SOLVING FORMATS

Groups meet to solve problems in a variety of settings and for a wide range of reasons. The formats they use are also varied. Some groups meet before an audience to address a problem. The onlookers may be involved in, and affected by, the topic under discussion, like the citizens who attend a typical city council meeting or voters who attend a candidates' debate. In other cases, the audience members are simply interested spectators, as occurs in televised discussions such as *Meet the Press* and *Face the Nation*.

This list of problem-solving formats and approaches is not exhaustive, but it provides a sense of how a group's structure can shape its ability to come up with high-quality solutions.

1. **Buzz groups**   When the number of members is too large for effective discussion, **buzz groups** can be used to maximize effective participation. In this approach, subgroups (usually consisting of five to seven members) simultaneously address an issue and then report back to the group at large. The best ideas of each buzz group are then assembled to form a high-quality decision.

2. **Problem census**   This approach is useful when groups want to identify important issues or problems. **Problem census** works especially well when some members are more vocal than others, because it equalizes participation. Members use a separate card to list each of their ideas. The leader collects all cards and reads them to the group one by one, posting each on a board visible to everyone. Because the name of the person who contributed each item isn't listed, issues are separated from personalities. As similar items are read, the leader posts and arranges them in clusters. After all items are read and posted, the leader and members consolidate similar items into a number of ideas that the group needs to address.

3. **Focus groups**   **Focus groups** are used as a market research tool to enable sponsoring organizations to learn how potential users or the public at large regards a new product or idea. Unlike other groups discussed here, focus groups don't include decision makers or other members who claim any ex-

UNDERSTANDING COMMUNICATION TECHNOLOGY

Mediated Meetings: Pros and Cons

Face-to-face meetings can be difficult. Just scheduling a session can be maddening: Almost every date or time that one person suggests doesn't work for someone else. If the participants come from different locations, the time and cost of a meeting can be significant. Challenges don't end after a meeting time is finally arranged. Some members may be late. Others have to leave early. And during the meeting distractions are common: Members are sidetracked by off-the-topic digressions and other distractions. One or more people dominate the conversation, whereas others rarely speak.

Given the drawbacks of meeting in person, the idea of using technology to create other ways of working together has strong appeal. One approach is teleconferencing: a multiway phone call in which members from several locations can collaborate. Other approaches involve computer conferencing, in which members exchange messages over digital networks. In a synchronous "chat room" computer conference members communicate in real time, as if they were talking over the phone or meeting in person. Asynchronous discussions resemble e-mail: Group members don't have to be online on at the same time. They can log on to the network at their convenience, check messages others have sent, and contribute their own ideas for other team members to read later.

In the 1990s, communication researchers began to sort out the advantages and disadvantages of computer-mediated meetings as compared to face-to-face interaction. Studies suggest that computer conferencing does have several advantages. Most obviously, it is much easier to schedule and "meet" online, because members don't need to travel any farther than their desktop PCs. Asynchronous meetings are especially convenient, because group members can log on at their convenience, independent of other participants. Furthermore, computer-mediated sessions encourage more balanced participation: Members who might have kept quiet in face-to-face sessions are more comfortable "speaking out" online. Also, online meetings generate a permanent record of the proceedings, which can be convenient.

Despite their advantages, computer-mediated groups aren't a panacea. The lack of nonverbal cues makes it difficult to convey and understand members' emotions and attitudes. Mediated meetings may be more convenient, but groups working at a distance take more time to reach decisions than those who meet face to face. Because typing takes more time and effort than speaking, messages conveyed via computer can lack the detail of spoken ones. In some cases, members may not even bother to type out a message online that they would have shared in person. Finally, the string of separate messages that is generated in a computerized medium can be hard to track, sort out, and synthesize in a meaningful way.

Research comparing the quality of decisions made by face-to-face and online groups is mixed. Some studies have found no significant differences. Others have found that computer-mediated groups generate more ideas than people meeting in person, although they take longer to reach agreement on which are best. The growing body of research suggests that certain types of mediated communication work better than others. For example, asynchronous groups seem to make better decisions than those functioning in a "chat" mode. Groups who have special decision-support software perform better than ones operating without this advantage. Having a moderator also improves the effectiveness of online groups.

What use does this information have for groups who want to decide how to meet? Perhaps the most valuable lesson is that online meetings should not replace face-to-face ones, but they can be a *supplement* to in-person sessions. Combining the two forms of interaction can help groups operate both efficiently and effectively.

For more information on computer-mediated meetings, see K. A. Graetz, E. S. Boyle, C. E. Kimble, P. Thompson, and J. L. Garloch, "Information Sharing in Face-to-Face, Teleconferencing, and Electronic Chat Groups," *Small Group Research* 29 (1998): 714–743.

pertise on a subject. Instead, their comments are used by decision makers to figure out how people in the wider world might react to ideas.

4. **Parliamentary procedure**   Problem-solving meetings can follow a variety of formats. A session that uses **parliamentary procedure** observes specific rules about how topics may be discussed and decisions made. The standard reference book for parliamentary procedure is the revised edition of *Robert's Rules of Order.* Although the parliamentary rules may seem stilted and cumbersome, when well used, they do keep a discussion on track and protect the rights of the minority against domination by the majority.

5. **Panel discussion**   Another common problem-solving format is the **panel discussion,** in which the participants talk over the topic informally, much as they would in an ordinary conversation. A leader (called a "moderator" in public discussions) may help the discussion along by encouraging the comments of some members, cutting off overly talkative ones, and seeking consensus when the time comes for making a decision.

6. **Symposium**   In a **symposium** the participants divide the topic in a manner that allows each member to deliver in-depth information without interruption. Although this format lends itself to good explanations of each person's decision, the one-person-at-a-time nature of a symposium won't lead to a

UNDERSTANDING COMMUNICATION TECHNOLOGY

Software to Aid Decision Making

Group software makes it easy for people to meet online when a face-to-face session isn't necessary or possible. As useful as these software programs are, they don't help groups come to conclusions. Online meetings can seem to go on forever, one e-mail after another. Because you can't see other members' nonverbal cues, it's often hard to get a sense of where the group stands in relation to the problem.

Software programs like Vroom (www.virtualwork-room.com) provide a framework designed to help groups move toward a decision. Instead of providing just a place for members to post their remarks formlessly, Vroom shows the status of the discussion: How many proposals are there? How close is the group to

making a decision? Are members tending toward one position, or is the group divided? Who is talking most, and who hasn't spoken up yet?

Vroom forces people to declare their views. It shows who keeps bringing up an idea that nobody else supports. Users can use the software to set a deadline or even to specify how many team members must declare themselves ready before a vote is held.

Software like this goes beyond re-creating face-to-face meetings. It helps team members better understand how their discussion is progressing (or not progressing) and hopefully helps them make better decisions.

B.C.

Source: By permission of John Hart and Creators Syndicate, Inc.

TABLE 9-1   Some Communication Factors Associated with Group Productivity

The group contains the smallest number of members necessary to accomplish its goals.

Members care about and agree with the group's goals.

Members are clear about and accept their roles, which match the abilities of each member.

Group norms encourage high performance, quality, success, and innovation.

The group members have sufficient time together to develop a mature working unit and accomplish its goals.

The group is highly cohesive and cooperative.

The group spends time defining and discussing problems it must solve and decisions it must make.

Periods of conflict are frequent but brief, and the group has effective strategies for dealing with conflict.

The group has an open communication structure in which all members may participate.

The group gets, gives, and uses feedback about its effectiveness.

Adapted from research summarized in S. A. Wheelan, D. Murphy, E. Tsumaura, and S. F. Kline, "Member Perceptions of Internal Group Dynamics and Productivity," *Small Group Research* 29 (1998): 371–393.

group decision. The contributions of the members must be followed by the give-and-take of an open discussion.

7. **Forum**   A **forum** allows nonmembers to add their opinions to the group's deliberations before the group makes a decision. This approach is commonly used by public agencies to encourage the participation of citizens in the decisions that affect them.

APPROACHES AND STAGES IN PROBLEM SOLVING

Groups may have the potential to solve problems effectively, but they don't always live up to this potential. What makes some groups succeed and others fail? Researchers spent much of the twentieth century asking this question. Two useful answers emerged from their work.

A Structured Problem-Solving Approach

Although we often pride ourselves on facing problems rationally, social scientists have discovered that much of the time logic and reason play little part in the way we make decisions.[5] The tendency to use nonrational approaches is unfortunate, because research shows that, to a great degree, a group's effectiveness is determined by whether or not it approaches a problem rationally and systematically.[6] Just as a poor blueprint or a shaky foundation can weaken a house, groups can fail by skipping one or more of the necessary steps in solving a problem.

As early as 1910, John Dewey introduced his famous "reflective thinking" method as a systematic method for solving problems.[7] Since then, other experts have suggested modifications of Dewey's approach. Some emphasize answering

CULTURAL IDIOM

the give-and-take: sharing

live up to: fulfill expectations

key questions, whereas others seek "ideal solutions" that meet the needs of all members. Research comparing various methods has clearly shown that, although no single approach is best for all situations, a structured procedure produces better results than "no pattern" discussions.[8]

The following problem-solving model contains the elements common to most structured approaches developed in the last eighty years:

1. Identify the problem
   a. What are the group's goals?
   b. What are individual members' goals?
2. Analyze the problem
   a. Word the problem as a probative question
   b. Gather relevant information
   c. Identify impelling and restraining forces
3. Develop creative solutions through brainstorming or the nominal group technique
   a. Avoid criticism at this stage
   b. Encourage "freewheeling" ideas
   c. Develop a large number of ideas
   d. Combine two or more individual ideas
4. Evaluate the solutions by asking which solution:
   a. Will best produce the desired changes
   b. Is most achievable
   c. Contains the fewest serious disadvantages
5. Implement the plan
   a. Identify specific tasks
   b. Determine necessary resources
   c. Define individual responsibilities
   d. Provide for emergencies
6. Follow up on the solution
   a. Meet to evaluate progress
   b. Revise approach as necessary

IDENTIFY THE PROBLEM   Sometimes a group's problem is easy to identify. The crew of a sinking ship, for example, doesn't need to conduct a discussion to understand that its goal is to avoid drowning or being eaten by a large fish.

There are many times, however, when the problems facing a group aren't so clear. As an example, think of an athletic team stuck deep in last place well into the season. At first the problem seems obvious: an inability to win any games. But a closer look at the situation might show that there are unmet goals—and thus other problems. For instance, individual members may have goals that aren't tied directly to winning: making friends, receiving acknowledgment as good athletes, not to mention the simple goal of having fun—of playing in the recreational sense of the word. You can probably see that if the coach or team members took a simplistic view of the situation, looking only at the team's win-lose record, analyzing player errors, training methods, and so on, some important problems would probably go overlooked. In this situation, the team's performance could probably be best improved by working on the basic problems—the frustration of the players about having their personal needs unmet. What's the moral here? That the way to start understanding a group's problem is to identify the concerns of each member.

What about groups who don't have problems? Several friends planning a surprise birthday party and a family deciding where to go for its vacation don't seem to be in the dire straits of a losing athletic team: They simply want to have fun. In cases like these, it may be helpful to substitute the word *challenge* for the more gloomy word *problem*. However we express it, the same principle applies to all task-oriented groups: The best place to start work is to identify what each member seeks as a result of belonging to the group.

ANALYZE THE PROBLEM   After you have identified the general nature of the problem facing the group, you are ready to look at the problem in more detail. There are several steps you can follow to accomplish this important job.

Word the Problem as a Probative Question   If you have ever seen a formal debate, you know that the issue under discussion is worded as a proposition: "The United States should reduce its foreign aid expenditures," for example. Many problem-solving groups define their task in much the same way. "We ought to spend our vacation in the mountains," suggests one family member. The problem with phrasing problems as propositions is that such wording invites people to take sides. Though this approach is fine for formal debates (which are contests rather like football or card games), premature side taking creates unnecessary conflict in most problem-solving groups.

A far better approach is to state the problem as a question. Note that this should be a **probative question**—an open one that encourages exploratory thinking. Asking, "Should we vacation in the mountains or at the beach?" still forces members to choose sides. A far better approach involves asking a question to help define the general goals that came out during the problem-identification stage: "What do we want our vacation to accomplish?" (that is, "relaxation," "adventure," "low cost," and so on).

Notice that this question is truly exploratory. It encourages the family members to work cooperatively, not forcing them to make a choice and then defend it. This absence of an either-or situation boosts the odds that members will listen openly to one another rather than listening selectively in defense of their own positions. There is even a chance that the cooperative, exploratory climate that comes from wording the question probatively will help the family arrive at consensus about where to vacation, eliminating the need to discuss the matter any further.

Gather Relevant Information   Groups often need to know important facts before they can make decisions or even understand the problem. We remember one group of students who determined to do well on a class presentation. One of their goals, then, was "to get an A grade." They knew that, to do so, they would have to present a topic that interested both the instructor and the students in the audience. Their first job, then, was to do a bit of background research to find out what subjects would be well received. They interviewed the instructor, asking what topics had been successes and failures in previous semesters. They tested some possible subjects on a few classmates and noted their reactions. From this research they were able to modify their original probative question—"How can we choose and develop a topic that will earn us an A grade?"—into a more specific one—"How can we choose and develop a topic that contains humor, action, and lots of information (to demonstrate our research skills to the instructor) and that contains practical information that will improve either the audience's social life, academic standing, or financial condition?"

Identify Impelling and Restraining Forces

After members understand what they are seeking, the next step is to see what forces stand between the group and its goals. One useful tool for this approach is the **force field analysis**—a list of the forces that help and hinder the group.[9] By returning to our earlier example of the troubled team, we can see how the force field operates. Suppose the team defined its problem-question as "How can we (1) have more fun and (2) grow closer as friends?"

One restraining force in Area (1) was clearly the team's losing record. But, more interestingly, discussion revealed that another damper on enjoyment came from the coach's obsession with winning and his infectiously gloomy behavior when the team failed. The main restraining force in Area (2) proved to be the lack of socializing among team members in nongame situations. The helping forces in Area 1 included the sense of humor possessed by several members and the confession by most players that winning wasn't nearly as important to them as everyone had suspected. The helping force in Area 2 was the desire of all team members to become better friends. In addition, the fact that members shared many interests was an important plus.

It's important to realize that most problems have many impelling and restraining forces, all of which need to be identified during this stage. This may call for another round of research. After the force field is laid out, the group is ready to move on to the next step—namely, deciding how to strengthen the impelling forces and weaken the restraining ones.

DEVELOP CREATIVE SOLUTIONS

After the group has set up a list of criteria for success, the next job is to develop a number of ways to reach its goal. Considering more than one solution is important, because the first solution may not be the best one. During this development stage, creativity is essential.[10] The biggest danger is the tendency of members to defend their own idea and criticize others'. This kind of behavior leads to two problems. First, evaluative criticism almost guarantees a defensive reaction from members whose ideas have been attacked. Second, evaluative criticism stifles creativity. People who have just heard an idea rebuked—however politely—will find it hard even to think of more alternatives, let alone share them openly and risk possible criticism. The following strategies can keep groups creative and maintain a positive climate.

A problem well stated is a problem half solved.

Charles Kettering

Source: FRANK & ERNEST reprinted by permission of Newspaper Enterprise Association, Inc.

Brainstorm   Probably the best-known strategy for encouraging creativity and avoiding the dangers just described is **brainstorming**.[11] There are four important rules connected with this strategy:

1. *Criticism Is Forbidden.* As we have already said, nothing will stop the flow of ideas more quickly than negative evaluation.
2. *"Freewheeling" Is Encouraged.* Sometimes even the most outlandish ideas prove workable, and even an impractical suggestion might trigger a workable idea.
3. *Quantity Is Sought.* The more ideas generated, the better the chance of coming up with a good one.
4. *Combination and Improvement Are Desirable.* Members are encouraged to "piggyback" by modifying ideas already suggested and to combine previous suggestions.

Although brainstorming is a popular creativity booster, it isn't a guaranteed strategy for developing novel and high-quality ideas. In some experiments, individuals working alone were able to come up with a greater number of high-quality ideas than were small groups.[12]

Use the Nominal Group Technique   Because people in groups often can't resist the tendency to criticize one another's ideas, the nominal group technique was developed to let members present ideas without being attacked but at the same

---

SKILL
BUILDER

Increasing Group Creativity

You can increase your skill at increasing creativity in group discussions by trying the approaches described in *Understanding Human Communication.* Your group should begin by choosing one of the following problems:

1. How can out-of-pocket student expenses (e.g., books, transportation) be decreased?
2. How can the textbook you are using in this (or any other) class be improved?
3. How could your class group (legally) earn the greatest amount of money between now and the end of the term?
4. What strategies can be used effectively when confronted with employer discrimination or harassment? (Assume you want to keep the job.)
5. Imagine that your group has been hired to develop a way of improving the course registration system at your institution. What three recommendations will be most effective?

Choose either brainstorming or the nominal group technique to develop possible solutions to your chosen problem. Explain why you chose the method. Under what conditions would the other method be more appropriate?

Creativity Killers in Group Discussion

Nothing squelches creativity like criticism. Although evaluating ideas is an important part of problem solving, judging suggestions too early can discourage members from sharing potentially valuable ideas. Here is a list of creativity-stopping statements that people should avoid making in the development phase of group work.

"That's ridiculous."
"It'll never work."
"You're wrong."

"What a crazy idea!"
"We tried it before, and it didn't work."
"It's too expensive."
"There's no point in talking about it."
"It's never been done like that."
"We could look like fools."
"It's too big a job."
"We could never do that."
"It's too risky."
"You don't know what you're talking about."

time to retain the key elements of brainstorming. As the following steps show, the pattern involves alternating cycles of individual work followed by discussion.

1. Each member works alone to develop a list of possible solutions.
2. In round-robin fashion, each member in turn offers one item from his or her list. The item is listed on a chart visible to everyone. Other members may ask questions to clarify an idea, but no evaluation is allowed during this step.
3. Each member privately ranks his or her choice of the ideas in order, from most preferable (five points) to least preferable (one point). The rankings are collected, and the top ideas are retained as the most promising solutions.
4. A free discussion of the top ideas is held. At this point critical thinking (though not personal criticism) is encouraged. The group continues to discuss until a decision is reached, either by majority vote or consensus.

EVALUATE POSSIBLE SOLUTIONS   After it has listed possible solutions, the group can evaluate the usefulness of each. One good way of identifying the most workable solutions is to ask three questions.

1. *Will This Proposal Produce the Desired Changes?* One way to find out is to see whether it successfully overcomes the restraining forces in your force field analysis.
2. *Can the Proposal Be Implemented by the Group?* Can the members strengthen impelling forces and weaken restraining ones? Can they influence others to do so? If not, the plan isn't a good one.
3. *Does the Proposal Contain Any Serious Disadvantages?* Sometimes the cost of achieving a goal is too great. For example, one way to raise money for a group is to rob a bank. Although this plan might be workable, it raises more problems than it solves.

IMPLEMENT THE PLAN   Everyone who makes New Year's resolutions knows the difference between making a decision and carrying it out. There are several important steps in developing and implementing a plan of action.

CULTURAL IDIOM

in round-robin fashion: go around in a circle, one after another

Identify Specific Tasks to Be Accomplished. What needs to be done? Even a relatively simple job usually involves several steps. Now is the time to anticipate all the tasks facing the group. Remember everything now, and you will avoid a last-minute rush later.

Determine Necessary Resources. Identify the equipment, material, and other resources the group will need in order to get the job done.

Define Individual Responsibilities. Who will do what? Do all the members know their jobs? The safest plan here is to put everyone's duties in writing, including the due date. This might sound compulsive, but experience shows that it increases the chance of having jobs done on time.

Provide for Emergencies. Murphy's Law states, "Whatever can go wrong, will." Anyone experienced in group work knows the truth of this law. People forget or welsh on their obligations, get sick, or quit. Machinery breaks down. (One corollary of Murphy's Law is "The copying machine will be out of order whenever it's most needed.") Whenever possible, you ought to develop contingency plans to cover foreseeable problems. Probably the single best suggestion we can give here is to plan on having all work done well ahead of the deadline, knowing that, even with last-minute problems, your time cushion will allow you to finish on time.

FOLLOW UP ON THE SOLUTION   Even the best plans usually require some modifications after they're put into practice. You can improve the group's effectiveness and minimize disappointment by following two steps.

Meet Periodically to Evaluate Progress. Follow-up meetings should be part of virtually every good plan. The best time to schedule these meetings is as you put the group's plan to work. At that time, a good leader or member will suggest: "Let's get together in a week (or a few days or a month, depending on the nature of the task). We can see how things are going and take care of any problems."

Revise the Group's Approach as Necessary. These follow-up meetings will often go beyond simply congratulating everyone for coming up with a good solution. Problems are bound to arise, and these periodic meetings, in which the key players are present, are the place to solve them.

Although these steps provide a useful outline for solving problems, they are most valuable as a general set of guidelines and not as a precise formula that every group should follow. As Table 9–2 suggests, certain parts of the model may need emphasis depending on the nature of the specific problem; the general approach will give virtually any group a useful way to consider and solve a problem.

Despite its advantages, the rational, systematic problem-solving approach isn't perfect. The old computer saying "Garbage in, garbage out" applies here: If the group doesn't possess creative talent, a rational and systematic approach to solving problems won't do much good. Despite its drawbacks, the rational approach does increase the odds that a group can solve problems successfully. Following the guidelines—even imperfectly—will help members analyze the problem, come up with solutions, and carry them out better than they could probably do without a plan.

Developmental Stages in Problem-Solving Groups

When it comes to solving problems in groups, research shows that the shortest distance to a solution isn't always a straight line. Communication scholar

TABLE 9-2   Adapting Problem-Solving Methods to Special Circumstances

Circumstances	Method
Members have strong feelings about the problem.	Consider allowing a period of emotional ventilation before systematic problem solving.
Task difficulty is high.	Follow the structure of the problem-solving method carefully.
Many possible solutions.	Emphasize brainstorming.
High level of member acceptance required.	Carefully define needs of all members, and seek solutions that satisfy all needs.
High level of technical quality required.	Emphasize evaluation of ideas; consider inviting outside experts.

Source: Adapted from "Adapting Problem-Solving Methods," *Effective Group Discussion,* 10th ed., John Brilhart and Gloria Galanes, p. 291. Copyright © 2001. Reprinted by permission of McGraw-Hill Companies, Inc.

Aubrey Fisher analyzed tape recordings of problem-solving groups and discovered that many successful groups seem to follow a four-stage process when arriving at a decision.[13] As you read about his findings, visualize how they have applied to problem-solving groups in your experience.

In the **orientation stage,** members approach the problem and one another tentatively. In some groups people may not know one another well, and even in ones where they are well acquainted they may not know one another's position on the issue at hand. For these reasons, people are reluctant to take a stand during the orientation stage. Rather than state their own position clearly and unambiguously, they test out possible ideas cautiously and rather politely. There is little disagreement. This cautiousness doesn't mean that members agree with one another; rather, they are sizing up the situation before asserting themselves. The orientation stage can be viewed as a calm before the storm.

After members understand the problem and become acquainted, a successful group enters the **conflict stage.** During this stage, members take strong positions and defend them against those who oppose their viewpoint. Coalitions are likely to form, and the discussion may become polarized. The conflict needn't be personal: It can focus on the issues at hand while preserving the members' respect for one another. Even when the climate does grow contentious, conflict seems to be a necessary stage in group development. The give-and-take of discussion tests the quality of ideas, and weaker ones may suffer a well-deserved death here.[14]

After a period of conflict, effective groups move to an **emergence stage.** One idea might emerge as the best one, or the group might combine the best parts of several plans into a new solution. As they approach consensus, members back off from their dogmatic positions. Statements become more tentative again: "I guess that's a pretty good idea," "I can see why you think that way."

Finally, an effective group reaches the **reinforcement stage.** At this point not only do members accept the group's decision, but also they endorse it. Whereas members used evidence to back up differing positions in the conflict stage, now

CULTURAL IDIOM

sizing up: assessing

they find evidence that will support the decision. Even if members disagree with the outcome, they do not voice their concerns. There is an unspoken drive toward consensus and harmony.

Ongoing groups can expect to move through this four-stage process with each new issue, so that their interaction takes on a cyclic pattern (see Figure 9–1). In fact, a group who deals with several issues at once might find itself in a different stage for each problem. In one series of studies, slightly less than 50 percent of the problem-solving groups examined followed this pattern.[15] The same research showed that a smaller percentage of groups (about 30 percent) didn't follow a cyclical pattern. Instead, they skipped the preliminary phases and focused on the solution.

What is the significance of the findings? They tell us that, like children growing toward adulthood, many groups can expect to pass through phases. Knowing that these phases are natural and predictable can be reassuring. It can help curb your impatience when the group is feeling its way through an orientation stage. It can also help you feel less threatened when the inevitable and necessary conflicts take place. Understanding the nature of emergence and reinforcement can help you know when it is time to stop arguing and seek consensus.

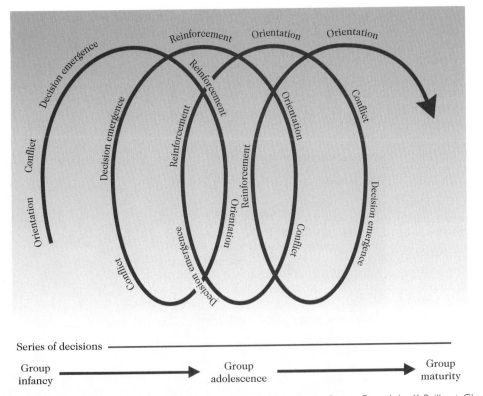

Figure 9–1 Cyclical Stages in an Ongoing Problem-Solving Group. *Source:* From John K. Brilhart, Gloria J. Galanes, and Katherine Adams, *Effective Group Discussion,* 10th ed. (New York: McGraw-Hill, 2001), p. 289.

CULTURAL IDIOM

boost the odds of:
increases the chances of
success

INVITATION
TO INSIGHT

Stages in Group Development

Identify a problem-solving group, either from your personal experience or from a book or film. Analyze the group's approach to problem solving. Does it follow the cyclical model pictured in Figure 9–1?
Does it follow a more linear approach? Or does the group follow
no recognizable pattern at all?

MAINTAINING POSITIVE RELATIONSHIPS

The task-related advice in the preceding pages will be little help if the members of a
group don't get along. We therefore need to look at some ways to maintain good relationships among members. Many of the principles described earlier in this book
apply here. Because these principles are so important, we will review them here.

Basic Skills

Groups are most effective when members feel good about one another.[16]
Probably the most important ingredient in good personal relationships is mutual
respect, and the best way to demonstrate respect for the other person is to listen
carefully. A more natural tendency, of course, is to assume you understand the
other members' positions and to interrupt or ignore them. Even if you are right,
however, this tendency can create a residue of ill feelings. On the other hand,
careful listening can at least improve the communication climate—and it may
even teach you something.

Groups are bound to disagree sooner or later. When they do, the win–win
problem-solving methods outlined in Chapter 6 boost the odds of solving the immediate issue in the most constructive way.[17] As you read in Chapter 8, taking
votes and letting the majority rule can often leave a sizable minority whose unhappiness can haunt the group's
future work. Consensus is
harder to reach in the short
term but far more beneficial in
the long term.

Building Cohesiveness

Cohesiveness can be defined
as the totality of forces that
causes members to feel themselves part of a group and
makes them want to remain in
that group. You might think of
cohesiveness as the glue that
bonds individuals together, giving them a collective sense of
identity.

Highly cohesive groups communicate differently than less

cohesive ones. Members spend more time interacting, and there are more expressions of positive feelings for one another. They report more satisfaction with the group and its work. In addition, cohesive groups have greater control over the behavior of their members.[18] With characteristics like these, it's no surprise that highly cohesive groups have the potential to be productive. In fact, one study revealed that cohesiveness proved to be the best predictor of a group's performance, both initially and over time.[19]

Despite its advantages, cohesiveness is no guarantee of success: If the group is united in supporting unproductive norms, members will feel close but won't get the job done. For example, consider members of a group of employees who have a boss they think is incompetent and unfair. They might grow quite cohesive in their opposition to the perceived tyranny, spending hours after (or during) work swapping complaints. They might even organize protests, work slowdowns, grievances to their union, or mass resignations. All these responses would boost cohesiveness, but they would not necessarily make the company more successful nor help the employees.

Research has disclosed a curvilinear relationship between cohesiveness and productivity: Up to a certain point, productivity increases as group members become a unified team. Beyond this point, however, the mutual attraction members feel for one another begins to interfere with the group's efficient functioning. Members may enjoy one another's company, but this enjoyment can keep them from focusing on the job at hand.

The goal, then, is to boost cohesiveness in a way that also helps get the job done. There are eight factors that can bring about these goals.

1. **Shared or Compatible Goals** People draw closer when they share a similar aim or when their goals can be mutually satisfied. For example, members of a conservation group might have little in common until a part of the countryside they all value is threatened by development. Some members might value the land because of its beauty; others, because it provides a place to hunt or fish; and still others, because the nearby scenery increases the value of their property; but as long as their goals are compatible, this collection of individuals will find that a bond exists that draws them together.

2. **Progress toward These Goals** While a group is making progress, members feel highly cohesive; when progress stops, cohesiveness decreases. All other things being equal, players on an athletic team feel closest when the team is winning. During extended losing streaks, it is likely that players will feel less positive about the team and less willing to identify themselves as members of the group.

3. **Shared Norms and Values** Although successful groups will tolerate and even thrive on some differences in members' attitudes and behavior, wide variation in the group's definition of what actions or beliefs are proper will reduce cohesiveness. If enough members hold different ideas of what behavior is acceptable, the group is likely to break up. Disagreements over values or norms can fall into many areas, such as humor, finance, degree of candor, and proportion of time allotted to work and play.

4. **Lack of Perceived Threat between Members** Cohesive group members see no threat to their status, dignity, and material or emotional well-being. When such interpersonal threats do occur, they can be very destructive. Often competition arises within groups, and as a result members feel threatened. Sometimes there is a struggle over who will be the nominal leader. At

other times, members view others as wanting to take over a functional role (problem solver, information giver, and so on), either through competition or criticism. Sometimes the threat is real, and sometimes it's only imagined, but in either case the group must neutralize it or face the consequences of reduced cohesiveness.

5. **Interdependence of Members** Groups become cohesive when their needs can be satisfied only with the help of other members. When a job can be done just as well by one person alone, the need for membership decreases. This factor explains the reason for food cooperatives, neighborhood yard sales, and community political campaigns. All these activities enable the participants to reach their goal more successfully than if they acted alone.

6. **Threat from outside the Group** When members perceive a threat to the group's existence or image (groups have self-concepts, just as individuals do), they grow closer together. Almost everyone knows of a family whose members seem to fight constantly among themselves—until an outsider criticizes one of them. At this point, the internal bickering stops, and for the moment the group unites against its common enemy. The same principle works on a larger scale when nations often bind up their internal differences in the face of external aggression.

7. **Mutual Perceived Attractiveness and Friendship** The factor of mutual attraction and friendship is somewhat circular because friendship and mutual attraction often are a result of the points just listed, yet groups often do become close simply because the members like each other.

8. **Shared Group Experiences** When members have been through some unusual or trying experience, they draw together. This explains why soldiers who have been in combat together often feel close and stay in touch for years after; it also accounts for the ordeal of fraternity pledging and other initiations. Many societies have rituals that all members share, thus increasing the group's cohesiveness.

It's important to realize that the eight factors just described interact with one another, often in contradictory ways. For instance, members of many groups are good friends who have been through thick and thin together (cohesiveness

---

CRITICAL THINKING PROBE

The Pros and Cons of Cohesiveness

1. Based on the information on pages 300–302 of this chapter and your own experiences, give examples of groups who meet each of the following descriptions:
   a. A level of cohesiveness so low that it interferes with productivity
   b. An optimal level of cohesiveness
   c. A level of cohesiveness so high that it interferes with productivity
2. For your answers to *a* and *c*, offer advice on how the level of cohesiveness could be adjusted to improve productivity.
3. Are there ever situations where maximizing cohesiveness is more important than maximizing productivity? Explain your answer, supporting it with examples.

builders), but they find themselves less dependent on each other than before and now struggle over playing certain roles. In cases like this, cohesiveness can be figured as the net sum of all attracting and dividing forces.

LEADERSHIP AND POWER IN GROUPS

Leadership . . . power . . . influence. For most of us, being in control of events ranks not far below parenthood in the hierarchy of values. "What are you, a leader or a follower?" we're asked, and we know which position is the better one. Even in groups without designated leaders, some members are more influential than others, and those who aren't out front at least some of the time are likely to feel frustrated.

The following pages will focus on how communication operates to establish influence. We will begin by looking at sources of power in groups, showing that not all influence rests with the person who is nominally in charge. We will then take a look at the communication behaviors that work best when one communicator is designated as the **leader**—or wants to acquire that role.

Power in Groups

We can begin by defining *power* as the ability to influence others. A few examples show that influence can appear in many forms.[20]

- In a tense meeting, apartment dwellers are arguing over crowded parking and late-night noise. One tenant cracks a joke and lightens up the tense atmosphere.
- A project team at work is trying to come up with a new way to attract customers. The youngest member, fresh from a college advertising class, suggests a winning idea.
- Workers are upset after the boss passes over a popular colleague and hires a newcomer for a management position. Despite their anger, they accept the decision after the colleague persuades them that she is not interested in a career move anyhow.
- A teacher motivates students to meet a deadline by awarding bonus points for projects that are turned in early and deducting points for ones turned in late.

These examples suggest that power comes in a variety of forms. We will examine each of them now.

LEGITIMATE POWER   Sometimes the ability to influence others comes from **legitimate power** (sometimes called *position power*). Legitimate power arises from the title one holds—supervisor, parent, or professor, for example. In many cases we follow the directions of others without knowing much about their qualifications, simply because we respect the role they occupy. In church we honor the request of the minister, and in courts we rise at judges' approach primarily because their positions confer authority on them.

Social scientists use the term **nominal leader** to label the person who is officially designated as being in charge of a group. Realize, however, that not all legitimate power resides with nominal leaders. The men and women with orange caps and vests who direct traffic at road repair sites are unlikely to be in charge of the project, yet they possess legitimate power in the eyes of motorists, who stop and start at their command.

The easiest way to acquire legitimate power is to have it conferred upon you by an outside authority. But being appointed isn't the only path to legitimate power: Even in groups who begin with no official leader, members can acquire legitimate power by the acknowledgment of others. Juries elect forepersons, and committees elect chairpersons. Teams choose a captain. Negotiating groups elect spokespeople. The subject of leadership emergence has been studied extensively.[21] Researchers have discovered several communicator characteristics that members who emerge as leaders possess: They speak up in group discussions without dominating others, they demonstrate their competence on the subject being discussed, they observe group norms, and they have the support of other influential members.

COERCIVE POWER   **Coercive power** occurs when influence comes from the threat or actual imposition of some unpleasant consequences. In school, at home, on the job, and in many other settings we sometimes do what others tell us, not because of any respect for the wisdom of their decisions but rather because the results of not obeying would be unpleasant. Economic hardship, social disapproval, undesirable work, even physical punishment—all are coercive forces that can shape behavior.

There are three reasons why coercion usually isn't the most effective type of power. First, it's likely to create a negative communication climate, because nobody likes to be threatened. Second, it can produce what has been called a "boomerang effect" in which a member who is threatened with punishment resists by doing exactly what the other members don't want. Third, coercion alone may tell others what *not* to do, but it doesn't tell them what you *do* want them to do. Telling an unproductive member, "If you can't contribute useful information, we'll kick you out of the group" doesn't offer much advice about what would count as "useful information."

Social scientists say that coercion has the best chance of success when it involves denial of an expected reward rather than the imposition of a negative consequence.[22] For example, canceling an upcoming vacation of a working group who doesn't meet its deadline is better than reducing employees' salaries. Even under circumstances like this, however, coercion alone is not as effective as the next kind of power, which involves rewards.

REWARD POWER   **Reward power** exists when others are influenced by the grant or promise of desirable consequences. Rewards come in a variety of forms. The most obvious are material reinforcers: money, awards, and so on. Other rewards can be social in nature. The praise of someone you respect can be a powerful motivator. Even spending time with people you like can be reinforcing.

Rewards don't come only from the official leader of a group. The goodwill of other members can sometimes be even more valuable. In a class group, for example, having your fellow students think highly of you might be a more powerful reward than the grade you could receive from the instructor. In fact, subordinates sometimes can reward nominal leaders just as much as the other way around. A boss might work hard to accommodate employees in order to keep them happy, for example.

EXPERT POWER **Expert power** exists when we are influenced by people because of what we believe they know or can do. For example, when a medical emergency occurs, most group members would gladly let a doctor, nurse, or paramedic make decisions because of that person's obvious knowledge. In groups it isn't sufficient to be an expert: The other members have to view you as one. This means that it is important to make your qualifications known if you want others to give your opinions extra weight.

INFORMATION POWER As its name implies, **information power** comes from a member's knowledge that he or she can help the group reach its goal. Not all useful information comes from experts with special credentials. For instance, a fundraising group seeking donations from local businesses might profit from the knowledge that one member has about which merchants are hospitable to the group's cause. Likewise, a class group working on a term project might benefit from the knowledge of one student who had taken other classes from the instructor who will be grading their work.

REFERENT POWER **Referent power** comes from the respect, liking, and trust others have for a member. If you have high referent power, you may be able to persuade others to follow your lead because they believe in you or because they are willing to do you a favor. Members acquire referent power by behaving in ways others in the group admire and by being genuinely likable. The kinds of confirming communication behaviors described in Chapter 7 can go a long way toward boosting referent power. Listening to others' ideas, honoring their contributions, and taking a win–win approach to meeting their needs lead to liking and respect.

After our look at various ways members can influence one another, three important characteristics of power in groups become clearer.[23]

- **Power Is Group-Centered.** Power isn't something an individual possesses. Instead, it is conferred by the group. You may be an expert on the subject being considered, but if the other members don't think you are qualified to talk, you won't have expert power. You might try to reward other people by praising their contributions; but if they don't value your compliments, then all the praise in the world won't influence them.
- **Power Is Distributed among Group Members.** Power rarely belongs to just one person. Even when a group has an official leader, other members usually have the power to affect what happens. This influence can be positive, coming from information, expertise, or social reinforcement. It can also be negative, coming from punishing behaviors such as criticizing or withholding the contributions that the group needs to succeed. You can appreciate how power is distributed among members by considering the effect just one member can have by not showing up for meetings or failing to carry out his or her part of the job.
- **Power Isn't an Either-Or Concept.** It's incorrect to assume that power is an either-or concept that members either possess or lack. Rather, it is a matter of degree. Instead of talking about someone as "powerful" or "powerless," it's more accurate to talk about how much influence he or she exerts.

TABLE 9–3 Methods for Acquiring Power in Small Groups

Power isn't the only goal to seek in a group. Sometimes being a follower is a comfortable and legitimate role to play. But when you do seek power, the following methods outline specific ways to shape the way others behave and the decisions they make.

Legitimate Authority

1. Become an authority figure. If possible, get yourself appointed or elected to a position of leadership. Do so by following Steps 2–5.

2. Speak up without dominating others. Power comes from visibility, but don't antagonize others by shutting them out.

3. Demonstrate competence on the subject. Enhance legitimate authority by demonstrating information and expertise power.

4. Follow group norms. Show that you respect the group's customs.

5. Gain support of other members. Don't try to carve out authority on your own. Gain the visible support of other influential members.

Information Power

1. Provide useful but scarce or restricted information. Show others that you possess information that isn't available elsewhere.

2. Be certain the information is accurate. One piece of mistaken information can waste the group's time, lead to bad decisions, and destroy your credibility. Check your facts before speaking up.

Expert Power

1. Make sure members are aware of your qualifications. Let others know that you have expertise in the area being discussed.

2. Don't act superior. You will squander your authority if you imply your expertise makes you superior to others. Use your knowledge for the good of the group, not ego building.

Reward and Coercive Power

1. Try to use rewards as a first resort and punishment as a last resort. People respond better to pleasant consequences than unpleasant ones, so take a positive approach first.

2. Make rewards and punishments clear in advance. Let people know your expectations and their consequences. Don't surprise them.

3. Be generous with praise. Let others know that you recognize their desirable behavior.

Referent Power

1. Enhance your attractiveness to group members. Do whatever you can to gain the liking and respect of other members without compromising your principles.

2. Learn effective presentation skills. Present your ideas clearly and effectively in order to boost your credibility.

Adapted from J. Dan Rothwell, *In Mixed Company: Small Group Communication*, 3rd ed. (Fort Worth, TX: Harcourt Brace, 1998), pp. 252–272. Reprinted with permission of Wadsworth, an imprint of the Wadsworth Group, a division of Thomson Learning. Fax 800-730-2215.

By now you can see that power is available to every member of a group. Table 9–3 outlines ways of acquiring the various types of power we have just examined.

What Makes Leaders Effective?

Even though power is distributed among members of a group, it is still important to explore the special role played by the nominal leader. In the next few pages we will describe the communication-related factors that contribute to leader effectiveness.

TRAIT ANALYSIS   Over two thousand years ago, Aristotle proclaimed, "From the hour of their birth some are marked out for subjugation, and others for command."[24] This is a radical expression of **trait theories of leadership,** sometimes labeled as the "great man" (or "great woman") approach. Social scientists began their studies of leader effectiveness by conducting literally hundreds of studies that compared leaders to nonleaders. The results of all this research were mixed. Yet, as Table 9–4 shows, a number of distinguishing characteristics did emerge in several categories.[25]

The majority of these categories involved social skills. For example, leaders talk more often and more fluently and are regarded as more popular, cooperative, and socially skillful.[26] Leaders also possess goal-related skills that help groups perform their tasks. They are somewhat more intelligent, possess more task-relevant information, and are more dependable than other members. Just as important, leaders want the role and act in ways that will help them achieve it. Finally, physical appearance seems to play a role in leadership. As a rule, leaders tend to be slightly taller, heavier, and physically more attractive than other members. They also seem to possess greater athletic ability and stamina. (Unfortunately there has been little research on whether female leaders possess any distinctive physical traits.)

Despite these general findings, trait theories have limited practical value. Later research has shown that many other factors are important in determining leader success and that not everyone who possesses these traits becomes a leader. Organizational researchers Warren Bennis and Burt Nanus interviewed ninety American leaders, including Ray Kroc, the founder of McDonald's; John Robinson, coach of the Los Angeles Rams; and John H. Johnson, publisher of *Ebony.* Their analysis led to the conclusion that the principle "leaders must be charismatic" is a myth.

> Some are, most aren't. Among the ninety there were a few—but damned few—who probably correspond to our fantasies of some "divine inspiration," that "grace under stress" we associated with J.F.K. or the beguiling capacity to spellbind for which we remember Churchill. Our leaders were all "too human"; they were short and tall, articulate and inarticulate, dressed for success and dressed for failure, and there was virtually nothing in terms of physical appearance, personality, or style that set them apart from their followers. Our guess is that it operates in the other direction; that is, charisma is the result of effective leadership, not the other way around, and that those who are good at it are granted a certain amount of respect and even awe by their followers, which increases the bond of attraction between them.[27]

LEADERSHIP STYLE   As researchers began to realize that traits aren't the key to effective leadership, they began to look in other areas. Some scholars theorized that

*A leader is best
When people barely know
that he exists,
Not so good when people
obey and acclaim him,
Worse when they despise
him.
"Fail to honor people,
They fail to honor you";
But of a good leader who
talks little,
When his work is done, his
aim fulfilled,
They will say, "We did it
ourselves."*

Lao-tzu

TABLE 9–4   Some Traits Associated with Leaders

Factor No.	Factors Appearing in Three or More Studies	Frequency
1	Social and interpersonal skills	16
2	Technical skills	18
3	Administrative skills	12
4	Leadership effectiveness and achievement	15
5	Social nearness, friendliness	18
6	Intellectual skills	11
7	Maintaining cohesive work group	9
8	Maintaining coordination and teamwork	7
9	Task motivation and application	17
10	General impression	12
11	Group task supportiveness	17
12	Maintaining standards of performance	5
13	Willingness to assume responsibility	10
14	Emotional balance and control	15
15	Informal group control	4
16	Nurturant behavior	4
17	Ethical conduct, personal integrity	10
18	Communication, verbality	6
19	Ascendance, dominance, decisiveness	11
20	Physical energy	6
21	Experience and activity	4
22	Mature, cultured	3
23	Courage, daring	4
24	Aloof, distant	3
25	Creative, independent	5
26	Conforming	5

good leadership is a matter of communication style—the way leaders deal with members. Three basic approaches were identified. The first approach was an **authoritarian leadership style** that relied on legitimate, coercive, and reward power to influence others. The second approach was a **democratic leadership style**, which invited other members to share in decision making. The third approach was the **laissez-faire leadership style**, in which the leader gave up the power to dictate, transforming the group into a leaderless collection of equals. Early research suggested that the democratic style produced the highest-quality results,[28] but later research showed that matters weren't so simple.[29] For instance, groups with autocratic leaders proved more productive under stressful conditions, but democratically led groups did better when the situation was nonstressful.[30]

Some researchers have focused on leadership style from a different perspective. Robert R. Blake and Jane S. Mouton developed an approach based on the relationship between the designated leader's concern with the task and with the relationships among members.[31] Their **Leadership Grid** consists of a two-dimensional model pictured in Figure 9–2. The horizontal axis measures the

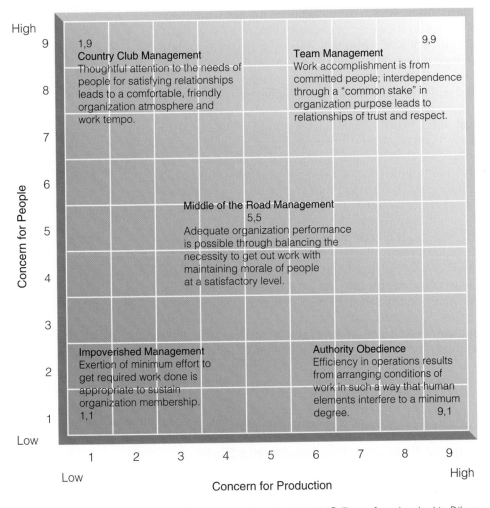

Figure 9–2 The Leadership Grid® *Source:* The Leadership Grid® Figure from *Leadership Dilemmas–Grid Solutions*, by Robert R. Blake and Anne Adams McCanse (Houston: Gulf Publishing Co.), p. 29. Copyright © 1991 by Scientific Methods, Inc. Reproduced by permission of the owners.

leader's concern for production. This involves a focus on accomplishing the organizational task, with efficiency being the main concern. The vertical axis measures the leader's concern for people's feelings and ideas. Blake and Mouton suggest that the most effective leader is the one who adopts a 9,9 style—showing high concern for both task and relationships.

Research showed that there is some merit to the styles approach. One extensive study of more than twelve thousand managers showed that a democratic approach to leadership correlated highly with success. Effective managers usually sought the advice and opinions of their subordinates, whereas average or unsuccessful ones were more authoritarian and less concerned with the welfare or ideas of the people who reported to them.[32] Despite this fact, a democratic approach isn't always the best one. For example, an autocratic approach gets the job done much more quickly, which can be essential in situations where time is of the essence. This explains experimental results showing that groups with autocratic leaders are more productive in stressful situations, whereas democratically led groups do better when conditions are less stressful.[33]

SITUATIONAL APPROACHES   Most contemporary scholars are convinced that the best style of leadership varies from one set of circumstances to another. In an effort to pin down which approach works best in a given type of situation, psychologist Fred Fiedler attempted to find out when a task-oriented approach was most effective and when a more relationship-oriented approach was most effective.[34] From his research, Fiedler developed a situational theory of leadership. Although the complete theory is too complex to describe here, the general conclusion of **situational leadership** is that a leader's style should change with the circumstances. A task-oriented approach works best when conditions are either highly favorable (good leader-member relations, strong leader power, and clear task structure) or highly unfavorable (poor leader-member relations, weak leader power, and an ambiguous task), whereas a more relationship-oriented approach is appropriate in moderately favorable or moderately unfavorable conditions.

More recently, Paul Hersey and Kenneth Blanchard have suggested that a leader's focus on task or relational issues should vary according to the readiness of the group being led (see Figure 9–3).[35] Readiness involves the members' level of motivation, willingness to take responsibility, and the amount of knowledge and experience they have in a given situation. For example, a new, inexperienced group would need more task-related direction, whereas a more experienced group might require more social support and less instruction about how to do the job. A well-seasoned group could probably handle the job well without much supervision at all. Because an employee's readiness changes from one job to another, Hersey and Blanchard suggest that the best way to lead should vary as well.

INVITATION TO INSIGHT   **Choosing the Most Effective Leadership Style**

Think of two effective leaders you have known. How would you describe the style of each one: autocratic, democratic, or laissez-faire? Task- or relationship-oriented? Imagine that the two leaders were transferred, so that each one was directing the other's group. Would the same style work equally well in each situation? Why or why not?

OVERCOMING DANGERS IN GROUP DISCUSSION

Even groups with the best of intentions often find themselves unable to reach satisfying decisions. At other times, they make decisions that later prove to be wrong. Though there's no foolproof method of guaranteeing high-quality group work, there are several dangers to avoid.

Information Underload and Overload

Information underload occurs when a group lacks information necessary to operate effectively. Sometimes the underload results from overlooking parts of a problem. We know of one group who scheduled a fund-raising auction without considering what other events might attract potential donors. They later found that their event was scheduled opposite an important football game, resulting in a loss of sorely needed funds. In other cases, groups suffer from underload because they simply don't conduct enough research. For example, a group of partners starting a new business has to be aware of all the startup costs to avoid going bankrupt in the first months of operation. Overlooking one or two important items can make the difference between success and failure.

Sometimes groups can suffer from too much information. **Information overload** occurs when the rate or complexity of material is too great to manage. Having an abundance of information might seem like a blessing, but anyone who has tried to do conscientious library research has become aware of the paralysis that can

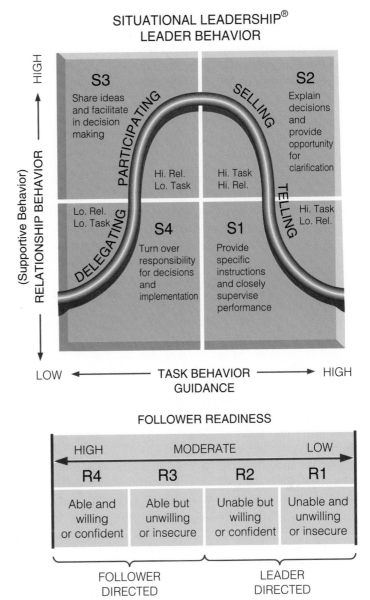

Figure 9–3   Hersey and Blanchard's Leadership Model
Source: "Situational Leadership Behavior." From *Management of Organizational Behavior, 8th edition,* © 2001. Adapted/Reprinted with permission of Center for Leadership Studies, Escondido, CA 92025. All Rights Reserved.

result from being overwhelmed by an avalanche of books, magazine and newspaper articles, reviews, films, and research studies. When too much information exists, it is hard to sort out the essential from the unessential information. Group expert J. Dan Rothwell offers several tips for coping with information overload.[36] First, specialize whenever possible. Try to parcel out areas of responsibility to each member instead of expecting each member to explore every angle of the topic. Second, be selective: Take a quick look at each piece of information to see whether it has real value for your task. If it doesn't, move on to examine more promising material. Third, limit your search. Information specialists have discovered that there is often a curvilinear relationship between the amount of information a group possesses and the quality of its decision. After a certain point, gathering more material can slow you down without contributing to the quality of your group's decisions.

Unequal Participation

The value of involving group members in making decisions—especially decisions that affect them—is great.[37] When people participate, their loyalty to the group increases. (Your own experience will probably show that most group dropouts were quiet and withdrawn.) Broad-based participation has a second advantage: It increases the amount of resources focused on the problem. As a result, the quality of the group's decisions goes up. Finally, participation increases members' loyalty to the decisions that they played a part in making.

The key to effective participation is balance. Domination by a few vocal members can reduce a group's ability to solve a problem effectively. Research shows that the proposal receiving the largest number of favorable comments is usually the one chosen even if it isn't the best one.[38] Furthermore, ideas of high-status members (who aren't always talkers) are given more consideration than those of lower-status members.[39] The moral to this story? Don't assume that quantity of speech or the status of the speaker automatically defines the quality of an idea: Instead, seek out and seriously consider the ideas of quieter members.

Not all participation is helpful, of course. It's better to remain quiet than to act out the kind of dysfunctional roles described in Chapter 8—cynic, aggressor, dominator, and so on. Likewise, the comments of a member who is uninformed can waste time. Finally, downright ignorant or mistaken input can distract a group.

You can encourage the useful contributions of quiet members in a variety of ways. First, keep the group small. In groups with three or four members, participation is roughly equal; but after size increases to between five and eight, there is a dramatic gap between the contributions of members.[40] Even in a large group you can increase the contributions of quiet members by soliciting their opinions. This approach may seem obvious, but in their enthusiasm to speak out, more verbal communicators can overlook the people who don't speak up. When normally reticent members do offer information, reinforce their contributions. It isn't necessary to go overboard by gushing about a quiet person's brilliant remark, but a word of thanks and an acknowledgment of the value of an idea increase the odds that the contributor will speak up again in the future. A third strategy is to assign specific tasks to normally quiet members. The need to report on these tasks guarantees that they will speak up. A fourth strategy is to use the nominal group technique, described in Chapter 8, to guarantee that the ideas of all members are heard.

Different strategies can help when the problem is one or more members talking too much—especially when their remarks aren't helpful. If the talkative member is at all sensitive, withholding reinforcement can deliver a diplomatic hint that it may be time to listen more and speak less. A lack of response to an idea or suggestion can work as a hint to cut back on speaking. Don't confuse lack of reinforcement with punishment, however: Attacking a member for dominating the group is likely to trigger a defensive reaction and cause more harm than good. If the talkative member doesn't respond to subtle hints, politely expressing a desire to hear from other members can be effective. The next stage in this series of escalating strategies for dealing with dominating members is to question the relevancy of remarks that are apparently off the wall: "I'm confused about what last Saturday's party has to do with the job we have to do today. Am I missing something?"

ETHICAL CHALLENGE

Dealing with Overly Talkative and Quiet Group Members

Balancing participation in group discussions can involve stifling some members and urging others to speak up when they would prefer to be silent. Explore the ethical justification for these actions by answering the following questions.

1. Are there any circumstances when it is legitimate to place quiet group members in the position of speaking up when they would rather remain quiet? When does it become unreasonable to urge quiet members to participate?

2. Does discouraging talkative members ever violate the principles of free speech and tolerance for others' opinions? Describe when it is and is not appropriate to limit a member's contributions.

After developing your ethical guidelines, consider how willing you would feel if they were applied to you.

Pressure to Conform

There's a strong tendency for group members to go along with the crowd, which often results in bad decisions. A classic study by Solomon Asch illustrated this point. College students were shown three lines of different lengths and asked to identify which of them matched with a fourth line. Although the correct answer was obvious, the experiment was a setup: Asch had instructed all but one member of the experimental groups to vote for the wrong line. As a result, fully one-third of the uninformed subjects ignored their own good judgment and voted with the majority. If simple tasks like this one generate such conformity, it is easy to see that following the (sometimes mistaken) crowd is even more likely in the much more complex and ambiguous tasks that most groups face.

Even when there's no overt pressure to follow the majority, more subtle influences motivate members—especially in highly cohesive groups—to keep quiet rather than voice any thoughts that deviate from what appears to be the consensus. "Why rock the boat if I'm the only dissenter?" members think. "And if everybody else feels the same way, they're probably right."

With no dissent, the group begins to take on a feeling of invulnerability: an unquestioning belief that its ideas are correct and even morally right. As its position solidifies, outsiders who disagree can be viewed as the enemy, disloyal to what is obviously the only legitimate viewpoint. Social scientists use the term **groupthink** to describe a group's collective striving for unanimity that discourages realistic appraisals of alternatives to its chosen decision.[41] Several group practices can discourage this troublesome force.[42] A first step is to recognize the problem of groupthink as it begins to manifest itself. If agreement comes quickly

---

Conformity and Nonconformity: Long and Short Views

When we look a little closer, we see an inconsistency in the way our society seems to feel about conformity (team playing) and nonconformity (deviance). For example, one of the great best-sellers of the 1950s was a book by John F. Kennedy called Profiles in Courage, *wherein the author praised several politicians for their courage in resisting great pressure and refusing to conform. To put it another way, Kennedy was praising people who refused to be good team players, people who refused to vote or act as their parties or constituents expected them to. Although their actions earned Kennedy's praise long after the deeds were done, the immediate reactions of their colleagues were generally far from positive. The nonconformist may be praised by historians or idolized in films or literature long after the fact of his nonconformity, but he's usually not held in high esteem, at the time, by those people to whose demands he refuses to conform.*

Elliot Aronson
The Social Animal

CULTURAL IDIOM

rock the boat: disturb a stable condition

and easily, the group may be avoiding the tough but necessary search for alternatives. Beyond vigilance, a second step to discourage groupthink is to minimize status differences. If the group has a nominal leader, he or she must be careful not to use various types of power that come with the position to intimidate members. A third step involves developing a group norm that legitimizes disagreement. After members recognize that questioning one another's positions doesn't signal personal animosity or disloyalty, a constructive exchange of ideas can lead to top-quality solutions. Sometimes it can be helpful to designate a person or subgroup as "devil's advocate" who reminds the others about the dangers of groupthink and challenges the trend toward consensus.

THE FAR SIDE   By GARY LARSON

Source: THE FAR SIDE © 1984 FARWORKS, INC. Used by permission. All Rights Reserved.

Laboratory peer pressure

CULTURAL IDIOM

"devil's advocate":
one who argues against
a widely held view in
order to clarify issues

SUMMARY

Despite the bad reputation of groups in some quarters, research shows that they are often the most effective setting for problem solving. They command greater resources, both quantitatively and qualitatively, than do either individuals or collections of people working in isolation; their work can result in greater accuracy; and the participative nature of the solutions they produce generates greater commitment from members.

Groups aren't always the best forum for solving problems. They should be used when the problem is beyond the capacity of one person to solve, when tasks are interdependent, when there is more than one desired solution or decision, and when the agreement of all members is essential.

Groups use a wide variety of discussion formats when solving problems. Some use parliamentary procedure to govern decision-making procedures. Others use moderated panel discussions, symposia, or forums. The best format depends on the nature of the problem and the characteristics of the group.

Groups stand the best chance of developing effective solutions to problems if they begin their work by identifying the problem, avoiding the mistake of failing to recognize the hidden needs of individual members. Their next step is to analyze the problem, including identification of forces both favoring and blocking progress. Only at this point should the group begin to develop possible solutions, taking care not to stifle creativity by evaluating any of them prematurely. During the implementation phase of the solution, the group should monitor the situation carefully and make any necessary changes in its plan.

Most groups can expect to move through several stages as they solve a problem. The first of these stages is orientation, during which the members sound each other out. The conflict stage is characterized by partisanship and open debate over the merits of contending ideas. In the emergence stage, the group begins to move toward choosing a single solution. In the reinforcement stage, members endorse the group's decision.

Groups who pay attention only to the task dimension of their interaction risk strains in the relationships among members. Many of these interpersonal problems can be avoided by using the skills described in Chapter 6 as well as by following the guidelines in this chapter for building group cohesiveness and encouraging participation.

Many naive observers of groups confuse the concepts of leader and leadership. We defined *leadership* as the ability to influence the behavior of other members through the use of one or more types of power—legitimate, coercive, reward, expert, or referent. We saw that many nominal leaders share their power with other members. Leadership has been examined from many perspectives—trait analysis, leadership style, and situational variables.

RESOURCES

Print

Adler, Ronald B., and Jeanne M. Elmhorst. *Communicating at Work: Principles and Practices for Business and the Professions,* 7th ed. New York: McGraw-Hill, 2002.

Chapter 9 offers a variety of tips on how to hold effective meetings: when to hold (and not hold) a meeting, how to prepare for an effective session, how to encourage balanced participation and keep discussion on track, and how to maintain a positive tone, even when members disagree.

Lippincott, Sharon M. *Meetings: Do's, Don'ts, and Donuts.* Pittsburgh, PA: Lighthouse Point Press, 2000.

This practical guide lives up to its title by offering tips on when to hold a meeting and what to do and not do in order to have a successful meeting.

Rothwell, J. Dan. *In Mixed Company: Small Group Communication,* 4th ed. Fort Worth, TX: Harcourt Brace, 2001.

This survey of small group communication combines readability with a comprehensive look at scholarship on the subject. Rothwell pays special attention to how gender and culture affect group work and discusses the features that distinguish effective teams.

Films
Conformity in Groups

Pleasantville (1998). Rated PG-13.

The film begins in present-day America, where teenage David (Tobey Maguire) escapes his mediocre social life by obsessively watching reruns of the 1950s sitcom *Pleasantville,* which depicts a wholesome town where every resident is happy. Through the intervention of a mysterious TV repairman (Don Knotts), David and his sister Jennifer (Reese Witherspoon) are transported back into the '50s, straight into Pleasantville, where they find themselves renamed as Bud and Mary Sue, members of the Parker family.

Pleasantville is a caricature of mid-twentieth-century U.S. society: Everyone is middle class, white, and relentlessly cheerful. "We're stuck in Nerdville!" Jennifer complains. We soon learn that Pleasantville also possesses characteristics of *The Twilight Zone.* The whole world is cast in black and white, just like a 1950s TV program. There is no world beyond the city limits: Take main street out of town, and soon you arrive back where you began.

A fundamental norm of Pleasantville culture is "don't challenge the status quo." But soon Bud/David and Mary Sue/Jennifer begin to introduce change. When Mary Sue teaches her mother how to please herself instead of always focusing on others, a tree bursts into colorful flame to signify Mrs. Parker's awakening. Soon color begins creeping in all over Pleasantville. As the story unfolds, we see that the black-and-white versus color debate is a metaphor for conformity versus change. We view the pressures nonconformists face, especially when they are outnumbered by group members who favor the status quo.

Creative Problem Solving

Apollo 13 (1995). Rated PG.

This is the gripping story of how teamwork and courage saved the lives of three astronauts who faced death when their spacecraft malfunctioned on its mission to the moon. After an onboard explosion, the three astronauts—Jim Lovell, Fred Haise, and Jack Swigert—were faced with the possibility of becoming marooned in space where the options were all grim: running out of oxygen, being poisoned by carbon dioxide, or freezing to death. The film chronicles how the engineers on the ground worked with the astronauts to devise a solution to this deadly challenge. The story shows how a dedicated team can work harmoniously to triumph over even apparently impossible challenges.

Kidco (1983). Rated G.

This is the story of a group of children, ages nine to sixteen, who triumph over the chores of cleaning out horse stables by creating the largest pest control and fertilizer service in San Diego County. State bureaucrats get wind of their scheme and attempt to shut the company down. The film—based on actual events—illustrates how a creative group can devise win–win solutions in an apparently win–lose or lose–lose situation.

Twelve Angry Men (1957/1997). Not rated.

A young ghetto-dwelling boy has been accused of stabbing his father to death. A jury deliberates his fate. At first only one juror (Henry Fonda/Jack Lemmon) votes for acquittal, but during the course of deliberations the opinion slowly shifts as the group reviews testimony from the trial. The film is an outstanding example of both the potential weaknesses and strengths of group problem solving; in keeping with the theme, this film is an exercise in ensemble acting rather than a showcase for a single performer.

Leadership

Chicken Run (2000). Rated G.

The inhabitants of a prison-like British chicken farm are mostly complacent despite the harsh management style of its owner, Mrs. Tweedy. One inmate refuses to accept her situation, though: Ginger (voiced by Julia Sawalha) makes one escape attempt after another. The situation

becomes more desperate when the chickens discover that their fate is to become the principal ingredient in Mrs. Tweedy's new line of chicken pies. Ginger gains an ally with the arrival of Rocky the Flying Rooster (voiced by Mel Gibson), an American bird who has fled from a circus. In a series of exciting events, Ginger and Rocky lead an escape plan.

The chickens in this clever cartoon feature exemplify the trait theory of leadership, illustrating how key members can help a group face long odds to solve daunting challenges. Rocky and Ginger show the value of spirit and energy in the face of adversity.

CONTENTS

KEY TERMS

attitude
audience analysis
belief
databases
demographics
general purposes
purpose statement
search engine
search string
specific purpose
survey research
thesis statement
value

**AFTER STUDYING
THE MATERIAL
IN THIS CHAPTER . . .**

YOU SHOULD UNDERSTAND:

1. The importance of defining a clear speech purpose.

2. The difference between a general and specific speech purpose.

3. The necessity of analyzing a speaking situation.

YOU SHOULD BE ABLE TO:

1. Choose an effective speaking topic.

2. Formulate a purpose statement that will help you develop that topic.

3. Analyze the three components of a speaking situation.

4. Gather information on your chosen topic from a variety of sources.

CHOOSING AND DEVELOPING A TOPIC

After the World Trade Center and the Pentagon were attacked by terrorists on September 11, 2001, President George W. Bush tried several times to reassure the nation and send a message of resolve to the world, but without much success. One observer noted of his public statements, "When Bush didn't seem lost, he often seemed scared. When he didn't seem scared, he often seemed angry. None of this soothed the public."[1]

The weekend after the attack, Bush knew he had to make a major speech. He went to Camp David and began working on it with his staff. By the following Thursday, he felt ready to address a joint session of Congress before a national and international television audience. The speech, a little less than three thousand words, was a huge success. Senator Ted Kennedy, a Democratic Party leader, said afterward, "The president's speech was exactly what the nation needed—a message of determination and hope, strength and compassion."[2]

Not many people will ever have to give a speech as important as the one President Bush gave that night, but a surprising number of people will give speeches that will change their lives. Some of these will be job-related speeches, like the presentation that gets your new company funded or wins you a promotion. Some will be personal, such as the toast at your best friend's wedding or a eulogy for a lost friend. And some will have the potential to change the world, perhaps locally, as you get a civic improvement project started in your hometown, or even globally, when you try to persuade listeners to deal more effectively with global problems like hunger, disease, or environmental threats.

You probably realize that the ability to speak well in public can benefit both your personal and professional life. You may also recognize that successful public speaking can be a liberating, transforming experience that boosts your self-confidence and helps you make a difference in the world. Yet most of us view the prospect of standing before an audience with the same enthusiasm we have for a trip to the dentist or the tax auditor. In fact, giving a speech seems to be one of the most anxiety-producing things we can do: *The Book of Lists* claims that Americans fear public speaking more than they do insects, heights, accidents, and even death.[3]

Despite the discomfort that speech giving causes, sooner or later most people will need to talk to an audience of some kind: while giving a class report, as part of the job, or as part of a community action group. And even in less "speechlike" situations, you will often need the same skills that are important in speech giving: the ability to talk with confidence, to organize ideas in a clear way, and to make those ideas interesting and persuasive.

Attaining a mastery of public speaking is at least partially a matter of practice. But practice doesn't always make perfect; without a careful analysis of what you are doing, practice has a tendency to make old public speaking habits permanent rather than perfect. The remaining chapters of this book will provide you with tools to analyze and improve your performance as a public speaker.

CHOOSING A TOPIC

Often the difference between a successful and an unsuccessful speech is the choice of topic. Your topic should be familiar enough for your audience to understand, yet be innovative enough to hold its attention. This chapter will discuss a number of approaches to choosing and developing an effective topic. The

I am at the boiling point! If I do not find some day the use of my tongue I shall die of an intellectual repression.

Elizabeth Cady Stanton

Public speaking can be a horror for the shy person, but it can also be the ultimate act of liberation. . . . I hadn't realized the transformative effect it could have on the speaker herself.

Susan Faludi

CULTURAL IDIOM

the toast: the speech given before a drink to honor someone

following guidelines will help you pick a topic that is right for you, your audience, and your assignment.

Look for a Topic Early

The best student speakers usually choose a topic as soon as possible after a speech is assigned by their instructor, and then they stick with it. One reason to look for a topic early is so that you will have plenty of time to complete the speech and practice it. Adequate practice time is essential to effective speech making, but the reasons for choosing a topic early run even deeper than that. Ideas seem to come automatically to speakers who have a topic in mind; things they read or observe or talk about that might have otherwise been meaningless suddenly relate to their topic, providing material or inspiration. The earlier you decide on a topic, the more you can take advantage of these happy coincidences.

Choose a Topic That Interests You

Your topic must be interesting to your audience, and the best way to accomplish that is to find a topic that is interesting to you. Your interest in a topic will also improve your ability to create the speech, and it will increase your confidence when it comes time to present it.

Sometimes it's difficult to pinpoint what your interests are—especially when you are being pressed to come up with a speech topic. If that happens to you, you might want to review your favorite media, discuss current events with your family and friends, or just contemplate your interests in solitude. The following checklist could be used as a guide.

REVIEW	DISCUSS CURRENT EVENTS	THINK ABOUT
■ newspapers	■ international	■ activities
■ magazines	■ national	■ hobbies
■ books	■ local	■ special interests
■ related Web sites	■ family	■ personal experience

> *A speech should not be just a sharing of information, but a sharing of yourself.*
>
> Ralph Archibold

SKILL BUILDER

Choosing a Topic

Using the preceeding checklist, spend a few minutes on each of the activities listed. For the "discussion" activities, pair up with another member of your class. Make a list of the possible speech topics that come to mind, based on this checklist. Compare your list for quantity and quality to others in your class. Which of the topics on your list interest you the most? Which do you know the most about? Which seems to you to be the most promising for your first speech?

CULTURAL IDIOM

stick with: continue with

being pressed: forced

After you choose your topic, you can begin developing it. Your first step in that task is defining your purpose.

DEFINING PURPOSE

CULTURAL IDIOM

boil down to: reduce
to the basic elements

No one gives a speech—or expresses *any* kind of message—without having a reason to do so. This is easy to see in those messages that ask for something: "Pass the salt" or "How about a movie this Friday?" or "Excuse me, that's my foot you're standing on." But even in subtler messages, the speaker always has a purpose: to evoke a response from the listener.

Sometimes purposes are misunderstood or confused by the speaker. This causes wasted time both in the preparation and in the presentation of the speech. It is essential, therefore, that the speaker keep in mind a clear purpose.

The first step in understanding the purpose is to formulate a clear and precise statement of that purpose. This requires an understanding of both *general purpose* and *specific purpose*.

General Purpose

Most students, when asked why they are giving a speech in a college class, will quickly cite course requirements. But you have to analyze your motives more deeply than that to develop an effective speech purpose. Even if you are giving your speech only for the grade, you still have to affect your audience in some way to earn that grade. If your motive for speaking is to learn effective speech techniques (as we hope it is), you still have to influence your audience to accomplish your goal because that is what effective speaking is all about.

When we say you have to influence your audience, we mean you have to change the audience in some way. If you think about all the possible ways you could change an audience, you'll realize that they all boil down to three options, which happen to be the three basic **general purposes** for speaking.

1. **To entertain.** To relax your audience by providing it with a pleasant listening experience
2. **To inform.** To enlighten your audience by teaching it something
3. **To persuade.** To move your audience toward a new attitude or behavior

A brief scrutiny of these purposes will reveal that no speech could ever have only *one* purpose. These purposes are interrelated because a speech designed for one purpose will almost always accomplish a little of the other purposes; even a

Dilbert   by Scott Adams

Source: DILBERT reprinted by permission of United Feature Syndicate, Inc.

speech designed purely to entertain might change audience attitudes or teach that audience something new. In fact, these purposes are cumulative in the sense that, to inform an audience, you have to make your remarks entertaining enough to hold its interest—at least long enough to convince it that your topic is worth learning about. And you certainly have to inform an audience (about your arguments) in order to persuade it.

Deciding your general purpose is like choosing the "right" answer on one of those multiple choice tests in which all the answers are right to a certain degree, but one answer is more right than the others. Thus, we say that any speech is primarily designed for one of these purposes. A clear understanding of your general purpose gets you on the right track for choosing and developing a topic. Understanding your specific purpose will keep you on that track.

The secret of success is constancy of purpose.

Benjamin Disraeli

Specific Purpose

Whereas your general purpose is only a one-word label, your **specific purpose** is expressed in the form of a **purpose statement**—a complete sentence that describes exactly what you want your speech to accomplish. The purpose statement usually isn't used word for word in the actual speech; its purpose is to keep you focused as you plan your speech.

There are three criteria for a good purpose statement.

1. **A Purpose Statement Should Be Receiver Oriented.** Having a *receiver orientation* means that your purpose is focused on how your speech will affect your audience members. For example, if you were giving an informative talk on how to sue someone in small claims court, this would be an inadequate purpose statement:

   My purpose is to tell my audience about small claims court.

   As that statement is worded, your purpose is "to tell" an audience something, which suggests that the speech could be successful even if no one listens. Your purpose statement should refer to the response you want from your audience: It should tell what the audience members will know or be able to do after listening to your speech. Thus, the preceding purpose statement could be improved in this way:

   After listening to my speech, my audience will know more about small claims court procedures.

   That's an improvement, because you now have stated what you expect from your audience. But this purpose statement could be improved more through the judicious application of a second criterion:

2. **A Purpose Statement Should Be Specific.** To be effective, a purpose statement should be worded specifically, with enough details so that you would be able to measure or test your audience, after your speech, to see if you had achieved your purpose. In the example given earlier, simply "knowing about small claims court" is too vague; you need something more specific, such as:

   After listening to my speech, my audience will know how to win a case in small claims court.

This is an improvement, but it can be made still better by applying a third criterion:

3. **A Purpose Statement Should Be Realistic.** You must be able to accomplish your purpose as stated. Some speakers insist on formulating purpose statements such as, "My purpose is to convince my audience to make federal budget deficits illegal." Unfortunately, unless your audience happens to be a joint session of Congress, it won't have the power to change U.S. fiscal policy. But any audience can write its congressional representatives or sign a petition. Similarly, an audience will not "learn how to play championship tennis" or "understand the danger of business regulation" in one sitting. You must aim for an audience response that is possible to accomplish. In your small claims court speech, it would be impossible for you to be sure that each of your audience members has a winnable case. So a better purpose statement for this speech might sound something like this:

After listening to my speech, my audience will be able to list the five steps for preparing a small claims case.

This purpose statement is receiver oriented, specific, and realistic. It also suggests an organizational pattern for the speech ("the five steps"), which can be a bonus in a carefully worded purpose statement.

Consider the following sets of purpose statements:

LESS EFFECTIVE	MORE EFFECTIVE
To talk about professional wrestling (not receiver oriented)	After listening to my speech, my audience will understand that kids who imitate professional wrestlers can be seriously hurt.
To tell my audience about textbook prices (not specific)	After my speech, the audience will understand the five reasons why textbooks cost more than mass market books.
After listening to my speech, my audience members will dedicate themselves to fighting cultural imperialism. (not realistic)	After listening to my speech, my audience will understand why some countries want to restrict the importation of American films and television programs.

The Thesis Statement

So far we have discussed how to select a topic, how partially to focus that topic through its general purpose, and how to focus it further through its specific purpose. Your next step in the focusing process is to formulate your thesis statement. The **thesis statement** tells you what the central idea of your speech is. It tells you the one idea that you want your audience to remember after it has forgotten everything else you had to say. The thesis statement for your small claims speech might be worded like this:

Arguing a case on your own in small claims court is a simple, five-step process that can give you the same results you would achieve with a lawyer.

SKILL
BUILDER
Formulating Purpose Statements

Write a specific purpose statement for each of the following speeches:

1. An after-dinner speech at an awards banquet in which you will honor a team who has a winning, but not championship, record. (You pick the team. For example: "After listening to my speech, my audience members will appreciate the individual sacrifices made by the members of the chess team.")

2. A classroom speech in which you explain how to do something. (Again, you choose the topic: "After listening to my speech, my audience members will know at least three ways to maximize their comfort and convenience on an economy class flight.")

3. A campaign speech in which you support the candidate of your choice. (For example, "After listening to my speech, my audience members will consider voting for Alexandra Rodman in order to clean up student government.")

Answer the following questions about each of the purpose statements you make up: Is it receiver oriented? Is it precise? Is it attainable?

Unlike your purpose statement, your thesis statement is usually delivered directly to your audience. The thesis statement is usually formulated later in the speech-making process, after you have done some research on your topic. The progression from topic to purpose to thesis is, therefore, another focusing process, as you can see in the following examples:

Topic: Grade inflation is good
General Purpose: To entertain
Specific Purpose: After listening to my speech, my audience members will be unafraid to march up to their professor and say, "Give me an 'A' or else."
Thesis Statement: Handing out high grades as if they were Halloween treats makes everybody look good, and it doesn't cause cavities.

Topic: Can the Internet cure the common cold?
General Purpose: To inform
Specific Purpose: After listening to my speech, my audience members will use the information available on the World Wide Web to be better informed before they see their doctors.
Thesis Statement: Online medical data can save you the cost and hassle of an unnecessary trip to the doctor.

Topic: Binge drinking on campus
General Purpose: To persuade
Specific Purpose: After listening to my speech, audience members will recognize binge drinking in themselves and others and know some realistic steps to take to deal with it.
Thesis Statement: Campus binge drinking is a serious problem that we can solve without having any less fun.

SKILL
BUILDER

Formulating Thesis Statements

Turn each of the following purpose statements into a statement that expresses a possible thesis. For example, if you had a purpose statement such as this:

After listening to my speech, my audience will recognize the primary advantages and disadvantages of home teeth bleaching.

you might turn it into a thesis statement such as this:

Home bleaching your teeth can significantly improve your appearance, but watch out for injury to the gums and damaged teeth.

1. At the end of my speech, the audience members will be willing to sign my petition supporting the local needle exchange program for drug addicts.
2. After listening to my speech, the audience members will be able to list five disadvantages of tattoos.
3. During my speech on the trials and tribulations of writing a research paper, the audience members will show their interest by paying attention and their amusement by occasionally laughing.

ANALYZING THE SPEAKING SITUATION

There are three components to analyze in any speaking situation: the audience, the occasion, and the speaker. To be successful, every choice you make in putting together your speech—your choice of purpose, topic, and all the material you use to develop your speech—must be appropriate to all three of these components.

The Listener: Audience Analysis

When you choose a gift, it's important to consider the person who will receive it; what would be an ideal gift for one person could be a disaster for another. In the same way, you need to use **audience analysis**—an examination of certain pertinent characteristics of your listeners—when planning a speech. Audience analysis is the purest form of receiver orientation. It allows you to adapt your speech to your listeners.

Audience adaptation—changing the way you say something so that it will be more meaningful or effective for a particular group of listeners—is something that we have a tendency to do naturally. Research suggests, for example, that in

"Good God! He's giving the white-collar voters' speech to the blue collars."

everyday conversations what we say to children and the elderly is simpler, more redundant, and less complex than what we say to other adults.[4] Your speeches will tend to be successful if you extend this principle of audience adaptation to your listeners.

There are several factors to consider in audience analysis.

AUDIENCE TYPE   There are at least three types of audience you are likely to encounter. We could call these types "passersby," "captives," and "volunteers." Each type suggests different audience interests. *Passersby,* as the name implies, are people who aren't much interested—at least not in advance—in what you have to say. A crowd milling around the student union or a shopping mall would fit into this type. With this type of audience, your first concern is to make it aware of you as a speaker, either by interesting it in the topic or in you as a speaker. You might have to pick a really sensational topic or begin developing your topic by using some kind of device or gimmick to get the audience's attention, such as the loud costumes or wild theatrics street speakers often rely on.

Captives are audience members who have gathered for some reason besides the joy of hearing you speak. Students in a required class often begin as a type of captive audience. So do military formations, mandatory work meetings, and other required gatherings. With captives you don't have to worry about devices and gimmicks to make them aware of you as a speaker; you do, however, have to use material that will get them interested and keep them interested in what you have to say.

Volunteers are audience members who have gathered together because of a common interest. Students in elective courses, especially those with long waiting lists, would fit into this type. So would gatherings of most clubs, social organization, and action groups. Even with an audience of volunteers, you still have to maintain the listeners' interests; you never lose that responsibility. But when the audience is informed and involved, as volunteers tend to be, you can treat your topic in greater depth without worrying about *losing* their interest.

Most college speech classes are a mixture of captives and volunteers, which means that you don't have to sensationalize your topic or use gimmicks, but you do have to maintain interest and provide depth.

AUDIENCE PURPOSE   Just as you have a purpose for speaking, the audience members have a purpose for gathering. Sometimes virtually all the members of your audience will have the same, obvious goal. Expectant parents at a natural childbirth class are all seeking a healthy, relatively painless delivery, and people attending an investment seminar are looking for ways to increase their net worth.

There are other times, however, when audience purpose can't be so easily defined. In some instances, different listeners will have different

> **CULTURAL IDIOM**
>
> **milling around:** moving around as a group
>
> **the student union:** a building on college and university campuses where students gather for purposes of dining, recreation, and other general student needs
>
> **gimmick:** a clever means of drawing attention

goals, some of which might not be apparent to the speaker. Consider a church congregation, for example. Whereas most members might listen to a sermon with the hope of applying religious principles to their lives, a few might be interested in being entertained or in merely appearing pious. In the same way, the listeners in your speech class probably have a variety of motives for attending. Becoming aware of as many of these motives as possible will help you predict what will interest them. Observing audience demographics helps you make that prediction.

DEMOGRAPHICS   **Demographics** are characteristics of your audience that can be labeled, such as number of people, age, gender, group membership, and so on. Demographic characteristics might affect your speech planning in a number of ways.[5] For example:

1. Number of People. Topic appropriateness varies with the size of an audience. With a small audience you can be less formal and more intimate—you can, for example, talk more about your own inner feelings and personal experiences. If you gave a speech before five people as impersonally as if they were a standing-room-only crowd in a lecture hall, they would probably find you stuffy. On the other hand, if you talked to three hundred people about your unhappy childhood, you'd probably make them uncomfortable. Also, the larger your audience, the broader the range of interests and knowledge; with a small audience you can choose a more specific topic.

2. Gender. Traditionally, men and women have tended to be interested in different topics. These differences are becoming less pronounced as time goes on because men and women are becoming conscious of sexual stereotypes and are rebelling against them. Still, the differences in interest that prevail are of concern to a speaker in choosing and developing a topic. There are still more men than women interested in automotive engineering and more women than men interested in cooking. The guideline here might be: *Do not exclude or offend any portion of your audience on the basis of gender.* Every speech teacher has a horror story about a student getting up in front of a class composed primarily, but not entirely, of men and speaking on a subject such as "Picking up Chicks." The women, after they realize that the speech is not about methods of handling poultry, are invariably offended. Most of the men will feel the same way.

   As with any of these demographic characteristics, the point is to analyze, not stereotype, your audience. If you talk down to any of your listeners, you have probably stereotyped them. The speaker who wants to speak to a mixed audience on how a man meets a woman, or vice versa, may still do so; the topic of the speech, however, should be "meeting people." That way it can be treated in a manner that would be appropriate for both men and women.

3. Age. In many areas younger people and older people have different interests. Topics such as Social Security, child rearing, and school success are all influenced by the age of the audience. These differences run relatively deep; Aristotle observed long ago that young people "have strong passions," that "their lives are spent not in memory but in expectation," and that they have high ideals because "they have not been humbled by life or learned its necessary limitations." Older people, on the other hand, tend to have more practical interests.

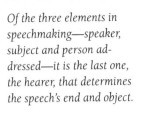

4. Group Membership. Organizations to which the audience members belong provide more clues to audience interests. By examining the groups to which they belong, you can surmise audience members' political leanings (Young Republicans, College Democrats, Campus Reform Party), religious beliefs (CYO or Hillel), or occupation (Bartender's Union or National Communication Association). Group membership is often an important consideration in college classes. Consider the difference between a "typical" college day class and a "typical" college night class. At many colleges the evening students are generally older and tend to belong to civic groups, church clubs, and the local chamber of commerce. Daytime students tend to belong to sororities and fraternities, sports clubs, and social action groups.

You have to decide which demographics of your audience are important for a particular speech. For example, when Stephanie Aduloju, a student at Creighton University in Nebraska, gave a speech on "Sexual Education for the Elderly," she knew age was an important demographic. She adapted to her college-aged audience this way:

> Get over the idea that older people don't have sex. They do have sex, they will continue to have sex, and hopefully, when we're all their age, we'll be having sex. But if you don't know any better, sex can kill you. We all have an older person close to our hearts, whether it's a grandparent, parent, or family friend. Think about that person.[6]

These four demographic characteristics are important examples, but the list goes on and on. Other demographic characteristics that might be important in a college classroom include ethnic background, educational level, economic status, hometown, year in school, and major subject.

A final factor to consider in audience analysis concerns members' attitudes, beliefs, and values.

ATTITUDES, BELIEFS, AND VALUES   Audience members' feelings about you, your subject, and your intentions for them are central issues in audience analysis. One way to approach these issues is through a consideration of attitudes, beliefs, and values.[8] These characteristics are structured in human consciousness like layers of an onion. They are all closely interrelated, but attitudes lie closer to the surface, whereas beliefs and values underlie them. An **attitude** is a predisposition to respond to something in a favorable or unfavorable way. A **belief** is an underlying conviction about the truth of something, which is often based on cultural training. A **value** is a deeply rooted belief about a concept's inherent worth or worthiness. An audience might, for example, hold the value that "freedom is a good thing." This value might be expressed in a belief such as "people should be free to choose their political leaders," which in turn will lead to the attitude that "voting is an important right and responsibility for all citizens." This in short leads to a predisposition to vote—in other words, a positive attitude toward voting.

Figure 10–1 shows the relationship among attitudes, beliefs, and values. Experts in audience analysis, such as professional speechwriters, often try to concentrate on values. As one team of researchers pointed out, "Values

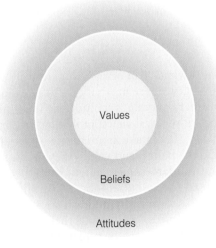

Figure 10–1   Structure of Values, Beliefs, and Attitudes

UNDERSTANDING DIVERSITY

The Age Demographic

When analyzing your audience in terms of age, remember that people of different generations will latch on to different concepts in a speech. These concepts might include memorable events, popular culture "icons" (i.e., symbols that strongly represent the times in which they lived), or types of music. Julie Hill, of *Presentations* magazine, says these kind of changes might play out as seen in the following chart[7]:

Traditionalists	Baby Boomers	Generation X	Generation Y
■ Born: 1922 to 1946	■ Born: 1946 to 1964	■ Born: 1965 to 1978	■ Born: 1979 to present
■ Population: 44.2 million	■ Population: 76.8 million	■ Population: 52.4 million	■ Population: 77.6 million
■ Memorable Events: Pearl Harbor bombing, World War II, the Great Depression, the New Deal, the Korean War	■ Memorable Events: John F. Kennedy assassination, the Vietnam War, the Civil Rights movement, women's liberation, the moon landing	■ Memorable Events: John Lennon murder, the *Challenger* disaster, the fall of the Berlin Wall, Operation Desert Storm	■ Memorable Events: The O. J. Simpson trial, the Columbine school shootings, the Clinton-Lewinsky scandal, the War on Terrorism
■ Icons: *Reader's Digest, Blondie,* the golden age of radio	■ Icons: television, *Doonesbury,* the peace symbol, fallout shelters, discos	■ Icons: the personal computer, *The Simpsons,* music videos, tattoos	■ Icons: the Internet, Nintendo and PlayStation, Beanie Babies, pagers, body piercing
■ Music: Benny Goodman, Tommy Dorsey, Frank Sinatra, Ella Fitzgerald, Billie Holliday, Charlie Parker	■ Music: Elvis Presley, the Beatles, Jimi Hendrix, the Rolling Stones, the Beach Boys, the Supremes	■ Music: The Cure, U2, Madonna, Guns N' Roses, Nirvana, Beck	■ Music: the Spice Girls, the Backstreet Boys, Offspring, Metallica, Matchbox 20

have the advantage of being comparatively small in number, and owing to their abstract nature, are more likely to be shared by large numbers of people."[9] Stable American values include the ideas of good citizenship, the work ethic, tolerance of political views, individualism, and justice for all.

You can often make an inference about audience members' attitudes by recognizing the beliefs and values they are likely to hold. For example, a group of religious fundamentalists might hold the value of "obeying God's word." This might lead to the belief—based on their interpretation of the Bible—that women are not meant to perform the same functions in society as men. This, in turn, might lead to the attitude that women ought not to pursue careers as firefighters, police officers, or construction workers.

You can also make a judgment about one attitude your audience members hold based on your knowledge of other attitudes they hold. If your audience is made up of undergraduates who have a positive attitude toward liberation movements, it is a good bet they also have a positive attitude toward civil rights and ecology. If they have a negative attitude toward collegiate sports, they probably also have a negative attitude toward fraternities and sororities. This should not only suggest some appropriate topics for each audience but should also suggest ways that those topics could be developed.

Few sinners are saved after the first twenty minutes of a sermon.

Mark Twain

CRITICAL THINKING PROBE   **Attitudes, Beliefs, and Values**

Find a persuasive appeal in an advertisement, newspaper editorial, or another source. Identify an attitude, belief, or value that the source of the message is appealing to. Explain why you have identified the appeal the way you have (i.e., why is it an attitude or belief rather than a value, etc.). Explain why, in your opinion, this appeal is or is not effective.

The Occasion

The second phase in analyzing a speaking situation focuses on the occasion. The occasion of a speech is determined by the circumstances surrounding it. Three of these circumstances are time, place, and audience expectations.

TIME   Your speech occupies an interval of time that is surrounded by other events. For example, other speeches might be presented before or after yours, or comments might be made that set a certain tone or mood. External events such as elections, the start of a new semester, or even the weather can color the occasion in one way or the other. The date on which you give your speech might have some historical significance. If that historical significance relates in some way to your topic, you can use it to help build audience interest.

The time available for your speech is also an essential consideration. You should choose a topic that is broad enough to say something worthwhile but brief enough to fit your limits. "Wealth," for example, might be an inherently interesting topic to some college students, but it would be difficult to cover such a broad topic in a ten-minute speech and still say anything significant. However, a topic like "How to Make Extra Money in Your Spare Time" could conceivably be covered in ten minutes in enough depth to make it worthwhile. All speeches have limits, whether they are explicitly stated or not. If you are invited to say a few words, and you present a few volumes, you might not be invited back.

PLACE   Your speech also occupies a physical space. The beauty or squalor of your surroundings and the noise or stuffiness of the room should all be taken into consideration. These physical surroundings can be referred to in your speech if appropriate. If you were talking about world poverty, for example, you could compare your surroundings to those that might be found in a poorer country.

The simplest way to customize a speech is to call members of the audience in advance and ask them what they expect from your session and why they expect it. Then use their quotes throughout your presentation.

Allan Pease

AUDIENCE EXPECTATION   Finally, your speech is surrounded by audience expectations. A speech presented in a college class, for example, is usually expected to reflect a high level of thought and intelligence. This doesn't necessarily

Sample Analysis of a Speaking Situation

Audience: Employees in the Production Department of my company

Situation: Training session on sexual harassment

Purpose: After I am finished speaking, I want audience members to view sexual harassment as a legitimate concern and to be careful to avoid communicating in a way that might be perceived as harassing.

Management has realized that our company is at risk of being slapped with a harassment lawsuit. The most likely offenders are several "good old boys" who have worked in the Production Department a long time. They are really nice guys, and I know they view their jokes and comments as good-natured fun and not harassment. On the other hand, several female employees have complained about being hassled by these men.

One of my duties as an intern in the Human Resources Department of my company is to share the latest information on sexual harassment with employees. My bosses know that this topic has been covered in my classes, and they decided I should pass it along.

This is a tricky situation for me: First of all, these guys will be a captive audience, forced to listen to a subject that they find annoying. Also, I am younger than anyone in my audience, and I'm a woman. In fact, I've been the target of some of the behavior I'm being asked to discourage! There's a strong risk that the men who are the target of my remarks won't take me seriously, so I have to change their attitude about the subject and me.

I know that scolding and threatening these men would be a big mistake. Even if they didn't object out loud, they would probably regard me as some sort of chip-on-the-shoulder feminist and consider the advice I offered as "politically correct" and out of touch with the way the real world operates.

To avoid this sort of negative reaction, I need to separate myself from the law that they dislike, taking the position of sharing with them "here's what I've learned about how it works." I might even give them a few examples of harassment suits that I think were frivolous, so we can agree that some people are much too sensitive. That common ground will help put us on the same side. Then I can emphasize that they don't have to *agree* with the law to follow it. I'll tell stories of people like them who suffered as targets of harassment suits, pointing out that even an unfair accusation of harassment could make all of our lives miserable. My basic argument will be that potentially harassing behavior "isn't worth it."

I also hope to use my age and gender as advantages. A couple of the men have told me that they have daughters my age. I could ask the group to imagine how they would feel if their daughters were the targets of suggestive comments and sexual jokes. I'll tell them that I know how angry and protective my dad would feel, and I'll tell them that I know that, as good fathers, they'd feel the same way. I could also ask them to think about how they would feel if their wives, sisters, or mothers were the targets of jokes that made those women feel uncomfortable.

I don't think any speech will totally reverse attitudes that were built over these men's lifetimes, but I do think that getting on their side will be much more effective than labeling them as insensitive sexist pigs and threatening them with lawsuits.

---

mean that it has to be boring or humorless; wit and humor are, after all, indicative of intelligence. But it does mean that you have to put a little more effort into your presentation than if you were discussing the same subject with friends over coffee.

When you are considering the occasion of your speech, it pays to remember that every occasion is unique. Although there are obvious differences among the occasion of a college class, a church sermon, and a bachelor party "roast," there are also many subtle differences that will apply only to the circumstances of each unique event.

CULTURAL IDIOM

a bachelor party: a men-only gathering of the groom and his friends

roast: an entertaining program where the guest of honor is teased and ridiculed

---

ETHICAL
CHALLENGE

Adapting to Speaking Situations

How much adaptation is ethical? How far would you go to be effective with an audience? Try the following exercise with your classmates.

1. Prepare, in advance, three index cards: one with a possible topic for a speech, one with a possible audience, and one with a possible occasion.
2. Form groups of three members each, and place your cards face down, with one member's "audience" matched with a second member's "topic" and a third member's "occasion," and so on.
3. Turn the cards over. For each set, decide which characteristics of the audience, topic, and occasion would most likely affect the way the speech was developed.
4. Discuss the adaptation that would be necessary in each situation and the role ethics would play in determining how far you would go.

GATHERING INFORMATION

This discussion about planning a speech purpose and analyzing the speech situation makes it apparent that it takes time, interest, and knowledge to develop a topic well. Much of the knowledge you present in your speech will be based on your own thoughts and experience. Setting aside a block of time to reflect on your own ideas is essential. However, you will also need to gather information from outside sources.

By this time you are probably familiar with both Internet searches and library research as forms of gathering information. Sometimes, however, speakers overlook some of the less obvious resources of the Internet and the library. More often they also overlook interviewing, personal observation, and survey research as equally effective methods of gathering information. We will review all these methods here and perhaps provide a new perspective on one or more of them.

Internet Research

SEARCH ENGINES Internet research generally begins with the use of a search engine or directory. These two devices are very similar, and in fact many of the people who use both of them never realize that they are different. *Search engines* like AltaVista send out electronic robots to identify key words. You supply a search engine with a key word or words, and it provides you with a list of Web sites that use those key words in their description. *Directories* like Yahoo! have been organized by actual humans. They return sites that are divided into categories. A directory is like a giant library catalog or electronic index. We'll use the term **search engine** for both of these devices.

Searching the Web is one of the most popular online activities. If you treat this activity like a game it can be fun, but under deadline pressure it can be frustrating unless you approach it systematically. The main problem with trying to find information on the Web is that it is unstructured and unguided—the user is usually unassisted by library professionals, mentors, or professors. A systematic

Knowledge is of two kinds: We know a subject ourselves, or we know where we can find information upon it.

Samuel Johnson

The content of the Web aspires to absolute variety. One might find anything there. It is like rummaging the forefront of the collective global mind. Somewhere, surely, there is a site that contains . . . everything we have lost?

William Gibson

search enables the user to make some sense of this amorphous mass. For example, if you were to enter the key words "television programming" on most search engines you would be presented with a list of some fifteen thousand sites.

Now, if you don't have the time to check out all these sites (remember that anyone with a computer can build a Web site), you might narrow your search by using a more specific term. In this case, however, even the term "MTV" will yield thousands of sites.

Some search engines allow plain English queries where the user can type in a regular question, such as "Where can I find information about sexuality on MTV?" Plain English searches, however, will return lists that include every key word in the question. On AltaVista, for example, the preceeding question recently returned 1,400,000 sites. The search became more usable, though, with the use of a carefully selected **search string,** the line of words you enter in the search box. You can string together several words to construct a very precise query. The techniques to use when doing so can vary depending on which search engine you are using, but there are some standard symbols that work with a majority of these devices. You could narrow your search by using terms such as AND, OR, or NOT,[10] such as "MTV AND sexuality AND rock music NOT criticism." Most popular search engines also allow the use of a plus symbol (+) in front of each word that you want in your search results. For example, if you were searching the Web for information about the causes of high blood pressure, you could type "+high +blood +pressure +causes." Just as the plus symbol, or AND, indicates that you want these words in the Web pages the engine finds for you, the minus symbol (−), or NOT, lets you eliminate words you don't want to see. If you find your blood pressure query is yielding results that show numerous pages about treatment instead of causes, you could type in "+high +blood +pressure +causes −treatment." Many search engines enter the plus symbol for you, but you have to enter the minus symbol for yourself. Others have another option that performs the same function. For example, Yahoo!, Excite, and AltaVista all allow a minus symbol. But in HotBot, you click on the "More Search Options" button and select "Must Not Contain" in the "Word Filter" section. You can sometimes also add NEAR, as in "Clinton near Gore and (not Starr)," which would return items that mention Bill Clinton close to Al Gore but do not mention Kenneth Starr.

Many search engines allow you to place quotation marks around a phrase so only that combination of words will be returned, rather than any combination that happens to include one of those words. Thus you could enclose "+high +blood +pressure" or even "+high +blood +pressure +causes" so that phrase would be treated like one word. Type in "Gettysburg Address," and you won't get the irrelevant vacation sites and real estate listings that you would have with +Gettysburg +Address without quotation marks. Again, some search engines have a box to click that says "Search for These Terms as a Phrase," which serves the same function.

Be careful about the spelling of the terms in your search string: Although some search engines now offer to check your spelling, it will still save time if the term you want is spelled exactly the same way on the Web site. And try alternate spellings, if necessary. For example, if "CD-ROM" was one of your terms, you should also try "CDROM" and "CD ROM." The OR command is useful for alternate spellings, as you could insert them, asking the search engine to look for either one, as in "CD-ROM" OR "CDROM" or "CD ROM."

No matter which search engine you use, be sure to read the instructions that can be found in the search engine's Help, Search Tips, and Frequently Asked Questions (FAQ) files.

> CULTURAL IDIOM
>
> **string together:**
> connect

UNDERSTANDING COMMUNICATION TECHNOLOGY

Search Engines

Even using a search engine, doing research on the Net requires time and patience. Remember that multiple tools (which is to say, multiple search engines) are available. If one frustrates you, move on to the next. Here's a list of some of the most popular and useful search engines and a description of each.

Search Engine	Address	Description
Yahoo!	www.yahoo.com	This was the first Web directory, and it's still the most popular search site on the Internet.
Google	www.google.com	This is fast becoming a favorite, because it is faster and more accurate than most other search engines.
Excite	www.excite.com	Excite looks and feels more like a general-purpose portal, but the search box interface lets you direct your search to specific indexes for news, photos, MP3/audio, and video.
AltaVista	www.altavista.com	One of the first search engines and once the biggest and fastest, although it has now given up that title to Google.
HotBot	www.hotbot.com	Now owned by Lycos, it remains an independent search engine with unique power search capabilities that allow you to define the style, date range, language, category, and results options for your search.
LookSmart	www.looksmart.com	LookSmart is a key Web directory that began as a specialized venture funded by *Reader's Digest.*
Northern Light	www.northernlight.com	A favorite of skilled researchers, it includes a convenient results format that sorts results into folders of related sites.
About	www.about.com	Consists of over seven hundred guide sites organized into thirty-six channels. Each site is run by a professional guide.
Open Directory Project	http://dmoz.org	Owned by Netscape, this is the largest, most comprehensive human-edited directory of the Web. Its 350,000 categories are managed by thirty-five thousand volunteer editors.
iwon	www.iwon.com	Not the largest or best organized, but it might be the most fun: It includes a number of lotteries, including an annual one with a $25 million prize.

EVALUATING WEB SITES   Students are sometimes so grateful for finding a Web site dealing with their topic that they forget to evaluate it. Like any information you would use, the Web site should be accurate and rational. Beyond that, there are three specific criteria that you can use to evaluate the quality of a Web site:

1. **Credibility**. Anyone can establish a Web site, so it is important to evaluate where your information is coming from. Who wrote the page? Anonymous sources should not be used. If the sources *are* listed, are their credentials listed? If so, are they qualified to write this document? Is some kind of contact information, such as an e-mail address, provided? What institution publishes the document? Remember that a handsome site design doesn't guarantee high-quality information, but misspellings and grammatical mistakes are good signs of low quality.

2. **Objectivity.** What opinions (if any) are expressed by the author? The domain names .edu, .gov, .org, or .net are generally preferable to .com because if the page is a mask for advertising, the information might be biased.

3. **Currency.** When was the page produced? When was it updated? How up-to-date are the links? If any of the links are dead, the information might not be current.

The "Print Resources" section at the end of this chapter contains references for books that offer more detailed guidelines for using the Web. Chapter 11 (page 350) offers some guidelines for citing Web sites in a bibliography.

Electronic discussion groups can also be used as a form of research. These discussion groups are formed by people with similar interests who are eager to share knowledge, so you can pose a question ("How is plastics recycling handled in your town?" "Any ideas about tax reform?") and collect a wide range of answers. However you use the Internet, remember that it is a good addition to, but *not* a substitute for, library research. Library experts help you make sense of and determine the validity of the information you find. Also, most of the important database indexes of archived newspaper, magazine, and journal articles—indexes such as *The Academic Index, The Magazine Index, Communication Abstracts,* and *The New York Times Index*—can be found at the library but are not yet available to the home user without a hefty subscription fee.

Library Research

Libraries, like people, tend to be unique. It's important to get to know your own library, to see what kind of special collections and services it offers, and just to find out where everything is. There are, however, a few resources that are common to most libraries, including the library catalog, reference works, periodicals, and nonprint materials.

THE LIBRARY CATALOG The library catalog is an ancient and noble information-storing device. Today most catalogs are computerized, but whatever its form, the library catalog is your key to all the books and other materials in the library, filed according to subject, author, and title, so that you can look for general topics as well as for specific books and authors.

REFERENCE WORKS Reference works will also be listed in the library catalog. There are wonders there that could turn you into an information maven for life. There are encyclopedias galore, even specialized ones such as *The Encyclopedia of Social Sciences* and *The Encyclopedia of American History;* there are statistical compilations such as *The*

A library is a sacred place. For four thousand years, humanity has gone through dreadful turmoils, varied glories. How do we distill the past? How do we retain the memories? Libraries.

Vartan Gregorian

World Almanac, Facts on File, and *The Guinness Book of World Records;* you can find out *Who's Who in America* or even *Who Was Who.* You can collect a lot of facts in a short time in the reference room. Reference works are good for uncovering basic information, definitions, descriptions, and sources for further investigation.

Of course, not all reference works are books. Several encyclopedias are available for personal computers equipped with CD-ROM drives. The current bestsellers are *Compton's,* Microsoft's *Encarta,* and *Grolier's,* all of which provide multimedia images and sound. There is a wide range of specialized references on CD-ROM also. Those who subscribe to online services such as America Online also have a wide range of reference materials available to them, and there are others available to anyone with Internet access (see boxes on pages 393 and 407).

PERIODICALS   Magazines, journals, and newspapers are good resources for finding recently published material on interesting topics. Indexes such as *The Readers' Guide to Periodical Literature* and *The Magazine Index* on CD-ROM will enable you to find popular magazine articles on just about any subject. Specialized indexes such as the *Education Index* and *Psychological Abstracts* can be used to find articles in specific fields, and newspaper indexes such as *The New York Times Index* can be used to find microfilmed newspaper articles. Periodicals are a good source of high-interest, up-to-date information on your topic.

NONPRINT MATERIALS   Most libraries are also treasuries of nonprint and audiovisual materials. Films, records, tapes, and videotapes can be used not only as research tools but also as aids during your presentation. Your library probably has an orientation program that will acquaint you with what it has to offer in the way of nonprint materials.

DATABASES   Most libraries have access to **databases,** which are computerized collections of information that can be searched from a computer terminal. As we mentioned earlier, most of these are not available over the World Wide Web without a subscription. One popular collection of databases is Dialog Information Retrieval Service. Dialog contains millions of articles from news services, magazines, scholarly journals, conference papers, books, and other sources. Other popular databases include Infotrac Academic Index, which covers popular journals for the last few years and the *New York Times* for the most recent six months; and Infotrac National Newspapers Index, which covers several major papers. With a conscientious search strategy (using the techniques we discussed for search engines on the Internet), you should be able to locate dozens of citations on your topic in just a few minutes. After you have located the items you want, it is possible to read abstracts or even entire articles on the screen of the library's computer terminal—or print out a list of citations for further review.

LIBRARIANS   If you have explored all the sources mentioned in the preceding section, and you still can't find exactly what you need, seek out a librarian. Today's librarians are trained in special search techniques, and their familiarity with the resources of their library is exhaustive. Of course, part of the effectiveness of your interaction with the librarian will depend on your communication skills: your ability to ask clear, specific questions; to be direct but polite; and to listen effectively. This is also true in other forms of information-gathering interviews.

Interviewing

The information-gathering interview is an especially valuable form of research on a college campus because so many experts of every stripe run loose there, from librarians to professors to lab technicians. The interview allows you to view your topic from an expert's perspective, to take advantage of that expert's years of experience, research, and thought. You can use an interview to collect facts and to stimulate your own thinking. Often the interview will save you hours of Internet or library research and allow you to present ideas that you could not have uncovered any other way. And because the interview is a face-to-face interaction with an expert, many ideas that otherwise might be unclear can become more understandable through questions and answers. If you do use an interview for research, you might want to read the section on that type of interview in Appendix A.

Personal Observation

Personal observation enables you to use current, local, first-hand research that you have done yourself. You can think of personal observation as a simple form of experimentation. For example, if you wanted to prove that removing televisions from the student union building would be beneficial, you might include a personal observation like this:

> Last Wednesday I spent 7 to 10 P.M. in the lounge of the student union. Only three times during the evening did anyone attempt to start a conversation. Two of those attempts were met with a request for silence in deference to the television.

If you wanted to prove your point further, you could go one step beyond and observe the same situation under different circumstances:

> This Wednesday I received permission to remove the television from the student union. During those same hours, 7 to 10 P.M., I observed the following behavior in that lounge, this time without television:
> 1. Thirty conversations were begun.
> 2. Twenty-four of these conversations continued, in depth, for more than ten minutes.
> 3. Seven groups of students decided on alternative entertainment for the evening, including going out to the gym, the mall, and the library.
> 4. Four new social acquaintances were made, one of which resulted in a TV date for the following Wednesday night.

Personal observation is used to collect information about your audience members. Because audience members love hearing information about themselves, observing their behavior in this way can be an extremely valuable form of investigation. Survey research is also valuable in this respect.

Survey Research

One advantage of **survey research**—the distribution of questionnaires for people to respond to—is that it can give you up-to-date answers concerning "the way things are" for a specific audience. For example, if you handed out ques-

I've been vaguely aware that what I'm searching for in some loony, unfathomable manner, are not the answers, but The Answers. Somewhere, sprinkled out amongst the best minds of the century, are clues. And someone's tongue is bound to slip.

Digby Diehl

CULTURAL IDIOM

stripe: kind, sort

tionnaires a week or so before presenting a speech on the possible dangers of body piercing, you could present information like this in your speech:

According to a survey I conducted last week, 90 percent of the students in this class believe that body piercing is basically safe. Only 10 percent are familiar with the scarring and injury that can result from this practice. Two of you, in fact, have experienced serious infections from body piercing: one from a pierced tongue and one from a simple pierced ear.

That statement would be of immediate interest to your audience members because *they* were the ones who were surveyed. Another advantage of conducting your own survey is that it is one of the best ways to find out about your audience: It is, in fact, *the* best way to collect the demographic data mentioned earlier. The one disadvantage of conducting your own survey is that, if it is used as evidence, it might not have as much credibility as published evidence found in the library. But the advantages seem to outweigh the disadvantages of survey research in public speaking.

No matter how you gather your information, remember that it is the *quality* rather than the quantity of the research that is most important. The key is to determine carefully what type of research will answer the questions you need to have answered. Sometimes only one type of research will be necessary; at other times every type mentioned here will have to be used.

SKILL BUILDER

Gathering Information

Break up into groups of eight or fewer. Select a topic of your own choosing or one of the following:

1. Who came up with the idea of latitude and longitude lines, and how do they work?
2. College athletes are exploited by the schools they play for.
3. Our jury system does not work.
4. U.S. schools are not safe.
5. What are the steps in the design and construction of the Macy's Thanksgiving Day parade balloons?
6. What do modern-day witches believe?
7. What does it mean to be innumerate, and how many people suffer from this problem?

Assign each member of your group a different research source:

1. Internet search engine
2. Library catalog
3. Reference works
4. Periodicals
5. Databases
6. Talk to a librarian.
7. Talk to a professor.
8. Conduct a survey of your other class members.

During the next class period, report back to the class on which research sources were most productive.

SAMPLE SPEECH

The following speech was given by Jake Gruber, a student at Northern Illinois University. Jake was coached by Judy Santacaterina and won fourth place in the 2001 Interstate Oratorical Association Annual Contest.

On his choice of topic, Jake says, "I knew it was truly important. My grandmother died of heart disease less than a year prior to choosing the topic, so I knew the issue was real. Further, this fact gave me the requisite passion for the subject—which is essential in being truly persuasive and invoking real change."[11]

His general purpose was to persuade, and his specific purpose could be worded as follows:

> After listening to my speech, my audience members will take steps to protect themselves and the women in their lives from heart disease.

As his research progressed, his thesis statement emerged:

> Heart disease is a special problem for women, and we can do something about it.

On the process of researching his speech, Jake says, "Like most students of my generation, I turned to the Internet for information about the topic. While the idea was taken from a copy of *Fortune* magazine, I quickly found the other information needed for the speech floating around the vast electronic wilderness of humanity's collective memory banks. I sniffed out most of it using my school's Lexis-Nexis database."

Jake found more research than he could use and then winnowed it down:

> Because heart disease in women is such a huge problem, finding information was very easy. Once you've got the information in hand (it's always best to grab more than what you'll think you need) the next difficult part is figuring out what to use. Research exists not just to enlighten you and your audience, but also to lend credibility to your words. So part of the process of research sorting is deciding not just what information is important, but the source of the information as well. The *Journal of the American Medical Association,* for example, carries a lot more weight than *Jungle John's Book of Healthy Hemp Products.*

Jake's speech isn't perfect. It would have benefited from an interview, but unfortunately he didn't save himself enough time to do one. As Jake admits,

> A general rule of thumb for interviews is that it is an exceedingly bad idea to wait to the last minute to do them. Most doctors generally don't like being woken at midnight by over-eager college students. I found it is not the best way to get answers—unless you're wondering if you're an idiot.

Analyzing his potential listeners, Jake realized that his audience wouldn't be made up entirely of females, so he made sure he established the importance of his topic to everyone (Paragraph 2). He also knew that the speech would be delivered to an audience of students and professors, so he used a blend of strong logic and emotional appeal. Jake points out that the process of audience analysis is never perfect. "Frequently," he says, "it relies on guesswork and some amount of stereotyping. The trick was in not taking it too far."

HEART DISEASE IN WOMEN[12]   Jake Gruber

1 A 76-year-old mother of four slices bread at her kitchen counter. In a moment, her life will be over—cut down by a culprit who has been lying quietly

in wait for almost two decades. In a way, she's lucky. This culprit frequently strikes women far younger than she. But nevertheless, in a moment, a family will begin to mourn. But who was this stealthy assassin? Some rare and untreatable virus? No. An incredibly patient serial killer? Uh-uh. The truth is, this villain is not only far deadlier than both of these, but also the most preventable.

2 Because "the truth," as stated in the *Pittsburgh Post Gazette* of December 12, 2000, "is that heart disease kills more women every year than all forms of cancer, chronic lung disease, pneumonia, diabetes, accidents and AIDS combined." Whereas one in 28 women will die of breast cancer, one in five will die of heart disease. And guys, before you take the next nine minutes to decide what you'll eat for lunch, ask yourself one question: what would my life be like if the women who make it meaningful were not there? Clearly, this is an issue that concerns us all.

3 To gain a better understanding about the problem of heart disease in women, a three-step approach must be used. First, we must pin down the problem, specifically. Second, analyze its cause, and finally, outline some solutions.

4 So heart disease is the number one killer of women. So what? It's the number one killer of men. Well, with women the issue is a little more complicated than that, and a two-sided problem surfaces. First, women simply don't know that heart disease is a problem. And second, they don't seek or receive the treatment they need.

5 According to *Time* from March 27, 2000, women typically don't present signs of heart disease until after menopause. Unfortunately, by that time the assassin has been at work for many years. The *Chicago Sun-Times* of March 5, 2001 reports that women are a full 50% more likely to die of their first heart attack. And according to the *New England Journal of Medicine* from July 6, 2000, you can double that number if you're under 50. Yet despite these staggering statistics, a full 80% don't know it's the number one threat to their health.

6 The second problem is that women usually don't seek or receive the treatment they need. Marianne Legato, coauthor of *The Female Heart: The Truth about Women and Heart Disease,* states that she's had patients who have known they were having a heart attack, and instead of going to the hospital, paid their bills and made sure their house was in order. On average, women tend to delay seeking treatment four hours longer than men.

7 But that's not to say they will even get that treatment when they do seek it. The November 22, 1999 edition of *Fortune* reports that women are far less likely to receive lifesaving drugs and surgeries after a heart attack. When Indiana State Representative Julia Carson insisted there was something wrong with her heart in 1996, her doctor brushed her off, handing her a book on healthy eating. And rather than run more sophisticated tests when her cholesterol turned up high, he offered the following advice: lay off the fried egg sandwiches and potato chips. Two weeks later, Julia Carson had emergency double-bypass surgery. One of her arteries was completely blocked, and another over 90% occluded. And this was not an isolated instance. A study conducted at the State University of New York in 1999 found that, by large margins, when a man complains of heart problems, he's sent to a cardiologist. But when a woman complains, she's sent to a psychiatrist.

8 Clearly, heart disease in women is a very real problem that is not getting the attention it deserves. But who and what is to blame? Broadly speaking, there are two classic perpetrators: misconception and stigma.

Jake's opening example comes from personal experience (see conclusion, Paragraph 17).

A newspaper article found in the Nexis database.

Jake's soundly logical approach shows his receiver orientation.

Magazine and newspaper articles found in the library database.

Notice how carefully he cites his sources. We'll have more to say about this in Chapter 14.

A book found in the library catalog.

This was the article that Jake ran across that gave him the original idea for his speech. His personal experience made it immediately appealing to him.

Clearly, Jake's thesis and purpose statement keep him on track.

9   Misconception is probably the largest reason why this problem has reached such proportions. You see, much of our knowledge about heart disease was gained through studies solely focused on men. But because women present symptoms of heart disease differently than men, they fell through the cracks and a fallacy was created. Today, according to the *Tufts University Health and Nutrition Letter* of February 2000, women are inclined to ignore the red flags of heart disease because they don't expect to get it. And this fallacy applies to doctors as well. A full 30% of doctors surveyed didn't know heart disease is the number one killer of women. States Elizabeth Ross, a Washington D.C. cardiologist in the previously cited *Fortune:* "I came out of training with the idea heart disease is a man's disease." And that's exactly what's causing the problem.

> Because Jake's argument runs the risk of sounding sexist, he takes great pains to be logical and to back up what he says.

10   Women don't get the treatment they need because neither they, nor the medical community, know enough about the issue. The *University of California, Berkeley Wellness Letter* of November 2000 reports the symptoms of heart attack for women are frequently far more subtle than with men. But because of this misconception, women are less likely to know this, less likely to take preventative measures, and less likely to get help when they need it. Such was the case with 40-year-old Judy Mingram. After dismissing earlier signs of a heart attack, only total "crushing chest pain" sent her to the hospital—38 hours later. On the way to the ER, her heart stopped twice and doctors had to use electric shocks to save her life. All because of a simple misconception.

> This would have been a good place for an interview with a local health-care professional.

11   The second reason why this problem exists is, believe it or not, the stigma attached to women with heart disease. *Prevention* of April 2000 points out that male heart attacks are perceived as an outcropping of a macho lifestyle, while in women it's perceived as a sign of frailty. The gender bias has broad ramifications for all women—especially those in high profile positions. While in the grip of a heart attack that would soon take her life, executive June Esserman instructed her business partner, Carole, to tell no one . . . fearing it would hurt business. Ridiculous? Unfortunately not. Remember Congresswoman Julia Carson? She wasn't even out of the hospital before hungry politicians were vying for her seat. Why? Because they assumed she wouldn't be coming back—even though dozens of congressmen have suffered heart attacks and few such assumptions are ever made. Unfortunately, these seemingly innocuous presumptions help perpetuate the stigma—and that stigma creates silence—and that silence is deadly.

> More articles found in his library databases.

12   So we've seen the problem and uncovered its causes, but we still need to ask ourselves the most important question: What can be done? And that's the really beautiful thing. Because solving this problem doesn't take a government agency and billion dollars of taxes. In the end, it is you who can save your life, and it is your voice that can save the lives of those you love. How? Through prevention and awareness.

> This appeal shows a strong receiver orientation with his audience.

13   The easiest and most effective solution for this problem is prevention. According to the *Tufts University Health and Nutrition Letter* previously cited, a full 66% of women who die of heart disease have no warning of any kind. But in a study presented by the *New England Journal of Medicine* of July 6, 2000, women who observed a healthy lifestyle of proper diet and exercise were at an 80% lower risk of developing coronary heart disease. Here, the rules are the same for men and women: proper diet, lots of exercise, and no smoking.

> We'll have more to say about the effective use of statistics in Chapter 11.

14 Awareness is a bit more complicated, and it hits on two levels. First, women themselves need to be aware not only of their risk for heart disease, but of its causes, its symptoms, and its treatments. WomenHeart.org, updated daily, asserts that simply being knowledgeable of one's own vulnerability is half the battle. Not only will it encourage women to seek help in the event of a crisis, but to recognize that crisis. Women need to learn about the disease, ask questions of their doctors, and evaluate their risk. More specific information is available in the pamphlet I'll be handing out at the end of the round. Ultimately, such efforts will not only raise a woman's awareness of the disease, but facilitate awareness in the medical community—which is the second step.

Web site found through search engine.

(A "round" consists of a few speeches at a tournament.)

15 Admittedly, medicine isn't doing enough to address this problem. But according to WomenHeart.org just cited, the best way to remedy the situation is for individuals to speak up. If your doctor isn't taking your heart concerns seriously, be insistent. If that doesn't work, find a new doctor, get a second opinion, do whatever it takes to be heard. A list of organizations beneficial toward this end is also listed on the pamphlet. In the end, if individuals take charge of their own health, and families persuade their loved ones to do the same, doctors, the medical community, and the media will take notice. But it begins, and ends, with personal responsibility.

Jake's realistic call to action is based on his specific purpose statement.

16 So today, we have learned about the problems of heart disease in women, traced its cause, and put forth some answers. As with anything, these solutions aren't perfect, and it's unlikely we'll be able to change society or stop this virulent disease in its tracks. We can, however, change ourselves. Through controlling risk on a personal level, lives will be saved. Not every life, but many.

He reviews his main points—an important organizational technique we will discuss in Chapter 11.

17 And that 76-year-old mother of four? She was my grandmother. She died last August. But the tragedy was not in the years we lost with her. It isn't even in the fact that those years could have been saved through different habits and greater understanding. The tragedy will only be if others do not learn from her example. Regret. That is the real tragedy.

In his conclusion, Jake reveals why this topic was so meaningful to him.

SUMMARY

This chapter dealt with your first tasks in preparing a speech: choosing and developing a topic. Some guidelines for choosing a topic include these: Look for a topic early and stick with it, choose a topic you find interesting, and choose a topic you already know something about.

One of your tasks is to understand your purpose so that you can stick to it as you prepare your speech. General purposes include entertaining, informing, and persuading. Specific purposes are expressed in the form of purpose statements, which must be receiver-oriented, specific, and realistic.

Your next task is to formulate a thesis statement, which tells what the central idea of your speech is.

Another early task is to analyze the speaking situation, including the audience and the occasion. When analyzing your audience, you should consider the audience type (passersby, captives, volunteers), purpose, demographics, attitudes, beliefs, and values. When analyzing the occasion, you should consider the time (and date) your speech will take place, the time available, the location, and audience expectations.

Although much of your speech will be based on personal reflection about your own ideas and experiences, it is usually necessary to gather some information from outside sources. Techniques for doing so include interpersonal research (such as interviewing), personal observation, and surveys, as well as Internet and library research.

Throughout all these preliminary tasks you will be organizing information and choosing support-ing material. These processes will be discussed in the next chapter.

RESOURCES

Print

Clark, Carol Lea. *Working the Web: A Student's Guide,* 2nd ed. Fort Worth, TX: Harcourt Brace, 2000.

A hands-on escort through the intricacies and mysteries of cyberspace research. Includes everything from a basic introduction to the Web to instructions on creating your own Web pages. See especially Chapter 4, "Doing Research on the World Wide Web," and Chapter 5, "Research Resource Sites."

Interstate Oratorical Association. *Winning Orations,* published annually.

This collection of top student speeches is available from the Interstate Oratorical Association, 107 Agency Road, Mankato, MN 56001.

Rodman, George, and Ronald B. Adler. *The New Public Speaker.* Fort Worth, TX: Harcourt Brace, 1997.

This classic text develops the theme that public speaking is especially important in the media/information age, with audiences who are bombarded with information from both the mass media and emerging technologies such as the World Wide Web. See especially Part II, "Fundamental Steps in Speech Development."

Sprague, Jo, and Douglas Stuart. *The Speaker's Handbook,* 5th ed. Fort Worth, TX: Harcourt Brace, 2000.

A comprehensive reference guide laid out in twenty-eight sections. See especially Section 2, "Topic Selection and Analysis," Section 3, "Audience Analysis," and Section 4, "Research."

Vincent, Ryan Ruggiero. *The Art of Thinking: A Guide to Critical and Creative Thought,* 6th ed. Longman, 2000.

Discusses the process of idea generation through techniques like brainstorming and then refining those ideas and preparing them to stand up to criticism.

Woodward, Jeannette A. *Writing Research Papers: Investigating Resources in Cyberspace.* Lincolnwood, IL: NTC Publishing Group, 1997.

In spite of its apparently restrictive title, this is an excellent and comprehensive guide to academic research, whether for research papers or speeches.

See especially Chapter 1, "Understanding the Research Process," Chapter 3, "Planning a Research Strategy," Chapter 5, "Investigating Library Resources," and Chapter 6, "Exploring the Internet."

Films

There have been no popular films made about college students seeking an interesting topic for a classroom speech. This oversight obviously leaves a gaping hole in American popular culture that one of the fledgling screenwriters reading this book might do something about. In the meantime, we'd like to suggest a few of our favorite films that make related points.

All the President's Men (1976). Rated PG.

Robert Redford and Dustin Hoffman, playing the real-life reporters Bob Woodward and Carl Bernstein, crack the Watergate case through a variety of research skills, including interviewing and library research. Many movies hinge on a scene in which the hero goes to the library and uncovers the pivotal piece of evidence (e.g., *The Hand that Rocks the Cradle,* 1992, rated R) or gets that evidence from a difficult interview (e.g., *Silence of the Lambs,* 1991, rated R). This movie, though, is *all* about research.

Erin Brockovich (2000). Rated R.

Based on true events, this is the inspirational story of a single mother (played by Julia Roberts) who discovers a cover-up involving contaminated water in a local community, which is causing devastating illnesses among its residents. Working as a lowly legal assistant, Brockovich researches the problem through old medical records and interviews. She focuses on the purpose of her message and gives several speeches straight from the heart. Her audience analysis enables her to connect with the people involved in the lawsuit in a way that high-priced lawyers could not. In the end, her efforts result in the largest settlement ever paid in a direct-action lawsuit in U.S. history, $333 million. Her research and speaking enable her to prove herself and turn her life around.

Lorenzo's Oil (1992). Rated PG-13.

Nick Nolte and Susan Sarandon are the parents of a son with an incurable degenerative disease. Desperate to keep him alive, they research the disease for themselves and present a series of speeches that turns the medical community upside down.

Shakespeare in Love (1998). Rated R.

A movie that imagines the young William Shakespeare experiencing a case of writer's block that is not unlike that of most college students when they are assigned their first speech. Shakespeare overcomes his block when he finds a topic, and a muse, he truly believes in. A wonderful love story, but on another level it is a story of the creative process and the power of words.

CONTENTS

KEY TERMS

analogies
anecdote
bar charts
basic speech structure
cause-effect patterns
citation
climax patterns
column charts
conclusion (of a speech)
diagram
example
formal outline
hypothetical examples
introduction (of a speech)
line chart
models
narration
number chart
pie charts
problem-solution pattern
space patterns
statistics
testimony
time (pattern)
topic pattern
transitions
visual aids
word chart
working outline

AFTER STUDYING THE MATERIAL IN THIS CHAPTER . . .

YOU SHOULD UNDERSTAND:

1. The importance of a clear speech organization.

2. The basic structure of a speech.

3. The steps involved in organizing the body of a speech.

4. The importance of effective introductions, conclusions, and transitions.

5. The functions and types of supporting material.

YOU SHOULD BE ABLE TO:

1. Construct an effective speech outline using the organizing principles described in this chapter.

2. Develop an effective introduction, conclusion, and transitions.

3. Choose supporting material for a speech to make your points clear, interesting, memorable, and convincing.

4. Choose appropriate visual aids for a presentation.

ORGANIZATION AND SUPPORT

Alexandra came up with a great topic for her speech. She also worked out a careful purpose statement:

> After listening to my speech, my audience members will know how and when to perform the Heimlich maneuver.

In addition she had an effective thesis:

> The Heimlich maneuver is easy to learn, and it can save lives.

But when it came time to present her speech, all of Alexandra's advance planning seemed to fizzle. She began her speech like this:

> Would you know how to save someone who is choking? Imagine that you were in a restaurant with that someone special, that one person in the world who you would most like to keep breathing, and suddenly he gets a huge piece of fettuccine stuck in his throat. Could I have a volunteer, please?

One of her classmates got up willingly, and Alexandra continued:

> Okay, first you stand behind the victim and put both your arms around him like this. Oh but wait, first you have to figure out if he really is choking. Because believe me it can be really embarrassing if you perform this procedure on someone who *isn't* choking, but just resting between bites or thinking about something. Unless of course you're trying to get to know him better.
>
> Anyway, the next thing you do is make a fist with one hand and place it against the abdomen, like this. No wait, that isn't the first thing. The first thing is to make sure that the victim is standing upright. Well, not upright exactly, but with their head, arms, and upper torso hanging forward like this. But wait, I forgot to give you the list of symptoms so you know the person is really choking. You see, if someone's choking they can't breathe or speak. They also could lose consciousness, but that could be caused by something else, such as a heart attack . . .

Alexandra's speech went on in pretty much the same style, and when it was over the only new thought her audience members had was that they hoped Alexandra wasn't anywhere near them if they ever started to choke.

As Alexandra demonstrated, *knowing* what you are talking about and *communicating* that knowledge aren't the same thing. It's frustrating to realize you aren't expressing your thoughts clearly, and it's equally unpleasant to know that a speaker has something worth saying, yet be unable to figure out just what it is because the material is too jumbled to understand.

In the following pages, you will learn methods of organizing your thoughts in a way that others can follow. And being clear to your audience isn't the only benefit of good organization: Structuring a message effectively will help you refine your own ideas and construct more persuasive messages.

STRUCTURING THE SPEECH

A good speech is like a good building: Both grow from a careful plan. In Chapter 10 you began this planning by analyzing your audience, formulating a purpose, and conducting research. You apply that information to the structure of the speech through outlining. Like any other form of plan, a speech outline is the framework on which your message is built. It contains your main ideas and shows how they relate to one another and your thesis. Virtually every speech outline ought to follow the basic structure outlined in Figure 11–1.

> **CULTURAL IDIOM**
>
> **worked out:**
> formulated
>
> **to fizzle:** to weaken
> quickly

Words differently arranged have a different meaning, and meanings differently arranged have a different effect.

Pascal

This **basic speech structure** demonstrates the old aphorism for speakers: "Tell what you're going to say, say it, and then tell what you said." Although this structure sounds redundant, the research on listening cited in Chapter 4 demonstrates that receivers forget much of what they hear. The clear, repetitive nature of the basic speech structure reduces the potential for memory loss, because audiences have a tendency to listen more carefully during the beginning and ending of a speech.[1] Your outline will reflect this basic speech structure.

Outlines come in all shapes and sizes, but the three types that are most important to us here are working outlines, formal outlines, and speaking notes.

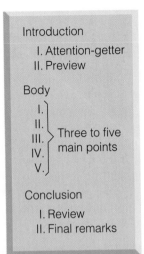

Figure 11–1   Basic Speech Structure

Working Outline

A **working outline** is a construction tool used to map out your speech. The working outline will probably follow the basic speech structure, but only in rough form. It is for your eyes only. No one else need understand it, so you can use whatever symbols and personal shorthand you find functional. Actually, it is probably a mistake to refer to a "working outline" in the singular form, because you will probably create several drafts as you refine your ideas. As your ideas solidify, your outline will change accordingly, becoming more polished as you go along.

Formal Outline

A **formal outline** such as the one shown on page 350 uses a consistent format and set of symbols to identify the structure of ideas.

A formal outline serves several purposes. In simplified form, it can be used as a visual aid (displayed while you speak or distributed as a handout). It can serve as a record of a speech that was delivered; many organizations send outlines to members who miss meetings at which presentations were given. Finally, in speech classes, instructors often use speech outlines to analyze student speeches. When one is used for that purpose, it is usually a full-sentence outline and includes the purpose, the thesis and topic, and/or title. Most instructors also require a bibliography of sources at the end of the outline. The bibliography should include full research citations, the correct form for which can be found in any style guide, such as Kate Turabian's *Student Guide for Writing College Papers.*[2] There are at least six standard bibliographic styles, and your instructor might assign one of them. Whichever style you use, you should be consistent in form and remember the two primary functions of a bibliographic citation: to demonstrate the credibility of your source and to enable the readers—in this case your professor or your fellow students—to find the source if they want to check its accuracy or explore your topic in more detail.

Another person should be able to understand the basic ideas included in your speech by reading the formal outline. In fact, that's one test of the effectiveness of your outline. See if the outline on p. 350 passes this test for you.

Speaking Notes

Like your working outline, your speaking notes are for your use only, so the format is up to you. Many teachers suggest that speaking notes should be in the form of a brief key-word outline, with just enough information listed to jog your

CULTURAL IDIOM

to jog your memory:
to remind yourself

UNDERSTANDING COMMUNICATION TECHNOLOGY

Citing Web Sources

The World Wide Web is becoming an increasingly important source for speech research, and listing the URL (uniform resource locator, or Web address) on your bibliography, including the date you found it, can establish the credibility of the source for your instructor and help people who want to follow up on the source. When you list a Web source, you should also include, if possible, the author of the page, the organization who supports it, and the last date it was updated. A complete citation might look something like this:

George Adler, "Citing Web Sites in Speech Bibliographies," Central States Communication Association Web site, updated July, 2001, available at www.csca-net.org. Accessed August 24, 2001.

The third item listed in the bibliography of the sample outline on page 351 is another example of a Web citation.

Speech Outline

The following outline is based on a speech by Wesley Schawe of Kansas State University.[3]

General purpose: To persuade

Specific purpose: After listening to my speech, audience members will be aware of diploma mills and take steps to help eliminate them.

Thesis: Phony online universities threaten our education and public safety.

Title: "Diploma Mills"

INTRODUCTION

I. Attention-Getter: Joke about professors "weighing" papers to grade them
II. Thesis statement
III. Preview of main points

BODY

I. Why are diploma mills a problem?
   A. Diploma mills are proliferating.
      1. There are more than 350 diploma mills worldwide.
      2. Hundreds of companies and organizations accept these degrees.
      3. Hundreds of thousands of students are involved.
   B. Diploma mills are dangerous.
      1. Some clients are cheated: They believe they are enrolling in legitimate degree programs.
      2. Some clients are cheaters: We lose pay raises, job offers, and promotions to people with fake degrees. Our own degrees are devalued by these fake diplomas.
II. What causes diploma mills to be so popular?
   A. We have accepted distance education as legitimate learning.
      1. A well-designed Web page can make an institution appear to be legitimate.
      2. Differences are hard to spot.
   B. We have automatically accepted the value of advanced degrees.
      1. There is too much emphasis on diplomas and not on the expertise they represent.
      2. Advanced degrees are automatically rewarded with promotions and pay raises.
III. What can we do about diploma mills?
   A. We should check for legitimate accreditation.
      1. There are eight regional accrediting agencies.
      2. Call your state Department of Education to see if a school is legitimate.
   B. We should help shut down illegal diploma mills.
      1. Be aware of false claims made online.
      2. Contact your state attorney general with your evidence.
   C. We should let employers know.

CONCLUSION

I. Review of main points
II. Final remarks: Refer back to our opening example, restate thesis. "Diploma mills may get a kick out of weighing your paper for a grade, but by shutting them down, we can finally tip the scales in our favor."

Speech Outline—cont'd

BIBLIOGRAPHY

Alexenia Dimitrova, "Honors for Sale," *World Press Review,* May 2002, p. 39.

Aimee Howd, "Will Cyber-School Pass or Fail?," *Insight on the News,* June 12, 2000, p. 22.

Illinois Online Network, "What Makes a Successful Online Student," available at http://Illinois.Online.Uillinois.edu/IONresources/onlineoverview/StudentProfile.html. Updated 4/27/01; Accessed 7/25/01. Site hosted by the Board of Trustees of the University of Illinois.

Mary Lord, "Sheepskin Fleecers: When Those Ivy-Clad Towers Are Nothing but a Diploma Mill," *U.S. News & World Report,* September 28, 1998, p. 72.

Bryon MacWilliams, "Diplomas for Sale on Moscow's Streets," *The Chronicle of Higher Education,* July 16, 1999, p. A43.

Genevieve Manna, "Attorney General Looks at Online Fraud," *Houston Chronicle,* February 11, 1999.

Gerald Redmond, *20/20* interview, December 12, 1998.

Anthony Zinga, "Online Diplomas Not What They Seem," *St. Louis Post Dispatch,* March 12, 1999.

memory but not enough to get lost in.

Many teachers also suggest that you fit your notes on one side of one three-by-five-inch note card. Other teachers recommend that you also have your introduction and conclusion on note cards, and still others recommend that your references and quotations be written out on note cards. Your notes for a speech on diploma mills might look like the ones in Figure 11–2.

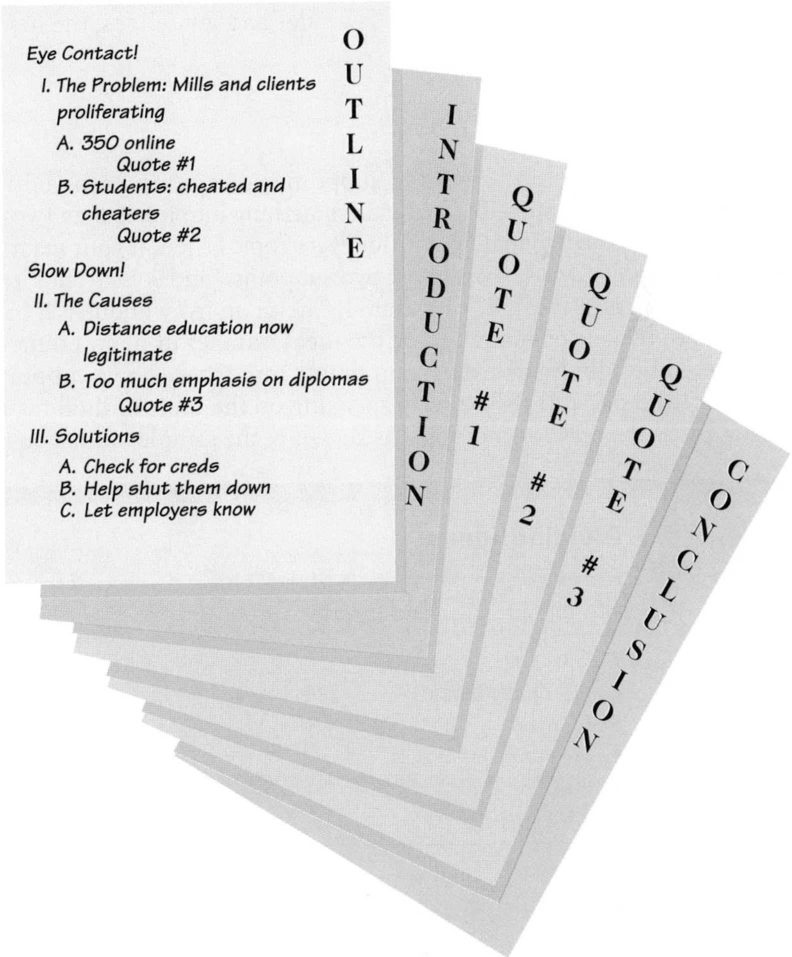

PRINCIPLES OF OUTLINING

Over the years, a series of rules or principles for the construction of outlines has evolved. These rules are based on the use of the standard symbols and format discussed next.

Standard Symbols

A speech outline generally uses the following symbols:

Figure 11–2 Speaking Notes

I. Main point (Roman numeral)
   A. Subpoint (capital letter)
      1. Sub-subpoint (standard number)
         a. Sub-subsubpoint (lowercase letter)

In the examples in this chapter, the major divisions of the speech—introduction, body, and conclusion—are not given symbols. They are listed by name, and the Roman numerals for their main points begin anew in each division. An alternative form is to list these major divisions with Roman numerals, main points with capital letters, and so on.

Standard Format

In the sample outlines in this chapter, notice that each symbol is indented a number of spaces from the symbol above it. Besides keeping the outline neat, the indentation of different-order ideas is actually the key to the technique of outlining; it enables you to coordinate and order ideas in the form in which they are most comprehensible to the human mind. If the standard format is used in your working outline, it will help you create a well-organized speech. If it is used in speaking notes, it will help you remember everything you want to say.

Proper outline form is based on a few rules and guidelines, the first of which is the rule of division.

The Rule of Division

In formal outlines main points and subpoints always represent a division of a whole. Because it is impossible to divide something into fewer than two parts, you always have at least two main points for every topic. Then, if your main points are divided, you will always have at least two subpoints, and so on. Thus, the rule for formal outlines is: Never a "I" without a "II," never an "A" without a "B," and so on.

Three to five is considered to be the ideal number of main points. It is also considered best to divide those main points into three to five subpoints, when necessary and possible. If you were speaking on the topic of diploma mills, you might divide the body of your topic as shown in the sample outline on page 350.

SKILL BUILDER

Dividing Ideas

For practice in the principle of division, divide each of the following into three to five subcategories:

1. Clothing
2. Academic studies
3. Crime
4. Health care
5. Fun
6. Charities

The Rule of Parallel Wording

Your main points should be worded in a similar, or "parallel," manner. For example, if you are developing a speech against capital punishment, your main points might look like this:

I.   Capital punishment is not effective: It is not a deterrent to crime.
II. Capital punishment is not constitutional: It does not comply with the Eighth Amendment.
III. Capital punishment is not civilized: It does not allow for a reverence for life.

Whenever possible, subpoints should also be worded in a parallel manner. For your points to be worded in a parallel manner, they should each contain one, and only one, idea. (After all, they can't really be parallel if one is longer or contains more ideas than the others.) This will enable you to completely develop one idea before moving on to another one in your speech. If you were discussing cures for indigestion, your topic might be divided incorrectly if your main points looked like this:

I.   "Preventive cures" help you before eating.
II. "Participation cures" help you during and after eating.

You might actually have three ideas there and thus three main points:

I.   Prevention cures (before eating).
II. Participation cures (during eating).
III. Postparticipation cures (after eating).

> *Control yourself when you have two things to say: say first one, then the other, not both at the same time.*
>
> George Polya

SKILL BUILDER

Building Outlines

Indicate which items would be main points and which would be subpoints in a speech entitled "World War II" by fitting them into the following outline form:

Japan desires an eastern empire
Shortage of rubber tires
Events of the war
Nazi policy of expansion
Japan seizes the Philippines
Sugar rationing
Effects of the war on America
Germany attacks France
Causes of the war
Germany attacks Soviet Union

I.
   A.
   B.
II.
   A.
   B.
   C.
III.
   A.
   B.

ORGANIZING YOUR POINTS IN A LOGICAL ORDER

An outline should reflect a logical order for your points. You might arrange them from newest to oldest, largest to smallest, best to worst, or in a number of other ways that follow. The organizing pattern you choose ought to be the one that best develops your thesis.

TIME PATTERNS   Arrangement according to periods of **time**, or chronology, is one of the most common patterns of organization. The period of time could be anything from centuries to seconds. In a speech on airline food, a time pattern might look like this:

I.   Early airline food: a gourmet treat
II. The middle period: institutional food at thirty thousand feet
III. Today's airline food: the passenger starves

Arranging points according to the steps that make up a process is another form of time patterning. The topic "Recording a Hit Song" might use this type of patterning:

I. Find an agent
II. Record the demo CD
III. Promote the song

Time patterns are also the basis of **climax patterns,** which are used to create suspense. For example, if you wanted to create suspense in a speech about military intervention, you could chronologically trace the steps that eventually led us into Korea, Vietnam, or Afghanistan in such a way that you build up your audience's curiosity. If you told of these steps through the eyes of a soldier who entered military service right before one of those wars, you would be building suspense as your audience wonders what will become of that soldier.

The climax pattern can also be reversed. When it is, it is called *anticlimactic* organization. If you started your military intervention speech by telling the audience that you were going to explain why a specific soldier was killed in a specific war, and then you went on to explain the things that caused that soldier to become involved in that war, you would be using anticlimactic organization. This pattern is helpful when you have an essentially uninterested audience, and you need to build interest early in your speech to get the audience to listen to the rest of it.

SPACE PATTERNS   **Space patterns** are organized according to area. The area could be stated in terms of continents or centimeters or anything in between. If you were discussing the Great Lakes, for example, you could arrange them from west to east:

I. Superior
II. Michigan
III. Huron
IV. Erie
V. Ontario

TOPIC PATTERNS   A topical arrangement or **topic pattern** is based on types or categories. These categories could be either well known or original; both have their advantages. For example, a division of college students according to well-known categories might look like this:

I. Freshmen
II. Sophomores
III. Juniors
IV. Seniors

Well-known categories are advantageous because audiences quickly understand them. But familiarity also has its disadvantages. One disadvantage is the "Oh, this again" syndrome. If the members of an audience feel they have nothing new to learn about the components of your topic, they might not listen to you. To avoid this, you could invent original categories that freshen up your topic by suggesting an original analysis. For example, original categories for "college students" might look like this:

I. Grinds—the students who go to every class and read every assignment before it is due and who are usually seen in dormitories telling everyone to turn their stereos down.

II. Renaissance students—the students who find a satisfying blend of scholarly and social pursuits. They go to most of their classes and do most of their assignments, but they don't let school get in the way of their social life.

III. Burnouts—the students who have a difficult time finding the classroom, let alone doing the work.

Sometimes topics are arranged in the order that will be easiest for your audience to remember. To return to our Great Lakes example, the names of the lakes could be arranged so their first letters spell the word "HOMES." Words used in this way are known as mnemonics. Carol Koehler, a professor of communication and medicine, uses the mnemonic "CARE" to describe the characteristics of a caring doctor:

C stands for *concentrate*. Physicians should hear with their eyes and ears . . .
A stands for *acknowledge*. Show them that you are listening . . .
R stands for *response*. Clarify issues by asking questions, providing periodic recaps . . .
E stands for *exercise emotional control*. When your "hot buttons" are pushed . . .[4]

PROBLEM-SOLUTION PATTERNS   The **problem-solution pattern,** as you might guess from its no-nonsense name, describes what's wrong and proposes a way to make things better. It is usually (but not always) divisible into these two distinct parts as in this example:

I. The Problem: Addiction (which could then be broken down into addiction to cigarettes, alcohol, prescribed drugs, and street drugs)

II. The Solution: A national addiction institute (which would study the root causes of addiction in the same way that the National Cancer Institute studies the root causes of cancer)

We will discuss this pattern in more detail in Chapter 14.

CAUSE-EFFECT PATTERNS
Cause-effect patterns are similar to problem-solution patterns in that they are basically two-part patterns: First you discuss something that happened, then you discuss its effects.

A variation of this pattern reverses the order and presents the effects first and then the causes. Persuasive speeches often have effect-cause or cause-effect as the first two main points. Elizabeth Hallum, a student at Arizona State University, organized the first two points of a speech on "workplace revenge"[5] like this:

UNDERSTANDING DIVERSITY

Nontraditional Patterns of Organization

In addition to the traditional patterns usually taught in public speaking classes, researchers are looking at other organizational patterns commonly used by women and ethnic speakers. For example, Cheryl Jorgenson-Earp is exploring a number of alternative patterns that women have used historically. She argues that many speakers are uncomfortable with the standard organization patterns because of cultural backgrounds or personal inclinations. As alternatives, she proposes several less direct and more "organic" patterns that provide a clear structure for a speech but have a less linear form.

One of these is the Wave pattern. In this pattern the speaker uses repetitions and variations of themes and ideas. The major points of the speech come at the crest of the wave. The speaker follows these with a variety of examples leading up to another crest where she repeats the theme or makes another major point.

Perhaps the most famous speech that illustrates this pattern is Martin Luther King, Jr.'s "I Have a Dream." King used this memorable line as the crest of a wave that he followed with examples of what he saw in his dream; then he repeated the line. He ended with a "peak" conclusion that emerged from the final wave in the speech—repetition and variation on the phrase "Let freedom ring."

An excerpt from Sojourner Truth's "Ain't I a Woman?" speech also illustrates this pattern.

That man over there says that women need to be helped into carriages, and lifted over ditches, and to have the best place everywhere. Nobody ever helps me into carriages, or over mud-puddles, or gives me any best place!

And ain't I a woman?

Look at me! Look at my arm! I have ploughed and planted, and gathered into barns, and no man could head me!

And ain't I a woman?

I could work as much and eat as much as a man—when I could get it—and bear the lash as well!

And ain't I a woman?

I have borne thirteen children and seen them most all sold off to slavery, and when I cried out with my mother's grief, none but Jesus heard me!

And ain't I a woman?

Clella Jaffe, *Public Speaking: A Cultural Perspective*, © 1995. Reprinted with permission of Wadsworth, an imprint of the Wadsworth Group, a division of Thomson Learning. Fax 800 730-2215.

I. The Effects of the Problem
  A. Lost productivity
  B. Costs of sabotage
II. The Causes of the Problem
  A. Employees feeling alienated
  B. Employers' light treatment of incidents of revenge

The third main point in this type of persuasive speech is often "solutions," and the fourth main point is often "the desired audience behavior." Elizabeth's final points were:

III. Solutions: Support the National Employee Rights Institute
IV. Desired Audience Response: Log on to *www.disgruntled.com*

MOTIVATED SEQUENCE   One variation of the problem-solution pattern contains five steps and has come to the known as the Motivated Sequence:[6]
  I. The Attention Step draws attention to your subject. ("Cheers for the urban guerillas of New York City, the dauntless men and women who let their dogs loose in the parks!"[7])
  II. The Need Step establishes the problem. ("In this country, we tend to think that freedom for dogs encourages bad behavior. Nothing could be further from the truth. Freedom actually improves a dog's conduct.")

III. The Satisfaction Step proposes a solution. ("The time has come for New York and other American cities to unleash their dogs.")

IV. The Visualization Step describes the results of the solution. ("In the splendid cities of Europe, well-mannered dogs are accepted almost everywhere as a normal part of life. In Milan, dogs are welcome in the best hotels, enjoy large play groups in the parks, and are seldom seen on leashes.")

V. The Action Step is a direct appeal for the audience to do something. ("Demand that parts of Central Park become leash-free. Dog lovers of New York, unite!")

Chapter 14 has more to say about the organization of persuasive speeches.

USING TRANSITIONS

Transitions keep your message moving forward. They perform the following functions:

They tell how the introduction relates to the body of the speech.
They tell how one main point relates to the next main point.
They tell how your subpoints relate to the points they are part of.
They tell how your supporting points relate to the points they support.

Transitions, to be effective, should refer to the previous point and to the upcoming point, showing how they relate to one another and to the thesis. They usually sound something like this:

"Like [previous point], another important consideration in [topic] is [upcoming point]."
"But _____ isn't the only thing we have to worry about. _____ is even more potentially dangerous."
"Yes, the problem is obvious. But what are the solutions? Well, one possible solution is . . ."

Sometimes a transition includes an internal review (a restatement of preceding points), an internal preview (a look ahead to upcoming points), or both:

"So far we've discussed _____, _____, and _____. Our next points are _____, _____, and _____."

You can find several examples of transitions in the sample speech at the end of this chapter.

BEGINNING AND ENDING THE SPEECH

The **introduction** and **conclusion** of a speech are vitally important, although they usually will occupy less than 20 percent of your speaking time. Listeners form their impression of a speaker early, and they remember what they hear last; it is, therefore, vital to make those few moments at the beginning and end of your speech work to your advantage.

The Introduction

There are four functions of the speech introduction. It serves to capture the audience's attention, preview the main points, set the mood and tone of the speech, and demonstrate the importance of the topic.

UNDERSTANDING COMMUNICATION TECHNOLOGY

Software for Organization and Outlining

Sometimes the best way to organize ideas is visually. Until recently, the best approach was to write ideas on note cards, spread them out on the table or floor, and rearrange them until a clear plan emerged. Now computers make the task quicker and easier. Any word processor can be used to cut and paste blocks of ideas so you can rearrange the structure of your speech, and more advanced ones include a document map or "outline view" that shows your organizational structure as you collect your notes.

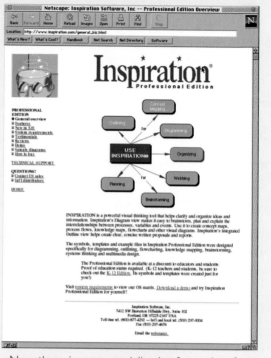

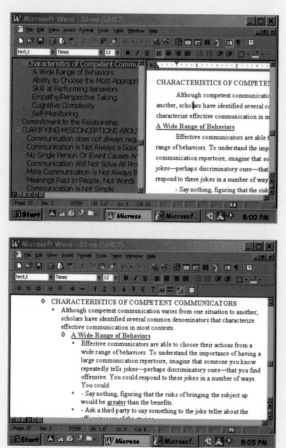

Word-processing programs like Microsoft Word include a document map, shown top, and an outline view, shown above, both of which show the organizational structure of the speech you are developing.

Now there is even specialized software just for organizing, outlining, and brainstorming as you go. Inspiration is a visual tool for developing ideas. The program's "diagram view" provides an easy-to-use equivalent to the note card approach. Each idea you type into the computer appears on-screen inside its own box or circle. You can click on these ideas with your mouse and rearrange them until they fall into patterns that seem clear and effective. Then, with a simple command, the visual map is turned into a traditional outline, suitable for conversion into speaker's notes, handouts, or visual aids.

Besides serving as an outlining tool, Inspiration makes it easy to create concept maps, process flows, knowledge maps, flow charts, and other visual diagrams.

You can find more information about Inspiration and download a demonstration version of the software by pointing your Web browser to http://www.inspiration.com/freetrial/index.csm

CAPTURING ATTENTION There are several ways to capture an audience's attention. The following discussion shows how some of these ways might be used in a speech entitled "Communication between Plants and Humans."

Refer to the Audience. The technique of referring to the audience is especially effective if it is complimentary: "Julio's speech last week about how animals communicate was so interesting that I decided to explore a related topic: Whether people can communicate with plants!"

Refer to the Occasion. A reference to the occasion could allude to the event of your speech, as in "Even though the focus of this course is *human* communication, it seems appropriate to talk about whether humans can communicate with plants."

Refer to the Relationship between the Audience and the Subject. "My topic, 'Communicating with Plants,' ties right in with our study of human communication. We can gain several insights into our communication with one another by examining our interactions with our little green friends."

Refer to Something Familiar to the Audience. The technique of referring to something familiar to the audience is especially effective if you are discussing a topic that might seem new or strange to that audience. Audience attention will be attracted to the familiar among the new in much the same way that we are able to pick out a friend's face in a crowd of strangers. For example, "See that lilac bush outside the window? At this very moment it might be reacting to the joys and anxieties that you are experiencing in this classroom."

Cite a Startling Fact or Opinion. A statement that surprises audience members is bound to make them sit up and listen. This is true even for a topic that the audience considers old hat; if the audience members think they've heard it all before about plant-human communication, you might mention, "There is now actual scientific evidence that plants appreciate human company, kind words, and classical music."

Ask a Question. A rhetorical question causes your audience to think rather than to answer out loud. "Have you ever wondered why some people seem able to grow beautiful, healthy plants effortlessly, whereas others couldn't make a weed grow in the best soil?" This question is designed to make the audience respond mentally, "Yeah, why is that?"

Tell an Anecdote. A personal story perks up audience interest because it shows the human side of what might otherwise be dry, boring information. "The other night, while taking a walk in the country, I happened on a small garden that was rich with lush vegetation. But it wasn't the lushness of the vegetation that caught my eye at first. There, in the middle of the garden, was a man who was talking quite animatedly to a giant sunflower."

Use a Quotation. Quotable quotes sometimes have a precise, memorable wording that would be difficult for you to say as well. Also, they allow you to borrow from the credibility of the quoted source. For example, "Thorne Bacon, the naturalist, recently said about the possibility of plants and humans communicating, 'Personally, I cannot imagine a world so dull, so satiated, that it should reject out of hand arresting new ideas which may be as old as the first amino acid in the chain of life on earth.'"

Tell a Joke. If you happen to know or can find a joke that is appropriate to your subject and occasion, it can help you build audience interest: "We once worried about people who talked to plants, but that's no longer the case. Now we only worry if the plants talk back." Be sure, though, that the joke is appropriate to the audience, as well as to the occasion and to you as a speaker.

PREVIEWING MAIN POINTS After you capture the attention of the audience, an effective introduction will almost always state the speaker's thesis and give the

> CULTURAL IDIOM
>
> **old hat:** not new or different

listeners an idea of the upcoming main points. Katherine Graham, the former chairperson of the board of the Washington Post Company, addressed a group of businessmen and their wives in this way:

> I am delighted to be here. It is a privilege to address you. And I am especially glad the rules have been bent for tonight, allowing so many of you to bring along your husbands. I think it's nice for them to get out once in a while and see how the other half lives. Gentlemen, we welcome you.
>
> Actually, I have other reasons for appreciating this chance to talk with you tonight. It gives me an opportunity to address some current questions about the press and its responsibilities—whom we are responsible to, what we are responsible for, and generally how responsible our performance has been.[8]

Thus, Ms. Graham previewed her main points:

1. To explain to whom the press is responsible
2. To explain what the press is responsible for
3. To explain how responsible the press has been

Sometimes your preview of main points will be even more straightforward:

> "I have three points to discuss: They are _____, _____, and _____."

Sometimes you will not want to refer directly to your main points in your introduction. Your reasons for not doing so might be based on a plan calling for suspense, humorous effect, or stalling for time to win over a hostile audience. In that case, you might preview only your thesis:

> "I am going to say a few words about _____."
> "Did you ever wonder about _____?"
> "_____ is one of the most important issues facing us today."

SETTING THE MOOD AND TONE OF YOUR SPEECH   Notice, in the example just given, how Katherine Graham began her speech by joking with her audience. She was speaking before an all-male organization; the only women in the audience were the members' wives. That is why Ms. Graham felt it necessary to put her audience members at ease by joking with them about women's traditional role in society. By beginning in this manner, she assured the men that she would not berate them for the sexist bylaws of their organization. She also showed them that she was going to approach her topic with wit and intelligence. Thus, she set the mood and tone for her entire speech. Imagine how different that mood and tone would have been if she had begun this way:

> Before I start today, I would just like to say that I would never have accepted your invitation to speak here had I known that your organization does not accept women as members. Just where do you Cro-Magnons get off, excluding more than half the human race from your little club?

DEMONSTRATING THE IMPORTANCE OF YOUR TOPIC TO YOUR AUDIENCE   Your audience members will listen to you more carefully if your speech relates to them as individuals. Based on your audience analysis, you should state directly *why* your topic is of importance to your audience members. This importance should be related as closely as possible to their specific needs at that specific time. For example, Stephanie Hamilton, a student at North Dakota State University, presented a speech about loopholes in the justice system when crimes of violence occur on cruise ships. After telling the story of a rape aboard ship, she established the importance of her topic this way:

> Each year, millions of people take to the seas on cruises. Many of us have taken cruises of our own or plan to take one someday and practically everyone knows at least someone who has taken a cruise. Even if we will never take a cruise, we are a part of society and a possible target for crime. If someone were found guilty of a crime, would we want them free? That is exactly what is happening without laws of recourse in place for our protection. We don't need to let our family, friends, neighbors or ourselves be taken advantage of and never given justice.[9]

The Conclusion

The conclusion, like the introduction, is an especially important part of your speech. Your audience members will have a tendency to listen carefully as your speech draws to a close; they will have a tendency to consider what you say at the end of your speech as important and to remember it. Because of this, the conclusion has three essential functions: to review the thesis, to review your main points, and to provide a memorable final remark.

You can review your thesis either by repeating it or by paraphrasing it. Either way, your conclusion should include a short summary statement:

> *And so, after listening to what I had to say this afternoon, I hope you agree with me that the city cannot afford to lose the services of the American Society for the Prevention of Cruelty to Animals.*

You will probably also want to review your main points. This can be done directly: "I made three main points about the ASPCA today. They are . . ." But your main points can also be reviewed artistically. For example, first look back at that example of an introduction by Katherine Graham; then read her conclusion to that speech:

> So instead of seeking flat and absolute answers to the kinds of problems I have discussed tonight, what we should be trying to foster is respect for one another's conception of where duty lies, and understanding of the real worlds in which we try to do our best. And we should be hoping for the energy and sense to keep on arguing and questioning, because there is no better sign that our society is healthy and strong.

Let's take a closer look at how and why this conclusion was effective. Ms. Graham posed three questions in her introduction. She dealt with those

A speech is like a love affair. Any fool can start it, but to end it requires considerable skill.

Lord Mancroft

questions in her speech and reminded her audience, in her conclusion, that she had answered the questions.

PREVIEW (FROM INTRODUCTION OF SPEECH)	**REVIEW (FROM CONCLUSION)**
1. To whom is the press responsible?	1. To its own conception of where its duty lies
2. What is the press responsible for?	2. For doing its best in the "real world"
3. How responsible has the press been?	3. It has done its best

Finally, you should devise a striking summary statement for your conclusion to help your audience remember your thesis. Ray Bramson, a student at California State University, Chico, gave a speech on the dangers of recycling medical devices and ended his conclusion with this statement: "It seems that in cutting costs, health care providers are ignoring one very important fact: human life cannot be recycled." That statement was concise but memorable.

You can make your final remarks most effective by avoiding the following mistakes:

DO NOT END ABRUPTLY   Make sure that your conclusion accomplishes everything it is supposed to accomplish. Develop it fully. You might want to use signposts such as "Finally . . .," "In conclusion . . .," or "To sum up what I've been talking about here . . ." to let your audience know that you have reached the conclusion of the speech.

BUT DON'T RAMBLE EITHER   Prepare a definite conclusion, and never, never end by mumbling something like, "Well, I guess that's about all I wanted to say . . ."

DON'T INTRODUCE NEW POINTS   The worst kind of rambling is "Oh, yes, and something I forgot to mention is . . ."

DON'T APOLOGIZE   Don't say, "I'm sorry I couldn't tell you more about this" or "I'm sorry I didn't have more time to research this subject" or any of those sad songs. They will only highlight the possible weaknesses of your speech, and there's a good chance those weaknesses were far more apparent to you than to your audience.

Instead, it is best to end strong. You can use any of the attention-getters suggested for the introduction to make the conclusion memorable. In fact, one kind of effective closing is to refer to the attention-getter you used in your introduction and remind your audience how it applies to the points you made in your speech.

INVITATION TO INSIGHT   **Organizational Effectiveness**

Take any written statement at least three paragraphs long that you consider effective. This statement might be an editorial in your local newspaper, a short magazine article, or even a section of one of your textbooks. Outline this statement according to the rules discussed here. Was the statement well organized? Did its organization contribute to its effectiveness?

CULTURAL IDIOM

sad songs: statements meant to elicit sympathy

SUPPORTING MATERIAL

It is important to organize ideas clearly and logically. But clarity and logic by themselves won't guarantee that you'll interest, enlighten, or persuade others; these results call for the use of supporting materials. These materials—the facts and information that back up and prove your ideas and opinions—are the flesh that fills out the skeleton of your speech.

Functions of Supporting Material

There are four functions of supporting material.

TO CLARIFY   As explained in Chapter 3, people of different backgrounds tend to attach different meanings to words. Supporting material can help you overcome this potential source of confusion by helping you clarify key terms and ideas. For example, when Ed Rubinstein, the economics analyst at the *National Review,* spoke at Hillsdale College in Michigan on "The Economics of Crime," he needed to clarify what he meant by a "career criminal." He used supporting material in this way:

> The career criminal, according to James Q. Wilson, was long ago identified as: "typically an impulsive young man who grew up in a discordant family where one or both parents had a criminal record, discipline was erratic, and human relations were cold and unpredictable. He had a low IQ and poor verbal skills. His behavioral problems appeared early, often by age eight, and included dishonesty and aggressiveness. Even in kindergarten or first grade he was disruptive, defiant, and badly behaved. He had few friends and was not emotionally close to those associates with whom he began stealing and assaulting."[10]

TO MAKE INTERESTING   A second function of support is to make an idea interesting or to catch your audience's attention. When Daniel White, a student at Marshall University in West Virginia, gave his speech on cloning, he might have simply said, "There's been a lot of interest in cloning in the media recently." Instead, he used supporting material to make the same point in a more interesting way:

> "British Scientists Clone the World's First Adult Mammal." On February 24 of this year, this headline, or something like it, was plastered on the front page of newspapers all across the nation. Coincidentally, the following weekend the new *Star Trek* episode revealed that Dr. Julian Bashere of Deep Space Nine was a product of genetic engineering, the *X-Files* ran a string of shows dealing with clones, and recently the movie *Multiplicity,* another cloning story, hit the new release section of local video stores.[11]

TO MAKE MEMORABLE   A third function of supporting materials, related to the preceding one, is to make a point memorable. We have already mentioned the importance of "memorable" statements in a speech conclusion; use of supporting material in the introduction and body of the speech provides another way to help your audience retain important information. When Amy Jones of Western Kentucky University wanted to help her audience remember that mosquitoes are a genuine health hazard, she used supporting material toward the end of her ten-minute speech this way:

> We must realize that mosquitoes are more than just a nuisance. In the past nine minutes, 75 more children have died of malaria.[12]

TO PROVE Finally, supporting material can be used as evidence, to prove the truth of what you are saying. When Brian Sosnowchik, a student at Pennsylvania State University, wanted to prove the point that chronic pain is a significant problem in the U.S. today, he used supporting material in this way:

> "I can't shower because the water feels like molten lava. Every time someone turns on a ceiling fan, it feels like razor blades are cutting through my legs. I'm dying." Meet David Bogan, financial advisor from Deptford, New Jersey. Porsche, boat, and home owner, and victim of a debilitating car accident that has not only rendered him two years of chronic leg pain, but a fall from the pinnacle of success. Bogan has nothing now. Life to him, life with searing pain, is a worthless tease of agony and distress.
>
> Unfortunately, according to the February 21, 2000 *St. Louis Post-Dispatch,* Bogan is one of 100 million Americans, nearly a third of the population, suffering from chronic pain due to everything from accidents to the simple daily stresses on our bodies. Moreover, in a personal telephone interview on March 30, 2000, Penny Cowan, founder and Executive Director of the American Chronic Pain Association, disclosed, "Chronic pain is the most expensive health care problem today, and it certainly doesn't get the appropriate amount of attention from the medical community."[13]

SKILL BUILDER

The Functions of Support

For practice in recognizing the functions of support, identify three instances of support in each of the speeches at the end of Chapters 13 and 14. Explain the function of each instance of support. (Keep in mind that any instance of support *could* perform more than one function.)

Types of Supporting Material

As you may have noted, each function of support could be fulfilled by several different types of material. Let's take a look at these different types of supporting material.

DEFINITIONS It's a good idea to give your audience members definitions of your key terms, especially if those terms are unfamiliar to them or are being used in an unusual way. A good definition is simple and concise. If you were giving a speech on binge drinking, you might define that term as follows:

> *Researchers consider a person who had had five drinks on one occasion during the previous two weeks to be a binge drinker.*

EXAMPLES An **example** is a specific case that is used to demonstrate a general idea. Examples can be either factual or hypothetical, personal or borrowed. Ben Crosby, a student at Southern Utah University, used three examples to back up his point that meningitis could be a dangerous disease on college campuses:

> Jessie Gardiner, formerly a freshman at Frostburg State University, spent a Thursday and Friday night partying at the campus Delta Chi fraternity with two hundred other people. According to the *Washington Post* of February 25, 1999, Gardiner woke up the following Sunday with fever, rash, and nausea. He died at 7:15 the following Tuesday, a day after being admitted to the hospital.

A definition is the enclosing of the wilderness of an idea within a wall of words.

Samuel Butler

Madison, Wisconsin's "Channel Three News" ran a story on October 28, 1998, reporting the death of Sarah Gornick, a junior Bio-Chemistry major at the University of Wisconsin. Sarah, too, spent a Friday night at a Greek party. After experiencing severe symptoms of the disease, she was rushed to the hospital at 7 A.M. Tuesday, and died a half-hour later.

Finally, Laura Tardiff was experiencing a sore throat on her way home from spring break festivities in Daytona Beach. Her temperature rose to 104 degrees. She woke the following morning vomiting. Only hours later, she was dead. The *Chronicle of Higher Education* of July 9, 1999 reported that the freshman University of Georgia student died, like the others, as a victim of bacterial meningitis.[14]

Hypothetical examples can often be more powerful than factual examples, because hypothetical examples ask audience members to imagine something—thus causing them to become active participants in the thought. Carrie A. Lydon of Ball State University used a hypothetical example in her speech on the relationship between universities and sweatshop labor:

> Imagine one day walking into class only to find children chained to desks, sewing t-shirts, jackets, and other products representing your school. This means one of two things: either Kathy Lee Gifford is the new chancellor of your university, or your university is utilizing sweatshop labor in order to turn a profit. In fact, the majority of companies that produce collegiate apparel violate standard working wages and conditions in at least one of their facilities.[15]

STATISTICS   **Statistics** are numbers that are arranged or organized to show that a fact or principle is true for a large percentage of cases. Statistics are actually collections of examples, which is why they are often more effective as proof than are isolated examples. Patricia Cook, a student at Southwestern University in Oklahoma, used statistics to prove that criminals bought weapons at gun shows:

> A 1999 report by the U.S. Department of Justice and the Bureau of Alcohol, Tobacco, and Firearms estimated that felons illegally bought weapons at gun shows in 46 percent of the 314 cases studied. Forty-six percent of illegally bought weapons in their survey came from gun shows.[16]

Because statistics can be powerful proof, you have certain rules to follow when using them. You should make sure that they make sense and that they come from a credible source. You should also cite the source of the statistic when you use it. A final rule is based on effectiveness rather than ethics. You should reduce the statistic to a concrete image if possible. For example, $1 billion in $100 bills would be about the same height as a sixty-story building. Using concrete images such as

"Tonight, we're going to let the statistics speak for themselves."

this will make your statistics more than "just numbers" when you use them. For example, one observer expressed the idea of Bill Gates's wealth this way:

> Examine Bill Gates' wealth compared to yours: Consider the average American of reasonable but modest wealth. Perhaps he has a net worth of $100,000. Mr. Gates' worth is 400,000 times larger. Which means that if something costs $100,000 to him, to Bill it's as though it costs 25 cents. So for example, you might think a new Lamborghini Diablo would cost $250,000, but in Bill Gates dollars that's 63 cents.[17]

ANALOGIES/COMPARISON-CONTRAST   We use **analogies,** or comparisons, all the time, often in the form of figures of speech, such as similes and metaphors. A simile is a direct comparison that usually uses *like* or *as,* whereas a metaphor is an implied comparison that does not use *like* or *as.* So if you said that the rush of refugees from a war-torn country was "like a tidal wave," you would be using a simile. If you used the expression "a tidal wave of refugees," you would be using a metaphor.

Analogies are extended metaphors. Here is the way Amanda Taylor, a student at the University of Florida, used an analogy between drunk driving and drowsy driving:

> For years now, programs to stop people who have been drinking from getting behind the wheel have been a top priority with government agencies and concerned communities. But the *London Times* of January 15, 2000 explains that sleepy drivers can be just as deadly as drunk drivers. The *Toronto Star* of July 17, 1998 reports a survey by the American Automobile Association, or Triple-A, and the results are astounding. Highway patrol officers in the United States were polled and each reported "stopping a motorist who appeared drunk only to find out that the driver was fatigued." But unlike drinking and driving, the *St. Louis Post-Dispatch* of March 29, 2000 explains that sleeping and driving does not have the same social stigma attached to it. According to the "2000 Sleep in America Poll," performed by the National Sleep Foundation, more than half of over 1000 adults responding to a telephone interview reported driving while feeling drowsy in the past year—and a majority of those polled were outraged when feeling drowsy was compared to consuming alcohol.[18]

Analogies can be used to compare or contrast an unknown concept with a known one. For example, if you had difficulty explaining to a public speaking class composed mostly of music majors why they should practice their speeches out loud, you might use this analogy:

> *We all realize that great masters often can compose music in their heads; Beethoven, for example, composed his greatest masterpieces after he had gone deaf and couldn't even hear the instruments play out his ideas. However, beginners have to sit down at a piano or some other instrument and play their pieces as they create them. It is much the same way for beginning public speakers. When composing their speeches, they need to use their instruments—their voices—to hear how their ideas sound.*

For an audience of music majors, this analogy might clarify the concept of practicing a speech. For a class of computer science majors who may not know Beethoven from the Beastie Boys, this analogy might confuse rather than clarify. It is important to remember to make your analogies, and all your supporting material, appropriate to your audience.

ANECDOTES   An **anecdote** is a brief story with a point, often (but not always) based on personal experience. (The word *anecdote* comes from the Greek, meaning "unpublished item.") Ronald Reagan was famous for his use of anecdotes. In his farewell address, when he wanted to make the point that America stood as a symbol of freedom to people in other lands, he used the following anecdote:

> It was back in the early eighties, at the height of the boat people, and a sailor was hard at work on the carrier Midway, which was patrolling the South China sea. The sailor, like most American servicemen, was young, smart and fiercely observant. The crew spied on the horizon a leaky little boat—and crammed inside were refugees from Indochina hoping to get to America. The Midway sent a small launch to bring them to the ship, and safety. As the refugees made their way through the choppy seas, one spied the sailor on deck, and stood up and called out to him. He yelled, "Hello American Sailor—Hello Freedom Man."
>
> A small moment with a big meaning, a moment the sailor, who wrote it in a letter, couldn't get out of his mind. And when I saw it, neither could I.[19]

QUOTATION/TESTIMONY   Using a familiar, artistically stated saying will enable you to take advantage of someone else's memorable wording. For example, if you were giving a speech on personal integrity, you might quote Mark Twain, who said, "Always do right. This will gratify some people, and astonish the rest." A quotation like that fits Alexander Pope's definition of "true wit": "What was often thought, but ne'er so well expressed."

You can also use quotations as **testimony,** to prove a point by using the support of someone who is more authoritative or experienced on the subject than you are. When Rajiv Khanna, a student at Newman University in Kansas, wanted to prove that the distortion of history was a serious problem, he used testimony this way:

> Eugene Genovese, Professor Emeritus of History at Emory University, states in the July 11 issue of the *Chronicle of Higher Education,* "The distortion of history remains a serious problem to the academic community and the country at large." He continues, "As individuals who are history-making animals, we remain rooted in the past, and we are shaped by our society's version of its history."[20]

Sometimes testimony can be paraphrased. For example, when one business executive was talking on the subject of diversity, he used a conversation he had with Jesse Jackson, Sr., an African-American leader, as testimony:

> At one point in our conversation, Jesse talked about the stages of advancement toward a society where diversity is fully valued. He said the first stage was emancipation—the end of slavery. The second stage was the right to vote and the third stage was the political power to actively participate in government—to be part of city hall, the Governor's office and Capitol Hill. Jesse was clearly focused, though, on the fourth stage—which he described as the ability to participate fully in the prosperity that this nation enjoys. In other words, economic power.[21]

Styles of Support: Narration and Citation

Most of the forms of support discussed in the preceding section could be presented in either of two ways: through narration or through citation. **Narration** involves telling a story with your information. You put it in the form of a small drama, with a beginning, middle, and end. For example, Jennifer Deem of Indiana University narrated an example in her speech on dangerous highway rest areas:

> This past summer Allison Garrett took her young sons, Kevin and Kyle, on a family vacation. Driving down a long stretch of Interstate 65, Ms. Garrett pulled into a rest

area just outside Atlanta. She allowed the boys to use the restroom by themselves. According to the March 1997 *Atlantic,* only Kyle returned. Kevin is still missing, presumably abducted, possibly dead.[22]

Citation, unlike narration, is a simple statement of the facts. Citation is shorter and more precise than narration, in the sense that the source is carefully stated. Citation will always include such phrases as "According to the July 25, 2001, edition of *Time* magazine," or "As Mr. Smith made clear in an interview last April 24." Jennifer Deem cited a statistic and a definition later in her speech on rest areas:

> An Associated Press Newswire from January 24, 1997 reports that state officials list 77% of all rest areas as "highly dangerous." Highly dangerous is defined as an area in which violent crimes such as murder, rape, and attacks are more likely to occur.

Some forms of support, such as anecdotes, are inherently more likely to be expressed as narration. Statistics, on the other hand, are nearly always cited rather than narrated. However, when you are using examples, quotation/testimony, definitions, and analogies, you often have a choice.

ETHICAL CHALLENGE

The Ethics of Support

Have you ever "stretched" supporting material to help it conform to a point you were trying to make? (An example might be citing an "expert" for an idea of your own when discussing a social issue with a friend.) How far can you stretch the facts without stepping onto thin ethical ice?

USING VISUAL AIDS

Visual aids are graphic devices used in a speech to illustrate or support ideas. They can show how things look (photos of your trek to Nepal or the effects of malnutrition). They can show how things work (a demonstration of a new ski binding, a diagram of how seawater is made drinkable). Visual aids can also show how things relate to one another (a graph showing the relationships among gender, education, and income). Finally, visual aids can be highly effective as evidence. A photograph of toxic waste in your community, a chart clearly delineating a rise in crime, or a sample of an incorrectly wired electric heater that caused a fire can all be striking evidence for a particular point.

Types of Visual Aids

There is a wide variety of types of visual aids. The most common types include the following.

OBJECTS AND MODELS   Sometimes the most effective visual aid is the actual thing you are talking about. This is true when the thing you are talking about is portable enough to carry and simple enough to use during a demonstration before an audience: a piece of sports equipment such as a lacrosse racket or a small piece of weight-training equipment. **Models** are scaled representations of the object you are discussing and are used when that object is too large (the new

CULTURAL IDIOM

thin ice: a dangerous area

campus arts complex) or too small (a DNA molecule) or simply don't exist any more (a *Tyrannosaurus rex*).

DIAGRAMS   A **diagram** is any kind of line drawing that shows the most important properties of an object. Diagrams do not try to show everything but just those parts of a thing that the audience most needs to be aware of and understand. Blueprints and architectural plans are common types of diagram, as are maps and organizational charts. A diagram is most appropriate when you need to simplify a complex object or event and make it more understandable to the audience. The diagram in Figure 11–3 shows the security devices in the U.S. $20 bill.

WORD AND NUMBER CHARTS   **Word and number charts** are visual depictions of key facts or statistics. Shown visually, these facts and numbers will be understood and retained better than if you just talked about them. Many speakers arrange the main points of their speech, often in outline form, as a word chart. Other speakers list their main statistics. Figure 11–4 shows a word chart listing

Figure 11–3   Diagram: $20 Bill

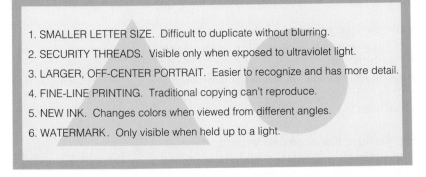

1. SMALLER LETTER SIZE. Difficult to duplicate without blurring.

2. SECURITY THREADS. Visible only when exposed to ultraviolet light.

3. LARGER, OFF-CENTER PORTRAIT. Easier to recognize and has more detail.

4. FINE-LINE PRINTING. Traditional copying can't reproduce.

5. NEW INK. Changes colors when viewed from different angles.

6. WATERMARK. Only visible when held up to a light.

Figure 11–4   Word Chart: Security Devices in $20 Bill

the security features of the U.S. $20 bill. This word chart could be used in conjunction with the diagram in Figure 11–3.

PIE CHARTS   **Pie charts** are shaped as circles with wedges cut into them. They are used to show divisions of any whole: where your tax dollars go, the percentage of the population involved in various occupations, and so on. Pie charts are often made up of percentages that add up to 100 percent. Usually, the wedges of the pie are organized from largest to smallest. The pie chart in Figure 11–5 represents the favorite colors of Americans.[23] It reflects the findings of one study that 44 percent of Americans like blue best, and so on proportionately.

BAR AND COLUMN CHARTS   **Bar charts,** such as the one shown in Figure 11–6, compare two or more values by stretching them out in the form of horizontal rectangles. **Column charts,** such as the one shown in Figure 11–7, perform the same function as bar charts but use vertical rectangles.

LINE CHARTS   A **line chart** maps out the direction of a moving point; it is ideally suited for showing changes over time. The time element is usually placed on the horizontal axis so that the line visually represents the trend over time. The average amount that U.S. citizens paid for healthcare over a 35-year period, for example, could be represented in the line chart in Figure 11–8.[2]

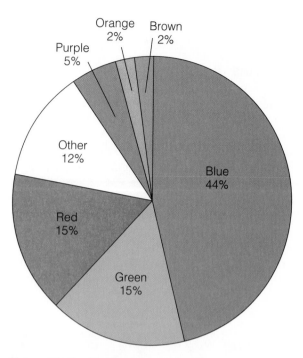

Figure 11–5   Pie Chart: America's Favorite Colors

Media for the Presentation of Visual Aids

Obviously, many types and variations of visual aids can be used in any speech. And a variety of materials can be used to present these aids.

CHALKBOARDS, WHITEBOARDS, AND POLYMER MARKING SURFACES
Chalkboards or whiteboards can be found in most classrooms. Polymer marking surfaces and their special marking pens can be bought in most bookstores and art supply shops and applied to the wall of a room that doesn't have a chalkboard or whiteboard.

The major advantage of these write-as-you-go media is their spontaneity. With them you can create your visual aid as you speak, including items generated from audience responses. Along with the odor of whiteboard markers and the squeaking of chalk, a major disadvantage of these media is the difficulty of preparing visual aids on them in advance, especially if several speeches are scheduled in the same room at the same hour.

FLIP PADS AND POSTER BOARD   Flip pads are like oversized writing tablets attached to a portable easel. As the name suggests, you reveal visuals on a flip pad one at a time by turning pages. Flip pads enable you to combine the spontaneity of the chalkboard (you can write on them as you go) with a portability that en-

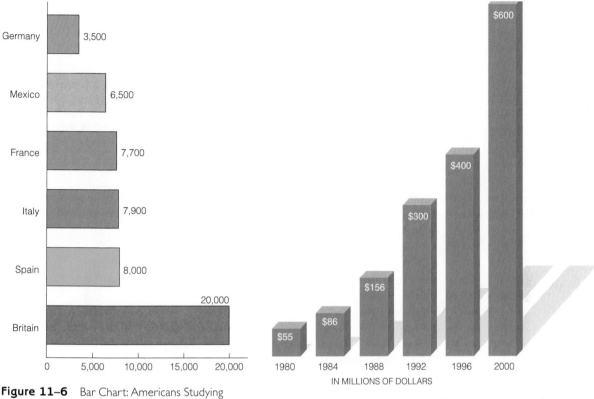

Figure 11–6   Bar Chart: Americans Studying Overseas

Figure 11–7   Column Chart: U.S. Olympic Committee Budgets

ables you to prepare them in advance. If you plan to use your visuals more than once you can prepare them in advance on rigid poster board and display them on the same type of easel.

Despite their advantages, flip pads and poster boards are bulky, and preparing professional-looking exhibits on them requires a fair amount of artistic ability.

HANDOUTS   The major advantage of handouts is that audience members can take away the information they contain after your speech. For this reason, handouts are excellent memory and reference aids. The major disadvantage is that they are distracting when handed out during a speech: First, there is the distraction of passing them out, and second, there is the distraction of having them in front of the audience members while you have gone on to something else. It's best, therefore, to pass them out at the end of the speech.

PROJECTORS   When your audience is too large to view handheld images, projectors are an ideal tool. Projectors come in several

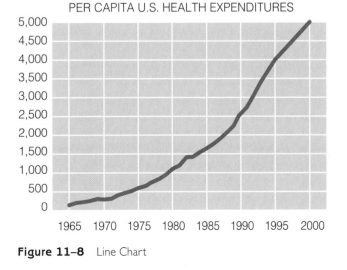

Figure 11–8   Line Chart

UNDERSTANDING COMMUNICATION TECHNOLOGY

Computer Presentation Software

Today's powerful computer programs make the production of visual aids quick and easy, once you take the time to learn a particular program. Take, for example, Corel's WordPerfect®.

To produce a professional quality chart, you click on "Graphics" on the menu bar. That makes the graphics menu appear, and you click on "Chart."

That brings up a sample chart that you can adapt to your own purposes by pointing, clicking, and typing in the data that you want your chart to demonstrate.

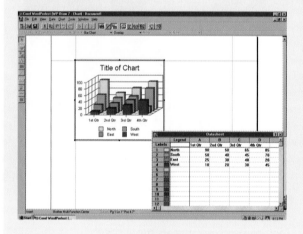

You can then click on the button on the tool bar that shows the types of chart. This allows you to con-

vert your chart to any of the types we've mentioned so far, along with some exotic versions such as the "radar chart" and the "scatter chart."

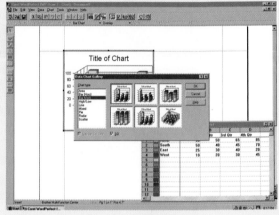

Several specialized programs exist just to produce visual aids. The most popular of these programs is Microsoft's PowerPoint®. In its simplest form, PowerPoint lets you build an effective slide show out of your basic outline. You can choose color-coordinated backgrounds and consistent formatting that match the tone and purpose of your presentation. PowerPoint contains a clip art library that allows you to choose images to accompany your words, and it al-

varieties, each of which works well for a specific purpose. *Overhead projectors* use transparencies—large, clear sheets of acetate—to cast an image on a screen. Most copy shops can transform ordinary pages into transparencies for a modest fee. If you have enough time to take a photograph of your visual aid with slide film, you can use a *slide projector* for an especially effective presentation. Slides can be projected large enough to be seen easily, and their brilliance and clarity can be superior to those of any printed image. *Computer projectors* allow you to use a screen image directly from a computer screen, making them the most direct way to use computer software presentations.

OTHER ELECTRONIC MEDIA   A wide range of other electronic media is available as presentation aids. Audio aids such as tape recordings and CDs can supply information that could not be presented any other way (comparing musical styles, for example, or demonstrating the differences in the sounds of gas and diesel engines), but in most cases you should use them sparingly. Remember that your presentation already relies heavily on your audience's sense of hearing; it's better to use a visual aid, if possible, than to overwork the audio.

lows you to import images from outside sources. To use PowerPoint, you can enter the program by clicking on the button for "Blank Presentation" or you can activate PowerPoint's "Wizard" function. Either way, the program will walk you through the stages of creating a slide show. It will, for example, show you a gallery of layout styles, and ask you which type you would like.

From this point on it is basically point, click, and follow directions. PowerPoint allows you to choose from several combinations of charts, text, and clip art. These visuals, like any type of computer-generated visual, can then be run directly from a computer projector, printed onto overhead transparencies, converted to

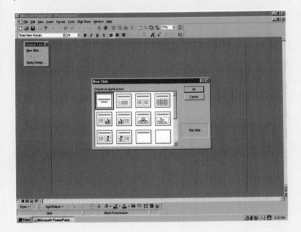

35mm slides at any photo shop or simply printed out in handout form. (See pages 370–372 for a discussion of the pros and cons of various presentation media.) Advanced uses of the program produce multimedia presentations with animated slide, sound, and video elements.

If you would like to learn more about using PowerPoint, there are several Web-based tutorial programs, which you can find easily by keying "PowerPoint" into your favorite search engine. As we go to press, the one we like best is:

http://www.utexas.edu/cc/training/handouts/
powerpoint.html

Of course, there are audiovisual aids, including films, videotapes, and sound-on-slide. These should also be used sparingly, however, because they allow audience members to receive information passively, thus relieving them of the responsibility of becoming active participants in the presentation. The general rule when using these media is: *Don't let them get in the way of the direct, person-to-person contact that is the primary advantage of public speaking.*

Rules for Using Visual Aids

It's easy to see that each type of visual aid and each medium for its presentation have their own advantages and disadvantages. No matter which type you use, however, there are a few rules to follow.

SIMPLICITY   Keep your visual aids simple. Your goal is to clarify, not confuse. Use only key words or phrases, not sentences. The "rule of seven" states that each exhibit you use should contain no more than seven lines of text, each with no more than seven words. Keep all printing horizontal. Omit all nonessential details.

SIZE   Visual aids should be large enough for your entire audience to see them at one time but portable enough for you to get them out of the way when they no longer pertain to the point you are making.

ATTRACTIVENESS   Visual aids should be visually interesting and as neat as possible. If you don't have the necessary skills—either artistic or computer—try to get help from a friend or at the computer or audiovisual center on your campus.

APPROPRIATENESS   Visuals must be appropriate to all the components of the speaking situation—you, your audience, and your topic—and they must emphasize the point you are trying to make. Don't make the mistake of using a visual aid that looks good but has only a weak link to the point you want to make—such as showing a map of a city transit system while talking about the condition of the individual cars.

RELIABILITY   You must be in control of your visual aid at all times. Test all electronic media (projectors, computers, and so on) in advance, preferably in the room where you will speak. Just to be safe, have nonelectronic backups ready in case of disaster. Be conservative when you choose demonstrations: Wild animals, chemical reactions, and gimmicks meant to shock a crowd can often backfire.

When it comes time for you to use the visual aid, remember one more point: Talk to your audience, not to your visual aid. Some speakers become so wrapped up in their props that they turn their backs on their audience and sacrifice all their eye contact.

CULTURAL IDIOM

gimmicks: clever means of drawing attention

wrapped up in: giving all one's attention to something

SKILL BUILDER

Inventing Visual Aids

Take any sample speech. Analyze it for where visual aids might be effective. Describe the visual aids that you think will work best. Compare the visuals you devise with those of your classmates.

SAMPLE SPEECH

The sample speech for this chapter was presented by Jennifer Sweeney, a student at Glendale Community College in Arizona. She was coached by Kirt Shineman and won first place at the 2000 Interstate Oratorical Association Annual Contest, held at Tallahassee Community College in Florida.

This speech uses an impressive array of supporting material: statistics, testimony, examples, and anecdotes. Jennifer used a modified problem-solution organizational plan in this speech.

The outline for this speech might look like this (the numbers in parentheses represent the corresponding paragraphs in the speech):

Introduction
  I. Attention-Getter (1)
      Definition: Racial profiling is the police practice of singling out minorities.
 II. Importance of topic (2)
      Quotation: Bill Clinton
III. Statement of thesis (3)
 IV. Preview of main points (3)

Body

I. The problem (4–8)
   A. Racial profiling exists as a national problem. (4–6)
      Testimony: Governor Whitman
      Example: Dr. Elmo Randolph
   B. Racial profiling is accepted as just the way things are. (7)

Transition: Now that we have examined the two main problems of racial profiling, we can move on to explore the causes of each of those problems. (8)

II. The causes (9–10)
   A. Racial profiling is caused in part by overextending the boundaries of ordinary profiling. (9)
      1. Profiling is an effective tool for law enforcement.
      2. Racial profiling is when race is the only factor.
   B. Racial profiling is also caused by the attitude that minorities are unequal. (10)

Transition: Now that we have examined the problem and its causes, we can move on to explore solutions on both the governmental and personal levels. (11)

III. The solution (12–16)
   A. On the governmental level (12), we must support appropriate legislation and enforce it.
      1. Data collection is a start.
      2. Accountability is the next step.
         a. Officers must be held responsible when they commit acts of racial profiling.
         b. Commanders must require officers to treat residents with respect.
            Example: Tallahassee Police Department (13)
   B. On the personal level, we must change the biased attitude that lies at the heart of racial profiling. (14–15)
      1. We should change our own attitudes. (16)
      2. We should influence others. (16)

Conclusion

I. Final remarks (16)
II. Review of main points (17)
III. Restatement of thesis (17)

RACIAL PROFILING
Jennifer Sweeney

1 Accusations of racial prejudice by police officers sparked riots in the 1960s, grand juries in the '70s and disorder in the '80s. Now, in the 21st Century, the prejudice has moved from accusation to blatant reality. A reality that unfortunately has always existed, but can no longer be ignored. In the past, terms for stereotyping of this nature included "prejudiced" or "racist," but now there is a new term. Minorities refer to it as "DWB," driving while black. Politicians call it racial profiling. According to the *Los Angeles Times,* March 10, 2000, racial profiling is the police practice of singling out minorities for questioning at airports, on highways, and on the street.

2 This problem is not isolated. It is a coast-to-coast epidemic, and anyone with any color is a potential victim. Former President Bill Clinton referred to racial profiling as "a morally indefensible, deeply corrosive practice that has affected members of Congress, students, doctors, even off-duty police officers."

Jennifer begins with a striking statement of fact.

She includes a quick definition.

Statement of importance of problem.

Quotation.

3 This speech is not about fixing the system at fault, it's about an attitudinal change that is necessary on a national scale. This issue should touch all of us, even those in the majority, because if it doesn't, that only reinforces the magnitude of the problem. In order to end these crimes against color, we must first paint an accurate picture of the problem, then explore the causes and finally establish solutions that will erase the practice of racial profiling.

Thesis statement.

Statement of importance: personal dimension.

Preview of main points.

4 Perhaps the most distressing fact about racial profiling is that we aren't shocked by it. Typical reactions include denying its existence or accepting it as a mere fact of life. Neither reaction is appropriate.

Begins first main point.

5 First, it does exist. According to the *Denver Post* of February 27, 2000, New Jersey Governor Christie Todd Whitman admitted after an internal investigation that State Troopers had engaged in racial profiling when deciding which cars to stop on the highway. New Jersey resident Dr. Elmo Randolph has been pulled over on his way to work fifty times, yet he has never been issued a ticket. The police approach his gold BMW and request his license and registration. The officers involved are always white and Dr. Randolph is always black. According to *Newsweek,* May 7, 1999, one group of officers parked along the road and shined their headlights into passing cars, looking for minorities to pull over. Then they radioed ahead to fellow officers that "a carload of coal," or "a group of porch monkeys" was headed their way.

First subpoint.

Citation of newspaper article.

Example.

Example.

6 However, racial profiling is not limited to local agencies and highways. The September 13, 1999, edition of the *New Republic* explains that after getting off a plane in Kansas City, a young man was taken into custody and questioned by DEA officers. When asked to explain their reasons for stopping him one officer declared, "the young man was black." According to the *Chicago Sun-Times,* March 12, 2000, "Blacks, Hispanics, or any people of color are five times more likely to be stopped than Whites." New Jersey and Kansas are not alone. Law enforcement agencies in Michigan, California, and even right here in Florida have openly admitted that some of their officers have specifically targeted minorities. Studies have been performed along highways across America. The NAACP has launched a campaign against it. Even President Clinton has been in support of abolishing racial profiling. *That's a lot of attention to something that doesn't exist.*

Example.

Statistic.

Examples.

A good summary statement for this subpoint (italics added).

7 The second aspect of the problem is the acceptance that racial profiling is just the way things are. How often have we been pulled over for apparently no reason? We weren't speeding or weaving. Maybe our car looked too expensive, maybe we didn't fit the norm for the neighborhood? Chances are, never, particularly if we are white. Docile acceptance comes from members of the majority. The *Chicago Sun-Times,* March 8, 2000, states that some reactions to racial profiling include, "if they're innocent, why should they worry about being stopped by police." This is a predictable response from people who never have to put up with it. Racial profiling cannot be accepted as a fact of life. It is a dangerous erosion of a basic American right, the right to be considered innocent until proven guilty. If this right was denied across the board to members of the majority, we would immediately be able to understand.

Second subpoint.

Analog.

Citation from newspaper article.

8 Now that we have examined the two main problems of racial profiling, we can move on to explore the causes of each of those problems.

Transition to next main point.

9 First, racial profiling is caused in part by overextending the boundaries of ordinary profiling. The *Los Angeles Times,* July 23, 1999, explains that profiling is an effective tool for law enforcement. Nuns are less likely to smuggle drugs than most people. The *New York Times Magazine,* June 18, 1999, clarifies:

First subpoint.

Citation from newspaper.

"Profiling means an officer using cumulative knowledge to identify certain indicators of criminal activity. Race may be one of those factors, but it cannot stand alone. Racial profiling is when race is the only factor. There is no other probable cause." It is the blurring of the line between the two types of profiling that is problematic.

10 Second, the cause of the apathetic attitude towards racial profiling is painfully easy to explain. Minorities are viewed as unequal. This is not a new attitude. It has been around for centuries. The relevance is that there is still a problem. The *Los Angeles Times,* March 5, 2000, explains that racial profiling is racism rationalized by a basic fear of "the other." There is a problem to be worked through and neither denial nor acceptance is part of the solution.

11 Now that we have examined the problem and its cause, we can move on to explore solutions on both the governmental and personal level, to erase the practice of racial profiling.

12 Current news like an article in the *National Journal,* March 4, 2000, suggests that the problem is under control. The article explains that the House Judiciary Committee recently approved legislation which directs state and local law enforcement agencies to collect race data from people they stop or arrest. However, don't be fooled. The *San Francisco Chronicle,* March 15, 2000, states that while this is clearly a move in the right direction, data collection is not enough to stop unfair police practices. Instead, the key on a governmental level is accountability. Officers in any law enforcement capacity, regardless of previous service history or time with the organization, must be held responsible when they commit acts of racial profiling. Within law enforcement agencies, there has to be the attitude that misconduct will not be tolerated. *U.S. News and World Report* explains in the March 29, 1999 edition that agencies in the South Bronx, Los Angeles, and Boston have seen a drop in racial profiling complaints since 1993. The drop is attributed to commanders of those divisions requiring their officers to treat residents with respect.

13 Even the Tallahassee Police Department is taking action to combat racial profiling. In a telephone interview yesterday afternoon, I discovered that Sergeant Cheryl Stewart organizes a group of officers that travel around to different schools in the area, explaining to students what racial profiling is and what it can do. The goal is both to educate potential offenders and change their mind-set early, as well as to explain to minorities that not all officers need to be feared. In both cases, these visits help bridge the gap between citizens and police. If you live here in the Tallahassee area or you just have more questions about the program, you can contact Sergeant Stewart at 904.891.4266. This type of leadership needs to spread throughout the country. Since law enforcement agencies are such a part of the problem, it seems fitting they would take an active role in the solution.

14 However, we cannot lay all the blame on the police. As members of society, we all shoulder some of the responsibility. The bottom line is that no amount of data collection, or legislation, or writing to our congressperson, or being cooperative if we're pulled over, will actually change the biased attitude that lies at the heart of racial profiling. Those solutions only work on paper. In the real world, ending racial profiling is dependent on individuals taking a stand against it.

15 In the beginning, I mentioned that this speech was about an attitudinal change on a national scale. Am I really up here tackling the enormous issue

of racism? Yes. It is the most offensive issue plaguing our society today and we have the power to end it.

16 The solution is simple. We have to change the way we think. We have a responsibility to act once we've been informed of the problem. Previous ambivalence can be forgiven in the wake of current action. We have the power to change our attitudes and influence the attitudes of the next generation, whether we are parents or teachers, friends or teammates. I know, in persuasion we look for an action step. In this case, the action is changing our minds. There is no kit I can pass out at the end of the speech. I don't have a magic 1-800 number that will end racism. However, this solution is one that can be implemented immediately, because it's so simple. We don't need preparation time or tools; this solution is only dependent on individuals taking action. See, modern racism is not about acting racist, it's about thinking that way, and changing the way we think is something we can all do on our own. Social change happens, not when millions of people gather together; it's before that, when all of those people decide individually that a change needs to occur.

Final main point.

Desired audience behavior.

Final remarks, memorable wording.

17 Today we have explored the crime of racial profiling and its causes. The main solution is simple: it relies on us. This community, this forensics community, has the potential to create change. Look at the number of people who can become aware today and start making a difference tomorrow. Make racial profiling unacceptable. In this case, the solution really is in our hands. Lead by example. Let changing our minds lead to changing our actions. Teach your children, hold a rally, tell a friend, vote. How we choose to create change is up to the individual. That a change is necessary, well, that should be understood.

Review of main points.

Repetition of thesis.

SUMMARY

This chapter dealt with speech organization and supporting material. Speech organization is a process that begins with the formulation of a thesis statement to express the central idea of a speech. The thesis is established in the introduction, developed in the body, and reviewed in the conclusion of a structured speech. The introduction will also gain the audience's attention, set the mood and tone of the speech, and demonstrate the importance of the topic to the audience. The conclusion will review your thesis and/or main points and supply the audience with a memory aid.

Organizing the body of the speech will begin with a list of points you might want to make. These points are then organized according to the principles of outlining. They are divided, coordinated, and placed in a logical order. Transitions from point to point help make this order apparent to your audience. Organization follows a pattern, such as time, space, topic, problem-solution, cause-effect, motivated sequence, or climax arrangements.

Supporting materials are the facts and information you use to back up what you say. Supporting material has four purposes: to clarify, to make interesting, to make memorable, and to prove. Any piece of support could perform any or all of these purposes, and any of the purposes could be fulfilled by any of the types of support.

Types of support include *definitions* of key terms; *examples,* which can be real or hypothetical; *statistics,* which show that a fact or principle is true for a large percentage of cases; *analogies,* which compare or contrast an unknown or unfamiliar concept with a known or familiar one; *anecdotes,* which add a lively, personal touch; *quotations and testimony,* which are used for memorable wording as well as ideas from a well-known or authoritative source;

and *visual aids,* which help clarify complicated points and keep an audience informed about where you are in the general scheme of things. Any piece of support might combine two or more of these types. Support may be narrated (told in story form) or cited (stated briefly).

RESOURCES

Print

The Oxford Dictionary of Quotations, 5th ed. New York: Oxford University Press, 2000.

A valuable reference for quotations and testimony. Contains more than twenty thousand quotations from over three thousand authors, from Woody Allen to Emile Zola. The quotations are arranged alphabetically by author with comprehensive topical and keyword indexes.

Gamble, Teri, and Michael Gamble. *Public Speaking in the Age of Diversity,* 2nd ed. Boston: Allyn and Bacon, 1998.

See especially Part III, "Putting It Together: The Plan Takes Shape."

Leeds, Dorothy. *Powerspeak: The Complete Guide to Persuasive Public Speaking and Presenting.* New York: Prentice Hall, 1988.

Chapter 5 presents an interesting perspective in which clear speech organization is presented as a necessary trait of leadership. Leeds also offers the "Powerspeak Outline," which includes her suggestions about how much time to spend on each section of a speech.

McCarthy, Edward. *Speechwriting: A Professional Step-by-Step Guide for Executives.* Dayton, OH: The Executive Speaker Co., 1989.

See especially "Step 3: Do Research for Supporting Material" for another perspective on finding and evaluating evidence.

Morreale, Sherwyn P., and Coutland L. Bovee. *Excellence in Public Speaking.* Fort Worth, TX: Harcourt Brace, 1998.

See especially Chapter 7, "Supporting Your Speech," Chapter 9, "Organizing Your Speech," and Chapter 11, "Outlining Your Speech."

Robbins, Jo. *High-Impact Presentations: A Multimedia Approach.* New York, NY: John Wiley & Sons, 1997.

Highlights the use of the computer as a presentation tool as well as a means of creating visual aids using Harvard Graphics, Microsoft PowerPoint, Lotus Freelance, and other popular software packages. Also gives confidence-building tips on speaking and encouraging audience participation.

Films

It is interesting to look at classic feature films as examples of organizational structure and how the human mind reacts to that structure. Consider the following:

Catch-22 (1970). Rated R.

This adaptation of Joseph Heller's classic novel flashes forward and backward, to scenes real and imaginary. The movie shows how confusing this type of narrative organization can be: Director Mike Nichols's intention was to make the structure of the film reflect the surrealist insanity of the Air Corps during World War II. Critics loved the complexity, but audiences were just confused. Recommended for those who have read the book, however.

Forrest Gump (1994). Rated PG-13.

Tom Hanks is a lovable slow-witted boy who floats through life, managing to encounter first-hand every major social and political phenomenon of his time, from the rise of Elvis to the fall of Nixon. This film uses a chronological order, with each segment of the film based on a major event in recent U.S. history.

Pulp Fiction (1995). Rated R

Starring John Travolta and Samuel L. Jackson as philosophical hitmen, this ultraviolent tale was a big hit at least partially because of its organization, which seems random at first, but then takes on a logic of its own that is intriguing.

CONTENTS

KEY TERMS

addition
articulation
debilitative stage fright
deletion
extemporaneous speech
facilitative stage fright
fallacy of approval
fallacy of catastrophic failure
fallacy of overgeneralization
fallacy of perfection
impromptu speech
irrational thinking
manuscript speeches
memorized speeches
pitch
rate
slurring
substitution
visualization

AFTER STUDYING
THE MATERIAL
IN THIS CHAPTER . . .

YOU SHOULD UNDERSTAND:

1. The difference between facilitative and debilitative stage fright.

2. The sources of debilitative stage fright.

3. The differences among the various types of delivery.

4. The visual and auditory aspects of delivery.

YOU SHOULD BE ABLE TO:

1. Overcome debilitative stage fright.

2. Choose the most effective type of delivery for a particular speech.

3. Follow the guidelines for effective extemporaneous, impromptu, manuscript, and memorized speeches.

4. Offer constructive criticism of others' presentations.

PRESENTING
YOUR MESSAGE

We know what you're thinking: You've developed a purpose, you've chosen and researched a topic that suits your own interests, your audience, and the occasion. You feel confident about your ability to organize your ideas in a logical, effective way, and you've built up a healthy reserve of supporting material. But all that doesn't solve your primary problem: When you think about the actual act of standing before a group, your self-confidence begins to erode. How will you act? Should you be formal or casual? Should you memorize your remarks, read from a script, or use notes? How loudly should you speak, and how quickly? Should you use visual aids? All of these questions make the prospect of talking to an audience seem threatening.

   Because the act of speaking before a group of listeners may be a relatively new one for you, we'll look at the process now. The purpose of this chapter is to make you feel more confident about yourself as a speaker and to give you a clearer idea of how to behave before an audience. We will begin with a look at the topic of stage fright.

> *All great speakers were bad speakers at first.*
>
> Ralph Waldo Emerson

> *Speeches are like babies—easy to conceive, hard to deliver.*
>
> Pat O'Malley

DEALING WITH STAGE FRIGHT

The terror that strikes the hearts of so many beginning speakers is called *communication apprehension* or *speech anxiety* by communication scholars, but it is more commonly known to those who experience it as *stage fright*.

Facilitative and Debilitative Stage Fright

Although stage fright is a very real problem for many speakers, it is a problem that can be overcome. In fact, research suggests that the problem can be overcome in basic communication courses such as the one you are taking now.[1] Interestingly enough, the first step in feeling less apprehensive about speaking is to realize that a certain amount of nervousness is not only natural but also facilitative. That is, **facilitative stage fright** is a factor that can help improve your performance. Just as totally relaxed athletes or musicians aren't likely to perform at the top of their potential, speakers think more rapidly and express themselves more energetically when their level of tension is moderate.

   It is only when the level of anxiety is intense that it becomes **debilitative**, inhibiting effective self-expression. Intense fear causes trouble in two ways. First, the strong emotion keeps you from thinking clearly.[2] This has been shown to be a problem even in the preparation process: Students who are highly anxious about giving a speech will find the preliminary steps, including research and organization, to be more difficult.[3] Second, intense fear leads to an urge to do something, anything, to make the problem go away. This urge to escape often causes a speaker to speed up delivery, which results in a rapid, almost machine-gun style. As you can imagine, this boost in speaking rate leads to even more mistakes, which only add to the speaker's anxiety. Thus, a relatively small amount of nervousness can begin to feed on itself until it grows into a serious problem.

> *According to most surveys, the number 1 fear for most people is public speaking. Number 2 is death. Now this means, to the average person, if you have to go to a funeral you're better off in the casket than giving the eulogy.*
>
> Jerry Seinfeld

Sources of Debilitative Stage Fright

Before we describe how to manage debilitative stage fright, it might be helpful to look at why people are afflicted with the problem.[4]

PREVIOUS NEGATIVE EXPERIENCE   People often feel apprehensive about speech giving because of unpleasant past experiences. Most of us are uncomfortable doing *anything* in public, especially if it is a form of performance in which our talents and abilities are being evaluated. An unpleasant experience in one type of performance can cause you to expect that a future similar situation will also be unpleasant.[5] These expectations can be realized through the self-fulfilling prophecies discussed in Chapter 2. A traumatic failure at an earlier speech and low self-esteem from critical parents during childhood are common examples of experiences that can cause later stage fright.

You might object to the idea that past experiences cause stage fright. After all, not everyone who has bungled a speech or had critical parents is debilitated in the future. To understand why some people are affected more strongly than others by past experiences, we need to consider another cause of speech anxiety.

IRRATIONAL THINKING   Cognitive psychologists argue that it is not events that cause people to feel nervous but rather the beliefs they have about those events. Certain irrational beliefs leave people feeling unnecessarily apprehensive. Psychologist Albert Ellis lists several such beliefs, or examples of **irrational thinking**, which we will call "fallacies" because of their illogical nature.[6]

1. **Catastrophic failure.** People who succumb to the **fallacy of catastrophic failure** operate on the assumption that if something bad can happen, it probably will. Their thoughts before a speech resemble these:

> "As soon as I stand up to speak, I'll forget everything I wanted to say."
> "Everyone will think my ideas are stupid."
> "Somebody will probably laugh at me."

Although it is naive to imagine that all your speeches will be totally successful, it is equally naive to assume they will all fail miserably. One way to escape the fallacy of catastrophic failure is to take a more realistic look at the situation. Would your audience members really hoot you off the stage? Will they really think your ideas are stupid? Even if you did forget your remarks for a moment, would the results be a genuine disaster? It helps to remember that nervousness is more apparent to the speaker than to the audience.[7] Beginning public speakers, when congratulated for their poise during a speech, are apt to make such remarks as "Are you kidding? I was *dying* up there."

2. **Perfection.** Speakers who succumb to the **fallacy of perfection** expect themselves to behave flawlessly. Whereas such a standard of perfection might serve as a target and a source of inspiration (like the desire to make a hole in one while golfing), it is totally unrealistic to expect that you will write and deliver a perfect speech—especially as a beginner. It helps to remember that audiences don't expect you to be perfect.

3. **Approval.** The mistaken belief called the **fallacy of approval** is based on the idea that it is vital—not just desirable—to gain the approval of everyone in the audience. It is rare that even the best speakers please everyone, especially on topics that are at all controversial. To paraphrase Abraham Lincoln, you can't please all the people all the time—and it is irrational to expect you will.

I have a slight inferiority complex still. I go into a room and have to talk myself into going up to people. If I'm the epitome of a woman who is always confident and in control, don't ever believe it of anyone.

Barbara Walters

| CULTURAL IDIOM |

bungled: done something imperfectly

hoot: express rude and disparaging remarks

a hole-in-one: hitting the golf ball in the hole with one swing of the club, a perfect shot

I don't know the key to success, but the key to failure is trying to please everyone.

Bill Cosby

4. Overgeneralization. The **fallacy of overgeneralization** might also be labeled the fallacy of exaggeration, because it occurs when a person blows one poor experience out of proportion. Consider these examples:

"I'm so stupid! I mispronounced that word."
"I completely blew it—I forgot one of my supporting points."
"My hands were shaking. The audience must have thought I was a complete idiot."

A second type of exaggeration occurs when a speaker treats occasional lapses as if they were the rule rather than the exception. This sort of mistake usually involves extreme labels, such as "always" or "never."

"I *always* forget what I want to say."
"I can *never* come up with a good topic."
"I can't do *anything* right."

Overcoming Debilitative Stage Fright

There are four fairly simple ways to overcome debilitative stage fright:

1. Be rational. Listen to your thought processes, your internal voice, and try to figure out if the basis for your stage fright is rational. Then dispute any irrational beliefs. Use the list of fallacies given earlier to discover which of your internal statements are based on mistaken thinking.
2. Be receiver oriented. Concentrate on your audience members rather than on yourself. Worry about whether they are interested, about whether they understand, and about whether or not you are maintaining human contact with them.
3. Be positive. Build and maintain a positive attitude toward your audience, your speech, and yourself as a speaker. Some communication consultants suggest that public speakers should concentrate on three statements immediately before speaking. The three statements are:

    I'm glad I'm here.
    I know my topic.
    I care about the audience.

    Keeping these statements in mind is supposed to help you maintain a positive attitude. Another technique for building a positive attitude is known as **visualization.**[8] This technique has been used successfully with athletes. It requires you to use your imagination to visualize the successful completion of your speech. Visualization can help make the self-fulfilling prophecy discussed in Chapter 2 work in your favor.
4. Be prepared. Researchers have determined that the highest level of speech anxiety occurs just before speaking, the second-highest level at the time the assignment is announced and explained, and the lowest level during the time you spend preparing your speech.[9] You should take advantage of this relatively low-stress time to think through the problems that would tend to make you nervous during the actual speech. In fact, preparation is so important that the rest of this chapter will be devoted to it. One of the first things to consider when preparing to present a speech is the style of delivery you choose.

CULTURAL IDIOM

blows...out of proportion: exaggerates

Courage is resistance to fear, mastery of fear—not absence of fear.

Mark Twain

I arrived a little early for the meeting and was greeted by an attractive lady who asked, "What are you doing here?"
She looked a little familiar. I thought perhaps I had met her at a convention two years earlier. "I'm here to give a speech to the Rotary Club," I replied.
"Do you do this often?" she asked.
"Quite often," I said.
"Are you nervous before you talk?" she demanded.
"I don't think so," I replied.
She retorted, "Then what are you doing in the ladies' washroom?"

Ross Smyth

CULTURAL IDIOM

"for the record":
word-for-word
documentation

spur of the moment:
occurring without
warning

**off the top of one's
head:** with little time to
plan or think about

INVITATION
TO INSIGHT

Stage Fright: A Personal Analysis

To analyze your own reaction to stage fright, think back to your last
public speech, and rate yourself on how rational, receiver oriented,
positive, and prepared you were. How did these attributes affect
your anxiety level?

TYPES OF DELIVERY

There are four basic types of delivery—extemporaneous, impromptu, manuscript, and memorized. Each type creates a different impression and is appropriate under different conditions. Any speech may incorporate more than one of
these types of delivery. For purposes of discussion, however, it is best to consider them separately.

Extemporaneous

An **extemporaneous speech** is planned in advance but presented in a direct, spontaneous manner. Extemporaneous speeches are conversational in tone, which means
that they give the audience members the impression that you are talking to them,
directly and honestly. Extemporaneous speeches *are* carefully prepared, but they are
prepared in such a way that they create what actors call "the illusion of the first
time"—in other words, the audience hears your remarks as though they were brand
new. This style of speaking is generally accepted to be the most effective, especially
for a college class. In a classroom, you generally speak before a small audience (five
to fifty people) made up of people with diverse backgrounds. Spontaneity is essential with this type of audience, but so is careful message planning. Extemporaneous
speaking allows you to benefit from both careful planning and spontaneous delivery.
A speech presented extemporaneously will be researched, organized, and practiced
in advance, but the exact wording of the entire speech will not be memorized or
otherwise predetermined. Because you speak from only brief, unobtrusive notes,
you are able to move and maintain eye contact with your audience.

Extemporaneous speaking is also the most common type of delivery in the
"outside" world. Most of those involved in communication-oriented careers find
that the majority of their public speaking is done before audiences who, in
terms of size and diversity of interests represented, resemble those found in a
college classroom. Professional public speakers recognize the advisability of
both careful planning and spontaneity with such an audience.

The extemporaneous speech does have some disadvantages. It is difficult to
keep exact time limits, to be exact in wording, or to be grammatically perfect
with an extemporaneous speech. Therefore, if you are speaking as part of a radio
or television broadcast or if your speech will be reproduced "for the record," you
might want to use a manuscript or memorize your speech. Also, an extemporaneous speech requires time to prepare. On spur-of-the-moment speaking occasions, you will need to deliver an impromptu speech.

Impromptu

An **impromptu speech** is given off the top of one's head, without preparation.
An impromptu speech is often given in an emergency, such as when a scheduled

speaker becomes ill and you are suddenly called upon. Lack of preparation is the main problem with impromptu speeches, but there are some advantages to this style of speaking. It is by definition spontaneous. It is the delivery style necessary for informal talks, group discussions, and comments on others' speeches. It also can be an effective training aid; it can teach you to think on your feet and organize your thoughts quickly. To take full advantage of an impromptu speaking opportunity, remember the following points:

1. Take advantage of the time between being called on to speak and actually speaking. Even if you have only a minute, you can still scribble a few brief notes to protect against mental blocks.

2. Don't be afraid to be original; you don't have to remember what every other expert says about your topic—what do *you* say about it? Review your personal experiences and use them. If nothing else, consider questions such as *Who? What? When? Where? How?* And formulate a plan to answer one or more of them.

3. Observe what is going on around you, and respond to it. If there were other speakers, you might agree or disagree with what they said. You can comment on the audience and the occasion, too, as well as on your topic.

4. Keep a positive attitude. Remember that audience expectations are low. Audience members know you have not prepared in advance, and they don't expect you to be Patrick Henry.

5. Finally, and perhaps most important, keep your comments brief. Especially do not prolong your conclusion. If you have said everything you want to say or everything you can remember, wrap it up as neatly as possible and sit down. If you forgot something, it probably wasn't important anyway. If it was, the audience will ask you about it afterward.

Manuscript

Manuscript speeches are read word for word from a prepared text. They are necessary when you are speaking for the record, as when speaking at legal proceedings or when presenting scientific findings. The greatest disadvantage of a manuscript speech is the lack of spontaneity that may result. Manuscript readers have even been known, to their extreme embarrassment, to

It usually takes me more than three weeks to prepare a good impromptu speech.

Mark Twain

CULTURAL IDIOM

Patrick Henry: a gifted orator

wrap it up: finish

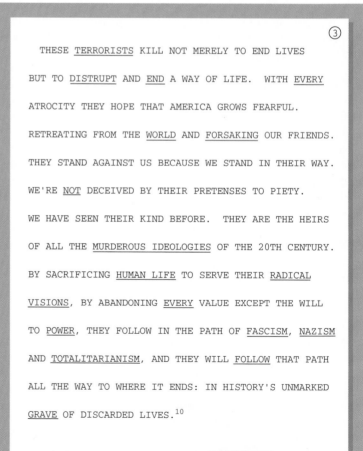

③

THESE <u>TERRORISTS</u> KILL NOT MERELY TO END LIVES

BUT TO <u>DISTRUPT</u> AND <u>END</u> A WAY OF LIFE. WITH <u>EVERY</u>

ATROCITY THEY HOPE THAT AMERICA GROWS FEARFUL.

RETREATING FROM THE <u>WORLD</u> AND <u>FORSAKING</u> OUR FRIENDS.

THEY STAND AGAINST US BECAUSE WE STAND IN THEIR WAY.

WE'RE <u>NOT</u> DECEIVED BY THEIR PRETENSES TO PIETY.

WE HAVE SEEN THEIR KIND BEFORE. THEY ARE THE HEIRS

OF ALL THE <u>MURDEROUS IDEOLOGIES</u> OF THE 20TH CENTURY.

BY SACRIFICING <u>HUMAN LIFE</u> TO SERVE THEIR <u>RADICAL</u>

<u>VISIONS</u>, BY ABANDONING <u>EVERY</u> VALUE EXCEPT THE WILL

TO <u>POWER</u>, THEY FOLLOW IN THE PATH OF <u>FASCISM</u>, <u>NAZISM</u>

AND <u>TOTALITARIANISM</u>, AND THEY WILL <u>FOLLOW</u> THAT PATH

ALL THE WAY TO WHERE IT ENDS: IN HISTORY'S UNMARKED

<u>GRAVE</u> OF DISCARDED LIVES.[10]

Figure 12–1 Part of a Sample Page from a Manuscript Speech (Reduced)

read their directions by mistake: "and so, let me say in conclusion, look at the audience with great sincerity . . . Oops!"

Manuscript speeches are difficult and cumbersome, but they are sometimes necessary. If you find occasion to use one, here are some guidelines:

1. When writing the speech, recognize the differences between written messages and speeches. Speeches are usually less formal, more repetitive, and more personal than written messages.[11] They use more adverbs, adjectives, and circumlocutions such as "well," and "as you can see." As one expert points out, "Speeches use more words per square thought than well-written essays or reports"[12]
2. Use short paragraphs. They are easier to return to after establishing eye contact with your audience.
3. Print out the manuscript triple spaced, in capital letters, with a dark ribbon. Underline the words you want to emphasize.
4. Use stiff paper so that it won't fold up or fly away during the speech. Print on only one side, and number the pages by hand with large, circled numbers.
5. Rehearse until you can "read" whole lines without looking at the manuscript.
6. Take your time, vary your speed, and try to concentrate on ideas rather than words.

Good results
Are seldom led to
When people feel
They're being read to.

Charles Osgood

Memorized

Memorized speeches—those learned by heart—are the most difficult and often the least effective. They often seem excessively formal. However, like manuscript speeches, they may be necessary on special occasions. They are used in oratory contests, and they are used as training devices for memory. They are also used in some political situations. For example, in televised debates between presidential candidates, the candidates are usually allowed to make prepared speeches, but they are not allowed to use notes. Thus, they have to memorize precise, for-the-record wording, and make it sound natural.

The legendary frontiersman Davy Crockett once gave an object lesson on the benefits and hazards of memorized speeches. When he was running for Congress, Crockett always extemporized, adapting to his audience, but his opponent always gave the same memorized speech. So for one debate Crocket memorized his opponent's entire speech and delivered it first, leaving the fellow with nothing to say.[13]

There is only one guideline for a memorized speech: Practice. The speech won't be effective until you have practiced it until you can present it with that "illusion of the first time" that we mentioned previously.

INVITATION
TO INSIGHT

Types of Delivery

Identify at least one speech you have seen presented using the four types of delivery: extemporaneous, impromptu, manuscript, or memorized. For this speech, decide whether the type of delivery was effective for the topic, speaker, and situation. Explain why or why not. If the speech was not effective, suggest a more appropriate type.

PRACTICING THE SPEECH

In most cases, a delivery that sounds smooth and natural is the result of extensive practice. After you choose the appropriate delivery type for the speech you are giving, the best way to make sure that you are on your way to an effective delivery is to practice your speech repeatedly and systematically. One way to do that is to go through some or all of the following steps:

1. First, present the speech to yourself. "Talk through" the entire speech, including your examples and forms of support (don't just say, "This is where I present my statistics" or "This is where I explain about photosynthesis").
2. Tape-record the speech, and listen to it. Because we hear our own voices partially through our cranial bone structure, we are sometimes surprised at what we sound like to others. Videotaping has been proven to be an especially effective tool for rehearsals, giving you an idea of what you look like, as well as sound like.[14]
3. Present the speech in front of a small group of friends or relatives.
4. Present the speech to at least one listener in the room in which you will present the final speech (or, if that room is not available, a similar room).

GUIDELINES FOR DELIVERY

The best way to consider guidelines for delivery is through an examination of the nonverbal aspects of presenting a speech. As you read in Chapter 5, nonverbal behavior can change, or even contradict, the meaning of the words a speaker utters. If audience members want to interpret how you *feel* about something, they are likely to trust your nonverbal communication more than the words you speak. If you tell them, "It's great to be here today," but you stand before them slouched over with your hands in your pockets and an expression on your face like you're about to be shot, they are likely to discount what you say. This might cause your audience members to react negatively to your speech, and their negative reaction might make you even more nervous. This cycle of speaker and audience reinforcing each other's feelings can work *for* you, though, if you approach a subject with genuine enthusiasm. Enthusiasm is shown through both the visual and auditory aspects of your delivery.

Visual Aspects of Delivery

Visual aspects of delivery include appearance, movement, posture, facial expression, and eye contact.

APPEARANCE   Appearance is not a presentation variable as much as a preparation variable. Some communication consultants suggest new clothes, new glasses, and new hairstyles for their clients. In case you consider any of these, be forewarned that you should be attractive to your audience but not flashy. Research suggests that audiences like speakers who are similar to them, but they prefer the similarity to be shown conservatively.[15] Fashionable dressers might not like someone dressed in dowdy, old-fashioned clothes, but they would also have problems with someone dressed in fashions that are too avant-garde. Speakers, it seems, are perceived to be more credible when they look businesslike.

Failure to prepare is preparing to fail.

Basketball coach John Wooden

CULTURAL IDIOM

flashy: showy, gaudy

MOVEMENT   Movement is an important visual aspect of delivery. The way you walk to the front of your audience, for example, will express your confidence and enthusiasm. And after you begin speaking, nervous energy can cause your body to shake and twitch, and that can be distressing both to you and to your audience. One way to control *involuntary* movement is to move *voluntarily* when you feel the need to move. Don't feel that you have to stand in one spot or that all your gestures need to be carefully planned. Simply get involved in your message, and let your involvement create the motivation for your movement. That way, when you move, you will emphasize what you are saying in the same way you would emphasize it if you were talking to a group of friends. If you move voluntarily, you will use up the same energy that would otherwise cause you to move involuntarily.

Movement can also help you maintain contact with *all* members of your audience. Those closest to you will feel the greatest contact. This creates what is known as the "action zone" in the typical classroom, within the area of the front and center of the room. Movement enables you to extend this action zone, to include in it people who would otherwise remain uninvolved. Without overdoing it, you should feel free to move toward, away, or from side to side in front of your audience.

Remember: Move with the understanding that it will add to the meaning of the words you use. It is difficult to bang your fist on a podium or take a step without conveying emphasis. Make the emphasis natural by allowing your message to create your motivation to move.

POSTURE   Generally speaking, good posture means standing with your spine relatively straight, your shoulders relatively squared off, and your feet angled out to keep your body from falling over sideways. In other words, rather than standing at military attention, you should be comfortably erect.

Of course, you shouldn't get *too* comfortable. There are speakers who are effective even though they sprawl on tabletops and slouch against blackboards, but their effectiveness is usually in spite of their posture rather than because of it. Sometimes speakers are so awesome in stature or reputation that they need an informal posture to encourage their audience to relax. In that case, sloppy posture is more or less justified. But because awesomeness is not usually a problem for beginning speakers, good posture should be the rule.

Good posture can help you control nervousness by allowing your breathing apparatus to work properly; when your brain receives enough oxygen, it's easier for you to think clearly. Good posture will also help you get a positive audience reaction because standing up straight makes you more visible. It also increases your audience contact because the audience members will feel that you are interested enough in them to stand formally, yet relaxed enough to be at ease with them.

FACIAL EXPRESSION   The expression on your face can be more meaningful to an audience than the words you say. Try it yourself with a mirror. Say, "You're a terrific audience," for example, with a smirk, with a warm smile, with a deadpan expression, and then with a scowl. It just doesn't mean the same thing. Remember also that it is just about impossible to control facial expressions from the outside. Like your movement, your facial expressions will reflect your involvement with your message. Don't try to fake it. Just get involved in your message, and your face will take care of itself.

Words represent your intellect. The sound, gesture and movement represent your feeling.

Patricia Fripp

CULTURAL IDIOM

squared off: evenly aligned

deadpan: an expressionless face

EYE CONTACT   Eye contact is perhaps the most important nonverbal facet of delivery. Eye contact not only increases your direct contact with your audience, but also can be used to help you control your nervousness. Direct eye contact is a form of reality testing. The most frightening aspect of speaking is the unknown. How will the audience react? What will it think? Direct eye contact allows you to test your perception of your audience as you speak. Usually, especially in a college class, you will find that your audience is more "with" you than you think. By deliberately establishing contact with any apparently bored audience members, you might find that they *are* interested; they just aren't showing that interest because they don't think anyone is looking.

To maintain eye contact, you could try to meet the eyes of each member of your audience squarely at least once during any given presentation. After you have made definite eye contact, move on to another audience member. You can learn to do this quickly, so you can visually latch on to every member of a good-sized class in a relatively short time.

The characteristics of appearance, movement, posture, facial expression, and eye contact are visual, nonverbal facets of delivery. Now consider the *auditory* nonverbal messages that you might send during a presentation.

> *Once you make good eye contact with a person in the audience, they will feel you are talking to them for the rest of the speech.*
>
> Ken Blanchard

CULTURAL IDIOM

squarely: directly

Auditory Aspects of Delivery

As you read in Chapter 5, your paralanguage—the way you use your voice—says a good deal about you, especially about your sincerity and enthusiasm. In addition, using your voice well can help you control your nervousness. It's another cycle: Controlling your vocal characteristics will decrease your nervousness, which will enable you to control your voice even more. But this cycle can also work in the opposite direction. If your voice is out of control, your nerves will probably be in the same state. Controlling your voice is mostly a matter of recognizing and using appropriate *volume, rate, pitch,* and *articulation.*

VOLUME   The loudness of your voice is determined by the amount of air you push past the vocal folds in your throat. The key to controlling volume, then, is controlling the amount of air you use. The key to determining the *right* volume is audience contact. Your delivery should be loud enough so that your audience members can hear everything you say but not so loud that they feel you are talking to someone in the next room. Too much volume is seldom the problem for beginning speakers. Usually they either are not loud enough or have a tendency to fade off at the end of a thought. Sometimes, when they lose faith in an idea in midsentence, they compromise by mumbling the end of the sentence so that it isn't quite coherent.

One contemporary speaker who has been criticized for inappropriate volume is Senator Ted Kennedy. One re-

"And now a correction: Portions of last night's story on diving mules which were read with an air of ironic detachment should actually have been presented with earnest concern."

searcher points out that "Kennedy tended to shout when an audience was small or uninterested or when he sensed he was losing them. Thus, his volume was often inappropriate to the time and place."[16]

RATE   Your speed in speaking is called your **rate.** There is a range of personal differences in speaking rate. Daniel Webster, for example, is said to have spoken at around 90 words per minute, whereas one actor who is known for his fast-talking commercials speaks at about 250. Normal speaking speed, however, is between 120 and 150 words per minute. If you talk much more slowly than that, you may tend to lull your audience to sleep. Faster speaking rates are stereotypically associated with speaker competence,[17] but if you speak too rapidly, you will tend to be unintelligible. Once again, your involvement in your message is the key to achieving an effective rate.

PITCH   The highness or lowness of your voice—**pitch**—is controlled by the frequency at which your vocal folds vibrate as you push air through them. Because taut vocal folds vibrate at a greater frequency, pitch is influenced by muscular tension. This explains why nervous speakers have a tendency occasionally to "squeak," whereas relaxed speakers seem to be more in control. Pitch will tend to follow rate and volume. As you speed up or become louder, your pitch will have a tendency to rise. If your range in pitch is too narrow, your voice will have a singsong quality. If it is too wide, you may sound overly dramatic. You should control your pitch so that your listeners believe you are talking *with* them rather than performing in front of them. Once again, your involvement in your message should take care of this naturally for you.

When considering volume, rate, and pitch, keep *emphasis* in mind. You have to use a variety of vocal characteristics to maintain audience interest, but remember that a change in volume, pitch, or rate will result in emphasis. If you pause or speed up, your rate will suggest emphasis. Words you whisper or scream will be emphasized by their volume. One student provided an example of how volume can be used to emphasize an idea. He was speaking on the way possessions like cars communicate things about their owners. "For example," he said, with normal volume, "a Cadillac says, 'I've got money!' but a Rolls-Royce says, *'I'VE GOT MONEY!'*" He blared out those last three words with such force the podium shook.

ARTICULATION   The final auditory nonverbal behavior, articulation, is perhaps the most important. For our purposes here, **articulation** means pronouncing all the parts of all the necessary words and nothing else.

It is not our purpose to condemn regional or ethnic dialects within this discussion. It is true that a considerable amount of research suggests that regional dialects can cause negative impressions,[18] but our purpose here is to suggest *careful,* not standardized, articulation. Incorrect articulation is usually nothing more than careless articulation. It is caused by (1) leaving off parts of words (deletion), (2) replacing parts of words (substitution), (3) adding parts to words (addition), or (4) overlapping two or more words (slurring).

Many a pair of curious ears had been lured by that well-timed pause.

Li Ang

A vessel is known by the sound, whether it be cracked or not.

Demosthenes

UNDERSTANDING DIVERSITY

A Compendium of American Dialects

The following is a short glossary of examples of regionalized pronunciation (with apologies to all residents who find them exaggerated).

Appalachian Hill Country

Bile To bring water to 212 degrees
Cowcumber Vittle you make pickles out of
Hern Not his'n
Tard Exhausted

Bawlamerese (Spoken around Baltimore)

Arn What you do with an arnin board
Blow Opposite of above
Pleece Two or more po-leece
Torst Tourist

Boston

Back The outer covering of a tree trunk
Had licka Hard liquor
Moa Opposite of less
Pahk To leave your car somewhere, as in "Pahk the cah in Haavaad Yahd"

Noo Yorkese

Huh Opposite of him

Mel pew? May I help you?
Reg you la caw fee Coffee with milk and sugar
Pock A place with trees and muggers

Philadelphia

Fluffya The name of the city
Mayan Opposite of yours
Pork A wooded recreational area
Tail What you use to dry off with after a shower

Southern

Abode A plank of wood
Bidness Such as, "Mistah Cottah's paynut bidness"
Shurf Local law enforcement officer
Watt The color of the Watt House in Wushinton

Texas

Ah stay Iced tea
Bayer A beverage made from hops
Pars A town in Texas. Also, the capital of France
Awful Tar Famous tall structure in Pars, France

Other interesting regionalisms can be found at the Slanguistics Web site, www.slanguage.com.

Deletion   The most common mistake in articulation is **deletion**, or leaving off part of a word. As you are thinking the complete word, it is often difficult to recognize that you are saying only part of it. The most common deletions occur at the ends of words, especially *-ing* words. *Going, doing,* and *stopping* become *goin', doin',* and *stoppin'*. Parts of words can be left off in the middle, too, as in *terr'iss* for *terrorist, Innernet* for *Internet,* and *asst* for *asked.*

Substitution   **Substitution** takes place when you replace part of a word with an incorrect sound. The ending *-th* is often replaced at the end of a word with a single *t,* as when *with* becomes *wit.* The *th-* sound is also a problem at the beginning of words, as *this, that,* and *those* have a tendency to become *dis, dat,* and *dose.* (This tendency is especially prevalent in many parts of the northeastern United States.)

Addition   The articulation problem of **addition** is caused by adding extra parts to words, such as *incentative* instead of *incentive, athalete* instead of *athlete,* and *orientated* instead of *oriented.* Sometimes this type of addition is caused by incorrect word choice, as when *irregardless,* which is not a word, is used for *regardless.*

Another type of addition is the use of "tag questions," such as *you know?* or *you see?* or *right?* at the end of sentences. To have every other sentence punctuated with one of these barely audible superfluous phrases can be maddening.

Probably the worst type of addition, or at least the most common, is the use of *uh* and *anda* between words. *Anda* is often stuck between two words when *and* isn't even needed. If you find yourself doing that, you might want just to pause or swallow instead.[19]

Slurring   **Slurring** is caused by trying to say two or more words at once—or at least overlapping the end of one word with the beginning of the next. Word pairs ending with *of* are the worst offenders in this category. *Sort of* becomes *sorta*, *kind of* becomes *kinda*, and *because of* becomes *becausa*. Word combinations ending with *to* are often slurred, as when *want to* becomes *wanna*. Sometimes even more than two words are blended together, as when *that is the way* becomes *thatsaway*. Careful articulation means using your lips, teeth, tongue, and jaw to bite off your words, cleanly and separately, one at a time.

> *Mend your speech a little, lest you may mar your fortune.*
>
> Shakespeare
> *King Lear*

SKILL
BUILDER

Articulation Exercises

Tongue twisters can be used to practice careful articulation out loud. Try these two classics:

- She sells seashells down by the seashore.
- Peter Piper picked a peck of pickled peppers.

Now make up some of your own and try them out. Make twisters for both consonant sounds ("Frank's friendly face flushed furiously") and vowel sounds ("Oliver oiled the old annoying oddity").

UNDERSTANDING COMMUNICATION TECHNOLOGY

Historic Speeches on the Web

"Streaming technology" enables you to listen to audio programming and watch video programming over the World Wide Web. This means that you can hear how speeches from history—at least twentieth-century history, since recording technology has been available—actually sounded. You can hear how speakers handled auditory nonverbal characteristics such as volume, rate, pitch, and articulation. When video clips are available, you can even observe how they handled the visual aspects of delivery discussed in this chapter.

Yahoo! has a site devoted to the world's great speeches at http://www.broadcast.com/publicaffairs/speeches/. Most are contained on a CD-ROM offered for sale, but twenty classics can be accessed here without charge. You can hear speeches such as Franklin D. Roosevelt's "War Message" (1941), Dr. Martin Luther King's "I Have a Dream" (1963), John F. Kennedy's inaugural speech (1962), Nixon's "Checkers Speech" (1952), Nixon's resignation speech (1974), and General Douglas MacArthur's "Old Soldiers Never Die" speech (1951).

The History Channel has a similar site at www.historychannel.com/speeches/index.html, featuring a vast collection drawn from the most famous broadcasts and recordings of the twentieth century, organized into three categories: Politics and Government (you can hear Hitler, following his occupation of Czechoslovakia in 1938, proclaim that "We now have arms to such an extent as the world has never seen before"); Science and Technology (with Amelia Earhart celebrating her solo trans-Atlantic flight in 1932); and Arts, Entertainment, and Culture (with Lou Gehrig saying farewell to baseball in 1939 and Gloria Steinem addressing the National Women's Political Caucus in 1971).

You'll need a player loaded onto your computer, such as RealPlayer from RealNetworks or Windows Media Player from Microsoft, which is part of Microsoft's Internet Explorer Web browser. If you don't have a player, the software can be downloaded from the Web free of charge (www.realnetwork.com or www.microsoft.com).

OFFERING CONSTRUCTIVE CRITICISM

In your public speaking class, you will do well to remember that everyone else is experiencing the same type of anxiety that you are. Your criticism of a classmate's speech is extremely important, but it can also be a sensitive area for that classmate. You should strive to make this criticism constructive, which means that it will be designed to help the speaker improve. To be constructive, the criticism has to be both positive and substantive.

"It was a little preachy."

When we say that criticism has to be positive, we mean that you should present it with the positive attitude mentioned earlier. The easiest way to do that is to point out what is *right* about the speech as well as what is *wrong* about it. In fact, negative criticism unaccompanied by positive criticism is often useless because the speaker might become defensive and block out your criticism completely. It is a good idea, therefore, to offer your positive criticism first and than tactfully offer your suggestions for improvement, using the various suggestions for creating a positive communication climate that were discussed in Chapter 7 (pages 227–231). For example, rather than saying, "Your ideas about the psychological aspects of diabetes were completely unclear and unsupported," you might say, "I found your explanation of the physical aspects of diabetes to be clearly stated and well backed up with details and examples. However, your explanation of the psychological aspects of the disease left me a little confused. It might be my own fault, but it just did not seem to be as well supported as the rest of your speech."

When we say that criticism has to be substantive, we mean two things: First, you need to criticize *what* was said as well as *how* it was said. Do not concentrate on delivery traits to the point where you lose track of the speaker's ideas. Second, you need to be specific. Rather than saying, "I liked this" or "I didn't like that," you should provide a detailed explanation of your reasons for liking or disliking parts of the speech.

SUMMARY

One of the most serious delivery problems is debilitative (as opposed to facilitative) stage fright. Sources of debilitative stage fright include irrational thinking, which might include a belief in one or more of the following fallacies: the fallacy of catastrophic failure (something is going to ruin this presentation), the fallacy of perfection (a good speaker never does anything wrong), the fallacy of absolute approval (*everyone* has to like you), and the fallacy of overgeneralization (you *always* mess up speeches). There are several methods of overcoming speech anxiety. The first is to refute the irrational fallacies just listed. The others include being receiver oriented, positive, and prepared.

There are four types of delivery: extemporaneous, impromptu, manuscript, and memorized. In each type, the speaker must be concerned with both visual and auditory aspects of the presentation. Visual aspects include appearance, movement, posture, facial expression, and eye contact. Auditory aspects include volume, rate, pitch, and articulation. The four most common articulation problems are deletion, substitution, addition, and slurring of word sounds.

Effective delivery is aided through the constructive criticism of speeches presented in class. Your criticism should include positive as well as nega-tive aspects of the speaker's behavior. It should also be substantive, which means that it should address what was said as well as how it was said, and it should be specific in terms of what you liked and didn't like about the speech.

RESOURCES

Print

Ayers, Joe, and Tim Hopf. *Coping with Speech Anxiety.* Norwood, NJ: Ablex, 1993.

A catalog and explanation of various "intervention procedures" that help people cope with communication anxiety, including rational-emotive therapy, visualization, systematic desensitization, rhetoritherapy, and anxiety reduction workshops.

Bremmer, Jan, and Herman Roodenburg, eds. *A Cultural History of Gesture.* Ithaca, NY: Cornell University Press, 1992.

Examines, in a historical/cultural analysis, why certain body movements mean what they do today. For example, Homer promoted the John Wayne walk in ancient Greece by constantly referring to heroes with "long strides."

Glenn, Ethel C., Phillip Glenn, and Sandra Forman. *Your Voice and Articulation,* 4th ed. Needham Heights, MA: Allyn and Bacon, 1998.

A comprehensive discussion of the anatomy and physiology of the human voice. Extensive vocal exercises are included for pitch, volume, rate, and "vocal color." Chapter 2 is devoted to dialects.

Lee, Charlotte, and Timothy Gura. *Oral Interpretation,* 10th ed. Boston: Houghton Mifflin, 2000.

A collection of prose, drama, and poetry pieces especially designed for oral presentation. See especially Chapter 3, "Voice Development for Oral Interpretation," and Chapter 4, "Use of the Body in Oral Interpretation."

Wells, Lynn K. *The Articulate Voice,* 3rd ed. Needham Heights, MA: Allyn and Bacon, 1999.

Provides basic information on voice production and techniques for improvement.

Films

The most interesting resource films for this chapter are those that portray characters whose personal delivery styles contribute to their success or failure. For example:

Saving Private Ryan (1998). Rated R.

Tom Hanks's nerves are shot, but he still manages a speech that rallies his men for a mission no one believes in at first.

As Good as It Gets (1997). Rated PG-13.

Jack Nicholson portrays a character with a slew of mental tics who manages to control his communication anxiety enough to win Helen Hunt.

Broadcast News (1987). Rated R.

This inside look at television news production shows how stage fright, in this case in front of the camera, changes the career of the character played by Albert Brooks. A smooth delivery makes the career for another character, this one played by William Hurt.

Contact (1998). Rated PG.

Based on a novel by the late Carl Sagan, starring Jodie Foster, directed by Robert Zemeckis. The title has multiple meanings—the main one being a scientist's contact with extraterrestrial life, but other meanings concern her contact with people, contact with God, and, of interest to us here, contact with a number of audiences, including a pitch session before a foundation board, testimony before Congress, and a lecture to a group of school children.

Four Weddings and a Funeral (1995). Rated PG.

Hugh Grant's breakthrough film is a catalog of social events that also happen to be speaking events. Delivery styles alter the effectiveness of the speeches considerably. For example, Grant "roasts" the groom at the first wedding with great success. At the second wedding one of his friends tries to imitate his style and fails miserably.

CONTENTS

KEY TERMS

audience involvement
audience participation
description
explanations
information hunger
informative purpose statement
instructions
signposts

AFTER STUDYING THE MATERIAL IN THIS CHAPTER . . .

YOU SHOULD UNDERSTAND:

1. The difference between an informative and a persuasive speech topic.

2. The importance of having a specific informative purpose.

3. The importance of creating information hunger.

4. The importance of using clear language.

5. The importance of generating audience involvement.

YOU SHOULD BE ABLE TO:

1. Formulate an effective informative purpose statement.

2. Create information hunger by stressing the relevance of your material to your listeners' needs.

3. Use the strategies outlined in this chapter to organize unfamiliar information in an understandable manner.

4. Emphasize important points in your speech.

5. Generate audience involvement.

INFORMATIVE SPEAKING

Information is all around us, and sometimes we seem to be drowning in it. Consider some of these facts:

- It is estimated that 108 million e-mail users receive more than 7 trillion e-mail messages each year, which works out to some 65,000 messages each.
- A weekday edition of *The New York Times* contains more information than the average person was likely to come across in a lifetime in seventeenth-century England.
- Americans buy more than a billion books a year. Fifty thousand new titles are published each year, and 1.5 million books are in print, from 20,000 different publishers.[1]

Informative speaking is especially important in our current "age of information," in which transmitting knowledge will account for most of the work we do and, in a large part, for the quality of our lives. Although much of the information of the future will be transmitted by machines—computers and electronic media—the spoken word will continue to be the best way to reach small audiences with messages tailored specifically for them. Whether it is teaching, coaching, or on-the-job training, informative speaking will provide the face-to-face, feedback-rich environment that helps people make sense of all the information around them.

Informative speaking seeks to increase the knowledge and understanding of an audience. This type of speaking goes on all around you: in your professors' lectures, in news reports on radio and TV, in a mechanic's explanation of how to keep your car from breaking down. You engage in this type of speaking frequently whether you realize it or not. Sometimes it is formal, as when you give a report in class. At other times, it is more casual, as when you tell a friend how to prepare your favorite dish. The main objective of this chapter is to give you the skills you need to enhance all of your informative speaking.

TYPES OF INFORMATIVE SPEAKING

There are several types of informative speaking. The primary types have to do with the content and purpose of the speech.

By Content

Informative speeches are generally categorized according to their content, including the following types:

SPEECHES ABOUT OBJECTS This type of informative speech is about anything that is tangible (that is, capable of being seen or touched). Speeches about objects might include an appreciation of the Grand Canyon (or any other natural wonder) or an informative speech about computer software (or any other product).

SPEECHES ABOUT PROCESSES A process is any series of actions that leads to a specific result. If you spoke on the process of aging, the process of learning to juggle, or the process of breaking into the accounting business, you would be giving this type of speech.

SPEECHES ABOUT EVENTS You would be giving this type of informative speech if your topic dealt with anything notable that happened, was happening, or might happen: the 1999 impeachment proceedings against President Clinton, the holiday Kwanzaa, or the prospects of your favorite team winning the championship.

SPEECHES ABOUT CONCEPTS   Concepts include intangible ideas, such as beliefs, theories, ideas, and principles. If you gave an informative speech about postmodernism, vegetarianism, or any other "ism," you would be giving this type of speech. Other topics would include everything from New Age religions to theories about extraterrestrial life to rules for making millions of dollars.

By Purpose

We also distinguish among types of informative speeches depending upon the speaker's purpose. We ask, "Does the speaker seek to describe, explain, or instruct?"

DESCRIPTIONS   A speech of **description** is the most straightforward type of informative speech. With your audience analysis in mind, you generally divide this type of speech into the components of the thing you are describing. You might introduce a new product to a group of customers, or you might describe what a career in nursing would be like. Whatever its topic, the speech of description builds a "word picture" of the essential details that make that thing what it is.

EXPLANATIONS   **Explanations** clarify ideas and concepts that are already known but not understood by an audience. For example, your audience members might already know that a U.S. national debt exists, but they might be baffled by the reasons why it has become so large. Explanations often deal with the question of *why*. Why do we have a national debt? Why do we have to wait until the age of twenty-one to drink legally? Why did tuition need to be increased this semester?

INSTRUCTIONS   **Instructions** teach something to the audience in a logical, step-by-step manner. They are the basis of training programs and orientations. They often deal with the question of *how to*. Speeches of instruction might deal with how to prepare for a test or how to prepare for a job interview. This type of speech often features a demonstration or a visual aid. Thus, if you were giving instructions on "The Perfect Golf Swing," you might demonstrate with your own club and/or use a mechanical model to show the physics involved. For instructions on "How to Perform CPR," you could use a volunteer or a dummy.

These types of informative speeches aren't mutually exclusive. There is considerable overlap, as when you give a speech about objects that has the purpose of explaining them. Still, even this imperfect categorization demonstrates how wide a range of informative topics is available. One final distinction we need to make, however, is the difference between an informative and a persuasive speech topic.

INFORMATIVE VERSUS PERSUASIVE TOPICS

There are many similarities between an informative and a persuasive speech. In an informative speech, for example, you are constantly trying to "persuade"

An individual without information cannot take responsibility.

Jan Carlzon

UNDERSTANDING DIVERSITY

How Culture Affects Information

Cultural background is always a part of informative speaking, although it's not always easy to spot. Sometimes this is because of ethnocentrism, *the belief in the inherent superiority of one's own ethnic group or culture. According to Larry Samovar and Richard Porter, authors of* Communication between Cultures, *ethnocentrism is exemplified by what is taught in schools.*

Schools in all cultures, whether they intend to or not, teach ethnocentrism. What is interesting are the manifest, invisible, and subtle ways in which it is taught. For instance, the next time you look at a world map, notice that the United States is prominently located in the center, unless, of course, you are looking at a Chinese or a Russian map. The teaching of history is common to all cultures, but which history do they teach? By teaching a culture's history to schoolchildren, a society is reinforcing all of its beliefs, values, and prejudices. Each culture attempts to glorify its historical and scientific accomplishments and to downplay the accomplishments of others.

Schools in the United States emphasize the English language and devote very little attention to teaching a second or third language. What subtle message does that give students about the position of English in the world and the importance of other languages?

Perhaps the most subtle forms of ethnocentrism appear in the selection of subjects and materials in the curriculum. In the United States, this selection has traditionally reflected the ideas generated by a male-dominated, Western point of view. Most of the works on a list of the great books of the world will almost certainly be by authors who are Western, white, and male. This leaves the impression that the rest of the world has or is doing nothing and therefore the dominant American culture is "the greatest."

From Larry Samovar and Richard Porter, *Communication between Cultures*, 2nd ed., © 1995. Reprinted with permission of Wadsworth, an imprint of the Wadsworth Group, a division of Thomson Learning. Fax 800 730-2215.

your audience to listen, understand, and remember. In a persuasive speech, you "inform" your audience about your arguments, your evidence, and so on. However, two basic characteristics differentiate an informative topic from a persuasive topic.

An Informative Topic Tends to Be Noncontroversial

In an informative speech, you generally do not present information that your audience is likely to disagree with. Again, this is a matter of degree. For example, you might want to give a purely informative talk on chiropractic medicine, simply describing what its practitioners believe and do. By contrast, a talk either boosting or criticizing chiropractic medicine would clearly be persuasive.

The noncontroversial nature of informative speaking does not mean that your speech topic should be uninteresting to your audience, but rather that your approach to it should not engender conflict. You could speak about the animal rights movement, for example, by explaining the points of view of both sides in an interesting but objective manner.

The Informative Speaker Does Not Intend to Change Audience Attitudes

The informative speaker does seek a response (such as attention and interest) from the listener and does try to make the topic important to the audience. But the speaker's primary intent is not to change attitudes or to make the audience members *feel* differently about the topic. For example, an informative speaker might explain how a microwave oven works but will not try to "sell" a specific brand of oven to the audience.

The speaker's intent is best expressed in a specific informative purpose statement, which brings us to the first of our techniques of informative speaking.

TECHNIQUES OF INFORMATIVE SPEAKING

The techniques of informative speaking are based on a number of principles of human communication in general, and public speaking specifically, that we have discussed in earlier chapters. The most important principles to apply to informative speaking include those that help an audience understand and care about your speech. Let's look at the way these principles apply to specific techniques.

"That dog is trying to tell us something."

Define a Specific Informative Purpose

As Chapter 10 explained, any speech must be based on a purpose statement that is audience oriented, precise, and attainable. When you are preparing an informative speech, it is especially important to define in advance, for yourself, a clear informative purpose. An **informative purpose statement** will generally be worded to stress audience knowledge, ability, or both:

> *After listening to my speech, my audience will be able to recall the three most important questions to ask when shopping for a VCR.*
>
> *After listening to my speech, my audience will be able to identify the four basic principles of aerodynamics.*
>
> *After listening to my speech, my audience will be able to discuss the idea of dramatic structure.*

Notice that in each of these purpose statements a specific verb such as *to recall, to identify,* or *to discuss* points out what the audience will be able to do after hearing the speech. Other key verbs for informative purpose statements include these:

Analyze	Contrast	Integrate	Operate	Review
Apply	Describe	List	Perform	Summarize
Choose	Explain	Name	Recognize	Support

A clear purpose statement will lead to a clear thesis statement. As you remember from Chapter 10, a thesis statement presents the central idea of your speech. Sometimes your thesis statement for an informative speech will just preview the central idea:

SKILL
BUILDER

Informative Purpose Statements

For practice in defining informative speech purposes, reword the following statements so that they specifically point out what the audience will be able to do after hearing the speech.

1. My talk today is about building a wood deck.
2. My purpose is to tell you about vintage car restoration.
3. I am going to talk about toilet training.
4. I'd like to talk to you today about sexist language.
5. There are six basic types of machines.
6. The two sides of the brain have different functions.
7. Do you realize that many of you are sleep deprived?

There are so many VCRs on the market that it is difficult for the uninformed consumer to make a choice.
Understanding the laws of aerodynamics could help save your life some day.
Every effective form of storytelling conforms to the rules of dramatic structure.

At other times, the thesis statement for an informative speech will delineate the main points of that speech:

When shopping for a VCR, the informed consumer seeks to balance price, dependability, and programmability.
The four basic principles of aerodynamics—lift, thrust, drag, and gravity—make it clear how an airplane flies.
Five components of dramatic structure—conflict, rising tension, climax, resolution, and denouement—are found in every effective form of storytelling.

Setting a clear informative purpose will help keep you focused as you prepare and present your speech. After you have a purpose in speaking, your next step is to give your audience a purpose in listening.

Create Information Hunger

An effective informative speech creates **information hunger:** a reason for your audience members to want to listen to and learn from your speech. The most effective way to do that is to respond in some way to their psychological needs. To do so, you can use the analysis of communication functions discussed in Chapter 1 (pages 8–10 as a guide. You read there that communication of all types helps us meet our physical needs, identity needs, social needs, and practical needs. In informative speaking, you could tap into your audience members' physical needs by relating your topic to their survival or to the improvement of their living conditions. If you gave a speech on food (eating it, cooking it, or shopping for it), you would be dealing with that basic need. If you gave a speech on water pollution, you could relate it to physical needs by listing the pollutants in one of your local lakes and explaining what each one could do to a human body. In the same way, you could appeal to identity needs by showing your audience members how to be respected—or simply by showing them that you respect them. You could relate to social needs by showing them how your topic could help them be well liked. Finally, you can relate your topic to practi-

Information's pretty thin stuff, unless mixed with experience.

Clarence Day

cal audience needs by telling your audience members how to succeed in their courses, their job search, or their quest for the perfect outfit.

We know more than we can tell.

Michael Polanyi

CRITICAL
THINKING
PROBE

Audience Needs and Information Hunger

Think about informative messages you receive, either from your professors or from other speakers. How closely do they connect with your needs? Can you provide an example of how even apparently unconnected topics can be linked to your needs by effective speakers?

Make It Easy to Listen

Remember the complex nature of listening discussed in Chapter 4, and make it easy for your audience members to hear, pay attention, understand, and remember. This means not only that you should speak loudly and clearly, but also that as you put your speech together you should take into consideration those techniques that recognize the way human beings process information. For example:

LIMIT THE AMOUNT OF INFORMATION YOU PRESENT Remember that you have become an expert on this topic and that you won't be able to transmit everything you know to your audience at one sitting. It's better to make careful choices about the three to five main ideas you want to get across and then develop those ideas fully. Too much information leads to overload, anxiety, and a lack of attention on the part of your audience.[2]

USE FAMILIAR INFORMATION TO INCREASE UNDERSTANDING OF THE UNFAMILIAR Move your audience members from information that you can assume, on the basis of your audience analysis, that they know about to your newer information. For example, if you are giving a speech about how the stock market works, you could compare the daily activity of a broker with that of a salesperson in a retail store, or you could compare the idea of capital growth (a new concept to some listeners) with interest earned in a savings account (a more familiar concept).

USE SIMPLE INFORMATION TO BUILD UP UNDERSTANDING OF COMPLEX INFORMATION Just as you move your audience members from the familiar to the unfamiliar, you can move them from the simple to the complex. An average

ETHICAL
CHALLENGE

The Ethics of Simplicity

Often, persuasive speakers use language that is purposely complicated or obscure in order to keep the audience uninformed about some idea or information. Informative rather than persuasive intent can often help clear the air. Find any sales message (a print ad or television commercial, for example) or political message (a campaign speech, perhaps) and see if you can transform it into an informative speech. What are the differences?

college audience, for example, can understand the complexities of gene splicing if you begin with the concept of inherited characteristics.

Emphasize Important Points

Along with defining a specific informative purpose and creating information hunger, you should stress the important points in your speech through repetition and the use of signposts.

REPETITION   Repetition is one of the age-old rules of learning. Human beings are simply more likely to comprehend information that is stated more than once. This is especially true in a speaking situation, because, unlike in writing, your audience members cannot go back to pick up something they have missed. If their minds have wandered the first time you say something, they just might pick it up the second time.

   Of course, simply repeating something in the same words might bore the audience members who actually are paying attention, so effective speakers learn to say the same thing in more than one way. Kathy Levine, a student at Oregon State University, used this technique in her speech on contaminated dental water:

> The problem of dirty dental water is widespread. In a nationwide *20/20* investigation, the water used in approximately 90% of dental offices is dirtier than the water found in public toilets. This means that 9 out of 10 dental offices are using dirty water on their patients.[3]

   Redundancy can be effective when you use it to emphasize important points.[4] It is ineffective only when (1) you are redundant with obvious, trivial, or boring points or (2) you run an important point into the ground. There is no sure rule for making certain you have not overemphasized a point. You just have to use your best judgment to make sure that you have stated the point enough that your audience members get it without repeating it so often that they want to give it back.

If you have an important point to make, don't try to be subtle or clever. Use a pile driver. Hit the point once. Then come back and hit it again. Then hit it a third time—a tremendous whack.

Winston Churchill

SKILL BUILDER

Effective Repetition

Create a list of three statements, or use the three that follow. Restate each of these ideas in three different ways.

1. The magazine *Modern Maturity* has a circulation of more than twenty million readers.
2. Before buying a used car, you should have it checked out by an independent mechanic.
3. One hundred thousand pounds of dandelions are imported into the United States annually for medical purposes.

SIGNPOSTS   Another way to emphasize important material is by using **signposts**: words or phrases that emphasize the importance of what you are about to say. You can state, simply enough, "What I'm about to say is important," or you can use some variation of that statement: "But listen to this . . .," or "The most important thing to remember is . . .," or "The three keys to this situation are . . .," and so on.

CULTURAL IDIOM

run a point into the ground: overelaboration of an idea to the point where the audience is tired of hearing about it

Use a Clear Organization and Structure

CULTURAL IDIOM

ironclad: meant to be
followed very specifically

Because of the way humans process information (that is, in a limited number of chunks at any one time),[5] organization is extremely important in an information speech. Rules for structure may be mere suggestions for other types of speeches, but for informative speeches they are ironclad.

Chapter 11 discusses some of these rules:

Limit your speech to three to five main points.
Divide, coordinate, and order those main points.
Use a strong introduction that previews your ideas.
Use a conclusion that reviews them and makes them memorable.
Use transitions, internal summaries, and internal previews.

The repetition that is inherent in strong organization will help your audience members understand and remember those points. This will be especially true if you use a well-organized introduction, body, and conclusion.

THE INTRODUCTION   The following principles of organization from Chapter 11 become especially important in the introduction of an informative speech:

1. Establish the importance of your topic to your audience.
2. Preview the thesis, the one central idea you want your audience to remember.
3. Preview your main points.

For example, Heather Pratt of Indiana University began her informative speech on St. John's Wort like this:

In the 1992 movie *Medicine Man,* Sean Connery searches the rainforest to find a cure for cancer. He tests a whole variety of leaves and roots until—prompted by a local medicine man—he discovers one magical herb. Much like Sean Connery, medical researchers in the last few years have waded through a jungle of supposedly all-natural remedies to focus in on one particular magical herb: St. John's Wort.

Recent discoveries have propelled St. John's Wort into the spotlight. As Jean Carper, former senior medical correspondent for CNN, reveals in the *Houston Chronicle* of August 15, 1997, "[For St. John's Wort] There is credibility at the top now, you never had that before."

The Herbal Information Center's Web site, last updated on March 28, 1998, adds that St. John's Wort already offers relief from depression, inflammation, sprains, bruises, incontinence, arthritis, and in the future may even provide a treatment for cancer.

The heroic little plant is a perennial herb that boasts brilliant yellow blossoms. The February 1998 issue of *Better Nutrition* explains that the herb grows wild in several Western states such as Colorado and California, but can be purchased as a pill or tea at virtually any health food store across the country. The little yellow flower is revolutionizing herbal medicine.

To better appreciate St. John's Wort we will first examine its history. Second, we will explore the current uses for St. John's Wort, and finally, we will determine what the future holds for this one magical herb.

THE BODY   In the body of an informative speech, the following organizational principles take on special importance:

1. Limit your division of main points to three to five subpoints.
2. Use transitions, internal summaries, and internal previews.

ɔ. Order your points in the way that they will be most easy to understand and remember.

Heather Pratt followed these principles for organizing her speech on St. John's Wort. Her first main point, "St. John's Wort has a long and ancient history," shows how carefully she structured it:

> First, where has this herb been all our lives? Well, in Ancient Greece, Aristotle prescribed it for one of his patients. In fact, the IHERB Web page last updated March 9,1998 reports that St. John's Wort proved popular with ancient physicians for treating infectious diseases such as syphilis, tuberculosis, and dysentery.
>
> In the Middle Ages, legend held that the herb possessed supernatural powers. The herb's name stems from the fact that the plant flowers on June 24th, the festival of St. John the Baptist. As Dr. Steve Bratman, in his 1997 book *Beating Depression with St. John's Wort,* explains, many believed the herb would drive evil spirits and demons away. Perhaps more realistically, according to London's *Independent* September 12, 1997, at a medieval hospital recently unearthed near Soutra, Scotland, monks prescribed St. John's Wort to treat chronic depression and insomnia.
>
> Approximately seven hundred years later we can realize the benefits of St. John's Wort are nothing new. However, discovering exactly how it affects the body? That's new! Like a good meatloaf, the secret lies in several special ingredients.

Notice that she ended this point with a transition that included an internal review and a preview of the next point.

THE CONCLUSION   Organizational principles are also important in the conclusion of an informative speech:

1. Review your main points.
2. Remind your audience members of the importance of your topic to them.
3. Provide your audience with a memory aid.

For example, here is the way Heather Pratt concluded her speech on Saint-John's-wort:

> After first examining the history of St. John's Wort, exploring its current application and determining what the future holds for St. John's Wort, it is clear that like Sean Connery in *Medicine Man,* herbal researchers have stumbled upon an incredible discovery. St. John's Wort holds within its small yellow petals the key to the future of herbal medicine, and perhaps the entire medical industry will benefit from this one magical herb.

Use Supporting Material Effectively

Another technique for effective informative speaking has to do with the supporting material discussed in Chapter 11. Three of the purposes of support (to clarify, to make interesting, and to make memorable) are essential to informative speaking. Therefore, you should be careful to support your thesis in every way possible. Notice the way in which Heather Pratt uses solid supporting material in the preceding examples.

Visual aids can grab your audience members' attention and keep them attuned to your topic throughout your speech. Heather might have used a slide showing what Saint John's wort looks like, along with charts listing its benefits and ingredients, to increase audience comprehension.

UNDERSTANDING COMMUNICATION TECHNOLOGY

Informative Resources on the Web

When researching an informative speech, you should be aware that several Web sites offer a wide variety of reference tools in one place. Sites like these provide an easy way to make sure your material is accurate.

Research-It!:

http://www.iTools.com/research-it/

Language, library, geographical, financial, and Internet tools all at one site.

The Reference Desk:

www.refdesk.com

A comprehensive "reference shelf."

Douglass Archives Reference Site:

http://douglass.speech.nwu.edu/

Reference links especially designed for students of public address. Includes links to a wide variety of other speech sites, as well as links to general reference works including encyclopedias, dictionaries, thesauri, translation tools, and citation guides.

There are also thousands of sites for specific types of information. For example, for quick statistics:

Fedstats: www.fedstats.gov
Census Bureau: www.census.gov
Bureau of Labor Statistics: stats.bls.gov/

For bills, laws, and other governmental actions, consult Thomas:

http://thomas.loc.gov

A site maintained by the Library of Congress that includes a wide range of legislative information.

Finally, a favorite site for newspaper and magazine articles:

www.gebbieinc.com

The Gebbie Press All-In-One Media Directory allows you to search hundreds of daily newspapers by state or magazines by topic. There are hundreds of links that lead you to the Web site of the paper or magazine of your choice.

Use Clear Language

Another technique for effective informative speaking is to use clear language—which means using precise, simple wording and avoiding jargon. Notice how Heather Pratt rewords the jargon of one of her pieces of support so her audience can understand it:

> In the treatment of cancer the all-important element of St. John's Wort is its carotenoids. According to the *Journal of the National Cancer Institute* of February 5, 1997 "A substantial body of evidence from subsequent laboratory and epidemiologic investigations indicates that dietary carotenoids are inhibitors of epithelial carcinogenesis."
>
> Carotenoids are antioxidants. Antioxidants destroy the molecules that damage our cells. In layman's terms, both laboratory and widespread studies have found that carotenoids, like the ones found in St. John's Wort, prevent the development of cancer by enhancing communication between healthy cells, restoring tumor suppression functions, inducing cancer cell death and preventing the growth of extraneous blood vessels related to the cancer cells. The same article also notes that researchers are investigating carotenoids for the treatment of neck cancers and even lung cancer.

Dictionaries and thesauri are handy tools for picking precise vocabulary. You should remember, though, that picking the right word, the most precise word, seldom means using a word that is difficult to find. In fact, just the opposite is true. Important ideas do not have to sound complicated.

Simply stated, it is sagacious to eschew obfuscation.

Norman Augustine

Generate Audience Involvement

The final technique for effective informative speaking is to get your audience involved in your speech. **Audience involvement** is the level of commitment and attention that listeners devote to a speech. Educational psychologists have long known that the best way to teach people something is to have them do it; social psychologists have added to this rule by proving, in many studies, that involvement in a message increases audience comprehension of, and agreement with, that message.

There are many ways to encourage audience involvement in your speech. One way is by following the rules for good delivery by maintaining enthusiasm, energy, eye contact, and so on. Other ways include personalizing your speech, using audience participation, using volunteers, and having a question-and-answer period.

PERSONALIZE YOUR SPEECH   One way to encourage audience involvement is to give audience members a human being to connect to. In other words, don't be afraid to be yourself and to inject a little of your own personality into the speech. If you happen to be good at storytelling, make a narration part of your speech. If humor is a personal strength, be funny. If you feel passion about your topic, show it. Certainly if you have any experience that relates to your topic, use it.

USE AUDIENCE PARTICIPATION   **Audience participation,** having your listeners actually do something during your speech, is another way to increase their involvement in your message. For example, if you were giving a demonstration on isometric exercises (which don't require too much room for movement), you could have the entire audience stand up and do one or two sample exercises. (Exercise not only involves audience members psychologically, but also keeps them more alert physically by increasing the flow of blood and adrenaline in their systems.) If you were explaining how to fill out a federal income-tax form, you could give each class member a sample form to fill out as you explain it. Outlines and checklists can be used in a similar manner for just about any speech.

The best way to send information is to wrap it up in a person.

J. Robert Oppenheimer

Here's how one student organization used audience participation to demonstrate the various restrictions that were once placed on voting rights:

CULTURAL IDIOM

zero in on: focus directly on

> Voting is something that a lot of us may take for granted. Today, the only requirements for voting are that you are a U.S. citizen aged 18 or older who has lived in the same place for at least 30 days—and that you have registered. But it hasn't always been that way. Americans have had to struggle for the right to vote. I'd like to illustrate this by asking everyone to please stand.
>
> [Wait, prod class to stand.]
>
> I'm going to ask some questions. If you answer no to any question, please sit down.
>
> Do you have $2 in your pocket right now? If not, sit down. Up until 1964, poll taxes existed in many states.
>
> Have you resided at the same address for at least one year? If not, sit down. Residency requirements of more than 30 days weren't abolished until 1970.
>
> Are you white? If not, sit down. The 15th Amendment gave non-whites the right to vote in 1870 but many states didn't enforce it until the late 1960s.
>
> Are you male? If not, sit down. The 19th Amendment gave women the right to vote in 1920.
>
> Do you own a home? If not, sit down. Through the mid-1800s only property owners could vote.
>
> Are you Protestant? If not, sit down. That's right. Religious requirements existed in the early days throughout the country.[6]

USE VOLUNTEERS If the action you are demonstrating is too expensive or intricate to allow all the class members to take part, you can select one or two volunteers from the audience to help you out. You will increase the psychological involvement of all the members, because they will tend to identify with the volunteers.

HAVE A QUESTION-AND-ANSWER PERIOD One way to increase audience involvement that is nearly always appropriate if time allows is to answer questions at the end of your speech. You should encourage your audience to ask questions. Solicit questions and be patient waiting for the first one. Often no one wants to ask the first question. When the questions do start coming, the following suggestions might increase your effectiveness in answering them:

1. Listen to the substance of the question. Don't zero in on irrelevant details; listen for the big picture—the basic, overall question that is being asked. If you are not really sure what the substance of a question is, ask the questioner to paraphrase it. Don't be afraid to let the questioners do their share of the work.
2. Paraphrase confusing questions. Use the active listening skills described in Chapter 4. You can paraphrase the question in just a few words: "If I understand your question, you are asking _____. Is that right?"
3. Avoid defensive reactions to questions. Even if the questioner seems to be calling you a liar or stupid or

Rubes® By Leigh Rubin

"In order to adequately demonstrate just how many ways there are to skin a cat, I'll need a volunteer from the audience."

biased, try to listen to the substance of the question and not to the possible personality attack.

4. Answer the question as briefly as possible. Then check the questioner's comprehension of your answer. Sometimes you can simply check his or her non-verbal response—if he or she seems at all confused, you can ask, "Does that answer your question?"

CRITICAL THINKING PROBE

Analyzing an Informative Message

Select an informative message from a textbook, an encyclopedia, an instruction manual, or any other source. Analyze the message in terms of its effectiveness, pointing out where the source used effective techniques. Use this chapter as a guide. If necessary, point out places where effective techniques are still needed, making specific suggestions for improvement. Finally, comment on the changes that would be necessary if the message was presented as a speech.

SPEECH EVALUATION FORM

Informative Speech

Name_____ Topic_____
Assignment #_____ Date_____
What did you especially like?_____
_____
In your opinion, how could the speech be improved?_____
_____

Please comment on the following areas:

Did the speaker seem to have a clear informative purpose?
Was "information hunger" created?
Were important points emphasized?
Was the speech clearly organized and structured?
   Did the introduction–
      establish importance of topic to audience?
      preview thesis?
      preview main points?
   Did the body of the speech–
      contain three to five main points?
      contain three to five subpoints per main point?
      contain transitions, internal summaries, internal previews?
      contain points ordered to be easy to understand and remember?
   Did the conclusion of the speech–
      review main points?
      remind audience members of the importance of the topic to them?
      provide audience with a memory aid?
Was supporting material used effectively?
Was the language clear?
Did the speaker seek to involve the audience?

Figure 13–1   Evaluation Form for an Informative Speech

SAMPLE SPEECH

The sample speech for this chapter was presented by Martin Note, a student at Bradley University in Illinois. Martin presented this speech at the 2001 National Forensics Association annual tournament, which was held at Western Kentucky University in Bowling Green, Kentucky. He won first place in Informative Speaking. His coach was Christine Smith.

This speech is informative rather than persuasive because the topic is non-controversial and Martin doesn't intend to change audience attitudes as much as to impart specific information. It could be categorized as an explanation of a concept, and a highly technical concept at that. Martin limits the amount of information he presents and uses simple language and comparisons to explain this difficult concept. He uses several personal signposts along the way, such as "real creative, I know," and "go figure." They suit his personality and are effective.

Martin's informative purpose might be stated like this:

After listening to my speech, my audience members will understand how DNA computing works, what its applications are, and its prospects for the future.

The thesis statement could be worded as follows:

DNA computers will someday be able to tackle problems that are impossible for today's best silicon supercomputers.

The organization and structure of the speech can be seen in the following outline (numbers in parentheses refer to paragraphs in speech):

Introduction
  I. Attention-Getter (1)
 II. Preview (2–3)

Body
  I. DNA computing works like today's computing, only better. (4–10)
     A. DNA computers replace standard 1s and 0s with nucleotides. (5–7)
     B. DNA computers become accessible by placing DNA on a computer chip. (8–10)
 II. DNA computing has some "killer applications." (11–16)
     A. Immediate applications deal with cryptography and information storage. (12–14)
        1. DNA computers can be used to crack codes. (13)
        2. DNA computers can be used for information storage. (14)
     B. Future applications deal with biotechnology. (15–16)
        1. Human engineered cells can target body malfunctions. (15)
        2. Building blocks can create microscopic wires. (16)
III. DNA computing has its pros and cons. (17–20)
     A. On the negative side, DNA computers are not yet available. (17–18)
        1. The technology to make them practical is far off. (17)
        2. This technology is difficult to control. (18)
     B. On the positive side, DNA computers will be inexpensive and powerful. (19–20)
        1. The base material is cost effective: DNA is everywhere. (19)
        2. The base material is compatible with humans: It can become part of our bodies. (20)

Conclusion
  I. Review (21)
 II. Final remarks (22)

DNA COMPUTING

Martin Note

1 In 1965, Intel founder Gordon Moore had an epiphany. He noticed that microprocessors doubled in speed yet got smaller every 18 months. After much contemplation, he decided to call this phenomenon "Moore's Law." Real creative, I know. But since then, Moore's Law has taken us from machines that used to fill rooms to machines that now fit into the palm of our hands. But as the July 3rd, 2000 *New York Times* reports, Moore's Law is running head first into the Law of Physics. Within the next 20 years, we will be reaching the physical limits of miniaturization. And in the microprocessor industry, where small size DOES matter, this is a problem.

Introduction is worded to be interesting, personal, and humorous, while still previewing the topic.

2 Fortunately, as the January 2nd, 2001 *Electronic Engineering Times* exclaims, scientists have discovered the most efficient computing system known to man. And our bodies have been using it for 4 billion years. DNA. By harnessing our very biological programming, DNA computing is quickly becoming the leading contender for new age supercomputers. DNA solves miniaturization. It's a rather difficult task to work more efficiently than the information that makes you live and breathe. To unravel the double helix mystery of DNA computing, we'll first see how DNA computers work, second find some killer apps for this technology, and finally examine the ons and offs of DNA computing. DNA: If it's good enough for God, it's good enough for Bill Gates.

A difficult concept presented in clear, simple terms, without jargon.

Preview of main points.

3 So by now, half of the audience is scared to death because "DNA" and "computing" are right next to each other in this topic. Don't worry—computers aren't going to come alive and take over the world. We're just making them faster.

More personalizing of the information creates information hunger.

4 To understand how DNA computers work, we need to look at both the coding and mainstreaming of DNA chips.

Preview of first main point.

5 First, while computers can do incredible things, they are actually stupid. All they can interpret are "ons" and "offs" represented by 1s and 0s. The binary code! [Show Visual Aid 1]

Repeats the concept in different ways.

6 This is what a strand of binary code looks like. As the March 15, 2001 *Computers Today* explains, to get a DNA computer, we just replace these 1s and 0s with the 2 complementary sets of nucleotides. C and G. A and T. Now we have two on/off switches, but DNA also likes to form the familiar double helix. [Show Visual Aid 2]

7 So we get four times the code in one strand. As the November 13th, 2000 *ComputerWorld* explains, this lends itself to "parallel processing"— nerdspeak for really, really fast computing. Until recently, this type of programming could only take place in a test tube. [Show Visual Aid 3]

8 However, as June 2000 *Popular Mechanics* describes, researchers at the University of Wisconsin-Madison have made this technology accessible to the mainstream by using an old techno-geek standby—a computer chip. On a small chip, scientists anchored two DNA strands at either end. These two strands stand for parts of an equation. The answer fits in between.

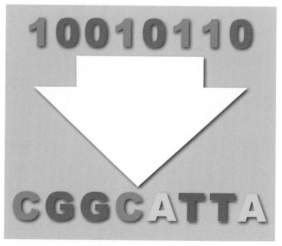

Visual Aid 1

9 While this resembles an ordinary silicon chip, it computes a little differently. Say Mo and Joe are computer chips. Their task is to find the Ace of Hearts in

Technical concept clarified with personal, clear language.

a pack of drawing cards. Mo, the silicon chip, does this by taking separate cards out of the deck until he finds the Ace. Long arduous process. Joe, the DNA chip, likes to play 52 card pickup and throws all the cards, or answers, out on the floor. Through a series of what are called enzyme washes, a chemical wash for DNA manipulation, he wipes away all the wrong cards (or answers) until only the correct one remains. While this might seem like a weird way for Joe to play Pinochle, multiply the deck by 53 billion and soon you'll want Joe as your Poker bud.

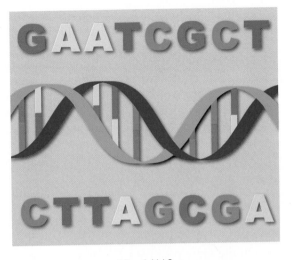

Visual Aid 2

10 As the January 17th, 2000 *Scotsman* contends, because of this powerful advantage, DNA computers can tackle mind boggling problems that would cause today's silicon supercomputers to crack under pressure.

11 So both molecular biology and computer scientists are excited about this concept. Go figure. But in order for a computer to be marketable, it needs some "killer applications." DNA computing has both immediate and future applications.

12 First, on the immediate side, scientists are attempting to harness DNA technology for cryptography and information storage.

13 Scientists want to use DNA computers to crack codes. As the February 14th, 2000 *Electronic Engineering Times* explains, DNA's parallel processing enables it to both crack current codes better and create new ones. This allows incredible advances in cryptography and security. In addition, they have the ability to find patterns in astronomical amounts of information. And if the Human Genome Project reminded us of anything, it is that DNA can store that—astronomical amounts of information.

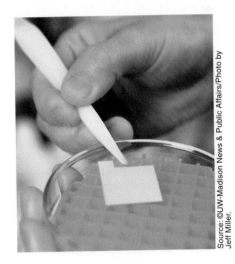

Visual Aid 3

14 Again, scientists are attempting to harness the information storage ability of DNA. So forget about floppy disks. The aforementioned *Electronic Engineering Times* estimates that 1 gram of DNA could hold more information than 1 trillion compact disks. Your grandfather's lifetime experience could be held in a device the size of his pocket watch.

Supporting material from a scientific journal is put to good use here.

15 But the most exciting application of DNA computing lies in its future, which includes biotechnology. Dr. Martyn Amos of Liverpool University reports in the September 4th, 2000 *London Financial Times* that within three years we will be able to custom program a cell's DNA. This paves the way for the creation of intelligent cells. Human engineered cells capable of targeting certain body malfunctions. These include blocked arteries, or brain damage in stroke victims.

Again, supporting material lends credibility to the ideas presented.

16 Scientists also envision tweaking DNA strands into their own building blocks. The May/June 2000 *Technology Review* reports on Erik Winfree's DNA Tiles. By programming DNA strands to wrap around each other, they form minute LEGO-like blocks that can only fit together in certain ways due to the bonds between certain nucleotides. Once put together, the tiles form

complex microscopic constructions. Scientists hope this will one day lead to potential conduction of electricity through DNA strands, like microscopic wires.

17 So DNA might seem the perfect choice to run Windows 2050. But there are still some critical issues surrounding DNA computing. First, on the negative side, the August 8th, 2000 *PC Magazine* explains that many of these concepts are still very distant on the horizon. Ability has not caught up with technology. As of yet, there is no nanomachine capable of reading the long lines of nucleotide readout.

Final main point: The pros and cons of this type of computing.

18 Second, as DNA computing inventor Leonard Aldeman regrets in the aforementioned *Technology Review,* don't expect DNA computers to replace the silicon PC. Molecular biology is still difficult to control. And when this technology becomes commonplace, the PC will be a thing of the past. Fifty years ago, we were still using punch cards and vacuum tubes. When was the last time any of us used those?

Comparison/contrast used to clarify point.

19 On the more positive side, Dr. Carter Bancroft in the November 2nd, 1999 *PC Magazine,* pointed out that DNA computers have a huge advantage. They are cost-effective. Unlike silicon based computers, the raw material of biological computing is cheap and plentiful. DNA is everywhere. And manipulation of DNA molecules requires only standard molecular biology equipment.

20 Further, DNA computers have another distinct advantage over silicon computers: evolution. DNA computers are made out of DNA. So are we. Therefore, they are more compatible with humans. As the November 28th, 2000 *New York Times* explains, this could lead to an ability to one day insert DNA chips to guide unnecessary biochemical reactions. Say you suffer from morning sickness. This will just start DNA program Puke Reducer 2.0.

This example clarifies the point for most college students.

21 So today we examined the double helix mystery of DNA based computing. We did this by first looking at how DNA computers work, second finding some killer applications for this technology, and finally discussing some critical issues surrounding DNA computing.

Review of main points.

22 Right now this technology stands at where the first computer did in 1945. Back then, IBM president Thomas Watson, Sr. said the world would only need 5 computers. Things have changed. So now I'll posit my own law, let's call it "Marty's Law": Really creative. In the future, it looks like computing might be happening . . . within ourselves.

Final comments.

SUMMARY

This chapter classified informative speaking based on content (speeches about objects, processes, events, and concepts) and purpose (descriptions, explanations, and instructions). It then suggested techniques for effective informative speaking. These techniques include using a specific informative purpose that stresses audience knowledge and/or ability; creating information hunger by tapping into audience needs; and making it easy to listen by limiting the amount of information you present, using familiar information to increase understanding of the unfamiliar, and using simple information to build up understanding of complex information. Other techniques include emphasizing important points through repetition and signposts; using clear organization and structure; using effective supporting materials, including visual aids; using clear language (language that uses precise, simple vocabulary and avoids jargon); and involving the audience through audience participation, the use of volunteers, and a question-and-answer period.

RESOURCES

Print

Hager, Peter. *Designing & Delivering Scientific, Technical, and Managerial Presentations.* New York: John Wiley & Sons, 1997.

Details how to design, prepare, and deliver informative presentations whose content, organization, style, and visuals will vary according to the informational needs, technical backgrounds, and uses of target audiences. Contains sample scripts of three professional presentations planned and delivered in work-world environments.

See also Cindy Todoroff, *Presenting Science with Impact,* New York: Trifolium Books, 1997, for more of the same.

Osborn, Michael, and Suzanne Osborn. *Public Speaking,* 5th ed. Boston: Houghton Mifflin, 2000.

See Chapter 12, "The Nature and Kinds of Informative Speaking," for a look at "major design options." These options include sequential, spatial, categorical, and comparison-contrast organizations of informative speeches.

Sprague, Jo, and Douglas Stuart. *The Speaker's Handbook,* 5th ed. Fort Worth, TX: Harcourt Brace, 2000.

Chapter 20, "Informative Strategies," gives a clear, concise treatment of how to design a speech around human information processing and principles of clear explanation.

Films

There is a subgenre of popular film that might be called "the teacher film," in which an idealistic teacher has to come up with ways to get through to a group of recalcitrant kids. The techniques that these teachers use to actually teach their students could be used as object lessons in innovative informative speaking. Here are some of our favorites.

Dangerous Minds (1995). Rated PG.

Michelle Pfeiffer stars as an English teacher in a tough inner-city high school who struggles to reach unruly students, mostly black and Latino, who don't see much point in learning anything. Based on LouAnne Johnson's memoir, *My Posse Don't Do Homework.* Johnson had to understand her students' needs before she could create information hunger. She also used every trick in the book (this book) to get them to listen.

Dead Poets Society (1989). Rated PG.

Robin Williams plays a charismatic English teacher at a staid New England prep school who inspires his students with his love of poetry. Among his many tricks, he uses audience participation, through the use of volunteers, to bring poetry to life.

Stand and Deliver (1987). Rated PG-13.

Edward James Olmos stars as a real-life tough, demanding teacher named Jaime Escalante, who inspires neglected East Los Angeles barrio students to pass an advanced calculus test for college credit. He breaks through to his students by learning to understand their needs. He also makes it easy for them to listen by limiting information and linking familiar, simple information to more complex concepts.

To Sir with Love (1967). Not rated.

A novice teacher (Sidney Poitier) is assigned to a classroom of thuggish students who couldn't care less about learning. He reaches them by caring about them as individuals. A breakthrough occurs when he learns how to listen to the substance of their questions and not answer defensively.

CONTENTS

KEY TERMS

actuate
ad hominem fallacy
anchor
argumentum ad populum
argumentum ad verecundiam
convince
credibility
direct persuasion
either-or fallacy
emotional evidence
ethical persuasion
evidence
fallacy
indirect persuasion
latitude of acceptance
latitude of noncommitment
latitude of rejection
Motivated Sequence
persuasion
post hoc fallacy
propositions of fact
propositions of policy
propositions of value
reductio ad absurdum
social judgment theory
straw man fallacy
target audience

AFTER STUDYING THE MATERIAL IN THIS CHAPTER . . .

YOU SHOULD UNDERSTAND:

1. That persuasion involves important ethical questions.

2. The differences among questions of fact, value, and policy.

3. The difference between the goals of convincing and actuating.

4. The difference between direct and indirect approaches.

5. The basic idea of persuasive strategy.

6. The importance of setting a clear persuasive purpose.

7. The importance of analyzing and adapting to your audience.

8. The components of personal credibility.

YOU SHOULD BE ABLE TO:

1. Formulate an effective persuasive strategy to convince or actuate an audience.

2. Formulate your persuasive strategy based on ethical guidelines.

3. Bolster your credibility as a speaker by enhancing your competence, character, and charisma.

4. Build persuasive arguments with common ground, solid evidence, and careful reasoning.

5. Organize a persuasive speech for greatest audience effect.

PERSUASIVE SPEAKING

Across the United States and the world, college students are speaking out. They are becoming increasingly engaged in a variety of issues, including global ones such as the gap between rich and poor and the international influence of American corporations. Students have staged hunger strikes at Purdue and clothing-optional protests at the University of North Carolina, where the theme was "I'd Rather Go Naked Than Wear Sweatshop." They have protested at the School of the Americas, a training center at Fort Benning in Columbus, Georgia, whose graduates include General Manuel Noriega of Panama and others connected to human rights abuses in their countries.

In 2001, students held campus demonstrations both for and against the U.S. war on terrorism. *The New York Times* reported that what both sides had in common was "an ardor not seen for several decades."[1] Robert Butler, the director of student activities at New York University, says that several factors have contributed to the new student activism. "One is the push for students to become involved in community service," Butler says. "There's probably a direct connection between seeing a problem and seeing constructive ways of getting involved in the problem."[2] Butler believes that today's students understand the issues and that they know how to work within the system to put pressure on those who can make change.

What is undeniable is that the students who are speaking out are engaged in the age-old activity of persuasion. How persuasion works and how to accomplish it successfully are complex topics. Our understanding of persuasion begins with classical wisdom and extends to the latest psychological research. We begin by looking at what we really mean by the term.

CHARACTERISTICS OF PERSUASION

Persuasion is the process of motivating someone, through communication, to change a particular belief, attitude, or behavior. Implicit in this definition are several characteristics of persuasion.

Persuasion Is Not Coercive

Persuasion is not the same thing as coercion. If you held a gun to someone's head and said, "Do this, or I'll shoot," you would be acting coercively. Besides being illegal, this approach would be ineffective. As soon as the authorities came and took you away, the person would stop following your demands.

The failure of coercion to achieve lasting results is also apparent in less dramatic circumstances. Children whose parents are coercive often rebel as soon as they can; students who perform from fear of an instructor's threats rarely appreciate the subject matter; and employees who work for abusive and demanding employers are often unproductive and eager to switch jobs as soon as possible. Persuasion, on the other hand, makes a listener *want* to think or act differently.

Persuasion Is Usually Incremental

Attitudes do not normally change instantly or dramatically. Persuasion is a process. When it is successful, it generally succeeds over time, in increments, and usually small increments at that. The realistic speaker, therefore, establishes goals and expectations that reflect this characteristic of persuasion.

Where wisdom is called for, force is of little use.

Herodotus

Communication scientists explain this characteristic of persuasion through **social judgment theory.**[3] This theory tells us that when members of an audience hear a persuasive appeal, they compare it to

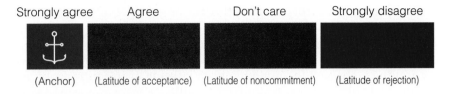

| Strongly agree | Agree | Don't care | Strongly disagree |
| (Anchor) | (Latitude of acceptance) | (Latitude of noncommitment) | (Latitude of rejection) |

Figure 14–1   Latitudes of Acceptance, Rejection, and Noncommitment

opinions that they already hold. The preexisting opinion is called an *anchor,* but around this anchor there exist what are called *latitudes of acceptance, latitudes of rejection,* and *latitudes of noncommitment.* A diagram of any opinion, therefore, might look something like Figure 14–1.

People who care very strongly about a particular point of view (called "highly ego-involved" by communication researchers) will have a very narrow latitude of noncommitment. People who care less strongly will have a wider latitude of noncommitment. Research suggests that audience members simply will not respond to appeals that fall within their latitude of rejection. This means that persuasion in the real world takes place in a series of small movements. One persuasive speech may be but a single step in an overall persuasive campaign. The best example of this is the various communications that take place during the months of a political campaign. Candidates watch the opinion polls carefully, adjusting their appeals to the latitudes of acceptance and noncommitment of the uncommitted voters.

Public speakers who heed the principle of social judgment theory tend to seek realistic, if modest, goals in their speeches. For example, if you were hoping to change audience views on the pro-life/pro-choice question, social judgment theory suggests that the first step would be to consider a range of arguments such as this:

Abortion should be considered simply a form of birth control.
Abortion should be available anytime to anyone.
Abortion should be discouraged but legal.
Abortion is a woman's personal decision.
A woman should not be required to have her husband's permission to have an abortion.
A girl under the age of eighteen should not be required to have a parent's permission before she has an abortion.
Abortion should be allowed during the first three months of pregnancy.
A girl under the age of eighteen should be required to have a parent's permission before she has an abortion.
A woman should be required to have her husband's permission to have an abortion.
Abortion should be allowed only in cases of rape and incest.
Abortion should be absolutely illegal.
Abortion is a sin.

You could then arrange these positions on a continuum, and estimate how listeners would react to each one. The statement that best represented the listeners' point of view would be their **anchor.** Other items that might also seem reasonable to them would make up their **latitude of acceptance.** Opinions that they would reject would make up their **latitude of rejection.** Those statements that are left would be the listeners' **latitude of noncommitment.**

Social judgment theory suggests that the best chance of changing audience attitudes would come by presenting an argument based on a position that fell somewhere within the listeners' latitude of noncommitment—even if this isn't the position that you ultimately wanted them to accept. If you pushed too hard by arguing a position in your audience's latitude of rejection, your appeals would probably backfire, making your audience *more* opposed to you than before.

INVITATION TO INSIGHT   ## Audience Latitudes of Acceptance

To better understand the concept of latitudes of acceptance, rejection, and noncommitment, formulate a list of perspectives on a topic of your choice. This list should contain eight to ten statements that represent a variety of attitudes, such as the list pertaining to the pro-life/pro-choice issue on page 419. Arrange this list from your own point of view, from most acceptable to least acceptable. Then circle the single statement that best represents your own point of view. This will be your "anchor." Underline those items that also seem reasonable. These make up your latitude of acceptance on this issue. Then cross out the numbers in front of any items that express opinions that you cannot accept. These make up your latitude of rejection. Those statements that are left would be your latitude of noncommitment. Do you agree that someone seeking to persuade you on this issue would do best by advancing propositions that fall within this latitude of noncommitment?

Persuasion Is Interactive

The transactional model of communication described in Chapter 1 makes it clear that persuasion is not something you do *to* audience members but rather that it is something you do *with* them. This mutual activity is best seen in an argument between two people, in which an openness to opposing arguments is essential to resolution. As one observer has pointed out,

> Arguments are not won by shouting down opponents. They are won by changing opponents' minds—something that can happen only if we give opposing arguments a respectful hearing and still persuade their advocates that there is something wrong with those arguments. In the course of this activity, we may well decide that there is something wrong with our own.[4]

Even in public communication, both source and receiver are active. This might be manifested in the source taking an audience survey *before* a speech, a sensitivity to audience reactions *during* a speech, or an open-minded question-and-answer period *after* a speech.

Persuasion Can Be Ethical

Even when they understand the difference between persuasion and coercion, some people are still uncomfortable with the idea of persuasive speaking. They

I know only that what is moral is what you feel good after and what is immoral is what you feel bad after.

Ernest Hemingway

see it as the work of high-pressure hucksters: salespeople with their feet stuck in the door, unscrupulous politicians taking advantage of beleaguered taxpayers, and so on. Indeed, many of the principles we are about to discuss have been used by unethical speakers for unethical purposes, but that is not what all—or even most—persuasion is about. Ethical persuasion plays a necessary and worthwhile role in everyone's life.

It is through ethical persuasion that we influence others' lives in worthwhile ways. The person who says, "I do not want to influence other people," is really saying, "I do not want to get involved with other people," and that is an abandonment of one's responsibilities as a human being. Look at the good you can accomplish through persuasion: You can convince a loved one to give up smoking or to not keep a firearm in the house; you can get members of your community to conserve energy or to join together to refurbish a park; you can persuade an employer to hire you for a job where your own talents, interests, and abilities will be put to their best use.

Persuasion is considered ethical if it conforms to accepted standards. But what are the standards today? If your plan is selfish and not in the best interest of your audience members, but you are honest about your motives—is that ethical? If your plan is in the best interest of your audience members, yet you lie to them to get them to accept the plan—is that ethical? Philosophers and rhetoricians have argued for centuries over questions like these.

There are many ways to define **ethical persuasion.**[5] For our purpose, we will consider it as *communication in the best interest of the audience that does not depend on false or misleading information to change an audience's attitude or behavior.* The best way to appreciate the value of this simple definition is to consider the many strategies listed in Table 14–1 that do not fit it. For example, faking enthusiasm about a speech topic, plagiarizing material from another source and passing it off as your own, and making up statistics to support your case are clearly unethical.

Besides being wrong on moral grounds, unethical attempts at persuasion have a major practical disadvantage: If your deception is uncovered, your credibility will suffer. If, for example, prospective buyers uncover your attempt to withhold a structural flaw in the condominium you are trying to sell, they will probably suspect that the property has other hidden problems. Likewise, if your speech instructor suspects that you are lifting material from other sources without giving credit, your entire presentation will be suspect. One unethical act can cast doubt on future truthful statements. Thus, for pragmatic as well as moral reasons, honesty really is the best policy.

INVITATION TO INSIGHT

Personal Persuasion

When was the last time you changed your attitude about something after discussing it with someone? In your opinion, was this persuasion interactive? Not coercive? Incremental? Ethical? Explain your answer.

TABLE 14-1   Unethical Communication Behaviors

1. Failing to Prepare Adequately
   a. Insufficient research (speaker does not know what he or she is talking about)
   b. Not meeting logical standards of proof

2. Sacrificing Convictions in Adapting to an Audience
   a. In propositions endorsed
   b. In style of presentation (for example, clothing)

3. Appearing to Be What One Is Not; Insincerity
   a. In words, saying what one does not mean or believe
   b. In delivery (for example, feigning enthusiasm)

4. Withholding Information; Suppression
   a. About self (speaker); not disclosing private motives or special interests
   b. About speech purpose
   c. About sources (not revealing sources; plagiarism)
   d. About evidence; omission of certain evidence (card stacking)
   e. About opposing arguments; presenting only one side

5. Relaying False Information
   a. Deliberate lying
   b. Ignorant misstatement
   c. Deliberate distortion and suppression of material
   d. Fallacious reasoning to misrepresent truth

6. Using Emotional Appeals to Hinder Truth
   a. Using emotional appeals as a substitute or cover-up for lack of sound reasoning and valid evidence
   b. Failing to use balanced appeals

7. Committing Plagiarism
   a. Claiming someone else's ideas as your own
   b. Quoting without citing the source

Adapted from Mary Klaaren Andersen, "An Analysis of the Treatment of Ethos in Selected Speech Communication Textbooks" (unpublished dissertation, University of Michigan, 1979), pp. 244–247.

CATEGORIZING TYPES OF PERSUASION

There are several ways to categorize the types of persuasive attempts you will make as a speaker. What kinds of subjects will you focus on? What results will you be seeking? How will you go about getting those results? In the following pages we will look at each of these questions.

By Types of Proposition

Persuasive topics fall into one of three categories, depending on the type of thesis statement (referred to as a "proposition" in persuasion) that you are advancing. The three categories are propositions of fact, propositions of value, and propositions of policy.

PROPOSITIONS OF FACT   Some persuasive messages focus on **propositions of fact:** issues in which there are two or more sides with conflicting evidence, where listeners are required to choose the truth for themselves. Some questions of fact are these:

> The United States does/does not give as much foreign aid to undeveloped nations as do other wealthy countries.
> Canada's nationalized health care is more/is less efficient than the U.S. system of health care.
> The local nuclear reactor does/does not emit an unacceptable level of radiation.

These examples show that many questions of fact can't be settled with a simple "yes" or "no" or with an objective piece of information. Rather, they are open to debate, and answering them requires careful examination and interpretation of evidence, usually collected from a variety of sources. That's why it is possible to debate questions of fact, and that's why these propositions form the basis of persuasive speeches and not informative ones.

PROPOSITIONS OF VALUE   **Propositions of value** go beyond issues of truth or falsity and explore the worth of some idea, person, or object. Propositions of value include the following:

> The United States is justified in attacking countries that harbor terrorist organizations.
> Cosmetic surgery is/is not a waste of medical facilities.
> The use of laboratory animals for scientific experiments is/is not cruel and immoral.

In order to deal with most propositions of value, you will have to explore certain propositions of fact. For example, you won't be able to debate whether the experimental use of animals in research is immoral—a proposition of value—until you have dealt with propositions of fact such as how many animals are used in experiments and whether experts believe they actually suffer.

PROPOSITIONS OF POLICY   **Propositions of policy** go one step beyond questions of fact or value; they recommend a specific course of action (a "policy"). Some questions of policy are these:

> Condoms should/should not be distributed in high schools.
> Genetic engineering of plants and livestock is/is not an appropriate way to increase the food supply.
> The United States should/should not intervene to prevent human rights abuses in other countries.

Looking at persuasion according to the type of proposition is a convenient way to generate topics for a persuasive speech, because each type of proposition suggests different topics. Selected topics could also be handled differently depending on how they are approached. For example, a campaign speech could be approached as a proposition of fact ("Candidate X has done more for this community than the opponent"), a proposition of value ("Candidate X is a better person than the opponent"), or a proposition of policy ("We should get out and vote for Candidate X"). Remember, however, that a fully developed persuasive speech is likely to contain all three types of propositions. If you were preparing a speech advocating that college athletes should be paid in cash for their talents (a proposition of policy), you might want to first prove that the practice is already widespread (a proposition of fact) and that it is unfair to athletes from other schools (a proposition of value).

SKILL BUILDER Propositions of Fact, Value, and Policy

Which of the following are propositions of fact, propositions of value, and propositions of policy?

1. Eldercare should/should not be the responsibility of government.
2. The mercury in dental fillings is/is not healthy for the dental patient.
3. Congressional pay raises should/should not be delayed until an election has intervened.
4. Third-party candidates strengthen/weaken American democracy.
5. National medical insurance should/should not be provided to all citizens of the United States.
6. Elderly people who are wealthy do/do not receive too many Social Security benefits.
7. Tobacco advertising should/should not be banned from all media.
8. Domestic violence is/is not on the rise.
9. Exposure to electromagnetic fields causes/does not cause cancer.
10. Pit bulls are/are not dangerous animals.
11. Part-time adjunct professors are/are not exploited under our current employment system.

By Desired Outcome

We can also categorize persuasion according to two major outcomes: convincing and actuating.

CONVINCING When you set about to **convince** an audience, you want to change the way its members think. When we say that convincing an audience changes the way its members think, we do not mean that you have to swing them from one belief or attitude to a completely different one. Sometimes audience members will already think the way you want them to, but they will not be firmly enough committed to that way of thinking. When that is the case, you reinforce, or strengthen, their opinions. For example, if your audience already believed that the federal budget should be balanced but did not consider the idea important, your job would be to reinforce members' current beliefs. Reinforcing is still a type of change, however, because you are causing an audience to adhere more strongly to a belief or attitude. In other cases, a speech to convince will begin to shift attitudes without bringing about a total change of thinking. For example, an effective speech to convince might get a group of skeptics to consider the possibility that bilingual education is/isn't a good idea.

ACTUATING When you set about to **actuate** an audience, you want to move its members to a specific behavior. Whereas a speech to convince might move an

The credit goes to the person who convinces the world, not to the one to whom the idea first occurs.

Sir Francis Darwin

audience to action based on the ideas you've convinced members of, it won't be any specific action that you have recommended. In a speech to actuate, you do recommend that specific action.

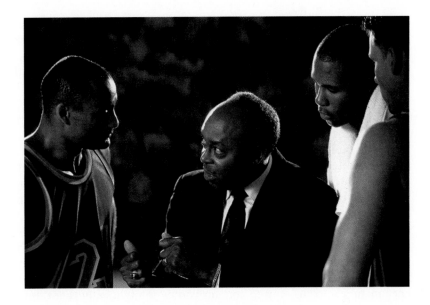

There are two types of action you can ask for—adoption or discontinuance. The former asks an audience to engage in a new behavior; the latter asks an audience to stop behaving in an established way. If you gave a speech for a political candidate and then asked for contributions to that candidate's campaign, you would be asking your audience to adopt a new behavior. If you gave a speech against smoking and then asked your audience members to sign a pledge to quit, you would be asking them to discontinue an established behavior.

By Directness of Approach

We can also categorize persuasion according to the directness of approach employed by the speaker.

DIRECT PERSUASION **Direct persuasion** does not try to disguise the speaker's persuasive purpose in any way. In direct persuasion the speaker will make his or her purpose clear, usually by stating it outright early in the speech. This is the best strategy to use with a friendly audience, especially when you are asking for a response that the audience is reasonably likely to give you. Direct persuasion is the kind we hear in most academic situations. Misty Williams, a student at Southwestern Oklahoma State University, used direct persuasion in her speech entitled "The Latest Buzz: Caffeine Labeling." Part of her introduction announced her intention to persuade in this way:

> Today, Americans are reaching new heights in caffeine consumption . . . This leads us to consider exactly what caffeine is and how it works. We will then discuss the health related and addictive effects of this harmful substance. Finally, I will illustrate how caffeine quantity specifications are necessary to inform Americans of this overlooked yet entrapping substance.[6]

INDIRECT PERSUASION **Indirect persuasion** disguises or deemphasizes the speaker's persuasive purpose in some way. The question "Is a season ticket to the symphony worth the money?" (when you intend to prove that it is) is based on indirect persuasion, as is any strategy that does not express the speaker's purpose at the outset.

Indirect persuasion is sometimes easy to spot. A television commercial that shows us attractive young men and women romping in the surf on a beautiful day and then flashes the product name on the screen is pretty indisputably indirect persuasion. Political oratory also is sometimes indirect persuasion, and it is sometimes more difficult to identify as such. A political hopeful might be ostensibly speaking on some great social issue when the real persuasive message is "Please—remember my name, and vote for me in the next election."

In public speaking, indirect persuasion is usually disguised as informative speaking. For example, a supposedly informative speech could be given on AIDS that actually has the intent of persuading audience members to remain celibate before marriage and monogamous after marriage. Indirect persuasion isn't necessarily unethical. In fact, it is probably the best approach to use when your audience is hostile to either you or your topic. It is also often necessary to use the indirect approach to get a hearing from listeners who would tune you out if you took a more direct approach. Under such circumstances, you might want to ease into your speech slowly.[7] You might take some time to make your audience feel good about you or the social action you are advocating. If you are speaking in favor of your candidacy for city council, but you are in favor of a tax increase and your audience is not, you might talk for a while about the benefits that a well-financed city council can provide to the community. You might even want to change your desired audience response. Rather than trying to get audience members to rush out to vote for you, you might want them simply to read a policy statement that you have written or become more informed on a particular issue. The one thing you cannot do in this instance is to begin by saying, "My appearance here today has nothing to do with my candidacy for city council." That would be a false statement. It is more than indirect; it is unethical.

CRITICAL THINKING PROBE

Direct or Indirect Persuasion?

Find a current political speech in *Vital Speeches of the Day, The New York Times,* or on the Internet (See the "Understanding Communication Technology" sidebar below). Which type of persuasive strategy is used in the speech: direct or indirect? Is the strategy used effectively? Why or why not?

UNDERSTANDING COMMUNICATION TECHNOLOGY

Persuasive Speeches On The Web

Chapter 12 (page 393) pointed out that the Web can be used to find audio and video clips of historical speeches. The Web can also be used to find a variety of persuasive speeches in transcript form, which is the best way to study them for attributes like strategy and ethics. Here are a few of our favorite sites.

The Douglass Archive
http://douglass.speech.nwu.edu/
An electronic archive of American oratory and related documents, maintained by Northwestern University. Has the most recent political speeches and reaches far back into history. Allows you to review speeches and related documents by speaker, by title, by time period, and by controversy or movement.

Congressional Record
http://www.access.gpo.gov/su_docs/aces/aces150.html
The *Congressional Record* is the official record of the proceedings and debates of the U.S. Congress. It is published daily when Congress is in session. Searchable.

Speech and Transcript Center
http://gwu.edu/~gprice/speech.htm
A wide range of speech transcripts and speeches in audio. Speeches from business leaders, television/radio programs, U.S. government, state officials, international government, professional organizations, and historical speeches. Maintained by George Washington University.

The test of the ethics of an indirect approach would be whether you would express your persuasive purpose directly if asked to do so. In other words, if someone in the audience stopped you and asked, "Don't you want us to vote for you for city council?" if you were ethical, you would admit to it rather than deny your true purpose.

CREATING THE PERSUASIVE MESSAGE

Preparing an effective persuasive speech isn't easy, but it can be made easier by observing a few simple rules. These include the following: Set a clear, persuasive purpose; structure the message carefully; use solid evidence; and avoid fallacies.

Set a Clear, Persuasive Purpose

Remember that your objective in a persuasive speech is to move the audience to a specific, attainable attitude or behavior. In a speech to persuade, the purpose statement will probably stress an attitude:

After listening to my speech, my audience members will agree that steps should be taken to save whales from extinction.

In a speech to actuate, the purpose statement will stress behavior:

After listening to my speech, my audience members will sign my petition.

As Chapter 11 explained, your purpose statement should always be specific, attainable, and worded from the audience's point of view. "The purpose of my speech is to save the whales" is not a purpose statement that has been carefully thought out. Your audience members wouldn't be able to jump up and save the whales, even if they were motivated into a frenzy. They might, however, be able to support a specific piece of legislation.

A clear, specific purpose statement will help you stay on track throughout all the stages of preparation of your persuasive speech. Because the main purpose of your speech is to have an effect on your audience, you have a continual test that you can use for every idea, every piece of evidence, and every organizational structure that you think of using. The question you ask is, "Will this help me to get the audience members to think/feel/behave in the manner I have described in my purpose statement?" If the answer is "yes," you forge ahead.

Structure the Message Carefully

A sample structure of the body of a persuasive speech is outlined in Figure 14–2. With this structure, if your objective is to convince, you

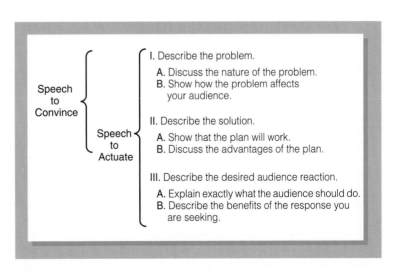

Figure 14–2   Sample Structure for a Persuasive Speech

concentrate on the first two components: Establishing the problem and describing the solution. If your objective is to actuate, you add the third component, describing the desired audience reaction.

There are, of course, other structures for persuasive speeches. This one can be used as a basic model, however, because it is easily applied to most persuasive topics.

DESCRIBE THE PROBLEM   In order to convince an audience that something needs to be changed, you have to show members that a problem exists. After all, if your listeners don't recognize the problem, they won't find your arguments for a solution very important. An effective description of the problem will answer two questions, either directly or indirectly.

What Is the Nature of the Problem?

Your audience members might not recognize that the topic you are discussing is a problem at all, so your first task is to convince them that there is something wrong with the present state of affairs. For example, if your thesis was "This town needs a shelter for homeless families," you would need to show that there are, indeed, homeless families and that the plight of these homeless families is serious.

Your approach to defining your problem will depend largely on your audience analysis, as discussed in Chapter 11. If your prespeech analysis shows that your audience may not feel sympathetic to your topic, you will need to explain why your topic is, indeed, a problem that your audience should recognize. In a speech about the plight of the homeless, you might need to establish that most homeless people are not lazy, able-bodied drifters who chose to panhandle and steal instead of work. You could cite respected authorities, give examples, and maybe even show photographs to demonstrate that some homeless people are hardworking but unlucky parents and innocent children who lack shelter owing to forces beyond their control.

How Does the Problem Affect Your Audience?

It's not enough to prove that a problem exists. Your next challenge is to show your listeners that the problem affects them in some way. This is relatively easy in some cases: the high cost of tuition, the lack of convenient parking near campus, the quality of food in the student center. In other cases, you will need to spell out the impact to your listeners more clearly. Jimmy Ficara, a student at the University of Texas at Austin, presented a speech on the high cost of prescription drugs overseas. After pointing out that residents of other countries could not afford the drugs needed to cure diseases like tuberculosis and cholera, he established the importance of this topic to his U.S. audience this way:

> Americans are at risk too. Epidemics simply don't stop at borders or bodies of water. Many of these nearly eradicated illnesses can quickly re-enter America because more and more immigrants are entering the United States with infectious diseases. The *Columbus Dispatch* of January 27, 2001 reports that over 40% of all new tuberculosis cases are found in foreign residents. Just last year in Virginia, a tuberculosis outbreak infected 78 people and was traced back to a Russian emigrant who was working at a Burger King. Dr. Lee Reichmann, a tuberculosis expert, told *60 Minutes* on July 23, 2000 that "a new tuberculosis drug has not been created in nearly 25 years and if an epidemic were to start in the U.S. there would not be enough drugs to stop it."[8]

The problem section of a persuasive speech is often broken up into segments discussing the cause and the effect of the problem. (The sample speech at the end of this chapter is an example of this type of organization.)

CULTURAL IDIOM

paint a...picture:
describe in detail

DESCRIBE THE SOLUTION   Your next step in persuading your audience members is to convince them that there is an answer to the problem you have just introduced. To describe your solution, you should answer two questions:

Will the Solution Work?   A skeptical audience might agree with the desirability of your solution but still not believe that it has a chance of succeeding. In the homeless speech discussed previously, you would need to prove that the establishment of a shelter can help unlucky families get back on their feet—especially if your audience analysis shows that some listeners might view such a shelter as a way of coddling people who are too lazy to work.

What Advantages Will Result from Your Solution?   You need to describe in specific terms how your solution will lead to the desired changes. This is the step where you will paint a vivid picture of the benefits of your proposal. In the speech proposing a shelter for homeless families, the benefits you describe would probably include these:

1. Families will have a safe place to stay, free of the danger of living on the street.
2. Parents will have the resources that will help them find jobs: an address, telephone, clothes washers, and showers.
3. The police won't have to apply antivagrancy laws (such as prohibitions against sleeping in cars) to people who aren't the intended target of those laws.
4. The community (including your listeners) won't need to feel guilty about ignoring the plight of unfortunate citizens.

DESCRIBE THE DESIRED AUDIENCE RESPONSE   When you want to go beyond simply a strategy to convince your audience members and use a strategy to actuate them to follow your solution, you need to describe exactly what you want them to do. This action step, like the previous ones, should answer two questions.

What Can the Audience Do to Put Your Solution into Action?   Make the behavior you are asking your audience members to adopt as clear and simple as possible for them. If you want them to vote in a referendum, tell them when and where to go to vote and how to go about registering, if necessary (some activists even provide transportation). If you're asking them to support a legislative change, don't expect them to write their congressional representative. *You* write the letter or draft a petition, and ask them to sign it. If you're asking for a donation, pass the hat at the conclusion of your speech, or give audience members a stamped, addressed envelope and simple forms that they can return easily.

What Are the Direct Rewards of This Response?   Your solution might be important to society, but your audience members will be most likely to adopt it if you can show that they will get a personal payoff. Show that supporting legislation to reduce acid rain will produce a wide range of benefits from reduced lung damage to healthier forests to longer life for their car's paint. Explain that saying "no" to a second drink before driving will not only save lives but also help your listeners avoid expensive court costs, keep their insurance rates low, and prevent personal humiliation. Show how helping to establish and staff a homeless shelter can lead to personal feelings of satisfaction and provide an impressive demonstration of community service on a job-seeking résumé.

ADAPT THE MODEL PERSUASIVE STRUCTURE   Describing the problem and the solution makes up the basic structure for any persuasive speech. However, you don't have to analyze too many successful persuasive speeches to realize that the best of them do far more than the basic minimum. One way to augment the basic persuasive structure is to use the organization suggested by Alan Monroe in his **Motivated Sequence**,[9] which we mentioned briefly in Chapter 11 (pages 356–357). In that pattern the problem is broken down into an attention step, and a satisfaction step, and the solution is broken down into a satisfaction step and a visualization step. In another adaptation of the basic model, the speaker will combine the "solution" with the "desired audience response." (See the sample speech at the end of this chapter.)

SKILL BUILDER

Structuring Persuasive Speeches

For practice in structuring persuasive speeches, choose one of the following topics, and provide a full-sentence outline that conforms to the outline in Figure 14–2, page 427.

It should/should not be more difficult to purchase a handgun.
Public relations messages that appear in news reports should/should not be labeled as advertising.
Newspaper recycling is/is not important for the environment.
Police should/should not be required to carry nonlethal weapons only.
Parole should/should not be abolished.
The capital of the United States should/should not be moved to a more central location.
We should/should not ban capital punishment.
Bilingual education should/should not be offered in all schools in which students speak English as a second language.

Use Solid Evidence

All the forms of support discussed in Chapter 12 can be used to back up your persuasive arguments.[12] Your objective here is not to find supporting material that just clarifies your ideas, but rather to find the perfect example, statistic, definition, analogy, anecdote, or testimony to establish the truth of your claim in the mind of this specific audience. You choose **evidence** that strongly supports your claim, and you should feel free to use **emotional evidence,** which is supporting material that evokes audience feelings such as fear, anger, sympathy, pride, or reverence. Whatever type of evidence you use, you should cite your sources carefully. It is important that your audience know that your sources are

The most savage controversies are about those matters as to which there is no good evidence either way.

Bertrand Russell

UNDERSTANDING DIVERSITY

Cultural Differences in Persuasion

Different individuals have a tendency to view persuasion differently, and often these differences are based on cultural background. Even the ability to recognize logical argument is, to a certain extent, culturally determined. Not all cultures use logic in the same way that the Euro-American culture does. The influence of the dominant culture is seen even in the way we talk about argumentation. When we talk about "defending" ideas and "attacking our opponent's position" we are using male-oriented militaristic/aggressive terms. Logic is also based on a trust in objective reality, on information that is verifiable through our senses. As one researcher points out, such a perspective can be culturally influenced:

Western culture assumes a reality that is materialist and limited to comprehension via the five senses. African culture assumes a reality that is both material and spiritual viewed as one and the same.[10]

The way logic is viewed differs between Eastern and Western Hemisphere cultures, also. As Samovar and Porter point out:

Westerners discover truth by active searching and the application of Aristotelian modes of reasoning. On the contrary, many Easterners wait patiently, and if truth is to be known it will make itself apparent.[11]

It is because of cultural differences such as these that speech experts have always recommended a blending of logical and emotional evidence.

credible, unbiased, and current. If you are quoting the source of an interview, give a full statement of the source's credentials:

According to Sean Wilentz, professor of history and director of the Program in American Studies at Princeton University and the author of several books on this topic . . .

If the currency of the interview is important, you might add, "I spoke to Professor Wilentz just last week . . ." If you are quoting an article, give a quick statement of the author's credentials and the full date and title of the magazine:

According to Professor Sean Wilentz of Princeton University, in an article in the June 25, 2002 New York Times Magazine *. . .*

You do not need to give the title of the article (although you may, if it helps in any way) or the page number. If you are quoting from a book, include a quick statement of the author's credentials:

According to Professor Sean Wilentz of Princeton University, in his book The Kingdom of Matthias *. . .*

You don't need to include the copyright date unless it's

important to authenticate the currency of the quotation, and you don't have to mention the publisher or city of publication unless it's relevant to your topic somehow. Generally, if you're unsure about how to cite your sources in a speech, you should err in the direction of too much information rather than too little.

Carefully cited sources are part of a well-reasoned argument. This brings us to our next step in creating a persuasive message.

Avoid Fallacies

A **fallacy** (from the Latin word meaning "false") is an error in logic. Although the original meaning of the term implied purposeful deception, most logical fallacies are not recognized as such by those who use them. Scholars have devoted lives and volumes to the description of various types of logical fallacies.[13] Here are some of the most common ones to keep in mind when building your persuasive argument:[14]

ATTACK ON THE PERSON INSTEAD OF THE ARGUMENT *(AD HOMINEM)* In an *ad hominem* **fallacy** the speaker attacks the integrity of a person in order to weaken the argument. At its most crude level, an *ad hominem* argument is easy to detect. "How can you believe that fat slob?" is hardly persuasive. It takes critical thinking to catch more subtle *ad hominem* arguments, however. Consider this one: "All this talk about 'family values' is hypocritical. Take Senator ————, who made a speech about the 'sanctity of marriage' last year. Now it turns out he was having an affair with his secretary, and his wife is suing him for divorce." Although the senator certainly does seem to be a hypocrite, his behavior doesn't necessarily weaken the merits of family values.

REDUCTION TO THE ABSURD *(REDUCTIO AD ABSURDUM)* A *reductio ad absurdum* **fallacy** unfairly attacks an argument by extending it to such extreme lengths that it looks ridiculous. "If we allow developers to build homes in one section of this area, soon we will have no open spaces left. Fresh air and wildlife will be a thing of the past." "If we allow the administration to raise tuition this year, soon they will be raising it every year, and before we know it only the wealthiest students will be able to go to school here." This extension of reasoning doesn't make any sense: Developing one area doesn't necessarily mean that other areas have to be developed, and one tuition increase doesn't mean that others will occur. Any of these policies might be unwise or unfair, but the *ad absurdum* reasoning doesn't prove it.

A **straw man argument** is a variation of the *ad absurdum* fallacy. In it, a speaker attacks a potentially valid argument by demolishing a weak example and suggesting that it represents the entire position. (The fallacy is so named because the arguer sets up a flimsy "straw man" and then knocks it down.) Consider this example: "The idea that the earth has been visited by beings from outer space is ridiculous. To show you just how lame it is, take a look at this headline from a trashy supermarket tabloid: 'I Was a Love Slave to Alien Sex Masters.' Maybe people with that kind of mentality believe in UFOs, but not anybody who is serious." What's wrong with this argument? Although stories in super market tabloids don't prove the existence of extraterrestrial visitors, these laughable stories don't rule out the possibility that other, more valid evidence might exist.

CULTURAL IDIOM

trashy supermarket tabloid: newspapers that are sold at supermarket checkout counters and known for articles that are attention-getting and not necessarily true

EITHER-OR   An **either-or fallacy** sets up false alternatives, suggesting that if the inferior one must be rejected, then the other must be accepted. An angry citizen used either-or thinking to support a proposed city ordinance: "Either we outlaw alcohol in city parks, or there will be no way to get rid of drunks." This reasoning overlooks the possibility that there may be other ways to control public drunkenness besides banning all alcoholic beverages. The old saying "America, love it or leave it" provides another example of either-or reasoning. For instance, when an Asian-born college professor pointed out examples of lingering discrimination in the United States, some suggested that if she didn't like her adopted country she should return to her native home—ignoring that it is possible to admire a country and still envision ways to make it a better place.

FALSE CAUSE (POST HOC ERGO PROPTER HOC)   A *post hoc* **fallacy** mistakenly assumes that one event causes another because they occur sequentially. An old (and not especially funny) joke illustrates the *post hoc* fallacy. Mac approaches Jack and asks, "Hey, why are you snapping your fingers?" Jack replies, "To keep the elephants away." Mac is incredulous: "What are you talking about? There aren't any elephants within a thousand miles of here." Jack smiles and keeps on snapping: "I know. Works pretty well, doesn't it?"

In real life, *post hoc* fallacies aren't always so easy to detect. For example, one critic of education pointed out that the increase in sexual promiscuity among adolescents began about the same time as prayer in public schools was prohibited by the courts. A causal link in this case may exist: Decreased emphasis on spirituality could contribute to promiscuity. But it would take evidence to establish a *definite* connection between the two phenomena.

APPEAL TO AUTHORITY (ARGUMENTUM AD VERECUNDIAM)   An *argumentum ad verecundiam* **fallacy** involves relying on the testimony of someone who is not an authority in the case being argued. Relying on experts is not a fallacy, of course. A movie star might be just the right person to offer advice on how to seem more glamorous, and a professional athlete could be the best person to comment on what it takes to succeed in organized sports. But an *ad verecundiam* fallacy occurs when the movie star promotes a political candidate or the athlete tells us why we should buy a certain kind of automobile. When considering endorsements and claims, it's smart to ask yourself whether the source is qualified to make them.

Ad verecundiam fallacies aren't restricted to advertising and politics: They can occur in everyday life. Salespeople with only a few weeks of experience advise customers on the purchase of expensive items such as computers or automobiles, and people who have been financially successful pontificate on other aspects of life as if their material wealth qualifies them in every area. When someone states or implies, "You can believe me on this," be sure to consider that person's credentials.

BANDWAGON APPEAL (ARGUMENTUM AD POPULUM)   An *argumentum ad populum* **fallacy** is based on the often dubious notion that, just because many people favor an idea, you should, too. Sometimes, of course, the mass appeal of an idea can be a sign of its merit. If most of your friends have enjoyed a film or a new book, there is probably a good chance that you will, too. But in other cases widespread acceptance of an idea is no guarantee of its validity. In the face of almost universal belief to the contrary, Galileo reasoned accurately that the earth is not the center of the universe, and he suffered for his convictions. The lesson here is simple to comprehend but often difficult to follow: When faced with an idea, don't just follow the crowd. Consider the facts carefully and make up your own mind.

CULTURAL IDIOM

follow the crowd: do what the majority does

SKILL BUILDER

Find the Fallacy

Test your ability to detect shaky reasoning by identifying which fallacy is exhibited in each of the following statements.

a. *ad hominem*   e. *post hoc*
b. *ad absurdum*   f. *ad verecundiam*
c. straw man   g. *ad populum*
d. either-or

_____ 1. Some companies claim to be in favor of protecting the environment, but you can't trust them. Businesses exist to make a profit, and the cost of saving the earth is just another expense to be cut.

_____ 2. How can you support abortion when some people use it as a form of after-the-fact birth control? They get one abortion after another instead of even thinking about sexual responsibility.

_____ 3. Rap music ought to be boycotted. After all, the number of assaults on police officers went up right after rap became popular.

_____ 4. Carpooling to cut down on the parking problem is a stupid idea. Look around—nobody carpools!

_____ 5. I know that staying in the sun can cause cancer, but if I start worrying about every environmental risk I'll have to stay inside a bomb shelter breathing filtered air, never drive a car or ride my bike, and I won't be able to eat anything.

_____ 6. The biblical account of creation is just another fairy tale. You can't seriously consider the arguments of those Bible-thumping, know-nothing fundamentalists, can you?

_____ 7. Take it from me, imported cars are much better than domestics. I used to buy only American, but the cars made here are all junk.

ADAPTING TO THE AUDIENCE

It is important to know as much as possible about your audience for a persuasive speech. For one thing, you should appeal to the values of your audience whenever possible, even if they are not *your* strongest values. This advice does not mean you should pretend to believe in something. According to our definition of *ethical persuasion,* pretense is against the rules. It does mean, however, that you have to stress those values that are felt most forcefully by the members of your audience.[15]

In addition, you should analyze your audience carefully to predict the type of response you will get. Sometimes you have to pick out one part of your audience—a **target audience,** the subgroup you must persuade to reach your goal—and aim your speech mostly at those members. Some of your audience members might be so opposed to what you are advocating that you have no hope of reaching them. Still others might already agree with you, so they do not need to be persuaded. A middle portion of your audience members might be undecided or uncommitted, and they would be the most productive target for your appeals.

Of course, you need not ignore that portion of your audience who does not fit your target. For example, if you were giving a speech against smoking, your target might be the smokers in your class. Your main purpose would be to get them to quit, but at the same time, you could convince the nonsmokers not to start and to use their influence to help their smoking friends quit.

All of the methods of audience analysis described in Chapter 11—surveys, observation, interviews, and research—are valuable in collecting information about your audience for a persuasive speech.

Establish Common Ground

It helps to stress as many similarities as possible between yourself and your audience members. This technique helps prove that you understand them: If not, why should they listen to you? Also, if you share a lot of common ground, it shows you agree on many things; therefore, it should be easy to settle one disagreement—the one related to the attitude or behavior you would like them to change.

The manager of public affairs for *Playboy* magazine gave a good demonstration of establishing common ground when he reminded a group of Southern Baptists that they shared some important values with him:

> I am sure we are all aware of the seeming incongruity of a representative of *Playboy* magazine speaking to an assemblage of representatives of the Southern Baptist convention. I was intrigued by the invitation when it came last fall, though I was not surprised. I am grateful for your genuine and warm hospitality, and I am flattered (although again not surprised) by the implication that I would have something to say that could have meaning to you people. Both *Playboy* and the Baptists have indeed been considering many of the same issues and ethical problems; and even if we have not arrived at the same conclusions, I am impressed and gratified by your openness and willingness to listen to our views.[16]

Organize According to the Expected Response

It is much easier to get an audience to agree with you if the members have already agreed with you on a previous point. Therefore, you should arrange your points in a persuasive speech so you develop a "yes" response. In effect, you get your audience into the habit of agreeing with you. For example, if you were giving a speech on the donation of body organs, you might begin by asking the audience members if they would like to be able to get a kidney if they needed one. Then you might ask them if they would like to have a major role in curbing tragic and needless dying. The presumed response to both questions is "yes." It is only when you have built a pattern of "yes" responses that you would ask the audience to sign organ donor cards.

An example of a speaker who was careful to organize material according to expected audience response was the late Robert Kennedy. Kennedy, when speaking on civil rights before a group of South Africans who believed in racial discrimination, arranged his ideas so that he spoke first on values that he and his audience shared—values like independence and freedom.[17]

If audience members are already basically in agreement with you, you can organize your material to reinforce their attitudes quickly and then spend most of your time convincing them to take a specific course of action. If, on the other hand, they are hostile to your ideas, you have to spend more time getting the first "yes" out of them.

Adapt to a Hostile Audience

One of the trickier problems in audience adaptation occurs when you face an audience hostile to you or your ideas. Hostile audiences are those who have a significant number of members who feel adversely about you, your topic, or the speech situation. Members of a hostile audience could range from unfriendly to violent. Two guidelines for handling this type of audience are (1) show that you understand their point of view and (2) if possible, use appropriate humor. A good example of a speaker who observed these guidelines was First Lady and literacy activist Barbara Bush when she was invited to speak at the commencement exercises at Wellesley College in 1990. After the invitation was announced, 150 graduating seniors at the prestigious women's college signed a petition in protest. They wrote, in part:

> We are outraged by this choice and feel it is important to make ourselves heard immediately. Wellesley teaches us that we will be rewarded on the basis of our own work, not on that of a spouse. To honor Barbara Bush as a commencement speaker is to honor a woman who has gained recognition through the achievements of her husband. . . .[18]

Mrs. Bush decided to honor her speaking obligation, knowing that these 150 students and others who shared their view would be in the audience of 5,000 people. Mrs. Bush diffused most of this hostility by presenting a speech that

Speech is power; speech is to persuade, to convert, to compel. It is to bring another out of his bad sense into your good sense.

Ralph Waldo Emerson

stressed that everyone should follow her personal dream and be tolerant of the dreams of others:

> For over fifty years, it was said that the winner of Wellesley's annual hoop race would be the first to get married. Now they say the winner will be the first to become a C.E.O. Both of these stereotypes show too little tolerance. . . . So I offer you today a new legend: the winner of the hoop race will be the first to realize her dream, not society's dream, her own personal dream.[19]

Hear the other side.

Saint Augustine

ETHICAL CHALLENGE

Adapting to a Hostile Audience

How far would you go in adapting to a hostile audience? What forms would that adaptation take? Discuss this question with your classmates, using a specific speech situation as an example. You can make up the speech situation or choose one of the following:

1. Speaking before a group of advertising executives about your firm belief that there should be heavy governmental penalties for false or deceptive advertising
2. Speaking before a group of Catholic bishops about your belief in reproductive choice
3. Speaking before a group of animal rights advocates about advances in interspecies (animal to human) organ transplants

BUILDING CREDIBILITY AS A SPEAKER

Credibility refers to the believability of a speaker. Credibility isn't an objective quality; rather, it is a perception in the minds of the audience. In a class such as the one you're taking now, students often wonder how they can build their credibility. After all, the members of the class tend to know each other well by the time the speech assignments roll around. This familiarity illustrates why it's important to earn a good reputation before you speak, through your class comments and the general attitude you've shown.

It is also possible for credibility to change during a speaking event. In fact, researchers speak in terms of initial credibility (what you have when you first get up to speak), derived credibility (what you acquire while speaking), and terminal credibility (what you have after you finish speaking). It is not uncommon for a student with low initial credibility to earn increased credibility while speaking and to finish with much higher terminal credibility.

Without credibility, you won't be able to convince your listeners that your ideas are worth accepting even if your material is outstanding. On the other hand, if you can develop a high degree of credibility in the eyes of your listeners, they will be likely to open up to ideas they wouldn't otherwise accept. Members of an audience form judgments about the credibility of a speaker based on their perception of many characteristics, the most important of which might be called the "Three Cs" of credibility: competence, character, and charisma.[20]

Competence

Competence refers to the speaker's expertise on the topic. Sometimes this competence can come from personal experience that will lead your audience to regard

---

CULTURAL IDIOM

roll around: occur, arrive

you as an authority on the topic you are discussing. If everyone in the audience knows you've earned big profits in the stock market, everyone will probably take your investment advice seriously. If you say that you lost twenty-five pounds from a diet-and-exercise program, everyone will almost certainly respect your opinions on weight loss.

The other way to be seen as competent is to be well prepared for speaking. A speech that is well researched, organized, and presented will greatly increase the audience's perception of the speaker's competence. Your personal credibility will therefore be enhanced by the credibility of your evidence, including the sources you cite, the examples you choose, the way you present statistics, the quality of your visual aids, and the precision of your language.

> *To be persuasive, we must be believable.*
> *To be believable, we must be credible.*
> *To be credible, we must be truthful.*
>
> Edward R. Murrow

Character

Competence is the first component of being believed by an audience. The second is being trusted, which is a matter of character. Character involves the audience's perception of at least two ingredients: honesty and impartiality. You should try to find ways to talk about yourself (without boasting, of course) that demonstrate your integrity. You might describe how much time you spent researching the subject or demonstrate your open-mindedness by telling your audience that you changed your mind after your investigation. For example, if you were giving a speech arguing against a proposed tax cut in your community, you might begin this way:

> *You might say I'm an expert on the municipal services of this town. As a lifelong resident, I owe a debt to its schools and recreation programs. I've been protected by its police and firefighters and served by its hospitals, roads, and sanitation crews.*
>
> *I'm also a taxpayer who's on a tight budget. When I first heard about the tax cut that's been proposed, I liked the idea. But then I did some in-depth investigation into the possible effects, not just to my tax bill but to the quality of life of our entire community. I looked into our municipal expenses and into the expenses of similar communities where tax cuts have been mandated by law.*

Charisma

Charisma is spoken about in the popular press as an almost indefinable, mystical quality. Even the dictionary defines it as "a special quality of leadership that captures the popular imagination and inspires unswerving allegiance and devotion." Luckily, communication scholars favor a more down-to-earth definition. For them, charisma is the audience's perception of two factors: the speaker's enthusiasm and likability. Whatever the definition, history and research have both shown us that audiences are more likely to be persuaded by a charismatic speaker than by a less charismatic one who delivers the same information.

Enthusiasm is sometimes called "dynamism" by communication scholars. Your enthusiasm will mostly be perceived from how you deliver your remarks, not from what you say. The nonverbal parts of your speech will show far better than your words that you believe in what you are saying. Is your voice animated and sincere? Do your gestures reflect your enthusiasm? Do your facial expression and eye contact show you care about your audience?

You can boost your likability by showing that you like and respect your audience. Insincere flattery will probably boomerang, but if you can find a way to give your listeners a genuine compliment, they'll be more receptive to your ideas.

Building your personal credibility through a recognition of the roles of competence, character, and charisma is an important component of your persuasive strategy. When combined with a careful consideration of audience adaptation, persuasive structure, and persuasive purpose, it will enable you to formulate the most effective strategy possible.

INVITATION TO INSIGHT

The Credibility of Persuaders

Identify someone who tries to persuade you via public speaking or mass communication. This person might be a politician, a teacher, a member of the clergy, a coach, a boss, or anyone else. Analyze this person's credibility in terms of the three dimensions discussed in the chapter. Which dimension is most important in terms of this person's effectiveness?

SAMPLE SPEECH

The following speech was given by Aaron Unseth, a student at the University of Wisconsin, Eau Claire. Aaron was coached by Karen Piercy and Kelly Jo Wright and won first place in the 2001 Interstate Oratorical Association Annual Contest, which was held at Solano Community College in Fairfield, California. Aaron came upon his topic while researching a different speech:

> I was looking up a reference for an informative speech in *The Scientific American* of June 2000 and while flipping through to the article I was searching for, came across a story on child warriors. I would have kept flipping the pages, but there was a startling picture of two African boys, about 10, with military rifles slung across their shoulders that caught my eye. After seeing that picture, I knew I had to read the rest of the article. After reading the complete story, I was really moved about the immensity and gravity of the problem of child warriors around the world. My main criteria for choosing the topic were that the topic was important to society, that it was solvable, and that it was something that I could believe strongly in and be passionate about. The topic of child warriors met all three of those criteria.[21]

His general purpose was to persuade, and his specific purpose could be worded as follows:

> After listening to my speech, my audience members will help me spread the word about the problem of child warriors.

This wording shows that Aaron understood the importance of adapting to his audience, as well as making the desired audience behavior as specific as possible. He explains it this way:

> I knew that I was probably not going to be giving this speech to a great number of foreigners whose countries were directly affected by this problem. That is why I immediately set forth in the speech to justify why child warriors are an important topic to all adult Americans. I also used a quotation from an American President to help cement the case that Americans were affected by the problem.

I also knew that when I delivered the speech in competition that practically every audience member would be either a college student or college professor. Therefore, I tailored the speech towards those involved in a campus community—especially my solutions. I discussed solutions that could be enacted on campus (such as hosting a forum on campus or writing an article in their school's newspaper), I gave them a website to visit that was geared toward college students, and I chose to encourage them to take the public service announcement I created to their college radio stations to play.[22]

Aaron's thesis statement might be worded as follows:

We should do what we can to stop the use of child warriors.

As this thesis statement makes clear, Aaron's speech is based on a proposition of policy. This speech is also a good example of how the "model" structure of a persuasive speech, as discussed in this chapter, can be adapted. His first two points deal with the problem in an effect-cause pattern. His final main point deals with solutions and includes his arguments for the desired audience behavior. Aaron's persuasive structure can be seen in the following outline. (Parenthetical numbers refer to paragraphs in the speech.)

Introduction
I. Attention-Getter (1–3)
II. Preview of main points (4)

Body
I. The problem is vast and international. (5–8)
   A. Children are being used as soldiers in 15 countries across 4 continents. (5)
   B. Children join military forces to find safety and acceptance, only to find themselves trapped. (6–7)
   C. Children are also forced to join. (7–8)
II. The problem is caused by children being in high demand as soldiers. (9–12)
   A. Children are inexpensive. (10)
   B. Children make good soldiers. (11)
   C. Children are not protected against this practice. (12)
III. The solution lies in raising awareness about this problem. (13–17)
   A. We should band together with other college students. (15–16)
   B. We should use the media to spread the message. (17)

Conclusion
I. Review of main points (18)
II. Final remarks (19)

As Aaron expands on this outline, he will prove his argument point by point.

CHILD WARRIORS: PAWNS IN INTERNATIONAL WARFARE
Aaron Unseth

1 "My commander gave me a gun, cocked it, and said, 'Kill him.' The prisoner was standing about five feet away. He was crying, begging, 'Don't shoot me, please don't shoot.' I had no feelings. I just fired."

The opening example grabs audience attention with emotional evidence.

2 These words are from an interview in the *World Press Review* of last December with veteran soldier Tejan Bockarie. A veteran soldier who happens to be 11 years old. Unfortunately, this young boy from Sierra Leone is not a rare ex-

The introduction previews Aaron's main argument.

ception. You see, Tejan is one of at least 300,000 children—both boys and girls—under the age of 18 who are actively participating in 36 ongoing or recently ended armed conflicts around the world. The *Scientific American* of June 2000 reports that many of these underage warriors are between the ages of 10 and 14, and there have even been documented cases of children as young as 7 years old entering armed combat. Although the atrocity of using child warriors is not being propagated in our own nation, all of us are being affected by these international evils.

3 Because the debate over how to stop these atrocities "shocks the conscience and shames humanity," as former President Clinton declared in a statement given on January 21, 2000, all of us must be concerned about this practice, which violates our natural and justifiable instinct to protect children.

4 Because we as adults—regardless of where we live—have an innate responsibility to protect children and therefore put an end to these atrocities, we must first take a look at the scope of this international issue. Second, we'll examine the conditions causing the prevalence of child warriors in our world today, and finally, we'll expound on some solutions that we as individuals can take to help bring about an end to this injustice.

5 Unfortunately, the problem of child warriors is not a localized problem. The previously cited *Scientific American* reports that minors are currently participating in or have participated recently in campaigns in at least 15 countries across 4 continents. One of these countries is Colombia, where the *World Press Review* of August 2000 claims that at least 6000 minors are fighting in various paramilitary and guerrilla groups.

6 One of these 6000 children is 15-year-old Adriana. Adriana joined a guerrilla group to escape the horrors of sexual abuse by one of her family members. She thought she could find safety and acceptance by joining an elite group of fighters, but all she has found are danger and fear. The rebels have filled her mind with stories about how the "enemy" Colombian army would torture her and eventually kill her if she was captured. After she joined, the rebels also made sure she realized the penalty for desertion: the firing squad. This rule applies to members of the group as young as 12 years old.

7 Although stories like Adriana's—of children joining military forces to find safety and acceptance, only to find themselves trapped in some of the most horrendous situations a human could ever imagine—are numerous, what's even more disturbing are stories of children forced against their will to join armed forces.

8 The *Christian Science Monitor* of March 30, 2000 reports that in Colombia, it is not uncommon for the various paramilitary groups to make sweeps of entire villages, kidnapping children as a kind of debt that families must pay. The previously cited *Scientific American* reports that over the last decade, in countries such as Mozambique, Sierra Leone, and Uganda, several thousand children per year have been kidnapped, physically abused and humiliated in order to train them for combat. In some countries, such as Cambodia, Liberia, and El Salvador, initiation for child soldiers has even included them being forced to kill captives and sometimes even to murder their own family members.

9 Unfortunately, the countries and children involved in the atrocity of child warriors are numerous. But before we can even begin to tackle this large problem, we first need to have an understanding of why child soldiers are in such high demand.

Margin notes:

Notice the careful but concise citation of the magazine article that was his primary inspiration for this speech.

(A blow up of the illustration from this article might have been an effective visual aid here.)

Statement of importance of topic to audience.

Preview of main points.

First main point: the effects of the problem.

First subpoint.

Second subpoint. Here a specific example is used for emotional effect.

Transition to third subpoint.

Again, evidence is carefully but concisely cited.

Specific details enhance the speaker's credibility by showing that he's done his homework.

Transition to second main point: the causes of the problem.

10 Child soldiers are a hot commodity for three main reasons. The first reason that these young warriors are in demand is that children—as awful as it is to say—are cheap. The *Times Educational Supplement* of March 31, 2000, reports that rebel agents in east Africa are paying as little as 500 U.S. dollars for every group of 150 Kenyan boys delivered to them. That's only $3.33 per child. Because of the cheap price for these young warriors, they are often considered to be more expendable than other resources.

Preview of subpoints.
First subpoint.

Repetition through paraphrasing drives home this point.

11 The second reason that military chiefs like child soldiers is that these "baby soldiers" are said to have no emotions and to obey orders without question—two attributes highly desired in any soldier. As one leader of the Khmer Rouge stated: "It usually takes time, but the younger ones become the most effective soldiers of all."

Second subpoint.

Quotation as evidence.

12 The third, and most unfortunate reason that military minors are used, is because they can be. There is currently no international retribution being brought against the cowardly leaders and groups that use children to fight their battles for them. In fact, the previously cited *Scientific American* states that child warriors have never been mentioned in any peace agreement or demobilization scheme ever. The United Nations has created an optional protocol that asks countries that sign it to oppose child warriors used by rebel forces within their own nation and to help end the practice in other countries. However, according to the Coalition to Stop the Use of Child Soldiers web page, last updated April 2001, there is absolutely no specific plan to enforce these requests. If countries were going to solve this problem on their own initiative, as this plan requires, it would have been done long ago. Signing a quick-fix feel-good treaty will not bring about change quickly enough. More specific international legislation must be implemented.

Third subpoint.

13 The problem of child warriors is vast, and no nation or United Nations seems to quite know how to address the issue in a meaningful way. So what can we in this room possibly do to quickly bring an end to something that is so contrary to some of our deepest instincts? Sadly, the answer is, "Not much." There simply is no magic course of action to be taken, no magic letters to send, no magic telephone numbers to call that will quickly erase these horrors for hundreds of thousands of children.

Transition to third main point: The solution.

14 However, what we *can* do right now is to help raise awareness on this little-known issue. Only then will any more than international lip service be paid to the problem. Just as world governments largely ignored the problems of land mines until Princess Diana forced the issue to the forefront, so world leaders today need to see a groundswell of informed citizens who strongly oppose the use of children in war. The February 1, 2000 *Wall Street Journal* was correct when it stated, "We need a global crusade against the use of children in war, not an occasional headline when the world seems dull."

Third main point.

Reasoning by analogy, comparing this issue to the land mine issue.

Quotation as testimony.

15 Each of us can be most effective by raising awareness in our own sphere of influence—which for most of us is our college campus. There are two ways we can help to raise awareness. First, by banding together with other college students and second, we need to use the media to spread the message.

First subpoint.

16 Here's what you can do to help. First, make sure to browse the USA4Action web site at www.USA, the numeral 4, action.org. At this site you can find a network of college and university students who are already banding together to stop the use of child soldiers, and you can even find information on lining up a speaker to come to your campus and host a forum on this issue.

A specific audience behavior is requested.

Visual aid: Web site address on chalkboard.

17 Second, there are some simple ways to raise awareness through the media. At the USA4Action web site, you can find information on publishing an article detailing the horrors of child warriors in your local or campus newspaper. Also, I have created a public service announcement for your local or campus radio station to play. I will have information on obtaining a copy of this announcement available after the round. But whatever you do, find a way to find a voice for these children who have none.

The requested behavior is made as simple as possible.

18 Today, we have examined the extent of child warriors in our world, considered the conditions causing the prevalence of child warriors, and finally, expounded on some solutions that we as individuals can take to help bring about an end to this injustice.

Review of main points.

19 It will be a long, tough process to raise enough awareness to cause world governments to take notice. However, as human beings who have a deep and innate sense to protect children, how can we do anything else but work to eradicate one of the last century's great tragedies and make sure this new century is rid of these horrors against children once and for all?

Final remarks to make the thesis memorable.

SUMMARY

Persuasion—the act of moving someone, through communication, toward a belief, attitude, or behavior—can be both worthwhile and ethical. Ethical persuasion requires that the speaker be sincere and honest and avoid such behaviors as poor preparation and plagiarism. It also requires that the persuasion be in the best interest of the audience.

Persuasion can be categorized according to the type of proposition (fact, value, or policy), outcome (convincing or actuating), or approach (direct or indirect). A persuasive strategy is put into effect through the use of several techniques. These include setting a specific, clear persuasive purpose, structuring the message carefully, using solid evidence (including emotional evidence), using careful reasoning, adapting to the audience, and building credibility as a speaker.

A typical structure for a speech to convince requires you to explain what the problem is and then propose a solution. For a speech to actuate, you also have to ask for a desired audience response. The basic three-pronged structure can be adapted to more elaborate persuasive plans, but the basic components will remain a part of any persuasive strategy. For each of these components, you need to analyze the arguments your audience will have against accepting what you say and then answer those arguments.

In adapting to your audience, you should establish common ground, organize your speech in such way that you can expect a "yes" response along each step of your persuasive plan, and take special care with a hostile audience. In building credibility, you should keep in mind the audience's perception of your competence, character, and charisma.

RESOURCES

Print

Cialdini, Robert B. *Influence: The Psychology of Persuasion.* Quill, 1994.

This inexpensive paperback looks at six human traits that can be triggered for effective persuasion. These traits are reciprocation, commitment and consistency, social proof, liking, authority, and scarcity.

Johannesen, Richard L. *Ethics in Human Communication,* 5th ed. Waveland Press, 2002

A comprehensive synthesis of key perspectives in communication ethics, this text relates the ethics of public speaking to interpersonal, small group, and mass communication.

Larson, Charles. *Persuasion: Reception and Responsibility*, 9th ed. Wadsworth, 2001.

Explains theories, research, and ethics of persuasion by looking at popular culture—politics, mass media, advertising, technology. Focuses on language and critical thinking from a consumer/receiver point of view. Contains current verbal and visual examples of persuasion in action.

Makau, Josina, and Ronald Arnett, eds. *Communication Ethics in an Age of Diversity*. University of Illinois Press, 1996.

Leading communication scholars blend research and practice in these considerations of how race, gender, ethnicity, affectional orientation, and technology affect communication ethics.

Pratkais, Anthony R., and Elliot Aronson. *Age of Propaganda: The Everyday Use and Abuse of Persuasion*. W.H. Freeman, 2001.

Looks at both the history of propaganda and modern research into its effectiveness. The focus is mass persuasion and manipulation in everything from advertising to political oratory.

Rottenberg, Annette T. *The Structure of Argument*, 3rd ed. Bedford/St. Martin's, 2000.

Explains how arguments are put together, stressing critical and analytical thinking. Interesting examples.

Rybacki, Donald, and Karyn Rybacki. *Advocacy and Opposition: An Introduction to Argumentation*, 4th ed. Allyn and Bacon, 2000.

Provides a practical approach to argumentation and critical thinking for the beginning student who needs to construct and present arguments on questions of fact, value, and policy—both orally and in writing. Offers a theoretical view of the nature of argument, a discussion of ethical principles of arguing as a form of communication, and a focus on how arguments are created.

Film

The Accused (1988). Rated R.

Jodie Foster as a rape victim and Kelly McGillis as the prosecutor who handles her case. Foster's character almost loses the case because of her low initial credibility, but in the end she wins over the jury with derived credibility based on her honesty and persistence. Based on a real-life case. Foster won an Oscar, although some critics felt the movie was marred by the graphic and unnecessary reenactment of the rape.

The Apostle (1997). Rated PG-13.

Robert Duvall directed and starred in this character study about a deeply flawed small-town southern minister who is forced to leave his home and find his way in the world mostly through the power of his oratory.

Boiler Room (2000). Rated R.

Giovanni Ribisi, Vin Diesel, and Ben Affleck are sales reps in a maverick brokerage house that provides a daily object lesson in unethical persuasion. These guys have no concerns about their customers' best interest and spin elaborate lies to get them to buy sure-loss investments.

Malcolm X (1996). Rated PG-13.

Directed by Spike Lee, starring Denzel Washington as the charismatic black leader who originally used his persuasive skills for criminal enterprises. Following a religious conversion in prison, however, he used those same skills first to preach the philosophy of Elijah Muhammad and eventually to create his own version of black Islam.

Network (1976). Rated R.

Writer Paddy Chayefsky's nightmare vision of television gone mad features the very persuasive ranting of an insane newscaster (Peter Finch), as well as a classic speech by a network executive (Ned Beatty) who manipulates the newscaster into ranting the way the executive wants him to.

Primary Colors (1998). Rated R.

John Travolta and Emma Thompson as thinly disguised Bill and Hillary Clinton during his 1992 run for president. Travolta plays Clinton as a naturally persuasive speaker with some serious ethical problems, not the least of which is that (1) he will make up supporting material for dramatic effect, if it's for a good cause and (2) he will lie to cover up his womanizing. In spite of these problems, Travolta's character truly wants to serve the people, which makes this another interesting study in speech ethics.

Wall Street (1987). Rated R.

Oliver Stone's morality tale about the demons of high finance features Michael Douglas (in an Oscar-winning performance) as a high roller who could convince anyone of anything. Pay careful attention to the classic speech "Greed Is Good."

INTERVIEWING

CONTENTS

KEY TERMS

closed questions
direct question
factual questions
hypothetical question
indirect questions
interviewing
leading question
neutral question
open questions
opinion questions
persuasive interview
primary question
probes
secondary questions
selection interview

- A potential employer greets a job applicant: "Let's begin by talking about exactly why you're interested in this opening."
- A student meets with a professor during office hours: "I wasn't very happy with my grade on the last paper. I'd like to see where the problem was so I can do better on the final."
- A customer replies to the salesperson's offer of help: "I've been thinking about buying a CD player, and I'd like to see what you have."
- One guest approaches another at a party: "I want to do some backpacking next summer, and I've heard that you've spent a lot of time in the mountains. I was hoping you could suggest some trails and tell me what to expect."

Mention the word *interview,* and most people will think of a news correspondent questioning some public figure or a job applicant facing a potential employer. Though these images are accurate, they tell only part of the story. We all take part in interviews. Some are work related, determining whether you will get the job you want and how you will do after you have landed the position. Others center on important personal relationships, focusing on everything from finding the perfect birthday gift to solving personal problems. Interviewing also comes into play when you want to learn important information from people with whom you aren't personally involved, perhaps about school, vacationing, how to fix a car, where to find a good restaurant, or what it was like to meet a famous person. Some interviews are formal, and others are casual. Sometimes you are the one who asks the questions; sometimes you are the person who responds. But in all these cases, the ability to get and give information is an important one.

THE NATURE OF INTERVIEWING

What is interviewing, and how does it differ from other kinds of communication? These are the questions the next few pages will answer.

TABLE 1   Types of Interviews

SELECTION
Hiring

Promotion

Placement

INFORMATION GATHERING
Investigating products and services

Research

Career exploration

On-the-job (caseworker, medical, and so on)

Personal interest

Survey (market, political, and so on)

Journalistic

PROBLEM AND EVALUATION
Appraisal/performance (employment and academic)

Counseling (personal and professional)

Complaint/grievance

PERSUASIVE
Selling products

Selling services

Quasi-commercial selling (charitable, political, religious, and so on)

Interviewing Defined

Most communication experts would agree with a definition of **interviewing** as a form of oral communication involving two parties, at least one of whom has a preconceived and serious purpose, and both of whom speak and listen from time to time. This description tells us several important characteristics of interviewing.

The phrase *oral communication* emphasizes the critical role of the spoken word. A verbal interview is far superior to a written one in several ways. A spoken exchange gives the interviewer a chance to follow up on ideas that emerge as important. Another advantage of face-to-face interviewing comes from the nonverbal messages that accompany a spoken exchange. Tone of voice, emphasis on certain words, disfluencies such as stammers and stutters, and the other paralinguistic clues we discussed in Chapter 5 add a new dimension to any interaction. For the same reason, in-person interviewing with its accompanying postures, gestures, facial expressions, and so on offers more information than does a written exchange or even one over the telephone.

The phrase *two parties* needs some explanation. There are certainly cases when one person is questioned by a panel of interviewers and other cases when two or more respondents face a single interviewer. But no matter how many participants are involved, in every case interviews are *bipolar:* One person or group is exploring issues with another person or group.

When we say that at least one party has a *preconceived and serious purpose,* we distinguish interviews from casual interactions in which the only goal is to pass the time. The fact that an interview has a serious purpose doesn't mean that enjoyment is against the rules—simply that the goal goes beyond sociability.

TABLE 2   Subjects of Interviews

JOB RELATED
Investigating career
Employment selection
Job performance
Employee grievance
Counseling
Sales
Other _____

SCHOOL
Investigating courses, major, and so on
Understanding coursework
Expressing dissatisfaction with course, program, and so on
Other _____

CONSUMER
Investigating products
Investigating services
Complaining about products or services
Other _____

FINANCIAL
Advice
Assistance (loans and so on)
Investigation (tax audit and so on)

OTHER
Personal problems
Information
Family
Recreation
Other _____

The words *both of whom speak and listen from time to time* make it clear that interviews are exchanges of messages. In most cases, these exchanges involve questions and answers. If either the speaker or the listener dominates the situation, then the interaction becomes a public-speaking situation even though there may be only one person in the audience.

How Interviewing Differs from Conversation

One way to understand the nature of interviewing is to see what it is not. There are several ways in which interviews differ from conversations.[1]

PURPOSE   We have already seen that conversations can occur without the participants having any serious preconceived purpose: Two people chat between floors in an elevator; friends swap jokes at a party; a boss and employees take a break around the coffee machine. An interview, on the other hand, always has a purpose.

STRUCTURE   Conversations can be aimless affairs in which neither person knows (or cares) when the exchange will end or exactly what topics will be covered. Any good interview, by contrast, has several distinct parts, which we'll discuss in a few pages.

CONTROL   Whereas conversations don't require any guidance from one of the parties, an interviewer should always be acting in ways that keep the exchange moving toward the preconceived purpose.

BALANCE   Though most conversations involve roughly the same amount of input from each person, authorities on interviewing suggest that participation ought to have a 70 to 30 percent ratio, with the interviewee doing most of the talking.

PLANNING THE INTERVIEW

A good interview begins long before you sit down to face the other person. There are several steps you can take to boost your chance for success.

The Interviewer's Role

Although the interviewee's responses will determine whether the interview is a success, drawing out that information is the interviewer's job. The following information will help you, as an interviewer, get the most out of the other person. As you read on, think about the personal interviewing situations you identified in the exercise you just completed. (If you haven't done the exercise, do so now before reading on.)

CLARIFY THE PURPOSE AND CONTENT AREAS   What do you want to accomplish in the interview? The answer to this question will often seem obvious. For example, in an information-gathering interview, you might want to find the best places to go on an upcoming vacation or to find out more about "the old days" from an older relative. But often a purpose that seems clear will prove too vague to get you what you want. For example, your questions about a vacation could result in a list of places too expensive for you or unrelated to your interests. In the same way, your request for information about the old days could bring on a string of stories about long-dead (and uninteresting) relatives when you are really interested in events rather than personalities.

The more clearly you can define the goal of your interview, the greater your chance for success will be. One way to set clear goals is to think about specific content areas you'll need to explore to achieve your general purpose. See how this process of focusing on a goal works in the following situations:

GENERAL GOAL	SPECIFIC CONTENT AREAS
Learn best place to go	Discover affordable, beautiful place that is different from home
Learn about old days	Learn how daily routines differed from now, how area looked before it was built up, what social relationships were like, what people did for recreation
Choose best roommate to fit with present occupants of apartment	Find person with similar or compatible study habits, dating life, ideas about neatness; also, person must be financially responsible
Get mechanic's opinion about whether I should fix up present car or get a newer one	Explore cost of repairing old one versus expense of fixing up newer one; determine life expectancy, performance, mileage of old versus new

DEVELOP TENTATIVE QUESTIONS   More than any other factor, the quality of the interviewer's questions and the way they are asked will determine the success or failure of an interview. Truly good questions rarely come spontaneously, even to the best of interviewers. After you define your goals and content objectives, the next step is to develop a list of questions. You need to think about several factors in planning questions:

1. *Relationship to Purpose* Your questions should cover all the content objectives you developed in the previous step. Furthermore, it's important to cover each area in the amount of depth that suits your needs. For example, in interviewing an instructor about how best to prepare for an exam, you should briefly cover the areas you feel confident about while spending enough time on tougher areas to be sure you're prepared. This suggestion may seem obvious, but many inexperienced interviewers find to their dismay that they have wasted most of their time discussing trivial areas and have failed to get their most important questions answered.

2. *Factual versus Opinion Questions* Some questions involve matters of fact: "What's the difference between an integrated amplifier and a preamplifier?" or "How many points will I need to earn an A for the course?" These can be called **factual questions.** In other cases, you'll want to ask **opinion questions:** "What occupations do you think will offer the best chance for advancement in the next few years?" or "How do you think I should go about apologizing?" When planning an interview, you should ask yourself whether you're more interested in facts or opinions and plan your questions accordingly.

In some cases, you can approach a question either factually or subjectively, often with quite different results. For example, imagine that you're interviewing two close friends, trying to resolve a conflict between them. Notice the difference between asking, "Where do you think the problem lies?" (a broad, subjective question that invites disagreement between the disputants) and "What are some of the things bothering each of you?" (a factual question that doesn't call for the parties to read each other's minds). Again, you need to think clearly about whether you're seeking facts or opinions.

3. *Open versus Closed Questions* You have almost certainly had the frustrating experience of trying to draw out an uncommunicative partner:

You: How've you been?
Other: Fine.
You: Up to anything new lately?
Other: Nope. Same old stuff.
You: You look good. Have you been getting a lot of exercise?
Other: Not really.

Although the respondent here could have certainly done better at holding up the other end of the conversation, much of the problem grew out of the type of questions being asked. All of them were closed: questions that could be answered in a word or two. Though some talkative subjects will freely amplify on a closed question, less outgoing ones will give you the briefest response possible. The best way to encourage interviewees to speak up is by asking **open questions,** which require the subject to answer in detail:

■ "If you had the chance to start your career over again, what things would you do differently?"
■ "What were some of the things you liked best about New York?"
■ "Start at the beginning and tell me just what happened."

Developing good open questions takes time and thought. Questions that are poorly worded or ones that are too broad or too narrow to get the information you seek can be a waste of time.[2] A good list of open-ended questions can help in several ways. First, you will almost certainly have enough lengthy responses to fill the allotted time, soothing a common fear of inexperienced interviewers. Your open questions, inviting comment as they do, will also make your subject feel more comfortable. Second, the way in which your subject chooses to answer your open questions will tell you more about him or her than you could probably learn by asking only more restrictive **closed questions,** which can be answered in a few words.

Closed questions aren't all bad: For one thing, they're easy for many subjects to answer, and you can ask many of them in a short period of time. Also, closed questions are appropriate for some subjects. For example, you wouldn't want long-winded replies to questions such as "What's the cost of part #1234?" or "What is your Social Security number?" As an interviewer, you should decide what type of information you need and then choose the combination of open and closed questions that will get it for you.

4. *Direct versus Indirect Questions* Most of the time the best way to get information is to ask a **direct question:**

■ "Have you had any experience in this kind of work?"
■ "How much were you planning to spend for a new coat?"
■ "What kinds of things are you looking for in an apartment and new roommates?"

There are times, however, when a subject won't be able to answer a direct question. At one time or another, most of us have been so confused that we've answered the question "What don't you understand?" by replying in exasperation, "Everything!" At other times, you've heard yourself or someone else sincerely answer the question "Do you understand?" in the affirmative, only to find out later that this wasn't true.

There are also times when a subject might be able to answer a question sincerely but isn't willing to do so. This sort of situation usually occurs when a candid answer would be embarrassing or risky. For instance, when interviewing a prospective roommate, you'd be naive to ask, "Do you always pay your share of the rent on time?" because a truly shifty person would probably answer "yes."

At times like these it's wise to seek information by using **indirect questions,** which do not directly request the information you are seeking. You could ask potential roommates whether their share of the rent money would be coming from current work (then check to see if they're employed) or from savings. In the same way, instead of asking, "Are you creative?" a prospective employer might present a job applicant with a typical or hypothetical situation, looking for an innovative solution.

5. *Primary versus Secondary Questions* Sometimes you will need to ask only an initial, **primary question** to get the fact or opinion you need in a given content area. But more often you will need to follow up your first question with others to give you all the information you need. These follow-ups are called **secondary questions.**

    Primary Question: "In your opinion, who are the best people for me to ask about careers in the computer field?"
    Secondary Questions: "How could I meet them?" "Do you think they'd be willing to help?" "How could each one help me?"

Sometimes an interviewer can follow up with secondary responses that aren't really questions. Simple **probes**—interjections, silences, and other brief remarks—can open up or direct an interviewee and uncover useful information.

Interviewer: What features are you looking for in a phone system?
Respondent: Flexibility is the most important thing for us.
Interviewer: Flexibility?
Respondent: Yes. We want to be able to add new phone lines in the future without having to replace the whole system.

Even silence or a well-timed nod of the head can trigger a good response:

Manager: How would you rate yourself in your first month on the job?
Employee: Oh, not bad.
Manager: Uh huh. *(pauses)*
Employee: I've learned a lot about the inventory system, but I'm having a hard time remembering the names of all our important customers.

It can be smart to develop a list of secondary questions to each primary one. In many cases, however, the best follow-ups will occur to you during the interview, depending on how the respondent answers your first question. As you ask and probe, be sure each secondary question you ask helps achieve your goal. It's easy to wind up taking an interesting digression, only to discover that you didn't get the information you were after.

6. *Neutral versus leading questions* A **neutral question** gives the interviewee a chance to respond without any influence from the interviewer. By contrast, a **leading question** is one in which the interviewer—either directly or indirectly—signals the desired answer.[3] A few examples illustrate the difference between these two types of questions:

NEUTRAL QUESTION

> Will you take the job if it's offered to you?
> What do you think about my idea?
> Do you think sexism is a problem at this college?

LEADING QUESTION

> You will take the job if it's offered, won't you?
> I've worked very hard on this idea, and I'm proud of it. What do you think?
> What examples of sexism have you seen at this college?

Although it seems hard to justify ever asking leading questions, there are a few situations where they serve a legitimate purpose. As Table 3 illustrates, they involve trying to either persuade or test the interviewee. Other than these situations, leading questions can distort the information you are seeking—hardly the outcome you're seeking in most interviews.

7. *Hypothetical Questions* A **hypothetical question** seeks a response by proposing a "what-if" situation. This type of question can be useful when you want to determine how an interviewee might think or act in the future. For example, if you aren't sure whether to enroll in a certain course due to the demands of your busy personal life, you might ask the professor, "How would you feel if I asked for a deadline extension for a major assignment?"

Hypothetical questions can also encourage interviewees to offer information they wouldn't volunteer if asked directly. For instance, a potential employer might get self-serving answers by asking job candidates about their strengths and weaknesses. But the hypothetical question "What would your last boss describe as your greatest strengths and weaknesses?" could reveal interesting information.

Hypothetical questions also are a good way to encourage respondents to think of a topic they haven't considered before. The coordinator of a crisis hot line invited prospective coaches to consider whether they were emotionally prepared to deal with a variety of difficult situations: child abuse, sexual violence, and so on. By thinking about the difficult parts of the job, the prospective coaches got a better sense of whether they were prepared to take on the responsibilities of being a coach.

ARRANGE THE SETTING Even the best questions won't help an interview that takes place in a bad setting. To avoid such problems, keep two considerations in mind as you arrange a meeting with your subject.

The first is *time*. Just as you should pick a time that is convenient for you, it's equally important for you to do the same for the interviewee. When arranging an appointment with your interviewee, be sure you've avoided predictably busy days or hours when the press of unfinished business may distract your interviewee. If you can, tactfully discover whether the interviewee is a morning or evening person—some people function especially well or poorly at certain times of the day. You should also make sure that the interviewee doesn't have appointments or other obligations that will overlap with your scheduled time.

CULTURAL IDIOM

a crisis hot line: an agency that provides telephone callers with immediate help for serious personal problems

TABLE 3 Uses of Question Types

OPEN AND CLOSED QUESTIONS
Use Open Questions To:
- Make the interviewee feel relaxed. (The question should be easy to answer and nonthreatening.)
- Discover the interviewee's opinions or feelings about the topic.
- Evaluate the communication skills of the interviewee.

Example
I see you're new in town. What brought you here? What do you think of the area?
What do you think about the way women are treated around here?
Suppose you had thirty seconds to persuade a prospective customer to buy this product. . . . What would you say?

Use Closed Questions To:
- Keep control over the interview.
- Gain specific information.
- Maximize information when time is scarce.
- Collect information from many respondents in a form that can be easily analyzed and reported.

Example
In a single word, would you describe the treatment you've received as fair or unfair?
When you left at 10:30 P.M., was there anyone remaining in the building?
I know you can only spare a few minutes. In your opinion, what are the two or three most important things I should do to improve my chances?
Which of the following best describes your level of education:
(a) high school graduate, (b) attended college, (c) received bachelor's degree?

PRIMARY AND SECONDARY QUESTIONS
Use Primary Questions To:
- Open up a new topic area.

Example
Now I'd like to change the topic and ask you to talk about what a vacation like this might cost.

Use Secondary Questions When:
- The previous answer was incomplete.
- You want to redirect the interviewee.
- You want to check a response that sounds inaccurate.

Example
You said the service you received was "fair." Can you explain what you meant?
When I asked about your education, I should have explained that I meant since high school. Can you tell me about your college coursework?
You said the cost was $19.95 per day. Does that include all charges, or is it a base rate?

NEUTRAL AND LEADING QUESTIONS
Use Neutral Questions When:
- You don't want to influence the interviewee's response.

Example
What kind of job do you think our company has been doing?

Use Leading Questions To:
- Guide the interviewee's thinking.
- Provoke or challenge an interviewee, in order to see whether she or he will accept your contentions.

Example
Have you thought about the cost of service after the warranty expires?
Are you sure that I could master everything about the software program in a half hour?

HYPOTHETICAL QUESTIONS
Use When:
- You want to know how the interviewee might react in the future.
- The interviewee might not volunteer the information directly.
- You want the interviewee to consider a new point of view.

Example
If I were your patient and I had an incurable disease, would you definitely tell me?
Suppose you knew that another employee—and I'm not mentioning any names—was turning in falsified time cards. What would you do?
What would you do if a student complained that a professor was failing students for expressing ideas that aren't "politically correct"?

The second is *place*. The most important consideration is to have a place that is free of distractions. A telephone constantly ringing or other people dropping by to ask questions or chat can throw you and your interviewee off track. If any of your questions call for confidential answers, the setting should be private. It's also important for the location to be convenient for both parties. Neither you nor the interviewee will do your best if you've had to struggle for a parking place or gotten lost trying to find the right place. Finally, your setting should be comfortable and attractive enough to put your interviewee at ease. Don't go overboard and choose too relaxed a setting: Too many beers or the pleasures of a beach might lead you or your interviewee to forget your main reason for meeting.

The Interviewee's Role

Because most of the responsibility for planning an interview rests with the interviewer, the interviewee has an easier time during the planning phase. There are, however, some things an interviewee can do in advance to make the interview a good one.

CLARIFY THE INTERVIEWER'S GOALS   It's important to know just what the interviewer is seeking from you. Sometimes the interviewer's goals are obvious. The insurance sales representative who wants "to see if you're paying too much for your present coverage" is trying to sell you a new policy, and a friend who wants to know how you've repaired an object or fixed a recipe is probably looking for your expertise.

At other times, the interviewer's goals aren't quite so obvious. Sometimes you know the general goal of the interview but need to understand the specific content areas more clearly. For example, suppose you are preparing for an employment interview. You know that the company is looking for the best applicant to fill the job. But just what kinds of qualities is it seeking? Are education and training the most important? Experience? Initiative? Knowing these criteria in advance will boost your chances of doing well in the interview.

There will be times when an interviewer has hidden goals, which you should do your best to discover. For instance, your boss's questions about your daily job routine might really be part of the managerial process of deciding whether to promote (or fire) you. An acquaintance's ostensible questions about factual information might really be aimed at building a friendship. This last example shows that not all hidden goals are malicious, but in any case you'll feel more comfortable and behave more effectively when you know what the interviewer wants from you.

CLARIFY YOUR OWN GOALS   Sometimes the interviewee's only role in an interview is to help the interviewer. But there are other times when you, as an interviewee, will have your own agenda. Although a sales representative might be trying to sell you an insurance policy, you could be interested in getting an education on the subject. When your boss conducts an interview assessing your performance, you might want to learn by observation how to do the same thing later in your career when you're a boss. Keep your own goals in mind when thinking about the upcoming interview.

DO YOUR HOMEWORK   There are many cases in which an interviewee can make an interview run quickly and well by preparing materials or answers in advance.

CULTURAL IDIOM

dropping by: making unannounced visits

go overboard: do so much as to be excessive

If you know that the interviewer will be seeking certain information, get it together before your meeting. Sometimes you'll need to bring facts and figures, as when you need to justify your claims during an income tax audit. At other times an interviewee should collect materials. For instance, an interviewee describing what college is like to a graduating high school senior might bring along class schedules, catalogs, textbooks, and exams.

CONDUCTING THE INTERVIEW

Preparation is an important step in interviewing. But after the interviewer and interviewee get together, there's more to do than simply ask and answer the prepared questions.

Stages of an Interview

An interview, like the speeches you read about in later Chapters 10–14, has three distinct stages.[4]

OPENING   This beginning stage serves two important functions. Most important, it establishes the tone of the relationship between interviewer and interviewee: formal or informal, relaxed or tense, serious or humorous. Just as the first stages of a date or party will generally shape what comes later, the success or failure of an interview is often determined in the first exchange.[5] Besides setting the tone, a good introduction will also give the interviewee a preview (or reminder) of the interviewer's goals and what subjects will be covered.

The usual format for an opening begins with some sort of greeting, which includes any introductions that are necessary. A period of informal conversation sometimes follows, in which the interviewer and interviewee talk about subjects of mutual interest not necessarily related to the interview topic. This period gives both people a chance to get settled and acquainted before getting down to business. This greeting stage may sound artificial—which it often is. But there's no need to discuss obviously trivial subjects or act phony here: The idea is to establish some common ground sincerely between interviewer and interviewee.

In the final stage of the opening, the interviewer should preview the goal of the interview, outline the topics of discussion, and brief the interviewee on plans for proceeding: "I appreciate your giving me the time. I expect my questions will take about forty-five minutes. I'd like to start by learning how you got started, then go on to talk about what you've learned during your career, and finish by asking for any suggestions you have that might help me in my career."

BODY   This middle stage of the interview is the longest. It's here that the interviewer asks the questions that were planned before the meeting.

Although the list of questions is important, it's sometimes a mistake to follow them precisely. Some areas will need more exploration, whereas others won't seem worth pursuing. The trick in the body of the interview is to focus on all the important content areas in a way that seems most comfortable to both interviewer and interviewee. (We'll have more to say about the roles of each party shortly.)

CLOSING   In many ways, the closing is similar to the opening. Instead of previewing, however, the closing is a time for reviewing what's occurred during the interview. This helps ensure that the interviewer has correctly understood any points that might be unclear and has gotten the general tone of the subject matter correctly.

The closing is also a time to establish the future of the relationship between interviewer and interviewee: to decide if any future meetings are necessary, possibly to set a date for them. Finally, it's usually good to conclude the interview with an exchange of sincere pleasantries. Table 4 is a checklist that summarizes the points to remember when planning, conducting, and evaluating an interview. This checklist can be used to rate both the interviewer and the interviewee in a variety of ways. It can be used before an interview by either party to prepare for a productive exchange. It can be used after an interview has been completed by either the interviewer, the interviewee, or a third party to evaluate the effectiveness of both communicators.

The Interviewer's Responsibilities

Most interviewers—at least those who haven't received training—are not especially effective at choosing the best candidate during employment interviews.[6] During the interview the interviewer has several responsibilities:

CONTROL AND FOCUS THE CONVERSATION

The interviewer's job is to ensure that each stage of the interview—opening, body, and closing—takes the right amount of time and that all important content areas are covered. It's easy to get off on a tangent and discover too late that the available time is up.

HELP THE INTERVIEWEE FEEL COMFORTABLE

In simplest terms, this includes making sure that the setting is physically comfortable. But it's just as important that the interviewer use the listening, relational, and nonverbal skills we discussed earlier in this book to help the interviewee feel at ease. For example, suppose the interviewee seems reluctant to share personal information in an im-

---

TABLE 4   Checklist for Evaluating Interviews

Opening
- Sincere, appropriate pleasantries are exchanged to help both parties feel comfortable.
- Proper tone is established (formal versus informal, serious versus casual).
- Interviewer previews subject and approach.

Body
- Interviewer's nonverbal behavior reflects interest and lack of threat to interviewee.
- Interviewer asks enough questions to cover all content areas established in advance.
- Interviewer uses probes to explore interviewee's responses (repetition, amplification, paraphrasing, silence).

- Interviewee gives clear, detailed answers.
- Interviewee keeps on subject.
- Interviewee corrects any misunderstandings of interviewer.
- Interviewee achieves own goals.

Closing
- Interviewer reviews results of interview.
- Future relationship between interviewer and interviewee is established.
- Sincere pleasantries are exchanged.

portant content area. The interviewer might then remember that self-disclosure is reciprocal and volunteer some information, such as the reasons for asking all the questions.

PROBE FOR IMPORTANT INFORMATION   Sometimes your first question in a certain area won't give you all the information you need. At times like this it's important to probe for the facts or beliefs you're seeking by asking secondary or follow-up questions. There are several types of probes you can use as an interviewer:

1. **Repeat.** Because of either evasiveness or fuzzy thinking, interviewees sometimes need to hear a question several times before giving a full answer.

Adult (*breaking up fight between two children*): Hey, what's this all about?
Child A: He's a jerk!
Adult: But what were you fighting about?
Child B: It's not my fault! She started it!
Adult: But what were you fighting about?
Child A: I did not start it. You started it!
Adult: I don't care who started it. I just want to find out what you're fighting about.

2. **Amplify.** When an answer is incomplete, you need to get more information.

Customer: I want to buy some running shoes.
Salesperson: What kind of running do you do?
Customer: Oh, mostly just for fun.
Salesperson: I mean how far do you run and on what kind of surfaces?
Customer: I mostly run on the track at the high school . . . a few miles.
Salesperson: When you say "a few miles," do you mean three or four each time you run or more?

3. **Paraphrase.** Paraphrasing, as discussed in Chapter 4, serves two purposes. First, it helps to clarify a vague answer. Second, it encourages the speaker to give more information about the topic.

A: I'm so fed up with that class that I'm ready to drop it. I just wanted to talk it over with you before I did.
B: So you're pretty sure that the right thing to do would be to quit because the class is giving you so much trouble.
A: Well, I'm just not sure. The semester is almost over, and if I did drop it now, I'd just have to repeat the class later.
B: So you're really not sure what to do, is that it?
A: Oh, I guess I ought to stick it out. It's just that I'm really tired. I'll sure be glad when the semester is over.

4. **Use Silence and Prods.** A bit of experimenting will show you the value of silence and prods—brief but encouraging phrases such as "Really?," "Uh-huh," "I see," and "Tell me more about it." Often an interviewee will be anxious to talk about a topic if simply given a sympathetic and interested ear.

The Interviewee's Responsibilities

There are several things you can do as an interviewee to make the interview a success.

GIVE CLEAR, DETAILED ANSWERS   Put yourself in the interviewer's shoes and be as specific and helpful as you hope others would be for you. Although the interviewer ought to draw you out skillfully, make that job easier by being helpful yourself.

KEEP ON THE SUBJECT   It is sometimes tempting to go overboard with your answers, sidetracking the discussion into areas that won't help the interviewer. It's often a good idea to ask the interviewer whether your answers are being helpful and then to adjust them accordingly.

CORRECT ANY MISUNDERSTANDINGS   Sometimes an interviewer will misinterpret your message. When this happens, be sure to correct the mistaken impression. Of course, one way to be certain that the message was received correctly is to invite the interviewer to paraphrase what he or she thinks you said. When an important issue is in question, any conscientious interviewer will be willing to do so.

COVER YOUR OWN AGENDA   As we pointed out earlier in this appendix, interviewees often have their own goals, which are sometimes different from those of the interviewer. It's important to keep these in mind during the interview so that you can satisfy your own needs in a way that is compatible with the interviewer's purpose.

THE SELECTION INTERVIEW

For many people the short time spent facing a potential employer is the most important interview of a lifetime. A **selection interview** may occur when you are being considered for employment, but it may also occur when you are being evaluated for promotion or reassignment. Being chosen for the position you seek depends on making a good impression on the person or people who can hire you, and your interviewing skills can make the difference between receiving a job offer and being an also-ran.

Employment Strategies

Most people naively believe that the person with the best qualifications will get a job. Although this principle might be fair and logical, research shows that selection interviews are not good predictors of career success. Interviewers are easily biased by their own mood and by irrelevant characteristics of applicants.[7] In reality, *the person who knows the most about getting hired* usually gets the desired position. Though job-getting skills are no substitute for qualifications after the actual work begins, they are necessary if you are going to be hired in the first place. The following guidelines will help your communication in interviews to give you the best chance of getting the job you deserve.

What is the best strategy for getting the job offer you want? The advice job seekers often get is certainly important: Scan sources of job announcements for positions, and prepare a thorough, professional résumé. But beyond these steps are other strategies that can often give you a critical boost over other applicants.

BACKGROUND RESEARCH   Your first step should be to explore the types of work and specific organizations for which you'd like to work. This step involves looking

CULTURAL IDIOM

put yourself in the interviewer's shoes: consider the situation from the point of view of the interviewer

an also-ran: an unsuccessful applicant

into all those areas that have interested you in the past. Through conducting library research, reading magazine and newspaper articles, taking classes, and simply fantasizing, find out as much as possible about jobs that might be interesting to you. The result of your research should be a list of organizations and of people who can tell you more about your chosen field and help you make contacts.

BACKGROUND INTERVIEWS   At this point arrange to meet the people on the list you have just developed. These meetings are not employment interviews in which you're specifically asking for the job. Rather, they serve three purposes:

1. To help you learn more about the fields and companies that interest you
2. To help you make contacts that might later lead to a job offer from your interviewer. It is hard to overstate the value of personal contacts in getting a job. According to a survey by the U.S. Department of Labor, over 70 percent of the respondents learned about the job they held through contacts with people in their personal networks: friends, coworkers, relatives, and teachers.[8]
3. To develop leads about other people you might contact for help in your job search

These background interviews are information gathering in nature, so it's wise to read the section of this appendix that deals with this subject before beginning this step.

Tips for the Interviewee

After you are in the interview itself, there are several important points to keep in mind.

MAKE A GOOD FIRST IMPRESSION   First impressions can make or break an interview. Research shows that many interviewers form their opinions about applicants within the first four minutes of conversation.[9] Physical attractiveness is a major influence on how applicants are rated, so it makes sense to do everything possible to look your best. The basic rules apply, no matter what the job or company: Be well groomed and neatly dressed. The proper style of clothing can vary from one type of job or organization to another. A good rule of thumb is to come dressed as you would for the first day of work. When in doubt it's best to dress formally and conservatively. It's unlikely that an employer will think less of you for being overdressed, but looking too casual can be taken as a sign that you don't take the job or the interview seriously.

COME PREPARED   Come to the interview with materials that will help the employer learn more about why you are ready, willing, and able to do the job. Bring extra copies of your résumé. Come prepared to take notes: You'll need something to write on and a pen or pencil. If appropriate, bring copies of your past work: reports you've helped prepare, performance reviews by former employers, drawings or designs you have created in work or school, letters of commendation, and so on. Besides demonstrating your qualifications, items like these demonstrate that you know how to sell yourself. Bring along the names, addresses, and phone numbers of any references you haven't listed in your résumé.

FOLLOW THE INTERVIEWER'S LEAD   Let the interviewer set the emotional tone of the session. If he or she is informal, you can loosen up and be yourself; but if he or she is formal and proper, you should act the same way. A great deal depends on the personal chemistry between interviewer and applicant, so try to match the interviewer's style without becoming phony. If the tone of the interview doesn't fit well with you, this may be a signal that you won't feel comfortable with this company. It may be smart to see whether the interviewer's approach represents the whole company, either by asking for a tour or speaking with other employees on your own. This desire to learn about the company shows that you are a thinking person who takes the job seriously, so your curiosity isn't likely to offend the interviewer.

> **CULTURAL IDIOM**
>
> **the personal chemistry:** how two people get along with or react to each other
>
> **pay off:** produce successful results

COME PREPARED TO ANSWER THE INTERVIEWER'S QUESTIONS   Whatever specific questions you might be asked, the employer is always asking, "How can you help us?" If you remember this fact, you can respond in ways that show how you can meet the employer's needs. Here's where your background research will pay off: If you've spent time learning about your potential employer, you'll be in a good position to talk about that company's concerns and how you can satisfy them. Knowing that you can, indeed, help the company can boost your self-confidence and lead you to feel most comfortable when facing a potential employer.[10]

1. **Tell me something about yourself.**
   This broad, opening question gives you a chance to describe what qualities you possess that can help the employer.

2. **What makes you think you're qualified to work for this company?**
   This question may sound like an attack, but it really is another way of asking, "How can you help us?" It gives you another chance to show how your skills and interests fit with the company's goals.

3. **What accomplishments have given you the most satisfaction?**
   The accomplishments you choose needn't be directly related to former employment, but they should demonstrate qualities that would help you be successful in the job for which you're interviewing. Your accomplishments might demonstrate creativity, perseverance in the face of obstacles, self-control, or dependability.

4. **Why do you want to work for us?**
   As the research cited in Table 5 shows, employers are impressed by candidates who have done their homework about the organization. This question offers you the chance to demonstrate your knowledge of the employer's organization and to show how your talents fit with its goals.

5. **What college subjects did you like most and least?**
   Whatever your answer, show how your preferences about schoolwork relate to the job for which you are applying. Sometimes the connection between college courses and a job is obvious. At other times, though, you can show how apparently unrelated subjects do illustrate your readiness for a job. For example, you might say, "I really enjoyed cultural anthropology courses because they showed me the importance of understanding different cultures. I think that those courses would help me a lot in relating to your overseas customers and suppliers."

6. **Where do you see yourself in five years?**
   This familiar question is really asking, "How ambitious are you?" "How well do your plans fit with this company's goals?" "How realistic are you?" If you have studied the industry and the company, your answer will reflect an understanding of the workplace realities and a sense of personal planning that should impress an employer.

TABLE 5   Communication Behaviors of Successful and Unsuccessful Interviewees

	Unsuccessful Interviewees	Successful Interviewees
Statements about the position	Had only vague ideas of what they wanted to do; changed "ideal job" up to six times during the interview.	Specific and consistent about the position they wanted; were able to tell why they wanted the position.
Use of company name	Rarely used the company name.	Referred to the company by name four times as often as unsuccessful interviewees.
Knowledge about company and position	Made it clear that they were using the interview to learn about the company and what it offered.	Made it clear that they had researched the company; referred to specific brochures, journals, or people who had given them information.
Level of interest, enthusiasm	Responded neutrally to interviewer's statements: "Okay," "I see." Indicated reservations about company or location.	Expressed approval of information provided by the interviewer nonverbally and verbally: "That's great!" Explicitly indicated desire to work for this particular company.
Picking up on interviewer's clues	Gave vague or negative answers even when a positive answer was clearly desired ("How are your math skills?").	Answered positively and confidently—and backed up the claim with a specific example of "problem solving" or "toughness."
Use of industry terms and technical jargon	Used almost no technical jargon.	Used technical jargon: "point of purchase display," "NCR charge," "two-column approach," "direct mail."
Use of specifics in answers	Gave short answers—ten words or fewer, sometimes only one word; did not elaborate. Gave general responses: "Fairly well."	Supported claims with specific personal experiences, comparisons, statistics, statements of teachers and employers.
Questions asked by interviewee	Asked a small number of general questions.	Asked specific questions based on knowledge of the industry and the company. Personalized questions: "What would my duties be?"
Control of time and topics	Interviewee talked 37 percent of the interview time, initiated 36 percent of the comments.	Interviewee talked 55 percent of the total time, initiated subjects 56 percent of the time.

Based on research reported by Lois J. Einhorn, "An Inner View of the Job Interview: An Investigation of Successful Communicative Behaviors," *Communication Education* 30 (July 1981): 217–228.

7. **What major problems have you faced, and how have you dealt with them?**

   The specific problems aren't as important as the way you responded to them. What (admirable) qualities did you demonstrate as you grappled with the problems you have chosen to describe? Perseverance? Calmness? Creativity? You may even choose to describe a problem you didn't handle well and to show what you learned from the experience that can help you in the future.

8. **What are your interests outside of work?**

   This can be a tricky question to answer. If you say you have no interests, you risk coming across as shallow. If you list too many interests, the interviewer may wonder if you have enough time and energy to focus on the job. Whatever answer you give, the best answer will show how your interests contribute to your effectiveness as an employee. At the very least, show that your interests won't detract from your dedication to the organization that will be writing you a paycheck.

9. **What are your greatest strengths and weaknesses?**

   The "strength" question offers another chance to sell yourself. As you choose an answer, identify qualities that apply to employment. "I'm a pretty good athlete" isn't a persuasive answer, *unless* you can show how your athletic skill is job related. For instance, you might talk about being a team player, having competitive drive, or having the ability to work hard and not quit in the face of adversity.

   Whatever answer you give to the "weakness" question, try to show how your awareness of your flaws makes you a desirable person to hire. There are four ways to respond to this question:[11]

- *Discuss a weakness that can also be viewed as a strength.*
  "When I'm involved in a big project I tend to work too hard, and I can wear myself out."
- *Discuss a weakness that is not related to the job at hand, and end your answer with a strength that is related to the job.*
  (for a job in sales) "I'm not very interested in accounting. I'd much rather work with people selling a product I believe in."
  (for a job in accounting) "I'm not great at sales and marketing. I'm at my best working with numbers and talking to people about them."
- *Discuss a weakness the interviewer already knows about from your résumé, application, or the interview.*
  "I don't have a lot of experience in multimedia design at this early stage of my career. But my experience in other kinds of computer programming and my internship in graphic arts have convinced me that I can learn quickly."
- *Discuss a weakness you have been working to remedy.*
  "I know being bilingual is important for this job. That's why I've enrolled in a Spanish course."

10. **What are your salary requirements?**

    Your answer should be based on a knowledge of the prevailing compensation rates in the industry and geography in question. Shooting too high can knock you out of consideration, whereas shooting too low can cost you dearly. Give your answer naming a salary range and backing up your numbers: "Based on the research I've done about compensation in this area, I'd expect to start somewhere between $25,000 and $28,500." As you give your answer, watch the interviewer. If he or she seems to respond favorably, you're in good shape.

CULTURAL IDIOM

shallow: superficial, having limited interests

If you notice signs of disapproval, follow up: ". . . depending, of course, on fringe benefits and how quickly I could expect to be promoted. However, salary isn't the most important criterion for me in choosing a job, and I won't necessarily accept the highest offer I get. I'm interested in going somewhere where I can get good experience and use my talents to make a real contribution."[12] It's important to know your "bottom line" for compensation in advance so you don't end up accepting an offer at a salary you can't afford to take.

BE PREPARED TO ASK QUESTIONS OF YOUR OWN   Near the end of almost every employment interview, you will be asked if you have any questions. It might seem as if you know all the important facts about the job, but a look at the following list suggests that a question or two can produce some useful information, as well as show the interviewer that you are also realistically assessing the fit between yourself and the organization:

1. Why is this position open now? How often has it been filled in the past five years? What have been the primary reasons for people leaving it in the past?
2. What is the biggest problem facing your staff now? How have past and current employees had trouble solving this problem?
3. What are the primary results you would like to see me produce?
4. How would you describe the management style I could expect from my supervisors?
5. Where could a person go who is successful in this position? Within what time frame?

KEEP YOUR ANSWERS BRIEF   It's easy to rattle on in an interview, either out of enthusiasm, a desire to show off your knowledge, or nervousness; but in most cases long answers are not a good idea. The interviewer probably has lots of ground to cover, and long-winded answers won't help this task. A good rule of thumb is to keep your responses under two minutes.

FOLLOW UP AFTER THE INTERVIEW   Follow up your interview with a note of thanks to the interviewer. Most candidates don't take this step, which will make your response especially impressive. Express your appreciation for the chance to get acquainted with the company, and let the interviewer know that the interview left you excited about the chance of becoming associated with it.

THE INFORMATION-GATHERING INTERVIEW

Although you might not label them as such, you can expect to take part in a great many information-gathering interviews during your career. Whenever you are seeking facts or opinions, you are conducting an informational interview: investigating an offer of goods or services, seeking advice about how to do your job better, collecting facts as part of an investigation, or conducting a survey of employees or customers. The following suggestions will help you do a good job.

Prepare for the Interview

Sometimes a period of research can pay dividends when the actual interview begins. Suppose, for instance, that you have decided to buy a new computer. Before you go shopping it would be smart to become knowledgeable about the various

> CULTURAL IDIOM
>
> **"bottom line":** minimum requirements
>
> **to rattle on:** to utter responses that are excessively wordy
>
> **ground to cover:** topics to discuss

types of systems available. What are the differences between the Windows and Macintosh operating systems, for example? Does your computer need to be compatible with computers already used by others? What software programs would best suit your needs, and what kind of system do they operate on? If you have answers to questions like these, your questions to dealers will be much more effective, and your chances of getting the best product will be greater.

CULTURAL IDIOM
warm up: stimulate the ability to converse
botched: done poorly

Choose the Right Interviewee

Sometimes the most obvious person for an information interview isn't the best person to answer your questions—or at least not the only person you should ask. Consider our example of shopping for a computer. It's certainly necessary to interview sales representatives from the companies you're considering, but you might also get useful information from people who use that kind of equipment. Likewise, if you are trying to figure out why employee turnover is too high, be sure to consider all the people who might be able to offer useful information: employees who have already left the company, those who haven't left, managers in your company, people in similar companies that don't suffer from the problem, and professors or other experts in the field. Sometimes knowing whom to ask is just as important as knowing what to ask.

Informational Interviewing Tips

In addition to the general suggestions on pages 458–459, follow these pointers when conducting informational interviews:

BE CURIOUS   Whereas ingredients like wording questions correctly and choosing the right environment are important, another essential ingredient for success in interviewing is honest curiosity, as shown by a willingness to follow a line of questioning until you're satisfied and to ask about points that interest you. Your sincere curiosity will often warm up an interviewee, who will be flattered by your interest. And an inquiring attitude will help you think of new and important questions during your interview, transforming it from what might be a sterile recitation of the questions you prepared in advance.

CHECK YOUR UNDERSTANDING   After reading Chapter 4, you know that much listening is inaccurate. Keeping this fact in mind, you will find it a good idea to check your understanding of important ideas with the interviewee. Sometimes the consequences of misunderstanding are fairly small: following a botched recipe (was it a tablespoon or a cup of vinegar?) or getting lost (were you supposed to turn right or left?). At other times, however, misunderstandings can be more serious. The fact that you thought that you understood an instructor's explanation won't change your low grade on a final exam, and the Internal Revenue Service won't forgive your tax penalties because you thought the local agent said something that turned out to be something else. Whenever there's a chance of misinterpretation, it's a good idea to use the active listening skills you learned earlier in this book.

USE THE BEST INTERVIEWING STRATEGY   In many cases, your best approach is to ask questions in the simplest, most straightforward manner. There are cases, however, when a more strategic approach will produce better results.

You have already read about the value of asking indirect questions when direct ones will be embarrassing or difficult to answer. Instead of asking a merchant, "Will your advice about products or service be any good?" you could ask about some product that you already know about.

There are also times when the personality of your interviewee calls for a strategic way of presenting yourself. For instance, if you are talking to someone whose self-image is one of being an authority or a wise person, you might take a naive approach: "Gee, I'm new at this, and you know so much." A little flattery never hurts. At other times you might want to act more like an interrogator, particularly when you think an interviewee is trying to treat you like a fool. For instance, you could show your knowledge and seriousness to a car mechanic by saying, "Why did you suggest a valve job without running a compression check?" (Here's one case where gathering background information on automotive repair could improve your interviewing and save you a healthy chunk of money.) In still other cases, a sympathetic or chummy approach can be helpful. Investing the time and money to chat over coffee or beers can shake loose information that an interviewee might be unwilling to share in a more formal setting.

CULTURAL IDIOM

chummy: friendly

shake loose: stimulate a free exchange of

OTHER INTERVIEW TYPES

The Persuasive Interview

A **persuasive interview** occurs when an interviewer's goal is to influence the thoughts or behaviors of an interviewee. The most recognizable type of persuasive interview involves the selling of some commercial product or service. But there are also noncommercial situations in which the interviewer aims at changing the attitudes or behavior of an interviewee. Candidates meet with prospective voters, either in person or via broadcast media; religious people try to influence the beliefs of others; and representatives of charitable organizations are constantly seeking more funds for their causes, often in interview settings.

There are several steps to follow for a successful persuasive interview:

DEFINE YOUR GOAL   Chapter 10 talked in detail about defining a public speaking goal. Some of the same principles apply here. You ought to have a clear idea of just what kind of change you're seeking in your interviewee. Your goal should be specifically worded, and it should be a realistically attainable one.

UNDERSTAND THE INTERVIEWEE   A persuasive approach that will convince one person will not convince others. Your best chance of success will come from understanding your interviewees—their interests, concerns, level of knowledge, and background.

USE PERSUASIVE STRATEGIES   Chapter 14 contains a list of persuasive strategies that is useful in both public speaking and interview settings. In addition to those strategies, you should consider these guidelines:[13]

1. Welcome the interviewee's questions and reactions. They tell you how the interviewee is responding to your approach, giving you a chance to adapt

and keep on target. It is important, however, for you to choose the time when the other person voices his or her concerns. You should keep control of the interview to avoid complicating the discussion.

2. Show that you understand the interviewee's position. The fact that you understand will leave the other person feeling more positive about you, diminishing the "hard-sell" image.

3. Keep your approach clear and simply stated. Bring up only one subject at a time, and organize your presentation logically. See Chapter 11 for more suggestions in this area.

THE PERFORMANCE APPRAISAL INTERVIEW   Performance appraisals are a fixture in most organizations after the number of employees grows beyond a handful. Their purpose is to acknowledge good performance, identify any areas where problems exist, resolve problems, improve productivity, and help develop the employee's talents.

At its best, the appraisal process is a valuable tool for helping employees feel better about work and for helping the organization. But in practice things often work out differently. More often than not, appraisal interviews result in lower productivity and greater apathy among employees.[14]

Performance appraisals have the greatest chance of success when the interviewer takes a supportive, constructive approach. This means acknowledging good work as well as pointing out problem areas. It is also helpful to set specific goals for improvement to aim for during the next evaluation period. The information in Chapter 3 on behavioral goals applies here. The interviewer needs to follow the descriptive approach described in Chapter 6, instead of using an excess of evaluative "you" language. Finally, it is essential for the interviewer to be a good listener who sincerely tries to understand the respondent's point of view. The surest way to get most employees to change is to involve them in the review process. Top-down, "I talk, you listen" approaches rarely work.[15]

As an interviewee, you can do plenty to make performance appraisals more successful, even with a superior who doesn't follow the advice in the preceding paragraph. Remember that criticism of your work in one area doesn't mean you are no good as a person, or even in other areas in which you interact with the interviewer. Approach the interview with a sincere desire to do better. View the interview as a chance to start improving your performance. This attitude will impress the interviewer and will help you grow.

When faced with vague descriptions of your behavior ("You're doing well" or "You're not keeping up"), ask the interviewer for specific examples. The goal here isn't to be argumentative, but rather to understand exactly what the interviewer is talking about. Finally, do your best to avoid acting defensively by counterattacking or withdrawing. Though reactions like these are understandable, they probably won't make you feel any better and are likely to lower your stature in the interviewer's eyes.

The Counseling Interview

Few people are professional counselors or therapists, but at one time or another we're all faced with the chance to help solve another person's problem: love, career, family, money—the list of problems is a long one.

There are two approaches to counseling others with problems—directive and nondirective. The directive approach includes a good deal of question asking, analysis, and advice. There are definitely situations in which this approach is the best one, most often when the counselor has greater knowledge than the interviewee. For example, a friend might approach you for advice on how to get help from some consumer protection agency. If you know the right procedure, you surely would share this information and suggest how your friend ought to proceed.

There are many other cases when a directive approach isn't the best one. Suppose your problem-ridden friend asks for advice about whether or not to get married. Even the best advice can be ignored or rejected at times like this. There is another risk in giving advice: If your friend follows your suggestions and things don't work out, you are the one who's likely to be held responsible.

The most important decision in counseling interviews, then, is whether to use a directive or nondirective approach. Be sure to base your decision on knowledge of the person seeking help and on the nature of the problem. In any case, it's essential to know just how much help and guidance one can give as a friend and when it's dangerous to begin playing counselor without the necessary training. It's better to say, "I don't know what to tell you" than to give bad advice to a person in need.

The Survey Interview

Surveys are a type of information gathering in which the responses of a sample of a population are collected to disclose information about the larger population. Surveys are used in government, business, and education. Interviews are a valuable way of surveying, because they provide greater respondent cooperation, depth of response, and flexibility than other means of gathering data, such as questionnaires.

In order to be effective, survey interviews must collect data from a representative sample of the population in question. A classic example of poor sampling occurred in the 1936 presidential election, when a popular magazine, *Literary Digest,* interpreted the results of over two million survey responses to predict that Alfred Landon would beat Franklin D. Roosevelt by a landslide. Hindsight showed that the incorrect prediction arose from the fact that the respondents were chosen from telephone directories and automobile registration lists. During the Great Depression, only upper- and middle-class people fell into these categories. Thus, the survey failed to give adequate representation to the millions of less affluent people who were to vote for Roosevelt.

Most survey interviews are highly structured, with respondents all being asked identical questions in identical order. This sort of structure ensures that all respondents are, in fact, being approached in the same way. Survey interviewers are trained to standardize their approach, even to the extent of repeating the same nonverbal behaviors from one situation to the next. For example, a smile in one interview might encourage responses that would differ from those elicited by a more restrained approach.

> **CULTURAL IDIOM**
>
> **by a landslide:** by an overwhelming majority

SUMMARY

Interviewing is a special kind of conversation, being more purposeful, structured, controlled, and one sided than other types of two-party interaction. There are many types of interviews—information gathering, selection, problem and evaluation, and persuasive. Each of these types contains several subcategories, which are listed in Table 1.

A successful interview begins with a planning phase before the parties meet. During that time, the interviewer should define the goal of the session, develop tentative questions, and arrange the setting. The questions should be closely related to the purpose of the interview. Thought should also be given to whether questions will be factual or opinion seeking, open or closed, and direct or indirect. When necessary, primary questions should be followed up by secondary questions. In the preparation stage, the interviewee should clarify the interviewer's goals as much as possible and do whatever planning will help the session run smoothly.

Interviews consist of three stages—opening, body, and closing. During the session, the interviewer should control and focus the conversation, help the subject feel comfortable, and probe for important information. The interviewee's role includes giving clear, detailed answers, keeping on the subject, and correcting any misunderstandings. In addition, interviewees should be sure to accomplish their own goals.

Though the steps outlined early in this appendix are useful in all contexts, specific types of interviews have their own requirements. Selection and information-gathering interviews were discussed in some detail; and persuasive, appraisal, counseling, and survey interviews were briefly described.

APPENDIX II

MEDIATED COMMUNICATION

CONTENTS

KEY TERMS

agenda setting
bullet theory
cultivation theory
cultural studies
cumulative effects theory
desensitization
diffusion of innovations theory
flow theories
gatekeepers
gender analysis
individual differences theory
mass communication
media
mediated communication
mediated interpersonal communication
medium
multistep flow
opinion leaders
political-economic analysis
social learning theory
two-step flow
uses and gratifications theory

Why study media? Most of us are inherently interested in the glamour and power of mass communication, and we enjoy learning about it in more depth. In addition, some want to explore the possibility of a media career. Others just want to be informed users of media. This appendix is designed to help you start analyzing how much mediated communication affects your life—sometimes for the better and sometimes for the worse. As informed users, we can also make better sense of the criticisms heard daily about the media. Those criticisms range from the nearsighted ("the media have no influence") to the exaggerated ("the media are in total control; people are manipulated to the point that they have no free will"). Obviously some middle ground is more likely the case, but where does that middle ground lie?

CULTURAL IDIOM

nearsighted:
understated

TYPES OF MEDIATED COMMUNICATION

When most people talk about "the media" they are referring to the channels of mass communication, such as television and radio. In fact, not all media are mass; so we need to clarify some key terms before going any further. For our purposes, mediated communication will consist of mass communication, mediated interpersonal communication, and communication through converged media that are both mass and interpersonal in nature.

Mass Communication

As Chapter 1 explained, **mass communication** consists of messages that are transmitted to large, usually widespread audiences via broadcast means (radio, television), print (newspapers, magazines, books), multimedia (CD-ROM, DVD, World Wide Web, etc.), and other forms of media such as recordings and movies.

As you read in Chapter 1, mass communication differs from the interpersonal, small group, and public varieties in several ways. A first important difference is that because mass messages are aimed at large audiences, there is *little or no interaction* between sender and receivers. For example, anyone who has attended a musical performance by a familiar artist recognizes how the contact between artist and audience creates an experience quite different from hearing the same material on a recording or watching it on television. That's one reason why people are willing to pay up to $100 for tickets to certain performances while complaining about the cost of a CD with the work of the same artist.

A second important difference between mass communication and face-to-face communication concerns *feedback*. In most forms of mass communication feedback is restricted. You might be able to write a letter to the editor of a newspaper and the author of your favorite Web site, but it could take a long time to receive a response. And if they didn't want to respond, they wouldn't feel the pressure to do so that they would in a face-to-face encounter.

A third important difference between mass and personal communication is that the messages sent via mass channels are usually developed, or at least financed by, *skilled professionals* working for *large organizations*. In this sense, mass communication is far less personal than the other types examined in this book. The producers of mass messages are often called **gatekeepers**, because they determine what messages will be delivered to media consumers, how those messages will be constructed, and when they will be delivered. Sponsors, editors, producers, reporters, and executives all have the power to influence mass messages.

Because of these and other unique characteristics, the study of mass communication raises special issues and deserves special treatment.

Mediated Interpersonal Communication

Although the nature of mass communication is reasonably easy to understand, the characteristics of communication media aren't quite so easy to grasp. The first step is to define two terms. A communication **medium** is any device that conveys a message. For example, radio is a communication medium, because technology is used to bridge the distance between the sender and receivers. **Mediated communication,** then, is any type of communication in which messages are conveyed via some medium, rather than face to face. Because **media** is the plural form of medium, we refer to the "print media" of books, magazines, and newspapers, the "broadcast media" of television and radio, the "entertainment media" of movies and recordings, and so on. In everyday use, the term *media* has taken on a second meaning, referring to the gatekeepers and decision makers in the mass media who determine what information will be conveyed to mass audiences and how it will be presented. For instance, in popular use we talk about how "the media" treat public figures such as politicians and celebrities and how "the media" address social issues like sex or violence.

Mediated communication, however, doesn't involve just mass messages. Today, much *interpersonal* communication is also mediated. We speak to friends over the telephone; we e-mail friends and business contacts across the nation and around the world; we might even send a videotape to far-off relatives. **Mediated interpersonal communication** does not involve face-to-face contact (in a teleconference, you're talking to only a facsimile of that other face), but it can possess all of the qualities of personal interaction described in Chapter 6.

There are differences between mediated interpersonal communication and mass communication. In the interpersonal variety, a message doesn't go out to a large audience, it isn't produced by professionals, and it allows a considerable amount of interaction and feedback.

Converging Communication Media

The distinction between mass and personal communication is much fuzzier today than in the past. In some respects, the World Wide Web resembles other forms of mass media. Both individuals and organizations can create Web sites that have the potential to reach thousands, or even millions of computer users. Also, many Web sites are created by professionals and are quite elaborate in nature, including the "portals" of major corporations such as Microsoft, AOL-Time Warner, and Yahoo!, which are part home page, part search engine, and part news service.

On the other hand, the Web also possesses characteristics of personal communication. Unlike most forms of mass communication, the Internet is a truly democratic medium: Anyone can set up a Web site and "broadcast" his or her opinions. Also, Web sites often invite visitors to submit queries and offer feedback via e-mail—just like a more personal medium.

Newsgroups offer another example of how the Internet blends mass and personal communication. These groups are organized by and for people with a specific interest. There are literally thousands of such groups, which address an astonishing range of topics, from antique cash registers to Lithuanian literature to hip-hop music. After joining a newsgroup, members can post their own messages and read the messages of others. An e-group or listserv with a large number of members certainly has some qualities of mass communication, but it also has much of the feel of more personal interaction.

THEORIES OF MEDIA EFFECTS

The media—whether mass, interpersonal, or convergent—are powerful forces in society. Interestingly enough, the average person will say that society is certainly affected by the media but that he or she, personally, is not. Still, most people remain extremely interested in media effects and equally confused about them. Do violent television and film cause violence in society? Does Internet use make us depressed? Do print media contribute to the moral decline in society? The best answer to these and most other media effects questions is, "It depends." Several researchers have pointed out that this answer is not as ambiguous as it might sound:

> The answer "it depends" should not be met with despair and a throwing up of the hands, however. The answer "it depends" does not mean that we do not know what is going on. In contrast to what we knew 40 or 50 years ago, we now have some more definite ideas of what "it" depends on.[1]

A quick look at some key theories will help explain the effects that media have both on societies and the people who compose those societies. Although these theories were all originally posed as theories of mass communication, they have been increasingly applied to interpersonal and converging media in recent research.[2]

Flow Theories

Some of the earliest theories of media effects, **flow theories,** dealt mainly with the way effects traveled, or "flowed," from the mass media to their audiences.

BULLET THEORY   Early mass media researchers, those who worked between the first and the second world wars, developed an approach later termed **bullet theory,** which implied that the media had direct, powerful effects—like a bullet.[3] According to bullet theory, people who watched violent movies, for example, would become violent, and those who read "immoral" comic books would become immoral. The problem was that these direct, powerful effects were very difficult to prove, especially over the long term. Eventually, a different theoretical model evolved.

TWO-STEP FLOW THEORY   Research during and after World War II suggested that media effects occurred in a **two-step flow,** meaning that media effects occurred mostly in interaction with interpersonal communication. Researchers characterized two-step flow like this: People would hear a message over the radio, perhaps a speech by a political candidate or a commercial message for a new type of laundry soap. Rather than immediately pledging their support for the candidate or buying the soap, they would discuss it with **opinion leaders**—people they knew whom they viewed as credible sources of information on a particular topic. If the opinion leaders were positive about the candidate or product, the people who heard the original message might become supporters of it.

MULTISTEP FLOW   The researchers who devised the two-step flow theory were moving in the correct direction—they just hadn't gone far enough. Today's researchers recognize a **multistep flow,** which implies that media effects are part of a complex interaction.[4] In that interaction, opinion leaders have opinion leaders, who in turn have their own opinion leaders. You might be your friend's opinion leader about what sort of computer to buy, for example, but that friend probably formed his or her own opinions from other people.

Besides demonstrating how theories become more sophisticated as they are explored over time, flow theories demonstrate the importance of interpersonal communication in the effects of mass communication. They show that the mass media don't operate on us in a vacuum: Rather, their effects are tempered by the way people react to them and communicate their reactions to one another. Also, even though the bullet theory is largely discredited today, we still have daily examples of some types of mediated messages having the direct, powerful effects that early researchers predicted. Many products become overnight successes through television advertising, without enough time passing to give interpersonal communication much time to operate. A new blockbuster movie, for example, can earn tens of millions of dollars in box office receipts in its first weekend, based purely on advertising and reviews that appeared in the mass media. But for the great majority of mediated messages, effects depend largely on how they interact with interpersonal communication. After the first weekend that a movie is in the theaters, its box office is determined largely by "word of mouth" communication.

Social Learning Theory

Flow theories aren't the only approach to studying media effects. **Social learning theory** is based on the assumption that people learn how to behave by observing others—often others portrayed in the mass media. The theory gained prominence from the experiments of Albert Bandura in the 1960s.[5] In Bandura's most famous studies, preschool children watched films in which an adult encountered Bobo, a three-foot-tall pop-up clown. One group of preschoolers saw a version in which the adult beat up Bobo and was then rewarded for being a "strong champion." Another group saw a version in which the adult assailant was scolded for being a bully and was spanked with a rolled-up magazine. After watching the films, the children themselves then had a chance to "play" with Bobo. Bandura discovered that the children who saw the adult model's aggression being rewarded treated the Bobo doll more violently than did those who saw the adult model punished.

The implications of social modeling are obvious. It's easy to imagine how a thirteen-year-old who has just seen one of the *Lethal Weapon* or *Terminator* movies might be inspired to lash out at one of his friends the first time a disagreement arises. However, the theory also suggests that viewing prosocial models can teach constructive behavior. The same thirteen-year-old, if he had just

CULTURAL IDIOM

operate ... in a vacuum: function as if there were no other individuals or influences

to lash out at: to react angrily

watched *Friends,* might be inspired to use one of those characters' nonviolent, communicative approaches to problem solving rather than using his fists.

Social learning theory makes sense, and the original laboratory studies produced impressive results. But in everyday life the theory doesn't hold up quite so well.[6] After all, behavior that is modeled from the media might not be successful in the real world. For example, thirteen-year-olds who try out their martial arts skills on the playground might be punched in the nose by tougher adversaries. The pain of that punch might do more in determining those children's attitude toward violence than all the television viewing they will ever do.

Besides the power of real-life rewards and punishments, all individuals are different, and that plays a role in determining how people are influenced by media. For example, boys seem to be more influenced by violent media than girls are, whereas girls seem to be more influenced by the "body image" of their media models—they often try to be as slim as fashion models, an influence that generally escapes boys. Observations such as these led to the development of the individual differences theory.

Individual Differences Theory

As its name suggests, **individual differences theory** looks at how media users with different characteristics are affected in different ways by the mass media.[7] Some types of users are more susceptible to some types of media messages than are others. For example, a viewer with a high level of education might be more susceptible to a message that includes logical appeals. Besides level of education, individual differences that help determine how the media affect individuals include age, sex, region, intellectual level, socioeconomic class, level of violence in the home, and a wealth of other characteristics that were referred to as demographics in Chapter 10.

There are also more subtle psychological characteristics that distinguish media users. **Diffusion of innovations theory,** for example, explains that there are five types of people who have different levels of willingness to accept new ideas from the media.[8] These types also predict who will be first to use and become competent in new media.[9]

1. Innovators—These are venturesome people who are eager to try new ideas. They tend to be extroverts and politically liberal. They are the first to try out and become competent in new media like the World Wide Web and new computer applications.
2. Early adopters—Less venturesome than innovators, these people still make a relatively quick but informed choice. This tendency makes them important opinion leaders within their social groups.
3. Early majority—These people make careful, deliberate choices after frequent interaction with their peers and with their opinion leaders. They seldom act as opinion leaders themselves, however.
4. Late majority—These people tend to be skeptical and accept innovations less often. When they do adopt an innovation, they often do so out of economic necessity or increasing peer pressure.
5. Laggards—These people tend to be conservative, traditional, and the most resistant to any type of change. Their point of reference tends to be the past,

and they tend to be socially isolated. Today, these are the people who are mystified by the World Wide Web and might not even own a computer.

Cultivation Theory

According to **cultivation theory,** the media shape how we view the world.[10] Cultivation theory therefore works hand in hand with the facets of perception discussed in Chapter 2. This theory helps explain how a person's perceptions of the world are shaped and sometimes distorted by media.

Cultivation theory was advanced by George Gerbner and his associates at the University of Pennsylvania. This theory predicts that media will teach a common worldview, common roles, and common values. Over time, media "cultivates" a particular view of the world within users. For example, Gerbner's research found that heavy television viewers had a markedly different view of reality than did light viewers. Heavy viewers overestimated their chances of being involved in some type of violence, overestimated the percentage of Americans who have jobs in law enforcement, and found people, in general, to be less trustworthy than did light viewers.

Cultivation theory suggests that the primary effect of television, therefore, is to give heavy viewers a perception that the world is less safe and trustworthy, and more violent, than it really is. Gerbner's findings help explain why society seems to be becoming more tolerant of violence, a process that is known as **desensitization**. Researchers suspect that desensitization has a profound effect on interpersonal communication by making people less caring about the feelings and reactions of other people.

Agenda-Setting Theory

Another important approach to media effects was posited by two researchers, Donald Shaw and Maxwell McCombs, in the 1970s. Studying the way political campaigns were covered in the media, Shaw and McCombs found the main effect of media to be **agenda setting:** The media tell people not what to think, but rather what to think *about*. In other words, the amount of attention given to an issue in the media affects the level of importance assigned to that issue by consumers of mass media. Shaw and McCombs explained their findings as follows:

> Perhaps more than any other aspect of our environment, the political arena—all those issues and persons about whom we hold opinions and knowledge—is secondhand reality. Especially in national politics, we have little personal or direct contact. Our knowledge comes primarily from the mass media. For the most part, we know only those aspects of national politics considered newsworthy enough for transmission through the mass media.[11]

The main thrust of agenda-setting theory is that the media might not change your point of view about a particular issue, but they will change your perception of what's important.[12] Although Shaw and McCombs concentrated on political issues and the news media, the idea of agenda setting can easily be expanded to all issues and to all the media. For many people, if a social problem is not on television, in the newspapers, or on a Web site, it may not exist—at least in the minds of media users. For today's researchers, the important point to make about agenda setting is that after issues get attention from the public they have a tendency to influence government policy.[13]

Cumulative Effects Theory

Not everyone agrees with the agenda-setting theory. Some point out that the media do, indeed, tell us *what* to think, but they do it slowly, over time. This has come to be called **cumulative effects theory**, which states that media messages are driven home through redundancy and have profound effects over time.

According to this theory, the media latch on to certain themes and messages and build them up over time. There is a bandwagon effect as various newspapers, magazines, television and radio networks, and other media take up the themes. Because the media are omnipresent and such a common part of most people's lives, the media view becomes the widely accepted one within society.

According to this theory, a "spiral of silence" occurs when individuals with divergent views become reluctant to challenge the consensus offered by the media. People form unconscious perceptions of the distribution of public opinion. If they feel that they are in the minority, they are less likely to express their opinions. People who hold majority viewpoints tend to speak out confidently. For example, in times of war some people might become concerned about civilian casualties inflicted on the other side, but they don't speak out about this issue if they feel that most people disagree.

CULTURAL STUDIES APPROACHES

All the theories we have discussed so far stress the media's effect on individuals; but these same media appear to have significant long-term effects on entire cultures. The role that the media play in changing us as a society is difficult to measure. Rather than rely on statistical analyses and controlled experiments, **cultural studies** rely on "close reading" of messages from the mass media. Media critics examine the meanings of these messages, both surface and hidden, and then use logic and insight to come to certain conclusions about the effect those messages might have on their audiences. Cultural studies examine the role that media play in reflecting and shaping society's most widely and deeply held values in areas such as class, race, and gender.

Cultural theorists explore the invisible ideology, or belief system, that is embodied in media programming and use. They ask questions about the nature of masculinity, femininity, individualism, capitalist economics, and education, among other topics. Does a television program affirm a particular lifestyle as natural? Does a movie advance a preferred way of viewing the world? Does an ad campaign make a statement about social roles? If a particular worldview is being advanced, who is being served by this view? In short, what *meanings* does this mediated message present? Some cultural theorists abandon the goal of impartiality that characterizes the social sciences, criticizing some social practices and suggesting what they believe are better alternatives.

There is a wide range of cultural approaches, including (but not limited to) political-economic analysis and gender analysis.

Gender Analysis

Gender analysis examines how the media construct and perpetuate gender roles. Our culture's assumptions about how males and females should think, act, and speak are continually presented in our mediated messages. The potential influence of these gender portrayals on our sense of who we are and who we should be is the gender critic's realm of consideration. These studies are concerned with the ways that gender stereotypes are confirmed and contradicted and with the way media legitimate the language we use to describe gender and sex roles.

For example, Caren Deming and Mercilee Jenkins examined the gender roles that were advanced in the classic television sitcom *Cheers*.[14] Their method was a close reading of just one episode of the series, which happened to be the premiere. These researchers found that the show contradicted certain gender stereotypes through dialogue and visual imagery. Their study showed how the character Diane Chambers (played by Shelley Long) used humor as a tool of resistance and succeeded in asserting her individuality in the face of attempted domination. Deming and Jenkins demonstrated how a sitcom like *Cheers* can refute the rules that subjugate people and therefore have a liberating effect on its audience.

Several other gender theorists have looked at the effects of media. Cheris Kramarae proposes a "Muted Group" theory, which she explains as follows:

> The language of a particular culture does not serve all its speakers equally, for not all speakers contribute in an equal fashion to its formulation. Women (and members of other subordinate groups) are not as free or as able as men are to say what they wish, when and where they wish, because the words and the norms for their use have been formulated by the dominant group, men.[15]

Kramarae examines the media to see how language is "man-made" and how it "aids in defining, depreciating and excluding women."[16] Another feminist scholar, Carol Gilligan, presents a theory that men and women speak in different ethical voices.[17] Her "Different Voice" theory posits that men define moral maturity in terms of justice, whereas women define it in terms of caring. Researchers who follow Gilligan's thinking look at mediated messages to see how those messages encourage these different voices.[18]

Political-Economic Analysis

Much of today's political-economic analysis is based on the work of the philosopher Karl Marx (1818–1883). To Marxist media critics, Marx was a humanist whose argument was essentially a moral one. Marx believed that the economic system of a nation (in the case of the United States, capitalism) influences the values of the entire culture (in our case, encouraging materialism, which is the craving for money and what it can buy). **Political-economic analysis** is a critical technique that focuses on the media's role in this influence. It looks at how media become the means by which the haves of society gain the willing support of the have-nots to maintain the status quo.

Marxist critics believe that media help create a "false consciousness" within the working/consuming class that enables the wealthy, who benefit most from the social arrangements in a capitalist country, to manipulate and exploit the working/consuming class. One expert on this type of analysis summed it up in this way:

The most frequent theme in Marxist cultural criticism is the way the prevalent mode of production and ideology of the ruling class in any society dominate every phase of culture, and at present, the way capitalist production and ideology dominate American culture, along with that of the rest of the world that American business and culture have colonized.[19]

According to Marxist theory, workers in a capitalist society are kept in a constant state of dissatisfaction. To escape from this dissatisfaction (which they do not recognize as a condition, but the symptoms of which they feel), they engage in various forms of consumption, all of which cost money, so that they are forced to work increasingly hard to escape from the effects of their work. The dissatisfaction generated by a capitalist system is therefore functional, because it encourages the impulsive consumption that enables capitalism to thrive.

In a Marxist analysis, the mass media perform the function of distracting people from the realities of their society (poverty, racism, sexism, and so on) by "clouding their minds" with the ideas that powerful commercial forces want them to have, ideas like "I feel better when I buy something." By doing so, the media perform the function of maintaining the dominance of those already in positions of power.

Marxist theory has led to many interesting insights about mass media. For example, two researchers looking at Muzak, the type of instrumental music we hear in elevators and department stores, pointed out that this type of "functional music," which was originally used in factories to control and regulate work, is now used in stores and malls to control and regulate consumption.[20]

One of the best-known political-economic critics is Stuart Hall. Hall's work attacks "the unknowing acquiescence to the dominant ideology of the culture"[21] and urges resistance to that acquiescence. He seeks to raise consciousness about the media's role. Hall does not claim a widespread establishment conspiracy to oppress the poor and the powerless; he accepts this oppression as a seldom-recognized part of the economic system of both the country and the media. In recent years, his work has sought to bring together various forms of cultural criticism, saying that gender, semiotics, and political economy are all part of the "representations" of the media, and that those representations are what produce the media's overall effect.[22]

HOW WE USE MEDIA

All of the theories we have explored so far have characterized media consumers as passive, being acted upon by various types of media, their content, and their creators. But instead of analyzing media effects, another group of scholars has developed **uses and gratifications theory:** the study of ways in which media consumers actively choose and use media to meet their own needs.[23] Uses and gratifications research doesn't regard consumers as passive creatures whose behaviors are controlled by the media industry. Instead, it regards them as decision makers who choose—sometimes consciously and sometimes less consciously—which media to use and how to use them.

Media Consumers as Active Agents

The difference between a uses and gratifications perspective and the other perspectives we have explored so far becomes clearer when we look at how each might explore a media phenomenon such as professional wrestling. Millions of people are devoted followers of this pseudosport. Media effects researchers concerned with violent behavior might study the relationship between watching wrestling and being aggressive. For example, they might study whether wrestling fans get in more fistfights or whether they are more likely to act violently toward their spouses or children. If researchers did discover a link between watching wrestling and perpetrating physical violence, they would try to sort out the causal relationship between the two phenomena: whether for example wrestling causes people to behave more violently, or whether people with violent personalities are attracted to wrestling. Cultural studies scholars might analyze how wrestling perpetuates violence in culture, how the wrestlers and their fans are exploited by corporate interests, or how the sport contributes to a male-dominated society.

By contrast, a uses and gratifications approach to wrestling would not concern itself with the effects of viewing the sport. Instead it would explore what motivates fans to watch wrestling in the first place and what needs wrestling fans are satisfying by watching matches. A uses and gratifications approach underscores the active role of media consumers. It regards them as decision makers rather than puppets who are driven by unconscious forces or manipulated by media producers.

Unless you are a wrestling fan yourself, you might wonder why anyone *would* watch more than a few minutes of this obviously phony "sport." A uses and gratifications perspective offers some answers to this question. Depending on their interests and attitudes, viewers might tune in to a match for a number of reasons. One reason might be *excitement:* Gullible viewers might find excitement, wondering which valiant combatant will win the contest. A second reason might be *amusement:* More sophisticated fans might watch the over-the-top costumes, names, and mock aggression as a joke instead of a genuine athletic event. A third might be *catharsis:* Watching muscular brutes slam one another to the canvas might be a better way of letting off steam than yelling at the family or kicking the cat. A fourth reason might be *escape:* For some fans, a wrestling match might be just the way to forget about the problems and challenges of the real world.

If you smugly dismissed the thought of watching phony wrestling for *any* reason, consider the fact that you probably consume other types of media for the same sorts of motives. Do you read novels? Surf the Web? Listen to sporting events on the radio or watch them on TV? Tune in to dramas or comedies? Watch films? If so, a little reflection will probably reveal that your reasons for consuming each type of media probably resemble some of the ones in the preceding list about wrestling.

Our brief look at professional wrestling should help you see the difference between the questions asked by media effects researchers and those asked by scholars who study uses and gratifications. The first group asks, "What effects do media have *on* people?" whereas the latter group asks "What do people do *with* media?"

Types of Uses and Gratifications

The uses and gratifications approach suggests several ways in which people use media:

SURVEILLANCE   Scholars use the word *surveillance* to describe our need to keep informed about the world. In earlier, simpler times surveillance needs could be met mostly through person-to-person contacts. But at the dawn of the twenty-first century, our fates are linked to people and forces that we cannot understand through direct personal experience. In this postindustrial world, mass media are an important tool in helping us understand what is going on around the world, as well as closer to home.

Newspapers, radio, television, and the Internet provide a variety of ways to meet surveillance needs: What are the latest developments in the Mideast? What will the weather be like tomorrow? How is the stock market doing? Does daylight saving time begin *this* weekend or next? What's the cost of an airline ticket to Mexico City? Media provide quick and easy ways to answer questions like these.

DIVERSION   Sometimes we use the media to *escape* from the pressures of the real world. Escape sometimes comes from *relaxation*. You might, for example, tune in to your favorite FM radio station seeking music that helps you calm down after a stressful day. At other times, we seek diversion by *excitement*, such as watching a suspenseful movie. Diversion also comes in the form of *amusement*, in forms such as television sitcoms.

IDLE TIME   On some occasions, we use media to fill idle time. Consider the way you browse through magazines while waiting in the doctor's or dentist's reception room: You probably aren't looking for news or diversion as much as filling the minutes until your appointment. Likewise, think about the times you use the radio in your car or at home to fill in time while you are commuting or doing chores.

SOCIAL INTEGRATION   In an age of Internet chat rooms and online romances, it shouldn't be a surprise that computer-mediated communication has the potential to bring people closer together. On the other hand, it might seem paradoxical or even downright wrong to suggest that watching the tube, listening to a CD, or reading a book promotes involvement with others. Uses and gratifications scholars suggest that the media can help us connect with others in several ways.

At the most obvious level, shared knowledge in media programming and publications provides what researchers have called an immediate "agenda for talk." Swapping news and opinions about current events can provide a useful way to develop relationships with strangers and to maintain them with acquaintances.

The ability of the media to provide conversational currency helps explain why movies are such a common first date. They provide an activity where two people who barely know one another can spend several hours together while minimizing the risk of running out of things to say. The first part of the date is spent in close proximity without the need to speak at all, and the second part of the date can be spent discussing the film.

Some research even indicates that television can be a tool for promoting family unity. For example, research suggests that TV viewing can bring family members together when they otherwise would have been apart.[24] Furthermore, television has the potential to reduce family conflict by providing a shared enjoyable experience ("Hey, we're all laughing together!"), by diverting attention from contentious issues, and by providing a neutral topic to discuss.

IDENTITY MANAGEMENT   Along with all their other functions, the media provide a tool for creating and managing our identities.[25] From an early age, children get a sense of who they are from the media. "Am I rich or poor, attractive or ugly, intelligent or not, similar to or different from others?" Questions like these are answered in part by consuming media that give children—and adults, too—a sense of how they fit into the world.

What we do with media also helps us define how we want to be seen by others. People often choose media to support a public identity. Imagine, for instance, how the choice of music you play when hosting company at home makes a statement about who you are. Perhaps you can recall how, as a young adolescent, you deliberately chose music, films, or television programming that would set you apart from your family and make the statement: "I'm my own person."

DIFFERENT THEORIES, DIFFERENT OBSERVATIONS

Different theories of media effects would explain changes in society in different ways. The way language is used, for example, has certainly changed in recent years. Terms that were once considered obscene have become commonplace. Most experts believe that the media have played a role in this transformation. Years ago, the media encouraged the use of only "proper" language. For many years, the word *pregnant* was not uttered on television, even by Lucille Ball, whose character on *I Love Lucy* was obviously in that condition. Today, words that used to be considered bad enough to get a kid kicked out of school—words such as *sucks, bites,* and *blows,* used as verbs of criticism—can be heard routinely on Saturday morning cartoons.

How would the various theories explain the media's role in the way language has changed?

- The findings from social learning research would suggest that these changes in language usage occurred as people imitated the language they heard in movies and on TV.
- Individual differences theory would suggest that the same language will affect different people in different ways and that perhaps only segments of the population who are predisposed to it would adopt the new language use.
- Cultivation theory would suggest that media language use slowly changes individuals' worldviews, perhaps convincing them that society in general has become more coarse and that such language use is therefore acceptable.
- Agenda-setting theory would suggest that news coverage of matters, such as President Clinton's affair with Monica Lewinsky, Lorena Bobbitt's attack on her husband in which his penis was severed, and the trial of sportscaster Marv Albert on sexual assault charges, made sexual affairs part of the national agenda and therefore grist for everyday conversation.
- Cumulative effects theory would suggest that language changed when those who believed in using only socially acceptable terms became silent in the face of the continual mediated use of obscenity.
- Uses and gratifications theory would suggest that people have attended to media messages with this type of language because it performs some function for them, perhaps freeing them from societal restraints that they found repressive.
- Gender analysts might see these changes in language use as a way for women to seek equality with men or perhaps as a form of oppression against women.
- Political-economic analysts might regard the new language use as a successful assault on the repressive status quo.

All of these theories provide insights into media effects. They might be different insights, but taken as a whole and mixed with logic, they begin to help make sense out of the question of how media affect behavior.

This variety of theories also demonstrates that it is usually ill advised to make blanket criticisms and blanket statements about media uses and effects. It is an oversimplification to say, "Watching television is a waste of time." It is not completely accurate to say, "Violent television causes violence in society" or "Skinny models encourage girls to be anorexic" without qualifying that statement with some form of "it depends." Each of the theories discussed in these pages (as well as many others) has revealed that the uses and the effects of media are many and complex. The study of mediated communication is in its relative infancy, and a growing body of scholarship will help us understand more about how we use the media and how it shapes us.

SUMMARY

Mediated communication is the sharing of messages that are conveyed through any type of device or medium. Mediated communication includes mass communication (such as television programming), mediated interpersonal communication (such as talking on the telephone), and communication through converged media that are both mass and interpersonal in nature (such as the various ways we use the Internet). Mass communication is transmitted to large audiences, usually by professional gatekeepers, and results in a lack of interaction and restricted feedback between source and receivers. Mediated interpersonal communication occurs through a medium, but the source and receiver still treat one another as unique individuals. In mediated interpersonal communication, feedback—at least the nonverbal kind—is still restricted. Converged media are combinations of mass and interpersonal media, such as we find on the World Wide Web, where either individuals or professionals can create Web sites, where portals can reach millions but friends can communicate one on one through e-mail, chat rooms, and instant messages.

A variety of theories helps explain the complex nature of media effects. An early theory now known as the bullet theory predicted that the media would have direct, powerful effects. Although this is true in some cases, in far more cases the media's effects are caused by a combination of mediated and interpersonal messages, especially interpersonal messages from those we consider to be opinion leaders on a particular topic. This explanation of media effects has come to be known as the multistep flow theory. Another influential theory, social learning theory, is based on the assumption that people learn how to behave by observing others, particularly role models in the media. The predictions that derive from social learning theory make the most sense when you also consider individual differences theory, which states that media users with different characteristics are affected in different ways by the mass media. A similar theory, diffusion of innovations, explains that different types of people will have different levels of willingness to accept new ideas from the media.

One of the more sophisticated theories of media effects, cultivation theory, states that the media shape our view of the world more than our behavior. Heavy viewers of television, for example, tend to see the world as less trustworthy than do light viewers. This theory helps explain why some people seem to be becoming more tolerant of violence within society, a process that is known as desensitization. Agenda setting is a theoretical approach that suggests that the main effect of the media is that they tell us what to think *about;* therefore, the amount of attention given to an issue in the press affects the level of importance assigned to that issue by consumers of mass media. Cumulative effects theory suggests that media have profound effects over time.

Cultural studies approaches look at the long-term effects of media on society in general. They are critical studies that rely on a close analysis of mediated messages rather than statistical studies.

There is a wide range of cultural studies, including (but not limited to) gender analysis and political-economic analysis. Gender analysis examines how the media construct and perpetuate gender roles. It looks at the way males and females think, act, and speak in mediated messages. Political-economic analysis provides studies into how media affect the relationship between the economic system of a nation and the values that the nation holds. It looks at how media become the means by which the haves of society gain the willing support of the have-nots to maintain the status quo.

Uses and gratifications theory looks at the ways media consumers actively choose and use media to meet their own needs. These needs include surveillance (keeping informed about the world), diversion (escaping from the pressures of the real world), passing time (filling idle moments), social integration (bringing people closer together), and identity management (creating and managing our sense of who we are).

All of these theories, when taken together, provide a broad understanding of the many different effects of media on the lives of individuals and on society overall. An understanding of these theories explains why the most accurate answer to the question of media effects is often "It depends."

NOTES

Chapter 1

1. For a discussion of the unique character of human communication, see J. Liska, "Bee Dances, Bird Songs, Monkey Calls, and Cetacean Sonar: Is Speech Unique?" in *Western Journal of Communication* 57 (1993): 1–26.

2. For an in-depth look at this topic, see S. B. Cunningham, "Intrapersonal Communication: A Review and Critique," in *Communication Yearbook* 15, S. Deetz, ed. (Newbury Park, CA: Sage, 1992).

3. L. Wheeler and J. Nelek, "Sex Differences in Social Participation." *Journal of Personality and Social Psychology* 35 (1977): 742–754.

4. J. John, "The Distribution of Free-Forming Small Group Size." *American Sociological Review* 18 (1953): 569–570.

5. Rudolph Verderber, Ann Elder, and Ernest Weiler, "A Study of Communication Time Usage among College Students" (Unpublished study, University of Cincinnati, 1976).

6. For a summary of the link between social support and health, see S. Duck, "Staying Healthy . . . with a Little Help from Our Friends?" in *Human Relationships,* 2nd ed. (Newbury Park, CA: Sage, 1992).

7. S. Cohen, W. J. Doyle, D. P. Skoner, B. S. Rabin, and J. M. Gwaltney, "Social Ties and Susceptibility to the Common Cold." *Journal of the American Medical Association* 277 (1997): 1940–1944.

8. Three articles in *Journal of the American Medical Association* 267 (January 22/29, 1992) focus on the link between psychosocial influences and coronary heart disease: R. B. Case, A. J. Moss, N. Case, M. McDermott, and S. Eberly, "Living Alone after Myocardial Infarction" (pp. 515–519); R. B. Williams, J. C. Barefoot, R. M. Calif, T. L. Haney, W. B. Saunders, D. B. Pryon, M. A. Hlatky, I. C. Siegler, and D. B. Mark, "Prognostic Importance of Social and Economic Resources among Medically Treated Patients with Angiographically Documented Coronary Artery Disease" (pp. 520–524); and R. Ruberman, "Psychosocial Influences on Mortality of Patients with Coronary Heart Disease" (pp. 559–560).

9. J. Stewart, *Bridges, Not Walls: A Book about Interpersonal Communication,* 8th ed. (New York: McGraw-Hill, 2001), p. 10.

10. R. Shattuck, *The Forbidden Experiment: The Story of the Wild Boy of Aveyron* (New York: Farrar, Straus & Giroux, 1980), p. 37.

11. For a fascinating account of Genie's story, see R. Rymer, *Genie: An Abused Child's Flight from Silence* (New York: HarperCollins, 1993). Linguist Susan Curtiss provides a more specialized account of the case in her book *Genie: A Psycholinguistic Study of a Modern-Day "Wild Child"* (San Diego: Academic Press, 1977).

12. A. M. Nicotera, "Where Have We Been, Where Are We, and Where Do We Go?" in *Interpersonal Communication in Friend and Mate Relationships,* A. M. Nicotera and associates, eds. (Albany: SUNY Press, 1993).

13. R. B. Rubin, E. M. Perse, and C. A. Barbato, "Conceptualization and Measurement of Interpersonal Communication Motives." *Human Communication Research* 14 (1988): 602–628.

14. W. Goldschmidt, *The Human Career: The Self in the Symbolic World* (Cambridge, MA: Basil Blackman, 1990).

15. *Job Outlook '99, National Association of Colleges and Employers.* Report on Internet at http://www.jobweb.org/pubs/joboutlook/report.htm (December 1998).

16. M. S. Peterson, "Personnel Interviewers' Perceptions of the Importance and Adequacy of Applicants' Communication Skills." *Communication Education* 46 (1997): 287–291.

17. M. W. Martin and C. M. Anderson, "Roommate Similarity: Are Roommates Who Are Similar in Their Communication Traits More Satisfied?" *Communication Research Reports* 12 (1995): 46–52.

18. E. Kirchler, "Marital Happiness and Interaction in Everyday Surroundings: A Time-Sample Diary Approach for Couples." *Journal of Social and Personal Relationships* 5 (1988): 375–382.

19. R. B. Rubin and E. E. Graham, "Communication Correlates of College Success: An Exploratory Investigation." *Communication Education* 37 (1988): 14–27.

20. R. L. Duran and L. Kelly, "The Influence of Communicative Competence on Perceived Task, Social and Physical Attraction." *Communication Quarterly* 36 (1988): 41–49.

21. C. E. Shannon and W. Weaver, *The Mathematical Theory of Communication* (Urbana, IL: University of Illinois Press, 1949).

22. K. R. Colbert, "The Effects of Debate Participation on Argumentativeness and Verbal Aggression." *Communication Education* 42 (1993): 206–214.

23. For a detailed discussion of the implications of channel selection, see P. B. O'Sullivan, "What You Don't Know Won't Hurt ME: Impression Management Functions of Communication Channels in Relationships." *Communication Monographs* 70 (2000). See also R. B. Adler and J. M. Elmhorst, *Communicating at Work: Principles and Practices for Business and the Professions,* 7th ed. (New York: McGraw-Hill, 2002).

24. S. A. Westmyer, R. I. DiCioccio, and R. B. Rubin, "Appropriateness and Effectiveness of Communication Channels in Competent Interpersonal Communication." *Journal of Communication* 12 (1998): 27–48.

25. See, for example, M. Dunne and S. H. Ng, "Simultaneous Speech in Small Group Conversation: All-Together-Now and One-at-a-Time?" *Journal of Language and Social Psychology* 13 (1994): 45–71.

26. The issue of intentionality has been a matter of debate by communication theorists. For a sample of the arguments on both sides, see J. O. Greene, ed., *Message Production: Advances in Communication Theory* (New York: Erlbaum, 1997); M. T. Motley, "On Whether One Can(not) Communicate: An Examination via Traditional Communication Postulates," *Western Journal of Speech Communication* 54 (1990) 1–20; J. B. Bavelas, "Behaving and Communicating: A Reply to Motley," *Western Journal of Speech Communication* 54 (1990): 593–602; and J. Stewart, "A Postmodern Look at Traditional Communication Postulates," *Western Journal of Speech Communication* 55 (1991): 354–379.

27. S. Duck, "Relationships as Unfinished Business: Out of the Frying Pan and into the 1990s." *Journal of Social and Personal Relationships* 7 (1990): 5. For another example of the contextual base of communication, see V. Manusov, "Reacting to Changes in Nonverbal Behaviors: Relational Satisfaction and Adaptation Patterns in Romantic Dyads," *Human Communication Research* 21 (1995): 456–477.

28. K. J. Gergen, *The Saturated Self: Dilemmas of Identity in Contemporary Life* (New York: Basic Books, 1991), p. 158.

29. T. P. Mottet and V. P. Richmond, "Student Nonverbal Communication and Its Influence on Teachers and Teaching: A Review of Literature," in J. L. Chesebro and J. C. McCroskey, eds., *Communication for Teachers* (Needham Heights, MA: Allyn & Bacon, 2001).

30. M. Dainton and L. Stafford, "The Dark Side of 'Normal' Family Interaction," in B. H. Spitzberg and W. R. Cupach, eds., *The Dark Side of Interpersonal Communication* (Hillsdale, NJ: Erlbaum, 1993).

31. For a thorough review of this topic, see B. H. Spitzberg and W. R. Cupach, *Handbook of Interpersonal Competence Research* (New York: Springer-Verlag, 1989).

32. See J. M. Wiemann, J. Takai, H. Ota, and M. Wiemann, "A Relational Model of Communication Competence," in B. Kovacic, ed., *Emerging Theories of Human Communication* (Albany, NY: SUNY Press, 1997).

33. For a review of the research citing the importance of flexibility, see M. M. Martin and C. M. Anderson, "The Cognitive Flexibility Scale: Three Validity Studies." *Communication Reports* 11 (1998): 1–9.

34. See G. M. Chen and W. J. Sarosta, "Intercultural Communication Competence: A Synthesis," in B. R. Burleson and A. W. Kunkel, eds., *Communication Yearbook* 19 (Thousand Oaks, CA: Sage, 1996).

35. See, for example, M. S. Kim, H. C. Shin, and D. Cai, "Cultural Influences on the Preferred Forms of Requesting and Re-Requesting." *Communication Monographs* 65 (1998): 47–66.

36. M. J. Collier, "Communication Competence Problematics in Ethnic Relationships." *Communication Monographs* 63 (1996): 314–336.

37. For an example of the advantages of cultural flexibility, see L. Chen, "Verbal Adaptive Strategies in U.S. American Dyadic Interactions with U.S. American or East-Asian Partners." *Communication Monographs* 64 (1997): 302–323.

38. For a discussion of the trait versus state assessments of communication, see D. A. Infante, A. S. Rancer, and D. F. Womack, *Building Communication Theory*, 3rd ed. (Prospect Heights, IL: Waveland Press, 1996), pp. 159–160. For a specific discussion of trait versus state definitions of communication competence, see W. R. Cupach and B. H. Spitzberg, "Trait versus State: A Comparison of Dispositional and Situational Measures of Interpersonal Communication Competence." *Western Journal of Speech Communication* 47 (1983): 364–379.

39. B. R. Burleson and W. Samter, "A Social Skills Approach to Relationship Maintenance," in D. Canary and L. Stafford eds., *Communication and Relationship Maintenance* (San Diego: Academic Press, 1994), p. 12.

40. L. K. Guerrero, P. A. Andersen, P. F. Jorgensen, B. H. Spitzberg, and S. V. Eloy. "Coping with the Green-Eyed Monster: Conceptualizing and Measuring Communicative Responses to Romantic Jealousy." *Western Journal of Communication* 59 (1995): 270–304.

41. See B. J. O'Keefe, "The Logic of Message Design: Individual Differences in Reasoning about Communication." *Communication Monographs* 55 (1988): 80–103.

42. See, for example, A. D. Heisel, J. C. McCroskey, and V. P. Richmond, "Testing Theoretical Relationships and Non-Relationships of Genetically-Based Predictors: Getting Started with Communibiology," *Communication Research Reports* 16 (1999): 1–9; and J. C. McCroskey and K. J. Beatty, "The Communibiological Perspective: Implications for Communication in Instruction," *Communication Education* 49 (2000): 1–6.

43. S. L. Kline and B. L. Clinton, "Developments in Children's Persuasive Message Practices." *Communication Education* 47 (1998): 120–136.

44. M. A. de Turck and G. R. Miller, "Training Observers to Detect Deception: Effects of Self-Monitoring and Rehearsal." *Human Communication Research* 16 (1990): 603–620.

45. R. B. Rubin, E. E. Graham, and J. T. Mignerey, "A Longitudinal Study of College Students' Communication Competence." *Communication Education* 39 (1990): 1–14.

46. See, for example, R. Martin, "Relational Cognition Complexity and Relational Communication in Personal Relationships," *Communication Monographs* 59 (1992): 150–163; D. W. Stacks and M. A. Murphy, "Conversational Sensitivity: Further Validation and Extension," *Communication Reports* 6 (1993): 18–24; and A. L. Vangelisti and S. M. Draughton, "The Nature and Correlates of Conversational Sensitivity," *Human Communication Research* 14 (1987): 167–202.

47. Research summarized in D. E. Hamachek, *Encounters with the Self,* 2nd ed. (Fort Worth, TX: Holt, Rinehart and Winston, 1987), p. 8. See also J. A. Daly, A. L. Vangelisti, and S. M. Daughton, "The Nature and Correlates of Conversational Sensitivity," in M. V. Redmond, ed. *Interpersonal Communication: Readings in Theory and Research* (Fort Worth, TX: Harcourt Brace, 1995).

48. D. A. Dunning and J. Kruger, *Journal of Personality and Social Psychology* (December 1999).

49. Adapted from the work of R. P. Hart as reported by M. L. Knapp in *Interpersonal Communication and Human Relationships* (Boston: Allyn & Bacon, 1984), pp. 342–344. See also R. P. Hart and D. M. Burks, "Rhetorical Sensitivity and Social Interaction," *Speech Monographs* 39 (1972): 75–91; and R. P. Hart, R. E. Carlson, and W. F. Eadie, "Attitudes toward Communication and the Assessment of Rhetorical Sensitivity," *Communication Monographs* 47 (1980); 1–22.

50. Adapted from J. C. McCroskey and L. R. Wheeless, *Introduction to Human Communication* (Boston: Allyn & Bacon, 1976), pp. 3–10.

51. R. K. Aune, "A Theory of Attribution of Responsibility for Creating Understanding." Paper delivered to the Interpersonal Communication Division of the 1998 International Communication Association Conference, Jerusalem, Israel. *Communication Monographs,* in press.

52. Cite CMM.

53. J. A. M. Meerloo, *Conversation and Communication* (Madison, CT: International Universities Press, 1952), p. 91.

54. E. Eisenberg, "Jamming: Transcendence through Organizing." *Communication Research* 17 (1990): 139–164.

55. Adapted from D. D. Thornburg, "Jamming, Technology and Learning." PBS Teacher Source Online. http://www.pbs.org/teachersource/thornburg/thornburg0701.shtm.

56. For a detailed rationale of the position argued in this section, see G. H. Stamp and M. L. Knapp, "The Construct of Intent in Interpersonal Communication," *Quarterly Journal of Speech* 76 (1990): 282–299. See also J. Stewart, "A Postmodern Look at Traditional Communication Postulates," *Western Journal of Speech Communication* 55 (1991): 354–379.

57. For a thorough discussion of communication difficulties, see N. Coupland, H. Giles and J. M. Wiemann, eds., *"Miscommunication" and Problematic Talk* (Newbury Park, CA: Sage, 1991).

58. McCroskey and Wheeless, p. 5.

Chapter 2

1. C. L. M. Shaw, "Personal Narrative: Revealing Self and Reflecting Other." *Human Communication Research* 24 (1997): 302–319.

2. P. M. Sias, "Constructing Perceptions of Differential Treatment: An Analysis of Coworkers' Discourse." *Communication Monographs* 63 (1996): 171–187.

3. J. M. Martz, J. Verette, X. B. Arriaga, L. F. Slovik, C. L. Cox, and C. E. Rusbult, "Positive Illusion in Close Relationships." *Personal Relationships* 5 (1998): 159–181.

4. J. C. Pearson, "Positive Distortion: 'The Most Beautiful Woman in the World,'" in K. M. Galvin and P. J. Cooper, eds., *Making Connections: Readings in Relational Communication,* 2nd ed. (Los Angeles: Roxbury, 2000), p. 186.

5. Summarized in Don E. Hamachek, *Encounters with Others* (New York: Holt, Rinehart and Winston, 1982), pp. 23–30.

6. For a review of these perceptual biases, see D. Hamachek, *Encounters with the Self,* 3rd ed. (Fort Worth, TX: Harcourt Brace Jovanovich, 1992). See also T. N. Bradbury and F. D. Fincham, "Attributions in Marriage: Review and Critique." *Psychological Bulletin* 107 (1990): 3–33. For an example of the self-serving bias in action, see R. Buttny, "Reported Speech in Talking Race on Campus," *Human Communication Research* 23 (1997): 477–506.

7. B. Sypher and H. E. Sypher, "Seeing Ourselves as Others See Us." *Communication Research* 11 (January 1984): 97–115.

8. Reported by D. Myers, "The Inflated Self." *Psychology Today* 14 (May 1980): 16.

9. See, for example, Penny Baron, "Self-Esteem, Ingratiation, and Evaluation of Unknown Others." *Journal of Personality and Social Psychology* 30 (1974): 104–109; and Elaine Walster, "The Effect of Self-Esteem on Romantic Liking." *Journal of Experimental and Social Psychology* 1 (1965): 184–197.

10. P. A. Mongeau and C. M. Carey, "Who's Wooing Whom II? An Experimental Investigation of Date-Initiation and Expectancy Violation." *Western Journal of Communication* 60 (1996): 195–213.

11. See, for example, D. E. Kanouse and L. R. Hanson, "Negativity in Evaluations," in E. E. Jones, D. E. Kanouse, H. H. Kelley, R. E. Nisbett, S. Valins, and B. Weiner, eds., *Attribution: Perceiving the Causes of Behavior* (Morristown, NJ: General Learning Press, 1972).

12. V. Manusov, "It Depends on Your Perspective: Effects of Stance and Beliefs about Intent on Person Perception." *Western Journal of Communication* 57 (1993): 27–41.

13. T. Adler, "Enter Romance, Exit Objectivity." *APA Monitor* (June 1992): 18.

14. S. B. Algoe, B. N. Buswell, and J. D. DeLamater, "Gender and Job Status as Contextual Cues for the Interpretation of Facial Expression of Emotion." *Sex Roles* 3 (2000): 183–197.

15. See D. H. Solomon and M. L. M. Williams, "Perceptions of Social-Sexual Communication at Work: The Effects of Message, Situation, and Observer Characteristics on Judgments of Sexual Harassment." *Journal of Applied Communication Research* 25 (1997): 196–216.

16. J. K. Alberts, U. Kellar-Guenther, and S. R. Corman, "That's Not Funny: Understanding Recipients' Responses to Teasing." *Western Journal of Communication* 60 (1996): 337–357.

17. J. W. Bagby, "A Cross-Cultural Study of Perceptual Predominance in Binocular Rivalry." *Journal of Abnormal and Social Psychology* 54 (1957): 331–334.

18. H. Giles, N. Coupland, and J. M. Wiemann, "'Talk Is Cheap . . .' but 'My Word Is My Bond': Beliefs about Talk," in K. Bolton and H. Kwok, eds., *Sociolinguistics Today: International Perspectives* (London: Routledge & Kegan Paul, 1992).

19. L. A. Samovar and R. E. Porter, *Communication between Cultures,* 2nd ed. (Belmont, CA: Wadsworth, 1995), p. 199.

20. Mary Jane Collier, "Rule Violations in Intercultural/Ethnic Advisement Contexts." Paper presented at the annual meeting of the Western Speech Communication Association, Tucson, AZ, 1986.

21. P. Andersen, M. Lustig, and J. Anderson, "Changes in Latitude, Changes in Attitude: The Relationship between Climate, Latitude, and Interpersonal Communication Predispositions." Paper presented at the annual convention of the Speech Communication Association, Boston, 1987. P. Andersen, M. Lustig, and J. Andersen, "Regional Patterns of Communication in the United States: Empirical Tests." Paper presented at the annual convention of the Speech Communication Association, New Orleans, 1988.

22. A. Fadiman, *The Spirit Catches You and You Fall Down* (New York: Farrar, Straus and Giroux, 1997), p. 33.

23. J. B. Stiff, J. P. Dillard, L. Somera, H. Kim, and C. Sleight, "Empathy, Communication, and Prosocial Behavior." *Communication Monographs* 55 (1988): 198–213.

24. D. Goleman, *Emotional Intelligence: Why It Can Matter More Than I.Q.* (New York: Bantam, 1995).

25. R. Lennon and N. Eisenberg, "Gender and Age Differences in Empathy and Sympathy," in N. Eisenberg and J. Strayer, eds., *Empathy and Its Development* (Cambridge, England: Cambridge University Press, 1987).

26. T. Adler, "Look at Duration, Depth in Research on Emotion." *APA Monitor* (October 1990): 10.

27. N. D. Feshbach, "Parental Empathy and Child Adjustment/Maladjustment," in N. Eisenberg and J. Strayer, eds., *Empathy*

and Its Development (Cambridge, England: Cambridge University Press, 1987).

28. D. T. Regan and J. Totten, "Empathy and Attribution: Turning Observers into Actors." *Journal of Personality and Social Psychology* 35 (1975): 850–856.

29. T. R. Peterson and C. C. Horton, "Rooted in the Soil: How Understanding the Perspectives of Landowners Can Enhance the Management of Environmental Disputes." *Quarterly Journal of Speech* 81 (1995): 139–166.

30. Hamachek (1982), op. cit., pp. 23–24.

31. D. Hamachek, *Encounters with the Self,* 3rd ed. (Fort Worth, TX: Holt, Rinehart and Winston, 1992), pp. 5–8. See also J. D. Campbell and L. F. Lavallee, "Who Am I? The Role of Self-Concept Confusion in Understanding the Behavior of People with Low Self-Esteem," in R. F. Baumeister, ed., *Self-Esteem: The Puzzle of Low Self-Regard* (New York: Plenum Press, 1993), pp. 3–20.

32. Arthur W. Combs and Donald Snygg, *Individual Behavior,* rev. ed. (New York: Harper & Row, 1959), p. 134.

33. Harry S. Sullivan, *The Interpersonal Theory of Psychiatry* (New York: Norton, 1953).

34. C. H. Cooley, *Human Nature and the Social Order* (New York: Scribner's, 1902). Contemporary research supports the power of reflected appraisal. See, for example, R. Edwards, "Sensitivity to Feedback and the Development of the Self." *Communication Quarterly* 38 (1990): 101–111.

35. See also J. Keltikangas, "The Stability of Self-Concept during Adolescence and Early Adulthood: A Six-Year Follow-Up Study." *Journal of General Psychology* 117 (1990); 361–369.

36. P. N. Myers and F. A. Biocca, "The Elastic Body Image: The Effect of Television Advertising and Programming on Body Image Distortions in Young Women." *Journal of Communication* 42 (1992): 108–134.

37. Adapted from Carol Padden and Tom Humphries, *Deaf in America: Voices from a Culture* (Cambridge, MA: Harvard University Press, 1988), pp. 16–17.

38. W. W. Wilmot, *Relational Communication* (New York: McGraw-Hill, 1995), pp. 35–54.

39. H. Giles and P. Johnson, "'Ethnolinguistic Identity Theory': A Social Psychological Approach to Language Maintenance." *International Journal of Sociology of Language* 68 (1987): 69–99.

40. S. P. Banks, "Achieving 'Unmarkedness' in Organizational Discourse: A Praxis Perspective on Ethnolinguistic Identity." *Journal of Language and Social Psychology* 6 (1982): 171–190.

41. T. M. Singelis and W. J. Brown, "Culture, Self, and Collectivist Communication." *Human Communication Research* 21 (1995): 354–389. See also H. R. Markus and S. Kitayama, "A Collective Fear of the Collective: Implications for Selves and Theories of Selves," *Personality and Social Psychology* 20 (1994): 568–579.

42. J. Servaes, "Cultural Identity and Modes of Communication," in J. A. Anderson, ed., *Communication Yearbook* 12 (Newbury Park, CA: Sage, 1989), p. 396.

43. A. Bharti, "The Self in Hindu Thought and Action," in *Culture and Self: Asian and Western Perspectives* (New York: Tavistock, 1985).

44. W. B. Gudykunst and S. Ting-Toomey, *Culture and Interpersonal Communication* (Newbury Park, CA: Sage, 1988).

45. L. A. Samovar and R. E. Porter, *Communication between Cultures,* 2nd ed. (Belmont, CA: Wadsworth, 1995), p. 91.

46. D. Klopf, "Cross-Cultural Apprehension Research: A Summary of Pacific Basin Studies," in J. Daly and J. McCroskey, eds.,

Avoiding Communication: Shyness, Reticence, and Communication Apprehension (Beverly Hills, CA: Sage, 1984).

47. S. Ting-Toomey, "A Face-Negotiation Theory," in Y. Kim and W. Gudykunst, eds., *Theory in Interpersonal Communication* (Newbury Park, CA: Sage, 1988).

48. T. M. Steinfatt, "Personality and Communication: Classical Approaches," in J. C. McCroskey and J. A. Daly, eds., *Personality and Interpersonal Communication* (Newbury Park, CA: Sage, 1987), p. 42.

49. G. W. Allport and H. W. Odbert, "Trait Names, a Psychological Study." *Psychological Monographs* 47 (1936).

50. J. Kagan, *Unstable Ideas: Temperament, Cognition, and Self* (Cambridge, MA: Harvard University Press, 1989).

51. J. C. McCroskey and V. Richmond, *The Quiet Ones: Communication Apprehension and Shyness* (Dubuque, IA: Gorsuch Scarisbrick, 1980). See also T. J. Bouchard, D. T. Lykken, M. McGue, and N. L. Segal, "Sources of Human Psychological Differences—The Minnesota Study of Twins Reared Apart," *Science* 250 (October 12, 1990): 223–228.

52. P. D. MacIntyre and K. A. Thivierge, "The Effects of Speaker Personality on Anticipated Reactions to Public Speaking." *Communication Research Reports* 12 (1995): 125-133.

53. J. Kolligan, Jr., "Perceived Fraudulence as a Dimension of Perceived Incompetence," in R. J. Sternberg and J. Kolligen, Jr., eds., *Competence Considered* (New Haven, CT: Yale University Press, 1990).

54. B. J. Zimmerman, A. Bandura, and M. Martinez-Pons, "Self-Motivation for Academic Attainment: The Role of Self-Efficacy Beliefs and Personal Goal Setting." *American Educational Research Journal* 29 (1992): 663–676.

55. G. Downey and S. I. Feldman, "Implications of Rejection Sensitivity for Intimate Relationships." *Journal of Personality and Social Psychology* 70 (1996): 1327–1343.

56. C. L. Kleinke, T. R. Peterson, and T. R. Rutledge, "Effects of Self-Generated Facial Expressions on Mood." *Journal of Personality and Social Psychology* 74 (1998): 272–279.

57. Robert Rosenthal and Lenore Jacobson, *Pygmalion in the Classroom* (New York: Holt, Rinehart and Winston, 1968).

58. For a detailed discussion of how self-fulfilling prophecies operate in relationships, see P. Watzlawick, "Self-Fulfilling Prophecies," in J. O'Brien and P. Kollock, eds., *The Production of Reality,* 3rd ed. (Thousand Oaks, CA: Pine Forge Press, 2001), pp. 411–423.

59. C. M. Shaw and R. Edwards, "Self-Concepts and Self-Presentation of Males and Females: Similarities and Differences." *Communication Reports* 10 (1997): 56–62.

60. E. Goffman, *The Presentation of Self in Everyday Life* (Garden City, NY: Doubleday, 1959), and *Relations in Public* (New York: Basic Books, 1971).

61. C. M. Scotton, "The Negotiation of Identities in Conversation: A Theory of Markedness and Code Choice." *International Journal of Sociological Linguistics* 44 (1983): 119–125.

62. J. Stewart and C. Logan, *Together: Communicating Interpersonally,* 5th ed. (New York: McGraw-Hill, 1998), p. 120.

63. M. R. Leary and R. M. Kowalski, "Impression Management: A Literature Review and Two-Component Model." *Psychological Bulletin* 107 (1990): 34–47.

64. V. Brightman, A. Segal, P. Werther, and J. Steiner, "Ethological Study of Facial Expression in Response to Taste Stimuli." *Journal of Dental Research* 54 (1975): 141.

65. N. Chovil, "Social Determinants of Facial Displays." *Journal of Nonverbal Behavior* 15 (1991): 141–154.

66. M. R. Leary and R. M. Kowalski, "Impression Management: A Literature Review and Two-Component Model." *Psychological Bulletin* 107: 34–47.

67. M. Snyder, "Self-Monitoring Processes," in L. Berkowitz, ed., *Advances in Experimental Social Psychology* (New York: Academic Press, 1979), and "The Many Me's of the Self-Monitor," *Psychology Today* (March 1983): 34+.

68. The following discussion is based on material in Hamachek, *Encounters with the Self,* pp. 24–26.

69. L. M. Coleman and B. M. DePaulo, "Uncovering the Human Spirit: Moving beyond Disability and 'Missed' Communications," in N. Coupland, H. Giles, and J. M. Wiemann, eds., *"Miscommunication" and Problematic Talk* (Newbury Park, CA: Sage, 1991), pp. 61–84.

70. J. W. Vander Zanden, *Social Psychology,* 3rd ed. (New York: Random House, 1984), pp. 235–237.

71. J. Brown, C. R. Dykers, J. R. Steele, and A. B. White, "Teenage Room Culture: Where Media and Identities Intersect." *Communication Research* 21 (1994): 813–827.

72. J. B. Walther, "Computer-Mediated Communication: Impersonal, Interpersonal, and Hyperpersonal Interaction." *Communication Research* 23 (1996): 3–43.

73. P. B. O'Sullivan, "What You Don't Know Won't Hurt ME: Impression Management Functions of Communication Channels in Relationships."

Chapter 3

1. W. S. Y. Wang, "Language and Derivative Systems," in W. S. Y. Wang, ed., *Human Communication: Language and Its Psychobiological Basis* (San Francisco: Freeman, 1982), p. 36.

2. O. Sacks, *Seeing Voices: A Journey into the World of the Deaf* (Berkeley: University of California Press, 1989), p. 17.

3. Adapted from J. O'Brien and P. Kollock, *The Production of Reality,* 3rd ed. (Thousand Oaks, CA: Pine Forge Press, 2001), p. 66.

4. M. Henneberger, "Misunderstanding of Word Embarrasses Washington's New Mayor." *New York Times* (January 29, 1999). Online at http://www.nyt.com.

5. C. K. Ogden and I. A. Richards, *The Meaning of Meaning* (New York: Harcourt Brace, 1923), p. 11.

6. S. Duck, "Maintenance as a Shared Meaning System," in D. J. Caharg and L. Stafford, eds., *Communication and Relational Maintenance* (San Diego: Academic Press, 1993).

7. D. Crystal, *Language and the Internet* (Cambridge, England: Cambridge University Press, 2001).

8. E. Graham, M. Papa, and G. P. Brooks, "Functions of Humor in Conversation: Conceptualization and Measurement." *Western Journal of Communication* 56 (1992): 161–183.

9. Genesis 2:19. This biblical reference was noted by D. C. Mader, "The Politically Correct Textbook: Trends in Publishers' Guidelines for the Representation of Marginalized Groups." Paper presented at the annual convention of the Eastern Communication Association, Portland, ME, May 1992.

10. G. W. Smith, "The Political Impact of Name Sounds." *Communication Monographs* 65 (1998): 154–172.

11. Research on the following pages is cited in M. G. Marcus, "The Power of a Name." *Psychology Today* 9 (October 1976): 75–77, 108.

12. K. M. Steele and L. E. Smithwick, "First Names and First Impressions: A Fragile Relationship." *Sex Roles* 21 (1989): 517–523.

13. T. Varadarajan, "Big Names, Big Battles." *New York Times* (July 26, 1999). Online at http://aolsvc.aol.com/computercenter/internet/index.adp.

14. J. M. Elmhorst, "Between Two Worlds: Communication Strategies for Managing Ethnic and Family Identity in Adult Korean Adoptees." Paper presented at the National Communication Association Convention, Seattle, WA, November 2000.

15. E-mail survey of adoptive parents (Albuquerque, NM, Parents of Intercultural Adoption), p. 6.

16. D. H. Naftulin, J. E. Ware, Jr., and F. A. Donnelly, "The Doctor Fox Lecture: A Paradigm of Educational Seduction." *Journal of Medical Education* 48 (July 1973): 630–635. See also C. T. Cory, ed., "Bafflegab Pays," *Psychology Today* 13 (May 1980): 12, and H. W. Marsh and J. E. Ware, Jr., "Effects of Expressiveness, Content Coverage, and Incentive on Multidimensional Student Rating Scales: New Interpretations of the 'Dr. Fox' effect, *Journal of Educational Psychology* 74 (1982): 126–134.

17. J. S. Armstrong, "Unintelligible Management Research and Academic Prestige." *Interfaces* 10 (1980): 80–86.

18. For a summary of research on this subject, see J. J. Bradac, "Language Attitudes and Impression Formation," in H. Giles and W. P. Robinson, eds., *The Handbook of Language and Social Psychology* (Chichester, England: Wiley, 1990), pp. 387–412.

19. H. Giles and P. F. Poseland, *Speech Style and Social Evaluation* (New York: Academic Press, 1975).

20. C. Miller and K. Swift, *Words and Women* (New York: HarperCollins, 1991) p. 27.

21. For a discussion of racist language, see H. A. Bosmajian, *The Language of Oppression* (Lanham, MD: University Press of America, 1983).

22. Mader, op cit., p. 5.

23. S. L. Kirkland, J. Greenberg, and T. Pysczynski, "Further Evidence of the Deleterious Effects of Overheard Derogatory Ethnic Labels: Derogation beyond the Target." *Personality and Social Psychology Bulletin* 12 (1987): 216–227.

24. For a review of the relationship between power and language, see J. Liska, "Dominance-Seeking Language Strategies: Please Eat the Floor, Dogbreath, or I'll Rip Your Lungs Out, O.K.?" in S. A. Deetz, ed., *Communication Yearbook* 15 (Newbury Park, CA: Sage, 1992). See also N. A. Burrell and R. J. Koper, "The Efficacy of Powerful/Powerless Language on Persuasiveness/Credibility: A Meta-Analytic Review," in R. W. Preiss and M. Allen, eds., *Prospects and Precautions in the Use of Meta-Analysis* (Dubuque, IA: Brown & Benchmark, 1994).

25. D. Tannen, *Talking from 9 to 5* (New York: Morrow, 1994), p. 101.

26. D. Geddes, "Sex Roles in Management: The Impact of Varying Power of Speech Style on Union Members' Perception of Satisfaction and Effectiveness." *Journal of Psychology* 126 (1992): 589–607.

27. L. A. Samovar and R. E. Porter, *Communication between Cultures,* 3rd ed. (Belmont, CA: Wadsworth ITP, 1998), pp. 58–59.

28. H. Giles, J. Coupland, and N. Coupland, eds., *Contexts of Accommodation: Developments in Applied Sociolinguistics* (Cambridge, England: Cambridge University Press, 1991).

29. See, for example, R. A. Bell and J. G. Healey, "Idiomatic Communication and Interpersonal Solidarity in Friends' Relational Cultures," *Human Communication Research* 18 (1992): 307–335, and R. A. Bell, N. Buerkel-Rothfuss, and

K. E. Gore, "Did You Bring the Yarmulke for the Cabbage Patch Kid?: The Idiomatic Communication of Young Lovers," *Human Communication Research* 14 (1987): 47–67.

30. M. Wiener and A. Mehrabian, *A Language within Language* (New York: Appleton-Century-Crofts, 1968).

31. E. S. Kubanyu, D. C. Richard, G. B. Bower, and M. Y. Muraoka, "Impact of Assertive and Accusatory Communication of Distress and Anger: A Verbal Component Analysis." *Aggressive Behavior* 18 (1992): 337–347.

32. T. L. Scott, "Teens before Their Time." *Time* (November 27, 2000): 22.

33. M. T. Motley and H. M. Reeder, "Unwanted Escalation of Sexual Intimacy: Male and Female Perceptions of Connotations and Relational Consequences of Resistance Messages." *Communication Monographs* 62 (1995).

34. T. Wallstein, "Measuring the Vague Meanings of Probability Terms." *Journal of Experimental Psychology: General* 115 (1986): 348–365.

35. T. Labov, "Social and Language Boundaries among Adolescents." *American Speech* 4 (1992): 339–366.

36. UCLA Slang. http://www.cs.rpi.edu/~kennyz/doc/humor/slang.humor. Accessed October 24, 2001.

37. M. Kakutani, "Computer Slang Scoffs at Wetware." *Santa Barbara News-Press* (July 2, 2000): D1.

38. M. Myer and C. Fleming, "Silicon Screenings." *Newsweek* (August 15, 1994): 63.

39. S. I. Hayakawa, *Language in Thought and Action* (New York: Harcourt Brace, 1964).

40. E. M. Eisenberg, "Ambiguity as Strategy in Organizational Communication," *Communication Monographs* 51 (1984): 227–242, and E. M. Eisenberg and M. G. Witten, "Reconsidering Openness in Organizational Communication," *Academy of Management Review* 12 (1987): 418–426.

41. J. K. Alberts, "An Analysis of Couples' Conversational Complaints." *Communication Monographs* 55 (1988); 184–197.

42. B. Streisand, Crystal Award speech delivered at the Crystal Awards Speech, Women in Film luncheon, 1992.

43. B. Morrison, "What You Won't Hear the Pilot Say." *USA Today* (September 26, 2000): A1.

44. For detailed discussions of the relationship between gender and communication, see D. J. Canary and T. M. Emmers-Sommer, *Sex and Gender Differences in Personal Relationships* (New York: Guilford, 1997); J. Wood, *Gendered Lives: Communication, Gender, and Culture* (Belmont, CA: Wadsworth, 1994); and J. C. Pearson, *Gender and Communication*, 2nd ed. (Madison, WI: Brown & Benchmark, 1994).

45. See, for example, A. Haas and M. A. Sherman, "Reported Topics of Conversation among Same-Sex Adults," *Communication Quarterly* 30 (1982): 332–342.

46. R. A. Clark, "A Comparison of Topics and Objectives in a Cross Section of Young Men's and Women's Everyday Conversations," in D. J. Canary and K. Dindia, eds., *Sex Differences and Similarities in Communication: Critical Essays and Empirical Investigations of Sex and Gender in Interaction* (Mawah, NJ: Erlbaum, 1998).

47. J. T. Wood, *Gendered Lives: Communication, Gender, and Culture*, 4th ed. (Belmont, CA: Wadsworth, 2001), p. 141.

48. M. A. Sherman and A. Haas, "Man to Man, Woman to Woman." *Psychology Today* 17 (June 1984): 72–73.

49. A. Haas and M. A. Sherman, "Conversational Topic as a Function of Role and Gender." *Psychological Reports* 51 (1982): 453–454.

50. Research summarized by D. Tannen, *You Just Don't Understand: Women and Men in Conversation* (New York: Morrow, 1990).

51. J. Sachs, "Young Children's Language Use in Pretend Play," in S. U. Philips, S. Steele, and C. Tanz, eds., *Language, Gender, and Sex in Comparative Perspective* (Cambridge, England: Cambridge University Press, 1987).

52. For a summary of research on the difference between male and female conversational behavior, see H. Giles and R. L. Street, Jr., "Communication Characteristics and Behavior," in M. L. Knapp and G. R. Miller, eds., *Handbook of Interpersonal Communication* (Beverly Hills, CA: Sage, 1985): 205–261, and A. Kohn, "Girl Talk, Guy Talk," *Psychology Today* 22 (February 1988): 65–66.

53. A. J. Mulac, J. M. Wiemann, S. J. Widenmann, and T. W. Gibson, "Male/Female Language Differences and Effects in Same-Sex and Mixed-Sex Dyads: The Gender-Linked Language Effect." *Communication Monographs* 55 (1988): 315–335.

54. L. L. Carli, "Gender, Language, and Influence." *Journal of Personality and Social Psychology* 59 (1990): 941–951.

55. D. J. Canary and K. S. Hause, "Is There Any Reason to Research Sex Differences in Communication?" *Communication Quarterly* 41 (1993): 129–144.

56. C. J. Zahn, "The Bases for Differing Evaluations of Male and Female Speech: Evidence from Ratings of Transcribed Conversation." *Communication Monographs* 56 (1989): 59–74. See also L. M. Grob, R. A. Meyers, and R. Schuh, "Powerful? Powerless Language Use in Group Interactions: Sex Differences or Similarities?" *Communication Quarterly* 45 (1997): 282–303.

57. J. T. Wood and K. Dindia, "What's the Difference? A Dialogue about Differences and Similarities between Women and Men." In Canary and Dindia, op cit.

58. D. L. Rubin, K. Greene, and D. Schneider, "Adopting Gender-Inclusive Language Reforms: Diachronic and Synchronic Variation." *Journal of Language and Social Psychology* 13 (1994): 91–114.

59. D. S. Geddes, "Sex Roles in Management: The Impact of Varying Power of Speech Style on Union Members' Perception of Satisfaction and Effectiveness." *Journal of Psychology* 126 (1992): 589–607.

60. For a thorough discussion of the challenges involved in translation from one language to another, see L. A. Samovar and R. E. Porter, *Communication between Cultures*, 4th ed. (Belmont, CA: Wadsworth, 2001), pp. 149–154.

61. The examples in this paragraph are taken from D. Ricks, *Big Business Blunders: Mistakes in International Marketing* (Homewood, IL: Dow Jones-Irwin, 1983), p. 41.

62. N. Sugimoto, "'Excuse Me' and 'I'm Sorry': Apologetic Behaviors of Americans and Japanese." Paper presented at the Conference on Communication in Japan and the United States, California State University, Fullerton, CA, March 1991.

63. A summary of how verbal style varies across cultures can be found in Chapter 5 of W. B. Gudykunst and S. Ting-Toomey, *Culture and Interpersonal Communication* (Newbury Park, CA: Sage, 1988).

64. E. Hall, *Beyond Culture* (New York: Doubleday, 1959).

65. P. Clancy, "The Acquisition of Communicative Style in Japanese," in B. B. Schieffelin and E. Ochs, eds., *Language Acquisition and Socialization across Cultures* (Cambridge, England: Cambridge University Press, 1986).

66. D. Tannen, *Talking from 9 to 5* (New York: Morrow, 1994), pp. 98–99.

67. Ibid., p. 99.
68. M. Morris, *Saying and Meaning in Puerto Rico: Some Problems in the Ethnology of Discourse* (Oxford, England: Pergamon, 1981).
69. L. Leets and H. Giles, "Words as Weapons—When Do They Wound?" *Human Communication Research* 24 (1997): 260–301, and L. Leets, "When Words Wound: Another Look at Racist Speech." Paper presented at the annual conference of the International Communication Association, San Francisco, May 1999.
70. A. Almaney and A. Alwan, *Communicating with the Arabs* (Prospect Heights, IL: Waveland, 1982).
71. K. Basso, "To Give Up on Words: Silence in Western Apache Culture." *Southern Journal of Anthropology* 26 (1970): 213–230.
72. J. Yum, "The Practice of Uye–ri in Interpersonal Relationships in Korea," in D. Kincaid, ed., *Communication Theory from Eastern and Western Perspectives* (New York: Academic Press, 1987).
73. L. Martin and G. Pullum, *The Great Eskimo Vocabulary Hoax* (Chicago: University of Chicago Press, 1991).
74. H. Giles and A. Franklyn–Stokes, "Communicator Characteristics," in M. K. Asante and W. B. Gudykunst, eds., *Handbook of International and Intercultural Communication* (Newbury Park, CA: Sage, 1989).
75. L. Sinclair, "A Word in Your Ear," in *Ways of Mankind* (Boston: Beacon Press, 1954).
76. B. Whorf, "The Relation of Habitual Thought and Behavior to Language," in J. B. Carrol, ed., *Language, Thought, and Reality* (Cambridge, MA: MIT Press, 1956). See also Harry Hoijer, "The Sapir-Whorf Hypothesis," in Larry A. Samovar and Richard E. Porter, eds., *Intercultural Communication: A Reader,* 7th ed. (Belmont, CA: Wadsworth, 1994), pp. 194–200.
77. N. Postman, *Crazy Talk, Stupid Talk* (New York: Delta, 1976), p. 122.
78. Ibid., pp. 123–124.
79. H. Hoijer, quoted in T. Seinfatt, "Linguistic Relativity: Toward a Broader View," in S. Ting-Toomey and F. Korzenny, eds., *Language, Communication, and Culture: Current Directions* (Newbury Park, CA: Sage, 1989).
80. H. Rheingold, *They Have a Word for It* (Los Angeles: J. P. Tarcher, 1988).
81. K. A. Foss and B. A. Edson, "What's in a Name? Accounts of Married Women's Name Choices." *Western Journal of Speech Communication* 53 (1989): 356–373.
82. See J. N. Martin, R. L. Krizek, T. K. Nakayama, and L. Bradford, "Exploring Whiteness: A Study of Self-Labels for White Americans," *Communication Quarterly* 44 (1996): 125–144.
83. T. Brown, "Predictors of Racial Label Preference in Detroit: Examining Trends from 1971 to 1992." *Sociological Spectrum* 19 (1999): 421–442. See also L. Harris, "On Our Own Terms: AJC Southern Focus Poll," *Atlanta Journal and Constitution* (July 25, 1999): 1F.
84. M. Hecht, M. J. Collier, and S. A. Ribeau, *African American Communication: Ethnic Identity and Cultural Interpretation* (Newbury Park, CA: Sage, 1993). See also L. K. Larkey, K. L. Hecht, and J. Martin, "What's in a Name? African American Ethnic Identity Terms and Self-Determination." *Journal of Language and Social Psychology* 12 (1993): 302–317.
85. D. Niven and J. Zilber, "Preference for African American or Black." *Howard Journal of Communications* 11 (2000): 267–277.

Chapter 4

1. L. Barker, R. Edwards, C. Gaines, K. Gladney, and F. Holley, "An Investigation of Proportional Time Spent in Various Communication Activities by College Students." *Journal of Applied Communication Research* 8 (1981): 101–109.
2. Research summarized in A. D. Wolvin and C. G. Coakley, "A Survey of the Status of Listening Training in Some Fortune 500 Corporations." *Communication Education* 40 (1991): 152–164.
3. K. W. Hawkins and B. P. Fullion, "Perceived Communication Skill Needs for Work Groups." *Communication Research Reports* 16 (1999): 167–174.
4. S. D. Johnson and C. Bechler, "Examining the Relationship between Listening Effectiveness and Leadership Emergence," *Small Group Research* 29 (1998): 452–471.
5. A. L. Vangelisti, "Couples' Communication Problems: The Counselor's Perspective." *Journal of Applied Communication Research* 22 (1994): 106–126.
6. A. D. Wolvin, "Meeting the Communication Needs of the Adult Learner." *Communication Education* 33 (1984): 267–271.
7. K. J. Prage and D. Buhrmester, "Intimacy and Need Fulfillment in Couple Relationships." *Journal of Social and Personal Relationships* 15 (1998): 435–469.
8. K. K. Hjalone and L. L. Pecchioni, "Relational Listening: A Grounded Theoretical Model." *Communication Reports* 14 (2001): 59–71.
9. B. D. Sypher, R. N. Bostrom, and J. H. Seibert, "Listening Communication Abilities and Success at Work." *Journal of Business Communication* 26 (1989): 293–303.
10. J. L. Winsor, D. B. Curtis, and R. D. Stephens, "National Preferences in Business and Communication Education: An Update." *Journal of the Association for Communication Administration* 3 (1997): 170–179.
11. R. G. Nichols, "Factors in Listening Comprehension." *Speech Monographs* 15 (1948): 154–163.
12. M. H. Lewis and N. L. Reinsch, Jr., "Listening in Organizational Environments." *Journal of Business Communication* 25 (1988): 49–67.
13. T. L. Thomas and T. R. Levine, "Disentangling Listening and Verbal Recall: Related but Separate Constructs?" *Human Communication Research* 21 (1994): 103–127.
14. Nichols, "Factors in Listening Comprehension."
15. J. Brownell, "Perceptions of Effective Listeners: A Management Study." *Journal of Business Communication* 27 (1990): 401–415.
16. N. Spinks and B. Wells, "Improving Listening Power: The Payoff." *Bulletin of the Association for Business Communication* 54 (1991): 75–77.
17. R. K. Aune, "A Theory of Attribution of Responsibility for Creating Understanding." Paper delivered to the Interpersonal Communication Division of the 1998 International Communication Association Conference, Jerusalem, Israel.
18. Reported by R. Nichols and L. Stevens, "Listening to People," *Harvard Business Review* 35 (September–October 1957): 85–92.
19. W. Winter, A. Ferreira, and N. Bowers, "Decision-Making in Married and Unrelated Couples." *Family Process* 12 (1973): 83–94.
20. A. L. Vangelisti, M. L. Knapp, and J. A. Daly, "Conversational Narcissism." *Communication Monographs* 57 (1990): 251–274.
21. K. B. McComb and F. M. Jablin, "Verbal Correlates of Interviewer Empathic Listening and Employment Interview Outcomes." *Communication Monographs* 51 (1984): 367.

22. R. G. Nichols, "Listening Is a Ten-Part Skill." *Nation's Business* 75 (September 1987): 40.

23. R. Drullman and G. F. Smoorenburg, "Audio-Visual Perception of Compressed Speech by Profoundly Hearing-Impaired Subjects." *Audiology* 36 (1997): 165–177.

24. A. Mulac, J. M. Wiemann, S. J. Widenmann, and T. W. Gibson, "Male/Female Language Differences and Effects in Same-Sex and Mixed-Sex Dyads: The Gender-Linked Language Effect." *Communication Monographs* 55 (1988): 315–335.

25. C. Kiewitz, J. B. Weaver III, JH. B. Brosius, and G. Weimann, "Cultural Differences in Listening Styles Preferences: A Comparison of Young Adults in Germany, Israel, and the United States." *International Journal of Public Opinion Research* 9 (1997): 233–248.

26. L. L. Barker and K. W. Watson, *Listen Up* (New York: St. Martin's Press, 2000).

27. J. L. Chesebro, "The Relationship between Listening Styles and Conversational Sensitivity." *Communication Research Reports* 16 (1999): 233–238.

28. K. W. Watson, L. L. Barker, and J. B. Weaver, "The Listening Styles Profile" (New Orleans: SPECTRA, 1995).

29. For a brief summary of ancient rhetoric, see E. Griffin, *A First Look at Communication Theory,* 4th ed. (New York: McGraw-Hill, 2000).

30. R. Remer and P. De Mesquita, "Teaching and Learning the Skills of Interpersonal Confrontation," in D. Cahn, ed., *Intimates in Conflict: A Communication Perspective* (Norwood, NJ: Erlbaum, 1991), p. 242.

31. Adapted from D. A. Infante, *Arguing Constructively* (Prospect Heights, IL: Waveland, 1988), pp. 71–75.

32. J. Sprague and D. Stuart, *The Speaker's Handbook,* 3rd ed. Fort Worth, TX: Harcourt Brace Jovanovich, 1992), p. 172.

33. For a detailed look at empathic listening, see S. Spacapan and S. Oskamp, *Helping and Being Helped: Naturalistic Studies* (Newbury Park, CA: Sage, 1992).

34. Research summarized in J. Pearson, *Communication in the Family* (New York: Harper & Row, 1989), pp. 272–275.

35. J. B. Weaver and M. D. Kirtley, "Listening Styles and Empathy." *Southern Communication Journal* 60 (1995): 131–140.

36. C. E. Currona, J. A. Suhr, and R. MacFarlane, "Interpersonal Transactions and the Psychological Sense of Support," in S. Duck, ed., *Personal Relationships and Social Support* (London: Sage, 1990).

37. D. J. Goldsmith and K. Fitch, "The Normative Context of Advice as Social Support." *Human Communication Research* 23 (1997): 454–476.

38. D. Goldsmith, "The Sequential Placement of Advice." Paper presented at the annual convention of the Speech Communication Association, New Orleans, November 1994.

39. D. Goldsmith, "Soliciting Advice: The Role of Sequential Placement in Mitigating Face Threat." *Communication Monographs* 67 (2000): 1–19.

40. See, for example, L. Pearlin and M. McCall, "Occupational Stress and Marital Support: A Description of Microprocesses," in J. Eckenrode and S. Gore, eds., *Stress between Work and Family* (New York: Plenum, 1990).

41. See research cited in B. Burleson, "Comforting Messages: Their Significance and Effects," in J. A. Daly and J. M. Wiemann, eds., *Communicating Strategically: Strategies in Interpersonal Communication* (Hillside, NJ: Erlbaum, 1990).

42. D. J. Goldsmith and K. Fitch, "The Normative Context of Advice as Social Support." *Human Communication Research* 23 (1997): 454–476.

43. M. Davidowitz and R. D. Myricm, "Responding to the Bereaved: An Analysis of 'Helping' Statements." *Death Education* 8 (1984): 1–10.

44. "Helping Adults, Children Cope with Grief." *Washington Post* (September 13, 2001). Online at http://www.washingtonpost.com/wp-dyn/articles/A23679-2001Sep13.html.

45. Adapted from B. R. Burleson, "Comforting Messages: Features, Functions, and Outcomes," in J. A. Daly and J. M. Wiemann, eds., *Strategic Interpersonal Communication* (Hillsdale, NJ: Erlbaum, 1994), p. 140.

46. J. M. Gottman, J. Coan, S. Carrere, and C. Swanson, "Predicting Marital Happiness and Stability from Newlywed Interactions." *Journal of Marriage & the Family* 60 (1998): 5–22.

47. C. R. Rogers, "Reflection of Feelings." *Person-Centered Review* 1 (1986): 375–377.

48. L. A. Hosman, "The Evaluational Consequences of Topic Reciprocity and Self-Disclosure Reciprocity." *Communication Monographs* 54 (1987): 420–435.

49. R. A. Clark and J. G. Delia, "Individuals' Preferences for Friends' Approaches to Providing Support in Distressing Situations." *Communication Reports* 10 (1997): 115–121.

50. See, for example, R. Silver and C. Wortman, "Coping with Undesirable Life Events," in J. Garber and M. Seligman, eds., *Human Helplessness: Theory and Applications* (New York: Academic Press, 1981), pp. 279–340, and C. R. Young, D. E. Giles, and M. C. Plantz, "Natural Networks: Help-Giving and Help-Seeking in Two Rural Communities." *American Journal of Community Psychology* 10 (1982): 457–469.

51. Clark and Delia, op cit.

52. Burleson, op cit.

Chapter 5

1. For a survey of the issues surrounding the definition of *nonverbal communication,* see M. Knapp and J. A. Hall, *Nonverbal Communication in Human Interaction,* 3rd ed. (Fort Worth, TX: Harcourt Brace Jovanovich, 1992), Chapter 1.

2. F. Manusov, "Perceiving Nonverbal Messages: Effects of Immediacy and Encoded Intent on Receiver Judgments." *Western Journal of Speech Communication* 55 (Summer 1991): 235–253.

3. For a discussion of intentionality, see Knapp, *Nonverbal Communication in Human Interaction,* pp. 8–10.

4. A. R. Dennis, S. T. Kinney, and Y. T. Hung, "Gender Differences in the Effects of Media Richness." *Small Group Research* 30 (1999): 405–437.

5. See S. W. Smith, "Perceptual Processing of Nonverbal Relational Messages," in D. E. Hewes, ed., *The Cognitive Bases of Interpersonal Communication* (Hillsdale, NJ: Erlbaum, 1994).

6. J. Burgeon, D. Buller, J. Hale, and M. de Turck, "Relational Messages Associated with Nonverbal Behaviors." *Human Communication Research* 10 (Spring 1984): 351–378.

7. J. K. Burgoon, T. B. Birk, and M. Pfau, "The Association of Socio-Communicative Style and Relational Type of Perceptions of Nonverbal Intimacy." *Communication Research Reports* 14 (1997): 339–349.

8. G. Y. Lim and M. E. Roloff, "Attributing Sexual Consent." *Journal of Applied Communication Research* 27 (1999): 1–23.

9. "Safeway Clerks Object to 'Service with a Smile.'" San Francisco *Chronicle* (September 2, 1998).

10. D. Druckmann, R. M. Rozelle, and J. C. Baxter, *Nonverbal Communication: Survey, Theory, and Research* (Newbury Park, CA: Sage, 1982).

11. M. T. Motley and C. T. Camden, "Facial Expression of Emotion: A Comparison of Posed Expressions versus Spontaneous Expressions in an Interpersonal Communication Setting." *Western Journal of Speech Communication* 52 (Winter 1988): 1–22.

12. See, for example, R. Rosenthal, J. A. Hall, M. R. D. Matteg, P. L. Rogers, and D. Archer, *Sensitivity to Nonverbal Communication: The PONS Test* (Baltimore, MD: Johns Hopkins University Press, 1979).

13. J. A. Hall, "Gender, Gender Roles, and Nonverbal Communication Skills," in R. Rosenthal, ed., *Skill in Nonverbal Communication: Individual Differences* (Cambridge, MA: Oelgeschlager, Gunn, and Hain, 1979), pp. 32–67.

14. R. Birdwhistell, *Kinesics and Context* (Philadelphia: University of Pennsylvania Press, 1970), Chapter 9.

15. P. Ekman, W. V. Friesen, and J. Baer, "The International Language of Gestures." *Psychology Today* 18 (May 1984): 64–69.

16. E. Hall, *The Hidden Dimension* (Garden City, NY: Anchor Books, 1969).

17. Ibid.

18. D. L. Rubin, "'Nobody Play by the Rule He Know': Ethnic Interference in Classroom Questioning Events," in Y. Y. Kim, ed., *Interethnic Communication: Recent Research* (Newbury Park, CA: Sage, 1986).

19. A. M. Warnecke, R. D. Masters, and G. Kempter, "The Roots of Nationalism: Nonverbal Behavior and Xenophobia." *Ethnology and Sociobiology* 13 (1992): 267–282.

20. S. Weitz, ed., *Nonverbal Communication: Readings with Commentary* (New York: Oxford University Press, 1974).

21. J. Eibl-Eibensfeldt. "Universals and Cultural Differences in Facial Expressions of Emotions," in J. Cole, ed., *Nebraska Symposium on Motivation* (Lincoln: University of Nebraska Press, 1972).

22. For a comparison of Japanese and Arab nonverbal communication norms, see D. G. Leathers, *Successful Nonverbal Communication* (New York: Macmillan, 1986), pp. 258–261.

23. M. Booth-Butterfield and F. Jordan, "'Act Like Us': Communication Adaptation among Racially Homogeneous and Heterogeneous Groups." Paper presented at the Speech Communication Association meeting, New Orleans, 1988.

24. B. Olaniran, "Computer-Mediated Communication: The Media and a Test of Social Cues in Misunderstandings." Paper presented at the annual meeting of the International Communication Association, Jerusalem, 1998.

25. M. T. Palmer and K. B. Simmons, "Communicating Intentions through Nonverbal Behaviors: Conscious and Nonconscious Encoding of Liking." *Human Communication Research* 22 (1995): 128–160.

26. Hall, op. cit.

27. C. R. Kleinke, "Compliance to Requests Made by Gazing and Touching Experimenters in Field Settings." *Journal of Experimental Social Psychology* 13 (1977): 218–233.

28. M. F. Argyle, F. Alkema, and R. Gilmour, "The Communication of Friendly and Hostile Attitudes: Verbal and Nonverbal Signals." *European Journal of Social Psychology* 1 (1971): 385–402.

29. D. B. Buller and J. K. Burgoon, "Deception: Strategic and Nonstrategic Communication," in J. Daly and J. M. Wiemann, eds., *Interpersonal Communication* (Hillsdale, NJ: Erlbaum, 1994).

30. J. K. Burgoon, D. B. Buller, L. K. Guerrero, and C. M. Feldman, "Interpersonal Deception: VI. Effects on Preinteractional and International Factors on Deceiver and Observer Perceptions of Deception Success." *Communication Studies* 45 (1994): 263–280, and J. K. Burgoon, D. B. Buller, and L. K. Guerrero, "Interpersonal Deception: IX. Effects of Social Skill and Nonverbal Communication on Deception Success and Detection Accuracy." *Journal of Language and Social Psychology* 14 (1995): 289–311.

31. R. G. Riggio and H. S. Freeman, "Individual Differences and Cues to Deception." *Journal of Personality and Social Psychology* 45 (1983): 899–915.

32. P. Andersen, *Nonverbal Communication: Forms and Functions* (Mountain View, CA: Mayfield, 1999).

33. M. G. Millar and K. U. Millar, "The Effects of Suspicion on the Recall of Cues to Make Veracity Judgments." *Communication Reports* 11 (1998): 57–64.

34. T. R. Levine and S. A. McCornack, "Behavior Adaptation, Confidence, and Heuristic-Based Explanations of the Probing Effect." *Human Communication Research* 27 (2001): 471–502. See also D. B. Buller, J. Comstock, R. K. Aune, and K. D. Stryzewski, "The Effect of Probing on Deceivers and Truth-tellers." *Journal of Nonverbal Behavior* 13 (1989): 155–170. See also D. B. Buller, K. D. Stryzewski, and J. Comstock, "Interpersonal Deception: I. Deceivers' Reactions to Receivers' Suspicions and Probing." *Communication Monographs* 58 (1991): 1–24.

35. T. H. Feely and M. J. Young, "Self-Reported Cues about Deceptive and Truthful Communication: The Effects of Cognitive Capacity and Communicator Veracity." *Communication Quarterly* 48 (2000): 101–119.

36. P. Rockwell, D. B. Buller, and J. K. Burgoon, "The Voice of Deceit: Refining and Expanding Vocal Cues to Deception." *Communication Research Reports* 14 (1997): 451–459.

37. P. Kalbfleisch, "Deceit, Distrust, and Social Milieu: Applications of Deception Research in a Troubled World." *Journal of Applied Communication Research* (1992): 308–334.

38. J. Hale and J. B. Stiff, "Nonverbal Primacy in Veracity Judgments." *Communication Reports* 3 (1990): 75–83, and J. B. Stiff, J. L. Hale, R. Garlick, and R. G. Rogan, "Effect of Cue Incongruence and Social Normative Influences on Individual Judgments of Honesty and Deceit," *Southern Speech Communication Journal* 55 (1990): 206–229.

39. J. K. Burgoon, T. Birk, and M. Pfau, "Nonverbal Behaviors, Persuasion, and Credibility." *Human Communication Research* 17 (1990): 140–169.

40. M. A. deTurck, T. H. Feeley, and L. A. Roman, "Vocal and Visual Cue Training in Behavior Lie Detection." *Communication Research Reports* 14 (1997): 249–259.

41. P. Kalbfleisch, "Deceit, Distrust, and Social Milieu: Applications of Deception Research in a Troubled World." *Journal of Applied Communication Research* (1992): 308–334.

42. S. A. McCornack and M. R. Parks, "What Women Know that Men Don't: Sex Differences in Determining the Truth behind Deceptive Messages." *Journal of Social and Personal Relationships* 7 (1990): 107–118.

43. S. A. McCornack and T. R. Levine, "When Lovers Become Leery: The Relationship between Suspicion and Accuracy in Detecting Deception." *Communication Monographs* 7 (1990): 219–230.

44. M. A. deTurck, "Training Observers to Detect Spontaneous Deception: Effects of Gender." *Communication Reports* 4 (1991): 81–89.

45. J. Pavlidis, N. L. Eberhardt, and J. A. Levine, "Seeing through the Face of Deception." *Nature* 415 (2002).

46. R. E. Maurer and J. H. Tindall, "Effect of Postural Congruence on Client's Perception of Counselor Empathy." *Journal of Counseling Psychology* 30 (1983): 158–163.

47. V. Manusov, "Reacting to Changes in Nonverbal Behaviors: Relational Satisfaction and Adaptation Patterns in Romantic Dyads." *Human Communication Research* 21 (1995): 456–477.

48. M. B. Myers, D. Templer, and R. Brown, "Coping Ability of Women Who Become Victims of Rape." *Journal of Consulting and Clinical Psychology* 52 (1984): 73–78. See also C. Rubenstein, "Body Language That Speaks to Muggers," *Psychology Today* 20 (August 1980): 20, and J. Meer, "Profile of a Victim," *Psychology Today* 24 (May 1984): 76.

49. J. M. Iverson, "How to Get to the Cafeteria: Gesture and Speech in Blind and Sighted Children's Spatial Descriptions." *Developmental Psychology* 35 (1999): 1132–1142.

50. P. Ekman, *Telling Lies: Clues to Deceit in the Marketplace, Politics, and Marriage* (New York: Norton, 1985), pp. 109–110.

51. W. Donaghy and B. F. Dooley, "Head Movement, Gender, and Deceptive Communication." *Communication Reports* 7 (1994): 67–75.

52. P. Ekman and W. V. Friesen, "Nonverbal Behavior and Psychopathology," in R. J. Friedman and M. N. Katz, eds., *The Psychology of Depression: Contemporary Theory and Research* (Washington, DC: J. Winston, 1974).

53. R. Sutton and A. Rafaeli, "Untangling the Relationship between Displayed Emotions and Organizational Sales: The Case of Convenience Stores." *Academy of Management Journal* 31 (1988): 463.

54. P. Ekman and W. V. Friesen, *Unmasking the Face* (Englewood Cliffs, NJ: Prentice Hall, 1975).

55. P. Edman, W. V. Friesen, and P. Ellsworth, *Emotion in the Human Face: Guidelines for Research and an Integration of Findings* (Elmsford, NY: Pergamon, 1972).

56. J. A. Starkweather, "Vocal Communication of Personality and Human Feeling." *Journal of Communication II* (1961): 69, and K. R. Scherer, J. Koiwunaki, and R. Rosenthal, "Minimal Cues in the Vocal Communication of Affect: Judging Emotions from Content-Masked Speech," *Journal of Psycholinguistic Speech I* (1972): 269–285. See also F. S. Cox and C. Olney, "Vocalic Communication of Relational Messages," paper delivered at annual meeting of the Speech Communication Association, Denver, 1985.

57. K. L. Burns and E. G. Beier, "Significance of Vocal and Visual Channels for the Decoding of Emotional Meaning." *The Journal of Communication* 23 (1973): 118–130. See also Timothy G. Hegstrom, "Message Impact: What Percentage Is Nonverbal?" *Western Journal of Speech Communication* 43 (1979): 134–143, and E. M. McMahan, "Nonverbal Communication as a Function of Attribution in Impression Formation," *Communication Monographs* 43 (1976): 287–294.

58. A. Mehrabian and M. Weiner, "Decoding of Inconsistent Communications." *Journal of Personality and Social Psychology* 6 (1967): 109–114.

59. D. Buller and K. Aune, "The Effects of Speech Rate Similarity on Compliance: Application of Communication Accommodation Theory." *Western Journal of Communication* 56 (1992): 37–53. See also D. Buller, B. A. LePoire, K. Aune, and S. V. Eloy, "Social Perceptions as Mediators of the Effect of Speech Rate Similarity on Compliance," *Human Communication Research* 19 (1992): 286–311, and J. Francis and R. Wales, "Speech a la Mode: Prosodic Cues, Message Interpretation, and Impression Formation," *Journal of Language and Social Psychology* 13 (1994): 34–44.

60. M. S. Remland and T. S. Jones, "The Influence of Vocal Intensity and Touch on Compliance Gaining." *Journal of Social Psychology* 134 (1994): 89–97.

61. Ekman, *Telling Lies,* p. 93.

62. C. E. Kimble and S. D. Seidel, "Vocal Signs of Confidence." *Journal of Nonverbal Behavior* 15 (1991): 99–105.

63. K. J. Tusing and J. P. Dillard, "The Sounds of Dominance: Vocal Precursors of Perceived Dominance during Interpersonal Influence." *Human Communication Research* 26 (2000): 148–171.

64. M. Zuckerman and R. E. Driver, "What Sounds Beautiful Is Good: The Vocal Attractiveness Stereotype." *Journal of Nonverbal Behavior* 13 (1989): 67–82.

65. Ashley Montagu, *Touching: The Human Significance of the Skin* (New York: Harper & Row, 1972), p. 93.

66. Ibid., pp. 244–249.

67. L. J. Yarrow, "Research in Dimension of Early Maternal Care." *Merrill-Palmer Quarterly* 9 (1963): 101–122.

68. For a review of research on this subject, see S. Thayer, "Close Encounters," *Psychology Today* 22 (March 1988): 31–36.

69. See, for example, C. Segrin, "The Effects of Nonverbal Behavior on Outcomes of Compliance Gaining Attempts," *Communication Studies* 11 (1993): 169–187.

70. C. R. Kleinke, "Compliance to Requests Made by Gazing and Touching Experimenters in Field Settings." *Journal of Experimental Social Psychology* 13 (1977): 218–223.

71. F. N. Willis and H. K. Hamm, "The Use of Interpersonal Touch in Securing Compliance." *Journal of Nonverbal Behavior* 5 (1980): 49–55.

72. A. H. Crusco and C. G. Wetzel, "The Midas Touch: Effects of Interpersonal Touch on Restaurant Tipping." *Personality and Social Psychology Bulletin* 10 (1984): 512–517.

73. S. E. Jones and E. Yarbrough, "A Naturalistic Study of the Meanings of Touch." *Communication Monographs* 52 (1985): 221–231.

74. R. Heslin and T. Alper, "Touch: The Bonding Gesture," in J. M. Wiemann and R. P. Harrison, eds., *Nonverbal Interaction* (Beverly Hills, CA: Sage, 1983).

75. V. J. Derlega, R. J. Lewis, S. Harrison, B. A. Winstead, and R. Costanza, "Gender Differences in the Initiation and Attribution of Tactile Intimacy." *Journal of Nonverbal Behavior* 13 (1989): 83–96.

76. D. K. Fromme, W. E. Jaynes, D. K. Taylor, E. G. Hanold, J. Daniell, J. R. Rountree, and M. Fromme, "Nonverbal Behavior and Attitudes toward Touch." *Journal of Nonverbal Behavior* 13 (1989): 3–14.

77. For a summary, see M. L. Knapp and J. A. Hall, *Nonverbal Communication in Human Interaction*, 3rd ed. (New York: Holt, Rinehart and Winston, 1992), pp. 93–132. See also W.

Hensley, "Why Does the Best Looking Person in the Room Always Seem to Be Surrounded by Admirers?" *Psychological Reports* 70 (1992): 457–469.

78. V. Ritts, M. L. Patterson, and M. E. Tubbs, "Expectations, Impressions, and Judgments of Physically Attractive Students: A Review." *Review of Educational Research* 62 (1992): 413–426.

79. L. Bickman, "The Social Power of a Uniform." *Journal of Applied Social Psychology* 4 (1974): 47–61.

80. S. G. Lawrence and M. Watson, "Getting Others to Help: The Effectiveness of Professional Uniforms in Charitable Fund Raising." *Journal of Applied Communication Research* 19 (1991): 170–185.

81. J. H. Fortenberry, J. Maclean, P. Morris, and M. O'Connell, "Mode of Dress as a Perceptual Cue to Deference." *The Journal of Social Psychology* 104 (1978).

82. L. Bickman, "Social Roles and Uniforms: Clothes Make the Person." *Psychology Today* 7 (April 1974): 48–51.

83. M. Lefkowitz, R. R. Blake, and J. S. Mouton, "Status of Actors in Pedestrian Violation of Traffic Signals." *Journal of Abnormal and Social Psychology* 51 (1955): 704–706.

84. L. E. Temple and K. R. Loewen, "Perceptions of Power: First Impressions of a Woman Wearing a Jacket." *Perceptual and Motor Skills* 76 (1993): 339–348.

85. T. F. Hoult, "Experimental Measurement of Clothing as a Factor in Some Social Ratings of Selected American Men." *American Sociological Review* 19 (1954): 326–327.

86. Y. K. Chan, "Density, Crowding, and Factors Intervening in Their Relationship: Evidence from a Hyper-Dense Metropolis." *Social-Indicators-Research* 48 (1999): 103–124.

87. E. T. Hall, op. cit., pp. 113–130.

88. M. Hackman and K. Walker, "Instructional Communication in the Televised Classroom: The Effects of System Design and Teacher Immediacy." *Communication Education* 39 (1990): 196–206. See also J. C. McCroskey and V. P. Richmond, "Increasing Teacher Influence through Immediacy," in V. P. Richmond and J. C. McCroskey, eds., *Power in the Classroom: Communication, Control, and Concern* (Hillsdale, NJ: Erlbaum, 1992).

89. C. Conlee, J. Olvera, and N. Vagim, "The Relationships among Physician Nonverbal Immediacy and Measures of Patient Satisfaction with Physician Care." *Communication Reports* 6 (1993): 25–33.

90. D. I. Ballard and D. R. Seibold, "Time Orientation and Temporal Variation across Work Groups: Implications for Group and Organizational Communication." *Western Journal of Communication* 64 (2000): 218–242.

91. R. Levine, *A Geography of Time: The Temporal Misadventures of a Social Psychologist* (New York: Basic Books, 1997).

92. See, for example, O. W. Hill, R. A. Block, and S. E. Buggie, "Culture and Beliefs about Time: Comparisons among Black Americans, Black Africans, and White Americans." *Journal of Psychology* 134 (2000): 443–457.

93. R. Levine and E. Wolff, "Social Time: The Heartbeat of Culture." *Psychology Today* 19 (March 1985): 28–35. See also R. Levine, "Waiting Is a Power Game," *Psychology Today* 21 (April 1987): 24–33.

94. Burgoon, Buller, and Woodall, p. 148.

95. Mehrabian, op. cit., p. 69.

96. E. Sadalla, "Identity and Symbolism in Housing." *Environment and Behavior* 19 (1987): 569–587.

97. A. H. Maslow and N. L. Mintz, "Effects of Esthetic Surroundings." *Journal of Psychology* 41 (1956): 247–254.

98. L. Festinger, S. Schachter, and K. Back, *Social Pressures in Informal Groups: A Study of Human Factors in Housing* (New York: Harper & Row, 1950).

99. Sommer, op. cit., p. 78.

100. Ibid., p. 35.

Chapter 6

1. For further discussion of the characteristics of impersonal and interpersonal communication, see A. P. Bochner, "The Functions of Human Communication in Interpersonal Bonding," in C. C. Arnold and J. W. Bowers, eds., *Handbook of Rhetorical and Communication Theory* (Boston: Allyn and Bacon, 1984), p. 550, S. Trenholm and A. Jensen, *Interpersonal Communication* (Belmont, CA: Wadsworth, 1987), p. 37, J. Stewart and C. Logan, *Together: Communicating Interpersonally,* 5th ed. (New York: McGraw-Hill, 1998).

2. See J. P. Dillard, D. H. Solomon, and M. T. Palmer, "Structuring the Concept of Relational Communication." *Communication Monographs* 66 (1999): 46–55.

3. See C. M. Rossiter, Jr., "Instruction in Metacommunication," *Central States Speech Journal* 25 (1974): 36–42, and W. W. Wilmot, "Metacommunication: A Reexamination and Extension," in *Communication Yearbook* 4 (New Brunswick, NJ: Transaction Books, 1980).

4. K. O'Toole, "Study Takes Early Look at Social Consequences of Net Use." *Stanford Online Report.* Accessed online February 16, 2000, at http://www.stanford.edu/dept/news/report/news/february16/internetsurvey-216.html.

5. Robert Kraut, Michael Patterson, Vicki Lundmark, Sara Kiesler, Tridas Mukophadhyay, and William Scherlis, "Internet Paradox: A Social Technology That Reduces Social Involvement and Psychological Well-Being?" *American Psychologist* 53 (1998): 1017–1031.

6. See J. B. Walther, "Computer-Mediated Communication: Impersonal, Interpersonal, and Hyperpersonal Interaction," *Communication Research* 23 (1996): 3–43.

7. B. G. Chenault, "Developing Personal and Emotional Relationships via Computer-Mediated Communication." *CMC Magazine.* Accessed online May 1998 at http://www.december.com/cmc/mag/1998/may/chenref.html.

8. UCLA Center for Communication Policy, "Surveying the Digital Future." Accessed online October 25, 2000, at www.ccp.ucla.edu.

9. Pew Charitable Trusts, "Pew Internet and American Life Project." Accessed online October 25, 2000, at http://www.pewinternet.org/.

10. D. Tannen, *Newsweek* (May 16, 1994): 41.

11. L. M. Register and T. B. Henley, "The Phenomenology of Intimacy." *Journal of Social and Personal Relationships* 9 (1992): 467–481.

12. D. Morris, *Intimate Behavior* (New York: Bantam, 1973), p. 7.

13. K. Floyd, "Meanings for Closeness and Intimacy in Friendship." *Journal of Social and Personal Relationships* 13 (1996): 85–107.

14. L. A. Baxter, "A Dialogic Approach to Relationship Maintenance," in D. Canar and L. Stafford, eds., *Communication and Relational Maintenance* (San Diego: Academic Press, 1994).

15. J. T. Wood and C. C. Inman, "In a Different Mode: Masculine Styles of Communicating Closeness." *Applied Communication Research* 21 (1993): 279–295.

16. See, for example, K. Dindia and M. Allen, "Sex Differences in Self-Disclosure: A Meta-Analysis," *Psychological Bulletin* 112 (1992): 106–124, Ivy and P. Backlund, *Exploring GenderSpeak* (New York: McGraw-Hill, 1994), p. 219, and J. C. Pearson, L. H. Turner and W. Todd-Mancillas, *Gender and Communication,* 2nd ed. (Dubuque, IA: W. C. Brown, 1991), pp. 170–171.

17. See, for example, K. Floyd, "Gender and Closeness among Friends and Siblings," *Journal of Psychology* 129 (1995): 193–202, and K. Floyd, "Communicating Closeness among Siblings: An Application of the Gendered Closeness Perspective," *Communication Research Reports* 13 (1996): 27–34.

18. C. Inman, "Friendships among Men: Closeness in the Doing," in J. T. Wood, ed., *Gendered Relationships* (Mountain View, CA: 1996). See also S. Swain, "Covert Intimacy in Men's Friendships: Closeness in Men's Friendships," in B. J. Risman and P. Schwartz, eds., *Gender in Intimate Relationships: A Microstructural Approach* (Belmont, CA: Wadsworth, 1989).

19. C. K. Reissman, *Divorce Talk: Women and Men Make Sense of Personal Relationships* (New Brunswick: Rutgers University Press, 1990).

20. For a useful survey of cultural differences in interpersonal communication, see W. B. Gudykunst, S. Ting-Toomey, and T. Nishida, eds., *Communication in Personal Relationships across Cultures* (Thousand Oaks, CA: Sage, 1996).

21. M. Argyle and M. Henderson, "The Rules of Relationships," in S. Duck and D. Perlman, eds., *Understanding Personal Relationships* (Beverly Hills, CA: Sage, 1985).

22. W. B. Gudykunst, "The Influence of Cultural Variability on Perceptions of Communication Behavior Associated with Relationship Terms." *Human Communication Research* 13 (1986): 147–166.

23. W. B. Gudykunst and S. Ting-Toomey, *Culture and Interpersonal Communication* (Newbury Park, CA: Sage, 1987), pp. 197–198.

24. C. W. Franklin, "'Hey Home—Yo Bro'. Friendship among Black Men," in P. M. Nardir, ed., *Men's Friendships* (Newbury Park, CA: Sage, 1992).

25. H. C. Triandis, *Culture and Social Behavior* (New York: McGraw-Hill, 1994), p. 230.

26. K. Lewin, *Principles of Topological Psychology* (New York: McGraw-Hill, 1936).

27. M. L. Knapp and A. L. Vangelisti, *Interpersonal Communication and Human Relationships,* 4th ed. (Boston: Allyn and Bacon, 2003).

28. D. J. Canary and L. Stafford, eds., *Communication and Relational Maintenance* (San Diego: Academic Press, 1994). See also J. Lee, "Effective Maintenance Communication in Superior-Subordinate Relationships." *Western Journal of Communication* 62 (1998): 181–208.

29. For a discussion of relational development in nonintimate relationships, see A. Jensen and S. Trenholm, "Beyond Intimacy: An Alternative Trajectories Model of Relationship Development." Paper presented at the Speech Communication Association annual meeting, New Orleans, 1988.

30. W. B. Gudykunst and S. Ting-Toomey, *Culture and Interpersonal Communication* (Newbury Park, CA: Sage, 1988), p. 193.

31. J. H. Tolhuizen, "Communication Strategies for Intensifying Dating Relationships: Identification, Use and Structure." *Journal of Social and Personal Relationships* 6 (1989): 413–434.

32. L. K. Guerrero and P. A. Andersen, "The Waxing and Waning of Relational Intimacy: Touch As a Function of Relational Stage, Gender and Touch Avoidance." *Journal of Social and Personal Relationships* 8 (1991): 147–165.

33. L. A. Baxter, "Symbols of Relationship Identity in Relationship Culture." *Journal of Social and Personal Relationships* 4 (1987): 261–280.

34. C. J. Bruess and J. C. Pearson, "Like Sands through the Hour Glass: These Are the Rituals Functioning in Day-to-Day Married Lives." Paper delivered at the Speech Communication Association convention, San Antonio, TX, November 1995.

35. H. Giles and P. F. Poseland, *Speech Style and Social Evaluation* (London: Academic Press, 1975).

36. M. Roloff, C. A. Janiszewski, M. A. McGrath, C. S. Burns, and L. A. Manrai, "Acquiring Resources from Intimates: When Obligation Substitutes for Persuasion." *Human Communication Research* 14 (1988): 364–396.

37. J. K. Burgoon, R. Parrott, B. A. LePoire, D. L. Kelley, J. B. Walther, and D. Perry, "Maintaining and Restoring Privacy through Different Types of Relationships." *Journal of Social and Personal Relationships* 6 (1989): 131–158.

38. J. A. Courtright, F. E. Millar, L. E. Rogers, and D. Bagarozzi, "Interaction Dynamics of Relational Negotiation: Reconciliation versus Termination of Distressed Relationships." *Western Journal of Speech Communication* 54 (1990): 429–453.

39. See, for example, L. A. Baxter and B. M. Montgomery, "A Guide to Dialectical Approaches to Studying Personal Relationships," in B. M. Montgomery and L. A. Baxter, eds., *Dialectical Approaches to Studying Personal Relationships* (New York: Erlbaum, 1998), and L. A. Ebert and S. W. Duck, "Rethinking Satisfaction in Personal Relationships from a Dialectical Perspective," in R. J. Sternberg and M. Hojjatr, eds., *Satisfaction in Close Relationships* (New York: Guilford, 1997).

40. Summarized by L. A. Baxter, "A Dialogic Approach to Relationship Maintenance," in D. J. Canary and L. Stafford, eds., *Communication and Relational Maintenance* (San Diego: Academic Press, 1994).

41. Morris, *Intimate Behavior,* pp. 21–29.

42. D. Barry, *Dave Barry Turns 40* (New York: Fawcett, 1990), p. 47.

43. C. A. VanLear, "Testing a Cyclical Model of Communicative Openness in Relationship Development." *Communication Monographs* 58 (1991): 337–361.

44. Adapted from Baxter and Montgomery, op. cit, pp. 185–206.

45. R. L. Conville, *Relational Transitions: The Evolution of Personal Relationships* (New York: Praeger, 1991), p. 80.

46. L. B. Rosenfeld and W. L. Kendrick, "Choosing to Be Open: Subjective Reasons for Self-Disclosing." *Western Journal of Speech Communication* 48 (Fall 1984): 326–343.

47. I. Altman and D. A. Taylor, *Social Penetration: The Development of Interpersonal Relationships* (New York: Holt, Rinehart and Winston, 1973).

48. J. Luft, *Of Human Interaction* (Palo Alto, CA: National Press, 1969).

49. W. B. Gudykunst and S. Ting-Toomey, *Culture and Interpersonal Communication* (Newbury Park, CA: Sage, 1987), pp. 197–198, S. Ting-Toomey, "A Comparative Analysis of the Communicative Dimensions of Love, Self-Disclosure, Maintenance, Ambivalence, and Conflict in Three Cultures: France, Japan, and the United States," paper presented at the

International Communication Association convention, Montreal, 1987.

50. S. Duck and D. E. Miell, "Charting the Development of Personal Relationships," in R. Gilmour and S. Duck, eds., *Studying Interpersonal Interaction* (Hillsdale, NJ: Erlbaum, 1991).

51. S. Duck, "Some Evident Truths about Conversations in Everyday Relationships: All Communications Are Not Created Equal," *Human Communication Research* 18 (1991): 228–67.

52. J. C. Pearson, *Communication in the Family,* 2nd ed. (New York: HarperCollins, 1993), pp. 292–296.

53. Summarized in J. Pearson, *Communication in the Family* (New York: Harper & Row, 1989), pp. 252–257.

54. E. M. Eisenberg and M. G. Witten, "Reconsidering Openness in Organizational Communication." *Academy of Management Review* 12 (1987): 418–428.

55. L. B. Rosenfeld and J. R. Gilbert, "The Measurement of Cohesion and Its Relationship to Dimensions of Self-Disclosure in Classroom Settings." *Small Group Behavior* 20 (1989): 291–301.

56. J. A. Jaksa and M. Pritchard, *Communication Ethics: Methods of Analysis,* 2nd ed. (Belmont, CA: Wadsworth, 1994), pp. 65–66.

57. D. O'Hair and M. J. Cody, "Interpersonal Deception: The Dark Side of Interpersonal Communication?" in B. H. Spitzberg and W. R. Cupach, eds., *The Dark Side of Interpersonal Communication* (Hillsdale, NJ: Erlbaum, 1993).

58. R. E. Turner, C. Edgley, and G. Olmstead, "Information Control in Conversation: Honesty Is Not Always the Best Policy." *Kansas Journal of Sociology* 11 (1975): 69–89.

59. S. A. McCornack and T. R. Levine, "When Lies Are Uncovered: Emotional and Relational Outcomes of Discov-ered Deception." *Communication Monographs* 57 (1990): 119–138.

60. See M. A. Hamilton and P. J. Mineo, "A Framework for Understanding Equivocation," *Journal of Language and Social Psychology* 17 (1998): 3–35.

61. S. Metts, W. R. Cupach, and T. T. Imahori, "Perceptions of Sexual Compliance-Resisting Messages in Three Types of Cross-Sex Relationships." *Western Journal of Communication* 56 (1992): 1–17.

62. J. B. Bavelas, A. Black, N. Chovil, and J. Mullett, *Equivocal Communication* (Newbury Park, CA: Sage, 1990), p. 171.

63. Ibid.

64. See, for example, W. P. Robinson, A. Shepherd, and J. Heywood, "Truth, Equivocation/Concealment, and Lies in Job Applications and Doctor-Patient Communication," *Journal of Language & Social Psychology* 17 (1998): 149–164.

65. Several of the following examples were offered by M. T. Motley, "Mindfulness in Solving Communicators' Dilemmas." *Communication Monographs* 59 (1992): 306–314.

66. D. B. Buller and J. K. Burgoon, "Deception," in *Communicating Strategically: Strategies in Interpersonal Communication* (Hillsdale, NJ: Erlbaum, 1994).

67. S. Bok, *Lying: Moral Choice in Public and Private Life* (New York: Pantheon, 1978).

Chapter 7

1. K. N. L. Cissna and E. Seiburg, "Patterns of Interactional Confirmation and Disconfirmation," in M. V. Redmond, ed., *Interpersonal Communication: Readings in Theory and Research.* (Fort Worth, TX: Harcourt Brace, 1995).

2. Ibid.

3. M. W. Allen, "Communication Concepts Related to Perceived Organizational Support." *Western Journal of Communication* 59 (1995): 326–346.

4. B. Bower, "Nice Guys Look Better in Women's Eyes." *Science News* (March 18, 1995): 165.

5. See, for example, J. Veroff, Douvan, T. L. Orbuch, and L. K. Acitelli, "Happiness in Stable Marriages: The Early Years," in T. N. Bradbury, ed., *The Development Course of Marital Dysfunction* (New York: Cambridge University Press, 1999), pp. 152–179.

6. D. J. Canary and T. M. Emmers-Sommer, *Sex and Gender Differences in Personal Relationships* (New York: Guildford, 1997).

7. J. J. Teven, M. M. Martin, and N. C. Neupauer, "Sibling Relationships: Verbally Aggressive Messages and Their Effect on Relational Satisfaction." *Communication Reports* 11 (1998): 179–186.

8. For a discussion of reactions to disconfirming responses, see A. L. Vangelisti and L. P. Crumley, "Reactions to Messages that Hurt: The Influence of Relational Contexts," *Communication Monographs* 64 (1998): 173–196. See also L. M. Cortina, V. J. Magley, J. H. Williams, and R. D. Langhout, "Incivility in the Workplace: Incidence and Impact," *Journal of Occupational Health Psychology* 6 (2001): 64–80.

9. A. L. Vangelisti, "Messages that Hurt," in W. R. Cupach and B. H. Spitzberg, eds., *The Dark Side of Interpersonal Communication* (Hillsdale, NJ: Erlbaum, 1994).

10. See W. W. Wilmot, *Dyadic Communication* (New York: Random House, 1987), pp. 149–158, and L. M. Andersson and C. M. Pearson, "Tit for Tat? The Spiraling Effect of Incivility in the Workplace," *Academy of Management Review* 24 (1999): 452–471.

11. C. Burggraf and A. L. Sillars, "A Critical Examination of Sex Differences in Marital Communication." *Communication Monographs* 54 (1987): 276–294. See also D. A. Newton and J. K. Burgoon, "The Use and Consequences of Verbal Strategies during Interpersonal Disagreements," *Human Communication Research* 16 (1990): 477–518.

12. J. L. Hocker and W. W. Wilmot, *Interpersonal Conflict,* 5th ed. (New York: McGraw-Hill, 1997), p. 32.

13. Ibid., p. 36.

14. J. Gibb, "Defensive Communication." *Journal of Communication* 11 (1961): 141–148. See also W. F. Eadie, "Defensive Communication Revisited: A Critical Examination of Gibb's Theory," *Southern Speech Communication Journal* 47 (1982): 163–177.

15. For a review of research supporting the effectiveness of "I" language, see R. F. Proctor II and J. R. Wilcox, "An Exploratory Analysis of Responses to Owned Messages in Interpersonal Communication," *Et Cetera: A Review of General Semantics* 50 (1993): 201–220. See also R. F. Proctor II, "Responsibility or Egocentrism?: The Paradox of Owned Messages," *Speech Association of Minnesota Journal* 16 (1989): 59–60.

16. T. C. Sabourin and G. H. Stamp, "Communication and the Experience of Dialectical Tensions in Family Life: An Examination of Abusive and Nonabusive Families." *Communication Monographs* 62 (1995): 213–243.

17. R. Vonk, "The Slime Effect: Suspicion and Dislike of Likeable Behavior toward Superiors." *Journal of Personality and Social Psychology* 74: 849–864.

18. Hocker and Wilmot, op. cit., p. 21.

19. See, for example, L. A. Baxter, W. W. Wilmot, C. A. Simmons, and A. Swartz, "Ways of Doing Conflict: A Folk Taxonomy of Conflict Events in Personal Relationships," in P. J. Kalbfleisch, ed., *Interpersonal Communication: Evolving Interpersonal Relationships* (Hillsdale, NJ: Erlbaum, 1993).

20. G. R. Birchler, R. L. Weiss, and J. P. Vincent, "Multimethod Analysis of Social Reinforcement Exchange between Maritally Distressed and Nondistressed Spouse and Stranger Dyads." *Journal of Personality and Social Psychology* 31 (1975): 349–360.

21. G. R. Bach and H. Goldberg, *Creative Aggression* (Garden City, NY: Doubleday, 1974).

22. See K. Kellermann and B. C. Shea, "Threats, Suggestions, Hints, and Promises: Gaining Compliance Efficiently and Politely," *Communication Quarterly* 44 (1996): 145–465.

23. J. Jordan and M. E. Roloff, "Acquiring Assistance from Others: The Effect of Indirect Requests and Relational Intimacy on Verbal Compliance." *Human Communication Research* 16 (1990): 519–555.

24. Research summarized by D. Tannen in *You Just Don't Understand: Women and Men in Conversation* (New York: William Morrow, 1989), pp. 152–157, 162–165.

25. N. Crick, "Relational and Overt Forms of Peer Victimization: A Multiinformant Approach." *Journal of Consulting and Clinical Psychology* 66 (1998): 337–347.

26. J. F. Benenson, S. A. Ford, and N. H. Apostoleris, "Girls' Assertiveness in the Presence of Boys."

27. M. J. Collier, "Conflict Competence within African, Mexican, and Anglo American Friendships," in S. Ting-Toomey and F. Korzenny, eds., *Cross-Cultural Interpersonal Communication* (Newbury Park, CA: Sage, 1991).

28. The information in this paragraph is drawn from research summarized by J. T. Wood in *Gendered Communication* (Mountain View, CA: Mayfield, 1996), pp. 157–158.

29. N. A. Klinetob and D. A. Smith, "Demand-Withdraw Communication in Marital Interaction: Tests of Interpersonal Contingency and Gender Role Hypotheses." *Journal of Marriage & the Family* 58 (1996): 945–957.

30. See M. J. Papa and E. J. Natalle, "Gender, Strategy Selection, and Discussion Satisfaction in Interpersonal Conflict," *Western Journal of Speech Communication* 52 (1989): 260–272.

31. See, for example, J. C. Pearson, *Gender and Communication,* 2nd ed. (Dubuque, IA: W. C. Brown, 1991): pp. 183–184.

32. For a more detailed discussion of culture, conflict, and context, see W. B. Gudykunst and S. Ting-Toomey, *Culture and Interpersonal Communication* (Newbury Park, CA: Sage, 1988), pp. 153–160.

33. B. L. Speicher, "Interethnic Conflict: Attribution and Cultural Ignorance." *Howard Journal of Communications* 5 (1995): 195–213.

34. S. Ting-Toomey, K. K. Yee-Jung, R. B. Shapiro, W. Garcia, and T. Wright, "Ethnic Identity Salience and Conflict Styles in Four Ethnic Groups: African Americans, Asian Americans, European Americans, and Latino Americans." Paper presented at the annual conference of the Speech Communication Association, New Orleans, November 1994.

35. See, for example, S. Ting-Toomey, "Rhetorical Sensitivity Style in Three Cultures: France, Japan, and the United States," *Central States Speech Journal* 39 (1988): 28–36.

36. K. Okabe, "Indirect Speech Acts of the Japanese," in L. Kincaid, ed., *Communication Theory: Eastern and Western perspectives* (San Diego: Academic Press, 1987), pp. 127–136.

37. The following research is summarized in Tannen, op. cit., p. 160.

38. M. J. Collier, op. cit.

39. T. Gordon, *Parent Effectiveness Training* (New York: New American Library, 1975), pp. 263–264.

Chapter 8

1. M. V. Redmond, "A Plan for the Successful Use of Teams in Design Education." *Journal of Architectural Education* 17 (May 1986): 27–49.

2. "Professional Occupations in Multimedia." *California Occupational Guide,* Number 2006 (Sacramento, CA: California State Employment Division, 1995), p. 4. See also "A Labor Market Analysis of the Interactive Digital Media Industry: Opportunities in Multimedia," San Francisco: Reagan & Associates, 1997, pp. 15–29.

3. L. Thompson, E. Peterson, and S. E. Brodt, "Team Negotiation: An Examination of Integrative and Distributive Bargaining." *Journal of Personality and Social Psychology* 70 (1996): 66–78.

4. For a more detailed discussion of the advantages and disadvantages of working in groups, see S. A. Beebe and J. T. Masterson, *Communicating in Small Groups: Principles and Practices,* 5th ed. (New York: Longman, 1997), pp. 11–14.

5. See, for example, S. Barnes and L. M. Greller, "Computer-Mediated Communication in the Organization," *Communication Education* 43 (1994): 129–142.

6. S. L. Herndon, "Theory and Practice: Implications for the Implementation of Communication Technology in Organizations." *Journal of Business Communication* 34 (January 1997): 121–129.

7. E. A. Marby, "The Systems Metaphor in Group Communication," in L. R. Frey, ed., *Handbook of Group Communication Theory and Research* (Thousand Oaks, CA: Sage, 1999).

8. J. D. Rothwell, *In Mixed Company: Small Group Communication,* 4th ed. (Belmont, CA: Wadsworth, 2001), pp. 27–29.

9. See, for example, J. R. Katzenbach and D. K. Smith, "The Discipline of Teams," *Harvard Business Review* 86 (March–April 1993): 111–120.

10. J. Hackman, "The Design of Work Teams," in J. Lorsch, ed., *Handbook of Organizational Behavior* (Englewood Cliffs, NJ: Prentice Hall, 1987), pp. 315–342.

11. Rothwell op. cit, pp. 40–45.

12. For a discussion of the relationship between individual and group goals, see L. Frey, "Individuals in Groups," in L. R. Frey and J. K. Barge, eds., *Managing Group Life: Communicating in Decision-Making Groups* (Boston: Houghton Mifflin, 1997).

13. J. Krakauer, *Into Thin Air* (New York: Anchor, 1997), pp. 212–213.

14. See D. Scheerhorn and P. Geist, "Social Dynamics in Groups," in L. R. Frey and J. K. Barge, op. cit.

15. S. B. Shimanoff, "Group Interaction via Communication Rules," in R. S. Cathcart and L. A. Samovar, eds., *Small Group Communication: A Reader,* 5th ed. (Dubuque, IA: W. C. Brown, 1988), pp. 50–64.

16. D. S. Gouran, R. Y. Hirokawa, K. M. Julian, and G. B. Leatham, "The Evolution and Current Status of the Functional Perspective on Communication in Decision-

Making and Problem-Solving Groups," in S. A. Deetz, ed., *Communication Yearbook 16* (Newbury Park, CA: Sage, 1992).

17. M. E. Mayer, "Behaviors Leading to More Effective Decisions in Small Groups Embedded in Organizations." *Communication Reports* 11 (1998): 123–132.

18. R. F. Bales and P. L. Strodbeck, "Phases in Group Problem Solving." *Journal of Abnormal and Social Psychology* 46 (1951): 485–495.

19. E. Bormann, *Small Group Communication: Theory and Practice* (New York: Harper & Row, 1990).

20. N. Postman, *Crazy Talk, Stupid Talk* (New York: Dell, 1976).

21. B. Steinzor, "The Spatial Factor in Face-to-Face Discussion Groups." *Journal of Abnormal and Social Psychology* 45 (1950): 522–555.

22. P. L. Strodtbeck and L. H. Hook, "The Social Dimensions of a Twelve-Man Jury Table." *Sociometry* 24 (1961): 397–415.

23. N. F. Russo, "Connotations of Seating Arrangements." *Cornell Journal of Social Relations* 2 (1967): 37–44.

24. Adapted from D. W. Johnson and F. P. Johnson, *Joining Together: Group Theory and Group Skills,* 7th ed. (Boston: Allyn and Bacon, 2000), pp. 289–297.

25. R. Hastle, *Inside the Jury* (Cambridge, MA: Harvard University Press, 1983).

26. B. Day, "The Art of Conducting International Business." *Advertising Age* (October 6, 1990): 48.

27. Adapted from R. B. Adler and J. M. Elmhorst, *Communicating at Work: Principles and Practices for Business and the Professions,* 7th ed. (New York: McGraw-Hill, 2002), pp. 261–262.

28. G. Hofstede, *Cultures and Organizations: Software of the Mind* (New York: McGraw-Hill, 1997), p. 158.

29. See H. C. Triandis, R. Bontempo, M. Villareal, M. Asai, and N. Lucca, "Individualism and Collectivism: Cross-Cultural Perspectives of Self-Ingroup Relationships." *Journal of Personality and Social Psychology* 54 (1988): 323–338.

30. Research supporting these differences is summarized in S. Ting-Toomey, "Identity and Interpersonal Bonding," in M. K. Asante and W. B. Gudykunst, eds., *Handbook of International and Intercultural Communication* (Newbury Park, CA: Sage, 1989), pp. 351–373.

31. Hofstede, op. cit., pp. 65–109.

32. Ibid., pp. 110–147.

33. Ibid., pp. 189–210.

Chapter 9

1. L. Tuck, "Meeting Madness." *Presentations* (May 1995): 20.

2. C. Downs, D. M. Berg, and W. A. Linkugel, *The Organizational Communicator* (New York: Harper & Row, 1977), p. 127.

3. S. L. Tubbs, *A Systems Approach to Small Group Interaction,* 5th ed. (New York: McGraw-Hill, 1995), pp. 328–329.

4. R. B. Adler and J. M. Elmhorst, *Communicating at Work: Principles and Practices for Business and the Professions,* 7th ed. (New York: McGraw-Hill, 2002), pp. 281–283.

5. M. Zey, ed., *Decision Making: Alternatives to Rational Choice Models* (Newbury Park, CA: Sage, 1992). For a discussion of how groups "muddle through" in organizational decision making, see H. Mintzberg and A. McHugh, "Strategy Formation in an Adhocracy," *Administrative Science Quarterly* 30 (1985): 160–197.

6. See, for example, A. L. Salazar, R. Y. Hirokawa, K. M. Propp, K. M. Julian, and G. B. Leatham, "In Search of True Causes:

Examination of the Effect of Group Potential and Group Interaction on Decision Performance," *Human Communication Research* 20 (1994): 529–599.

7. J. Dewey, *How We Think* (New York: Heath, 1910).

8. M. S. Poole, "Procedures for Managing Meetings: Social and Technological Innovation," in R. A. Swanson and B. O. Knapp, eds., *Innovative Meeting Management* (Austin, TX: 3M Meeting Management Institute, 1991). See also M. S. Poole and M. E. Holmes, "Decision Development in Computer-Assisted Group Decision Making," *Human Communication Research* 22 (1995): 90–127.

9. K. Lewin, *Field Theory in Social Science* (New York: Harper & Row, 1951), pp. 30–59.

10. See S. Jarboe, "Group Communication and Creativity Processes," in L. R. Frey, ed., *Handbook of Group Communication Theory and Research* (Thousand Oaks, CA: Sage, 1999).

11. A. Osborn, *Applied Imagination* (New York: Scribner's, 1959).

12. See, for example, M. Diehl and W. Strobe, "Productivity Loss in Brainstorming Groups: Toward the Solution of a Riddle," *Journal of Personality and Social Psychology* 53 (1987): 497–509, and V. Brown, M. Tumero, T. S. Larey, and P. B. Paulus, "Modeling Cognitive Interactions during Group Brainstorming," *Small Group Research* 29 (1998): 495–526.

13. B. A. Fisher, "Decision Emergence: Phases in Group Decision Making." *Speech Monographs* 37 (1970): 53–66.

14. C. R. Frantz and K. G. Jin, "The Structure of Group Conflict in a Collaborative Work Group during Information Systems Development." *Journal of Applied Communication Research* 23 (1995): 108–127.

15. M. Poole and J. Roth, "Decision Development in Small Groups IV: A Typology of Group Decision Paths." *Human Communication Research* 15 (1989): 323–356. Also, M. Poole and J. Roth, "Decision Development in Small Groups V: Test of a Contingency Model." *Human Communication Research* 15 (1989): 549–589.

16. S. A. Wheelan, D. Murphy, E. Tsumaura, and S. F. Kline, "Member Perceptions of Internal Group Dynamics and Productivity." *Small Group Research* 29 (1998): 371–393.

17. S. M. Farmer and J. Roth, "Conflict-Handling Behavior in Work Groups: Effects of Group Structure, Decision Process, and Time." *Small Group Research* 29 (1998): 669–713.

18. B. Mullen and C. Cooper, "The Relation between Group Cohesiveness and Performance: An Integration." *Psychological Bulletin* 115 (1994): 210–227.

19. R. T. Keller, "Predictors of the Performance of Project Groups in R & D Organizations." *Academy of Management Journal* 29 (1986): 715–726. See also B. A. Welch, K. W. Mossholder, R. P. Stell, and N. Bennett, "Does Work Group Cohesiveness Affect Individuals' Performance and Organizational Commitment?" *Small Group Research* 29 (1998): 472–494.

20. The following types of power are based on the categories developed by J. R. French and B. Raven, "The Basis of Social Power," in D. Cartright and A. Zander, eds., *Group Dynamics* (New York: Harper & Row, 1968), p. 565.

21. For a detailed discussion of leadership emergence, see E. Bormann, *Small Group Communication: Theory and Practice* (New York: Harper & Row, 1990).

22. C. Conrad, *Strategic Organizational Communication: An Integrated Perspective,* 2nd ed. (Fort Worth, TX: Holt, Rinehart and Winston, 1990), p. 139.

23. J. D. Rothwell, *In Mixed Company: Small Group Communication,* 4th ed. (Fort Worth, TX: Harcourt Brace, 2001), pp. 227–228.

24. Aristotle, *Politics* (New York: Oxford University Press, 1958), Book 7.

25. For a discussion of situational theories, see G. L. Wilson, *Groups in Context,* 6th ed. (New York: McGraw-Hill, 2002), pp. 190–194.

26. See B. L. Kelsey, "The Dynamics of Multicultural Groups." *Small Group Research* 29 (1998): 602–623.

27. W. Bennis and B. Nanus, *Leaders: The Strategies for Taking Charge* (New York: Harper & Row, 1985), cited in Tubbs, op. cit., p. 164.

28. K. Lewin, R. Lippitt, and R. K. White, "Patterns of Aggressive Behavior in Experimentally Created Social Climates." *Journal of Social Psychology* 10 (1939): 271–299.

29. G. Cheney, "Democracy in the Workplace: Theory and Practice from the Perspective of Communication." *Journal of Applied Communication Research* 23 (1995): 167–200.

30. L. L. Rosenbaum and W. B. Rosenbaum, "Morale and Productivity Consequences of Group Leadership Style, Stress, and Type of Task." *Journal of Applied Psychology* 55 (1985): 343–358.

31. R. R. Blake and A. A. McCanse, *Leadership Dilemmas Grid Solutions* (Houston: Gulf Publishing Co., 1991).

32. J. Hall and S. Donnell, "Managerial Achievement: The Personal Side of Behavioral Theory." *Human Relations* 32 (1979): 77–101.

33. L. L. Rosenbaum and W. B. Rosenbaum, "Morale and Productivity Consequences of Group Leadership Style, Stress, and Type of Task." *Journal of Applied Psychology* 55 (1971): 343–358.

34. F. E. Fiedler, *A Theory of Leadership Effectiveness* (New York: McGraw-Hill, 1967).

35. P. Hersey and K. Blanchard, *Management of Organizational Behavior: Utilizing Human Resources* (Englewood Cliffs, NJ: Prentice Hall, 1993), pp. 184–212.

36. Rothwell, op. cit., pp. 161–162.

37. M. E. Mayer, "Behaviors Leading to More Effective Decisions in Small Groups Embedded in Organizations." *Communication Reports* 11 (1998): 123–132.

38. L. R. Hoffman and N. R. F. Maier, "Valence in the Adoption of Solutions by Problem-Solving Groups: Concept, Method, and Results." *Journal of Abnormal and Social Psychology* 69 (1964): 264–271.

39. E. P. Torrence, "Some Consequences of Power Differences on Decision Making in Permanent and Temporary Three-Man Groups." *Research Studies, Washington State College* 22 (1954): 130–140.

40. R. F. Bales, F. L. Strodtbeck, T. M. Mills, and M. E. Roseborough, "Channels of Communication in Small Groups." *American Sociological Review* 16 (1951): 461–468.

41. I. Janis, *Groupthink: Psychological Studies of Policy Decisions and Fiascoes.* (Boston: Houghton Mifflin, 1982).

42. Adapted from Rothwell, op. cit., pp. 184–186.

Chapter 10

1. D. T. Max, "The Making of the Speech." *The New York Times Magazine* (October 7, 2001), p. 32.

2. Ibid., p. 35.

3. D. Wallenchinsky and A. Wallace, *The Book of Lists* (New York: Little Brown, 1995).

4. G. Asburn and A. Gordon, "Features of Simplified Register in Speech to Elderly Conversationalists." *International Journal of Psycholinguistics* 8, 3 (1981): 7–31.

5. For an example of how demographics have been taken into consideration in great speeches, see Gregory Stephens, "Frederick Douglass' Multiracial Abolitionism: 'Antagonistic Cooperation' and 'Redeemable Ideals' in the July 5 Speech," *Communication Studies,* 48 (Fall 1997): 175–194. On July 5, 1852, Douglass gave a speech entitled "What to the Slave Is the 4th of July," attacking the hypocrisy of Independence Day in a slaveholding republic. It was one of the greatest antislavery speeches ever given, and part of its success stemmed from the way Douglass sought common ground with his multiracial audience.

6. Stephanie Anuloju, "It's Never Too Late: Sexual Education for the Elderly," in *Winning Orations, 2001* (Interstate Oratorical Association, 2001), p. 55. Stephanie was coached by Susan Hellbusch.

7. Examples form Julie Hill, "Changing Faces, Facing Changes," *Presentations* (November, 2000): 42.

8. For example, see Jenifer E. Kopfman and Sandi Smith, "Understanding the Audiences of a Health Communication Campaign: A Discriminant Analysis of Potential Organ Donors Based on Intent to Donate," *Journal of Applied Communication Research* 24 (February 1996): 33–49.

9. R. K. Stutman and S. E. Newell, "Beliefs versus Values: Silent Beliefs in Designing a Persuasive Message." *Western Journal of Speech Communication* 48, 4 (Fall 1984): 364.

10. In information science parlance, these are referred to as Boolean terms.

11. All quotations from Jake Gruber are via personal correspondence, September 2001.

12. Jake Gruber, "Heart Disease in Women," in *Winning Orations, 2001* (Interstate Oratorical Association, 2001), p. 16. Jake was coached by Judy Santacaterina.

Chapter 11

1. See, for example, L. Stern, *The Structures and Strategies of Human Memory* (Homewood, IL: Dorsey Press, 1985). See also C. Turner, "Organizing Information: Principles and Practices," *Library Journal* (June 15, 1987).

2. K. L. Turabian, *Student's Guide for Writing College Papers* (Chicago: University of Chicago Press, 1987).

3. Wesley Schawe, "Diploma Mills," in *Winning Orations, 2000* (Interstate Oratorical Association, 2000), p. 47. The outline and bibliography have been adapted for demonstration purposes. Wesley was coached by Craig Brown.

4. Carol Koehler, "Mending the Body by Lending an Ear: The Healing Power of Listening." *Vital Speeches of the Day* (June 15, 1998): 543.

5. Elizabeth Hallum, "Untitled," in *Winning Orations, 1998* (Interstate Oratorical Association, 1998), p. 4. Elizabeth was coached by Clark Olson.

6. A. H. Monroe, *Principles and Types of Speech* (Glenview, IL: Scott, Foresman, 1935).

7. The examples of the steps of the motivated sequence are adapted from Elizabeth Marshall Thomas, "Canine Liberation," *The New York Times* (May 1, 1996), p. A19.

8. K. Graham, "The Press and Its Responsibilities." *Vital Speeches of the Day* 42 (April 15, 1976).

9. Stephanie Hamilton, "Cruise Ship Violence," in *Winning Orations, 2000* (Interstate Oratorical Association, 2000), p. 92. Stephanie was coached by Angela Hatton.

10. Ed Rubinstein, "The Economics of Crime: The Rational Criminal." *Vital Speeches of the Day* (October 15, 1995): 19.

11. Daniel White, "Cloning: When Is Enough Enough?" in *Winning Orations, 1997* (Interstate Oratorical Association, 1997), p. 145. Daniel was coached by Kristine Greenwood.

12. Amy Jones, "The Big Sting," in *Winning Orations, 1998* (Interstate Oratorical Association, 1998), p. 52. Amy was coached by Judy Woodring.

13. Brian Sosnowchik, "The Cries of American Ailments," in *Winning Orations, 2000* (Interstate Oratorical Association, 2000), p. 114. Brian was coached by Steve Blivess.

14. Ben Crosby, "The New College Disease," in *Winning Orations, 2000* (Interstate Oratorical Association, 2000), p. 131. Ben was coached by Terry West.

15. Carrie A. Lydon, "Higher Exploitation: Universities Profiting from Sweatshop Labor," in *Winning Orations, 2000* (Interstate Oratorical Association, 2000), p. 34. Carrie was coached by Jennifer Talbert and Keith Karlson.

16. Patricia Cook, "Gun Shows: Playgrounds for Criminals," in *Winning Orations 2000* (Interstate Oratorical Association, 2000), p. 105. Patricia was coached by Robin Jones.

17. Don Sherriff, "Bill Gates—Too Rich." Posted on CRTNET discussion group, April 1, 1998.

18. Amanda Taylor, "Drowsy Driving: A Deadly Epidemic," in *Winning Orations, 2000* (Interstate Oratorical Association, 2000), p. 12. Amanda was coached by Kellie Roberts and Slade Dukes.

19. Ronald Reagan, "President's Farewell Address to the American People." *Vital Speeches of the Day* (February 1, 1989): 226.

20. Rajiv Khanna, "Distortion of History," in *Winning Orations, 2000* (Interstate Oratorical Association, 2000), p. 46. Rajiv was coached by Alexis Hopkins.

21. Richard C. Notebaert, "Leveraging Diversity: Adding Value to the Bottom Line." *Vital Speeches of the Day* (November 1, 1998): 47.

22. Jennifer Deem, "Untitled," in *Winning Orations, 1998* (Interstate Oratorical Association, 1998), p. 31. Jennifer was coached by Andy Billings.

23. From JoAnn Wypiejewski, ed., *Painting by Numbers: Komar and Melamid's Scientific Guide to Art* (New York: Farrar, Straus & Giroux, 1997).

Chapter 12

1. R. B. Rubin, A. M. Rubin, and F. F. Jordon, "Effects of Instruction on Communication Apprehension and Communication Competence." *Communication Education* 46 (1997): 104–114. See also Peter D. MacIntyre and J. Renee MacDonald, "Public Speaking Anxiety: Perceived Competence and Audience Congeniality," *Communication Education* 47, 4 (October 1998): 359–365. In this study, the group with the highest anxiety showed the largest improvement in perceived competence and perception of audience pleasantness. The speaker's perception of the audience is a key factor in public speaking anxiety.

2. See, for example, J. Borhis and M. Allen, "Meta-Analysis of the Relationship between Communication Apprehension and Cognitive Performance," *Communication Education* 41 (January 1992): 68–76.

3. John A. Daly, Anita L. Vangelisti, and David J. Weber, "Speech Anxiety Affects How People Prepare Speeches: A Protocol Analysis of the Preparation Process of Speakers." *Communication Monographs* 62 (December 1995).

4. Researchers generally agree that speech anxiety has three causes: genetics, social learning, and inadequate skills acquisition. See, for example, Michael J. Beatty and Kristin Marie Valencic, "Context-Based Apprehension versus Planning Demands: A Communibiological Analysis of Anticipatory Public Speaking Anxiety," *Communication Education* 49, 1 (January 2000): 58.

5. See, for example, Chris R. Sawyer and Ralph R. Behnke, "Communication Apprehension and Implicit Memories of Public Speaking State Anxiety," *Communication Quarterly* 45, 3 (Summer 1997): 211–222.

6. Adapted from A. Ellis, *A New Guide to Rational Living* (North Hollywood, CA: Wilshire Books, 1977). Gerald M. Philips listed a different set of beliefs that he believed contributes to reticence. The beliefs are: (1) an exaggerated sense of self-importance. (Reticent people tend to see themselves as more important to others than others see them.) (2) Effective speakers are born, not made. (3) Skillful speaking is manipulative. (4) Speaking is not that important. (5) I can speak whenever I want to; I just choose not to. (6) It is better to be quiet and let people think you are a fool than prove it by talking (they assume they will be evaluated negatively). (7) What is wrong with me requires a (quick) cure. See James A. Keaten, Lynne Kelly, and Cynthia Finch, "Effectiveness of the Penn State Program in Changing Beliefs Associated with Reticence," *Communication Education* 49, 2 (April 2000): 134.

7. R. R. Behnke, C. R. Sawyer, and P. E. King, "The Communication of Public Speaking Anxiety." *Communication Education* 36 (April 1987): 138–141.

8. See, for example, Joe Ayres and Brian L. Heuett, "The Relationship between Visual Imagery and Public Speaking Apprehension," *Communication Reports* 10, 1 (Winter 1997): 87–94. Besides visualization, treatments for speech anxiety include skills training (such as a public speaking class), systematic desensitization (such as having practice sessions until you feel more comfortable with the real thing), rational-emotive therapy (recognizing irrational beliefs, as discussed earlier in this chapter), interpersonal support (such as coaching), and physical exercise. Students tend to do best when selecting their own treatment. See, for example, Karen Kangas Dwyer, "The Multidimensional Model: Teaching Students to Self-Manage High Communication Apprehension by Self-Selecting Treatments." *Communication Education* 49, 1 (January 2000): 72.

9. Ralph R. Behnke and Chris R. Sawyer, "Milestones of Anticipatory Public Speaking Anxiety." *Communication Education* 48, 2 (April 1999): 165.

10. From "President Bush's Address on Terrorism before a Joint Meeting of Congress," *The New York Times* (September 21, 2001), p. B4. President Bush delivered his speech from a TelePrompTer.

11. Speeches are also easier to understand than written text. See, for example, Donald L. Rubin, Teresa Hafer, and Kevin Arata, "Reading and Listening to Oral-Based versus Literate-Based Discourse," *Communication Education* 49, 2 (April 2000): 121. An interesting study in this area is D. P. Hayes's "Speaking and Writing: Distinct Patterns of Word Choice," *Journal of Memory*

and Language 27 (October 1988): 572–585. This extensive study of written/spoken language differences found these differences so pronounced that "conversations between college graduates more closely resemble a preschool child's speech to its parents than texts from newspapers."

12. J. Tarver, "Can't Nobody Here Use This Language? Function and Quality in Choosing Words." *Vital Speeches of the Day* (May 1, 1979): 420–423.

13. M. A. Lofaro and J. Cummings, eds., *Crockett at Two Hundred: New Perspectives on the Man and the Myth* (Knoxville: University of Tennessee Press, 1989).

14. J. S. Hinton and Michael W. Kramer, "The Impact of Self-Directed Videotape Feedback on Students' Self-Reported Levels of Communication Competence and Apprehension." *Communication Education* 47, 2 (April 1998): 151–161. Significant increases in competency and decreases in apprehension were found using this method.

15. See, for example, L. R. Rosenfeld and J. M. Civikly, *With Words Unspoken* (New York: Holt, Rinehart and Winston, 1976), p. 62. Also see S. Chaiken, "Communicator Physical Attractiveness and Persuasion," *Journal of Personality and Social Psychology* 37 (1979): 1387–1397.

16. L. P. Devlin, "An Analysis of Kennedy's Communication in the 1980 Campaign." *Quarterly Journal of Speech* 68 (November 1982): 397–417.

17. A study demonstrating this stereotype is R. L. Street, Jr., and R. M. Brady, "Speech Rate Acceptance Ranges as a Function of Evaluative Domain, Listener Speech Rate, and Communication Context," *Speech Monographs* 49 (December 1982): 290–308.

18. See, for example, A. Mulac and M. J. Rudd, "Effects of Selected American Regional Dialects upon Regional Audience Members," *Communication Monographs* 44 (1977): 184–195. Some research, however, suggests that nonstandard dialects do not have the detrimental effects on listeners that were once believed. See, for example, F. L. Johnson and R. Buttny, "White Listener's Responses to 'Sounding Black' and 'Sounding White': The Effect of Message Content on Judgments about Language," *Communication Monographs* 49 (March 1982): 33–39.

19. Victoria Smith, Susan A. Siltanen, and Lawrence A. Hosman, "The Effects of Powerful and Powerless Speech Styles and Speaker Expertise on Impression Formation and Attitude Change." *Communication Research Reports* 15, 1 (Fall 1998): 27–35. In this study, a powerful speech style was defined as one without hedges and hesitations such as "uh" and "anda."

Chapter 13

1. Shirley Duglin Kennedy, "Finding a Cure for Information Anxiety." *Information Today* (May 2001): 40.

2. One book that explains the problems of information overload is R. S. Wurman, *Information Anxiety* (New York: Doubleday, 1989). Wurman makes a strong case that information overload is an increasingly significant problem.

3. Kathy Levine, "The Dentist's Dirty Little Secret," in *Winning Orations, 2001* (Interstate Oratorical Association, 2001), p. 77. Kathy was coached by Trischa Goodnow.

4. J. T. Cacioppo and R. E. Petty, "Effects of Message Repetition and Position on Cognitive Response, Recall, and Persuasion." *Journal of Personality and Social Psychology* 37 (1979): 97–109.

5. See K. D. Fransden and D. A. Clement, "The Functions of Human Communication in Informing: Communicating and Processing Information," in C. C. Arnold and J. W. Bowers, eds., *Handbook of Rhetorical and Communication Theory* (Boston: Allyn and Bacon, 1984), pp. 338–399.

6. Voter registration project, New York Public Interest Research Group, Brooklyn College chapter, 1998.

Chapter 14

1. Abby Ellin, "The Making of a Student Activist." *The New York Times* online (November 11, 2001).

2. Ibid.

3. For an explanation of social judgment theory, see E. Griffin, *A First Look at Communication Theory,* 4th ed. (New York: McGraw-Hill, 2000).

4. C. Lasch, "Journalism, Publicity and the Lost Art of Argument." *Gannett Center Journal* (Spring 1990): 1–11.

5. See, for example, James A. Jaska and Michael S. Pritchard, *Communication Ethics: Methods of Analysis,* 2nd ed. (Wadsworth, 1994).

6. Misty Williams, "The Latest Buzz: Caffeine Labeling," in *Winning Orations, 2001* (Interstate Oratorical Association, 2001), p. 69. Misty was coached by Jeff Gentry and Robin Jones.

7. Some research suggests that audiences may perceive a direct strategy as a threat to their freedom to form their own opinions. This perception hampers persuasion. See J. W. Brehm, *A Theory of Psychological Reactance* (New York: Academic Press, 1966).

8. Jimmy Ficaro, "The Cost of Our Conscience: Changing Patent Laws for Overpriced Prescription Drugs," in *Winning Orations 2001* (Interstate Oratorical Association, 2001), p. 88. Jimmy was coached by Chris Lacy.

9. A. Monroe, *Principles and Types of Speech* (Glenview, IL: Scott, Foresman, 1935).

10. Linda James Myers, "The Nature of Pluralism and the African American Case." *Theory into Practice* 20 (1981): 3–4. Cited in Larry A. Samovar and Richard E. Porter, *Communication between Cultures,* 2nd ed. (New York: Wadsworth, 1995), p. 251.

11. Samovar and Porter, *Communication between Cultures,* pp. 154–155.

12. For an excellent review of the effects of evidence, see J. C. Reinard, "The Empirical Study of Persuasive Effects of Evidence: The Status after Fifty Years of Research," *Human Communication Research* (Fall 1988): 3–59.

13. There are, of course, other classifications of logical fallacies than those presented here. See, for example, Barbara Warnick and Edward Inch, *Critical Thinking and Communication: The Use of Reason in Argument,* 2nd ed. (New York: Macmillan, 1994), pp. 137–161.

14. J. Sprague and D. Stuart, *The Speaker's Handbook,* 3rd ed. (Fort Worth, TX: Harcourt Brace Jovanovich, 1992), p. 172.

15. For an example of how one politician failed to adapt to his audience's attitudes, see Michael J. Hostetler, "Gov. Al Smith Confronts the Catholic Question: The Rhetorical Legacy of the 1928 Campaign," *Communication Quarterly* 46, 1 (Winter 1998): 12–24. Smith was reluctant to discuss religion, attributed bigotry to anyone who brought it up, and was impatient with the whole issue. He lost the election. Many years later,

John F. Kennedy dealt with "the Catholic question" more reasonably and won.

16. A. Mount, speech before the Southern Baptist Convention, in W. A. Linkugel, R. R. Allen, and R. Johannessen, eds., *Contemporary American Speeches*, 3rd ed. (Belmont, CA: Wadsworth, 1973).

17. H. J. Rudolf, "Robert F. Kennedy at Stellenbosch University." *Communication Quarterly* 31 (Summer 1983): 205–211.

18. Preface to Barbara Bush's speech, "Choices and Change," in O. Peterson, ed., *Representative American Speeches, 1990–1991* (New York: H. W. Wilson Co., 1991), p. 162.

19. B. Bush, "Choices and Change," speech presented to the graduating class of Wellesley College in Wellesley, MA, on June 1, 1990. Reprinted in Peterson, *Representative American Speeches, 1990–1991*, p. 166.

20. J. A. DeVito, *The Communication Handbook: A Dictionary* (New York: Harper & Row, 1986), pp. 84–86.

21. Personal correspondence with Aaron Unseth. November 2001.

22. Ibid.

Appendix I

1. C. J. Stewart and W. B. Cash, Jr., *Interviewing: Principles and Practices*, 9th ed. (New York: McGraw-Hill, 2000), pp. 1–4.

2. J. G. Geer, "Do Open-Ended Questions Measure 'Salient' Issues?" *Public Opinion Quarterly* 55 (1991): 360–371.

3. G. L. Wilson and H. L. Goodall, Jr., *Interviewing in Context* (New York: McGraw-Hill, 1992), pp. 86–87.

4. M. Gotlieb, *Interview* (New York: Longman, 1986), pp. 16–40.

5. J. Jorgenson, "Communication, Rapport, and the Interview: A Social Perspective." *Communication Theory* 2 (1992) 148–157.

6. For an assessment of interview effectiveness, see W. G. Kirkwood and S. M. Ralston, "Inviting Meaningful Applicant Performance in Employment Interviews," *Journal of Business Communication* 66 (1999): 55–76.

7. R. D. Avery and J. E. Campion, "The Employment Interview: A Summary and Review of Recent Research." *Personnel Psychology* 35 (1982): 284–288.

8. *Tips for Finding the Right Job.* U.S. Department of Labor Employment and Training Administration, 1996.

9. Avery and Campion, pp. 290, 303. See also S. Forsythe, M. F. Drake, and C. Cox, "Influence of Applicant's Dress on Interviewer's Selection Decisions," *Journal of Applied Psychology* 70 (1985): 374–378, and H. Carl, "Nonverbal Communication during the Employment Interview," *ABCA Bulletin* (December 1980): 14–18.

10. R. C. Linden, C. L. Martin, and C. K. Parsons, "Interviewer and Applicant Behaviors in Employment Interviews." *Academy of Management Journal* 36 (1993): 372–386.

11. Adapted from K. O. Locker, *Business and Administrative Communication*, 5th ed. (Homewood, IL: Irwin, 2000), pp. 574–575.

12. Ibid., p. 680.

13. C. Downs, W. Linkugel, and D. M. Berg, *The Organizational Communicator* (New York: Harper & Row, 1977), pp. 120–121.

14. See, for example, K. Loraine, "How Effective Are Work Evaluations?" *Supervision* 45 (1983): 7–8, 13, and M. Zippo and M. Miller, "Performance Appraisal: Current Practices and Techniques," *Personnel* 61 (1984): 57–59.

15. See R. N. F. Maier, *The Appraisal Interview: Objectives, Methods, and Skills* (New York: Wiley, 1958).

Appendix II

1. Werner J. Severin and James W. Tankard, Jr., *Communication Theories: Origins, Methods, and Uses in the Mass Media*, 4th ed. (New York: Longman, 1997), p. 322.

2. Patrick B. O'Sullivan, "Bridging the Mass-Interpersonal Divide: Synthesis Scholarship." *Human Communication Research* 25 (1999): pp. 569–588.

3. The name "bullet theory," also referred to as "hypodermic needle theory" or "transmission belt theory," was not used by the early researchers who performed these studies but rather by later theorists. See Melvin L. DeFleur and Sandra Ball-Rokeach, *Theories of Mass Communication*, 5th ed. (New York: Longman, 1989), pp. 145–166. See also Severin and Tankard, pp. 297–298.

4. See, for example, Peter M. Sandman, David M. Rubin, and David B. Sachsman, *Media: An Introductory Analysis of American Mass Communications*, 3rd ed. (Englewood Cliffs, NJ: Prentice Hall, 1982), pp. 4–5.

5. These and other social learning experiments are reported in Bandura's seminal book, *Social Learning Theory* (Englewood Cliffs, NJ: Prentice Hall, 1977). See Melvin L. DeFleur and Sandra Ball-Rokeach, *Theories of Mass Communication*, 5th ed. (New York: Longman, 1989), pp. 112–116, for more on this study and social learning and modeling theory.

6. See, for example, Stanley J. Baran and Dennis K. Davis, *Mass Communication Theory: Foundations, Ferment, and Future* (Belmont, CA: Wadsworth, 1995), p. 206.

7. DeFleur and Ball-Rokeach, pp. 172–186.

8. Diffusion of innovations theory is attributed primarily to Everett Rogers, *Diffusion of Innovations*, 3rd ed. (New York: Free Press, 1983). See also Severin and Tankard, pp. 238–239. This research perspective continues to be the foundation for important research. See, for example, Thomas W. Valente, "Diffusion of Innovations and Policy Decision-Making," *Journal of Communication* 43, 1 (Winter 1993): 30–45, or Marcy Meyer, J. David Johnson, and Caroline Ethington, "Contrasting Attributes of Preventive Health Innovations," *Journal of Communication* 47, 2 (Spring 1997): 112–131.

9. See, for example, Leo Jeffres and David Atkin, "Predicting Use of Technologies for Communication and Consumer Needs," *Journal of Broadcasting and Electronic Media* 40, 3 (Summer 1996): 318–330. See also Tyrone Adams, "Follow the Yellow Brick Road: Using Diffusion of Innovations Theory to Enrich Virtual Organizations in Cyberspace," *Southern Communication Journal* 62, 2 (Winter 1997): 133–148.

10. G. Gerbner, L. Gross, M. Morgan, and N. Signorielli, "Living with Television: The Cultivation Perspective," in J. Bryant and D. Zillmann, eds., *Media Effects: Advances in Theory and Research* (Hillsdale, NJ: Lawrence Erlbaum, 1994), pp. 17–41. See also Severin and Tankard, pp. 299–303.

11. Donald Shaw and Maxwell McCombs, *The Emergence of American Political Issues: The Agenda-Setting Function of the Press* (St. Paul, MN: West Publishing Co., 1977), p. 7.

12. The way these theories converge can be seen in studies such as Hans-Bernd Brosius and Gabriel Weimann, "Who Sets the Agenda? Agenda-Setting as a Two-Step Flow," *Communication*

Research 23, 5 (October 1996): 561–580. This research examined news items on German television and found that issues tend to flow from the public to the media and within the public.

13. See, for example, James W. Dearing and Everett M. Rogers, *Agenda-Setting* (Thousand Oaks, CA: Sage, 1996), especially Chapter 5.

14. Caren Deming and Mercilee Jenkins, "Bar Talk: Gender Discourse in *Cheers,*" in Leah R. Vande Berg and Lawrence A. Wenner, eds., *Television Criticism: Approaches and Applications* (New York: Longman, 1991), pp. 47–57. A similar type of study can be found in Jocelyn Steinke, "Connecting Theory and Practice: Using Women Scientist Role Models in Television Programming," *Journal of Broadcasting and Electronic Media* 42, 1 (Winter 1998): 142–151.

15. Cheris Kramarae, *Women and Men Speaking* (Rowley, MA: Newbury House Publishers, 1981), p. 1. Cited in Griffin, p. 459.

16. Griffin, p. 459.

17. Carol Gilligan, *In a Different Voice: Psychological Theory and Women's Development* (Cambridge, MA: Harvard University Press, 1982).

18. See, for example, Jonathon Cohen, "Parasocial Relations and Romantic Attraction: Gender and Dating Status Difference," *Journal of Broadcasting and Electronic Media* 41, 4 (Fall 1997): 516–529.

19. Donald Lazere, "Mass Culture, Political Consciousness and English Studies." *College English* 38 (April 1977): 755–766.

20. Simon Jones and Thomas Shumacher, "Muzak: On Functional Music and Power." *Critical Studies in Mass Communication* 9 (June 1992): 156–169.

21. Griffin, p. 365.

22. See, for example, Stuart Hall, ed., *Representation: Cultural Representations and Signifying Practices* (Thousand Oaks, CA: Sage, 1997).

23. Baran and Davis provide a concise, readable overview of uses and gratifications theory. See Chapter 10, "Using Media: Theories of the Active Audience," pp. 210–275.

24. J. Lull, *Inside Family Viewing* (London: Routledge, 1990), pp. 35–46.

25. D. Grodin, Debra Lindlof, and T. Lindlof, eds., *Constructing the Self in a Mediated World* (Thousand Oaks, CA: Sage, 1996).

Abstract language   Language that lacks specificity or does not refer to observable behavior or other sensory data. See also *Behavioral description.*

Abstraction ladder   A range of more- to less-abstract terms describing an event or object.

Action-oriented listening   A listening style that is primarily concerned with accomplishing the task at hand.

Actuating   *See Strategy to actuate.*

Ad absurdum fallacy   Fallacious reasoning that unfairly attacks an argument by extending it to such extreme lengths that it looks ridiculous.

Ad hominem fallacy   Fallacious argument that attacks the integrity of a person to weaken his or her position.

Ad populum fallacy   Fallacious reasoning based on the dubious notion that because many people favor an idea, you should, too.

Ad verecundiam fallacy   Fallacious reasoning that tries to support a belief by relying on the testimony of someone who is not an authority on the issue being argued.

Addition   The articulation error that involves adding extra parts to words.

Advising response   Helping response in which the receiver offers suggestions about how the speaker should deal with a problem.

Affect blend   The combination of two or more expressions, each showing a different emotion.

Agenda setting   A communication theory that suggests that, rather than telling us what to *think,* the media tells us what to think *about.*

All-channel network   A communication network in which all parties have equal access to one another.

Ambushing   A style in which the receiver listens carefully to gather information to use in an attack on the speaker.

Analogy   Extended comparison that can be used as supporting material in a speech.

Analyzing response   A helping style in which the listener offers an interpretation of a speaker's message.

Anecdote   A brief personal story used to illustrate or support a point in a speech.

Articulation   The process of pronouncing all the necessary parts of a word.

Assertion   Direct expression of the sender's needs, thoughts, or feelings, delivered in a way that does not attack the receiver's dignity.

Attending   The process of focusing on certain stimuli from the environment.

Attitude   Predisposition to respond to an idea, person, or thing favorably or unfavorably.

Attribution   The process of attaching meaning to behavior.

Audience analysis   A consideration of characteristics including the type, goals, demographics, beliefs, attitudes, and values of listeners.

Audience involvement   Level of commitment and attention that listeners devote to a speech.

Audience participation   Listener activity during speech; technique to increase audience involvement.

Authoritarian leadership style   A leadership style in which the designated leader uses legitimate, coercive, and reward power to dictate the group's actions.

Bar chart   Visual aid that compares two or more values by showing them as elongated horizontal rectangles.

Basic speech structure   The division of a speech into introduction, body, and conclusion.

Behavioral description   An account that refers only to observable phenomena.

Belief   An underlying conviction about the truth of an idea, often based on cultural training.

Brainstorming   A method for creatively generating ideas in groups by minimizing criticism and encouraging a large quantity of ideas without regard to their workability or ownership by individual members.

Breadth (of self-disclosure)   The range of topics about which an individual discloses. See also *Depth.*

Briefing   Type of informative speech that condenses large amounts of information, often providing facts that people need to do their jobs.

Bullet theory   An early theory of media effects that predicted direct, powerful effects from media use.

Buzz groups   A group discussion strategy used when the number of members is too large for effective discussion. Subgroups simultaneously address an issue and then report back to the group at large.

Causal reasoning   See *Cause-effect pattern.*

Cause-effect pattern   Organizing plan for a speech that demonstrates how one or more events result in another event or events.

Certainty   Messages that dogmatically imply that the speaker's position is correct and that the other person's ideas are not worth considering. Likely to generate a defensive response.

Chain network   A communication network in which information passes sequentially from one member to another.

Channel   Medium through which a message passes from sender to receiver.

Character   The dimension of credibility that involves traits such as honesty and impartiality.

Charisma   The dimension of credibility that is a combination of a speaker's enthusiasm and likability.

Chronemics   The study of how humans use and structure time.

Citation   Brief statement of supporting material in a speech.

Cliché   A ritualized, stock response to a social situation.

Climax pattern   Organizing plan for a speech that builds ideas to the point of maximum interest or tension.

Closed question   Interview question that can be answered in a few words.

Coercive power   The power to influence others by the threat or imposition of unpleasant consequences.

Cohesiveness   The totality of forces that causes members to feel themselves part of a group and makes them want to remain in that group.

Collectivistic orientation   A cultural orientation focusing on the welfare of the group as a whole, rather than a concern by individuals for their own success. See also *Individualistic orientation*.

Column chart   Visual aid that compares two or more values by showing them as elongated vertical rectangles.

Common ground   A persuasive strategy stressing similarities between speaker and audience.

Communication   A continuous, irreversible, transactive process involving communicators who occupy different but overlapping environments and are simultaneously senders and receivers of messages, many of which are distorted by physical and psychological noise.

Communication climate   The emotional tone of a relationship as it is expressed in the messages that the partners send and receive.

Communication competence   Ability to maintain a relationship on terms acceptable to all parties.

Communication networks   Systems of stable person-to-person relationships through which information flows in an organization.

Competence   The dimension of credibility that involves the speaker's expertise in the topic area.

Compromise   An approach to conflict resolution in which both parties attain at least part of what they seek through self-sacrifice.

Conclusion (of a speech)   The final structural unit of a speech, in which the main points are reviewed and final remarks are made to motivate the audience to act or help listeners remember key ideas.

Conflict   An expressed struggle between at least two interdependent parties who perceive incompatible goals, scarce rewards, and interference from the other party in achieving their goals.

Conflict of interest   The unauthorized use of one's professional position for personal gain.

Conflict stage   A stage in problem-solving groups when members openly defend their positions and question those of others.

Connotation   The emotional associations of a term.

Consensus   Agreement between group members about a decision.

Content message   A message that communicates information about the subject being discussed. See also *Relational message*.

Content-oriented listening   A listening style that focuses on the content of a message.

Contextual interpersonal communication   Any communication that occurs between two individuals. See also *Qualitative interpersonal communication*.

Control   The social need to influence others.

Controlling communication   Messages in which the sender tries to impose some sort of outcome on the receiver, usually resulting in a defensive reaction.

Convincing   A speech goal that aims at changing audience members' beliefs, values, or attitudes. See also *Strategy to convince*.

Coordination   Interaction in which participants interact smoothly, with a high degree of satisfaction but without necessarily understanding one another well.

Crazymaking   Passive-aggressive messages sent in indirect ways that frustrate and confuse the recipient.

Credibility   The believability of a speaker or other source of information.

Critical listening   Listening in which the goal is to judge the quality or accuracy of the speaker's remarks.

Cultivation theory   A theory of media effects that suggests that the media shape how certain users view the world.

Cultural studies   A group of theories that explores the effects of mass media society, relying on close readings rather than statistical experiments.

Database   A computerized collection of information that can be searched in a variety of ways to locate information that the user is seeking.

Debilitative stage fright   Intense level of anxiety about speaking before an audience, resulting in poor performance.

Decoding   The process in which a receiver attaches meaning to a message.

Deduction   Reasoning from a generality to a specific conclusion.

Deescalatory conflict spiral   A communication spiral in which the parties slowly lessen their dependence on one another, withdraw, and become less invested in the relationship.

Defensive listening A response style in which the receiver perceives a speaker's comments as an attack.

Deletion Articulation error that involves leaving off parts of words.

Democratic leadership style A style in which the nominal leader invites the group's participation in decision making.

Demographics Audience characteristics that can be analyzed statistically, such as age, gender, education, group membership, and so on.

Denotation The objective, emotion-free meaning of a term. See also *Connotation*.

Depth (of self-disclosure) The level of personal information a person reveals on a particular topic. See also *Breadth*.

Descriptive communication Messages that describe the speaker's position without evaluating others. Synonymous with *"I" language*.

Desensitization The process by which people who have encountered large amounts of media violence become less concerned about violence in society.

Developmental models (of relational maintenance) These models propose that the nature of communication is different in various stages of interpersonal relationships.

Diagram A line drawing that shows the most important components of an object.

Dialectical model (of relational maintenance) A model claiming that, throughout their lifetime, people in virtually all interpersonal relationships must deal with equally important, simultaneous, and opposing forces such as connection and autonomy, predictability and novelty, and openness versus privacy.

Diffusion of innovations A theory of media effects describing how different types of people have different levels of willingness to accept new ideas from the media.

Direct aggression An expression of the sender's thoughts or feelings or both that attacks the position and dignity of the receiver.

Direct persuasion Persuasion that does not try to hide or disguise the speaker's persuasive purpose.

Direct question Interview question that makes a straightforward request for information.

Disconfirming response A message that expresses a lack of caring or respect for another person.

Disfluency A nonlinguistic verbalization. For example, *um, er, ah*.

Divergence A linguistic strategy in which speakers emphasize differences between their communicative style and others' in order to create distance.

Downward communication Communication from a superior to one or more subordinates.

Dyad A two-person unit.

Dysfunctional roles Individual roles played by group members that inhibit the group's effective operation. See also *Functional roles*.

Either-or fallacy Fallacious reasoning that sets up false alternatives, suggesting that if the inferior one must be rejected, then the other must be accepted.

Emblems Deliberate nonverbal behaviors with precise meanings, known to virtually all members of a cultural group.

Emergence phase A stage in problem solving when the group moves from conflict toward a single solution.

Emotional evidence Evidence that arouses emotional reactions in an audience.

Emotive language Language that conveys the sender's attitude rather than simply offering an objective description.

Empathic listening Listening in which the goal is to help the speaker solve a problem.

Empathy The ability to project oneself into another person's point of view, so as to experience the other's thoughts and feelings.

Encoding The process of putting thoughts into symbols, most commonly words.

Enthymeme Compressed version of a syllogism in which the underlying premises are not stated.

Environment Both the physical setting in which communication occurs and the personal perspectives of the parties involved.

Equality A type of supportive communication suggesting that the sender regards the receiver as worthy of respect.

Equivocal words Words that have more than one dictionary definition.

Equivocation A vague statement that can be interpreted in more than one way.

Escalatory conflict spiral A communication spiral in which one attack leads to another until the initial skirmish escalates into a full-fledged battle.

Ethical persuasion Persuasion in an audience's best interest that does not depend on false or misleading information to induce change in that audience.

Euphemism A pleasant-sounding term used in place of a more direct but less pleasant one.

Evaluative communication Messages in which the sender judges the receiver in some way, usually resulting in a defensive response.

Evidence Material used to prove a point, such as testimony, statistics, and examples.

Example A specific case that is used to demonstrate a general idea.

Expected response The audience reaction predicted on the basis of audience analysis; used in planning a speech.

Expert power The ability to influence others by virtue of one's perceived expertise on the subject in question. See also *Information power*.

Expressive communication Communication of emotional information. See also *Instrumental communication*.

Extemporaneous speech A speech that is planned in advance but presented in a direct, conversational manner.

External noise Factors outside the receiver that interfere with the accurate reception of a message.

Face   The socially approved identity that a communicator tries to present. See also *Impression management*.

Facework   Verbal and nonverbal behavior designed to create and maintain a communicator's face and the face of others.

Facilitative stage fright   A moderate level of anxiety about speaking before an audience that helps improve the speaker's performance.

Factual question   Interview question that investigates matters of fact. See also *Opinion question*.

Factual statement   Statement that can be verified as being true or false.

Fallacy of approval   The irrational belief that it is vital to win the approval of virtually every person a communicator deals with.

Fallacy of catastrophic failure   The irrational belief that the worst possible outcome will probably occur.

Fallacy of overgeneralization   Irrational beliefs in which (1) conclusions (usually negative) are based on limited evidence or (2) communicators exaggerate their shortcomings.

Fallacy of perfection   The irrational belief that a worthwhile communicator should be able to handle every situation with complete confidence and skill.

Flow theories   Early theories of media effects that dealt with the way effects traveled from the mass media to their audiences.

Focus group   Used in market research by sponsoring organizations to survey potential users or the public at large regarding a new product or idea.

Force field analysis   A method of problem analysis that identifies the forces contributing to resolution of the problem and the forces that inhibit its resolution.

Formal communication networks   Management's idea of who should talk to whom in order to accomplish the organization's mission.

Formal outline   A consistent format and set of symbols used to identify the structure of ideas.

Formal role   A role assigned to a person by group members or an organization, usually to establish order.

Forum   A discussion format in which audience members are invited to add their comments to those of the official discussants.

Functional roles   Member roles (usually unstated) that must be carried out if the group is to accomplish its task-related goals. See also *Informal role; Task functions; Social functions*.

Gatekeepers   Producers of mass messages, who determine what messages will be delivered to consumers, how those messages will be constructed, and when they will be delivered.

Gender analysis   A critical approach that examines how the media construct and perpetuate gender roles.

General needs   Needs that are shared by all humans. See also *Maslow's needs*.

General purpose   One of three basic ways a speaker seeks to affect an audience: to entertain, inform, or persuade.

Gibb categories   Six sets of contrasting styles of verbal and nonverbal behavior. Each set describes a communication style that is likely to arouse defensiveness and a contrasting style that is likely to prevent or reduce it. Developed by Jack Gibb.

Group   A small collection of people whose members interact with each other, usually face to face, over time in order to reach goals.

Group goals   Goals that a group collectively seeks to accomplish. See also *Individual goals*.

Groupthink   A group's collective striving for unanimity that discourages realistic appraisals of alternatives to its chosen decision.

Growth group   A group whose goal is to help members learn more about themselves.

Haptics   The study of touch.

Hearing   The process wherein sound waves strike the eardrum and cause vibrations that are transmitted to the brain.

Hidden agendas   Individual goals that group members are unwilling to reveal.

High-context culture   A culture that avoids direct use of language to express information, especially about relational matters. Instead, members of the culture rely on the context of a message to convey meaning. See also *Low-context culture*.

Homeostasis   A form of equilibrium that keeps a system following its established standards of behavior.

Horizontal communication   Communication between people who are not connected vertically on an organization chart.

Hypothetical example   Example that asks an audience to imagine an object or event.

Hypothetical question   Seeks a response by proposing a "what-if" situation.

"I" language   Language that describes the speaker's position without evaluating others. Synonymous with *Descriptive communication*.

Illustrators   Nonverbal behaviors that accompany and support verbal messages.

Impersonal communication   Behavior that treats others as objects rather than as individuals. See also *Interpersonal communication*.

Impression management   Strategies used by communicators to influence the way others view them.

Impromptu speech   A speech given "off the top of one's head," without preparation.

Indirect communication   Hinting at a message instead of expressing thoughts and feelings directly. See also *Passive aggression; Assertion*.

Indirect question   Interview question that does not directly request the information being sought. See also *Direct question*.

Individual differences   A theory of media effects that predicts that media users with different characteristics will be affected in different ways by mediated messages.

Individual goals   The motives of individual members that influence their behavior in groups. See also *Group goals*.

Individualistic orientation   A cultural orientation focusing on the value and welfare of individual members, as opposed to a concern for the group as a whole. See also *Collectivistic orientation*.

Induction   Reasoning from specific evidence to a general conclusion.

Inferential statement   Conclusion arrived at from an interpretation of evidence. See also *Factual statement*.

Informal roles   Roles usually not explicitly recognized by a group that describe functions of group members, rather than their positions. Sometimes called "functional roles." See also *Formal role*.

Information hunger   Audience desire, created by a speaker, to learn information.

Information overload   Decline in efficiency that occurs when the rate of complexity of material is too great to manage.

Information power   The ability to influence others by virtue of the otherwise obscure information one possesses. See also *Expert power*.

Information underload   Decline in efficiency that occurs when there is a shortage of the information that is necessary to operate effectively.

Informational interview   Interview intended to collect facts and opinions from the respondent.

Informational listening   Listening in which the goal is to receive accurately the same thoughts the speaker is trying to convey.

Informative purpose statement   A complete statement of the objective of a speech, worded to stress audience knowledge and/or ability.

Insensitive listening   Failure to recognize the thoughts or feelings that are not directly expressed by a speaker, instead accepting the speaker's words at face value.

Instrumental communication   Communication of functional, practical information. See also *Expressive communication*.

Insulated listening   A style in which the receiver ignores undesirable information.

Interactive communication model   A characterization of communication as a two-way event in which the sender and the receiver exchange messages in response to one another.

Interpersonal communication   Communication in which the parties consider one another as unique individuals rather than as objects. It is characterized by minimal use of stereotyped labels; unique, idiosyncratic social rules; and a high degree of information exchange.

Interpersonal relationship   An association in which the parties meet each other's social needs to some degree.

Interview   A structured form of oral communication involving two parties, at least one of whom communicates in ways designed to achieve a preconceived purpose.

Intimacy   A state of closeness between two (or sometimes more) people. Intimacy can be manifested in several ways: physically, intellectually, emotionally, and via shared activities.

Intimate distance   One of Hall's four distance zones, ranging from skin contact to eighteen inches.

Intrapersonal communication   Communication that occurs within a single person.

Introduction (of a speech)   The first structural unit of a speech, in which the speaker captures the audience's attention and previews the main points to be covered.

Irrational thinking   Beliefs that have no basis in reality or logic; one source of debilitative stage fright.

Irrelevant response   A disconfirming response in which one communicator's comments bear no relationship to the previous speaker's ideas.

Jargon   The specialized vocabulary that is used as a kind of shorthand by people with common backgrounds and experience.

Johari Window   A model that describes the relationship between self-disclosure and self-awareness.

Judging response   A reaction in which the receiver evaluates the sender's message either favorably or unfavorably.

Kinesics   The study of body movement, gesture, and posture.

Knowledge gap hypothesis   The prediction that members of higher socioeconomic groups and those with more education will acquire and make use of more knowledge from the media than other groups.

Laissez-faire leadership style   A style in which the designated leader gives up his or her formal role, transforming the group into a loose collection of individuals.

Language   A collection of symbols, governed by rules, and used to convey messages between individuals.

Latitude of acceptance   In social judgment theory, statements that a receiver would not reject.

Latitude of noncommitment   In social judgment theory, statements that a receiver would not care strongly about one way or another.

Latitude of rejection   In social judgment theory, statements that a receiver could not possibly accept.

Leader   See *Nominal leader*.

Leadership   The ability to influence the behavior of others in a group.

Leading question   A question in which the interviewer—either directly or indirectly—signals the desired answer.

Learning group   A group whose goal is to expand its knowledge about some topic other than itself or its individual members. See also *Growth group.*

Legitimate power   The ability to influence a group owing to one's position in a group. See also *Nominal leader.*

Linear communication model   A characterization of communication as a one-way event in which a message flows from sender to receiver.

Line chart   Visual aid consisting of a grid that maps out the direction of a trend by plotting a series of points.

Linguistic determinism   Theory that a culture's world-view is unavoidably shaped and reflected by the language its members speak.

Linguistic relativism   A moderate form of linguistic determinism that argues that language exerts a strong influence on the perceptions of the people who speak it.

Listening   Process wherein the brain reconstructs electro-chemical impulses generated by hearing into representations of the original sound and give them meaning.

Logical fallacy   An error in reasoning that can lead to false conclusions.

Lose–lose problem solving   An approach to conflict resolution in which neither party achieves its goals.

Low-context culture   A culture that relies heavily on language to make messages, especially of a relational nature, explicit. See also *High-context culture.*

Maintenance functions   See *Social functions.*

Managerial grid   A two-dimensional model that describes the various combinations of a leader's concern with task-related and relational goals.

Manipulators   Movements in which one part of the body grooms, massages, rubs, holds, fidgets, pinches, picks, or otherwise manipulates another part.

Manuscript speech   A speech that is read word for word from a prepared text.

Maslow's needs   A hierarchy of needs that motivates humans, that is, physical, safety, social, self-esteem, and self-actualization needs, in that order.

Mass communication   The transmission of messages to large, usually widespread audiences via broadcast means (such as radio and television), print (such as newspapers, magazines, and books), multimedia (such as CD-ROM, DVD, and the World Wide Web), and other forms of media such as recordings and movies.

Media   Plural form of (communication) *medium.* Also used to refer to the organizations that produce and deliver messages through channels of mass communication.

Mediated communication   The exchange of messages through an interposed device, including mass communication, mediated interpersonal communication, and communication through converged media that are both mass and interpersonal in nature.

Medium   Any device that conveys a message. See *Channel.*

Memorized speech   A speech learned and delivered by rote without a written text.

Message   A sender's planned and unplanned words and nonverbal behaviors.

Metacommunication   Messages (usually relational) that refer to other messages; communication about communication.

Mixed messages   Contradiction between a verbal message and one or more nonverbal cues.

Motivated sequence   A five-step plan used in persuasive speaking; also known as "Monroe's Motivated Sequence."

Narration   Presentation of speech supporting material as a story with a beginning, middle, and end.

Narrative   The stories people create and use to make sense of their personal worlds.

Negotiation   A process in which two or more parties discuss specific proposals in order to find a mutually acceptable agreement.

Networks   Patterns that individual channels of communication form between group members.

Neutral question   A question that gives the interviewee a chance to respond without any influence from the interviewer.

Neutrality   A defense-arousing behavior in which the sender expresses indifference toward a receiver.

Noise   External, physiological, and psychological distractions that interfere with the accurate transmission and reception of a message.

Nominal leader   The person who is identified by title as the leader of a group.

Nonassertion   The inability or unwillingness to express one's thoughts or feelings when necessary.

Nonverbal communication   Messages expressed by other than linguistic means.

Norms   Shared values, beliefs, behaviors, and procedures that govern a group's operation.

Number chart   Visual aid that lists numbers in tabular form in order to clarify information.

One-way communication   Communication in which a receiver provides no feedback to a sender.

Open question   Interview question that requires the interviewee to respond in detail. See also *Closed question.*

Open system   A system that is influenced by the environment in which it operates.

Opinion leaders   People who are known by receivers of a mediated message, with whom they interpersonally communicate for advice on the topic of those messages.

Opinion question   Interview question seeking the interviewee's opinion. See also *Factual question.*

Opinion statement   Statement based on the speaker's beliefs. See also *Factual statement.*

Orientation stage   A stage in problem-solving groups when members become familiar with one another's position and tentatively volunteer their own.

Panel discussion A discussion format in which participants consider a topic more or less conversationally, without formal procedural rules. Panel discussions may be facilitated by a moderator.

Paralanguage Nonlinguistic means of vocal expression: rate, pitch, tone, and so on.

Parallel relationship One in which the balance of power shifts from one party to the other according to the situation.

Paraphrasing Feedback in which the receiver rewords the speaker's thought and feelings. Can be used to verify understanding, demonstrate empathy, and help others solve their problems.

Parliamentary procedure A problem-solving method in which specific rules govern the way issues may be discussed and decisions made.

Participative decision making Development of solutions with input by the people who will be affected.

Passive aggression An indirect expression of aggression, delivered in a way that allows the sender to maintain a façade of kindness.

People-oriented listening A listening style that is primarily concerned with creating and maintaining positive relationships.

Perceived self The person we believe ourselves to be in moments of candor. It may be identical with or different from the presenting and ideal selves.

Perception checking A three-part method for verifying the accuracy of interpretations, including a description of the sense data, two possible interpretations, and a request for confirmation of the interpretations.

Performance appraisal interview An interview intended to acknowledge good performance, identify areas where problems exist, resolve problems, improve productivity, and help develop the employee's talents.

Personal distance One of Hall's four distance zones, ranging from eighteen inches to four feet.

Personality A relatively consistent set of traits a person exhibits across a variety of situations.

Persuasion The act of motivating a listener, through communication, to change a particular belief, attitude, value, or behavior.

Persuasive interview Occurs when an interviewer's goal is to influence the thoughts or behaviors of an interviewee.

Phonological rules Linguistic rules governing how sounds are combined to form words.

Physical need Identified by Maslow as the most fundamental type of human need. Includes sufficient food, air, rest, and the ability to reproduce as a species.

Physiological noise Biological factors in the receiver that interfere with accurate reception of a message.

Pictograph A visual aid that artistically modifies a chart or graph in order to make it more interesting.

Pie chart A visual aid that divides a circle into wedges, representing percentages of the whole.

Pitch The highness or lowness of one's voice.

Plagiarism Appropriating someone else's creative work as one's own without crediting the source.

Political-economic analysis A critical technique that focuses on media's role in influencing how the economic system of a nation determines the values of the entire culture.

***Post hoc* fallacy** Fallacious reasoning that mistakenly assumes that one event causes another because they occur sequentially.

Power The ability to influence others.

Power distance The degree to which members are willing to accept a difference in power and status between members of a group.

Pragmatic rules Rules that govern the everyday use of language. Unlike syntactic and semantic rules, pragmatic rules are rarely written down or discussed.

Presenting self The image a person presents to others. It may be identical to or different from the perceived and ideal selves. See also *Face*.

Primary question The first question asked to elicit information on an interview topic. See also *Secondary question*.

Probative question An open question used to analyze a problem by encouraging exploratory thinking.

Probe An interjection, silence, or other brief remark designed to open up or direct an interviewee.

Problem census Used to equalize participation in groups when the goal is to identify important issues or problems. Members first put ideas on cards, which are then compiled by a leader to generate a comprehensive statement of the issue or problem.

Problem orientation A supportive style of communication in which the communicators focus on working together to solve their problems instead of trying to impose their own solutions on one another.

Problem-solution pattern Organizing pattern for a speech that describes an unsatisfactory state of affairs and then proposes a plan to remedy the problem.

Problem-solving group A task-related group whose goal is to resolve a mutual concern of its members.

Procedural norms Norms that describe rules for the group's operation.

Prod Word or phrase that encourages a speaker to continue talking.

Proposition of fact Claim bearing on issue in which there are two or more sides of conflicting factual evidence.

Proposition of policy Claim bearing on issue that involves adopting or rejecting a specific course of action.

Proposition of value Claim bearing on issue involving the worth of some idea, person, or object.

Provisionalism A supportive style of communication in which the sender expresses a willingness to consider the other person's position.

Proxemics The study of how people and animals use space.

Pseudolistening An imitation of true listening in which the receiver's mind is elsewhere.

Psychological noise Forces within a communicator that interfere with the ability to express or understand a message accurately.

Public communication Communication that occurs when a group becomes too large for all members to contribute. It is characterized by an unequal amount of speaking and by limited verbal feedback.

Public distance One of Hall's four distance zones, extending outward from twelve feet.

Purpose statement A complete sentence that describes precisely what a speaker wants to accomplish.

Qualitative interpersonal communication Interaction in which people treat one another as unique individuals, regardless of the context in which the interaction occurs or the number of people involved. Contrasted with impersonal communication. See also *Contextual interpersonal communication.*

Quantification The use of numbers to clarify a concept.

Questioning Feedback that usually requests the speaker to supply additional information in order to clarify or expand the receiver's understanding. Also, a style of helping in which the receiver seeks additional information from the sender. Some questioning responses are really disguised advice.

Rate The speed at which a speaker utters words.

Reasoning by analogy An argument based on the similarity between two ideas.

Receiver One who notices and attends to a message.

Referent power The ability to influence others by virtue of the degree to which one is liked or respected.

Reflected appraisal The theory that a person's self-concept matches the way the person believes others regard him or her.

Reinforcement stage A stage in problem-solving groups when members endorse the decision they have made.

Relational maintenance Communication aimed at keeping relationships operating smoothly and satisfactorily.

Relational message A message that expresses the social relationship between two or more individuals.

Relationship See *Interpersonal relationship.*

Relative words Words that gain their meaning by comparison.

Remembering The act of recalling previously introduced information. Recall drops off in two phases: short- and long-term.

Report Type of informative speech that presents information from any type of investigation.

Residual message The part of a message a receiver can recall after short- and long-term memory loss.

Reward power The ability to influence others by the granting or promising of desirable consequences.

Role fixation Acting out a specific role whether or not the situation requires it.

Roles The patterns of behavior expected of group members.

Rule Explicit, officially stated guideline that governs group functions and member behavior.

Secondary question Follow-up question used in an interview to elicit information not revealed by a primary question.

Selection interview Interview in which a candidate is evaluated for a new position, either initial employment, promotion, or reassignment.

Selective listening A listening style in which the receiver responds only to messages that interest him or her.

Self-actualization One of five of Maslow's needs. The desire to reach one's maximum potential.

Self-concept The relatively stable set of perceptions each individual holds of himself or herself.

Self-disclosure The process of deliberately revealing information about oneself that is significant and that would not normally be known by others.

Self-esteem The part of the self-concept that involves evaluations of self-worth.

Self-fulfilling prophecy A prediction or expectation of an event that makes the outcome more likely to occur than would otherwise have been the case.

Self-serving bias The tendency to interpret and explain information in a way that casts the perceiver in the most favorable manner.

Semantic rules Rules that govern the meaning of language as opposed to its structure. See also *Syntactic rules.*

Semiotic analysis A body of media criticism technique that looks at the way symbols are used in the media, especially nonverbal symbols such as camera angles, lighting, and editing.

Sex role the social orientation that governs behavior, in contrast to a person's biological gender.

Significant other A person whose opinion is important enough to affect one's self-concept strongly.

Signpost A phrase that emphasizes the importance of upcoming material in a speech.

Sign reasoning Reasoning from specific evidence to a specific conclusion without explaining how the evidence and conclusion are related.

Situational leadership A theory that argues that the most effective leadership style varies according to leader-member relations, the nominal leader's power, and the task structure.

Slang Language used by a group of people whose members belong to a similar coculture or other group.

Slurring The articulation error that involves overlapping the end of one word with the beginning of the next.

Small group A group of a size such that every member can participate actively with the other members.

Social distance   One of Hall's distance zones, ranging from four to twelve feet.

Social functions   Functional roles concerned with maintaining smooth personal relationships among group members. Also termed "Maintenance functions." See also *Task functions.*

Social goals   Motives of individual group members related to satisfying their social needs, for example, inclusion, control, affection. See also *Task-related goals.*

Social group   A group whose goal is to meet the social needs of its members rather than to meet task-related goals.

Social judgment theory   Explanation of attitude change that posits that opinions will change only in small increments and only when the target opinions lie within the receiver's latitudes of acceptance and noncommitment.

Social learning   A theory of media effects that states that people learn how to behave by observing and imitating models.

Social learning theory   Explanation of broad range of human behavior based on the assumption that people learn how to behave by observing others.

Social needs   Identified by Maslow as needs associated with one's interpersonal relationships.

Social penetration model   A model describing how intimacy can be achieved via the breadth and depth of self-disclosure.

Social roles   Emotional roles concerned with maintaining smooth personal relationships among group members. Also termed "Maintenance functions." See also *Task functions.*

Socialization   Process through which children learn how to become productive members of adult society.

Sociogram   Graphic representation of the interaction patterns in a group.

Space pattern   Organizing plan in a speech that arranges points according to their physical location.

Specific needs   The needs of a particular audience as opposed to general needs.

Specific purpose   The precise effect that the speaker wants to have on an audience. Expressed in the form of a *purpose statement.*

Spiral   Reciprocal communication pattern in which each person's message reinforces the other's.

Spontaneity   Supportive communication behavior in which the sender expresses a message without any attempt to manipulate the receiver.

Stage hogging   A listening style in which the receiver is more concerned with making his or her own point than with understanding the speaker.

Statistic   Numbers arranged or organized to show how a fact or principle is true for a large percentage of cases.

Strategy   A defense-arousing style of communication in which the sender tries to manipulate or trick a receiver; also, the general term for any type of plan, as in the plan for a persuasive speech.

Strategy to actuate   Persuasive plan that seeks to move an audience to immediate action.

Strategy to convince   Persuasive strategy that seeks to change the way an audience thinks.

Straw man argument   Fallacious reasoning that attacks a potentially valid argument by demolishing a weak example and suggesting that it represents the entire position. See also *Ad absurdum fallacy.*

Substitution   The articulation error that involves replacing part of a word with an incorrect sound.

Superiority   A defense-arousing style of communication in which the sender states or implies that the receiver is inferior.

Supporting response   A response style in which the receiver reassures, comforts, or distracts the person seeking help.

Survey research   Information gathering in which the responses of a sample of a population are collected to disclose information about the larger group.

Syllogism   Arguments made up of two premises and a conclusion.

Symbol   An arbitrary sign used to represent a thing, person, idea, event, or relationship in ways that make communication possible.

Symposium   A discussion format in which participants divide the topic in a manner that allows each member to deliver in-depth information without interruption.

Syntactic rules   Rules that govern the ways in which symbols can be arranged as opposed to the meanings of those symbols. See also *Semantic rules.*

System   A group of people whose members interact with one another to form a whole greater than the sum of its parts.

Target audience   That part of an audience that must be influenced in order to achieve a persuasive goal.

Task functions   Functional roles of group members concerned with accomplishing the group's stated task.

Task-related goals   Goals related to accomplishing the group's stated purpose for operating.

Territory   Fixed space that an individual assumes some right to occupy.

Testimony   Supporting material that proves or illustrates a point by citing an authoritative source.

Thesis statement   A complete sentence describing the central idea of a speech.

Time-oriented listening   A listening style that is primarily concerned with minimizing the time necessary to accomplish the task at hand.

Time pattern   Organizing plan for a speech based on chronology.

Topic pattern   Organizing plan for a speech that arranges points according to logical types or categories.

Trait theories of leadership   The belief that it is possible to identify leaders by personal traits, such as intelligence, appearance, or sociability.

Transactional communication model   A characterization of communication as the simultaneous sending and receiving of messages in an ongoing, irreversible process.

Transition   Phrase that connects ideas in a speech by showing how one relates to the other.

Two-step flow   A theory that states that media effects occur mostly in interaction with interpersonal communication.

Two-way communication   Exchange of information in which the receiver deliberately provides feedback to a sender.

Uncertainty avoidance   The cultural tendency to seek stability and honor tradition instead of welcoming risk, uncertainty, and change.

Understanding   The act of interpreting a message by following syntactic, semantic, and pragmatic rules.

Uses and gratifications theory   The study of ways in which media consumers actively choose and use media to meet their own needs.

Value   A deeply rooted belief about a concept's inherent worth.

Visual aids   Graphic devices used in a speech to illustrate or support ideas.

Visualization   Technique for behavior rehearsal (for example, for a speech) that involves imagining the successful completion of the task.

Wheel network   A communication network in which a gatekeeper regulates the flow of information from all other members.

White lie   Deception intended to be unmalicious, or even helpful, to the person to whom it is told.

Whorf-Sapir hypothesis   Theory that the structure of a language shapes the worldview of its users.

Win–lose problem solving   An approach to conflict resolution in which one party reaches its goal at the expense of the other.

Win–win problem solving   An approach to conflict resolution in which the parties work together to satisfy all their goals.

Word chart   Visual aid that lists words or terms in tabular form in order to clarify information.

Working outline   Constantly changing organizational aid used in planning a speech.

Y network   A communication network in which a gatekeeper conveys information from one member to all other members.

"You" language   Language that judges another person, increasing the likelihood of a defensive reaction. See also *Evaluative communication*.

CREDITS

Literary

Page 4: "The Many Meanings of Communication" adapted from *Communication and Human Behavior, 2e* by Brent Ruben. Copyright ©1988 by Allyn & Bacon. Reprinted/adapted by permission.

Page 41: "We and They" by Rudyard Kipling.

Page 47: "Today's Lesson: Empathy" by Julie Irwin, *The Cincinnati Enquirer,* 2/10/95. Used with permission.

Page 49: "Premier Artiste" by Lenni Shender Goldstein. Reprinted by permission of the author.

Page 72: Excerpt from "Burnt Norton" from FOUR QUARTERS by T.S. Elliot, copyright 1936 by Harcourt, Inc. and renewed 1964 by T.S. Elliot, reprinted by permission of the publisher.

Page 84: "In the Name of Love" by Suzanne Scholosberg. Reprinted by permission of the author.

Page 121: "Deafness Lite" by Sal Parlato, Jr. from *Silent News*. Reprinted courtesy of *Silent News*.

Page 122: "What Good Is Free Speech if No One Listens?" by Kurt Luedtke. Reprinted by the permission of the author.

Page 132: "Finding Common Ground through Listening" by Ellen Goodman in *The Boston Globe*, 6/2/92. Copyright ©1992, The Boston Globe Newspaper Co./Washington Post Writers GroupPage. Reprinted with permission.

Page 135: "Council: Reviving the Art of Listening" by Jack Zimmerman and Virginia Coyle. Reprinted by permission of the authors. For further information on this topic, the reader is referred to *The Way of Council*, by Jack Zimmerman and Virginia Coyle, published by Bramble Books, 1996.

Page 165: "Expressive Italians Let Hands Do the Talking" by Brian Murphy, 12/17/94. Reprinted by permission.

Page 168: "Ideal Speaker's Voice Types in Mexico and the United States" adapted from C.A. Valentine and B. Saint Damian, "Communicative Power: Gender and Culture as Determinants of the Ideal Voice" in C.A. Valentine and N. Hoar, eds., *Women and Communicative Power: Theory, Research, and Practice*, Speech Communication Association, ©1988. Used by permission of the National Communication Association.

Page 173: "Marked: Women in the Workplace" by Deborah Tannen in *Talking from 9 to 5*, pages 107–113. Copyright © 1994 by Deborah Tannen. Reprinted by permission of HarperCollins Publishers Inc. and William Morrow & Co., Inc.

Page 190: Excerpt from "The Death of the Hired Man" by Robert Frost in *The Poetry of Robert Frost*, Edward Connery Lathem, ed. Reprinted by permission of Henry Holt and Company, Inc.

Page 200: Excerpt from THE PROPHET by Kahlil Gibran. Copyright ©1923 by Kahlil Gibran and renewed 1951 by Administrators C.T.A of Kahlil Gibran Estate and Mary G. Gibran. Used by permission of Alfred A. Knopf, Inc. and © Gibran National Committee, e-mail: k.gibran@cyberianet.pub.

Page 229: "A Comparison of Dialogue and Debate" adapted from *Dialogue: Turning Controversy into Community* by Rachel Poliner and Jeffrey Benson. © 1997 Educators for Social Responsibility. For more information call ESR at (800) 370-2515.

Page 287: "Once upon a September Day?" by Thomas DiBacco. Reprinted by permission of the author.

Page 320: Excerpt from SPEAK FOR YOURSELF by Susan Faludi, from *The New York Times*, January 26, 1992, pages 10 and 29.

Page 372: TWO LINE POEM from OSGOOD ON SPEAKING by Charles Osgood. Copyright 1988 by Charles Osgood. Reprinted by permission of HarperCollins Publishers Inc. and William Morrow & Co., Inc.

Page 374: "Racial Profiling" by Jennifer Sweeney from *Winning Orations,* 2001. With permission from the Interstate Oratorical Association, Mankato, MN, Winning Orations, 2001.

Page 411: "DNA Computing" by Martin Note. Used by the permission of the author.

Page 440: "Child Warriors: Pawns in International Warfare" by Aaron Unseth from *Winning Orations,* 2001. With permission from the Interstate Oratorical Association, Mankato, MN, Winning Orations, 2001.

Art

Page 1: © Chuck Keeler/CorbisStockmarket

Page 5: © John Berry/Syracuse Newspapers/The Image Works

Page 8: © Michael Newman/Photoedit/PictureQuest

Page 18: © Charles Gatewood/The Image Works

Page 31: © Charles Gupton/Stone/Getty Images

Page 35: © Daniel Aubry Photography/Stock Direct

Page 40: © Dilip Mehta/Contact Press Images/PictureQuest

Page 42: © Robert Essel/CorbisStockmarket

Page 49: © Alon Reininger/Contact Press Images/PictureQuest

Page 60: © Lea Atherton/SuperStock

Page 71: © Pierre-Yves Goavec/The Image Bank/Getty Images

Page 72: © Will & Deni McIntyre/Photo Researchers

Page 79: © David Falconer/SuperStock

Page 85: © Todd Elert

Page 88: © Paul Eekhoff/Masterfile

Page 96: © Tom & DeeAnn McCarthy/CorbisStockmarket

Page 101: © Walter Bibikow/FPG/Getty Images

Page 101: © Paul Eekhoff/Masterfile

Page 115: © I. Zotin/Sovfoto/Eastfoto/PictureQuest

Page 119: © Vedros & Associates, Inc./Picturesque/PictureQuest

Page 127: © Mike Mazzaschi/Stock, Boston, Inc./PictureQuest

Page 133: © Alon Reininger/Contact Press Images/PictureQuest

Page 137: © Syracuse Newspapers/The Image Works

Page 149: © Ray Massey/Stone/Getty Images

Page 151: © Angela Cappetta/Stone/Getty Images

Page 154: © The Hackensack Record

Page 160: © Andrew Kolb/Masterfile.

Page 164: © Dick Luria/FPG/Getty Images

Page 183: © Tony Savino/The Image Works

Page 186: © Bill Market/Stock Connection/PictureQuest

INDEX